Introducing *Practice Spanish: Study Abroad*

Practice Spanish: Study Abroad, created exclusively by McGraw-Hill Education, is the first 3-D immersive language game designed to put students' developing language skills to the test through real-world communicative scenarios. Students travel virtually to Colombia, where they problem-solve, communicate, and navigate through a variety of cultural scenarios and adventures in a fictional Colombian town.

Players begin by playing Mini-games—fast-paced games designed to help master the vocabulary and grammar needed to successfully complete the Quest that follows. Whether dragging and dropping words into meaningful sentences, accurately moving cascading words into specified categories, or labeling visual images, the students' goal is to earn as many points as possible in the limited time available. Once completed, they unlock the corresponding Quest and begin the adventure.

Students begin the Quest experience by creating their very own, personalized avatar. Selecting their gender, physical characteristics, and clothing, students are encouraged to enter a world of their own making.

Within each Quest, students are given clear objectives, such as finding a fellow student in the sprawling plaza, assisting a friend in medical need, navigating their local campus, and even solving a series of mysteries incorporating elements of the magical realism that plays such a significant role in Latin American culture and literature. Performance is measured by completing the required tasks successfully while also managing the students' four key variables: money, time, health, and mystery. Students can play the game through different parts of the city and meet interesting people along the way.

Practice Spanish: Study Abroad is accessible online via laptops and tablets through McGraw-Hill Connect or directly through www.mhpractice.com. *Practice Spanish: Mini-games* are optimized for smartphones.

Conéctate **develops students' critical thinking skills as they explore cultural perspectives and interactions.**

Students learn more, faster when they can apply the material to real-life situations. Conéctate and Practice Spanish: Study Abroad mirror what can be a real-life experience.

Ana Vicente
Indiana University Perdue University Indianapolis

Conéctate **is enhanced by Connect Spanish's mobile-friendly platform, giving students and instructors access to stellar resources anytime and from anywhere.**

In this modern world with our increased use of technology throughout our lives, I welcome this up-to-date approach that is in-tune with students' needs and desires to improve their learning.

Jorge W. Suazo
University of Southern Georgia

CONÉCTATE

Introductory Spanish

CONÉCTATE

Introductory Spanish

Grant Goodall
University of California, San Diego

Darcy Lear
University of North Carolina, Chapel Hill

McGraw Hill Education

CONÉCTATE

Published by McGraw-Hill Education, 2 Penn Plaza, New York, NY 10121. Copyright © 2016 by McGraw-Hill Education.
All rights reserved. Printed in the United States of America. No part of this publication may be reproduced or distributed in any
form or by any means, or stored in a database or retrieval system, without the prior written consent of McGraw-Hill Education,
including, but not limited to, in any network or other electronic storage or transmission, or broadcast for distance learning.

Some ancillaries, including electronic and print components, may not be available to customers outside the United States.

This book is printed on acid-free paper.

1 2 3 4 5 6 7 8 9 0 DOW/DOW 1 0 9 8 7 6 5

Student Edition
ISBN: 978-0-07-338525-9
MHID: 0-07-338525-5

Instructor's Edition (not for resale)
ISBN: 978-0-07-721135-6
MHID: 0-07-721135-9

Senior Vice President, Products & Markets: *Kurt L. Strand*
Vice President, General Manager, Products & Markets:
  Michael Ryan
Vice President, Content Design & Delivery:
  Kimberly Meriwether David
Managing Director: *Katie Stevens*
Brand Manager: *Kim Sallee*
Director, Product Development: *Meghan Campbell*
Product Developer: *Sadie Ray/Misha MacLaird*
Executive Marketing Manager: *Craig Gill*
Marketing Manager: *Chris Brown*
Senior Faculty Development Manager: *Jorge Arbujas*

Director of Digital Content: *Janet Banhidi*
Digital Product Analyst: *Sarah Carey*
Digital Product Developer: *Laura Ciporen*
Director, Content Design & Delivery: *Terri Schiesl*
Program Manager: *Kelly Heinrichs*
Content Project Managers: *Erin Melloy/Amber Bettcher*
Buyer: *Susan K. Culbertson*
Design: *Matt Backhaus*
Content Licensing Specialists: *Lori Hancock/Rita Hingtgen*
Cover Image: *Ferran Traite Soler/Getty Images*
Compositor: *Aptara®, Inc.*
Printer: *R. R. Donnelley*

All credits appearing on page or at the end of the book are considered to be an extension of the copyright page.

Library of Congress Cataloging-in-Publication Data

Goodall, Grant, author.
  Conéctate : introductory Spanish / Grant Goodall, University of California, San Diego; Darcy Lear, University of
North Carolina, Chapel Hill. — 1 Edition.
       pages cm
  Includes bibliographical references and index.
  ISBN 978-0-07-338525-9 (Student Edition : alk. paper) — ISBN 0-07-338525-5 (Student Edition : alk. paper) —
ISBN 978-0-07-721135-6 (Instructor's Edition (not for resale) : alk. paper) — ISBN 0-07-721135-9 (Instructor's Edition
(not for resale) : alk. paper) 1. Spanish language—Textbooks for foreign speakers—English. 2. Spanish language—
Grammar. 3. Spanish language—Spoken Spanish. I. Lear, Darcy, author. II. Title.
  PC4129.E5G58 2014
  468.2'421—dc23
                                                                                          2014038964

The Internet addresses listed in the text were accurate at the time of publication. The inclusion of a website does not indicate
an endorsement by the authors or McGraw-Hill Education, and McGraw-Hill Education does not guarantee the accuracy of the
information presented at these sites.

Dedications

For their patient support and encouragement, I thank el amor de mi vida, Armando Vargas Matus, and my parents, Frank and Lois Goodall. My father did not live to see the book in print, but he felt pride knowing that his son would be published by McGraw-Hill, the company that he devoted his professional life to for more than 30 years. This book is for him.
—Grant

To my two Nancys and my two Bills. I am because of them.
—Darcy

CONTENTS

*See the **Instructors Manual** for more resources and information on integrating film and music into lessons.

	COMUNICACIÓN	VOCABULARIO

ESTRUCTURA

CONÉCTATE

PARA SABER MÁS

*See the **Instructors Manual** for more resources and information on integrating film and music into lessons.

	COMUNICACIÓN	VOCABULARIO

ESTRUCTURA

CONÉCTATE

PARA SABER MÁS

*See the **Instructors Manual** for more resources and information on integrating film and music into lessons.

	COMUNICACIÓN	VOCABULARIO

ESTRUCTURA

CONÉCTATE

PARA SABER MÁS

*See the **Instructors Manual** for more resources and information on integrating film and music into lessons.

COMUNICACIÓN

VOCABULARIO

ESTRUCTURA

CONÉCTATE

PARA SABER MÁS

*See the **Instructors Manual** for more resources and information on integrating film and music into lessons.

ESTRUCTURA

CONÉCTATE

*See the **Instructors Manual** for more resources and information on integrating film and music into lessons.

PREFACE

Students of Introductory Spanish learn best when they are connecting—with authentic culture, with each other as a community, and with the language as used in real-world settings. *Conéctate* sparks the curiosity that builds these connections as students drive toward communicative and cultural confidence and proficiency.

The *Conéctate* program's distinctive approach is built around the following principles.

- **Focused approach:** *Conéctate* concentrates on what Introductory Spanish students can reasonably be expected to learn, allowing for sustained engagement with the material that respects the natural process of language acquisition. An intentional focus, first on meaning and then on form, puts in action the best practices of second language pedagogy. Plus, *Conéctate*'s reduced grammar scope leaves more time for the systematic review and recycling of vocabulary and grammar required for students to achieve mastery of first-year skills. Fortifying this process at every turn is LearnSmart™, a powerful, super-adaptive learning program that guides students on an individualized path toward mastery of all the vocabulary and grammar in *Conéctate*.

- **Active learning:** *Conéctate* gives students the opportunity to explore language and culture through interactive activities that keep them focused and engaged. Vocabulary and grammar in *Conéctate* are taught using an active learning approach, nudging students to discover new vocabulary and language rules through a carefully balanced mix of inductive and explicit presentations and hands-on learning. Students are similarly asked to take an active role in an immersive online game, *Practice Spanish: Study Abroad,* designed around a study abroad experience in which they leverage their language and cultural skills to accomplish tasks and solve problems in various real-world scenarios.

- **Integration of culture:** Building on the active learning theme, students develop and apply critical thinking skills as they draw personal conclusions about the rich culture presented throughout *Conéctate*. Culture is embedded within the language activities themselves, included in notes that expand on the activity at hand, and seen through the integrated video that forms the basis for many activities in each chapter of the text. This authentic, unscripted video introduces students to useful chunks of language, real-world Spanish, and a wide range of topics related to cultural themes. *Conéctate*'s stunning video was shot in Spain, Panama, Miami, Argentina, Costa Rica, and Mexico, and exposes students to a wide variety of people in each country who discuss topics that are familiar and engaging to students.

- **Mobile tools for digital success:** The digital tools available in the Connect Spanish platform with *Conéctate* also successfully promote student progress by providing extensive opportunities to practice and hone their developing skills. These learning opportunities include online communicative activities, instant feedback, peer editing, sophisticated reporting, an immersive game, and an interactive eBook with embedded video and audio. The mobile-friendly platform allows students to engage in the course material anytime and everywhere.

A Focused Approach

Many instructors tell us that it's a challenge to "get through all the grammar" in their Introductory Spanish courses. From day one, it's a race to the finish line—and at what cost? Students get only superficial coverage, without adequate opportunities for review or cultural exploration—there simply isn't time.

Conéctate takes a distinctive approach to this issue by respecting the natural process of language acquisition and concentrating on what Introductory Spanish students can be reasonably expected to learn. Each chapter presents the most important concepts, allowing students to focus and engage more fully with a few crucial pieces, rather than aim to have a cursory understanding of many. This means that more advanced structures are located in the **Para saber más** section that follows **Capítulo 16**. These supplemental grammatical presentations expand and develop the chapter's content and their practice activities may be found in Connect Spanish or the print Workbook / Laboratory Manual. By situating the more typically late-acquired concepts in the **Para saber más** section, *Conéctate* gives instructors the freedom to easily adapt and expand their presentations of these structures for learners who can move more rapidly through the sequence. By focusing on a realistic and reasonable scope and sequence, *Conéctate* promotes a deeper comprehension and a more well-rounded experience.

Because instructors aren't having to race to the finish line, a more focused pace affords the opportunity to review and recycle the material that's been covered previously, allowing students to practice putting it together and to truly acquire this language. Beginning in **Capítulo 3,** a recycling section appears before each new grammar point, pulling in a related point from earlier in the sequence and showing students how concepts are interrelated. This interweaving of the old with the new allows for better retention and more fluid opportunities to tie it all together.

With LearnSmart, precious study time is focused and directed, maximizing the impact of each minute a student devotes to studying. With over 2.5 billion probes answered since its launch in 2011, LearnSmart has proven to enhance students' learning and improve course outcomes significantly—by as much as a full letter grade. As each student works through a chapter's vocabulary and grammar modules, LearnSmart identifies the learning objectives behind each question and indicates the areas that warrant more practice based on that student's performance. Then it provides an individualized study program, one that is unique and tailored to that particular student's strengths and weaknesses. LearnSmart reports provide students with details about their own learning and give instructors the ability to understand the strengths and weaknesses of individual students as well as of the entire class.

Reciclaje

Plural forms of *ser, tener, estar,* and *ir*

Complete each sentence using a verb from the following list that would make sense in the context. Then indicate whether each sentence is **cierto** (*true*) or **falso** (*false*).

estar   ir   ser   tener

	CIERTO	FALSO
1. Los españoles <u>son</u> de Asia.	☐	☑
2. Nosotros <u>somos</u> estudiantes.	☑	☐
3. Los profesores de español <u>van</u> a muchas clases de química.	☐	☑
4. Mis amigos <u>están</u> muy contentos hoy.	☑	☑
5. Las universidades <u>tienen</u> muchas clases.	☑	☐
6. Nosotros <u>vamos</u> a la clase de español los sábados y los domingos.	☐	☑

3.2   Desayunamos a las siete.

Present indicative: Plural forms

Para empezar...

PASO 1. In many cultures, the daily schedule of activities is organized around the schedule of meals. In Mexico, families typically have breakfast (**desayunar**) at around 7:00, eat their midday meal (**comer**) at around 2:00, and dinner (**cenar**) at around 8:00. Use this information to complete the following sentences about meals in Mexico and about your own personal habits.

Active Learning

Conéctate puts students in the driver's seat, engaging them in their own learning process and inspiring them to learn more and do more with Spanish. The vocabulary and grammar presentations do not simply provide translations or explain the rules, rather they challenge students to pause, think critically, and use meaning-based, contextual clues to figure things out. In this way, students' attention is directed toward their expanding vocabulary, the *why* behind the grammar presentations, and the functions these phrases and structures serve in the language. There is no room for passive standers-by in *Conéctate*!

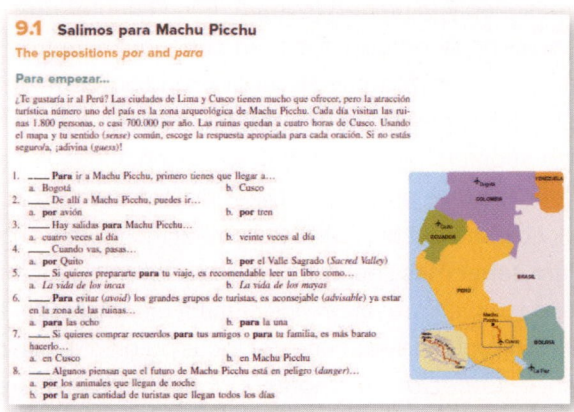

And students won't stand by while playing *Practice Spanish: Study Abroad,* the market's first 3-D immersive language game designed exclusively by McGraw-Hill Education. Students "study abroad" virtually in Colombia, where they will create their very own avatar, live with a host family, make new friends, and navigate a variety of real-world scenarios using their quickly developing language skills. Students will earn points and rewards for successfully accomplishing these tasks via their smartphones, tablets, and computers, and instructors will have the ability to assign specific tasks, monitor student achievement, and incorporate the game into the classroom experience.

> **This will 100% improve my Spanish. I'm always intimidated to practice in real life because I don't want to sound silly, but this is perfect!**
> —**Susana Sánchez,** student at San Diego Mesa College

Integration of Culture

Conéctate is built around an extensive video program that serves a dual purpose: to introduce new language structures and common expressions, as well as to provide a window into the cultures of the Spanish-speaking world. This focus on cultural exploration has the additional advantage of making the communicative activities in the classroom more meaningful. The emphasis throughout is on culture "from the inside," that is, from the perspective of Spanish speakers themselves. This perspective often includes comparisons with the students' own lives and leads students to the discovery that Spanish speakers are in many ways similar to themselves. Activities and **notas** further encourage self-reflection, as students are asked to consider how their own cultural perspectives might look to people from other cultures.

Culture is integrated throughout each chapter, embedded in presentations and activities, notes and videos. This integration culminates in the end-of-chapter section called **Conéctate,** where students bring together what they have learned thus far to further develop their abilities in listening, reading, writing, and speaking.

Each **Conéctate** section contains the following integrative sections.

- **¡Leamos!** provides students with authentic readings from the very beginning of their language studies. Activities ensure comprehensibility by supporting students' language abilities, enabling students to be successful at building their receptive skills.

- **¡Escuchemos!** Another video-based activity, this feature presents authentic language that incorporates many of the chapter's linguistic and cultural topics together into a cohesive activity that builds confidence and further promotes cultural exploration. Follow-up activities put students in the active-communicator role as they deliver similar information in spoken situations.

- **¡Escribamos!** This activity integrates a process-approach to writing, in which students focus on real-life and academic writing tasks, such as developing an online profile or writing a descriptive paragraph. The process starts with a unique writing strategy in every chapter, followed by a brainstorming and drafting stage, and ending with a careful editing of student work using a peer review system.

- **¡Hablemos!** This section pulls together the chapter theme, grammar, vocabulary, and culture, and encourages students to talk extensively in pairs and group-based activities. These fun, engaging, oral-based activities can be used for oral exams, in-class culminating conversations, and/or oral presentations.

- **Conéctate a la música** and **Conéctate al cine:** In these sections that alternate chapters, students listen to a Spanish-language song or watch a scene from a Spanish-language film that relates to some cultural, thematic, and/or linguistic aspect of the chapter. Information on the artists, background information on the films, and vocabulary support are provided, as well as pre- and post-listening and viewing activities. *All songs are readily available online through iTunes and/or YouTube. All films are available at major online and in-store video retailers, including Netflix (whose timestamps are provided for the selected clips). Due to permissions limitations, songs and films are not provided by McGraw-Hill Education.*

**Get Connected.
Get Engaged.**

With our media rich eBook, course content comes alive with videos, interactive elements, and even the instructor's own notes.

Mobile Tools for Digital Success

Connect Spanish: Used in conjunction with *Conéctate,* Connect Spanish provides a mobile-friendly digital solution to meet the needs of any course format. Some of the key features of Connect Spanish include:

- an interactive eBook, the complete Workbook / Laboratory Manual exercises, grammar tutorials, and all audio and video materials.

- additional interactive activities using drag-and-drop functionality, embedded audio, voice recorders, and videos targeting key vocabulary, grammar, and cultural content for extra practice.

- *Practice Spanish: Study Abroad,* our immersive online game for Introductory Spanish available online and as an mobile-ready app.

- a comprehensive gradebook, including time-on-task measurements, the ability to quick-grade, to drop the lowest score, and to view calculations of students' grades to date.

- the ability to customize assignments using the Assignment Builder's user-friendly filtering system, allowing instructors to create unique assignments that target specific skills, learning objectives, ACTFL standards, and more.

- access to all instructor's resources, including pre-made exams and a test bank for online delivery of exams.

- Tegrity™, McGraw-Hill's unique video capture software, which allows instructors to post short videos, tutorials, and lessons for student access outside of class.

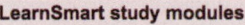

LearnSmart, the only super-adaptive learning tool on the market, is proven to significantly enhance students' learning and improve course outcomes. Available within Connect Spanish and as a mobile app, LearnSmart provides students with targeted feedback specific to their individual performance, and additional practice in areas where they need help the most. As students work on each chapter's grammar and vocabulary modules, LearnSmart identifies the main grammatical structures and vocabulary words that warrant more practice and provides a unique study program based on each individual student's performance, that pinpoints the student's strengths and weaknesses.

Voice Board and Blackboard IM, two powerful tools integrated into Connect Spanish, promote communication and collaboration outside of the classroom. Voice Board activities allow students to participate in threaded oral discussion boards, while Blackboard IM activities facilitate real-time interaction via text instant messaging and voice or video chat. The white board and screen sharing tools provide opportunities for collaboration, and virtual office hours allow instructors to meet online with students either one-on-one or in groups. Instructors can deliver voice presentations, voice emails, or podcasts as well. Whether for an online, hybrid, or face-to-face course seeking to expand oral communication practice and assessment, these tools allow student-to-student or student-to-instructor virtual oral chat functionality.

MH Campus and Blackboard simplify and facilitate course administration by integrating with any Learning Management System. With features such as single sign-on for students and instructors, gradebook synchronization, and easy access to all of

McGraw-Hill's language content (even from other market-leading titles not currently adopted for your course), teaching an introductory language course has never been more streamlined.

Acknowledgements

We would like to thank the overwhelming number of friends and colleagues who served on boards of advisors or as consultants, completed reviews or surveys, and attended symposia or focus groups. Their feedback was indispensable in creating the *Conéctate* program. The appearance of their names in the following lists does not necessarily constitute their endorsement of the program or its methodology.

Symposia and Focus Groups

Daniel Anderson, *University of Kentucky*

Enrica Ardemagni, *Indiana University—Purdue University Indianapolis*

Angela Bailey de las Heras, *Illinois State University*

Ann Baker, *University of Evansville*

Adam Ballart, *Ball State University*

Adoracion Berry, *University of Memphis*

Amy Bomke, *Indiana University—Purdue University*

Daniel Briere, *University of Indianapolis*

Nancy Broughton, *Wright State University—Celina*

Patricia Cabrera, *University of Indianapolis*

Maribel Campoy, *University of Indianapolis*

Doug Canfield, *University of Tennessee—Knoxville*

Deanne Cobb-Zygadlo, *Kutztown University of Pennsylvania*

Kelly Conroy, *Western Kentucky University*

Manuel Cortes-Castaneda, *Eastern Kentucky University*

Darren Crasto, *Houston Community College—Northwest College*

Richard Curry, *Texas A & M University*

Allen Davis, *Indiana University*

Ana Vives de Girón, *Collin College*

Esther Domenech, *University of Redlands*

Dorian Dorado, *Louisiana State University—Baton Rouge*

Paula Ellister, *University of Oregon*

Idoia Elola, *Texas Tech University*

Jason Fetters, *Purdue University—West Lafayette*

Gayle Fielder-Vierma, *University of Southern California, Los Angeles*

Ruth Flores, *California Baptist University*

William Flores, *California Baptist University*

Leah Fonder-Solano, *University of Southern Mississippi*

Luz Font, *Florida State College South Campus*

Robert Fritz, *Ball State University*

Muriel Gallego, *Ohio University—Athens*

Alejandro Garces, *Coastal Carolina University*

Scott Gibby, *Austin Community College—Northridge*

Inma Gómez Soler, *University of Memphis*

Antonio Martín Gómez, *University of Kentucky*

Melissa Groenewold, *University of Louisville—Louisville*

Patricia Harrigan, *Community College of Baltimore County*

Mary Hartson, *Oakland University*

Greg Helmick, *University of North Florida*

Eda Henao, *Borough of Manhattan Community College*

Alex Herrera, *Cypress College*

Cristina Kowalski, *University of Cincinnati—Cincinnati*

Ryan LaBrozzi, *Bridgewater State University*

Debbie Lee-DiStefano, *Southeast Missouri State University*

Melissa Logue, *Columbus State Community College*

Steve Lombardo, *Purdue University Calumet Hammond*

Nuria López-Ortega, *University of Cincinnati—Cincinnati*

Christopher Luke, *Ball State University*

Jillian Markus, *Vincennes University*

Ivan Martínez, *Ball State University*

Leticia McGrath, *Georgia Southern University*

Ivalise Méndez, *Ball State University*

Wendy Méndez-Hasselman, *Palm Beach State College*

Montserrat Mir, *Illinois State University*

Cheryl Moody, *Pulaski Technical College*

Juan Carlos Moraga, *Folsom Lake College*

Rosa-María Moreno, *Cincinnati State Technical & Community College*

Danae Orlins, *University of Cincinnati—Cincinnati*

Sandra Yelgy Parada, *Los Angeles City College*

Federico Pérez-Pineda, *University of South Alabama*

Lee Ragsdale, *Ivy Tech Community College of Indiana—Indianapolis*

Noris Rodríguez, *University of Cincinnati—Cincinnati*

Aaron Roggia, *Northern Illinois University*

Daniel Runnels, *University of Louisville*

Aaron Salinger, *Mount San Antonio College*

Jacquelyn Sandone, *University of Missouri—Columbia*

Eduardo Santa Cruz, *Hanover College*

Daniela Schuvaks-Katz, *IUPUI—Indianapolis*

Steven Sheppard, *University of North Texas*

Efila Jzar Simpson, *Vincennes University*

Leah Solano, *University of Southern Mississippi*

Alfredo J. Sosa-Velasco, *Southern Connecticut State University*

Melissa Stewart, *Western Kentucky University*

Jorge Suazo, *Georgia Southern University*

Alysha Timmons, *California State University—San Bernardino*

Ana Vicente, *IUPUI—Indianapolis*

Michael Vrooman, *Grand Valley State University*

Amber Workman, *California Lutheran University*

Carlota Yetter, *Moreno Valley College*

Elizabeth Zúñiga Irvin, *University of North Carolina—Wilmington*

Reviewers

Maria Akrabova, *Metropolitan State University of Denver*

Tim Altanero, *Austin Community College*

Aleta Anderson, *Grand Rapids Community College*

Enrica J. Ardemagni, *Indiana University—Purdue University Indianapolis*

Silvia Arroyo, *Mississippi State University*

Sandra Barboza, *Trident Technical College*

Shaun A. Bauer, *University of Central Florida*

Fleming L. Bell, *Valdosta State University*

Maritza Bell-Corrales, *Middle Georgia State College*

Amy Bomke, *Indiana University—Purdue University Indianapolis*

Herbert Brant, *Indiana University—Purdue University Indianapolis*

Cathy Briggs, *North Lake College*

Kristy Britt, *University of South Alabama*

Isabel Zakrzewski Brown, *University of South Alabama*

Suzanne M. Buck, *Central New Mexico Community College*

Adolfo Campoy-Cubillo, *Oakland University*

Beth Buckingham Cardon, *Georgia Perimeter College*

Esther Castro, *San Diego State University*

Marco Tulio Cedillo, *Lynchburg College*

Irene Chico-Wyatt, *University of Kentucky*

Christine E. Cotton, *University of Arkansas at Little Rock*

Jacqueline Daughton, *University of North Carolina at Greensboro*

Luis M. Delgado, *Olive-Harvey College*

Kent L. Dickson, *California State Polytechnic University—Pomona*

Margaret Rose Don, *University of San Diego*

Dorian Dorado, *Louisiana State University*

Megan Echevarria, *University of Rhode Island*

Ronna S. Feit, *Nassau Community College*

María Ángeles Fernández, *University of North Florida*

Sandra Fernández-Tardani, *Grand Valley State University*

Erin S. Finzer, *University of Arkansas at Little Rock*

Leah Fonder-Solano, *University of Southern Mississippi*

Joan H. Fox, *University of Washington*

Marianne Franco, *Modesto Junior College*

Ellen Lorraine Friedrich, *Valdosta State University*

Diana García-Denson, *San Francisco City College*

Susana García Prudencio, *Pennsylvania State University*

Audrey Gertz, *Indiana University—Purdue University Indianapolis*

Ransom Gladwin, *Valdosta State University*

Jesse Gleason, *University of Florida*

Inmaculada Gómez Soler, *University of Memphis*

Christine Pratt Gonzales, *Salt Lake Community College*

Kenneth A. Gordon, *Winthrop University*

Melissa Guzmán Groenewold, *University of Louisville*

Marta C. Gumpert, *Southeastern Louisiana University*

Agnieszka Gutthy, *Southeastern Louisiana University*

Angela Haensel, *Cincinnati State Technical and Community College*

Shannon W. Hahn, *Durham Technical Community College*

Patricia Harrigan, *Community College of Baltimore County*

Mary Hartson, *Oakland University*

Richard A. Heath, *Kirkwood Community College— Iowa City*

Greg Helmick, *University of North Florida*

Eda Henao, *Borough of Manhattan Community College*

Yolanda Hernández, *College of Southern Nevada*

Michael J. Horswell, *Florida Atlantic University*

Nuria Ibáñez Quintana, *University of North Florida*

Jennifer Erin Irish, *Coastal Carolina Community College*

Bernard Issa, *University of Illinois at Chicago*

Douglas A. Jackson, *University of South Carolina Upstate*

Natalia Jacovkis, *Xavier University*

Becky S. Jaimes, *Austin Community College*

Qiu Y. Jiménez, *Bakersfield College*

Dallas Jurisevic, *Metropolitan Community College*

Anne Kelly-Glasoe, *South Puget Sound Community College*

Kelly C. Kingsbury Brunetto, *University of Nebraska—Lincoln*

Julie Kleinhans-Urrutia, *Austin Community College*

Dora Cecilia Mezzich Kress, *Florida State College at Jacksonville*

Kajsa Larson, *Northern Kentucky University*

Rachele Lawton, *Community College of Baltimore County*

Vanessa Lazo-Wilson, *Austin Community College*

David Leavell, *College of Southern Nevada*

Lance Lee, *Durham Technical Community College*

Talia Loaiza, *Austin Community College*

Soumaya B. Long, *Community College of Baltimore County*

Nuria Lopez-Ortega, *University of Cincinnati*

Jude Thomas Manzo, *Saint Philip's College*

Laura Manzo, *Modesto Junior College*

Karen R. Martin, *Texas Christian University*

Lornaida McCune, *University of Missouri—Columbia*

Leticia McGrath, *Georgia Southern University*

Mary Newcomer McKinney, *Texas Christian University*

Peggy McNeil, *Louisiana State University*

Mercedes Meier, *Coastal Carolina Community College*

Mandy R. Menke, *Grand Valley State University*

Dennis Miller, *Clayton State University*

Cheryl Moody, *Pulaski Technical College*

María Yazmina Moreno-Florido, *Chicago State University*

Sandra Mulryan, *Community College of Baltimore County*

Esperanza Muñoz Pérez, *Kirkwood Community College*

Alicia Muñoz-Sánchez, *University of California— San Diego*

Ruth Fátima Navarro, *Grossmont College*

Benjamin J. Nelson, *University of South Carolina Beaufort*

Christine Coleman Núñez, *Kutztown University of Pennsylvania*

Martha T. Oregel, *University of San Diego*

William Otáñez, *Coastal Carolina Community College*

Ignacio Pérez-Ibáñez, *Moses Brown School*

Anne Prucha, *University of Central Florida*

Yaneth Ramírez, *Fresno City College*

Claire L. Reetz, *Florida State College at Jacksonville*

Terri Rice, *University of South Alabama*

Angelo Rodríguez, *Kutztown University of Pennsylvania*

Teresa Roig-Torres, *University of Cincinnati*

Mevelyn Romay Fernández, *University of Mississippi*

Latasha Lisa Russell, *Florida State College at Jacksonville*

Maritza Salgueiro-Carlisle, *Bakersfield College*

Mariela Sánchez, *Southeastern Louisiana University*

José Sandoval, *Coastal Carolina Community College*

Jason Steve Sarkozi, *Central Michigan University*

Dora Schoebrun-Fernandez, *San Diego Mesa College*

Daniela Schuvaks Katz, *Indiana University—Purdue University Indianapolis*

Alfredo J. Sosa-Velasco, *Southern Connecticut State University*

Sabrina Spannagel Bradley, *University of Washington*

Linda S. Stadler, *Cincinnati State Technical and Community College*

Nancy Stucker, *Cabrillo College*

Jorge W. Suazo, *Georgia Southern University*

Joe Terantino, *Kennesaw State University*

Rosa Tezanos-Pinto, *Indiana University—Purdue University Indianapolis*

Linda Tracy, *Santa Rosa Junior College*

Norma Urrutia, *Xavier University*

Gloria Vélez-Rendón , *Purdue University Calumet*

Ana Vicente, *Indiana University—Purdue University Indianapolis*

Rosario P. Vickery, *Clayton State University*

Gayle Vierma, *University of Southern California*

Paul Vincent, *Grossmont College*

Michael Vrooman, *Grand Valley State University*

Joseph A. Wieczorek, *Community College of Baltimore County, Notre Dame of Maryland University*

Kelley L. Young, *University of Missouri— Kansas City*

Author Acknowledgments

Conéctate would not be possible without the hard work of a hugely talented and creative group of people. I thank the entire editorial team at McGraw-Hill, especially Katie Crouch, who got us started, and Kim Sallee, Sadie Ray, and Misha MacLaird, who led us through to a successful completion; our wonderful video crew led by Hugo Krispyn, David Murray, Lamar Owen, and Rocío Barajas; my co-author, Darcy Lear, who has been a great friend and companion along this amazing journey; and to the hundreds of people in Spain and Latin America who agreed to speak to us on camera. Getting to hear their stories and their perspectives on the world was an immense privilege and an unforgettable experience. My approach to education has been greatly influenced by my colleagues here at UC San Diego, including Leonard Newmark and David Perlmutter, who taught me so much in so many ways; our language coordinators Alicia Muñoz Sánchez, Peggy Lott, Elke Riebeling, and Françoise Santore, four of the most inspiring language teachers one could ever hope to meet; and the many other instructors and teaching assistants here whose influence is spread throughout these pages.

—Grant Goodall

First, I thank Katie Crouch for bringing me into this project, and for pairing me with Grant Goodall. The "arranged marriage" we joked of has blossomed into all the very best of arranged relationships. I am grateful for that. It has been a pleasure to work with everyone else at McGraw-Hill who has helped us along the way, including Susan Blatty, Kim Sallee, Misha MacLaird, Allen Bernier, Pennie Nichols, and Sadie Ray. The international travel was truly a thrilling once-in-a-lifetime experience, thanks in a large part to our crew: Hugo Krispyn, David Murray, Lamar Owen, and Rocío Barajas. I owe my career in language education to some amazing mentors—all textbook authors themselves—starting with the late Graciela Ascarrunz Gilman who saved me years of handwringing by telling me: *¡Naciste para enseñar!* Then I had the great good luck to work with Janice Macián and Donna Reseigh Long at The Ohio State University. They always lovingly put me where I belonged, pushed me when I needed it, and told me the truth. Glynis Cowell's warmth, kindness, and support together with Larry King being a great boss made my entire stay at the University of North Carolina a pleasure. My work at the University of Illinois brought me close Diane Musumeci— half of the *Avanti!* team—who always offered good advice about everything textbook- and work-related. And that is also where I met my closest colleague and dear friend, Ann Abbott, who has supported me in all my professional endeavors.

—Darcy Lear

We would also like to gratefully acknowledge all of the people who worked tirelessly to produce the entire *Conéctate* program.

Contributing Writers
Student Edition: Maria Akrabova, Misha MacLaird
Workbook / Laboratory Manual: Maria Akrabova, Allen Bernier, Dorian Delgado, Gayle Fiedler-Vierma, Eileen Francher, Kristina Gibby, Misha MacLaird, Nuria López Ortega, Pennie Nichols, Alfonso J. Quiñones-Rodriguez

Product Team
Editorial and Marketing: Jorge Arbujas, Caitlin Bahrey, Janet Banhidi, Jessica Becker, Allen Bernier, Susan Blatty, Leslie Briggs, Chris Brown, Sarah Carey, Laura Chastain, Laura Ciporen, Katie Crouch, Craig Gill, Lorena Gómez Mostajo, Helen Greenlea, Misha MacLaird, Pennie Nichols, Sadie Ray, Kim Sallee, Katie Stevens
Art, Design, and Production: Matt Backhaus, Harry Briggs, Sue Culbertson, Lori Hancock, Danielle Havens, Kelly Heinrichs, Rita Hingtgen, Lynne Lemley, Erin Melloy, Terri Schiesl, Preston Thomas.
Media Partners: Aptara, Eastern Sky Studios, Laserwords, Truth-Function

ABOUT THE AUTHORS

Grant Goodall is Professor of Linguistics and Director of the Language Program at the University of California, San Diego, where he is also affiliated with the Center for Iberian and Latin American Studies. An internationally recognized scholar of Spanish syntax, he has a longstanding commitment to the development and implementation of highly effective, research-based practices in language teaching. He brings a rich international background to the *Conéctate* project: He was educated in both the United States and Mexico, has spent much of his life along the border between the two, and has taught or lectured in twenty countries.

Darcy Lear holds a Ph.D. in Foreign and Second-Language Education from The Ohio State University. She has been the director of the Spanish basic-language program at the University of Illinois, Urbana-Champaign; the inaugural coordinator of the minor program in Spanish for the professions at the University of North Carolina at Chapel Hill; and, most recently, a lecturer at the University of Chicago. She devotes most of her professional time to career coaching, which includes workshops for foreign-language students navigating the campus-to-career transition.

En la clase

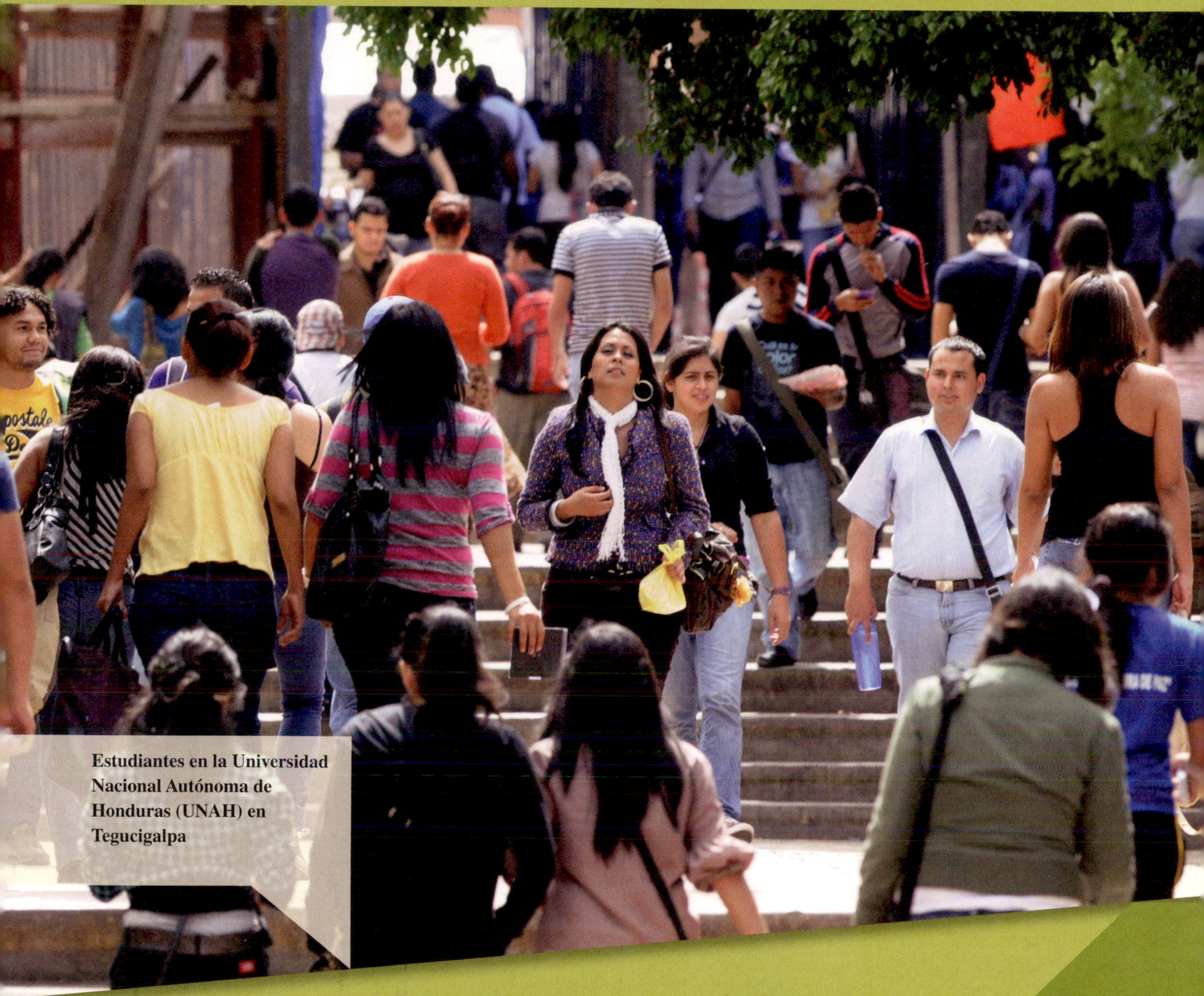

Estudiantes en la Universidad Nacional Autónoma de Honduras (UNAH) en Tegucigalpa

Objetivos

In this chapter you will learn how to:

- greet someone, find out his/her name, how he/she is doing, where he/she is from, and say good-bye
- pronounce the letters and sounds of the alphabet
- express the date, months, and seasons of the year
- say the numbers 0–99
- identify people and things
- express possession by talking about the objects people have
- say the names of the Spanish-speaking countries

connect SPANISH
http://www.connectspanish.com

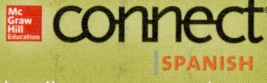

COMUNICACIÓN LARIO UCTURA ATE

¡Hola!
Greeting people in Spanish

A. A ver (*Let's see*): ¡Hola!   Watch and listen as the following people say hello. Indicate which greeting each person uses. Some speakers use more than one greeting. **¡Atención!** The video in this program shows everyday people speaking at a natural rate. This may seem challenging at first, but allow yourself to listen as many times as you need, and what used to seem fast will start to seem normal. For now, listen for words you know and try to get the gist of what you hear.

		BUENOS DÍAS / BUEN DÍA	BUENAS TARDES	¿CÓMO ANDA?	HOLA
1.	Adolfo, de México	☐	☐	☐	☐
2.	Marlén, de México	☐	☐	☐	☐
3.	Rodrigo, de Argentina	☐	☐	☐	☐
4.	Maritza, de la República Dominicana	☐	☐	☐	☐
5.	Manuel, de Cuba	☐	☐	☐	☐
6.	Mariana, de Costa Rica	☐	☐	☐	☐
7.	Esteban, de Costa Rica	☐	☐	☐	☐
8.	Keylin, de Costa Rica	☐	☐	☐	☐

B. Los saludos (*Greetings*)   Check all the Spanish greetings you have heard before. Do you know what they mean? Are you familiar with any other greetings in Spanish? Just like in English, there are many!

☐ Buenos días.   ☐ ¿Cómo anda?   ☐ ¿Qué tal?

☐ Buenas tardes.   ☐ Hola.

Vocabulario

To say hello to someone before noon, use **buenos días,** which translates as *good morning* (literally, *good days*). In the afternoon, use **buenas tardes,** which means *good afternoon* or *good evening*. After dark, use **buenas noches.** This means *good night*, and may be used to greet people or to wish them well as they turn in for the night.

Notice how all three of these expressions use the Spanish word for *good* (**buenos/buenas**) and yet they appear with different endings depending on what they describe. We'll explain this in the next chapter, but in the meantime, take a guess. Why might these endings vary?

C. ¡Buenos días!   Decide whether you would use **buenos días, buenas tardes,** or **buenas noches** in each of the following situations.

	BUENOS DÍAS	BUENAS TARDES	BUENAS NOCHES
1. as you walk into your first class of the morning	☐	☐	☐
2. in the school cafeteria at dinner	☐	☐	☐
3. in line for a cup of morning coffee	☐	☐	☐
4. on your way to the library for an all-nighter	☐	☐	☐
5. as you leave your last class of the afternoon	☐	☐	☐
6. just before bedtime	☐	☐	☐

CONÉCTATE AL MUNDO HISPANO

At social gatherings, approaching and greeting people is important. Spanish-speakers often engage in a formal, physical greeting, such as a handshake combined with a slap on the back, or kisses on one or both cheeks. Not doing so may be considered rude, so it is always a good idea to observe what others are doing and follow their example!

¿Cómo te llamas? / ¿Cómo se llama?

Asking someone his/her name

A. A ver: ¿Cómo te llamas? / ¿Cómo se llama usted?

PASO 1. Watch and listen as Spanish speakers say their names. Match each photo with the correct name.

1. _____   4. _____

2. _____   5. _____

3. _____   6. _____

a. Bertha Lara
b. Víctor Rodrigo
c. Marlina Rodríguez
d. Natalia López
e. Paul Reid
f. Pedro Alberto Jiménez Mancilla

PASO 2. Watch and listen again. Indicate which expression each person uses to say their name.

	(YO) ME LLAMO	MI NOMBRE ES
1. Marlina Rodríguez	☐	☐
2. Natalia López	☐	☐
3. Pedro Alberto Jiménez Mancilla	☐	☐
4. Paul Reid	☐	☐
5. Víctor Rodrigo	☐	☐
6. Bertha Lara	☐	☐

En español...

The verb **llamarse** is used to give your name in Spanish. It literally means *to call oneself*. The question **¿Cómo te llamas?** means *What do you call yourself?* and the answer **Me llamo...** means *I call myself* . . .

To literally say *My name is . . .* in Spanish, use **Mi nombre es...**

—Hola, me llamo Jorge.
—Mucho gusto. Mi nombre es Iván.

To introduce yourself and ask someone's name, you could use the following expressions.

INFORMAL (**TÚ**)	FORMAL (**USTED**)
¡Hola! Me llamo Pablo.	**Buenas tardes. Me llamo Marta Campillos.**
¿Cómo te llamas?	**¿Cómo se llama?**

You can also introduce yourself in the following way.

INFORMAL	FORMAL
¡Hola! Mi nombre es Pablo.	**Buenas tardes. Mi nombre es Marta Campillos.**

To ask *And you?*, simply add the question after you've introduced yourself.

¿Y tú?   **¿Y usted?**

One way to say *Nice to meet you* is **Mucho gusto,** to which you could reply **Igualmente** (*Likewise*).

INFORMAL (**TÚ**)	FORMAL (**USTED**)
—**¿Cómo te llamas?**	—**¿Cómo se llama usted?**
—**Me llamo Elena. ¿Y tú?**	—**Raúl Fuentes. ¿Y usted?**
—**Marina.**	—**Soy** (*I am*) **Ana Freire.**
—**Mucho gusto.**	—**Mucho gusto.**
—**Igualmente.**	—**Igualmente.**

B. ¿Cómo se llaman los otros estudiantes?

PASO 1. Walk around the room and greet at least five other students using appropriate expressions. Introduce yourself and find out their names.

PASO 2. See if you can remember and repeat your classmates' names. Follow the model as you point to the desk where each person is seated. **¡Atención!** With the below pronouns **él** and **ella,** you're getting a sneak peek at a grammar point that soon we'll present at length. For now, simply follow the model and see if you can detect the pattern. What might be the difference between the pronouns **él** and **ella**?

MODELO: Él se llama Christopher. Ella se llama Miranda. Ella se llama Gloria. Él se llama Jason.

Christopher

Miranda

Gloria

Jason

En español...

The use of **tú** and **usted (Ud.)** can vary from region to region, so when in doubt, use **usted.** The person you are addressing will usually invite you to use **tú** if it is appropriate.

Watch the video that accompanies **Actividad A** again. Can you tell why **tú** and **usted** were used in each case in the video?

C. ¿Cómo te llamas? ¿Cómo se llama usted?   Read the following questions.
Based on the question's level of formality, select the person who is being addressed appropriately.

1. ¿Cómo se llama usted?

   a.    b.

2. ¿Cómo te llamas?

   a.    b.

3. ¿Cómo te llamas?

   a.    b.

4. ¿Cómo se llama usted?

   a.    b.

CONÉCTATE AL MUNDO HISPANO

Residents of Spain and most Latin American countries usually have two last names (**dos apellidos**): the first one is inherited from the father, and the second one from the mother. The first of these names, the paternal family name, is considered primary, and is the one passed on to future generations. For example, when we look at the name of Mexican actor Gael García Bernal we know that García is his father's family name (that is, inherited from his father), and Bernal is his mother's family name (that is, inherited from his mother). When Gael García Bernal and Argentine actress Dolores Fonzi had a son, they named him Lázaro García Fonzi. Their daughter is Libertad García Fonzi. What would your last name look like if you were to adopt this custom?

When moving to a country that doesn't practice this custom, some Spanish speakers choose to drop their mother's last name in order to avoid confusion. Others prefer to hyphenate the two last names to maintain this important part of their identity.

D. Los apellidos

PASO 1.   Based on what you read in the **Conéctate al mundo hispano** box about dual last names in Spanish, what would the last names be of the following children?

1. Father: Marco Ruiz Cortés   Mother: Josefa Martín González
    Son: Andrés _____ _____
2. Father: Alberto Esquivel Muñoz   Mother: Liliana Andrade Arbujas
    Daughter: Jana _____ _____
3. Mother: Emilia Barajas Bermúdez   Father: Alfonso Silva Arce
    Son: Enrique _____ _____

 PASO 2.   In groups, use the above pattern to introduce yourselves, saying what your last names would be if you used both your father's and mother's last names.

¿Cómo estás? / ¿Cómo está?
Asking people how they are

To find out how someone is doing, you might ask the following questions.

¿Cómo estás? for informal (**tú**)   or   **¿Cómo está usted?** for formal (**usted**)

When addressing someone informally, you can also use the Spanish equivalent of *How is it going?*: **¿Qué tal?**

In English, *How are you?* can be another way to just say *hello,* but in the Spanish-speaking world an answer is expected. Common responses for **¿Cómo está(s)?** include: **Bien** (*Good*), **Más o menos** (*Okay*), **Mal** (*Bad*).

When someone asks how you are, it is polite to say **gracias** after you answer. Return the question by asking, **¿y tú?** or **¿y usted?**

—**Buenos días. ¿Cómo estás?**   —**Buenas tardes. ¿Cómo está?**
—**Bien, gracias. ¿Y tú?**   —**Muy bien, gracias. ¿Y usted?**
—**Muy bien.**   —**Bien, gracias.**

If someone answers with anything less positive than **bien,** you can inquire further by asking *What's the matter?* using **¿Qué te pasa?** (**tú**) / **¿Qué le pasa?** (**usted**)

Hola, ¿cómo estás?

 A. ¿Formal o informal?

PASO 1. Indicate whether each expression you hear is formal (**usted**) or informal (**tú**).

	INFORMAL	FORMAL	
1.	☐	☐	_____
2.	☐	☐	_____
3.	☐	☐	_____
4.	☐	☐	_____
5.	☐	☐	_____

PASO 2. Listen a second time to the expressions in **Paso 1** and jot down the words that let you know if each expression is informal or formal.

B. ¿Cómo estás? How would you greet the following people and ask how they are? Write the appropriate answers next to the image of each person, then share your responses to check for accuracy.

MODELO:    *¡Hola! ¿Cómo estás?*

■ The audio files for in-text listening activities are available in the eBook, within Connect Plus activities, and on the Online Learning Center.

1.    2.    3.    4.    5.

C. ¿Y tú?   Greet at least three different classmates by name, and ask how they are. See how many remember to ask how you are in return!

¿De dónde eres? / ¿De dónde es?
Asking where someone is from

A. A ver: ¿De dónde eres? / ¿De dónde es usted?   Watch and listen to people from all over the Spanish-speaking world say where they are from. For each group of speakers, check the names of all the countries you hear.

1. ____ Argentina ____ Panamá
   ____ Colombia ____ Paraguay
   ____ Ecuador ____ Perú
   ____ El Salvador ____ la República Dominicana
   ____ España ____ Uruguay
   ____ México ____ Venezuela

2. ____ Argentina ____ España
   ____ Bolivia ____ Honduras
   ____ Chile ____ México
   ____ Colombia ____ Nicaragua
   ____ Costa Rica ____ Panamá
   ____ Ecuador ____ Venezuela

To ask a person where he/she is from, use one of the following questions.

INFORMAL (**TÚ**)		FORMAL (**USTED**)
¿De dónde eres?	or	**¿De dónde es?**

To say *I am from* . . . in Spanish, say: **Soy de…**

—Elena, ¿de dónde eres? —¿De dónde es usted, señora Gallegos?
—Soy de México. —Soy de El Salvador.

If you want to know where someone currently lives, ask one of the following questions.

—**¿Dónde vives?** —**¿Dónde vive usted?**
—**Vivo en Village Hall.** —**Vivo en Puebla.**

B. Los orígenes y la geografía   Read the following statements about people's origins. Then, using your knowledge of geography (and the map at the back of your book), select the country that each speaker could be from.

1. «Soy de Centroamérica.»
   a. Venezuela b. Honduras c. España

2. «Soy de Europa.»
   a. Ecuador b. Guatemala c. España

3. «Soy del Caribe.»
   a. Honduras b. Argentina c. Bolivia

4. «Somos de Norteamérica.»
   a. Nicaragua b. México c. Paraguay

5. «Somos de Sudamérica.»
   a. Chile b. Panamá c. Cuba

C. Soy de...   Circulate around the room asking **¿De dónde eres?** Can you find two classmates from different cities than you? Can you find a classmate from another state? Ask at least five classmates.

MODELO: ESTUDIANTE 1: Hola, me llamo Gabriela y soy de Miami. ¿De dónde eres?
ESTUDIANTE 2: Hola, Gabriela. Me llamo Jason. Soy de Miami, también (*also*).

ESTUDIANTE 1: Hola, mi nombre es Gabriela y soy de Miami. ¿De dónde eres?
ESTUDIANTE 3: Buenos días, Gabriela. Me llamo Dana y soy de Atlanta.

¡Adiós!
Saying good-bye

 A. A ver: ¡Adiós!   Watch and listen as the people in the video say good-bye. How many times do you hear each expression? Which expression isn't used?

1. ____ Adiós.
2. ____ Chau chau.
3. ____ Hasta mañana.
4. ____ ¡Bye-bye!
5. ____ Hasta luego.
6. ____ Chau.

There are several ways to say good-bye in Spanish.

Adiós is commonly used throughout the Spanish-speaking world.

Chau (or **chau chau**) is used more in Latin America than in Spain and is commonly used among people who address each other informally (as **tú**).

Hasta luego literally means *Until later* but conveys the sense of *See you later* or *Until we meet again*. If you know when you will see the person again, you can give a specific time instead of **luego**.

Hasta mañana.	*See you tomorrow.*
Hasta el jueves.	*See you (on) Thursday.*
Hasta pronto.	*See you soon.*

B. Presentaciones (*Introductions*)

PASO 1.   Make a short list of expressions you would use to do the following. **¡Atención!** Don't forget that there are often several ways to say the same thing!

… say *Hello* in Spanish
… say what your name is
… ask another person what their name is
… express that you are pleased to meet someone
… ask someone how he or she is doing
… ask someone where he or she is from
… say where you are from
… say *good-bye* in Spanish

Dos amigos vestidos de Superhombre

 PASO 2.   Find a classmate you haven't yet met or whom you don't know very well, and use your list to have a conversation and get to know one another better.

 PASO 3.   Act out your conversation for the class.

¿Cómo se escribe?°

The Spanish alphabet and campus vocabulary

How do you spell . . . ?

(a)
el **a**ula

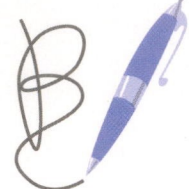
(be)
el **b**olígrafo

(ce)*
la **c**omputadora /
las **ci**encias

(de)
el **d**iccionario

(e)
el **e**scritorio

(efe)
la **f**ilosofía

(ge)*
la **g**raduación /
el **g**imnasio

(hache)
la **h**oja de papel

(i *or* i latina)
la **i**dea

(jota)
el **j**oven

(ka)
el **k**ilo

(ele)
el **l**ibro

(elle *or* doble, ele)†
la **ll**ave

(eme)
la **m**ochila

(ene)
los **n**úmeros

(eñe)
el a**ñ**o

(o)
la **o**ficina

(pe)
la **p**uerta

(cu)
la **q**uímica

(ere)
el **r**eloj

(erre *or* doble erre)†
la piza**rr**a

(ese)
la **s**illa

(te)
la **t**area

(u)
la **u**niversidad

(uve)
la **v**entana

(doble ve)
la página **w**eb

(equis)
el e**x**amen

(i griega *or* ye)
el pro**y**ector

(zeta)
el lápi**z**

---

*The letters **c** and **g** each have two examples because they are pronounced differently depending on which letters follow them. When followed by a consonant or the vowels **a, o,** or **u,** these letters make hard **c** and **g** sounds. The soft **c** and **g** sounds are followed by the vowels **e** or **i.**
†The clusters **ll** and **rr** are not actually letters of the Spanish alphabet, but they are included here because of their unique pronunciation.

A. El alfabeto español y las capitales   Each of the following sequences of letters spells the name of a capital city. Identify the city, then spell out its country's name. The map at the back of your book will help you.

> **MODELO:**   Ele - i - eme - a: Lima.
> Lima es la capital del Perú: pe - e - ere - u con acento.

1. eme - a - de - ere - i - de
2. ese - a - ene - te - i - a - ge - o
3. be - o - ge - o - te - a con acento
4. ce - a - ere - a - ce - a - ese
5. eme - a - ene - a - ge - u - a

B. A ver: ¿Cómo se escribe?

PASO 1.   Watch and listen as the following people spell their names, then match each photo with the correct name. **¡Atención!** One person uses the phrase **Mi nombre se deletrea…** , which is simply another way to say **Mi nombre se escribe…**

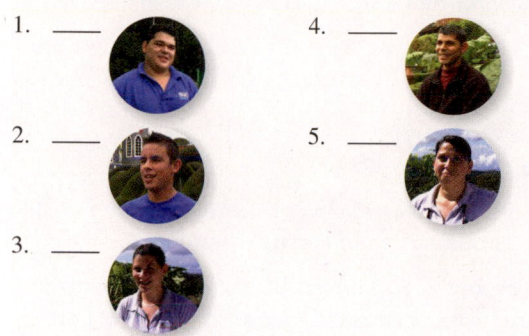

1. ___
2. ___
3. ___
4. ___
5. ___

a. Anlluly
b. Juan Andrés
c. Keylin*
d. Olman
e. William

PASO 2.   Watch and listen as the following people spell their names then write each name beside the corresponding photo.

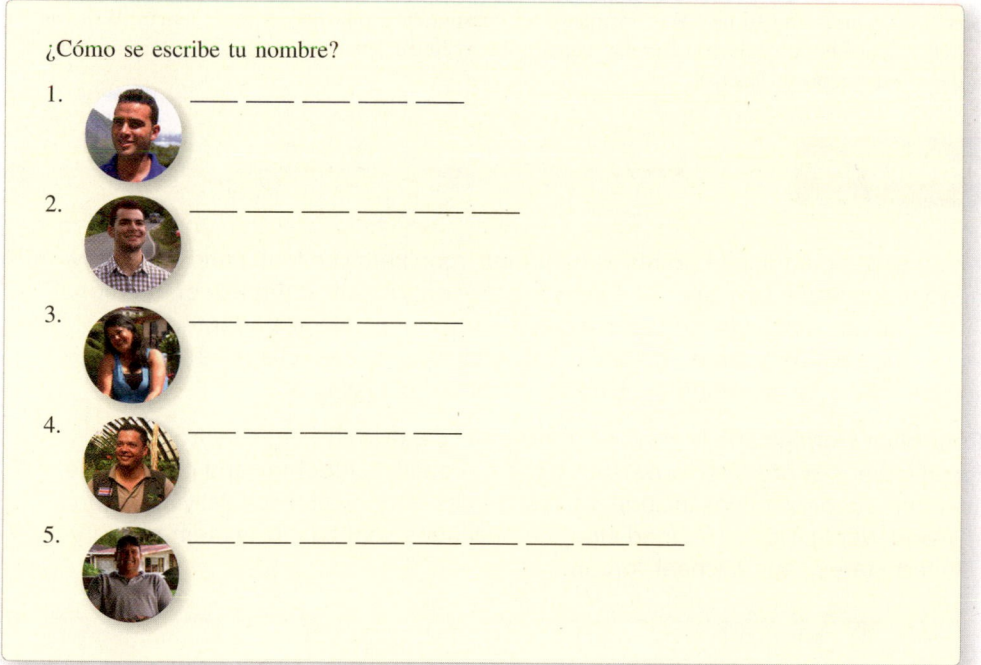

¿Cómo se escribe tu nombre?

1. ___ ___ ___ ___ ___ ___
2. ___ ___ ___ ___ ___ ___
3. ___ ___ ___ ___
4. ___ ___ ___ ___ ___
5. ___ ___ ___ ___ ___ ___ ___ ___

(Continues)

(Continues)

---

*When Keylin spells her name, she distinguishes between **y griega** and **i latina.** Many people use the term **i latina** to make it clear they are talking about **i** and not **y** (**y griega**).

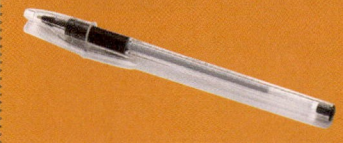

PASO 3. Working in small groups, take turns spelling your names out loud while the others write them down. Did everyone spell your name correctly?

> **MODELO:** Mi nombre es Ana: a-ene-a, y mi apellido (*last name*) es Peña: pe-e-eñe-a.

PASO 4. Working in small groups, spell out your email addresses (**direcciones de correo electrónico**) for each other. (See the **Vocabulario** box below for spelling tips.) Be sure to write down your classmates' addresses so you can contact each other about homework and other assignments. **¡Atención!** If you need to include numbers, look ahead to their vocabulary presentation in this chapter. Also, note that common domain names such as *com* and *edu* are normally pronounced as words rather than spelled out.

> **MODELO:** Mi dirección de correo electrónico es ache - o - ele - a - arroba - gmail - punto - com.

Vocabulario

Some important words and phrases for sharing your e-mail or web address in Spanish include:

> **arroba** = @
> **punto com** = .com
> **punto edu** = .edu
> **doble ve, doble ve, doble ve** (*or* **triple doble ve**) = www

As in English, many Spanish speakers choose to eliminate the "www" when giving a web address because it is generally understood as part of the address.

While the expression **email** is generally accepted by Spanish speakers (and pronounced mostly the same in Spanish), you will often hear the term **correo electrónico** (*electronic mail*) as well.

C. ¿Cómo se escribe... ? Meet and greet a new partner (*Hello!, How are you?, What is your name?,* and so on). Your instructor will assign each pair one or more letters. Write as many Spanish words as you can that contain the assigned letter(s). Finally, take turns spelling the words aloud in Spanish.

CONÉCTATE AL MUNDO HISPANO

Dominican baseball player Robinson Canó was named after his father's hero, baseball great Jackie Robinson.

When most people think of **nombres hispanos,** monikers like María and Juan may come to mind. While they are still common, in recent decades, the use of traditional Catholic names such as these has become less frequent. Names adopted from other languages are gaining popularity, though they are often changed to adapt to Spanish spelling conventions, such as Deivi instead of Davy.

La República Dominicana is known for this practice, drawing not only from the **santoral** (*calendar of saints' days*), but also from political ideology and pop culture. Some interesting examples include the first names Roosevelt (especially common after World War II), Usmail (named after the packages sent by family members in the United States), and Michael Jordan.

Vocabulario

Los meses y las estaciones
Months and seasons

A. Los meses y las estaciones   Match each month to the appropriate season, based on where you live.

marzo	agosto	mayo	febrero	abril	octubre
septiembre	diciembre	junio	noviembre	julio	enero

la primavera   el verano   el otoño   el invierno

B. El hemisferio norte (*northern*) y el hemisferio sur (*southern*)   For each of the following countries, tell whether it is located in the northern or southern hemisphere. **¡Atención!** Remember that the equator divides the two hemispheres.

1. México
2. Argentina
3. Venezuela
4. Costa Rica
5. España
6. Bolivia

C. Las estaciones en los dos hemisferios

 PASO 1.   You will hear the months of the year in Spanish. Write down the month and then add the appropriate season in the northern hemisphere: **primavera, verano, otoño, invierno.**

	MES	ESTACIÓN		MES	ESTACIÓN
1.	_____	_____	5.	_____	_____
2.	_____	_____	6.	_____	_____
3.	_____	_____	7.	_____	_____
4.	_____	_____	8.	_____	_____

PASO 2.   Now look at the months in **Paso 1** and say the corresponding season in the southern hemisphere. How would your daily life in those months be different if you lived in the southern hemisphere?

En español…

In Spanish, the months begin with a lower case letter, unlike English, where they begin with an upper case letter. You'll notice that this also applies to the days of the week and nationalities, which you'll see in **Capítulo 2.**

CONÉCTATE AL MUNDO HISPANO

About half of the world's Spanish-speaking countries are in the southern hemisphere and therefore have opposite seasons from the northern hemisphere. For example, when it's summer in Mexico, it's winter in Argentina and Chile.

■ The audio files for in-text listening activities are available in the eBook, within Connect Plus activities, and on the Online Learning Center.

Vocabulario

Los números y las fechas
Numbers and dates

0 **cero**			
1 **uno***	11 **once**	21 **veintiuno***	31 **treinta y uno***
2 **dos**	12 **doce**	22 **veintidós**	32 **treinta y dos**
3 **tres**	13 **trece**	23 **veintitrés**	33 **treinta y tres**
4 **cuatro**	14 **catorce**	24 **veinticuatro**	34 **treinta y cuatro**
5 **cinco**	15 **quince**	25 **veinticinco**	35 **treinta y cinco**
6 **seis**	16 **dieciséis**	26 **veintiséis**	36 **treinta y seis**
7 **siete**	17 **diecisiete**	27 **veintisiete**	37 **treinta y siete**
8 **ocho**	18 **dieciocho**	28 **veintiocho**	38 **treinta y ocho**
9 **nueve**	19 **diecinueve**	29 **veintinueve**	39 **treinta y nueve**
10 **diez**	20 **veinte**	30 **treinta**	40 **cuarenta**

...
50 **cincuenta**
60 **sesenta**
70 **setenta**
80 **ochenta**
90 **noventa**

Use **y** (*and*) to build any number between 31 and 99: **cuarenta y uno, setenta y cuatro, noventa y seis.**

A. ¿Cuántos?

PASO 1. Write the numerals as you hear them.

1. _____   3. _____   5. _____   7. _____   9. _____

2. _____   4. _____   6. _____   8. _____   10. _____

PASO 2. Tell how many of the specified unit there are in each of the following things.

MODELO: los días en septiembre:

Hay treinta días en septiembre.

1. los días en diciembre
2. los días en junio
3. los días en mayo
4. los segundos en un minuto
5. los minutos en una hora
6. los días en una semana (*week*)
7. las semanas en un año (*year*)
8. las letras en tu nombre (¿y cómo se deletrea?)

B. Las fechas
In Spanish, the day and month are written left to right, as one would say them. For instance, 7/6 in Spanish is the 7th of June (**el siete de junio**). Based on this information, how would you write numerically the 6th of July? _____

Look at the following images representative of important days and match them with their numerical date.

a. 17/3   b. 25/12   c. 14/2   d. 7/4   e. 4/7

1. _____   2. _____   3. _____   4. _____

Vocabulario

---

*When identifying the number of specific things, use **un** before something that ends with **-o** or **-os** (**un libro, treinta y un libros**) and **una** before something that ends with **-a** or **-as** (**una puerta, cuarenta y una sillas**). The reasons and variations for this will be explained in more detail in **Estructura 1.1.** Note the one-word form to indicate twenty-one of something (**veintiún meses, veintiuna semanas**).

C. Nuestro calendario

Working in pairs, take turns consulting the course syllabus and asking about important dates. Write them down and check each other's answers. Be sure to plan your studying, projects, and travel for the semester.

MODELO: ESTUDIANTE 1: ¿Cuál es la fecha del examen final?
ESTUDIANTE 2: Es el 7 de diciembre.

¿Cuál es la fecha

1. ...del primer (*first*) examen?
2. ...del primer día festivo (*holiday*) del semestre?
3. ...del primer día de vacaciones?
4. ...del último (*last*) día de vacaciones durante el semestre?
5. ...del último día de clase?
6. ...del examen final?

D. Mi número de teléfono

PASO 1. In groups, take turns introducing yourself and dictating your phone number. Write down the numbers of other group members.

MODELO: Buenos días. Me llamo Elena. Mi número de teléfono es el cuatro, cincuenta y seis, noventa y ocho, trece (456-9813).

PASO 2. Your instructor will give one group member a phone number on it—this is the only person who can look at the written number. The person with the number dictates it to a second person, the second to a third, and so on. The last person writes the number on the board. How many teams ended with the same number they started with?

E. Las tarjetas de presentación

Choose one of the identities shown on the business cards. Your partner will close his or her book while you introduce yourself, providing some of the information on your business card. When you've finished, check your partner's notes for accuracy, then switch roles.

MODELO: Me llamo Eva Pintor. Mi número de teléfono es el cincuenta y cinco - cincuenta y cuatro - treinta y tres - cincuenta y tres.

Vocabulario

In Spanish it is most common to divide the seven digits of telephone numbers into four groups: the single first digit followed by three groups of two. Note that the article **el** may be used before the first number.

—¿Cuál es tu número de teléfono?
—Es el cinco, cincuenta y cinco, ochenta y siete, sesenta y dos. (5-55-87-62)

Similar strategies are used in countries where telephone numbers have more or fewer digits.

Las Lupitas

Eva Pintor

Plaza Sta. Catarina No 4
Col. Barrio de Sta. Catarina
Coyoacán, México
55 54 33 53

El Centro Latino

Ben Balderas
Executive Director

110 West Main Street
Suite 2F
Carrboro, NC 27510

Phone: (919) 929-7633
Fax: (919) 929-7632
E-mail: bbccentol@bellsouth.net
www.elcentrolatino.org

Samuel Pérez "El Peseta"

SERVICIO TAXI
SI NO CONTESTO, MANDA 1 SMS   TLFNOS.: 618 054 501

Tete Depetris
Producción Audiovisual

Tel: 011-15-5523-4228
Exterior 0054-9-11-5523-4228
tetedepetris@gmail.com

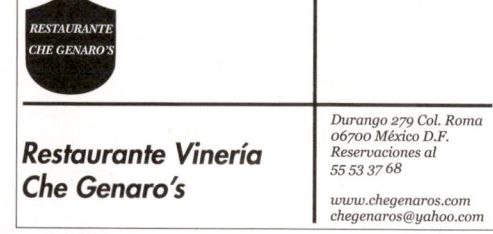

RESTAURANTE
CHE GENARO'S

**Restaurante Vinería
Che Genaro's**

Durango 279 Col. Roma
06700 México D.F.
Reservaciones al
55 53 37 68

www.chegenaros.com
chegenaros@yahoo.com

COMUN VOCABUL **ESTRUCTURA** ATE

■ Answers to these activities are in Appendix 2 at the back of your book.

¿Por qué?

Why do Spanish and hundreds of other languages divide their nouns up into different genders? One main reason is that gender on nouns makes it easier for our brains to process speech. As we listen to language spoken to us, our brains are constantly trying to predict what the next word or syllable will be. When we hear an article with gender like **el** or **la,** this gives our brains an important clue about what the next word will be, and this leads to quicker and more efficient processing of the incoming message. This efficiency is a big advantage, and it helps explain why so many languages in the world have gender on nouns.

■ For more tips on determining the gender of nouns that end in letters other than **-o** or **-a,** see **Para saber más** (*To find out more*) **1.1** at the back of your book.

1.1 Un lápiz en la mochila

Singular nouns and articles

Para empezar (*To start*)...

Which of the following items might you expect to find in a backpack?

☐ **un** bolígrafo   ☐ **un** escritorio   ☐ **una** puerta

☐ **una** computadora   ☐ **un** libro   ☐ **una** silla

☐ **un** diccionario   ☐ **una** mesa

Actividades analíticas

1 Words such as **computadora, diccionario, libro,** and **mesa** are *nouns* (**sustantivos**). The words **un** and **una,** like the English words *a* and *an*, are *indefinite articles* (**artículos indefinidos**). Based on the pattern that you see in **Para empezar,** choose the appropriate indefinite article for each noun.

UN	UNA	
☐	☐	mochila
☐	☐	gimnasio
☐	☐	año
☐	☐	pizarra

2 Nouns in Spanish are classified by *gender* (**género**). Those that use **un** are called *masculine* (**masculino**), and those that use **una** are *feminine* (**femenino**). As a general rule of thumb, nouns that end in **-o** are masculine and those that end in **-a** are feminine. Do all the nouns in **Para empezar** obey this generalization?

Sí ☐   No ☐

3 More than 90% of the nouns that end in **-o** or **-a** have the gender that you would expect, but you will occasionally run into nouns that don't.

un día   *a day*   **una** mano   *a hand*

With nouns that end in letters other than **-o** or **-a**, some are masculine and some are feminine.

un reloj   *a clock*   **una** universidad   *a university*

The article or other surrounding words can tell you the gender of the noun.

En español...

For most nouns, the gender is unrelated to the noun's meaning. That is, some words (such as **libro** [*book*]) are masculine and others (such as **mesa** [*table*]) are feminine even though there is nothing inherently masculine or feminine about the nouns. With other nouns, however, the gender corresponds to the biological or natural gender (**género natural**) of the object being described. For example, **un hombre** (*man*) is masculine and **una mujer** (*woman*) is feminine.

4 Spanish also uses *definite articles* (**artículos definidos**), which function like English *the*. These also have a separate form for each gender.

	masculino	femenino
artículos definidos	el	la
	el libro *the book*	la mesa *the table*
artículos indefinidos	un	una
	un libro *a book*	una mesa *a table*

Actividades prácticas

A. En la clase   Look at the image of the classroom and respond in complete sentences to the questions that follow.

> **MODELO:**   ¿Hay una puerta en el salón de clase?
> Sí, hay una puerta.
> ¿Hay un proyector en el salón de clase?
> No, no hay un proyector.

1. ¿Hay un reloj en el salón de clase?
2. ¿Hay un profesor en el salón de clase?
3. ¿Hay una pizarra en el salón de clase?
4. ¿Hay una mesa en el salón de clase?
5. ¿Hay una mochila en el salón de clase?
6. ¿Hay una puerta en el salón de clase?
7. ¿Hay un libro en el salón de clase?

B. Categorías

PASO 1. Write the indefinite article (**un** or **una**) before each noun in column **A**.

<table>
<tr><td>**A**</td><td>**B**</td></tr>
<tr><td>1. ____ número ____</td><td>a. *Conéctate*</td></tr>
<tr><td>2. ____ bolígrafo ____</td><td>b. arquitectura</td></tr>
<tr><td>3. ____ computadora ____</td><td>c. enero</td></tr>
<tr><td>4. ____ mes ____</td><td>d. dieciséis</td></tr>
<tr><td>5. ____ materia ____</td><td>e. Yale</td></tr>
<tr><td>6. ____ universidad ____</td><td>f. Mac</td></tr>
<tr><td>7. ____ libro ____</td><td>g. Bic</td></tr>
</table>

PASO 2. Match each item in column **B** to the correct category in **A**.

C. Más categorías

PASO 1. Write the definite article (**el** or **la**) for each of the following nouns.

1. ____ otoño
2. ____ economía
3. ____ primavera
4. ____ historia

5. ____ profesor de la clase
6. ____ verano
7. ____ profesora de la clase
8. ____ química

PASO 2. Using **es** (*is*), say whether each of the above items is **una estación del año, un hombre, una materia,** or **una mujer.**

> **MODELO:** El otoño es una estación del año.

D. ¡Adivina! (*Guess!*) Working with a partner, try to guess what is in his/her backpack using the vocabulary you learned in this chapter. How many of your guesses are correct?

> **MODELO:** ESTUDIANTE 1: ¿Hay un teléfono?
> ESTUDIANTE 2: ¡Sí!

1.2 Los estudiantes y la universidad

Plural nouns and articles

Para empezar...

How many of each of the following can you find in this picture?

■ Answers to these activities are in Appendix 2 at the back of your book.

1. ____ libros
2. ____ mochilas

3. ____ borradores (*erasers*)
4. ____ mujeres

5. ____ hombres
6. ____ relojes

Actividades analíticas

1 All of the nouns in **Para empezar** have a *plural ending* (**una terminación plural**): **-s** or **-es**. Place the singular form of each of these nouns into the appropriate column here, depending on which ending it takes.

-s	-es
hombre	_____
_____	_____
_____	reloj

When you're finished, take a look at the two columns. How are the words in these two columns different? What pattern can you detect? See if you can formulate a hypothesis about pluralization before you read the next grammar segment, because you may be on the right track already.

2 There is a simple rule that determines which plural ending a noun takes: If the noun ends in a vowel (**una vocal**), it takes **-s**, and if it ends in any consonant (**una consonante**), it takes **-es**.

Use this rule to create the plural form of these nouns.

singular	plural
estudiante	_____
mes	_____
universidad	_____
bolígrafo	_____

3 For nouns that end in **-z**, change the **-z** to **-c** and add **-es.**

singular	plural
lápiz	_____
luz (*light*)	_____

4 The definite and indefinite articles also come in both singular and plural forms.

	masculino	femenino
artículos definidos		
singular	el	la
plural	los	las
artículos indefinidos		
singular	un	una
plural	unos	unas

Which definite articles would you use for these words?

_____ lápiz   _____ computadoras   _____ escritorios   _____ mochila

Which indefinite articles would you use for these words?

_____ gimnasio   _____ sillas   _____ pizarra   _____ bolígrafos

En español…

The plural indefinite articles are equivalent to *some* in English.

unos estudiantes
some students
unas mochilas
some backpacks
unos relojes
some clocks/watches

Actividades prácticas

A. ¡Escucha bien!   Listen to the plural nouns and write down how many there are in your classroom. If there is only one, use **un** or **una** and change the noun to singular.

> **MODELO:**   You hear: *estudiantes*
> You write: *Hay veinticinco estudiantes.*
>
> You hear: *escritorios*
> You write: *Hay un escritorio.*

1. _____
2. _____
3. _____
4. _____

5. _____
6. _____
7. _____
8. _____

B. Categorías

PASO 1.   Write the appropriate definite article (**los** or **las**) for the items in column **A,** then complete the lists in column **B,** if necessary. Finally, match the items in column **A** with the lists in column **B.**

A

1. _____ estaciones del año _____ en el hemisferio norte
2. _____ meses del verano _____ en el hemisferio norte
3. _____ números del uno al (*to*) cinco _____
4. _____ edificios (*buildings*) del campus _____
5. _____ materias de ciencias _____

B

a. uno, dos, tres, _____, _____
b. el gimnasio, la biblioteca (*library*),
   _____
   _____
c. la biología, la física, la química
d. la primavera, el verano, _____,
   _____
e. junio, _____, _____

PASO 2.   Write the appropriate indefinite article (**un, una, unos,** or **unas**) for each category in **A**, then choose the item(s) in **B** that go with each category in **A.**

A

1. _____ mujeres: _____, _____
2. _____ año: _____
3. _____ hombres: _____, _____
4. _____ universidad: _____
5. _____ número de teléfono: _____
6. _____ materias: _____, _____, _____

B

a. Salma Hayek
b. filosofía
c. Mario Vargas Llosa
d. Notre Dame
e. 1492
f. literatura
g. Cristina Fernández de Kirchner
h. química
i. Diego Luna
j. 735-394-9065

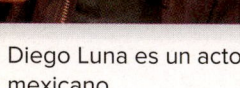

Diego Luna es un actor mexicano.

C. ¿Cuáles son las diferencias?   Working with a partner, create two lists. In one, write sentences saying what image A (**dibujo A**) and image B (**dibujo B**) have in common. In the other, write sentences saying how they are different. Begin your sentences with **hay** (*there is/are*), and mention these people and objects: **puerta(s), ventana(s), escritorio(s), estudiante(s), profesor(es), computadora(s), reloj(es), pizarra(s), hombre(s), mujer(es).**

MODELOS: En dibujo A y dibujo B, hay un profesor.
En dibujo A, hay una pizarra, pero (*but*) en dibujo B, hay dos pizarras.

Dibujo A

Dibujo B

1.3   Son estudiantes. Tienen mochilas.

The verbs *ser* (to be) and *tener* (to have)

Para empezar...

Find the best ending for each incomplete sentence. The first is done for you.

1. Los estudiantes __e__
2. Un libro ____
3. Juanes y Shakira ____
4. Zoe Saldaña y América Ferrera ____
5. Enero ____
6. Octubre ____
7. Un año ____
8. Los diccionarios ____

a. **es** un mes de otoño.
b. **son** de los Estados Unidos.
c. **tiene** doce meses.
d. **tienen** las definiciones de muchas palabras (*words*).
e. **tienen** mochilas, bolígrafos, libros y cuadernos (*notebooks*).
f. **tiene** páginas (*pages*).
g. **es** un mes de invierno en el hemisferio norte.
h. **son** de Colombia.

■ Answers to these activities are in Appendix 2 at the back of your book.

América Ferrera es de Los Ángeles.

En español...

Actividades analíticas

1 In **Para empezar,** you saw some forms of the verbs **ser** (*to be*) and **tener** (*to have*). You may have noticed that the form of the verb changes depending on what the subject is. Use the forms from **Para empezar** to complete this chart.

	ser	tener
yo (*I*)	soy	tengo
tú (*you* [*informal, singular*])	eres	tienes
él/ella, usted (*he/she, you* [*formal*])	_____	_____
nosotros/nosotras (*we* [*masculine/feminine*])	somos	tenemos
vosotros/vosotras* (*you* [*informal, plural, m./f.*])	sois	tenéis
ellos/ellas, ustedes (*they* [*m./f.*], *you* [*formal, plural*])	_____	_____

You will see that the conjugation of **ser** in particular shows many changes from form to form. Keep in mind that this verb has irregularities in English, as well: *I am,* You *are,* He/She *is* . . . .

2 The conjugations in **Parte 1** list the verb forms according to the pronoun (**el pronombre**) that corresponds to the subject. This pronoun is often not used, however, since the verb form itself frequently makes the subject clear.

Soy de los Estados Unidos.	*I am from the United States.*
¿Eres estudiante?	*Are you a student?*
Somos de Canadá.	*We are from Canada.*
Tengo un amigo de Venezuela.	*I have a friend from Venezuela.*
¿Tienes libros en la mochila?	*Do you have books in the backpack?*
Tenemos una profesora del Perú.	*We have a teacher from Peru.*

3 **Usted** uses the same verb form as do **él** and **ella.** If you were speaking to someone more formally, then, how would you say the following?

(**INFORMAL, TÚ**)

a. ¿De dónde eres?
¿Tienes un lápiz?

(**FORMAL, USTED**)

b. ¿De dónde _____ usted?
¿_____ usted un lápiz?

Actividades prácticas

A. Preguntas y respuestas For each question, choose the best answer and write its letter in the corresponding space. The first is done for you. **¡Atención!** Questions with **tú** are always addressed to a single person, while those with **ustedes** are to a group.

Preguntas	Respuestas
1. ¿Tienes amigos en la clase? __b__	a. No, soy de los Estados Unidos.
2. ¿De dónde eres? _____	b. Sí, tengo dos. Son Melissa y Steve.
3. ¿De dónde son Uds.? _____	c. No, es de España.
4. ¿Tienen un diccionario? _____	d. Sí, tengo una Mac.
5. ¿Tienes una computadora? _____	e. Somos de Paraguay.
6. ¿Penélope Cruz es de México? _____	f. Sí, tenemos dos.
7. ¿Eres de Canadá? _____	g. Soy de Costa Rica.

*****Vosotros** and **vosotras** are informal plural forms of *you,* and are used only in Spain. Latin America uses **ustedes** for both formal and informal plural *you.*

B. ¿De dónde eres?

PASO 1.   Ask as many of your classmates as possible where they're from. Keep track of the answers by writing down their names grouped according to the part of your city or country that they are from. If you don't know your classmates' names, you will need to ask them.

> **MODELO:**   ESTUDIANTE 1: ¿Cómo te llamas? ¿De dónde eres?
> *or*   ¿Cómo se llama? ¿De dónde es?
> ESTUDIANTE 2: Me llamo Marisa. Soy de Atlanta.

PASO 2.   Tell the class where your classmates are from.

> **MODELO:**   ESTUDIANTE 1: Mis compañeros son de Colorado y de Utah.
> ESTUDIANTE 2: Son de Atlanta.

> **MODELO:**   Somos de Nebraska.

 C. Gente famosa (*Famous people*)   How well do you know these Spanish-speaking celebrities? With a partner, alternate asking each other questions about where they are from. **¡Atención!** When asking about one person, use the singular form **es.** When asking about a group, use **son.** If you don't know the answer, say **no sé** (*I don't know*).

> **MODELO:**   ESTUDIANTE 1: ¿De dónde es Rafael Nadal?
> ESTUDIANTE 2: Es de España. (No sé.)

1. Javier Bardem y Penélope Cruz
2. Gael García Bernal y Salma Hayek
3. Lionel Messi
4. Daddy Yankee
5. Juanes y Shakira
6. Rosario Dawson y Jennifer López

Lionel Messi juega en el equipo nacional de su país (*country*). ¿Sabes (*Do you know*) de dónde es?

D. ¿Qué tienes?

PASO 1.   Check off those items in the list that you have with you in class today.

	YO	MI COMPAÑERO/A
1. un bolígrafo	☐	☐
2. una computadora	☐	☐
3. un cuaderno	☐	☐
4. un lápiz	☐	☐
5. un reloj	☐	☐
6. un teléfono	☐	☐

 PASO 2.   Ask a partner whether he or she has each of these items, and complete the chart in Paso 1.

> **MODELO:**   ESTUDIANTE 1: ¿Tienes un bolígrafo?
> ESTUDIANTE 2: Sí, tengo un bolígrafo. (No, no tengo un bolígrafo.)

Puerto Rico   **los Estados Unidos**

E. Cultura: La vida bilingüe en los Estados Unidos y Puerto Rico

PASO 1. Read the following text about the United States and Puerto Rico.

Puerto Rico… ¿Es un país[a]? ¿O es una parte de los Estados Unidos? En realidad Puerto Rico se llama «el Estado Libre Asociado de Puerto Rico». Es un territorio no incorporado de los Estados Unidos con estatus de autogobierno.[b]

Pero en los Estados Unidos, las personas hablan inglés[c] y en Puerto Rico hablan español, ¿no? La verdad[d] es que[e] en los dos países hay muchas personas bilingües y cada[f] día hay más. En los dos países, hay personas que hablan un idioma[g] en la casa y toman[h] clases para estudiar otro idioma.

Hay muchas palabras en el español de Puerto Rico que tienen influencia del inglés. Por ejemplo,[i] una persona puede decir[j] «No te panikees» for *Don't panic*. Otros anglicismos son **parquear** (*to park*), **gufear** (*to goof around*) y **hanguear** (*to hang out*). ¿Sabes[k] algunas palabras en inglés que son del español?

[a]*country*   [b]*estatus… self-governing status*   [c]*hablan… speak English*   [d]*truth*   [e]*that*   [f]*each*   [g]*language*   [h]*take*
[i]*Por… For example*   [j]*puede… can say*   [k]*Do you know*

PASO 2. Indicate whether the following statements are true (**cierto**) or false (**falso**), according to information presented in the reading.

	CIERTO	FALSO
1. Hay personas en los Estados Unidos que hablan español.	☐	☐
2. Hay muchas personas bilingües en Puerto Rico.	☐	☐
3. Cada día hay menos (*fewer*) personas bilingües en los Estados Unidos.	☐	☐
4. Puerto Rico es un estado de los Estados Unidos.	☐	☐
5. En Puerto Rico, los estudiantes toman clases de inglés.	☐	☐

PASO 3. With a partner, answer the following questions and discuss the ideas behind your responses.

1. ¿Por qué (*Why*) hablan inglés en los Estados Unidos y español en Puerto Rico?
2. ¿Cuáles son los cuatro idiomas europeos que ahora hablan más (*the most*) en América (*the Americas*)?
3. ¿Qué otras partes de los Estados Unidos fueron (*were*) colonias españolas? ¿Hay huellas (*traces*) de esto todavía (*still*)?

San Juan, la ciudad capital de Puerto Rico

1.4 Nuestra (*Our*) clase de español
Possessive adjectives

Para empezar...

Choose the appropriate response for each question, then provide the information needed to complete the answer.

Preguntas	Respuestas
1. ____ ¿Cómo se llama **nuestra** universidad?	a. **Nuestro** libro de español se llama ____.
2. ____ ¿Cómo se llama **nuestro** profesor / **nuestra** profesora de español?	b. **Nuestro** profesor / **Nuestra** profesora de español se llama ____.
3. ____ ¿Cómo se llama **nuestro** libro de español?	c. **Mis** (*My*) otras clases son ____.
4. ____ ¿Cuáles son **tus** (*your*) otras clases?	d. **Nuestra** universidad se llama ____.
5. ____ ¿Cuál es **tu** clase favorita?	e. **Mi** clase favorita es ____.

■ Answers to these activities are in Appendix 2 at the back of your book.

Actividades analíticas

1 Possessive adjectives (**adjetivos posesivos**), such as **mi** and **nuestro**, show who possesses a noun. Using what you saw in **Para empezar**, complete this chart of possessive adjectives.

____(s)	*my*	**nuestro(s)/____(s)**	*our*	
____(s)	*your* (informal, singular)	**vuestro(s)/vuestra(s)**	*your* (informal, plural, Spain)	
su(s)	*your* (formal, singular), *his/her*	**su(s)**	*your* (formal, plural), *their*	

2 The ending **-s** is added to any possessive adjective when it is used with a plural noun.

mis amigos	*my friends*
tus teléfonos	*your* (informal, singular) *telephones*
sus bolígrafos	*his/her, your* (formal, singular and plural), *their pens*

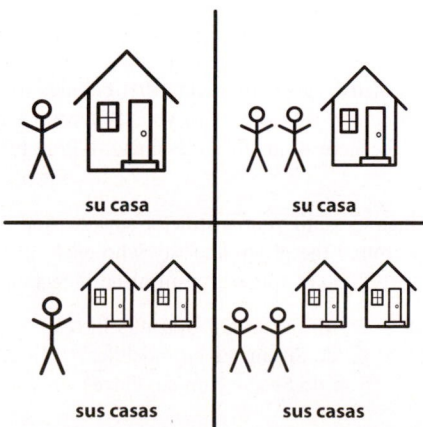

su casa su casa

sus casas sus casas

You may think of possessive adjectives as consisting of two parts: the beginning agrees with the owner, and the ending agrees with the possession.

(*Continues*)

En español...

The subject pronoun **tú** is spelled with an accent mark and the possessive adjective **tu** is not.

Tú eres mi amigo.
You are my friend.

Tu profesora es de Colombia.
Your teacher is from Colombia.

Similarly, the subject pronoun **él** is spelled with an accent mark, but the definite article **el** is not.

Él es mi compañero de clase.
He is my classmate.

Tengo **el** libro.
I have the book.

When using **nuestro(s)/nuestra(s)** and **vuestro(s)/vuestra(s),** the ending of the possessive must show agreement with the gender (masculine/feminine) and number (singular/plural) of the noun that follows it.

nuestros profesores	*our teachers*
nuestra clase	*our class*
vuestras mochilas	*your* (informal, plural, Spain) *backpacks*

Actividades prácticas

A. Mis cosas

PASO 1. Check off all of the objects in the **yo** column that you have with you. If you have more than one of any item, add **-s** to the possessive and the noun. Then see how many objects your partner has and add **-s** where appropriate in the **mi compañero/a** column.

YO	MI COMPAÑERO/A
☐ mi____ computadora____	☐ su____ computadora____
☐ mi____ libro____	☐ su____ libro____
☐ mi____ llave____	☐ su____ llave____
☐ mi____ teléfono____	☐ su____ teléfono____

PASO 2. For each item that both you and your partner have, answer the question **¿Cuál pesa más?** (*Which weighs more?*) by comparing both, and then indicating the heavier one.

MODELO: Mi computadora pesa más.

B. Nuestro salón de clase (*classroom*)   Working with a partner, make a list of five objects that are an integral part of your classroom, preceding each with the correct form of **nuestro(s)/nuestra(s).** One item is partially done for you.

1. nuestr____ pizarra
2. _____
3. _____
4. _____
5. _____

C. ¡Una prueba!   Give your partner a vocabulary quiz! Point to an object or objects in his or her possession and ask **¿Es tu ____?** for something singular or **¿Son tus ____?** for something plural. Use the wrong word sometimes and see if your partner can catch you.

MODELOS: ESTUDIANTE 1: ¿Es tu lápiz?
ESTUDIANTE 2: Sí, es mi lápiz.

ESTUDIANTE 1: ¿Son tus libros?
ESTUDIANTE 2: No, ¡son mis bolígrafos!

D. ¿De quién es?

PASO 1. Working in groups of five, give something that belongs to you, such as your backpack or your keys, to the person sitting next to you. Tell your neighbor what the object is. Now your neighbor will pass the item to another classmate, telling him/her who it belongs to and what it is.

PASO 2. Continue in this manner until your instructor says to stop. You should now be holding someone else's object(s). Go around the group and say who each object belongs to. Did the message get transmitted properly? Don't forget to return the objects to their owners!

MODELO: ESTUDIANTE 1: Es mi mochila. / Son mis llaves.
ESTUDIANTE 2: Es de Susan. Es su mochila. /
Son de Susan. Son sus llaves.

¡Leamos!

Tu puerta° al mundo   *doorway*

Antes de leer (*Before reading*)

The following reading is an advertisement for the **Universidad del Valle de México.** Looking at the visual cues, what do you think the heading **Tu puerta al mundo** means?

_____ Your window to Paris   _____ Your door to the world   _____ Your big door

A leer (*Start reading*)

Read the advertisement from **la Universidad del Valle de México** and answer questions 1–6.

1. _____ La UVM quiere atraer a (*wants to attract*)…
   a. estudiantes.   b. familias.   c. profesores.   d. turistas.

Tu puerta al mundo.

La UVM te abre la puerta al mundo para enfrentar los retos de la globalización, ya que es la única Universidad Global de México porque forma parte integral de *Laureate International Universities*, la red de universidades más importante del mundo.

- **Preparatoria**
- **Preparatoria Bicultural**

- **Licenciaturas**
  - Administración de Empresas
  - Administración de Empresas Turísticas
  - Arquitectura
  - Ciencias de la Comunicación
  - Comercio Internacional
  - Contaduría Pública y Finanzas
  - Derecho
  - Diseño de la Moda e Industria del Vestido
  - Diseño Gráfico
  - Diseño Industrial
  - Ingeniería Industrial y de Sistemas
  - Ingeniería Mecatrónica
  - Mercadotecnia
  - Negocios Gastronómicos
  - Psicología
  - Relaciones Internacionales

- **Maestrías**

- **Licenciaturas Ejecutivas**

Llámanos al
01800-888-6010 o visítanos:
www.saltillo.uvmet.edu

Campus Saltillo
Tels.: (01 844) 4 85 17 86 al 89
En el D.F. y 13 estados más
www.uvmnet.edu

La única Universidad Global de México

■ Have you ever wondered what it would be like to study abroad and live with a host family? *Practice Spanish: Study Abroad* is an immersive, 3-D, virtual game in which you take on the role of a foreign exchange student in Colombia. You will interact in Spanish with your host family, local residents, and students from around the world while you problem-solve, communicate, and navigate through a variety of fun and engaging cultural scenarios and adventures. You might even forget you are practicing Spanish! Access the first Quest for free on *Connect* or at MHPractice.com.

(*Continues*)

2. _____ ¿Qué tipo de universidad es la UVM?
   a. científica   b. doméstica   c. global   d. psicológica

3. _____ La estudiante en la foto quiere estudiar (*wants to study*) en...
   a. Buenos Aires.   b. Nueva York.   c. París.   d. Roma.

4. ¿En cuántas materias se ofrecen licenciaturas (*undergraduate degrees*) en la UVM? _____

5. ¿Cuál es el número de teléfono que debemos llamar (*we should call*) para saber más (*to find out more*) sobre este programa? _____

6. ¿Cuál es la dirección de internet URL que debemos visitar para saber más sobre el programa?
   _____

En español...

American students often want to know how to say *What's your major?* in Spanish. While you can translate it directly as **¿Cuál es tu carrera?,** it is more common to ask **¿Qué estudias?** (*What do you study?*).

Después de leer (*After reading*)

PASO 1. Make a chart to say what you study, where you study for your classes, and where you would like to study abroad, if given the opportunity. Besides the Spanish-speaking countries you have learned, some other popular countries for study abroad include **Alemania** (*Germany*), **Australia, Brasil, China, Francia, Irlanda, Italia, Japón,** and **el Reino Unido** (*United Kingdom*).

   MODELO:

Nombre	¿Qué estudias?	¿Dónde estudias para tus clases?	Quiero viajar a (*I want to travel to*)...
Gustavo	ciencias políticas	la biblioteca, la residencia (*dorm*)	Bolivia, Ecuador, Perú

PASO 2. Pass your chart along to a classmate and, in turn, fill in your own information on your fellow students' sheets as they come your way. When your own chart comes back to you, read the information provided by all other students. If you think you have found a match (someone with similar academic interests, study habits, and travel interests), find that person and stand up together. How many students found a match?

CONÉCTATE AL MUNDO HISPANO...

When you think about studying abroad, you probably imagine students from the United States or Canada going to Europe, Latin America, or Asia. Consider that students from other countries also travel around the globe. Students from Latin America may go to Europe, European students may travel to Asia, Asian students may be interested in studying in North America, and so forth.

As you study a foreign language, it is important to think of things from the perspective of other people. Americans often think of the word *immigrant,* for instance, as referring to people coming into the United States, but in the Spanish-speaking world, there have been many immigrants from Japan to Peru, or from Italy to Argentina. More recently, there have been many immigrants from China to Spain and from Honduras to Mexico.

¡Escuchemos!

¿De dónde son?

 ## Antes de escuchar (*listening*)

Work in pairs to make a list of all the Spanish-speaking countries you know. Then combine your list with that of another group. Together, see if you can sort the countries by the region of the world: **África, Centroamérica, el Caribe, Europa, Norteamérica, Sudamérica.** Finally, listen to the names of the various countries and write down the ones you missed.

 ## A escuchar

Watch and listen as the following people tell you their names and where they're from. Complete the sentences to tell which country each person is from.

1.

   Juan Péndola _____.

2.

   Santiago Mariscal _____.

3.

   Andrea Suárez _____.

4.

   Sabrina Vélez _____.

5.

   Hérley Alegría González _____.

Después de escuchar

Look at the map at the back of the book and name the capital of each country mentioned in **A escuchar.** Then say in which hemisphere (northern or southern) that country is located. What season is it there now?

MODELO: Juan Péndola es de Chile. Santiago es la capital de Chile. Chile está en el hemisferio sur. Ahora en Chile es… (*the season depends on time of year you respond to this question*).

¡Escribamos!

La información de contacto

On the first day of class, you might have filled out an information card for your instructor. It's also a good idea to get some contact information from classmates so you can communicate outside of class.

Antes de escribir (*writing*)

Use the images to help you write the questions you will have to ask to elicit the information needed to complete **A escribir.**

1. ¿_____ _____
   _____?

2. ¿ Cuál es la _____
   de tu cumpleaños
   (*birthday*)?

3. ¿Cuál es tu dirección
   de _____
   _____?

4. ¿Qué _____
   tomas (*do you take*)?

5. ¿Cuál es tu _____
   _____ _____?

 ### A escribir

Ask and answer three classmates' questions to complete the contact sheets provided. Don't peek at each other's sheet.

MODELO: ESTUDIANTE 1: ¿Cómo te llamas?
              ESTUDIANTE 2: Me llamo Marcos.

              ESTUDIANTE 1: ¿Cómo se escribe?
              ESTUDIANTE 2: Eme - a - ere - ce - o - ese.

              ESTUDIANTE 1: ¿Eme - a - ere - ce - o - ese?
              ESTUDIANTE 2: ¡Sí!

	ESTUDIANTE 1	ESTUDIANTE 2	ESTUDIANTE 3
Nombre			
Número de teléfono			
Correo electrónico			
Clases			
Cumpleaños			

Después de escribir

In your groups, compare your contact lists and check your own contact information on your classmates' lists for accuracy. Are your first and last names spelled correctly? Are all necessary numbers, including area codes, included for the phone numbers? Is your e-mail address correct and does it include the **arroba** and at least one **punto**?

☐ nombre correcto   ☐ la dirección de correo electrónico correcta

☐ número de teléfono correcto

¡Hablemos!

Una charla°   *A chat*

Antes de hablar (*speaking*)

In groups, make a list of all the questions you have learned so far. Use the vocabulary list at the end of the chapter if you need help coming up with more questions.

A hablar

Now, in the same groups, create the longest conversation you can with the expressions you have learned so far. One student should start by asking a question of the person on his or her left. That person should answer the question and then ask another question of the person to his or her left, continuing clockwise around the circle until the group is unable to come up with any more questions. Include as many of the expressions you learned in this chapter as possible. Have someone keep track of how many questions were asked in your group.

Después de hablar

Which group came up with the longest conversation? Try to recreate it for the rest of the class.

Conéctate a la música

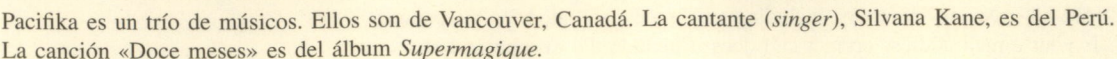

Canción (*Song*): «Doce meses» (2010)
Artista: Pacifika (Canadá)

Pacifika es un trío de músicos. Ellos son de Vancouver, Canadá. La cantante (*singer*), Silvana Kane, es del Perú. La canción «Doce meses» es del álbum *Supermagique*.

Antes de escuchar

What do you associate with each season? Does it depend on the weather? Write whether each of the following items is a season or a month.

	¿ESTACIÓN O MES?
diciembre	_____
verano	_____
abril	_____
otoño	_____

■ For copyright reasons, the songs referenced in **Conéctate a la música** have not been provided by the publisher. The video for this song can be found on YouTube, and it is available for purchase at the iTunes store.

A escuchar

First read through the phrases below, then listen to the song "**Doce meses**." You won't understand the meaning of every word, but pay attention to the names of seasons and months that you recognize. Match each month with the actions that occur in that month.

1. enero _____
2. febrero _____
3. abril _____
4. mayo, junio, julio _____
5. septiembre _____
6. octubre _____
7. noviembre _____
8. diciembre _____

a. ...abrí (*I opened*) mi ventana...
b. ...cantan (*sing*) los pajaritos (*little birds*)...
c. ...mandaste (*you sent*) flores...
d. ...no estás en mi mente...
e. ...perdí la mente (*I lost my mind*)...
f. ...sentí (*I felt*) tus besos (*kisses*)...
g. ...te conocí (*I met you*) por el parque...
h. ...te perseguí (*I pursued you*)...

Después de escuchar

Which statement best summarizes the song?

a. _____ Después de doce meses, la cantante está contenta (*happy*) porque está enamorada (*in love*).
b. _____ Después de doce meses, la cantante está triste (*sad*) porque perdió (*lost*) su amor (*love*).

VOCABULARIO

Comunicación

¡Hola!	Hello!
Buenos días. / Buen día.	Good morning.
Buenas tardes.	Good afternoon/ evening.
Buenas noches.	Good evening/night.
¿Cómo te llamas? / ¿Cómo se llama?	What is your name? (*informal/formal*)
Me llamo / Mi nombre es...	My name is . . .
¿Y tú? / ¿Y usted?	And you? (*informal/formal*)
Mucho gusto.	Nice to meet you.
Igualmente.	Likewise.
¿Cómo estás? / ¿Cómo está?	How are you? (*informal/formal*)
¿Qué tal?	How's it going?
¿Qué te pasa? / ¿Qué le pasa?	What's happening with you? / What's the matter? (*informal/formal*)
(Muy) bien.	(Very) well.
Más o menos.	OK.
(Muy) mal.	(Very) bad.
Gracias.	Thank you.
¿De dónde eres? / ¿De dónde es?	Where are you from? (*informal/formal*)
Soy de...	I am from . . .
¿Dónde vives? / ¿Dónde vive?	Where do you live? (*informal/formal*)
Vivo en ... + *place*	I live in . . . + *place*
¡Adiós!	Good-bye!
Chau.	Good-bye.
Hasta luego.	See you later.
Hasta mañana / el jueves.	See you tomorrow / (on) Thursday.
Hasta pronto.	See you soon.

Los meses y las estaciones / The months and the seasons

el año	year
las estaciones	seasons
la primavera	spring
el verano	summer
el otoño	autumn, fall
el invierno	winter

los meses: enero, febrero, marzo, abril, mayo, junio, julio, agosto, septiembre, octubre, noviembre, diciembre

Los números y las fechas / Numbers and dates

cero, uno, dos, tres, cuatro, cinco, seis, siete, ocho, nueve, diez, once, doce, trece, catorce, quince, dieciséis, diecisiete, dieciocho, diecinueve, veinte, veintiuno, veintidós, veintitrés, veinticuatro, veinticinco, veintiséis, veintisiete, veintiocho, veintinueve, treinta, treinta y uno... , cuarenta, cuarenta y dos, cincuenta, sesenta, setenta, ochenta, noventa

¿Cuál es la fecha de hoy?	What is today's date?
el día	day
Hoy es...	Today is . . .
el primero de mayo.	the first of May.
el cinco de noviembre.	November fifth.

En la universidad / At the university

el amigo / la amiga	friend
el aula	classroom
la biblioteca	library
el bolígrafo	pen
el borrador	eraser
la cosa	thing
el cuaderno	notebook
el diccionario	dictionary
el escritorio	desk
el/la estudiante	student
el examen	exam, test
el gimnasio	gymnasium
la hoja de papel	sheet of paper
el hombre	man
el/la joven	young person
el lápiz (*pl.* lápices)	pencil
la librería	bookstore
el libro	book
la llave	key
la mesa	table
la mochila	backpack
la mujer	woman
la página web	web page
la pizarra	chalkboard; whiteboard
la puerta	door
el reloj	clock; watch
el salón de clase	classroom
la silla	chair
la tarea	homework
la ventana	window

Los cognados: la clase, la computadora, el curso, el/la estudiante, la graduación, la idea, el kilo, la oficina, el profesor / la profesora, el proyector, la universidad

(Continues)

Las materias — Subjects

la arquitectura, la biología, las ciencias (políticas),
las comunicaciones, el diseño, la economía, la filosofía,
la física, el francés, la historia, las humanidades,
la ingeniería, el inglés, las matemáticas, la psicología,
la química, las relaciones internacionales

Verbos — Verbs

hay	there is, there are
ser (*irreg.*)	to be
soy, eres, es, somos, sois, son	
tener (*irreg.*)	to have
tengo, tienes, tiene, tenemos, tenéis, tienen	

Para dar y pedir información — Giving and asking for information

arroba	@ (at, *in an e-mail address*)
¿Cómo se escribe... ?	How do you spell . . . ?
¿Cuál es tu... ?	What is your . . . ?
carrera	major
(dirección de) email / correo electrónico	e-mail (address)
número de teléfono	phone number
¿Cuántos/as... ?	How many . . . ?
¿Puede / Puedes repetir... ?	Can you (*formal/informal*) repeat . . . ?
punto com	dot com (*in an e-mail address*)
¿Qué estudias?	What do you study? / What's your major?
Un número / Una letra a la vez, por favor.	One number / letter at a time, please.

Otras palabras y expresiones útiles — Other words and useful expressions

antes (de)	before
de	of; from
después (de)	after
diferente	different
el, la, los, las	the
en	at; in
igual	same
más	more
no	no
un, una, / unos, unas	a, an / some
sí	yes
también	also
y	and

Mis amigos y yo

A estos jóvenes argentinos les gusta ([*they*] *like*) el fútbol. Y a ti, ¿qué te gusta (*do you like*)?

Objetivos

In this chapter you will learn how to:

- talk about your age
- say where you are going
- express likes and dislikes
- describe people, places, and things

2

COMUNICACIÓN ~~LARIO~~ ~~UCTURA~~ ~~ATE~~

¿Cuántos años tienes? / ¿Cuántos años tiene Ud.?

Finding out someone's age

A. A ver: ¿Cuántos años tienes? / ¿Cuántos años tiene?   Watch and listen as the following people say their age, then choose the correct answer.

1. Tengo _____ años.
   a. nueve
   b. diecinueve
   c. veintinueve

2. Tengo _____ años.
   a. veinte
   b. veintiséis
   c. treinta

3. Tengo _____ años.
   a. seis
   b. diecisiete
   c. sesenta

4. Tengo _____ años.
   a. dieciocho
   b. diecinueve
   c. veinte

5. Tengo _____ años.
   a. cuatro
   b. catorce
   c. cuarenta

6. Tengo _____ años.
   a. quince
   b. once
   c. nueve

7. Tengo _____ años.
   a. diecisiete
   b. veintisiete
   c. siete

8. Tengo _____ años.
   a. dieciocho
   b. veintiún
   c. veinte

9. Tengo _____ años.
   a. veinte
   b. veintitrés
   c. veintiséis

10. Tengo _____ años.
    a. veinticinco
    b. cuarenta y siete
    c. sesenta y seis

11. Tengo _____ años.
    a. veinte
    b. veintitrés
    c. veintiséis

12. Tengo _____ años.
    a. treinta y tres
    b. cuarenta y tres
    c. cincuenta y tres

¡Anticipa!

What does the verb **tener** mean in English? _____
This is an important verb in Spanish as there are many expressions that work with it. Here are a few.

tener hambre to be hungry (*lit.*, to have hunger)

What could the following expressions mean?

tener sed: **Tengo sed. ¿Hay agua** (*water*)**?**
tener frío: **Tenemos frío en el invierno.**
tener calor: **¿No tienes calor en la sauna?**

Respuestas: *to have; to be thirsty, to be cold, to be hot*

To ask someone's age in Spanish, you can say the following.

¿Cuántos años tienes? (*informal*)   **¿Cuántos años tiene (Ud.)?** (*formal*)

To answer that question, say: **Tengo _____ años.**

—Alicia, ¿cuántos años tienes?   —Señora Beltrán, ¿cuántos años tiene?
—Tengo 18 años.   —Tengo 40 años.

¡Atención! Before the word **años,** use **un** (instead of **uno**) for any age ending in *one* (*one, twenty-one, thirty-one,* and so on).

Tengo 21 (veintiún) años.
Tengo 61 (sesenta y un) años.

B. ¿Cuántos años tienen (*How old are*) **los estudiantes de la clase?**

PASO 1. In groups of four, take turns asking each other's ages. Individually complete the following form to note your age and the age of each group member. Then calculate the average (**el promedio**) for the group. Did you all get the same average? What is the average age for the whole class?

NOMBRE	EDAD (*AGE*)
yo	

MODELO: ESTUDIANTE 1: ¿Cuántos años tienes?
ESTUDIANTE 2: Tengo 20 años.

Total: _____ / el número de personas en el grupo = _____ (el promedio del grupo)
El promedio de la clase es de _____ años.

PASO 2. Who are the youngest and oldest members of your group? Share this information with the rest of the class. Based on the information provided by each group, who is the oldest in your class? Who is the youngest?

La persona mayor (*oldest*) del grupo / de la clase tiene (*is*) _____ años.
La persona menor (*youngest*) del grupo / de la clase tiene _____ años.

¿Adónde vas? / ¿Adónde va?

Finding out where someone is going

 A. A ver: ¿Adónde vas? / ¿Adónde va?

PASO 1. Watch and listen as people say where they go on a typical weekday, then check the appropriate boxes.

			LAS CLASES	EL GIMNASIO	LA OFICINA	EL TRABAJO	LA UNIVERSIDAD
1.		Elisabeth	☐	☐	☐	☐	☐
2.		Enrique	☐	☐	☐	☐	☐
3.		Nuria	☐	☐	☐	☐	☐
4.		Cinthya	☐	☐	☐	☐	☐
5.		Esteban	☐	☐	☐	☐	☐
6.		Lourdes	☐	☐	☐	☐	☐
7.		Diego	☐	☐	☐	☐	☐

(*Continues*)

¡Anticipa!

Can't and *I'll* are examples of common contractions in English. What others can you think of? What words fuse to form them?

As you now know, **al** is a contraction of the words **a** and **el** in Spanish. We'll introduce more contractions soon, but here's a sneak peek. Read the following sentences and see if you can detect the contraction and discern its formation pattern.

Ella es mi amiga *de la* universidad.
Ella es mi amiga *del* colegio.

En español...

Just like in English, where *picture* becomes *pic*, *refrigerator* becomes *fridge*, and *biography* becomes *bio*, in Spanish, long words also often get shortened. For example, people might say **el súper** instead of **el supermercado.** Other examples include **la uni (la universidad), la moto (la motocicleta), el/la profe (el profesor / la profesora)** and **la foto (la fotografía).**

PASO 2.   Where do the following people say they go on a typical weekend?

1.   Sabrina: «Voy al _____.»

2.   Benjamín: «Voy al _____.»

3.   María José: «Voy al _____.»

4.   Angélica: «Voy al _____.»

To ask where someone is going, use one of the following questions.

¿Adónde vas? (*informal*)   **¿Adónde va?** (*formal*)

To answer, say: **Voy a** + *name of place.*

Note the contraction **al** (**a** + **el**): Voy a + el gimnasio = Voy al gimnasio.

Voy al gimnasio.   I go to the gym.
Voy a la oficina.   I go to the office.

B. ¿Adónde vas en un día típico?

PASO 1.   Check all the places that you go to on a typical day (**un día típico**) and all the places that you go to on the weekend (**el fin de semana**).

	UN DÍA TÍPICO	EL FIN DE SEMANA
1. el cine (*the movies*)	☐	☐
2. la clase	☐	☐
3. el gimnasio	☐	☐
4. la oficina	☐	☐
5. el supermercado	☐	☐
6. el trabajo (*work*)	☐	☐
7. la universidad	☐	☐

PASO 2.   Now ask a classmate if what he or she does is the same or different than what you do.

MODELO: ESTUDIANTE 1: Yo voy al gimnasio en un día típico. ¿Y tú?
ESTUDIANTE 2: Yo no. Yo voy al gimnasio solo los (*only on*) fines de semana.

C. ¿Adónde van los otros estudiantes?

PASO 1.   Write down one place where you go on a typical weekday and one place you go on the weekend. Then find out where three of your classmates go, and fill out the chart.

MODELO: ESTUDIANTE 1: En un día típico / un fin de semana típico, ¿adónde vas?
ESTUDIANTE 2: Voy al gimnasio.
ESTUDIANTE 1: Gracias.

NOMBRE	EN UN DÍA TÍPICO	EN UN FIN DE SEMANA TÍPICO
yo	voy a/al...	
	va a/al...	

PASO 2. If two or more people on your chart have a place in common, write it on the board. Answer the following questions based on the final list created by the class.

1. En un día típico, ¿adónde va la mayoría (*the majority*) de la clase?
2. En un fin de semana típico, ¿adónde va la mayoría de la clase?

CONÉCTATE AL MUNDO HISPANO

Though large supermarket chains and big box stores can be found in many cities in the Spanish-speaking world, most people do not go to one supermarket location to do all their shopping for the week. It is more typical to go to smaller, specialized markets and local stores throughout the week.

Visiting small, family-owned grocery stores in Spanish-speaking countries is a cultural experience in itself. Even the words used for *grocery store* differ between countries. In Central America and Mexico you might hear **abarrotería** (Honduras), **abastecedor** (Costa Rica), **pulpería** (El Salvador, Honduras), and **tienda de abarrotes** (México); in South America, you can find **almacén** (Uruguay), **boliche** (Argentina), **tienda** (Colombia), **tienda de abastos** (Venezuela), and **tienda de barrio** (Bolivia); in the Caribbean, you might hear **bodega** (Cuba) and **colmado** (Puerto Rico); and in Spain you'll buy at the **tienda de comestibles.**

Keep in mind that not all Spanish speakers shop in the same way and many U.S. cities have a lot of small markets similar to those in Spanish-speaking communities.

Me gusta...
Expressing likes and dislikes

To talk in Spanish about activities you like to do, use **me gusta** + *activity*.

Me gusta tocar la guitarra.	I like to play the guitar.

To say you don't like to do something, just add **no** to the beginning.

No me gusta jugar* los videojuegos.	I don't like to play video games.

To ask someone else about what activities he or she likes to do, use **te gusta** (*informal*) or **le gusta** (*formal*).

INFORMAL	FORMAL
¿Te gusta + *verb*?	**¿Le gusta** + *verb*?
Do you like to . . . ?	Do you like to . . . ?
—¿Te gusta nadar?	**—¿Le gusta ir al cine?**
"Do you like to swim?"	"Do you like to go to the movies?"
—Sí, me gusta nadar.	**—No, no me gusta ir al cine.**
"Yes, I like to swim."	"No, I don't like to go to the movies."

---

*If you have studied Spanish before, you may have learned the construction **jugar a** + *sport/activity*. Many native speakers of Spanish omit the **a,** as you will see and hear on the video.

Un consejo (*Advice*)…

When learning a new language it is easy to get caught up in translating and become frustrated when expressions do not translate literally. Remember that there is no master language from which all other languages are derived. You have to think of different languages as separate systems that have evolved over centuries—and continue to evolve as they come into contact with each other. In the **Comunicación** sections of each chapter you will learn Spanish expressions that you can use immediately to communicate successfully, but it is best to try to use them as fixed expressions without attempting to translate every nuance to English.

For example, in English you might say *What's up?* to which the literal answer would be *the sky* or *the ceiling*, yet it is understood as a common greeting. Likewise in Spanish, **¿Qué onda?** is the equivalent of *What's up?*, even though **onda** literally means *wave*.

 A. A ver: Me gusta… Watch and listen. Then check which activities each person likes.

	JULIÁN	NASLY	YENARO	HENRY
1. andar/correr en bicicleta	☐	☐	☐	☐
2. hacer ejercicio	☐	☐	☐	☐
3. ir a la playa	☐	☐	☐	☐
4. ir al cine	☐	☐	☐	☐
5. ir de compras	☐	☐	☐	☐
6. jugar fútbol/bola	☐	☐	☐	☐
7. jugar los videojuegos	☐	☐	☐	☐
8. montar a caballo	☐	☐	☐	☐
9. nadar	☐	☐	☐	☐
10. tocar la guitarra	☐	☐	☐	☐

B. El tiempo libre

PASO 1. Read the list of activities and check all the ones that you enjoy.

☐ andar/correr en bicicleta (*to ride a bike*)
☐ hacer ejercicio (*to exercise*)
☐ ir a la playa (*to go to the beach*)
☐ ir al cine
☐ ir de compras (*to go shopping*)

☐ jugar fútbol/bola (*to play soccer*)
☐ jugar los videojuegos
☐ montar a caballo (*to ride horses*)
☐ nadar
☐ tocar la guitarra

PASO 2. At this point your vocabulary is still limited, but take a look at the phrases from **Paso 1** and see if you can add a detail (with whom? where?) or an example to each of your answers.

> **MODELOS:** Me gusta jugar los videojuegos, especialmente Halo.
> Me gusta montar a caballo. Mi caballo se llama Silver.
> Me gusta hacer ejercicio en el parque.
> Me gusta ir de compras con mi mamá.

 C. ¿Qué te gusta hacer (*to do*)? Find a partner and take turns asking each other what you like to do. Use the list of activities in **Actividad A.** Does your partner have more in common with Julián, Nasly, Yenaro, or Henry?

> **MODELO:** ESTUDIANTE 1: ¿Te gusta hacer ejercicio?
> ESTUDIANTE 2: Sí, me gusta hacer ejercicio.
> ESTUDIANTE 1: ¿Te gusta ir de compras?
> ESTUDIANTE 2: No, no me gusta ir de compras.
> ESTUDIANTE 1: Entonces (*Well then*), tienes más en común con Julián.

COMUN **VOCABULARIO** UCTURA ATE

¿Cómo somos?°

What are we like?

Describing people, places, and things with adjectives and colors

A. ¿Cómo somos?

PASO 1. Here are some common adjectives used to describe people, places, and things. Look at the images and match the pairs of opposites.

alto

animado

bajo

contenta

débil

delgada

fuerte

gordo

grande

joven (*pl.* **jóvenes**)

lento

pequeño

perezoso

pobre

rápido

reservada

rica

trabajador

triste

vieja

(*Continues*)

Vocabulario

As with any language, there are often many synonyms for a frequently used adjective. Here are a few examples in Spanish.

bello/a = **bonito/a** = **lindo/a** = **hermoso/a** = **precioso/a**
contento/a = **alegre** = **feliz**
delgado/a = **flaco/a**
pequeño/a = **chico/a**

¡Anticipa!

You'll notice here how the endings of adjectives change according to whom or what they describe. We'll explain this at length later in this chapter, but for now, see if you can predict the pattern. The following examples will help you.

Rita Moreno es *vieja.*
Carlos Saura es *viejo.*

Carlos Slim es *rico.*
Jennifer López es *rica.*
Jennifer López y Cameron Díaz son *ricas.*
Jennifer López y Carlos Slim son *ricos.*

Vocabulario

To talk about hair (**el pelo**) color and sometimes complexion (**la piel**), use the following color adjectives.

castaño/a brown
moreno/a dark brown or black
negro/a black
rubio/a blond
trigueño/a light brown

Also, use **tengo, tienes,** or **tiene** to describe these features.

Tengo los ojos azules.

Marcela tiene el pelo castaño y los ojos verdes. Su esposo, Ricardo, tiene la piel morena. (*but* **Ricardo es moreno.**)

Ricardo tiene los ojos negros.

PASO 2. Select at least three of the adjectives from **Paso 1** and name a well-known person or fictional character who fits each one.

> **MODELO:** rápido → Usain Bolt es rápido.
> vieja → Betty White es vieja.
> bajo → Bilbo Baggins es bajo.

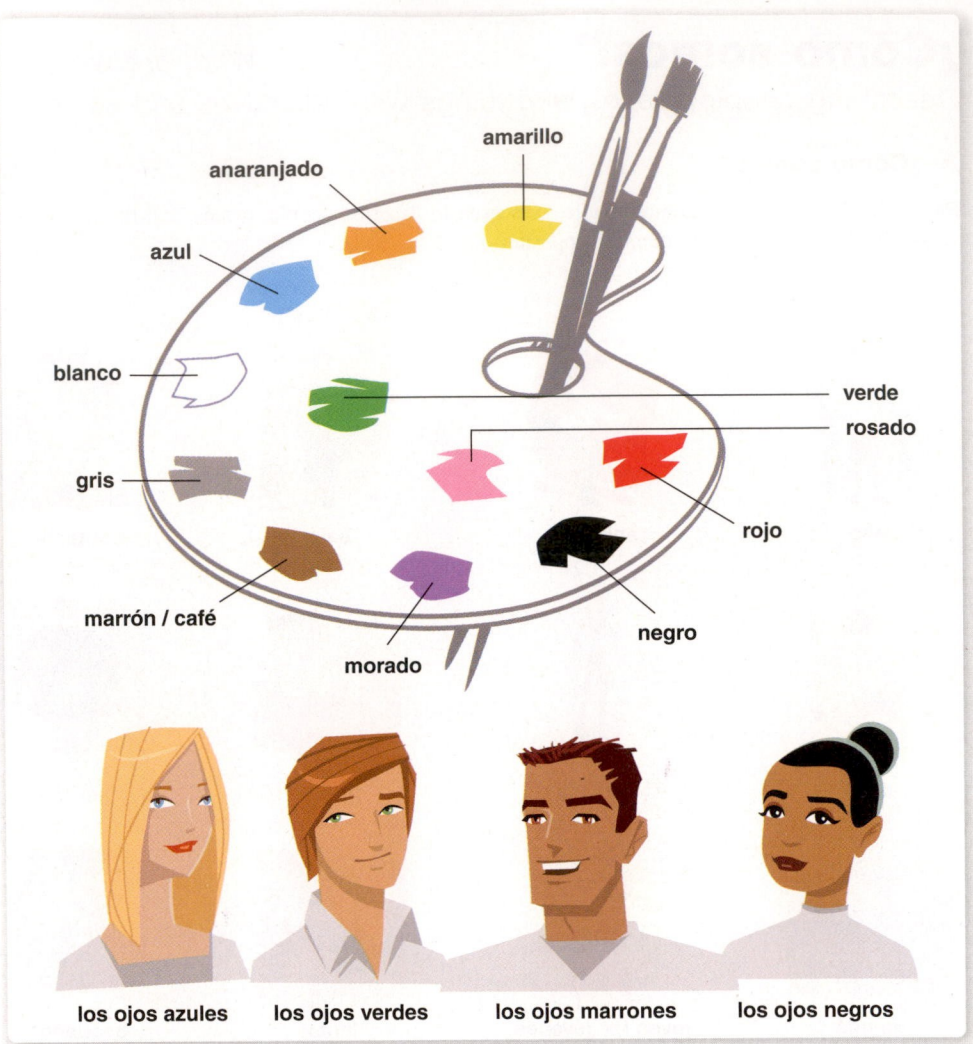

anaranjado   amarillo   azul   blanco   gris   marrón / café   morado   verde   rosado   rojo   negro

los ojos azules   los ojos verdes   los ojos marrones   los ojos negros

B. ¿De qué color es?

PASO 1. What color(s) do you associate with these objects?

1. el amor
2. la bandera (*flag*) de este país (*this country*)
3. el café (*coffee*)
4. el equipo de fútbol americano de tu universidad o ciudad (*university or city football team*)
5. el mar (*sea*)
6. el otoño
7. la pizza
8. el sol
9. la rosa

PASO 2. In groups of three or four, take turns playing "I Spy" (**Yo veo**) based on colors. Look around the room and select an item, then give a hint, naming the color of the item. Your group will take turns trying to guess what it is.

MODELO: ESTUDIANTE 1: Yo veo algo (*something*) blanco.
ESTUDIANTE 2: ¿Es la pizarra?
ESTUDIANTE 1: No, no es la pizarra.
ESTUDIANTE 3: ¿Es tu libro?
ESTUDIANTE 1: ¡Sí!

C. Ese fulano de tal (*Whatshisface*)   Study the picture. Then for each item, indicate if the sentence is describing **Fulano A** or **Fulano Z.**

	FULANO A	FULANO Z
1.	☐	☐
2.	☐	☐
3.	☐	☐
4.	☐	☐
5.	☐	☐
6.	☐	☐
7.	☐	☐
8.	☐	☐
9.	☐	☐
10.	☐	☐
11.	☐	☐

Fulano A   Fulano Z

■ The audio files for in-text listening activities are available in the eBook, within Connect Plus activities, and on the Online Learning Center.

Vocabulario

You learned about cognates (**cognados**) in **Capítulo 1.** Can you recognize these adjectives?

ansioso/a
bilingüe
excelente
extrovertido/a
famoso/a
generoso/a
inteligente
introvertido/a
maravilloso/a
motivado/a
optimista
organizado/a
pesimista
tranquilo/a

¡Atención! Some adjectives are false cognates. For example, **blanco/a** means *white* and **largo/a** means *long.*

En español...

Fulano roughly translates as *guy, whatshisname, so-and-so,* and can refer to any imaginary or indeterminate person. In some parts of the Spanish-speaking world, **fulano** can have a negative connotation, as in *fool.*

As you use Spanish outside of class, you will be able to pick up a lot of slang words, but be careful! Not only can the meaning vary in different parts of the Spanish-speaking world, but as with any language, slang words often have multiple meanings and only sound appropriate when certain people use them (think of your parents trying to use the same slang you use!).

D. A ver: ¿Cómo es? (*What's it like?*)

PASO 1. Watch and listen. Which adjective(s) does each person use to describe his or her family?

		BONITA	EXCELENTE	FELIZ	GRANDE	LINDA	PEQUEÑA
1.	Juan Andrés	☐	☐	☐	☐	☐	☐
2.	Andrea	☐	☐	☐	☐	☐	☐
3.	Mayra	☐	☐	☐	☐	☐	☐
4.	Delano	☐	☐	☐	☐	☐	☐
5.	Tania	☐	☐	☐	☐	☐	☐
6.	Ricardo	☐	☐	☐	☐	☐	☐
7.	Lourdes	☐	☐	☐	☐	☐	☐
8.	Óscar	☐	☐	☐	☐	☐	☐

PASO 2. In small groups, take turns describing your family in at least two adjectives just as the speakers did in **Paso 1. ¡Atención!** Remember the different adjective endings (**vieja** or **viejo, ricos** or **ricas**) you observed in **Activity A** depending on the the nouns they describe? We'll lay out the rule soon, but if you already detected a pattern—try to apply it here!

MODELO: Mi familia es pequeña y feliz.

CONÉCTATE AL MUNDO HISPANO

You know that Spanish (**el español**) used as a noun can refer to the language or, as a plural noun (**los españoles**), to the people of Spain. But remember that when you use the word Spanish (**español**) as an adjective (**español[a]**), it refers exclusively to people, things, and traditions of Spain. Spanish people live in or are from the European country of Spain. Spanish food is very different from Mexican food, typical Spanish music is different from typical Argentine music, and traditional Spanish dances are very different from traditional Puerto Rican dances.

Vocabulario

Here are some words that describe the countries that people or things are from.

argentino/a
(Argentina)

boliviano/a
(Bolivia)

canadiense
(Canadá)

chileno/a
(Chile)

colombiano/a
(Colombia)

costarricense
(Costa Rica)

cubano/a
(Cuba)

dominicano/a
(la República
Dominicana)

ecuatoriano/a
(Ecuador)

español(a)
(España)

**estadounidense /
norteamericano/a**
(los Estados Unidos)

guatemalteco/a
(Guatemala)

hondureño/a
(Honduras)

mexicano/a
(México)

nicaragüense
(Nicaragua)

panameño/a
(Panamá)

paraguayo/a
(Paraguay)

peruano/a
(el Perú)

puertorriqueño/a
(Puerto Rico)

salvadoreño/a
(El Salvador)

uruguayo/a
(Uruguay)

venezolano/a
(Venezuela)

E. Es peruano; son chilenas.

PASO 1. Match the following famous people with their nationality.

1. _____ Julieta Venegas
2. _____ Isabel Allende y Violeta Parra
3. _____ Julio y Enrique Iglesias
4. _____ Mario Vargas Llosa

a. españoles
b. mexicana
c. chilenas
d. peruano

 PASO 2. In pairs, take turns reviewing **Paso 1** by saying where the people are from and responding with the correct nationality.

MODELO: ESTUDIANTE 1: ¿De dónde es Isabel Allende?
ESTUDIANTE 2: Es de Chile. Es chilena.

Mario Vargas Llosa, escritor peruano y ganador del Premio Nobel de la Literatura

2.1 Una estudiante alta

Adjectives

- Answers to these activities are in Appendix 2 at the back of your book.

Para empezar...

Match each picture to the appropriate description.

1. ____

2. ____

3. ____

4. ____

5. ____

6. ____

7. ____

8. ____

a. altos
b. contenta
c. contentos, jóvenes, guapos
d. contento, viejo
e. alta
f. tristes
g. triste
h. alto

¿Por qué?

Why does Spanish have two different plural endings, **-s** and **-es?** Before we answer, think about how English also has an **-es** ending for words that end in **-s,** such as *bus* and *boss,* and words that end in **-ch,** such as *church* and *switch.* In Spanish, the rule is similar. For nouns that already end in a consonant, we use **-es** for the plural. The **e** of that ending breaks up what would otherwise be a sequence of two consonants.

Actividades analíticas

1 Words such as **alto, triste,** and **joven** are *adjectives* (**los adjetivos**), and they describe nouns. In Spanish, adjectives often change their form to agree with the noun that they describe. What two other forms of **alto** do you see in **Para empezar?**

alto ____ ____

2 Adjectives that end in **-o** like **alto** must agree with both the gender (masculine/feminine) and the number (singular/plural) of the noun. Masculine gender is indicated by **-o,** feminine by **-a,** and plural by **-s.**

	singular	plural
masculine	el hombre alt**o**	los hombres alt**os**
feminine	la mujer alt**a**	las mujeres alt**as**

3 Adjectives that end in **-e,** such as **triste,** or that end in a consonant, like **joven,** agree only with the number of the noun. The ending **-s** or **-es** is added to indicate plural, but the masculine and feminine forms are exactly the same.

	singular	plural
masculine	el hombre triste el hombre joven	los hombres triste**s** los hombres jóven**es**
feminine	la mujer triste la mujer joven	las mujeres triste**s** las mujeres jóven**es**

The rule for choosing between **-s** and **-es** is just like what you saw in **Estructura 1.2** for nouns: add **-s** if it ends in a vowel, and add **-es** if it ends in a consonant.

4 Now try this yourself! For each of the following phrases, adjust the adjective in parentheses as needed so that it agrees with the noun.

a. los libros _____ (nuevo)
b. las profesoras _____ (joven)
c. una mochila _____ (viejo)
d. la niña _____ (inteligente)

Actividades prácticas

A. ¿Cómo son? (*What are they like?*) Finish each sentence in column **A** with an item from column **B**.

<table>
<tr><td align="center">**A**</td><td align="center">**B**</td></tr>
<tr><td>1. El cálculo y la física son materias _____.</td><td>a. famosas de los Estados Unidos</td></tr>
<tr><td>2. Hillary Clinton y Oprah Winfrey son mujeres _____.</td><td>b. difícil</td></tr>
<tr><td>3. La química avanzada (*advanced*) es una materia _____.</td><td>c. pequeños</td></tr>
<tr><td>4. Penélope Cruz y Rafael Nadal son personas _____.</td><td>d. grandes</td></tr>
<tr><td>5. En general, un perro Chihuahua es _____.</td><td>e. famosas de España</td></tr>
<tr><td>6. Barack Obama y Brad Pitt son hombres _____.</td><td>f. grande</td></tr>
<tr><td>7. La Universidad Nacional Autónoma de México es una universidad muy _____.</td><td>g. famosos de los Estados Unidos</td></tr>
<tr><td>8. Los Estados Unidos y Canadá son muy _____.</td><td>h. difíciles</td></tr>
<tr><td>9. En general, los teléfonos celulares son _____.</td><td>i. pequeño</td></tr>
</table>

B. ¿Quién es? Listen as your instructor describes various people in your class. Guess who they are and write down their names here.

1. _____   3. _____   5. _____
2. _____   4. _____   6. _____

C. Una comparación Working in a group, create two lists: one of what everyone in your group has in common, and another of the ways in which you are different from each other. Use adjectives (p. 41) and colors, including hair and eye color (p. 42).

MODELO: Somos inteligentes y jóvenes.
Yo tengo el pelo negro. Kathy y Mark tienen el pelo rubio.

D. Más listas In each of the lists below, eliminate the item that doesn't belong. Then say what the remaining items have in common, using the correct form of the following adjectives. ¡Atención! Make sure the adjective's ending matches the noun that it is describing.

académico/a	**azul**	**electrónico/a**	**rojo/a**
amarillo/a	**blanco/a**	**famoso/a**	

MODELO: Shakira, ~~Mary Smith,~~ Lady Gaga, Eva Longoria
Son mujeres *famosas.*

1. La bandera (*flag*) española, la bandera guatemalteca, la bandera hondureña, la bandera nicaragüense
   Son banderas _____ y _____.

2. Un bolígrafo, una computadora, un teléfono, un iPad
   Son cosas _____.

3. Antonio Banderas, Javier Bardem, Penélope Cruz, Gael García Bernal
   Son españoles _____.

(Continues)

■ For more on the placement of adjectives in Spanish, see **Para saber más 2.1** at the back of your book.

Típicamente, los perros Gran Danés son grandes y los perros Chihuahua son pequeños.

4. El café, el oso (*bear*) polar, una hoja de papel, la luna (*moon*)
   Son cosas _____.

5. La bandera colombiana, la bandera ecuatoriana, la bandera mexicana, la bandera venezolana
   Son banderas _____, _____ y _____.

6. La biología, la televisión, la literatura, la química
   Son materias _____.

Panamá

E. Cultura: La diversidad de Panamá

PASO 1. Read the following text about Panama.

¿Cómo son los panameños? No es fácil describirlos[a] porque son muy diversos. Las familias panameñas son de diferentes orígenes étnicos y nacionales. Este fenómeno tiene que ver[b] con dos eventos importantes en la historia de Panamá: la conquista de América y la construcción del canal.

En 1501 (mil quinientos uno), los primeros exploradores de España llegan[c] a Panamá. Durante ese siglo,[d] llegan muchos españoles y se mezclan[e] con los habitantes[f] indígenas. Varios siglos después, en 1850 (mil ochocientos cincuenta), empieza[g] la construcción del ferrocarril[h] y luego del canal. En este periodo llegan ingenieros[i] de Francia y trabajadores antillanos,[j] por ejemplo de Jamaica, Barbados y Cuba. Llegan trabajadores chinos, colombianos y eventualmente estadounidenses. A Panamá, durante los últimos[k] siglos, han llegado[l] inmigrantes de países árabes, como Líbano, Palestina y Siria, y también del sur de Asia, como la India y Paquistán.

[a]*to describe them* [b]*tiene... has to do* [c]*arrive* [d]*century* [e]*se... they mix* [f]*inhabitants* [g]*begins* [h]*railroad* [i]*engineers* [j]*West Indian (from the Antilles)* [k]*last* [l]*han... have arrived*

PASO 2. Using information from the reading, complete the list of nationalities and countries of origin.

1. franceses, de _____
2. jamaicanos, de _____
3. libaneses, de _____
4. palestinos, de _____
5. paquistanís, de _____

6. _____, de China
7. _____, de Colombia
8. _____, de España
9. _____, de los Estados Unidos
10. _____, de Panamá

PASO 3. With a partner, answer the following questions and discuss the ideas behind your responses.

1. Los trabajadores que llegan a Panamá durante la construcción del canal enfrentan (*face*) muchos problemas: un viaje costoso (*costly trip*), un idioma (*language*) nuevo, la malaria, etcétera. ¿Por qué crees que lo hacen (*do you think that they do it*)?
2. Los latinoamericanos son de muchas razas (*races*) diferentes, igual que (*just like*) los norteamericanos. ¿Cómo pasó eso (*how did that happen*)?
3. Llegan muchos trabajadores a Panamá durante la construcción del canal entre 1881 y 1914. En tu país, ¿también hay mucha inmigración en este periodo? ¿Tu familia llega en este periodo?

Una de las esclusas (*locks*) del Canal de Panamá.

2.2   ¿Estás triste?

The verbs *estar* (to be) and *ir* (to go)

Para empezar...

Match each problem to the most likely solution. Some solutions can be used more than once since certain problems can have more than one solution.

1. _____ **Estás** (*You are*) cansado/a (*tired*).
2. _____ **Estamos** nerviosos/as.
3. _____ **Estás** solo/a (*alone*).
4. _____ **Estás** ansioso/a.
5. _____ **Estamos** aburridos/as (*bored*).
6. _____ **Estás** enfermo/a (*sick*).
7. _____ **Estás** triste.

a. **Vas** a un consejero (*counselor*).
b. **Vas** a la cama (*bed*).
c. **Vas** a una fiesta con amigos.
d. **Vas** a la farmacia.
e. **Vamos** al cine.
f. **Vamos** a una clase de yoga.

Estoy enferma.

■ Answers to these activities are in Appendix 2 at the back of your book.

Actividades analíticas

1 In **Para empezar,** you saw examples of two new verbs: **estar** (*to be*) and **ir** (*to go*). Use these examples to complete the conjugations here.

	estar	ir
SINGULAR		
yo	estoy	voy
tú		
él/ella, Ud.	está	va
PLURAL		
nosotros/as		
vosotros/as	estáis	vais
ellos/ellas, Uds.	están	van

As with other verbs in Spanish, the subject is usually left unexpressed unless it is needed for clarification.

Estoy contenta.	*I'm happy.*
Están aburridos.	*They are bored.*
Vamos a la fiesta.	*We're going to the party.*
¿**Vas** a clase?	*Are you going to class?*

2 As you saw in **Estructura 1.3,** the form of the verb used to address someone formally (with **Ud.**) is different from the form used to address someone informally (with **tú**). Change the following questions from the **tú** form to the **Ud.** form.

¿Cómo estás?   →   ¿Cómo _____ usted?

¿Vas a la fiesta?   →   ¿ _____ usted a la fiesta?

■ To learn how to use the verb **tener** to express how you are feeling, see **Para saber más 2.2** at the back of your book.

3 The verb **estar** expresses characteristics that are not necessarily lasting. For example, the state of being tired or being sick could change at any time, so you express this with **estar.**

Estamos cansados.	*We are tired.*
¿**Estás** enferma?	*Are you sick?*

Characteristics that are not likely to change are expressed with the verb **ser**, which you saw in **Estructura 1.3.**

Soy de Guatemala.	*I'm from Guatemala.*
UCLA **es** una universidad.	*UCLA is a university.*

You will learn more about the differences between **ser** and **estar** in **Estructura 4.4** and **5.3.**

¡Anticipa!

Sometimes the same adjectives can have very different meanings, depending on whether they are used with **estar** or **ser.** We'll explain at length later, but for now, based on the description in point 3, what do you think the difference in meaning could be in each of these pairs of sentences?

Ella *está* nerviosa.
Ella *es* nerviosa.

Él *está* borracho (*drunk*).
Él *es* borracho.

Mis amigas *están* bonitas.
Mis amigas *son* bonitas.

Make a mental note and we'll explain soon!

Actividades prácticas

A. En orden   The following sentences form a simple conversation, but they are out of order. Put them in an order that makes sense. The first one is done for you.

_____ a. Porque mañana tengo un examen.
__1__ b. ¿Cómo estás?
_____ c. Buena idea. Voy. ¿Adónde vas tú?
_____ d. ¿Por qué?
_____ e. Ansioso.
_____ f. ¿Por qué no vas a la biblioteca a estudiar?
_____ g. Voy a la casa (*home*) a dormir (*to sleep*). Tengo sueño (*I'm sleepy*).

B. ¿Estoy o soy?   Select the correct form to complete the sentences.

1. (Estoy / Soy) frustrado (*frustrated*).
2. (Estoy / Soy) de Panamá.
3. (Estoy / Soy) una chica alta.
4. (Estoy / Soy) triste.
5. (Estoy / Soy) profesor.
6. (Estoy / Soy) cansada.

En español…

By now you have seen many ways of asking questions. Here are some useful question words.

¿Qué?	**¿Cómo?**
¿Quién?	**¿Cuándo?**
¿Cuál?	**¿Cuántos/as?**
¿Dónde?	**¿Por qué?**
¿Adónde?	

Notice that **dónde** and **adónde** are both translated as *where* in English, but **dónde** is used to ask where you *are* and **adónde** to ask where you are *going.*

Questions with **por qué** are often answered with **porque** (*because*), which is spelled as one word and has no accent mark.

What do all of the above question words have in common?

What do you notice about the punctuation that is different from English?

C. Preguntas y respuestas   Match each question with the appropriate answer.

1. _____ ¿Cómo estás?
2. _____ ¿Dónde estás?
3. _____ ¿Adónde vas?
4. _____ ¿Por qué van al cine?
5. _____ ¿Adónde va Julia?
6. _____ ¿Quién va a la biblioteca?
7. _____ ¿Por qué vas a la farmacia?
8. _____ ¿Por qué estás ansioso?
9. _____ ¿Adónde van?
10. _____ ¿Dónde están?

a. Porque estoy enferma.
b. Voy a una fiesta.
c. Porque voy a un examen.
d. Estamos en el gimnasio.
e. Vamos al cine.
f. Bien, gracias.
g. Estoy en el restaurante.
h. María Elena.
i. Porque estamos aburridos.
j. Va al gimnasio.

D. ¿Adónde vas?

PASO 1.   Where do you go in the following situations? Choose one of the answers provided or think of an alternative and mark your answer with an X.

1. ¿Adónde vas cuando (*when*) estás enfermo/a?
   ☐ al médico (*doctor*)   ☐ a la clínica de la universidad   ☐ a la farmacia
   ☐ otra (*another*) respuesta: _____

2. ¿Adónde vas para estudiar?
   ☐ a la casa   ☐ a la biblioteca   ☐ a la casa de un amigo
   ☐ a un café   ☐ otra respuesta: _____

3. ¿Adónde vas cuando tienes hambre a mediodía (*at midday*)?
   ☐ a la casa   ☐ a un restaurante   ☐ al comedor (*dining area*) de la universidad
   ☐ otra respuesta: _____

4. ¿Adónde vas cuando estás triste?
   ☐ a un parque   ☐ a la casa   ☐ a una iglesia (*church*)
   ☐ otra respuesta: _____

Now, for each of the questions, circle the box next to the answer you think will be the most common among your classmates.

PASO 2.   Your instructor will assign you one of the four questions. Interview as many of your classmates as you can, and keep a tally of the results (using the area to the left of each answer, if you wish). Some possible answers are given, but keep in mind that there may be others.

MODELO: ESTUDIANTE 1: ¿Adónde vas cuando estás triste?
             ESTUDIANTE 2: Voy a la casa de una amiga.

PASO 3.   Report your results to the class. **¡Atención!** If the answer you are reporting applies to you also, use the **nosotros/as** form of the verb: **Vamos a la biblioteca.** If the answer does not necessarily apply to you, use the **ellos/as** form of the verb: **Van a la casa.** If you wish to report a split response, use numbers: **Tres van a la biblioteca. Cinco van a la casa.**

Others will report their results, so you should now get a good picture of how the class answered each of the four questions. How good were your predictions from **Paso 1?**

Normalmente voy a la biblioteca para estudiar.

E. La clase de actuación

PASO 1. Working in a team of three students, read through this list of adjectives and choose one that you will act out as a team in front of the class.

aburrido/a	cansado/a	loco/a (*crazy*)	solo/a
ansioso/a	contento/a	malo/a (*bad*)	triste
antipático/a (*disagreeable*)	enfermo/a	serio/a	
bueno/a (*good*)	enojado/a (*angry*)	simpático/a (*nice*)	

PASO 2. Act out your adjective as a team, while the other students try to describe your psychological state.

> **MODELO:** ESTUDIANTE 1: ¿Están cansadas?
> ESTUDIANTE 2: No, no estamos cansadas.
> ESTUDIANTE 3: ¿Están enojadas?
> ESTUDIANTE 2: ¡Sí! Estamos enojadas.

¡Atención! As you watch other teams act, pay attention to their gender in order to know which form of the adjective to use.

2.3 ¿Te gusta la clase de español?

The verb *gustar*

Para empezar...

PASO 1. Below you see four people and their **hobbies** (this word has been borrowed from English). Write the name of the person most likely to say each of the quotes that follow. **¡Atención!** One sentence doesn't belong to any of these four. Which is it?

Agustina, de Argentina
Hobby: música metal progresivo

Javier, de España
Hobby: el cine (*film*)

Esther, de España
Hobby: novelas

Pedro, de México
Hobby: fútbol

■ Answers to these activities are in Appendix 2 at the back of your book.

Persona

_____ 1. «Me gustan las películas (*movies*).»
_____ 2. «Me gusta la música.»
_____ 3. «Me gustan los deportes (*sports*).»
_____ 4. «Me gusta la biología.»
_____ 5. «Me gustan los libros.»

PASO 2. Now apply the same procedure to yourself. Which of the above sentences apply to you? Can anyone in the class say that all of these sentences apply to them?

Actividades analíticas

1 In **Para empezar,** you saw examples of both **me gusta** and **me gustan.** They both mean *I like,* so what is the difference between the two? To help you decide, write down here which things from **Paso 1** take **me gusta** and which take **me gustan.**

me gusta	me gustan
	las películas

What conclusion can you come to? In the table below, place the words **singular** and **plural** in the appropriate places.

me gusta	con un sustantivo (*noun*) _____
me gustan	con un sustantivo _____

2 **Te gusta** and **te gustan** work the same way as **me gusta** and **me gustan.** They both mean *you like,* but which form you use depends on whether the noun is singular or plural. Which would you use to ask if someone likes the following things?

¿_____ los deportes?   ¿_____ la historia?

3 **Le gusta** and **le gustan** mean *he / she likes* or *you* (formal) *like.* If you want to clarify who you are talking about, you may use *a + name or pronoun.*

¿A usted _____ las novelas gráficas?

A Carolina no _____ el chocolate.

Actividades prácticas

A. Preguntas y respuestas   Match each question with the answer that makes the most sense.

1. ____ ¿Te gustan los deportes?
2. ____ ¿A usted le gusta el cine español?
3. ____ ¿Te gusta la música hip hop?
4. ____ ¿A Jerónimo le gusta la televisión?
5. ____ ¿A Ana le gusta el jazz?
6. ____ ¿Te gusta la música clásica?
7. ____ ¿A usted le gusta el café?
8. ____ ¿Te gusta nadar (*to swim*)?
9. ____ ¿A tu madre le gusta ir al gimnasio?

a. Sí, me gusta mucho Bach.
b. Sí, me gusta mucho el fútbol.
c. No, me gusta más el té (*tea*).
d. Sí, le gusta la música de Miles Davis.
e. Sí, me gustan las películas de Almodóvar.
f. No, le gustan más las películas.
g. No, no le gusta hacer ejercicio (*to exercise*).
h. Sí, me gusta Pitbull.
i. No, no me gusta estar en el agua (*water*).

B. Las banderas   Many people like certain flags because of their colors rather than where they are from. Using the list of flags on page 45, match each description with the appropriate flag(s). **¡Atención!** Notice whether the statements in the first column end in **me gusta** or **me gustan.**

____ 1. Me gusta el color rojo. Me gusta…
____ 2. Me gusta el color blanco. Me gustan…
____ 3. Me gusta el color azul. Me gusta…
____ 4. Me gusta el color verde. Me gustan…
____ 5. Me gusta el color amarillo. Me gustan…

a. las banderas de Bolivia y México.
b. la bandera de Honduras.
c. la bandera de Perú.
d. las banderas de Ecuador y Venezuela.
e. las banderas de Chile y Costa Rica.

C. Tus clases

PASO 1.   What classes are you taking this term and how do you feel about them? Create two sentences: one that lists classes you like, and another that lists any you don't like.

MODELO: Me gustan las clases de español y química. No me gusta la clase de historia.

 PASO 2.   Ask a partner which classes he or she has (**¿Qué clases tienes?**). Then find out whether he or she likes each one.

MODELO: ESTUDIANTE 1: ¿Qué clases tienes?
ESTUDIANTE 2: Tengo clases de historia, español y biología.
ESTUDIANTE 1: ¿Te gusta la clase de español?
ESTUDIANTE 2: Sí, mucho.
ESTUDIANTE 1: A mí, también. (*I do, too.*) Es muy buena.

¡Anticipa!

Just like **me, te,** and **le,** the words **nos, os,** and **les** are also used with **gustar** to express preferences of different people. These pronouns will be explained fully in **Chapter 7,** but for now, be on the lookout for them used with **gustar.**

■ For more on how to say what different people like or don't like in Spanish, see **Para saber más 2.3** at the back of your book.

D. Una encuesta (*survey*) People often make assumptions about what students like, such as the items in the list below. Is there any truth to these stereotypes?

PASO 1. Circulate throughout the classroom and ask classmates **¿Qué te gusta?** (*What do you like?*). Your classmates should use the items on the list to respond.

> **MODELO:** ESTUDIANTE 1: ¿Qué te gusta?
> ESTUDIANTE 2: Me gustan el café, el chocolate y las películas de terror.

＿＿ el café	＿＿ las computadoras	＿＿ la música
＿＿ la cerveza (*beer*)	＿＿ las fiestas	＿＿ las películas de terror (*horror*)
＿＿ el chocolate	＿＿ las hamburguesas	＿＿ la pizza

PASO 2. Now present your results! Who likes each of the items from **Paso 1?**

> **MODELO:** A Sarah le gusta el café. Pero a Jaime le gustan las computadoras y la música.

Me gusta el chocolate.

2.4 ¿Qué te gusta hacer? ¿Qué vas a hacer?

Infinitives with *gustar* and *ir*

Para empezar...

PASO 1. Here are some activities that many people enjoy doing. Rank them in order of preference (1–9) for you. Write **no me gusta** for any activity that you do not like to do.

Me gusta...

＿＿ bailar (*dance*)	＿＿ dormir	＿＿ leer (*read*)
＿＿ comer (*eat*)	＿＿ hablar (*talk*) por teléfono	＿＿ nadar
＿＿ correr (*run*)	＿＿ hacer ejercicio	＿＿ usar la computadora

PASO 2. Which of these activities are you going to do over the next eight hours? Write those verbs here.

Voy a ＿＿＿＿＿＿＿＿＿＿＿＿＿＿＿＿＿＿＿＿＿＿＿＿＿＿＿

Actividades analíticas

1 In the examples in **Para empezar**, **me gusta** is followed by the infinitive (**el infinitivo**), the unconjugated form of the verb. Infinitives in Spanish always end in **-ar, -er,** or **-ir.** Find an example from **Para empezar** of each of these three types.

Infinitive ending	-ar	-er	-ir
Example			

You will find out more about these three types of verbs in **Capítulo 3.**

■ Answers to these activities are in Appendix 2 at the back of your book.

2 **Gustar** is always in the singular form when used with one or more infinitives.

Me **gusta ir** al cine.	*I like to go to the movies.*
A José le **gusta escuchar** música y bailar.	*José likes to listen to music and dance.*

3 Infinitives are also used after **ir a,** as a way of expressing a future event.

ir a + *infinitive*

Voy a estudiar.	*I am going to study.*
Van a nadar.	*They are going to swim.*
¿**Vas a** correr?	*Are you going to run?*
Ana **va a** usar la computadora.	*Ana is going to use the computer.*

Actividades prácticas

A. ¿Dónde estás? ¿Qué vas a hacer?   If you are in the place stated in column **A,** which activity in column **B** are you most likely going to do?

A

1. ＿＿＿ Estoy en la biblioteca.
2. ＿＿＿ Estoy en la cama (*bed*).
3. ＿＿＿ Estoy en un restaurante.
4. ＿＿＿ Estoy en un gimnasio.
5. ＿＿＿ Estoy en la clase de español.
6. ＿＿＿ Estoy en la playa.
7. ＿＿＿ Estoy en una discoteca.
8. ＿＿＿ Estoy en la universidad.

B

a. Voy a hablar español.
b. Voy a bailar.
c. Voy a nadar.
d. Voy a asistir a clase (*attend class*).
e. Voy a dormir.
f. Voy a leer.
g. Voy a hacer ejercicio.
h. Voy a comer.

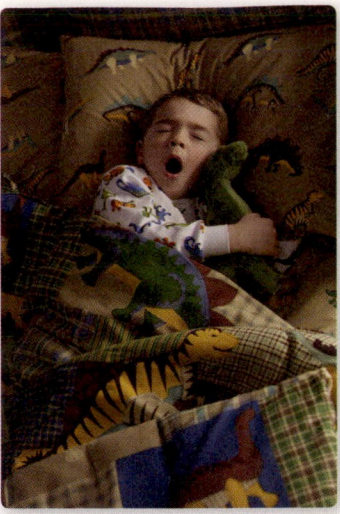

El niño está en la cama.

 B. ¿Dónde te gusta... ?   Do your classmates like to do things on campus, at home, or somewhere else? Think of three common activities and ask a partner where he/she likes to do them.

MODELO: ESTUDIANTE 1: ¿Dónde te gusta estudiar?
ESTUDIANTE 2: Me gusta estudiar en casa.

C. ¡Me gusta!

PASO 1.   Complete each of these sentences with either **gusta** or **gustan.**

1. «Me ＿＿＿ ir al cine.»
2. «Me ＿＿＿ leer.»
3. «Me ＿＿＿ las películas norteamericanas.»
4. «Me ＿＿＿ los gimnasios.»
5. «Me ＿＿＿ la música de Juanes.»
6. «Me ＿＿＿ los libros de Carlos Ruiz Zafón.»
7. «Me ＿＿＿ ir a conciertos (*concerts*).»
8. «Me ＿＿＿ hacer ejercicio y bailar.»

PASO 2.   Now look at the sentences in **Paso 1** and find the pairs that relate to the same topic and would likely have been spoken by the same person. Use the sentence numbers to identify the pairs of sentences that go together.

＿＿＿ y ＿＿＿   ＿＿＿ y ＿＿＿   ＿＿＿ y ＿＿＿   ＿＿＿ y ＿＿＿

 D. ¿Qué vas a hacer?

PASO 1.   Ask as many classmates as possible what they are going to do this weekend (**este fin de semana**). Keep track of their answers. If another student asks you what you are going to do, give that person up to three activities.

MODELO: ESTUDIANTE 1: ¿Qué vas a hacer este fin de semana?
ESTUDIANTE 2: Voy a ir a una fiesta, hacer ejercicio y estudiar.

PASO 2.   Now tally up the answers. What were the top three activities in your class?

¡Leamos!

¿Cómo son los profesionales?

Antes de leer

PASO 1. Write down a list of adjectives you might expect to see in an advertisement for the services offered by a group of people working at a small business.

> **MODELO:** Es un grupo *motivado*.

 PASO 2. In groups, take turns describing individuals pictured in the ad (without using any names). Can the other members of the group name the person being described?

> **MODELO:** ESTUDIANTE 1: Es baja, delgada y rubia.
> ESTUDIANTE 2: ¿Es Elizabeth Wexler?

A leer

Examine the ad for the law firm Hale & Hopkins run by two lawyers (**abogados**). Based on the text of the ad, answer each of the following questions using an appropriate adjective.

1. ¿Cómo son los abogados?
2. ¿Cuánto cuesta (*costs*) una consulta (*consultation*)?
3. ¿Qué tipo de asistente es Elizabeth Wexler?
4. Hablan inglés y español. ¿Qué adjetivo describe a una persona que habla dos idiomas?

 ## Después de leer

Working in groups, use the nouns and the adjectives to prepare another ad for Hale & Hopkins. Take turns presenting your ads to the class. **¡Atención!** Make sure the adjectives agree with the subjects in both gender and number.

En Hale & Hopkins...

el equipo (*team*)	animado/a	inteligente	pequeño/a
los abogados	bilingüe	motivado/a	simpático/a
los asistentes legales	fuerte	organizado/a	trabajador(a)

¡Escuchemos!

¿Cómo son las familias hispanas?

Antes de escuchar

Organize the following adjectives into three categories based on what they could describe: a family (**una familia**), a girl (**una niña**), and a boy (**un niño**). **¡Atención!** Use the gender of the adjective as clues wherever possible.

alto	delgado	grande	maravillosa
baja	gorda	hermosa	pequeña

una familia					
una niña					
un niño					

(*Continues*)

En español...

A escuchar

Watch and listen, then fill in the descriptions as the following people describe their family member(s).

Óscar

1. El hijo tiene
_____ años.
La niña tiene
_____ años.

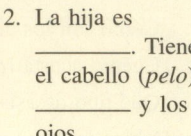

María Luz

2. La hija es
_____. Tiene
el cabello (*pelo*)
_____ y los
ojos _____.

Zulay

3. Su hijo, Luis
Miguel, tiene
_____ años.
Él es _____,
_____ y
_____.

Guadalupe

4. Su padre es
_____ y
_____.
Su madre es
_____ y
_____. Sus
hermanos son
_____ y
_____.

Después de escuchar

Use the adjectives you have studied in this chapter and pick three that you think best describe your personality and the three that describe your siblings, parents, or guardians. Use the family vocabulary words you can draw from these video clips to formulate your answers.

MODELO: Soy graciosa, simpática y alta. Mi madre es baja y trabajadora. Mis hermanitos son altos y delgados y muy animados.

¡Escribamos!

El perfil electrónico°

Online profiles

Being able to present yourself succinctly in Spanish to others will be an invaluable skill as you get to know more native speakers, study, travel, work, and explore the Spanish-speaking world. An online profile is one way to do this, allowing you to connect with people who share your interests so you can develop personal or professional relationships.

Antes de escribir

PASO 1.   To get started on your online profile (for Facebook, a blog, a networking site, or an online dating site) in Spanish, answer the following questions.

¿Cómo te llamas?

¿Cómo eres? (cinco adjetivos)

¿De dónde eres?

¿Cuántos años tienes?

¿Qué te gusta hacer (*to do*)? (¿esquiar? ¿leer?) (cuatro actividades)

PASO 2.   Choose the audience for your profile.

☐ mi familia

☐ mis colegas de trabajo (*work*)

☐ todos mis contactos

☐ todos (*all*) mis amigos

☐ un grupo de amigos: _____

(Continues)

PASO 3. Look at the information you listed in **Paso 1** and cross off the items you wouldn't want to share with your selected audience.

> **MODELO:** (Audience: *todos mis contactos*)
> Soy ~~pesimista~~, trabajadora, ~~ansiosa~~,..
> Me gusta ir al gimnasio.
> ~~Me gusta ir a las fiestas todas las noches~~.
> Me gustan los videojuegos.

A escribir

Use the information you compiled in **Antes de escribir** to write a clear, simple, compelling profile that is appropriate for your selected audience. Use complete sentences, and add details where appropriate.

 ### Después de escribir

Check your own work, then exchange profiles with a classmate and use the following checklist to edit your classmate's work. (Proofreading your own work and that of your classmates is an important way to improve your language skills!)

☐ hay concordancia (*agreement*) de género (*gender*) entre los adjetivos y los sustantivos (*nouns*)

☐ hay concordancia de número (singular o plural) entre los adjetivos y los sustantivos

☐ ha usado (*he/she has used*) **soy** con adjetivos para describir la personalidad

☐ ha usado **me llamo** o **mi nombre es** para indicar el nombre

☐ ha usado **tengo** _____ **años** para indicar la edad (*age*)

☐ ha usado **me gusta** para nombrar los pasatiempos (*hobbies*)

When you are finished, make corrections to your own papers based on each other's feedback.

¡Hablemos!

A conocernos°   *Getting to know each other*

Antes de hablar

Prepare a list of seven questions you can use to get to know your classmates better. Be strategic: Ask about personality traits and activities that they do not like as well as ones that they do like.

> **MODELO:** ¿Eres extrovertido/a?
> ¿Te gusta + *activity*... ? / ¿Te gusta(n) + *noun(s)*... ?

 ## A hablar

Use your questions from **Antes de hablar** as a checklist to quickly interview three or more classmates. **¡Atención!** Don't forget to take notes.

Después de hablar

Use your notes from **A hablar** to find the person in the class with whom you have the most in common. Write a few sentences about that person and what you have in common. Share this with the class.

> **MODELO:** Tengo mucho en común con Alicia. Ella es muy extrovertida y le gusta nadar y cantar. Yo también soy extrovertida y me gusta nadar.

Conéctate al cine

Película: *El laberinto del fauno* (*Pan's Labyrinth*, drama, México/España, 2006)
Director: Guillermo del Toro

Sinopsis:

Several years after the end of the Spanish Civil War, Ofelia and her mother arrive at the rural home of Captain Vidal, an officer loyal to Francisco Franco. Ofelia's mother is married to Captain Vidal and pregnant with his son. On arriving, the two meet Mercedes, the captain's head maid. Amid the cruelty and violence of her new home, where the captain kills and tortures members of the continuing resistance movement, Ofelia discovers a secret world of mythical creatures.

Escena (DVD, Scene 6, 00:24:50 to 00:29:14):

In the first of these three scenes, Captain Vidal orders Mercedes to clean some rabbits and taste his coffee. In the second scene, Ofelia's mother gives her a new dress to wear at a special dinner with the captain. In the third scene, Mercedes and the other maids see Ofelia in her new dress.

Antes de ver

El laberinto del fauno contrasts a world of magic with a world of harsh realities. It also contrasts very kind characters with very cruel characters. Read the following list of adjectives and circle the words you consider to be positive traits of a person. Underline the words you consider to be negative.

aburrido/a	feo/a	malo/a	simpático/a
antipático/a	gracioso/a	organizado/a	trabajador(a)
bueno/a	hermoso/a	serio/a	triste

A ver

PASO 1.   Review the **Expresiones útiles,** then watch the film clip. Don't worry about understanding every word, but try to make guesses about what is happening in each scene based on the words you do understand and the actions and expressions of the characters.

PASO 2.   Complete the sentences with the correct form of the following adjectives.

castaño	fuerte	negro	trabajador
débil	joven	organizado	verde
estricto	largo	serio	viejo

1. El capitán Vidal es un hombre _____ y _____.
2. Mercedes dice (*says*) que los conejos son muy _____.
3. Dos de las mujeres que trabajan en la cocina son _____.
4. Mercedes y las otras mujeres son muy _____; ellas hacen muchas cosas.
5. La madre de Ofelia es _____, pero su esposo (*husband*) es _____.
6. Mercedes maneja (*manages*) todas las actividades de la casa. Es muy _____.
7. La madre de Ofelia tiene el pelo _____ y _____.
8. El vestido de Ofelia es _____ y sus zapatos son _____.

Después de ver

Use your own adjectives to describe the following characters. **¡Atención!** Try not to repeat the adjectives used for each person in **A ver, Paso 2.**

   MODELO: La madre de Ofelia es guapa y generosa.

1. Ofelia es _____.
2. El capitán Vidal es _____.
3. Mercedes es _____.
4. Las cocineras (*cooks*) son _____.

Expresiones útiles

conejos	rabbits
café	coffee
está quemado	is burnt
el vestido	dress
los zapatos	shoes
date prisa	hurry up (*you, informal*)
gallinas	hens
limpias	clean
leche con miel	milk and honey

■ For copyright reasons, the feature-film clips referenced in **Conéctate al cine** have not been provided by the publisher. Each of these films is readily available through retailers or online rental sites such as Amazon, iTunes, or Netflix.

VOCABULARIO

Comunicación

¿Cuántos años tienes? / ¿Cuántos años tiene?	How old are you (informal/formal)?
Tengo + number + años.	I'm + number + years old.
¿Adónde vas? / ¿Adónde va?	Where are you (informal/formal) going?
Voy a/al + place	I'm going to . . .
Me gusta + infinitive/noun	I like + infinitive/noun
No me gusta + infinitive/noun	I don't like + infinitive/noun
¿Te gusta + activity?/ ¿Le gusta + activity?	Do you (informal/formal) like + infinitive?
¿Cómo se dice... ?	How do you say . . . ?

Las descripciones — Descriptions

aburrido/a	boring
alto/a	tall
animado/a	lively
antipático/a	disagreeable
bajo/a	short
bueno/a	good
cansado/a	tired
débil	weak
difícil	difficult
enojado/a	angry
fácil	easy
feo/a	ugly
fuerte	strong
gordo/a	fat
gracioso/a	funny
grande	big
guapo/a	good-looking
hermoso/a	pretty
joven (pl. jóvenes)	young
largo/a	long
lento/a	slow
loco/a	crazy
malo/a	bad
nuevo/a	new
perezoso/a	lazy
pobre	poor
rico/a	rich
serio/a	serious
simpático/a	nice
solo/a	alone
trabajador(a)	hard-working
triste	sad
viejo/a	old

Sinónimos

bello/a, bonito/a, hermoso/a, lindo/a, precioso/a	pretty
alegre, contento/a, feliz (pl. felices)	happy
delgado/a, flaco/a	thin
chico/a, pequeño/a	small

Cognados: ansioso/a, bilingüe, excelente, extrovertido/a, famoso/a, generoso/a, horrible, inteligente, interesante, introvertido/a, maravilloso/a, motivado/a, optimista, organizado/a, pesimista, rápido/a, reservado/a, tranquilo/a

¿De qué color es?   What color is it?

amarillo/a, anaranjado/a, azul, blanco/a, gris, marrón, morado/a, negro/a, rojo/a, rosado/a, verde

los colores del pelo y de la piel

castaño/a	brown
moreno/a	dark brown
negro/a	black
rubio/a	blond
trigueño/a	light brown

Las nacionalidades

argentino/a, boliviano/a, canadiense, chileno/a, colombiano/a, costarricense, cubano/a, dominicano/a, ecuatoriano/a, español(a), estadounidense / norteamericano/a, guatemalteco/a, hondureño/a, mexicano/a, nicaragüense, panameño/a, paraguayo/a, peruano/a, puertorriqueño/a, salvadoreño/a, uruguayo/a, venezolano/a

Los verbos

asistir (a)	to attend
bailar	to dance
comer	to eat
correr	to run
dormir	to sleep
estar (irreg.)	to be
estudiar	to study
hablar	to speak
hacer (irreg.) ejercicio	to do exercise
ir (irreg.)	to go
ir a + infinitive	to be going to (do something)
ir de compras	to go shopping

(Continues)

jugar	to play
leer	to read
nadar	to swim
tocar la guitarra	to play the guitar
usar	to use

la música	music
la película (de terror)	(horror) film
la playa	beach
el supermercado (el súper)	supermarket
el trabajo	work

Los sustantivos — Nouns

la bandera	flag
el café	coffee
la casa	house; home
la cerveza	beer
el cine	movies; movie theater; film (*in general*)
el deporte	sport
la fiesta	party
la hamburguesa	hamburger

Las palabras interrogativas

¿Adónde?	Where to?
¿Cómo?	How?
¿Cuál?	Which?
¿Cuándo?	When?
¿Cuánto/a/os/as?	How much / many?
¿Dónde?	Where?
¿Por qué?	Why?
¿Qué?	What?
¿Quién(es)?	Who?

¿Qué haces?

Tomando el sol en la orilla (*shore*) del lago Villarrica en Chile

Objetivos

In this chapter you will learn how to:

- ask and tell time
- say when events occur
- get someone's attention
- say what you do in your free time
- talk about daily schedules in the Spanish-speaking world

3

COMUNICACIÓN LARIO UCTURA ATE

Disculpa, ¿qué hora es?

Getting someone's attention, asking for the time

A. A ver: ¿Qué hora es? Watch and listen as the following people say the time. Then choose the correct answer.

1. _____ Alexander   a. 5:00   b. 6:00   c. 7:00   d. 8:00

2. _____ Victorino   a. 9:00   b. 9:15   c. 9:30   d. 9:45

3. _____ Olman   a. 4:00   b. 4:05   c. 4:15   d. 4:25

4. _____ Óscar   a. 4:55   b. 5:00   c. 5:05   d. 5:15

5. _____ Noel   a. 12:05   b. 12:15   c. 12:25   d. 12:55

6. _____ Juan Andrés   a. 9:02   b. 9:22   c. 9:32   d. 9:42

Vocabulario

If you want to get someone's attention before asking a question, use a form of the verb **disculpar** (*to excuse, pardon*) or **oír** (*to hear, listen*).

Disculpa or **Oye, ¿...?** (if you address the person as **tú**)

Disculpe or **Oiga, ¿...?** (if you address the person as **Ud.***)

Disculpen or **Oigan, ¿...?** (if you address more than one person [**Uds.***])

Disculpe, ¿qué hora es?

Son las dos.

Oye, ¿qué hora es?

Son las seis y media.

---

*The words **usted** and **ustedes** are abbreviated as **Ud.** and **Uds.**, respectively. You will see them appear with this abbreviation throughout *Conéctate*.

To ask the time in Spanish, say: **¿Qué hora es?**

> —**¿Qué hora es?**
> —**Son las cinco.**

To tell the time in Spanish, use the verb **ser.**

> **Es + la una.**
> **Son + las dos, las tres, las cuatro...**

INFORMAL (TÚ)

—**Disculpa** (*Excuse me*), **¿qué hora es?**
—**Son las tres.**

FORMAL (USTED)

—**Disculpe, ¿qué hora es?**
—**Es la una.**

You can say *noon* in Spanish two ways.

> **Es mediodía.** *or* **Son las doce del día.**

You can also say *midnight* in Spanish two ways.

> **Es medianoche.** *or* **Son las doce de la noche.**

To say *half-past* or *thirty*, use either **y media** or **(y) treinta.**

> **Es la una y media. = Es la una (y) treinta.**

To say *quarter-past* or *fifteen*, use either **y cuarto** or **y quince.**

> **Son las dos y cuarto. = Son las dos (y) quince.**

For times after the half-hour, it is common to use **menos** or **para.**

> **Son las ocho y cincuenta. / Son las nueve menos diez. / Son diez para las nueve.**

Vocabulario

B. Son las...

PASO 1. Match each clock with the appropriate time.

1. ____

2. ____

3. ____

4. ____

5. ____

6. ____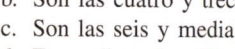

a. Son las tres.
b. Son las cuatro y trece.
c. Son las seis y media.
d. Es medianoche. (Son las doce.)
e. Son las tres menos diez.
f. Es la una.

(Continues)

PASO 2. In pairs, take turns asking and answering questions about the time. When asked what the time is, pick randomly one of the pictures below, and give your partner the time shown on that picture. Can the student who asked for the time point to the correct clock?

MODELO: E1: ¿Qué hora es?
E2: Son las tres de la tarde.
[*Estudiante 1 points to 3:00.*]

1.

2.

3.

4.

5.

6.

7.

¿A qué hora... ?
Asking at what time events occur

To ask at what time something happens, say: **¿A qué hora?**

Answer with **a**: *a* **la una**, *a* **las dos y media**, *a* **las tres menos cuarto**, *a* **las cuatro y cinco...**

—**¿A qué hora es la clase de español?**

—**Es a las diez.**

A. Preguntas sobre la hora

1. Check all the possible answers to the question **¿Qué hora es?**
   ☐ Es medianoche.   ☐ Son las diez menos veinte.
   ☐ A las tres y media.   ☐ A las cinco de la tarde.

2. Check all the possible answers to **¿A qué hora es la clase de español?**
   ☐ Es a mediodía.   ☐ Son las dos menos cinco.
   ☐ Es a las cinco de la tarde.   ☐ No sé. No tengo el horario (*schedule*).

3. Now answer each question yourself: **¿Qué hora es? ¿A qué hora es la clase de español?**

B. A ver: ¿A qué hora se levantan?

Watch and listen. Then write down the time each person says they get up in the morning.

¿A qué hora te levantas?

1. Belén se levanta a las _____.
2. Diana se levanta a las _____.
3. Marlén se levanta a las _____.
4. Abril se levanta a las _____.

¿A qué hora se levanta Ud.?

5. Pudenciano se levanta a las _____.
6. Isabel Baña se levanta a las _____.
7. Víctor Peralta se levanta a las _____.
8. Erick Solís Morales se levanta a las _____.
9. Sabrina Amezcua se levanta a las _____.

C. A ver: ¿A qué hora... ?   Watch and listen as various Spanish-speakers from around the world describe their daily routines. Then choose the correct time.

1. _____ Jorge entra en clase…
   a. a las 6:00 de la mañana.
   b. a las 7:30 de la mañana.
   c. a las 8:00 de la mañana.
   d. a las 8:30 de la mañana.

2. _____ Javier entra a la escuela (*school*)…
   a. a las 6:00 de la tarde.
   b. a las 6:30 de la tarde.
   c. a las 3:00 de la tarde.
   d. a las 3:30 de la tarde.

3. _____ Carolina empieza (*starts*) las clases…
   a. a las 11:00 de la mañana.
   b. a mediodía.
   c. a la 1:00 de la tarde.
   d. a las 2:00 de la tarde.

4. _____ Eduardo sale (*leaves*) de la universidad…
   a. a las 11:00 de la mañana.
   b. a mediodía.
   c. a la 1:00 de la tarde.
   d. a las 2:00 de la tarde.

5. _____ Abril entra a la escuela…
   a. a las 6:00 de la mañana.
   b. a las 7:30 de la mañana.
   c. a las 8:00 de la mañana.
   d. a las 8:30 de la mañana.

6. _____ Florencio Fernández Labrador está en su oficina…
   a. a las 6:00 de la mañana.
   b. a las 7:30 de la mañana.
   c. a las 8:00 de la mañana.
   d. a las 8:30 de la mañana.

D. ¿A qué hora abre (*does it open*)... / cierra (*does it close*)... ?

PASO 1.   In pairs, decide which of you will be **Estudiante 1,** and which will be **Estudiante 2.** Ask and respond to the questions about what time each business opens and closes, based only on your particular image. The image and questions for **Estudiante 2** are on page 68.

MODELO: E1: Oye. ¿A qué hora abre la panadería Los Cielos?
E2: A las seis y media.
E1: ¿A qué hora cierra?
E2: A las cinco.
E1: Gracias.

Estudiante 1   Ask your partner for the hours of operation of the establishments listed here. Then use the following image to answer your partner's questions about the hours of operation of the businesses pictured.

1. la peluquería (*hair salon / barber shop*)
2. el veterinario
3. el museo
4. la agencia de viajes (*travel agency*)

(*Continues*)

Estudiante 2   Use the following image to answer your partner's questions about the hours of operation of the businesses pictured. Then ask your partner for the hours of operation of the establishments listed here.

1. la papelería
2. el restaurante
3. la farmacia
4. la biblioteca

PASO 2.   Using the questions you learned in **Paso 1** (**¿A qué hora abre?** / **¿A qué hora cierra?**), take turns formulating and answering questions based on the situations below.

> **MODELO:**   You have a headache and need medicine, but it's getting late.
> E1: ¿A qué hora cierra la farmacia?
> E2: A las doce y media.

1. You want the first appointment to get your hair cut.
2. You have a long drive tomorrow and want to get some coffee and pastries for the trip as early as possible.
3. You would like to study at the library as late as possible this weekend.
4. Your have to pick up your dog from his medical procedure before the office closes.

CONÉCTATE AL MUNDO HISPANO...

In parts of the Spanish-speaking world the **siesta** is scheduled as part of workday. Where the **siesta** is practiced, actual times may vary, but businesses often operate from 7:00 A.M. to 1:00 P.M. and then again from 3:00 or 4:00 P.M. to 7:00 P.M. This gives people time to go home for lunch, rest, and spend time with their families. While a nap might be part of **siesta,** it is not the definition of the practice.

¿Cómo es tu rutina diaria?

Your daily routine and the days of the week

A. ¿Qué haces?

PASO 1. Match each activity pictured with the appropriate description.

1. ____   a. mirar la televisión
2. ____   b. asistir a clase
3. ____   c. practicar el fútbol
4. ____   d. leer el periódico (*newspaper*)
5. ____   e. hablar por teléfono
6. ____   f. estudiar en la biblioteca
7. ____   g. trabajar en una oficina
8. ____   h. comer con mi familia
9. ____   i. cantar en el coro (*choir*)

(*Continues*)

PASO 2. Check all the activities you like to do on a regular basis, then compare activities with your partner.

MODELO: E1: Solo me gusta desayunar los fines de semana (*on weekends*).
E2: A mí me gusta desayunar todos los días (*every day*).

E1: Me gusta cenar en casa.
E2: A mí me gusta cenar en la cafetería o en restaurantes. No me gusta cenar en casa.

_____ desayunar   _____ almorzar / comer   _____ cenar

_____ bailar   _____ ir a la playa   _____ ir al cine   _____ ir de compras / comprar

_____ correr en el parque   _____ hacer ejercicio / practicar yoga   _____ montar a caballo   _____ jugar básquetbol   _____ nadar

_____ dormir   _____ jugar los videojuegos   _____ leer   _____ usar la computadora

B. Los estilos de vida de dos estudiantes

Tomás Teleadicto   Adela Atleta

En
español...

Spanish uses the single verbs **desayunar, almorzar,** and **cenar** where English uses the multi-word expressions *to have breakfast, to have lunch,* and *to have dinner.* **Comer** may be used in a general sense to mean *to eat,* but in some places it is used more specifically to mean *to have lunch.* For many speakers, then, **almorzar** and **comer** are interchangeable. Meal times vary greatly across the Spanish-speaking world, although lunch and dinner often occur much later than is common in English-speaking countries.

PASO 1. Who is more likely to make each of the following statements, **Tomás Teleadicto** or **Adela Atleta?**

	TOMÁS TELEADICTO	ADELA ATLETA
1. Me gusta ir de compras en bicicleta (*bicycle*).	☐	☐
2. Me gusta usar la computadora para comprar.	☐	☐
3. Me gusta comer pizza.	☐	☐
4. Me gusta desayunar, almorzar y cenar comida saludable (*healthy food*).	☐	☐
5. Me gusta jugar videojuegos de básquetbol.	☐	☐
6. Me gusta comer la comida chatarra (*junk food*).	☐	☐

PASO 2. Identify each of the following activities and tell who probably likes to do each one, **Tomás Teleadicto** or **Adela Atleta.**

MODELO:  A *Adela Atleta* le gusta *jugar fútbol.*

1.

2.

3.

4.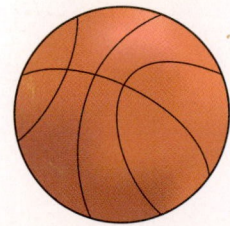

5.

6.

Vocabulario

To talk about the morning, afternoon, and evening in general, use:

por la mañana   in the morning
por la tarde   in the afternoon
por la noche   at night

Estudio por la tarde.   I study at night.

¡Atención! To refer to a specific time of day, use **de: de la mañana, de la tarde,** and **de la noche.**

Voy al gimnasio a las cinco de la tarde.

See the **Vocabulario** box on page 65.

C. A ver: ¿Cómo es tu rutina diaria?

PASO 1. Watch and listen as the following university students describe their daily routines. Then for each one put the list of activities in the correct order. Then decide when each person does each activity: **por la mañana, por la tarde,** or **por la noche.**

		MAÑANA	TARDE	NOCHE
1. Andrea	_____ Asistir a clase.	☐	☐	☐
	_____ Cenar en casa.	☐	☐	☐
	_____ Ir al gimnasio.	☐	☐	☐
	_____ Levantarse (*to get up*).	☐	☐	☐
2. Nicolás	_____ Asistir a clase.	☐	☐	☐
	_____ Dormir.	☐	☐	☐
	_____ Estudiar.	☐	☐	☐
	_____ Levantarse.	☐	☐	☐
	_____ Trabajar.	☐	☐	☐
3. Guadalupe	_____ Ir a los jardines (*gardens*).	☐	☐	☐
	_____ Ir a las oficinas.	☐	☐	☐
	_____ Ir al trabajo.	☐	☐	☐
	_____ Regresar a la casa.	☐	☐	☐
4. Noel	_____ Almorzar.	☐	☐	☐
	_____ Empezar la práctica (*internship*).	☐	☐	☐
	_____ Levantarse.	☐	☐	☐
	_____ Viajar hacia (*Travel to*) la práctica en bus.	☐	☐	☐

PASO 2. Look again at the breakdown of the daily routines of the speakers in **Paso 1.** With a partner, express whose routine is most like your own and why. Be sure to tell why.

    MODELO: Mi horario es parecido (*similar*) al horario de _____ porque también me gusta…

PASO 3. Use complete sentences to answer each question about the daily routines of the speakers in the video and your own routine.

1. a. ¿Se levanta temprano (*early*) o tarde (*late*) Noel?
    b. ¿Y a ti? ¿Te gusta levantarte temprano o tarde?
2. a. ¿A Andrea qué le gusta hacer (*to do*) por la mañana?
    b. ¿Y a ti? ¿Qué te gusta hacer por la mañana?
3. a. ¿Qué tiene que (*have to*) hacer Nicolás entre las dos y las ocho de la tarde?
    b. ¿Y tú? ¿Qué tienes que hacer entre las dos y las ocho de la tarde normalmente?

 D. Tu rutina   With a partner, take turns asking each other the general time of day that you prefer to do the following activities. Say **No lo hago** if you don't do the activity at all.

MODELO: E1: ¿Cuándo prefieres (*do you prefer*) trabajar?
  E2: Prefiero (*I prefer to*) trabajar por la mañana. / No lo hago.

1. Asistir a clase.
2. Cenar con mi familia.
3. Comer en el comedor (*dining area*).
4. Correr en el parque.
5. Desayunar.
6. Estudiar en la biblioteca.
7. Hablar por teléfono.
8. Leer el periódico.
9. Mirar la televisión.
10. Jugar básquetbol / **los** videojuegos.

Vocabulario

The calendar week begins on Monday in the Spanish-speaking world. Starting with Monday, these are **los días de entre semana** (*weekdays*).

lunes   martes   miércoles   jueves   viernes

Here are the days that make up **el fin de semana.**

sábado   domingo

To express *on* a day, use **el** (no preposition).

This works for plurals, too.

el lunes = on Monday   **los lunes** = on Mondays

Tengo un examen **el** lunes.   Trabajo **los** lunes.

Note that days of the week are not capitalized in Spanish.

M A Y O
7
VIERNES
Sta. Gisela

 E. La rutina diaria de tu compañero/a de clase

PASO 1.   With a partner, choose an activity you will plan to do together (**ir a bailar, ir al cine, ir de compras, ir al gimnasio, ir a jugar, ir a la playa…**).

MODELO: E1: ¿Vamos a bailar?
  E2: No me gusta bailar. ¿Vamos al cine?
  E1: Sí. Me gusta ir al cine.

PASO 2.   Now use your real schedules to find a day that you are both available. Once you have agreed on a day, find a time that works for the two of you, then report your findings to the class.

MODELO: E1: ¿El viernes?
  E2: No. ¿El jueves? (Sí, el viernes.)
  E1: ¿A las siete?
  E2: No. ¿A las nueve? (Sí, a las siete.)
  E1: Sí, está bien.

COMUN VOCABU **ESTRUCTURA** ATE

Reciclaje

Singular forms of **estar, ir, ser,** and **tener**

Complete the sentences in column **A** by choosing the best match in column **B.** Then complete column **B** by choosing one of the verbs given and writing the appropriate form of the verb in the blank.

estar   ir   ser   tener

■ Answers to this activity are in Appendix 2 at the back of your book.

A

1. Voy a clases porque ___d___
2. Ricky Martin _____
3. Mario se acuesta (*goes to bed*) temprano (*early*) porque _____
4. Son las dos y media. _____
5. Paula bailó toda la noche (*danced all night long*). Ahora, ella _____

B

a. _____ una clase de física mañana a las siete y media de la mañana.
b. ¿Tú _____ a la clase de inglés a las tres?
c. _____ de Puerto Rico.
d. _____ estudiante.
e. _____ muy cansada.

3.1   Vivo en España

Present indicative: Singular forms

Para empezar...

PASO 1.   Over the past decade, Gael García Bernal and Javier Bardem have become international movie stars. Based on the descriptions below, which statement could be uttered by which actor? Which could be uttered by both? **¡Atención!** For languages spoken, the names of some of their films will help you!

GAEL GARCÍA BERNAL

Es de México.

En las películas:

> *Y tu mamá también*
> *Diarios de motocicleta*
> *La science des rêves* (Francia)
> *No*
> *The Loneliest Planet*

JAVIER BARDEM

Es de España.

En las películas:

> *Mar adentro*
> *Before Night Falls*
> *No Country for Old Men*
> *Skyfall*

	GAEL GARCÍA BERNAL	JAVIER BARDEM
1. «**Soy** español.»	☐	☐
2. «**Soy** mexicano.»	☐	☐
3. «**Hablo** francés.»	☐	☐
4. «**Hablo** inglés.»	☐	☐
5. «**Vivo** en México, D.F.»	☐	☐
6. «**Vivo** en Madrid».	☐	☐
7. «**Trabajo** en el cine».	☐	☐
8. «**Leo** muchos guiones (*screenplays*)».	☐	☐

■ Answers to these activities are in Appendix 2 at the back of your book.

PASO 2.   Now answer the following questions about yourself. You can answer **sí** to at least one of them, but can anyone in the class answer **sí** to more than one?

¿Y TÚ?	SÍ	NO
1. ¿**Eres** español?	☐	☐
2. ¿**Eres** mexicano?	☐	☐
3. ¿**Hablas** francés?	☐	☐
4. ¿**Hablas** inglés?	☐	☐
5. ¿**Vives** en México, D.F.?	☐	☐
6. ¿**Vives** en Madrid?	☐	☐
7. ¿**Trabajas** en el cine?	☐	☐
8. ¿**Lees** muchos guiones?	☐	☐

Actividades analíticas

1 Using what you saw in **Para empezar,** complete these partial conjugations of **trabajar, leer,** and **vivir.**

	trabajar	leer	vivir
SINGULAR			
yo			
tú			
él/ella, Ud.	trabaja	lee	vive

2 Verbs like these are known as *regular verbs* (**los verbos regulares**), because their conjugations follow a predictable pattern. For example, what ending do all of these regular **yo** forms have in common?

La forma **yo** siempre (*always*) termina en (*ends in*) _____.

The rest of the verb form (the part without this ending) is known as the *root* or *stem* (**la raíz del verbo**). For the three verbs here, the stems are **trabaj-, le-, viv-.**

3 The ending for the **él/ella** and **Ud.** form is always a vowel (**una vocal**). For **-ar** verbs like **trabajar,** this vowel is **-a,** and for **-er** and **-ir** verbs like **leer** and **vivir,** it is **-e.** What single letter can you then add to this to create the **tú** form?

La forma **tú** siempre termina en _____.

Actividades prácticas

A. Gael y Javier   Gael García Bernal and Javier Bardem know each other, and in fact, Gael has said that Javier is his favorite actor. Based on this and the information in **Para empezar,** write **G** for each sentence that Gael might say to Javier and **J** for each sentence that Javier might say to Gael. If it is something that they could both say, write **G/J.**

1. _____ Vives en México.
2. _____ Eres mi actor favorito.
3. _____ Trabajo en el cine.
4. _____ Vivo en España.
5. _____ Trabajas en el cine.
6. _____ Vivo en México.
7. _____ Vives en España.

B. Preguntas y respuestas Match the questions on the left with the most reasonable answer on the right.

1. ¿Estudias en la biblioteca? __h__
2. ¿Estudias mucho? ____
3. ¿Tomas mucho café? ____
4. ¿Trabajas? ____
5. ¿Corres mucho? ____
6. ¿Cantas? ____
7. ¿Y tu amiga canta? ____
8. ¿Tu amigo corre mucho? ____

a. Sí canto, pero mal.
b. Sí, corre todos los días (*every day*).
c. Sí canta, pero mal.
d. Sí, estudio todos los días.
e. Tomo café de vez en cuando (*every once in a while*), pero no mucho.
f. Sí, trabajo en la biblioteca de la universidad.
g. Sí, corro todos los días.
h. No, estudio en casa.

C. Cuatro colombianos

PASO 1. With a partner, look at the chart about four well-known Colombians and some of the things they are known for. Ask your partner whether he or she does these activities and keep track of the answers in the column on the right.

MODELO: E1: ¿Cantas?
E2: Sí, canto. (No, no canto.)

¡Anticipa!

You have already detected the patterns for regular **-ar, -er,** and **-ir** verbs in several conjugations: **yo, tú,** and **él/ella, Ud.** We'll explain this soon, but for now, can you predict what letter combinations are added to the stem to form the **ellos/ellas, Uds.** form of regular verbs?

Take a look at the following sentences and see if you can find the pattern.

Shakira habla árabe. Juanes, Camilo Villegas y Sofía Vergara no hablan árabe.

Camilo Villegas no lee mucho. Juanes, Shakira y Sofía Vergara leen mucho.

Camilo Villegas y Sofía Vergara viven en los Estados Unidos. Juanes vive en Colombia.

	Juanes CANTANTE DE MÚSICA ROCK	Shakira CANTANTE DE MÚSICA POP	Camilo Villegas JUGADOR DE GOLF	Sofía Vergara ESCRITOR DE NOVELAS	tu compañero/a
Canta.	☑	☑	☐	☐	☐
Baila mucho.	☐	☑	☐	☐	☐
Practica mucho deporte.	☑	☐	☑	☐	☐
Toca (*He/ She plays*) la guitarra.	☑	☑	☐	☐	☐
Habla árabe.	☐	☑	☐	☐	☐
Practica el golf.	☐	☐	☑	☐	☐
Trabaja en la televisión.	☐	☐	☐	☑	☐
Lee mucho.	☑	☑	☐	☑	☐
Vive en Colombia.	☑	☐	☐	☐	☐
Vive en los Estados Unidos.	☐	☐	☑	☑	☐

PASO 2.   By comparing check marks, with which person does your partner have the most in common? How many things does he or she have in common with this person?

_____ tiene _____ cosas en común con _____.

D. ¿Miras la televisión?

PASO 1.   With a partner, take turns asking each other whether you do the activities listed below. Tell your partner whether you do them **todos los días, a veces** (*sometimes*), or **nunca** (*never*).

MODELO: E1: ¿Miras la televisión?
E2: No, nunca miro la televisión.

cocinar	estudiar	mirar la televisión
comer comida mexicana	hablar por teléfono	practicar un deporte
correr	ir al cine	trabajar
desayunar	ir al gimnasio	

Miro la televisión los fines de semana.

PASO 2.   Create two statements about your partner: one about what he or she does *every day* and another about what he or she *never* does.

MODELO: Mike cocina todos los días. Nunca baila.

Reciclaje

Plural forms of *ser, tener, estar,* and *ir*

Complete each sentence using a verb from the following list that would make sense in the context. Then indicate whether each sentence is **cierto** (*true*) or **falso** (*false*).

estar   ir   ser   tener

	CIERTO	FALSO
1. Los españoles _____ de Asia.	☐	☐
2. Nosotros _____ estudiantes.	☐	☐
3. Los profesores de español _____ a muchas clases de química.	☐	☐
4. Mis amigos _____ muy contentos hoy.	☐	☐
5. Las universidades _____ muchas clases.	☐	☐
6. Nosotros _____ a la clase de español los sábados y los domingos.	☐	☐

■ Answers to this activity are in Appendix 2 at the back of your book.

3.2   Desayunamos a las siete.

Present indicative: Plural forms

Para empezar...

PASO 1.   In many cultures, the daily schedule of activities is organized around the schedule of meals. In Mexico, families typically have breakfast (**desayunar**) at around 7:00, eat their midday meal (**comer**) at around 2:00, and dinner (**cenar**) at around 8:00. Use this information to complete the following sentences about meals in Mexico and about your own personal habits.

En México en general...

1. **desayunan** a las _____.
2. **comen** a las _____.
3. **cenan** a las _____.

Yo en general...

1. desayuno a las _____.
2. como a las _____.
3. ceno a las _____.

PASO 2.   What is the general schedule for meals for most people in your country?

En nuestro (*our*) país en general...

1. **desayunamos** a las _____.
2. **comemos / almorzamos** a las _____.
3. **cenamos** a las _____.

Actividades analíticas

1 Use the examples that you saw in **Para empezar,** as well as what you already know about verbs in Spanish, to complete the following conjugations.

	cenar	comer	vivir
SINGULAR			
yo			
tú			
él/ella, Ud.	cena	come	vive
PLURAL			
nosotros/as			vivimos
vosotros/as	cenáis	coméis	vivís
ellos/ellas, Uds.			viven

2 In **Estructura 3.1** you saw the pattern for the singular forms of regular verbs.

		ENDINGS	EXAMPLES
yo		-o	trabajo leo vivo
tú	-ar verbs -er, -ir verbs	-as -es	trabajas lees vives
él/ella, Ud.	-ar verbs -er, -ir verbs	-a -e	trabaja lee vive

In the **tú** and the **él/ella** and **Ud.** forms, the vowel that is added to the stem is **-a** (for **-ar** verbs) or **-e** (for **-er** and **-ir** verbs).

Now complete this chart of endings for *plural* verb forms, basing your answers on the examples given.

		ENDINGS	EXAMPLES
nosotros/as	-ar verbs -er verbs -ir verbs	-amos _____mos -imos	cenamos comemos vivimos
vosotros/as	-ar verbs -er verbs -ir verbs	_____is -éis -ís	cenáis coméis vivís
ellos/ellas, Uds.	-ar verbs -er, -ir verbs	-an _____n	cenan comen viven

3 As you saw in the charts in **2**, verb endings vary slightly depending on whether the verb is of the **-ar, -er,** or **-ir** type. Despite these differences, what do the three **nosotros/as** endings all have in common?

> La forma **nosotros/as** siempre termina en _____.

What about the **vosotros/as** and **ellos/ellas/Uds.** endings?

> La forma **vosotros/as** siempre termina en _____.
>
> La forma **ellos/ellas/Uds.** siempre termina en _____.

4 You can now conjugate any regular verb in Spanish. Practice this by completing the conjugations for these regular verbs.

	bailar	correr	asistir
SINGULAR			
yo	bailo		
tú		corres	
él/ella, Ud.			asiste
PLURAL			
nosotros/as			
vosotros/as	bailáis		
ellos/ellas, Uds.		corren	asisten

Actividades prácticas

A. La vida (*life*) en nuestro país

PASO 1. When interacting with Spanish-speakers, you may be asked what life is like in your country. Which of these statements do you think are true for most people in your country?

	CIERTO	FALSO

En general…

1. Trabajamos de lunes a viernes. ☐ ☐
2. Hablamos inglés. ☐ ☐
3. Cenamos muy temprano (*early*). ☐ ☐
4. Leemos muchos libros. ☐ ☐
5. Bailamos muy bien. ☐ ☐
6. Vivimos en casas. ☐ ☐
7. Practicamos muchos deportes. ☐ ☐
8. Cocinamos todos los días. ☐ ☐

 PASO 2. Compare your answers with those of two classmates. Do you disagree about any of the statements? Report these disagreements to the class using **según** (*according to*).

> **MODELO:** Según Mary, bailamos muy bien. Según yo, no bailamos muy bien.

En este país, ¿leemos muchos libros?

Nosotros…

B. Una mexicana habla Given what you saw in **Para empezar** about meal times, which of the following would be reasonable things for a Mexican woman to say when comparing her own country with this country? For each sentence, write **C** for **cierto** or **F** for **falso**. ¡Atención! Use the verb endings to know whether she is referring to people in her own country (**nosotros**) or to most people in this country (**los estadounidenses/canadienses**).

En general…

1. _____ comemos a las dos.
2. _____ comen a las dos.
3. _____ cenamos a las ocho.

4. _____ cenan a las ocho.
5. _____ comemos a mediodía.
6. _____ comen a mediodía.

7. _____ cenamos a las seis.
8. _____ cenan a las seis.

C. ¿Tomas café?

PASO 1. In many parts of the world, coffee is a traditional part of the early morning routine, but does everyone drink it at that time, or at all? Ask as many classmates as possible whether they drink coffee, and if so, at what times. Keep track of the responses that you get.

MODELO:

¿cuándo?	número de personas
7:00–8:00	
8:00–10:00	
10:00–12:00	
12:00–15:00	
15:00–19:00	
19:00–	
todo el día	
nunca	

E1: ¿Tomas café?
E2: Sí.
E1: ¿Cuándo?
E2: A las ocho y media.

PASO 2. Now report to the class what you have found. What statements can you make about the habits of the people in your class?

MODELOS: Todos (*Everyone*) tomamos café.
Catorce personas toman café de las siete a las ocho.
Nadie (*No one*) toma café.
Nadie toma café por la noche.

D. ¿Qué hacen todos los estudiantes de la clase?

PASO 1. Working in groups, take five minutes to create as many sentences as possible using **todos** (*everyone; all of us*) to express what you think everyone in the class does every day (**todos los días**). Use the following list of activities to get you started, but you may think of others as well.

MODELO: Todos desayunamos todos los días.

asistir a clase	desayunar	leer
cenar	dormir	mirar la televisión
cocinar	escuchar música	practicar un deporte
comer	estudiar	trabajar
correr	hablar por teléfono	

PASO 2.   Now report your results from **Paso 1** to the class. Can any student in the class contradict your claims?

> **MODELO:**   Grupo 1: Todos desayunamos todos los días.
> Grupo 2: ¡No es cierto! Cathy no desayuna.

E. Cultura: El café de Nicaragua y El Salvador

PASO 1.   Read the text about Nicaragua and El Salvador.

¿Tomas café cuando desayunas? ¿Tomas café antes de ir a tus clases? ¿Cuando estudias? ¿Después de cenar? A muchos de nosotros nos gusta tomar café. Es parte de la rutina diaria. Pero en varios países de Centroamérica, como en Nicaragua y El Salvador, cultivar, producir y exportar el café es la rutina diaria de muchas personas.

¿Cómo es la rutina diaria del agricultor de café? Él se levanta muy temprano, desayuna y toma su café. Va a los campos y recolecta[a] las bayas de café rojas. Descansa[b] para almorzar y entonces vuelve a[c] recolectar más bayas de café. Finalmente camina[d] a la planta donde procesan el café y entrega[e] las bayas que tiene.

En la planta, el café tiene su propia[f] rutina. Los trabajadores lavan[g] el café. Entonces procesan las bayas para separar la pulpa de los granos. Dejan[h] el café en agua por un día y entonces secan[i] los granos. Procesan el café otra vez para quitarle la cáscara.[j] Entonces tienen que tostar el café y meterlo en costales.[k] Venden[l] el café a un distribuidor y el distribuidor exporta el café a otros países.

[a]he picks   [b]He rests   [c]vuelve... he goes back to   [d]he walks   [e]he delivers   [f]own   [g]wash   [h]They leave   [i]They dry   [j]quitarle... remove the shell   [k]meterlo... put it into sacks   [l]They sell

PASO 2.   Number the first set of sentences from 1–5 to show a coffee farmer's daily routine. Then, number the second set of sentences from 1–8 to show the process for preparing raw coffee beans once they arrive at the processing plant.

La rutina del agricultor

_____ Almuerza y luego recolecta más café.

_____ Camina a la planta para entregar su café.

_____ Recolecta el café toda la mañana.

_____ Se levanta y desayuna.

_____ Va a los campos de café.

El proceso del café en la planta

_____ Dejan los granos en agua durante un día.

_____ El distribuidor exporta el café a muchos países.

_____ Primero, lavan las bayas.

_____ Procesan las bayas para separar la pulpa de los granos.

_____ Procesan los granos de café para quitar la cáscara.

_____ Secan el café.

_____ Tuestan el café y lo meten en costales.

_____ Venden el café al distribuidor.

 PASO 3.   With a partner, answer the following questions and discuss the ideas behind your responses.

1. El arbusto (*bush*) del café necesita lluvia (*rain*) todo el año y temperaturas moderadas o altas. Además de (*in addition to*) El Salvador y Nicaragua, ¿en qué países hispanos crees (*do you think*) que cultivan el café?
2. En el mundo hispano, hay países relativamente ricos y países relativamente pobres. Muchos de los países donde cultivan el café son relativamente pobres. ¿Por qué crees?
3. Cultivan el café comercialmente en solo un estado (*state*) de los Estados Unidos. ¿Qué estado es? ¿Por qué crees que es muy caro el café de ese estado?

Nicaragua   **El Salvador**

Vocabulario útil

el agricultor / la agricultora	farmer
las bayas	coffee berries/cherries
el campo	field
los granos	coffee beans
tostar (o → ue)	to roast

Unas bayas de café

■ Answers to this activity are in Appendix 2 at the back of your book.

○ Reciclaje

Infinitives

Complete each verb with its infinitive ending: **-ar, -er,** or **-ir.** Then indicate whether you prefer to do the activity **en la biblioteca (B)**, **en la casa (C)**, or **en otro lugar (O)** (*in another place*).

	B / C / O		B / C / O
1. almorz____	_____	7. estudi____	_____
2. cen____	_____	8. le____	_____
3. corr____	_____	9. mir____ la televisión	_____
4. desayun____	_____	10. nad____	_____
5. dorm____	_____	11. tom____ café	_____
6. hac____ ejercicio	_____		

3.3 Podemos nadar.

Stem-changing verbs: *o → ue*

Para empezar...

The daily lives of university students in the Spanish-speaking world are sometimes different than those of students in this country. Some primary reasons for these differences are that university students in the Spanish-speaking world typically do not live on campus, and beginning in their first year of studies they typically focus on a specialized area, such as law, pharmacy, or dentistry.

PASO 1. The following is a list of things that students can do on the campus of the **Universidad de Panamá,** but one item on the list is incorrect. Basing your answer on the information in the paragraph above, select which things can students most likely do.

EN LA UNIVERSIDAD DE PANAMÁ...

- ☐ **pueden** (*they can*) tomar café.
- ☐ **pueden** estudiar medicina.
- ☐ **pueden** nadar.
- ☐ **pueden** leer en la biblioteca.
- ☐ **pueden** vivir en la universidad.

PASO 2. Now compare what you just saw for the **Universidad de Panamá** with your own university. Which of these things can you do? Can you do all of these things? Any of them?

EN NUESTRA UNIVERSIDAD...

- ☐ **podemos** (*we can*) tomar café.
- ☐ **podemos** estudiar medicina.
- ☐ **podemos** nadar.
- ☐ **podemos** leer en la biblioteca.
- ☐ **podemos** vivir en la universidad.

■ Answers to these activities are in Appendix 2 at the back of your book.

En la universidad, podemos aprender mucho.

Actividades analíticas

1 Use the verb forms that you saw in **Para empezar** to complete the conjugation of **poder** (*can, to be able to*).

	poder (o → ue)
SINGULAR	
yo	**pue**do
tú	**pue**des
él/ella, Ud.	**pue**de
PLURAL	
nosotros/as	
vosotros/as	podéis
ellos/ellas, Uds.	

Poder is typically followed by a verb in the infinitive form.

A veces **puedo** estudiar en la biblioteca.	*Sometimes I can study in the library.*
¿**Puedes** llegar a las once?	*Can you arrive at 11:00?*
Graciela **puede** correr muy rápido.	*Graciela can run very fast.*

2 The endings that you see in the conjugation of **poder** are exactly what you would expect of an **-er** verb. The *stem*, on the other hand, is sometimes **pod-** and sometimes **pued-**. Complete the following list of the three instances where the stem is **pod-**, and write the conjugated form of **poder** associated with each.

1. el infinitivo: **poder**
2. la forma _____: _____
3. la forma **vosotros/as** : _____

In all other instances, the stem is **pued-**.

3 **Poder** is a *stem-changing verb* (**un verbo que cambia de raíz**). In this particular type of stem-changing verb, the vowel **o** of the stem changes to **ue** in all forms except **nosotros/as** and **vosotros/as.** Some other verbs of this type in Spanish are **almorzar, dormir,** and **soñar** (*to dream*).

José **almuerza** a la una.	*José has lunch at 1:00.*
¿Cuántas horas **duermes**?	*How many hours do you sleep?*
¿**Sueñas** todas las noches?	*Do you dream every night?*

Following the pattern with **poder,** write the **yo** and the **nosotros/as** forms for these verbs here.

	almorzar (o → ue)	dormir (o → ue)	soñar (o → ue)
yo			
nosotros/as			

Verbs of this type belong to the **o → ue** family of stem-changing verbs; you will see some other families of stem-changing verbs in **Capítulo 4.**

■ For additional *o → ue* stem-changing verbs, see **Para saber más 3.3** at the back of your book.

¿Por qué?

Why do verbs like **poder** change their stem in this way? To see this, compare where the stress falls in forms like **puedo** and **podemos.**

PUE-do   po-DE-mos   po-DER

The syllable containing **ue** is stressed, while the **o** is not stressed. This is characteristic of verbs like **poder:** the **o → ue** change occurs when the syllable is stressed. In many languages, vowels tend to change their pronunciation when they are stressed, and that is exactly what happens to the **o** in verbs like **poder.**

Un consejo...

This **o → ue** change happens in many words in Spanish, not just in verbs. One result is that cognates are sometimes hard to recognize, because the vowel in Spanish has become **ue,** while in English it has remained **o** (sometimes in combination with other letters). Here are some examples.

acuerdo *accord, agreement*
escuela *school*
fuente *fountain*
fuerza *force*
puerco *pork, pig*
puerto *port*

There are many cognate pairs like this in Spanish and English, so you may find it helpful to keep this **o → ue** change in mind when you encounter new words with **ue** in Spanish.

Actividades prácticas

A. ¿Qué puedes hacer? Write the correct form of the verb **poder** next to activities that you are able to do. Then ask others in the class whether they can do the remaining activities (**¿Puedes... ?**). Write the name of the person who can do each activity along with the correct form of **poder**. **¡Atención!** You can have more than one name on each line.

> MODELO: _____ hablar francés.
> **Puedo** hablar francés. (**Stephanie puede** hablar francés.)

¿QUIÉN PUEDE?   ¿QUÉ PUEDE HACER?

1. _____ correr cuatro millas (*miles*).
2. _____ cocinar comida china.
3. _____ dormir bien en una silla en la biblioteca.
4. _____ hablar dos o más idiomas (*languages*).
5. _____ leer en el autobús (*bus*).
6. _____ mirar la televisión y estudiar al mismo tiempo (*at the same time*).
7. _____ nadar estilo mariposa (*butterfly*).
8. _____ tocar la guitarra, cantar y bailar.

B. ¿Durante (*During*) el día o por la noche? When do you usually do each of the following activities, during the day or at night? Or never? Place each activity in the appropriate category.

> **Actividades:** almuerzo, sueño, duermo, juego los videojuegos

DURANTE EL DÍA:	_____	_____	_____
POR LA NOCHE:	_____	_____	_____
NUNCA:	_____	_____	_____

C. ¿Cuántas horas duermes?

PASO 1. In a group of three or four, find out how many hours each of you sleeps on a normal night and on a night when circumstances are ideal (that is, with a quiet environment, no alarm clock, and so on). Keep track of each person's answer.

> MODELO: ¿Cuántas horas duermes en una noche normal?
> ¿Cuántas horas duermes en una noche ideal?

PASO 2. Calculate the average for your group for the normal night and for the ideal night. Report your results in two separate sentences and state whether the situation is good (**bien**) or bad (**mal**).

> MODELO: En una noche normal, dormimos 5,6 (cinco coma seis) horas.
> En una noche ideal, dormimos 9,5 (nueve coma cinco) horas.
> (La situación) Está muy mal.

D. ¿A qué hora... ? In small groups, ask your classmates when they usually do the following activities. Then use the **nosotros** form to say whether you do the activity at the same time or at different times. **¡Atención!** All of these verbs belong to the **o → ue** family.

> **almorzar**   **dormir**   **volver a casa** (*return home*)

> MODELO: E1: ¿A qué hora almuerzas?
> E2: Almuerzo a las doce y media.
> E1: Yo también. Almorzamos a la misma (*same*) hora. (Yo almuerzo a la una. Almorzamos a horas diferentes.)

Reciclaje

Gender and definite articles

Write the correct article (**el** or **la**) for each word. Then circle the words related to *time*.

1. ____ teléfono
2. ____ noche
3. ____ día
4. ____ mes
5. ____ deporte
6. ____ televisión
7. ____ semana
8. ____ parque
9. ____ profesor
10. ____ hora
11. ____ mañana
12. ____ biblioteca

■ Answers to this activity are in Appendix 2 at the back of your book.

3.4 ¿A qué hora es esa clase?

Demonstrative adjectives

Para empezar...

In many countries, university students choose a specialized major from the beginning of their studies and all students in that major take the same classes. Here, for example, you see a class schedule for first-semester pharmacy students at the **Universidad Central de Venezuela.** Use this schedule to complete the sentences that follow.

HORA	LUNES	MARTES	MIÉRCOLES	JUEVES	VIERNES
7–8 A.M.	Física Prof. Michael Mijares		Química General Profa. Carmen Chirinos	Física Prof. Michael Mijares	Química General Profa. Carmen Chirinos
8–9 A.M.		Salud (*Health*) Pública Prof. Jaime Charris			
9–10 A.M.	Formación General Prof. Carlos Ayala		Química Orgánica I Profa. Ingrid Merchán		Química Orgánica I Profa. Ingrid Merchán
10–11 A.M.					
11–12 A.M.	Prácticas (*Laboratory*)	Prácticas		Prácticas	Prácticas
12–1 P.M.					
1–2 P.M.					
2–3 P.M.		Talleres (*Workshops*)		Química Orgánica I Prof. Carlos Ayala	

1. Tienen una clase a las siete de la mañana los lunes. **Esa** (*That*) clase se llama _____.
2. Uno de los profesores se llama Jaime Charris. Tienen la clase con **ese** profesor los _____.
3. Los martes, no tienen muchas clases. **Ese día,** solo tienen la clase de _____.
4. Los miércoles tienen dos clases. **Esas** clases son _____ y _____.
5. Los lunes y jueves tienen la clase de Física a las siete. También tienen la clase de _____ a **esa** hora los miércoles y viernes.
6. Dos de los profesores son Michael Mijares y Carlos Ayala. Tienen clases con **esos** profesores los _____ y _____.

■ Answers to these activities are in Appendix 2 at the back of your book.

Actividades analíticas

1 Words like **este, esta, estos,** and **estas** are *demonstrative adjectives* (**los adjetivos demostrativos**). They indicate that something is close or nearby, in the same way you would use English *this* or *these*. **Ese, esa, esos,** and **esas** are also demonstrative adjectives, but they refer to something that is farther away, similar to English *that* or *those*.

Esta mochila es vieja, pero me gusta.	*This backpack is old, but I like it.*
Este libro es muy bueno.	*This book is very good.*
Me gustan **esas revistas.**	*I like those magazines.*

2 Demonstrative adjectives, like other adjectives in Spanish, agree with the noun that they modify in both number and gender. Complete the following chart by correctly placing the above demonstrative adjectives in the chart.

	DEMONSTRATIVE ADJECTIVES			
	SINGULAR		**PLURAL**	
MASCULINE	**est**e libro	*this book*	**est**os libros	*these books*
	_____ libro	*that book*	_____ libros	*those books*
FEMININE	**est**a clase	*this class*	**est**as clases	*these classes*
	_____ clase	*that class*	_____ clases	*those classes*

■ For more on demonstrative adjectives and demonstrative pronouns see **Para saber más 3.4** at the back of your book.

3 Choose the correct demonstrative adjective for these nouns, assuming that they are close to you.

_____ bolígrafo   _____ señoras   _____ niños   _____ mochila

Actividades prácticas

A. ¿Cierto o falso?   Listen to the sentences and write **C** for **cierto** or **F** for **falso.**

1.___   2.___   3.___   4.___   5.___   6.___   7.___   8.___

■ The audio files for in-text listening activities are available in the eBook, within Connect Plus activities, and on the Online Learning Center.

B. Preguntas   For each of the following items, first answer the question in (a), then provide the correct form of **ese, esa, esos,** or **esas.** Finally, answer the question in (b).

RESPUESTAS

1. a. ¿Cómo se llama el actor favorito de Gael García Bernal?   _____
   b. ¿De qué país es ___ actor?   _____
2. a. ¿Cuántos colombianos hay en la **Actividad práctica C** de **3.1**?   _____
   b. ¿De qué país son ___ personas?   _____
3. a. ¿Cómo se llama el país al norte (*north*) de Guatemala?   _____
   b. ¿A qué hora comen en ___ país?   _____
4. a. ¿Cómo se dice *to work* en español?   _____
   b. ¿Cuál es la forma *yo* de ___ verbo?   _____
5. a. ¿Cuál es la palabra para *five* en español?   _____
   b. ¿Cuántas letras tiene ___ palabra?   _____
6. a. ¿Cuántos bolígrafos tienes en tu mochila?   _____
   b. ¿De qué color son ___ bolígrafos?   _____

C. En la sala de computación   Imagine that you are the student in the doorway. What is nearest him is nearest you, and what is far from him is far from you. With a partner, write four sentences comparing and contrasting what you see in the lab.

MODELO: Esta chica tiene el pelo castaño, pero esa chica tiene el pelo rubio.

D. Las cosas de la clase   Create five sentences, some true and some false, about objects in the classroom. Choose some objects that are in your possession (such as **este libro**) and others that are far away (such as **ese libro**). Read the sentences to a partner and ask him/her to reply **cierto** or **falso** to each one.

MODELOS: Estos bolígrafos son rojos.
Esos libros son de Mary.
Esa mochila es muy grande.

¡Leamos!

Un día en la vida° de la presidenta   *life*

Antes de leer

PASO 1. You're going to read about the work schedule of Cristina Fernández de Kirchner, the president of Argentina from 2007 to 2015. First, read the following elements of a typical work day and put them in the order you would expect from a president.

_____ comer con la familia

_____ hacer ejercicio

_____ informarse de las noticias (*to find out about news*)

_____ reunirse con (*to meet with*) colegas

_____ reunirse con representantes de otras (*other*) organizaciones

_____ trabajar en el despacho (la oficina)

PASO 2. The activities in **Paso 1** come from a professional's work life schedule. For each element in that schedule, write on a separate piece of paper an equivalent for the life of a student.

> **MODELO:** Para una persona profesional **trabajar en el despacho** es como (*is like*) **estudiar en la biblioteca** para un(a) estudiante.

1. comer con la familia
2. hacer ejercicio
3. informarse de las noticias
4. reunirse con colegas
5. reunirse con representantes de otras organizaciones

A leer

PASO 1. Read over the questions in **Paso 2 on** page 89, then read the article about the daily activities of the President of Argentina, Cristina Fernández de Kirchner.

Un día en la vida de la presidenta

La presidenta, Cristina Fernández de Kirchner, comienza[a] su día en la Quinta de Olivos, donde vive…

Su primera actividad de la mañana es leer los diarios[b] y hacer algo de ejercicio antes de tomar el helicóptero que la traerá[c] a su despacho en la Casa Rosada. …

Normalmente su actividad empieza[d] con reuniones[e] internas junto al Secretario General u otros miembros del Gabinete.[f]

A media mañana es habitual que la presidenta participe de algún[g] acto en el Salón Blanco o en distintas localidades del país. Habitualmente se trata de firma de acuerdos,[h] inauguraciones o anuncios de obras[i] que el gobierno lleva adelante.[j]

Siempre que[k] puede, vuelve[l] a la residencia de Olivos para almorzar junto a su familia. Después regresa a su despacho para seguir[m] con la actividad de gobierno.

Durante la tarde suele[n] tener reuniones en su despacho y otras actividades públicas. …

También es frecuente que la presidenta viaje a otros países para participar en encuentros[ñ] internacionales o reunirse con otros gobernantes y firmar acuerdos entre naciones o simplemente estrechar vínculos.[o] …

Tanto cuando viaja como[p] en Buenos Aires, su actividad suele terminar tarde por la noche.

Muchos fines de semana se traslada[q] a su provincia, Santa Cruz, donde descansa junto a su familia en (la provincia de) Río Gallegos…

[a]*begins* [b]*periódicos* [c]*la… will take her* [d]*comienza* [e]*meetings* [f]*Cabinet* [g]*some* [h]*firma… signing agreements* [i]*public works projects* [j]*lleva… takes forward* [k]*Siempre… As often as* [l]*she returns* [m]*continue* [n]*she tends* [ñ]*conferences* [o]*estrechar… strengthen connections* [p]*Tanto… Both when she travels and when she's* [q]*se… she goes*

PASO 2.   Now answer the questions and complete the activity.

1. ¿Cómo se llama la casa de la presidenta de Argentina?

2. ¿Qué hace la presidenta antes de (*before*) trabajar?

3. ¿Cómo llega (*does she arrive*) al trabajo?

4. ¿Dónde está la oficina de la presidenta?

5. Indica las actividades que hace la presidenta.

   ☐ anuncia obras del gobierno   ☐ tiene reuniones con sus empleados
   ☐ asiste a inauguraciones   ☐ participa en actos públicos
   ☐ escribe las leyes (*writes laws*) del país   ☐ tiene reuniones con líderes de otros países
   ☐ firma acuerdos   ☐ viaja a otros países

6. ¿Cuándo termina el día de trabajo?

Después de leer

PASO 1.   Look again at the activities you put in order in **Antes de leer, Paso 1**. This time, order them according to what you just read about Fernández de Kirchner's schedule and compare the lists. Does the president's schedule differ from how you envisioned a typical work day? If so, how?

PASO 2.   Now work in pairs to interview each other about your own daily routines following the model from the reading.

   1. ¿Cuál es tu primera actividad de la mañana?

   2. ¿Cómo empiezan las actividades del trabajo o de la universidad?

   3. ¿Qué haces a media mañana?

   4. ¿Qué haces para almorzar?

   5. Normalmente, ¿cuándo termina el día?

   6. ¿Qué haces los fines de semana?

PASO 3.   Prepare a presentation of your classmate's day using format and structures from the reading as models.

   MODELO: (*Nombre*) comienza su día en… Normalmente su actividad empieza con…

   A media mañana…

   Para almorzar…

   Su día termina…

   Los fines de semana…

¡Escuchemos!

El horario para comer

 Antes de escuchar

Fill in the first row of the table below with the times you typically eat. Then ask three of your classmates when they tend to eat, and include their information in the table.

MODELO: E1: ¿A qué hora desayunas?
E2: A las nueve y media. ¿y tú?
E1: A las ocho.

 A escuchar

Now watch the video of Isabel, Claudia, Roberto, and María and fill in the times they say they eat.

NOMBRE	EL DESAYUNO	EL ALMUERZO/ LA COMIDA	LA CENA
yo			
Isabel (México)			
Claudia (Argentina)			
Roberto (Costa Rica)			
María (España)			

Después de escuchar

PASO 1.   Compare the schedules of Isabel, Claudia, Roberto, and María and say whether they are **muy diferentes, similares** or **iguales.**

1. Los horarios de desayunar de Isabel, Claudia, Roberto y María son…

2. Los horarios de comer/almorzar de Isabel, Claudia, Roberto y María son…

3. Los horarios de cenar de Isabel, Claudia, Roberto y María son…

PASO 2.   Now compare your schedule and those of your classmates to the schedules of the people in the video. Present your conclusions to the class.

MODELO: Mi horario y el horario de Isabel son iguales porque desayunamos a las nueve, comemos a las dos y cenamos a las nueve.
Los horarios de cenar de los estudiantes de esta clase y los de Isabel y María son muy diferentes porque nosotros cenamos a las seis de la tarde y ellas cenan a las nueve o diez de la noche.

En español…

In many parts of the Spanish-speaking world, **la comida** and **el almuerzo** refer to the same midday meal, but that isn't true everywhere. In Mexico, for instance, **el almuerzo** is a morning meal. As you may notice in the video, in Argentina, as in many other Spanish-speaking countries, some people eat **la merienda** regularly between lunch and dinner.

CONÉCTATE AL MUNDO HISPANO:

The schedules of Isabel, Claudia, Roberto, and María represent common patterns in the Spanish-speaking world, where a large family meal is often eaten at midday and a light supper is eaten later in the evening. But be careful not to jump to conclusions about a whole country based on one person—schedules vary widely and Isabel, Claudia, Roberto, and María are just four individuals. Think of your schedule at college, which is probably quite different than your parents' schedule; neither one can be said to represent all of this country's culture.

¡Escribamos!

Las rutinas diarias

Comparing daily routines with others is a great way to make cross-cultural connections while traveling or studying abroad. You may find that you have activities in common, and can plan to do them together, allowing you to meet new people and experience the culture from a more intimate perspective. Or, you may find that your routines are very different, which provides an opportunity to learn and try new things.

You've worked a lot in this chapter with your own schedule, so for this activity you'll focus on the schedule of someone who is not a student.

Antes de escribir

Prepare a timeline of at least four activities in a family member's routine on a typical day. (Ideally, select someone who is not a student.)

> **MODELO:** mi madre
>
> | 6:30 | 7:00 | 8:00 | | 3:00 |
> |------|------|------|---|------|
> | desayunar | ir a | trabajar | | comer |
> | | la oficina | | | |

A escribir

PASO 1. Use the timeline to guide you as you convert these isolated activities into at least four complete sentences.

> **MODELOS:** Mi madre desayuna a las seis y media de la mañana.
> A las siete de la mañana, ella va a la oficina.

PASO 2. Next, flesh out each sentence by adding more description to help turn them into a more cohesive paragraph. Try to anticipate questions your readers might have (such as **¿dónde?** and **¿con quién?**), and incorporate the answers into your paragraph.

> **MODELO:** Todos los días a las seis y media de la mañana mi madre desayuna cereal en casa (*at home*) con mi hermanito. Los días de entre semana, él va en autobús (*bus*) a la escuela y ella va en coche (*car*) a la oficina.

Después de escribir

PASO 1. Check your own work, then exchange paragraphs with a classmate. Read the content of your classmate's essay carefully. Are there any important pieces of information missing? If so, be sure to point that out. Next, read the essay again, using the following checklist to edit the grammar.

Verifica que (*Check that*)…

☐ hay concordancia (*agreement*) de género (*gender*) entre los adjetivos y lo que describen (*what they describe*)

☐ hay concordancia de número (singular o plural) entre los adjetivos y lo que describen

☐ hay concordancia entre los sustantivos (*nouns*) y verbos

☐ los verbos con cambio de raíz tienen los cambios correctos

When you are finished, return the paper to your classmate and make corrections to your own, based on your classmate's feedback.

PASO 2. Now exchange essays with another classmate. Read your classmate's paragraph, then ask at least two follow-up questions about the content. Together, compare your paragraphs. Do your family members' schedules have anything in common? Do their schedules have anything in common with your own schedules as students? Talk about the similarities and differences with your partner.

¡Hablemos!

La rutina de la familia Ramírez

Antes de hablar

Based on the illustrations of this family's daily routine, indicate which of the invitations below would make sense (**Es lógico**) and which would not (**No es lógico**). Can you explain why?

	ES LÓGICO	NO ES LÓGICO
1. Jaime, ¿corremos a las ocho y quince de la mañana?	☐	☐
2. Elena, ¿vamos de compras a las diez de la mañana?	☐	☐
3. Marisol, ¿montamos a caballo por la tarde?	☐	☐
4. Ignacio, ¿corremos a las dos de la tarde?	☐	☐
5. Marisol, ¿jugamos fútbol a las nueve de la noche?	☐	☐

 ### A hablar

Make plans with at least two different classmates to do some of the activities the family pictured does.

MODELO: E1: Claire, ¿montamos a caballo a las cinco?
E2: No puedo. Tengo clase hasta las seis. ¿Montamos a caballo mañana a las diez de la mañana?
E1: Sí.

 ### Después de hablar

In groups, take turns describing something from the pictures without naming the item. Can the others guess what you are describing? **¡Atención!** Use vocabulary from **Capítulos 1** and **2**.

MODELO: E1: Es pequeño y blanco. Tiene números.
E2: ¿Es el reloj?
E1: ¡Sí!

En español…

Just as you might say *Joe, are we going running at 2:00?* as a way to invite someone to do something or to confirm plans, you can also use present tense to invite in Spanish.

Carmen, ¿vamos al comedor a las 6:30?
Carmen, do you want to go to the cafeteria at 6:30?
(Carmen, we're going to the cafeteria at 6:30, right?)

Conéctate a la música

Canción: «Ella tiene fuego (*fire*)» (2010)
Artistas: Celia Cruz (Cuba) y El General (Panamá)

Celia Cruz (1925–2003) era (*was*) una cantante muy famosa de Cuba. Era muy conocida (*well known*) en Cuba y en los Estados Unidos. La canción «Ella tiene fuego» es del álbum *Regalo del alma* (*Gift from the Soul*). Es el último (*last*) álbum de estudio que ella hizo antes de su muerte (*made before her death*) en 2003. La canción (*song*) incluye la voz (*voice*) del cantante panameño El General, quien es conocido por su música reggae.

Antes de escuchar

PASO 1. Music is a very important aspect of Cuban culture. **Tiene fuego** is a slang expression to describe someone who is dancing. What do you think it could mean?

PASO 2. Circle the verbs that you associate with music.

almorzar	comer	**mover** to move
bailar	escuchar	**tocar la guitarra**
cantar	**jugar los videojuegos**	viajar

A escuchar

> **Expresiones útiles**
>
> **las caderas** hips   **la fiesta** party
>
> **el ciclón** cyclone   **todo el mundo** everyone
>
> **las piernas** legs   **pregunta de qué está hecha** asks what she is made of

Read the text below, then listen once to the song all the way through. Then listen again, paying attention to the chorus. Fill in the blanks with the correct form of the verb **tener, ser,** or **mover** (*to move,* o → ue).

Ella _____ fuego cuando _____ las caderas.

Ella _____ fuego; _____ un ciclón en las piernas.

Ella _____ fuego; _____ la atracción de la fiesta.

Ella _____ fuego y todo el mundo pregunta de qué está hecha.

Después de escuchar

PASO 1. **¿Cierto o falso?** Indicate whether the following statements are true or false.

	CIERTO	FALSO
1. La mujer de la canción no puede bailar bien.	_____	_____
2. A ella le gusta bailar.	_____	_____
3. Se mueve lentamente (*slowly*) cuando baila.	_____	_____
4. Ella atrae (*attracts*) mucha atención en las fiestas.	_____	_____

 PASO 2. Work with a partner to ask and answer the following questions. Be sure to use complete sentences in your answers.

¿A ti te gustan las fiestas? ¿Te gusta bailar? ¿Bailas bien? ¿Tus amigos «tienen fuego» cuando ellos bailan? ¿Qué otras actividades haces (*do you do*) en las fiestas? (¿Comes? ¿Tocas la guitarra? ¿Hablas con amigos? ¿Juegas videojuegos? ¿ ?)

La cantante cubana, Celia Cruz

■ For copyright reasons, the songs referenced in **Conéctate a la música** have not been provided by the publisher. The video for this song can be found on YouTube, and it is available for purchase from the iTunes store.

■ The video for this song can be found on YouTube, and it is available for purchase from the iTunes store.

VOCABULARIO

Comunicación

¿Qué hora es?	What time is it?
Es la una.	It's 1:00.
Es la una y media.	It's 1:30.
Son las dos y cuarto.	It's 2:15.
Son diez para las nueve. /	
Son las nueve menos diez.	It's 8:50.
Es mediodía.	It's noon.
Es medianoche.	It's midnight.
¿A qué hora... ?	At what time . . . ?
Es a la/las...	It's at . . .
de la mañana	in the morning
de la tarde	in the afternoon/ evening
de la noche	at night
de la madrugada	in the early A.M. hours
por la mañana	(*generally*) during the morning
por la tarde	(*generally*) during the afternoon/ evening
por la noche	(*generally*) during the night
Disculpa... / Disculpe... / Disculpen...	Excuse me . . . (*inform. / form. / pl.*)
Oye... / Oiga... / Oigan...	Listen . . . (*inform. / form. / pl.*)

Los días de la semana — The days of the week

los días de entre semana	weekdays
lunes, martes, miércoles, jueves, viernes	
el fin de semana	weekend
sábado, domingo	

Los sustantivos

la comida	food; (midday) meal
la escuela	school
el horario	schedule
la vez (*pl.* veces)	time; instance
una vez	once
dos veces	twice
el país	country

La rutina diaria — The daily routine

almorzar (ue)	to eat lunch
asistir (a)	to attend

cantar	to sing
cenar	to eat dinner
cocinar	to cook
comer (comida mexicana)	to eat (Mexican food)
comprar	to buy
correr (en el parque)	to run (in the park)
desayunar	to eat breakfast
escuchar	to listen (to)
hablar (por teléfono)	to talk (on the phone)
hacer (*irreg.*) ...	to do
ejercicio	to exercise
la tarea	to do homework
ir (*irreg.*) al gimnasio	to go to the gym
jugar (ue)...	to play . . .
básquetbol	basketball
fútbol	soccer
los videojuegos	video games
leer (el periódico)	to read (the paper)
mirar (la televisión)	to watch (television)
montar a caballo	to go horseback riding
nadar	to swim
poder (ue)	can, to be able to
practicar...	to practice/do/play . . .
un deporte	a sport
yoga	yoga
regresar	to return
soñar (ue)	to dream
tocar (la guitarra)	to play (guitar)
tomar...	
café	to drink coffee
el tren	to take the train
trabajar	to work
viajar	to travel
vivir	to live
volver (ue)	to return

Los adjetivos demostrativos — Demonstrative adjectives

ese/esa, esos/esas	that, those
este/esta, estos/estas	this, these

Expresiones útiles

a veces	sometimes
nunca	never
siempre	always
todo/a; todos/as	all; everyone; all of us
todo el día / toda la noche	all day / night
todos los días	every day

¡Qué bonita familia!

Una niña guatemalteca con su familia

Objetivos

In this chapter you will learn how to:

- ask what people do for a living
- comment on things and compliment people
- talk about your family members and their activities
- compare and contrast people and things
- talk about what you want or plan to do

4

connect
| SPANISH

http://www.connectspanish.com

COMUNICACIÓN LARIO UCTURA ATE

¿A qué te dedicas? / ¿A qué se dedica?

Asking what people do for a living

A. A ver: Introducciones

PASO 1. First, work in pairs to ask and answer the questions that you will hear answered in the video clips.

> **MODELO:** E1: ¿Cómo te llamas?
> E2: Mónica.

¿Cómo te llamas?
¿De dónde eres?
¿Cuántos años tienes?

PASO 2. Watch and listen as Spanish-speakers introduce themselves, then complete the chart.

En español...

Just as English speakers use fillers such as *uh, um,* and *OK* in spontaneous speech, Spanish speakers use expressions such as **pues, bueno, eh,** and **OK.** If you watch and listen to the speakers in **Actividad A** again you will notice that almost all of them use one of those fillers when they begin to speak.

¿Quién es?	¿Cómo se llama?	¿Cuántos años tiene?	¿De dónde es?	¿A qué se dedica?
1.	_____ Chavarría Mora			
2.		X		
3.		X		
4.	Kadín Eliecer Morán		Panamá	
5.	Yazmín Lyons	X		
6.	_____ Sequeira Chávez		_____, Costa Rica	
7.				trabaja en banca privada

You have learned how to introduce yourself by providing the answers to the following questions.

¿Cómo te llamas? / ¿Cómo se llama?
¿De dónde eres? / ¿De dónde es?
¿Cuántos años tienes? / ¿Cuántos años tiene?

An additional piece of information that people may offer when introducing themselves is the answer to these questions.

¿Cuál es tu profesión? / ¿Cuál es su profesión? ⎫
¿A qué te dedicas? / ¿A qué se dedica? ⎭ What do you do (for a living)?

—**Mavi, ¿a qué te dedicas?**   —**Señora Serna, ¿cuál es su profesión?**
—**Estudio ciencias políticas.**   —**Soy ingeniera** (*engineer*).

Here are some common professions. Can you figure out all the cognates?

abogado/a	attorney	**periodista**	journalist
ama de casa	housewife	**pintor(a)**	painter
chofer		**policía**	
doctor(a) / médico/a		**psicólogo/a**	
guía naturalista		**sociólogo/a**	

B. ¿A quién conoces? (*Whom do you know?*) Draw a grid with nine cells, like tic-tac-toe: three columns of three rows each. Fill each cell with a profession you know how to say in Spanish. For each cell in the table, try to find a classmate who knows someone who practices that profession and circle it. When you have three circles in a row, sit down.

> **MODELO:** E1: ¿Conoces a (*Do you know*) un policía?
> E2: No. ¿Conoces a un ingeniero?
> E1: ¡Mi padre es ingeniero!

¡Qué lindo!
Commenting on things and complimenting people

To express the equivalent of *How* + adjective*!* or *What a* + noun*!* use: **¡Qué... !**

¡Qué + adjective**!**
  ¡Qué guapo/a!   How cute! / How handsome! (*to a friend who is dressed up for a special occasion*)

¡Qué + noun**!**
  ¡Qué lío!   What a mess!
  ¡Qué frío/calor!   It's so cold/hot! (*when it's noticeably or unusually cold/hot*)

¡Atención! Remember, whenever you use an adjective, it must agree in number and gender with the noun it refers to.

A. No estamos de acuerdo. (*We don't agree.*) Work in pairs, using the list of adjectives as a starting point. For each word your partner gives, say the opposite. How many more adjectives can you add to the list?

> **MODELOS:** E1: ¡Qué bueno!
> E2: ¡Qué malo!
>
> E1: ¡Qué feo!
> E2: ¡Qué lindo!

> alto/a bajo/a bello/a
> débil delgado/a feo/a frío/a
> gordo/a gracioso/a guapo/a
> joven lento/a lindo/a
> pequeño/a rápido/a

■ The audio files for in-text listening activities are available in the eBook, within Connect Plus activities, and on the Online Learning Center.

En español...

Here are some more expressions that use **¡Qué... !**

¡Qué cara (tiene)!
What nerve!

¡Qué coraje! / ¡Qué rabia!
How frustrating/annoying!

¡Qué feo/a!
How ugly! / How horrible!
(*weather, behavior, situation, and so on*)

¡Qué pesado!
What a pain! / How annoying!

¡Qué rico/a!
How delicious!

B. Las reacciones Look at the following images and listen for expressions with **¡Qué... !** Does the expression fit the image? React by using «es lógico» or «no es ilógico». If it's not logical, suggest a reaction that would be logical.

MODELO:

You hear: ¡Qué triste! *You say:* Es lógico.

1.
2.

3.
4.

5.
6.

C. ¡Qué bueno!

PASO 1. Write an example of each of the following. Try to include examples from the Spanish-speaking world.

1. el nombre de un actor
2. el nombre de una actriz
3. el título de una película
4. el título de un libro
5. el nombre de un grupo musical
6. el título de una canción (*song*)
7. el nombre de un restaurante
8. el nombre de un curso
9. el nombre de una ciudad
10. el nombre de una universidad

PASO 2. Now express your opinions! Working in pairs, take turns naming things from your list. Your partner will react using **¡Qué... !** expressions.

MODELO: E1: La clase de biología.
E2: ¡Qué aburrida! ¡Qué pesada! *or* ¿La biología? ¡Qué interesante!

COMUN **VOCABULARIO** UCTURA ATE

¿Cómo es la familia de Camila?

Describing family members

Carmen
la abuela
72 años

Ricardo
el abuelo
75 años

Antonio
el padre
52 años

María
la madre
50 años

Jaime
el tío
42 años

Aurelia
la tía
39 años

Gustavo
el tío
42 años

Chispa
el perro

Camila
16 años

Reina
la gata

Hernán
el pez

Sebastián
el primo
13 años

Isabel
la prima
10 años

■ **Note:** More family vocabulary is listed later in this chapter.

El padre de Camila se llama Antonio. María es **la madre** de Camila.
Camila es **hija única:** Ella no tiene **hermanos.**
El tío de Camila se llama Jaime. Él es soltero (no tiene **mujer**).
Aurelia es **la tía** de Camila. Su **marido** se llama Gustavo.
Jaime tiene otra **sobrina** además de (*in addition to*) Camila: Isabel.
Aurelia y Gustavo tienen dos **hijos: un hijo,** Sebastián, y **una hija,** Isabel.
La abuela de Camila se llama Carmen; Ricardo es **el abuelo** de Camila.
Sebastián es **el nieto** de Carmen y Ricardo.
Camila tiene **un perro,** Chispa, y **una gata,** Reina.
Sebastián (**el primo** de Camila) e Isabel (**la prima** de Camila) tienen **un pez,** Hernán.
La familia tiene tres **mascotas** en total: un perro, un gato y un pez.

A. La familia de Camila
Look at the family tree on page 99 and read the statements below it. Then answer the following questions about Camila.

1. ¿Quiénes son **los padres** de Camila?
2. ¿Cuántos años tiene **la madre** de Camila? ¿Y **el padre** de Camila?
3. ¿Cómo se llaman **los hijos** de Aurelia y Gustavo?
4. ¿Cómo se llaman las dos **sobrinas** de Jaime?
5. ¿Cuántos años tiene **el sobrino** de Jaime?
6. ¿Quiénes son **los abuelos** de Camila?
7. ¿Cuántos **nietos** tienen Carmen y Ricardo?
8. ¿Quién es **el nieto** de Carmen y Ricardo?
9. ¿Cómo se llaman las dos **nietas** de Ricardo y Carmen?
10. ¿Cuántas **mascotas** hay en la familia?

B. Definiciones
Provide the family term that corresponds to each definition.

1. La madre de mi padre es mi…
2. La hermana de mi madre es mi…
3. El hijo de mi hijo es mi…
4. La hija de mi hermano es mi…
5. La esposa de mi padre es mi…
6. El marido de mi abuela es mi…
7. Los hijos de mi tía son mis…
8. La madre de mi sobrina es mi…
9. El padre de mi nieto es mi…
10. Los hermanos de mi padre son mis…

C. Noticias sobre mi familia

PASO 1. Read the following statements about the speaker's family and react accordingly using the **¡Qué… !** structure. The following words will help you.

bueno	horrible	terrible
emocionante (*exciting*)	interesante	triste (*sad*)
fabuloso	malo	
fantástico	maravilloso	

> **MODELO:** Mi primo ganó una beca (*won a scholarship*) para asistir a la universidad. →
> ¡Qué maravilloso!

1. Mi padre perdió (*lost*) su trabajo.
2. Mi tía está embarazada (*pregnant*).
3. Mi prima tiene 16 años y quiere casarse con (*marry*) su novio.
4. Mi hermana acaba de empezar su propio negocio (*own business*).
5. Mis abuelos están de vacaciones en Puerto Rico.
6. Mi hermano está enfermo (*sick*).

PASO 2. Now share at least two pieces of news about your own family (or be creative and invent news) with a partner. Your partner will react using the **¡Qué… !** structure.

¿Tienen una nueva mascota? ¡Qué bueno!

Vocabulario

Relatives are **los familiares** or **los parientes**.
Here are some more relatives.

el/la bisabuelo/a	great-grandfather/great-grandmother
el/la cuñado/a	brother-in-law/sister-in-law
el/la esposo/a	spouse
la nuera	daughter-in-law
el/la suegro/a	father-in-law/mother-in-law
el yerno	son-in-law

Step-relationships use the suffix **-astro/a.**

el/la hermanastro/a	stepbrother/stepsister
el/la hijastro/a	stepson/stepdaughter
la madrastra	stepmother
el padrastro	stepfather

Las mascotas are also part of many families.

el/la gato/a	cat
el/la perro/a	dog
el pez (*pl.* **los peces**)	fish

D. A ver: Los miembros de la familia

PASO 1. Watch and listen as the following people describe their families. For each family member they mention, there are two terms provided. Circle the one used in the video.

1.
   Francisco

   a. padre   papá
   b. madre   mamá
   c. hermano   hermana
   d. abuelo   abuelos
   e. tíos   hermanos de mi mamá

2. Angélica

   a. padres   papás
   b. hermanas   hermanos
   c. madre   mamá
   d. hija   hijo

3. Michael

   a. madre   mamá
   b. padre   papá
   c. abuelo   abuelos
   d. tíos   hermanos de mi mamá
   e. hermano   hermana

4. Guadalupe

   a. padre   papá
   b. madre   mamá
   c. hermanas   hermanos
   d. sobrino   sobrinos

PASO 2. Make a list indicating a) the family members you see most often and b) the family members you see only once in a while. Make sure you use two ways of describing your relative (for example: madre/mamá; tía/hermana de mi mamá, etc.). Are there occasions that usually bring your whole family together? What are they?

E. ¿Quién soy? Identify the family member relationships for each of the following.

1. SILVIA: Me casé con (*married*) Julio, pero la relación fue (*went*) muy mal y nos divorciamos. Luego, me casé con Ramón. Ramón ya tenía (*already had*) un hijo, Esteban. Ahora soy la _____ de Esteban. Esteban es mi _____.

2. EFRAÍN: Mi esposa se llama Carla. La madre de Carla se llama Liliana. Liliana es mi _____. Yo soy el _____ de Liliana.

3. JOSEFA: Mi esposo se llama Carlos. El hermano de Carlos se llama Guillermo. Yo soy la _____ de Guillermo. Guillermo es mi _____.

F. ¿Cómo es la familia de Pedro y Manuela?

PASO 1. Work in pairs to complete Pedro and Manuela's family tree. One partner should consult only the family tree labeled **Estudiante 1,** while the other should consult only the family tree labeled **Estudiante 2.**

> **MODELO:** E1: ¿Cómo se llama la esposa de Pedro?
> E2: Manuela.
>
> E2: ¿Cuántos años tiene?
> E1: 65 años.

PASO 2. Compare your finished products. Do you both have the same family tree and correct ages?

Para **Estudiante 1**

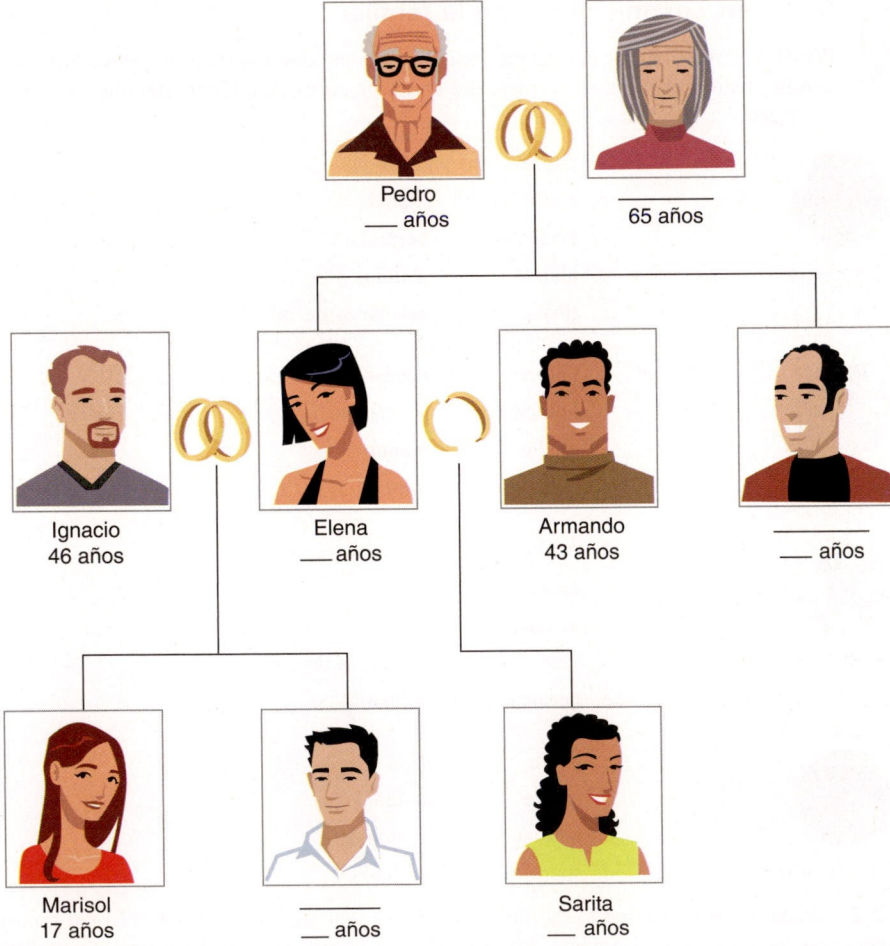

Para Estudiante 2

Pedro
70 años

Manuela
___ años

___ años

Elena
45 años

___ años

José Manuel
39 años

___ años

Jorge
22 años

25 años

G. ¡Qué bonita familia!

PASO 1. Work in pairs to interview each other and find out more about your family members and pets. (You can make up an imaginary family if you prefer.) Draw your partner's family tree as you go and react to what you find out about your partner using **¡Qué… familia!**

Sample questions:
¿Con quién vives?
¿Cómo se llaman los padres de tu mamá/papá?
¿Tienes hermanos? ¿Cuántos? ¿Cómo se llaman? ¿Cómo son?
¿Quién es tu pariente favorito? ¿Por qué?
¿Tienes primos?

PASO 2. Report to the class your reaction about your partner's family. Use the family tree you created and any other details you learned during your interview to support your reaction.

> **MODELO:** ¡Qué pequeña familia tiene Joe! Es hijo único. Vive con su mamá y papá y no tiene mascotas.

En español…

In Spanish, *godmother* and *godfather* are **la madrina** and **el padrino** (*godparents* = **los padrinos**). The *godchild* is **el ahijado** or **la ahijada**.

Comadre refers to the close relationship between the parents and the godmother of a child.
Compadre is the relationship between the parents and godfather.

Elena es mi comadre; es la madrina de mi hijo.

Fernando y yo somos compadres.

Compadres can also sometimes be close family friends.

COMUN VOCABU ESTRUCTURA ATE

 Reciclaje

Adjectives

The Grammy award–winning Mexican singer Julieta Venegas has an identical twin sister Yvonne, an accomplished and very successful photographer whose work has been exhibited at several major museums. Given this information, and given the photo here, how would you describe the two sisters? Choose from the adjectives provided. **¡Atención!** Be sure to make the adjectives agree!

bonito/a delgado/a feo/a gordo/a joven pobre rico/a viejo/a

Las hermanas Venegas son…

——————, ——————, y ——————.

■ Answers to this activity are in Appendix 2 at the back of your book.

4.1 Es más alto que su padre

Comparatives

Para empezar…

As in some other European countries with monarchies, Spain's **familia real** (*royal family*) has played a prominent but mainly ceremonial role in the country. Members of the family include **el rey** (*king*) Felipe VI, **la reina** (*queen*) Letizia, and the king's parents **el rey** Juan Carlos I and **la reina** Sofía.* King Felipe and Queen Letizia have two daughters, **la princesa** Leonor and **la princesa** Sofía. Match each of the statements below to a member of the royal family. **¡Atención!** Some items have more than one possible answer.

■ Answers to these activities are in Appendix 2 at the back of your book.

	LA REINA LETIZIA	EL REY FELIPE	EL REY JUAN CARLOS	LA REINA SOFÍA	LA PRINCESA SOFÍA	LA PRINCESA LEONOR
1. Es más (*more*) alto que su padre.	☐	☐	☐	☐	☐	☐
2. Es más delgada que su esposo.	☐	☐	☐	☐	☐	☐
3. Es más bajo que su hijo.	☐	☐	☐	☐	☐	☐
4. Es más alta que sus nietas.	☐	☐	☐	☐	☐	☐
5. Es más alto que su esposa.	☐	☐	☐	☐	☐	☐
6. Es más baja que su mamá.	☐	☐	☐	☐	☐	☐

———————
*With King Juan Carlos' abdication of the throne in 2014, **el príncipe** (*prince*) Felipe became king and his wife became queen. The former king and queen retain their titles for life.

Actividades analíticas

1 In English, to make comparisons in which one person has *more* of a given quality, *-er* may be added to the adjective: *Mary is taller than Catherine.*

The word *more* may also be used: *Mary is more intelligent than Catherine.*

What word is used to make these comparisons in Spanish? _____

Where English uses the word *than*, Spanish uses **que.**

José es **más** alto **que** Antonio.	*José is taller than Antonio.*
Mónica y Julia son **más** delgadas **que** José.	*Mónica and Julia are thinner than José.*

You can see in these comparisons that the adjective agrees with the subject, just as it would in any other sentence.

2 To express a comparison in which one person has *less* of a given quality than the other, use **menos.**

Antonio es **menos** alto **que** José.	*Antonio is less tall than (not as tall as) José.*

Now try converting the following statements with **más** into ones with **menos. ¡Atención!** Be sure the adjective agrees with the subject.

María es más rica que Celia. → Celia es _____ que María.

Juan es más alto que Marisela. → Marisela es _____ que Juan.

Patricia es más alta que los niños. → Los niños son _____ que Patricia.

José es más alto que Antonio.

■ For more on making comparisons in Spanish, see **Para saber más 4.1** at the back of your book.

En español…

For the adjectives **bueno** and **malo**, there are special comparative forms.

mejor	*better*	Mi hermano juega a fútbol **mejor** que yo.
		My brother plays soccer better than I do.
peor	*worse*	El lunes es **peor** que el martes.
		Monday is worse than Tuesday.

When comparing people's ages, it is common to use **mayor** (*older*) and **menor** (*younger*).

Ana es **mayor** que su hermana.	*Arturo is older than his sister.*
Yo soy **menor** que tú.	*I'm younger than you.*
Nosotros somos **menores** que nuestros amigos.	*We're younger than our friends.*

Note that these comparative forms do not change based on gender, but they do show number agreement: **mejores, peores, mayores, menores.**

Actividades prácticas

A. ¿Cómo son mis compañeros/as? Listen as your instructor reads statements comparing two of your classmates. For each statement, write **C** for **cierto** or **F** for **falso.**

1. ____   2. ____   3. ____   4. ____   5. ____   6. ____

B. ¿Quién es más famoso? Here are some Spanish-speaking celebrities who have become famous outside their home countries. In your country, are some better known than others? Complete each of the following sentences with **más famoso/a** or **menos famoso/a.**

En mi país…

1. Juanes es _____ que Shakira.
2. Penélope Cruz es _____ que Javier Bardem.
3. Antonio Banderas es _____ que Diego Luna.
4. Julieta Venegas es _____ que Gael García Bernal.
5. Daddy Yankee es _____ que Plácido Domingo.
6. Salma Hayek es _____ que Sofía Vergara.

Sofía Vergara, actriz colombiana

C. ¿Qué te dice una foto?

PASO 1.   In pairs, look at the photos and read the descriptions of each person. Then write a statement comparing each person to someone else.

> **MODELO:**   Angélica es menos seria que Carolina.
> Diego es más estudioso que Ignacio y Erick.

Denise, de Argentina

Estudia teatro. Canta y baila mucho.

Carolina, de Colombia

Estudia cine. Lee mucho, ve películas y viaja (*travel*).

Angélica, de Costa Rica

Trabaja en un hotel. Cocina y pasa tiempo con la familia y con amigos.

Diego, de México

Estudia derecho (*law*). Va a fiestas con amigos y baila.

Erick, de Nicaragua

Trabaja en un parque nacional. Sale a comer con amigos y va al cine.

Ignacio, de España

Trabaja en un banco. Viaja mucho a otros países.

PASO 2.   Now match up people who you think have something in common, such as classes, activities, or interests. Share your answers with the class.

> **MODELOS:**   Carolina y Ignacio tienen mucho en común porque los dos (*both of them*) viajan.

D. Una clasificación

PASO 1.   With a partner, rank the items in each list from 1 to 4 (1 = **máximo,** 4 = **mínimo**), according to the criterion given.

CARO/A (*expensive*)

_____ un Ford
_____ un Kia
_____ un Mercedes
_____ un Rolls-Royce

DIFÍCIL

_____ un curso de español
_____ un curso de historia
_____ un curso de matemáticas
_____ un curso de química

PEOR

_____ un examen de matemáticas
_____ una cita (*appointment*) con el dentista
_____ un día sin (*without*) hablar con amigos
_____ una noche sin dormir

DIVERTIDO/A

_____ un concierto
_____ un examen
_____ una noche con la familia
_____ una película

MAYOR

_____ un abuelo
_____ un padre
_____ un hijo
_____ un bisabuelo

MEJOR

_____ una película de acción
_____ una película cómica
_____ una película romántica
_____ una película de terror

PASO 2.   For each category, create a statement that compares the top-ranked member (number 1) with the lowest ranked member (number 4).

> **MODELO:**   Una película romántica es mejor que una película de terror.

¡Anticipa!

The superlative structure is explained in this chapter's **Para saber más** section, but before taking a look, see if you can anticipate the structure.

Un Rolls Royce es el coche más caro de la lista (*of the list*).

Tomar un examen es la actividad menos divertida de la lista.

Note the agreement and use of the definite article in these sentences—these will be important!

E. La familia de tu compañero/a
Interview a classmate about his/her family. Select four family members (for example, **abuelo/a, tío/a, hermano/a, primo/a**) and then find out how they compare. In addition to the obvious information (who is older, younger, taller, or shorter), find out more interesting information as well (such as, who is more intelligent, who is funnier, and so on). Take good notes so you can share your findings with the class!

F. Cultura: La planificación (*planning*) familiar en Guatemala

PASO 1.   Read the following text about Guatemala.

En ciertas comunidades del altiplano[a] guatemalteco, las familias son muy grandes. En esta región, la tasa de fertilidad[b] es muy alta. Muchas veces las madres tienen hasta[c] diez u once hijos.

Hay organizaciones internacionales que se dedican a ofrecerles alternativas a estas familias. Los trabajadores de estas organizaciones están preocupados por[d] las familias, en particular por la salud[e] de las madres y sus hijos. Las mujeres pueden tener problemas de salud porque sus cuerpos[f] no tienen mucho tiempo para descansar entre cada embarazo.[g] Otro problema en las familias con muchos hijos es que todos necesitan comer. Muchas veces los padres no tienen suficiente dinero y los hijos sufren hambre[h] o malnutrición.

Sin embargo,[i] no todas las mujeres del altiplano quieren[j] usar contraceptivos para limitar el número de hijos que tienen. La mayoría de las familias son mayas católicas. Según sus tradiciones culturales y religiosas, no es normal controlar o planificar[k] el número de hijos en una familia. En algunos[l] casos, las mujeres sí quieren usar contraceptivos, pero sus maridos no están de acuerdo.[m] Las organizaciones de salud continúan ofreciendo a las mujeres programas educativos sobre[n] la salud femenina y la planificación familiar.

[a]*high plains* [b]*tasa... fertility rate* [c]*up to* [d]*preocupados... worried about* [e]*health* [f]*bodies* [g]*pregnancy* [h]*sufren... suffer from hunger* [i]*Sin... However* [j]*want* [k]*to plan* [l]*some* [m]*no... don't agree* [n]*about*

PASO 2.   Complete the sentences with **más… que** or **menos… que** to create logical comparisons according to the information found in the reading.

1. El altiplano de Guatemala tiene una tasa de fertilidad _____ alta _____ la tasa de fertilidad de otros países.
2. Las familias de otras partes de Latinoamérica son _____ grandes _____ las familias del altiplano guatemalteco.
3. La malnutrición es _____ frecuente en las familias grandes _____ en las familias pequeñas.
4. La planificación familiar es _____ común en las familias mayas católicas _____ en familias de otras tradiciones culturales y religiosas.

PASO 3.   With a partner, answer the following questions and discuss the ideas behind your responses.

1. En algunos países hispanos, hay mujeres que quieren tener muchos hijos por razones (*reasons*) prácticas. ¿Puedes pensar en una de esas razones prácticas?
2. En Guatemala y en muchos otros países, en general las mujeres en las áreas urbanas tienen menos hijos que las mujeres en las áreas rurales. ¿Por qué crees?
3. En Guatemala, las mujeres con más acceso a la educación tienen menos hijos. ¿Es así en los Estados Unidos también?

Guatemala

Una mujer guatemalteca

Reciclaje

Present indicative

Categorize these activities into those that you do with your family together (**juntos**), those that you do alone (**solo/a**), and those that you don't do at all.

almorzar	cocinar	jugar al fútbol
cantar	correr	mirar la televisión
cenar	desayunar	nadar

> **MODELO:**   Mis amigos y yo cenamos juntos. Almuerzo solamente y no desayuno.

4.2   ¿Qué dices para contestar el teléfono?

Stem-changing verbs: e → i

Para empezar...

When you answer the phone (**contestar el teléfono**), what do you say? Here is what people from around the Spanish-speaking world say.

Nadia Angélica, de México:
Decimos «bueno».

Luis, de Nicaragua:
Decimos «hola».

María, de Argentina:
Decimos «hola».

Mario, de España:
Decimos «diga».

Edgardo, de Venezuela:
Decimos «aló».

Now complete the following sentences, then say how you answer the telephone.

1. Los argentinos **dicen** (*say*) _____ para contestar el teléfono.
2. Los españoles **dicen** _____ para contestar el teléfono.
3. Los mexicanos **dicen** _____ para contestar el teléfono.
4. Los nicaragüenses **dicen** _____ para contestar el teléfono.
5. Los venezolanos **dicen** _____ para contestar el teléfono.
6. En mi país, **decimos** _____ para contestar el teléfono.

Actividades analíticas

1 In the **Para empezar** activity, you saw two forms of the verb **decir** (*to say*). Use these forms and what you know about verb endings in general to complete the conjugation in the chart.

You may notice that the **yo** form (**digo**) has a **g,** which might seem unexpected. This is because **decir** has an irregular **yo** form, a trait we will discuss in depth in **Capítulo 5.** For now, we'll focus on the other forms.

decir (e → i)	
SINGULAR	
yo	d**i**go
tú	
él/ella, Ud.	d**i**ce
PLURAL	
nosotros/as	
vosotros/as	d**e**cís
ellos/ellas, Uds.	

¡Anticipa!

In this **Para empezar** activity you see the use of the stem-changing verb **decir** (e → i). Without looking ahead, and based on the pattern you detected for o → ue stem-changing verbs, in which conjugations do you anticipate this verb to change its stem? In which conjugations will the **e** in the stem not change? Refer back to the presentation of the verb **poder** in **Capítulo 3** if you need a refresher.

■ Answers to these activities are in Appendix 2 at the back of your book.

2 The endings on the verb forms of **decir** are completely regular, but the stem vowel (**la vocal de la raíz**) changes: sometimes it is **e** (as in **decir**) and sometimes it is **i** (as in **dice**). The stem vowel **e** is used in the infinitive **decir** and in the **nosotros/as** and **vosotros/as** forms. In all other forms, the stem vowel changes to **i.**

3 There are other verbs that behave in a similar way. Two examples are **servir** (*to serve*) and **pedir** (*to ask for*). These verbs have an **e** in the infinitive and the **nosotros/as** and **vosotros/as** forms, and this vowel becomes **i** in all other forms. Use this information to complete the conjugations of these verbs.

	servir (e → i)	pedir (e → i)
SINGULAR		
yo	sirvo	
tú		pides
él/ella, Ud.	sirve	
PLURAL		
nosotros/as		pedimos
vosotros/as	servís	pedís
ellos/ellas, Uds.	sirven	

Both of these verbs are very common in everyday Spanish.

Sirven desayuno en ese restaurante. — *They serve breakfast at that restaurant.*

¿**Pedimos** café? — *Shall we ask for coffee?*

Servir is often used in the sense of *to work* (as in whether something functions or not) or *to be good at* something.

¿Tu computadora **sirve?** — *Does your computer work?*

No **sirvo** para jugar al fútbol. — *I'm no good at playing soccer.*

The rest of this chapter will concentrate on **decir, servir,** and **pedir,** but now that you know how these verbs work, you can conjugate any member of this family of verbs. Some other common verbs in this family are **repetir** (*to repeat*) and **seguir** (*to follow*).

Repito las palabras difíciles. — *I repeat the difficult words.*

Paula siempre **sigue** las instrucciones. — *Paula always follows the instructions.*

¿Por qué?

Why does the stem vowel change from **e** to **i** in some parts of the conjugation but not in others? You may recall from **Estructura 3.3** that with verbs like **poder,** the stem vowel **o** changes to **ue** when it is stressed. The same thing happens with verbs like **decir,** but the stem vowel **e** changes to **i.** This is one more example of how vowels can change their pronunciation when stressed in Spanish.

Autoprueba

Repetir (e → i) and **competir (e → i)** are other examples of stem-changing verbs. Although you haven't worked with these verbs yet, since you know the pattern, you already know how to conjugate and use them. Try it! (Remember that the stem change usually occurs in the next-to-last syllable.)

Repetir (*to repeat*)

1. yo _____
2. tú _____
3. nosotras _____

Competir (*to compete*)

4. Uds. _____
5. vosotros _____
6. ella _____

Respuestas: 1. repito **2.** repites **3.** repetimos **4.** compiten **5.** competís **6.** compite

■ For additional **e → i** stem-changing verbs, see **Para saber más 4.2** at the back of your book.

Actividades prácticas

A. ¿Para qué sirve? A family, like any group, is a mix of people with varying strengths and weaknesses. Think of those things that individuals in your own family are *not* especially good at and complete the following sentences, adding or subtracting family members as needed.

1. No sirvo para _____
2. Mi padre no sirve para _____
3. Mi madre no sirve para _____
4. Mi hermano/a no sirve para _____
5. _____ no sirve para _____
6. En general en mi familia, no servimos para _____

B. ¿Qué piden para tomar? You have probably observed that in some families, everyone is remarkably alike, whereas in others, each family member is very different from the others. In your family, what does everyone order to drink when you go out to eat? Using the following list of beverages, state what your family's preferences are. Do you all ask for the same thing (**lo mismo**) or for different things (**cosas diferentes**)? Answer using complete sentences.

> **MODELOS:** En mi familia, todos pedimos lo mismo.
> Pedimos leche.
> Pedimos cosas diferentes. Mi papá pide cerveza, mi mamá pide jugo, mis hermanas piden soda y yo pido leche.

> **café   cerveza**
> **jugo** (*juice*)   **leche** (*milk*)
> **soda   té** (*tea*)
> **vino** (*wine*)

C. Saludar a los padres de los amigos How do you greet a parent of one of your friends? When you say *hi* or *hello* to him/her, do you add anything else, such as *sir/ma'am, Mr./Mrs.,* or use a first name? What do you think people generally say in Spanish? For each sentence, in the first blank write the correct form of **decir,** then on the second line write the greeting you would say. **¡Atención!** In cases where you don't say anything, mark an X.

Para saludar a uno de los padres de un amigo o una amiga,...

1. Yo _____ (decir), «*Hello/Hi,* _____».
2. Otros _____ (decir), «*Hello/Hi,* _____».
3. En general, en nuestro país _____ (decir), «*Hello/Hi,* _____».
4. En general, los hispanohablantes _____ (decir), «Hola, _____».

D. ¿Qué dices? You have already seen examples where there is more than one way to say something in Spanish. The same phenomenon occurs in English. Here are three well-known cases, as they might be described in a textbook for Spanish-speakers learning English.

- Para decir **¡salud!** o **¡Jesús!** cuando una persona estornuda (*sneezes*), dicen *bless you* o *gesundheit*, o no dicen nada.
- Para decir **mamá** (cuando hablan con ella), dicen *Mom, Mommy, Momma, Mother* o *Ma*.
- Para decir **papá** (cuando hablan con él), dicen *Dad, Daddy, Pop, Father* o *Pa*.

PASO 1. Are these statements about English accurate? To find out, choose one of these cases, ask at least five classmates what they say, and keep track of the results.

> **MODELO:** Para decir **mamá** en inglés, ¿qué dices tú?

PASO 2. If a Spanish-speaker who was learning English asked you about one of these cases, what would you say? Use the information you gathered in **Paso 1** to create a statement describing which words your classmates actually say. **¡Atención!** If your statement includes yourself, use **decimos.** If it does not include you, use **dicen.**

E. El trabajo de la casa

PASO 1. In many parts of Latin America, middle-class families often employ full-time domestic help, which means that multiple people are available to do any household chore: the parent(s), the children, or the employee (**el empleado / la empleada**). Imagine that you are the head of
a household in Latin America and you need to make a list of who is going to do which task. Place each task in the list below under the appropriate heading, keeping in mind that no single person can do everything. **¡Atención!** You will need to conjugate each verb according to who is doing that task.

lavar la ropa (*wash clothes*)	**preparar el desayuno**	**servir el café /**
lavar los platos (*dishes*)	**preparar la cena**	**la leche por la mañana**
limpiar (*clean*) **la casa**	**servir el almuerzo**	**servir el desayuno**
preparar el almuerzo		**servir la cena**

YO	MIS HIJOS	EL EMPLEADO / LA EMPLEADA

PASO 2. Now compare your answers with those of a classmate. Do the two of you have anything in common in your choices? Report this to the class. Is there anything that the whole class has in common?

> **MODELO:** Lavamos la ropa y servimos el almuerzo. Los hijos preparan la cena.
> La empleada sirve la cena.

↻ Reciclaje

The infinitive of the verb

For many people, the weekends are when they have the most free time, but even then, it's difficult to squeeze in everything they want to do. Make two lists: one with what you *are* able to get done on weekends (**Puedo…**) and one with what you generally are *not* able to get done on weekends (**No puedo…**).

4.3   ¿Adónde quieren ir?

Stem-changing verbs: e → ie

Para empezar…

Some friends are visiting from out of town, and you need to find out what they want to do. For each question that you ask them from column **A,** choose an answer that makes sense from column **B.**

A	**B**
1. _____ ¿**Quieren** (*do you* [*pl.*] *want*) comer en un restaurante?	a. Sí, **queremos** ver una película de terror.
2. _____ ¿Adónde **quieren** ir?	b. Sí, ¡vamos a la playa!
3. _____ ¿**Quieren** ver la universidad?	c. No, no tenemos hambre.
4. _____ ¿**Quieren** ir a nadar?	d. **Queremos** ir al parque.
5. _____ ¿**Quieren** ir al cine?	e. Sí, **queremos** ver dónde estudias.

■ Answers to these activities are in Appendix 2 at the back of your book.

Actividades analíticas

1 In **Para empezar**, you saw two forms of the verb **querer** (*to want*). Add these forms to the conjugation below.

querer (e → ie)	
SINGULAR	
yo	qu**ie**ro
tú	qu**ie**res
él/ella, Ud.	qu**ie**re
PLURAL	
nosotros/as	
vosotros/as	qu**er**éis
ellos/ellas, Uds.	

2 In the infinitive of **querer,** the stem vowel is **e,** as it is also in the **nosotros/as** and **vosotros/as** forms. In all of the other conjugated forms, this vowel changes to **ie.** Everything else about the conjugation of **querer** is completely regular.

■ For additional **e → ie** stem-changing verbs, see **Para saber más 4.3** at the back of your book.

¡**Quiero** dormir!	*I want to sleep!*
Mañana **queremos** jugar fútbol.	*We want to play soccer tomorrow.*

There is a whole family of verbs that behave like **querer,** including **empezar** (*to begin*) and **pensar** (*to think, to plan*).

Nuestra clase **empieza** a las once.   *Our class begins at 11:00.*

¿**Piensas** ir a la biblioteca esta noche?   *Are you planning to go to the library tonight?*

Following the pattern with **querer,** complete the conjugations for **empezar** and **pensar.**

	empezar (e → ie)	pensar (e → ie)
SINGULAR		
yo	empi**e**zo	
tú		pi**e**nsas
él/ella, Ud.	empi**e**za	
PLURAL		
nosotros/as		p**e**nsamos
vosotros/as	emp**e**záis	p**e**nsáis
ellos/ellas, Uds.	empi**e**zan	

The verb **tener,** which you already know, is also a member of this family.

¿**Tienes** un diccionario?   *Do you have a dictionary?*

Tenemos un examen el martes.   *We have a test on Tuesday.*

3   We have now seen three families of verbs in which the vowel in the stem changes.

	o → ue	e → i	e → ie
Ejemplos:	**poder**	**decir**	**querer**
	dormir	**servir**	**pensar**
	almorzar	**pedir**	**empezar**

The vowel change that occurs is different in each family, but the change always occurs in the same forms: everywhere except the infinitive and the **nosotros/as** and **vosotros/as** forms.

Actividades prácticas

A. Empiezas a vivir

PASO 1.   Working with a partner, place the following events on a timeline based on the age at which they occur for *most people* in your country. Then, report your results to the class. Can you all reach a consensus on what is typical for most people in your country?

   MODELO: A los 28 años, quieres empezar a tener hijos.

1. Quieres empezar a tener hijos.
2. Empiezas a pensar que tus padres no son perfectos.
3. Empiezas a vivir fuera (*away*) de la casa de tus padres.
4. Empiezas a salir con chicos/chicas y tener citas (*dates*).
5. Quieres casarte (*get married*).
6. Piensas que eres más inteligente que tus padres.

PASO 2.   In many parts of the Spanish-speaking world, and especially in Latin America, children typically live with their parents until they get married, which for many people means until at least their late 20s. Select the answer below to compare this to what your class put on its timeline.

En general, los latinoamericanos empiezan a vivir fuera de la casa de sus padres…

a. más tarde que nosotros.
b. más temprano que nosotros.
c. a la misma edad (*age*) que nosotros.

En español...

Many of the verbs that we see in this section are often followed by an infinitive.

Juan **quiere tener** una bicicleta.
Juan wants to have a bike.
Angélica **piensa comprar** un coche.
Angélica is thinking about / planning to buy a car.

Some verbs are followed by another word and then the infinitive.

To express that somebody starts an action, use

empezar a + *inf.*
Los niños **empiezan a comer** a las dos.
The children begin to eat at 2:00.

To express that somebody needs to do an action, use

tener que + *inf.*
Tenemos que leer ese libro.
We have to read that book.

Si quieres ir a la fiesta, tienes que hacer la tarea.

B. Unos consejos   Parents are known for giving lots of advice to their children, and Spanish-speaking parents are no exception. Match the information in the two columns to create sensible advice (and commands disguised as advice!).

1. _____ Si (*If*) quieres sacar (*get*) buenas notas (*grades*), …
2. _____ Si piensas comprar un auto, …
3. _____ Si no quieres ser tan (*so*) delgado/a, …
4. _____ Si quieres ir al cine con tus amigos, …
5. _____ Si pensamos comprar una casa, …
6. _____ Si tus amigos quieren sacar buenas notas, …
7. _____ Si empezamos a limpiar todos, …
8. _____ Si empiezas a estudiar hoy, …

a. vas a estar listo/a (*ready*) para el examen mañana.
b. podemos tener la casa muy limpia.
c. tienes que estudiar mucho.
d. tienes que comer más.
e. primero tienes que limpiar (*clean*) la casa.
f. tienes que empezar a ahorrar (*save*) más.
g. tenemos que empezar a ahorrar más.
h. tienen que estudiar mucho.

C. ¿Qué tienes que hacer? ¿Qué quieres hacer?

PASO 1.   Time is precious and responsibilities often take precedence over things we want to do . . . and vice versa! Think about your average weekend. What do you have to do? What do you want to do? What about your family members? What do they have to do and want to do? What can you normally get done?

MODELO: Los fines de semana tengo que estudiar y trabajar, pero quiero dormir y ver películas (*movies*).
Mi padre quiere mirar la televisión los fines de semana, pero tiene que hacer ejercicio.
Normalmente puedo dormir y también estudiar, pero no puedo mirar muchas películas.

 PASO 2.   With a classmate, compare weekends. Whose do you prefer?

D. Tu vida en el futuro

PASO 1.   We all have ideas of how we would like to live in the future, but do we all think the same? First, ask yourself the following questions about your life over the next several years and write your answers on a separate piece of paper.

1. ¿Quieres tener hijos? ¿Cuántos?
2. ¿Quieres vivir en la ciudad o en el campo (*countryside*)?
3. ¿Piensas estudiar más para sacar la maestría (*master's*) o el doctorado (*doctorate*)?
4. ¿Quieres tener un perro o un gato?

PASO 2.   Now ask three or four of your classmates the same questions and keep track of their answers, then share your findings with the class. Did anyone answer two of the questions the same as you? Three of the questions? All four?

 E. Tu familia y el fin de semana   Many Spanish-speakers have the idea that North Americans are not very close to their families and don't interact with them much. To what extent is this true? In this spirit, ask your partner what he/she plans to do this weekend (or on the next school break) that involves his/her family (parents, siblings, spouse, children, and so on).

MODELO: E1: ¿Qué piensas hacer con tu familia este fin de semana / durante (*during*) las vacaciones?
E2: Pienso cenar con mis padres el sábado. El domingo, quiero jugar al fútbol con mi hermano.

⟳ Reciclaje

The verbs *ser* and *estar*

Read through these statements and check off those that are true for you. Then, talk to a classmate and find out which statements are true for him/her.

MODELO: ¿Eres de los Estados Unidos?

	YO	MI COMPAÑERO/A
1. Soy de los Estados Unidos.	☐	☐
2. Soy de Canadá.	☐	☐
3. Soy de otro país.	☐	☐
4. Mi madre es de otro país.	☐	☐
5. Mi padre es de otro país.	☐	☐
6. Estoy contento/a hoy (*today*).	☐	☐
7. Estoy muy ansioso/a hoy.	☐	☐

4.4   Es su mamá; está en Argentina.

Ser and *estar* for identity and location

Para empezar...

Cecilia Roth is an Argentinian actress, partly raised in Spain, who now works in both countries. Her mother and brother are also well-known entertainers, but all three have adopted stage names (**nombres artísticos**) so you might not know that they are related. Choose the right ending for each of these sentences. **¡Atención!** In Spanish, everyone has both **un apellido paterno** and **un apellido materno** and women often continue to use their birth name after marriage.

La actriz Cecilia Roth y el músico Fito Páez

1. Cecilia Roth **es** ____.
2. Dina Rot **es** ____ y ____.
3. Ariel Rot **es** ____ y ____.
4. Martín Páez Rotenberg **es** ____.
5. Fito Páez **es** ____.
6. Dina Rot **está** ____.
7. Fito Páez **está** ____.
8. Cecilia Roth trabaja mucho en España pero sus padres **están** ____ y viven en diferentes países.
9. Cecilia Roth, Dina Rot y Ariel Rot **son** ____, pero **están** ____.

a. el hijo de Cecilia Roth y Fito Páez
b. el nombre artístico de Dina Gutkin, la cantante
c. el nombre artístico de Cecilia Rotenberg Gutkin
d. el nombre artístico del músico español Ariel Rotenberg Gutkin
e. el hermano de Cecilia Roth
f. la madre de Cecilia Roth
g. muy orgulloso de su ex esposa
h. un músico argentino y el ex esposo de Cecilia Roth
i. familiares
j. en diferentes países
k. muy orgullosa de su hija
l. divorciados

■ Answers to these activities are in Appendix 2 at the back of your book.

Actividades analíticas

1 In **Para empezar,** you saw these forms of the verbs **ser** and **estar.**

es   está   están   son

Circle those that are forms of **ser**; underline those that are forms of **estar.**

2 Many of the forms of **estar** are followed by a phrase indicating location (**ubicación**). Find an example of this in **Para empezar.** _____

3 The forms of **ser** in **Para empezar** are always followed by a person, thing, or nationality.

Es el hermano de Cecilia Roth.   **Es** un músico argentino.
Son familiares.

This use of **ser** indicates the identity (**identidad**) of the subject.

4   This chart summarizes everything that you have seen so far about **ser** and **estar,** including the information from **Capítulos 1** and **2.**

ser	estar
Origin	Location
Soy de Los Ángeles.	Los hijos **están** en casa.
Identity	Property that could change
Ese señor **es** mi papá.	**Estamos** cansados.

Now for each of the following sentences, identify the infinitive of the verb and say which of these four uses it exemplifies.

	VERBE	USE
a. Argentina está en América del Sur.		
b. Los niños están tristes.		
c. Mario es de Venezuela.		
d. María y Vicente son estudiantes.		

Buenos Aires, Argentina

¿Por qué?

You may have noticed that the **yo** forms of **ser, estar,** and **ir** end in **-oy,** rather than the usual **-o.**

Soy estudiante.   **Estoy** en la universidad.   **Voy** a la biblioteca.

This might seem like an irregularity, but in fact there is a simple rule behind it. When the present tense **-o** ending is stressed, it is pronounced **-oy.** This is one more example of how vowels in Spanish change their form when they are stressed.

Actividades prácticas

A. ¡Adivinanzas!

PASO 1.   Work with a partner or small group to see if you can solve these riddles about cities or countries in the Spanish-speaking world. **¡Atención!** The four photos below provide clues to solving the riddles. If necessary, you can also consult the maps at the back of the book.

Hay hermosas playas en El Salvador.

El cerro Santa Ana es un barrio bonito de Guayaquil.

La Casa Milà de Antoni Gaudí está en Barcelona.

Se baila mucha bachata en la República Dominicana.

1. Estoy en un país.
   Es uno de los países de América Central.
   Está en la costa del Pacífico.
   Tiene frontera (*border*) con Guatemala y Honduras.
   ¿En qué país estoy? _____

2. Estoy en una ciudad.
   Está en Ecuador, pero no es la capital.
   Es más grande que la capital.
   Está en la costa del Pacífico.
   ¿En qué ciudad estoy? _____

3. Estoy en una ciudad.
   No es la capital, pero es muy grande.
   Está en la costa del Mediterráneo.
   Está en España, muy cerca (*close*) de la frontera con Francia.
   ¿En qué ciudad estoy? _____

4. Estoy en un país.
   El país está en una isla (*island*).
   La isla está en el Caribe.
   El país tiene frontera con Haití.
   ¿En qué país estoy? _____

(Continues)

PASO 2.   Pick a recognizable location on your school's campus and write four clues (similar to those in **Paso 1**) so your partner can guess it. Be sure to include at least one use of **ser** and one use of **estar.** The following phrases will help you describe the location.

al lado de	beside	**estar lejos de**	to be far from
el edificio	building	**un lugar**	a place
estar cerca de	to be close to		

MODELO: E1: Es un edificio viejo.
Está cerca de la librería.
Está lejos del gimnasio.
Es un lugar donde podemos estudiar.
E2: ¿Es la biblioteca?
E1: ¡Sí!

El padre de Carmelo Anthony es puertorriqueño.

B. Cuatro hispanos de los Estados Unidos   There are many very famous Hispanics in the United States, but many people don't know what their family origins are (that is, whether they are Mexican-American, Cuban-American, and so on). Here you will find out about a few.

PASO 1.   The following are descriptions of four different people. Fill in each blank with a form of **ser** or **estar.**

1. Sus padres ____ de la República Dominicana.
   ____ actriz (*actress*) en las películas de *Star Trek* y *Avatar*.

2. Su padre ____ de Puerto Rico.
   ____ jugador de básquetbol.
   Su equipo (*team*) ____ en Nueva York.

3. Sus padres ____ de Cuba.
   ____ cantante (*singer*) de reggaetón y hip hop.
   ____ en un video musical con Jennifer López.

4. Sus abuelos ____ de México.
   ____ astronauta.
   Su casa ____ en Houston.

PASO 2.   Match each person to the corresponding description.

Armando Pérez (Pitbull) ____   Ellen Ochoa ____

Zoe Saldaña ____   Carmelo Anthony ____

C. ¿Dónde están tus familiares?   Another impression that Spanish speakers often have of North Americans is that our families are very dispersed, with many family members living very far from their birthplace and very far from each other. Is there any truth to this? To explore this question, interview a classmate about his/her family (parents, uncles and aunts, grandparents) and find out where each one is from (**¿De dónde es?**) and where each one is now (**¿Dónde está?**).

MODELO: E1: ¿Tienes tíos?
E2: Sí, tengo una tía y un tío.
E1: ¿De dónde es tu tía?
E2: Es de Minnesota.
E1: ¿Y ahora dónde está?
E2: Está en Nueva York.

D. ¡Más adivinanzas!   Create a riddle about a famous person using **Actividad B** as a model, then try it out on your classmates. Be sure to give enough facts that the other person will be able to guess whom you're talking about.

¡Leamos!

La edad dorada°: de 25 a 34   *golden*

Antes de leer

Answer the questions about the ideal age to embark on different aspects of adulthood.

¿A qué edad (*age*)…

piensas viajar sin (*without*) tus padres? _____

quieres irte de (*leave*) la casa de tus padres? _____

quieres comprar un coche (*car*)? _____

empiezas a disponer de una tarjeta de crédito propia (*have your own credit card*)? _____

empiezas a ahorrar para la jubilación (*save for retirement*)? _____

quieres comprar una casa? _____

piensas convertirte en (*to become*) padre/madre? _____

A leer

PASO 1.   Read the results of **un sondeo** (*survey*) **internacional** about the ideal age to embark on different aspects of adulthood.

PASO 2.   ¿Estás de acuerdo? (*Do you agree?*) Compare the ideal ages from the survey with the ideal ages you wrote in **Antes de leer.** For each item, indicate whether you agree with the survey results or not.

	ESTOY DE ACUERDO	NO ESTOY DE ACUERDO
Viajar sin los padres:	☐	☐
Irse de la casa de los padres:	☐	☐
Comprar un coche:	☐	☐
Disponer de una tarjeta de crédito propia:	☐	☐
Ahorrar para la jubilación:	☐	☐
Comprar una casa:	☐	☐
Convertirse en padre/madre:	☐	☐

Después de leer

PASO 1.   Write three comparisons between your ideal ages and those in the survey (**sondeo**) in **A leer.**

> **MODELO:**   Para mí, la edad ideal para ahorrar para la jubilación es mayor que la edad del sondeo, pero la edad ideal para irse de la casa de los padres es menor que la edad del sondeo.

PASO 2.   Compare your answers to **Paso 1** with those of at least three other classmates and decide which of the following statements is most true for you. Then see if the whole class agrees.

_____ En general, la edad ideal para nosotros es menor que la edad del sondeo.

_____ En general, estamos de acuerdo con el sondeo.

_____ En general, la edad ideal para nosotros es mayor que la edad del sondeo.

VIVIR A LOS...

19 La edad escogida para comenzar a viajar sin los padres.

22 La edad perfecta para irse de casa, emanciparse de los padres y comprarse un coche.

23 Un buen momento para empezar a disponer de una tarjeta de crédito propia.

26 Ideal para disfrutar del amor, y también el momento de empezar a ahorrar para la jubilación.

27 La etapa idónea para lanzarse a la compra de una casa y también para convertirse en padres.

¡Escuchemos!

¿De dónde son sus antepasados°?   *ancestors*

Antes de escuchar
Where are your ancestors from? Check all the places that apply.

☐ África   ☐ Japón

☐ América   ☐ México

☐ Asia   ☐ otro: _____

☐ Europa

 A escuchar

Lourdes and Abigaíl are sisters from Mexico. Lourdes will describe their large family, then Abigaíl will speak about their ethnic heritage.

PASO 1.   Watch and listen, then answer the questions.

1. ¿Es grande o pequeña la familia de Lourdes y Abigaíl?

2. ¿Cuántos abuelos vivos (*alive*) tienen?

3. ¿Cuántas hermanas tiene su mamá?

4. ¿Cuántos primos tienen?

5. ¿Cuántas tías viven en los Estados Unidos?

Abigaíl y Lourdes

PASO 2.   Lourdes and Abigaíl have a rich ethnic past. Out of four great-grandparents Abigaíl mentions, one is **indígena** (*Native American*). What does she say about the nationality of the other three?

1. El bisabuelo materno (de parte de la mamá) es _____.

2. La bisabuela materna es _____.

3. El bisabuelo paterno (de parte del papá) es _____.

4. La bisabuela paterna es ___*indígena* (*mexicana*)___.

 Después de escuchar

Working with a classmate, take turns using **¡Qué... la familia!** to comment on Lourdes and Abigaíl's family. Use adjectives such as: **grande, interesante, diverso, divertido, internacional, típico/atípico,** etc. Make sure you use the correct gender/number. Can you think of more adjectives?

CONÉCTATE AL MUNDO HISPANO

Lourdes and Abigaíl's family shows that immigration is an international phenomenon. Did you know that the Mexican actress, Salma Hayek, has Lebanese ancestors? And that the large influx of Italian immigrants to Argentina in the early twentieth century is still evident in the many Italian restaurants and pizzerias there? Because of this immigration, there is no one "look" for Spanish speakers from any country. Throughout this book you will see Spanish speakers in the video from many countries with ancestors from all over the world.

¡Escribamos!

Una familia famosa

In this activity, you will write a description of a family without naming it. Can your instructor and classmates figure out which family you are describing?

Antes de escribir

Brainstorm a list of famous families that you can describe. They can be historical, political, or from literature, film, television, or pop culture. Choose the best one to write about. List the nationality, each person's age, profession, and adjectives that describe each person. Include both physical and personality descriptions.

> **MODELO:** familia: los Bush
> descripción: una familia norteamericana; el padre es político (ex presidente) y es conservador, la madre es bibliotecaria, el abuelo es político (ex presidente) y es muy viejo, una hija es rubia, otra hija tiene el pelo castaño…

A escribir

Write a description of the family you chose. Be careful not to mention any names, but include the number of family members, their relationships to each other, their ages, what they do, and comparisons of their appearances and personalities. Be sure to use complete sentences.

Después de escribir

 PASO 1. Exchange descriptions with a classmate and check each other's work using the following list. Then share your edited description with the class to see if they can guess who it is.

- hay concordancia (*agreement*) de género (*gender*) entre los artículos y los sustantivos
- hay concordancia de número (singular o plural) entre los adjetivos y lo que describen
- hay concordancia entre los sustantivos (*nouns*) y verbos
- los verbos con cambio de raíz tienen los cambios correctos
- hay comparaciones con **más/menos… que** (o **mayor/menor… que**)

 PASO 2. In groups, share your descriptions. Can everyone identify the families that are described?

¡Hablemos!

¡Esta es mi familia!

Antes de hablar

What if you were trying to locate family members and only had a few pieces of information? Your instructor will give you information about an imaginary person (e.g., **nombre, estado civil** [*marital status*], **lugar de origen, profesión**). Read the information and prepare to talk to others about your new identity.

 ### A hablar

Circulate around the room to ask and answer questions in Spanish and find the other members of your imaginary family. When you've found everyone, sit down together in a group.

Después de hablar

When everyone is seated, be prepared to introduce your family member(s) to the rest of the class.

Conéctate al cine

Película: *Cautiva (Captive,* drama, Argentina, 2005)
Director: Gastón Biraben

Sinopsis:

Cristina is in high school when she is called to a judge's office. The judge tells her that the parents she knows are not her real parents, but that they adopted her illegally when she was a baby. This was a common practice in Argentina's Dirty War (1976–1983), when babies were born to political prisoners, taken away, and then placed with families supportive of the military dictatorship. The judge introduces Cristina to Elisa, the mother of her biological mother, Leticia.

Escena (Netflix 00:32:34 to 00:34:34):

Cristina and Elisa have just recently met. Cristina is still very confused about who her parents are. Elisa shows Cristina photos of her biological parents (Leticia and her husband, Agustín) and tells her stories about them. She explains that they disappeared during the military dictatorship. A psychologist sits nearby and observes them.

Expresiones útiles

recién empezaban a salir	they had just started dating
un asado en casa	a barbeque at home
no decía nada	he didn't talk
era muy tímido	he was very shy
habían elegido los nombres	they had picked out names
varón	boy/male
nena	(baby) girl
desaparecieron	they disappeared
no supimos nada más de ellos	we never heard from them again
déjame sola	leave me alone

■ For copyright reasons, the feature film clips referenced in **Conéctate al cine** have not been provided by the publisher. Each of these films is readily available through retailers or online rental sites such as Amazon, iTunes, or Netflix.

Antes de ver

In *Cautiva,* Cristina learns that her parents are not related to her biologically and that her name at birth was not Cristina, but Sofía. How would you feel if you found out news that changed your perception of yourself and your identity? Write at least three adjectives.

Estaría (*I would be*) _____ y _____. Probablemente estaría _____, también.

A ver

PASO 1.   Use the film summaries and the **Expresiones útiles** to begin to make a list of the names and relationships of the characters in *Cautiva.* As you watch the clip, add more names and family relationships to the list.

PASO 2.   Complete the sentences with the family relationship. Include the definite article (**el/la/los/las**).

1. Agustín y Leticia son _____ biológicos de Cristina.
2. Cristina es _____ de Elisa.
3. Leticia es _____ de Elisa y Beto.

4. Beto es _____ de Elisa.
5. Leticia es _____ de Agustín.
6. Beto y Elisa son _____ de Agustín.

Después de ver

Use the following questions to discuss your own family with a classmate.

¿Eres similar a tus padres? ¿O eres muy diferente? ¿Físicamente eres más similar a tu madre oa tu padre? En cuanto a (*regarding*) tu personalidad, ¿con cuál de tus padres tienes más en común? ¿Ellos forman una parte importante de tu identidad? Explica.

VOCABULARIO

Comunicación

¿A qué te dedicas? / ¿A qué se dedica?	What do you do (*occupation*)?
¿Cuál es tu/su profesión?	What is your profession?
Las profesiones	**Professions**
el/la abogado/a	attorney
el ama de casa	housewife
el/la guía naturalista	nature guide
el/la médico/a	doctor
el/la periodista	journalist

el/la chofer, el/la doctor(a), el/la ingeniero/a, el/la pintor(a), el/la policía, el/la psicólogo/a, el/la sociólogo/a

¡Qué + *adj.*!	
¡Qué feo/a!	How ugly! / How horrible!
¡Qué guapo/a!	How handsome/ beautiful!
¡Qué lindo/a!	How cute/pretty!
¡Qué pesado!	What a pain! / How annoying!
¡Qué rico/a!	How delicious!
¡Qué + *n*.!	
¡Qué coraje! / ¡Qué rabia!	How aggravating / annoying!
¡Qué frío/a!	How cold!
¡Qué lío!	What a mess!
¡Qué + *adj.* + *n*.!	
¡Qué bonita familia!	What a beautiful family!

La familia

el/la abuelo/a	grandfather/grandmother
el/la bisabuelo/a	great-grandfather/ great-grandmother
el/la cuñado/a	brother-in-law/ sister-in-law
el/la esposo/a	husband/wife
el/la gato/a	cat
el/la hermanastro/a	stepbrother/stepsister
el/la hermano/a	brother/sister
el/la hijastro/a	stepson/stepdaughter
el/la hijo/a	son/daughter
el/la hijo/a único/a	only child
la madrastra	stepmother
la madre/mamá	mother
el marido	husband
la mascota	pet
la mujer	woman; wife
el/la nieto/a	grandson/granddaughter
la nuera	daughter-in-law
el padrastro	stepfather
el padre/papá	father
los padres	parents
los parientes	relatives
el/la perro/a	dog
le pez (*pl.* peces)	fish
el/la primo/a	cousin
el/la sobrino/a	nephew/niece
el/la suegro/a	father-in-law/ mother-in-law
el/la tío/a	uncle/aunt
el yerno	son-in-law

Las comparaciones

más/menos + *adj.* + que	more/less (-er) (+ *adj.*) than
más alto que	taller than
menos alto que	less tall than
mayor	older
mejor	better
menor	younger
peor	worse

Los verbos

decir (i) (g)	to say; to tell
empezar (ie)	to begin
empezar a + *inf.*	to begin (*to do something*)
lavar	to wash
los platos / la ropa	the dishes/clothes
limpiar	to clean
pedir (i)	to ask for
pensar (ie)	to think; to plan
preparar	to prepare
el desayuno / el almuerzo / la cena	breakfast/lunch/dinner
querer (ie)	to want
querer + *inf.*	to want (*to do something*)
repetir (i)	to repeat
seguir (i)	to follow
servir (i)	to serve; to be useful; to work
servir para + *inf.*	to be good at/for (*doing something*)
tener (ie) (g) que + *inf.*	to have (*to do something*)

Por la ciudad

El tráfico en la avenida 18 de Julio, Montevideo, Uruguay

Objetivos

In this chapter you will learn how to:

- express gratitude
- ask for and give directions
- describe cities and towns
- compare urban and rural life
- use numbers from 100–9,999
- talk about your daily routine
- describe people and places
- express negation and indefinite quantities of people and things

Muchas gracias

Expressing gratitude

 A. A ver: ¡Gracias!

PASO 1. Mira y escucha, luego indica si cada (*if each*) persona contesta con **gracias, muchas gracias** o **muchísimas gracias.**

	GRACIAS	MUCHAS GRACIAS	MUCHÍSIMAS GRACIAS			GRACIAS	MUCHAS GRACIAS	MUCHÍSIMAS GRACIAS
1.	☐	☐	☐		5.	☐	☐	☐
2.	☐	☐	☐		6.	☐	☐	☐
3.	☐	☐	☐		7.	☐	☐	☐
4.	☐	☐	☐		8.	☐	☐	☐

 PASO 2. Mira y escucha, luego empareja (*match*) la persona que habla con lo que dice.

1. _____    3. _____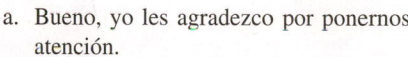

2. _____   4. _____

a. Bueno, yo les agradezco por ponernos atención.
b. Muchísimas gracias, gracias por entrevistarme. Es un honor.
c. Pues, muchas gracias por este tiempo.
d. Bueno, muchas gracias por la entrevista, muchas gracias por venir, ustedes aquí con nosotros. Muy agradecida de parte mía (*I am very grateful*).

To thank someone in Spanish, you can use one of these expressions.

Gracias.	Thank you.
Muchas/Muchísimas gracias.	Thank you very much.
Gracias por + *noun/infinitive*.	
Gracias por la entrevista.	Thank you for the interview.
Gracias por venir.	Thank you for coming.
Te/Le/Les agradezco por…	I appreciate that you . . .
	I thank you for . . .

¡Atención! To say *Yes, please* in Spanish, say **Sí, gracias.** To say *You're welcome,* use **De nada** or **No hay de qué.**

B. Sí, gracias. Para cada situación, escoge (*choose*) la expresión más apropiada.

	MUCHAS GRACIAS.	SÍ, GRACIAS.
1. ¿Quieres un café?	☐	☐
2. Tu profesor te ayuda (*helps you*) con el proyecto.	☐	☐
3. Estás perdido/a (*lost*) en una ciudad nueva. Una persona te pregunta: "¿Necesita ayuda?"	☐	☐
4. Un amigo te da (*gives you*) un regalo (*gift*).	☐	☐
5. Una persona te da información sobre la ciudad que visitas.	☐	☐

C. ¡Gracias! En parejas (*With a partner*), túrnense (*take turns*) para regalarse (*give each other*) las siguientes (*following*) cosas y darse las gracias (*thank each other*) usando las expresiones en **Comunicación.**

> **MODELO:** E1: Muchas gracias por el reloj.
> E2: ¡De nada! (No hay de qué.)

1.  2.  3.

4.  5.  6.

D. ¿Quieres... ? Circula por el salón de clase, pídeles y ofréceles algo (*something*) de la lista a cinco compañeros. Agradéceles (*thank*) a tus compañeros por lo que te ofrecen a ti.

algo de comer	una curita (*band-aid*)	gel antibacterial
un soda	chicle (*gum*)	hojas de papel
un bolígrafo	un diccionario	el libro de texto

> **MODELOS:** E1: ¿Quieres ayuda con la tarea?
> E2: No, gracias. (Sí, gracias.)
>
> E1: ¿Tienes un lápiz?
> E2: Sí. (No.)
> E1: Gracias por el lápiz. (Gracias de todas maneras. [*Thanks anyway.*])
> E2: No hay de qué.

¿Dónde está... ?

Asking for and giving directions

To ask where something is located, use **¿Dónde está... ?** or **¿Dónde queda... ?**

¿Dónde está / ¿Dónde queda el supermercado?	Where is the supermarket?

To say *here* and *there*, use **aquí** and **allí**.

De aquí no está muy lejos.	From here, it's not very far.
Allí está el mercado.	The market is over there.

To give directions, you can use **Siga** (*Go / Keep going / Continue*).

Siga derecho/recto ____ cuadras.	Keep going straight (for) ____ blocks.

For long distances, you can add references to intersections.

Siga hasta llegar a la esquina de ____ y ____.	Continue until you get to the corner of ____ and ____.

These are more expressions you might need when giving directions.

Doble/Gire...	Turn...
a la derecha/izquierda.	(to the) right/left.
Suba/Baje...	Go up / Go down . . .
por esta calle.	along this street.
hasta llegar al parque.	until you get to the park.
Está... / Queda...	It is . . .
a la derecha/izquierda.	on/to the right/left.
enfrente	across from
detrás de ____.	behind ____.
al lado de ____.	next to ____.

To say *block(s)* in Spanish, use **cuadra(s)**.

—**Perdone, ¿dónde está el gimnasio?**
—**Siga derecho dos cuadras, doble a la izquierda y siga una cuadra. El gimnasio está a la derecha, en la esquina de la calle San Martín y la avenida 18 de Septiembre.**
—**Gracias.**

Note that the formal **Ud.** is used in all of these examples because asking for directions often involves talking to someone you don't know and therefore would not want to treat informally.

En español...

The expressions presented in **¿Dónde está?** will be understood anywhere in the Spanish-speaking world, but you may hear other expressions as well when people are giving directions. For instance, instead of the verbs **doblar** or **girar** for *to turn,* some people use **dar la vuelta** or **virar.** In Spain and some South American countries, the word **manzana** is used for *block.*

«Siga todo derecho por tres cuadras...»

A. Cómo llegar

PASO 1. Escoge (*Choose*) la respuesta que mejor describe cada imagen. **¡Atención!** En cada una, la «x» marca tu punto de partida (*starting point*).

1. _____

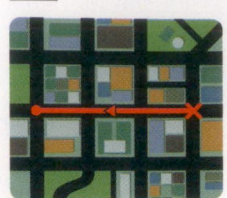

   a. Siga recto tres cuadras.
   b. Siga recto una cuadra, gire a la izquierda y siga recto tres cuadras.
   c. Siga recto una cuadra, gire a la derecha y siga recto tres cuadras.

2. _____

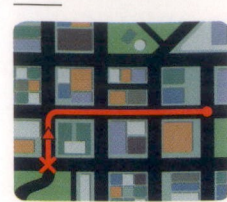

   a. Siga derecho una cuadra, doble a la derecha y siga derecho dos cuadras.
   b. Siga derecho tres cuadras, doble a la derecha y siga derecho una cuadra.
   c. Siga derecho una cuadra, doble a la derecha y siga derecho tres cuadras.

3. _____

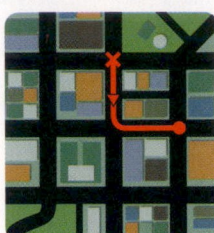

   a. Siga recto una cuadra, doble a la derecha y siga recto una cuadra.
   b. Doble a la derecha y siga recto una cuadra.
   c. Siga recto una cuadra, doble a la izquierda y siga recto una cuadra.

4. _____

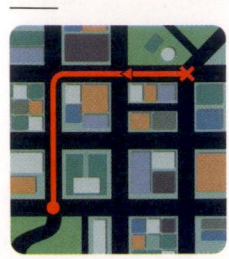

   a. Siga derecho dos cuadras, gire a la izquierda y siga derecho dos cuadras.
   b. Siga derecho dos cuadras, gire a la derecha y siga derecho dos cuadras.
   c. Siga derecho dos cuadras, gire a la derecha y siga derecho tres cuadras.

5. _____

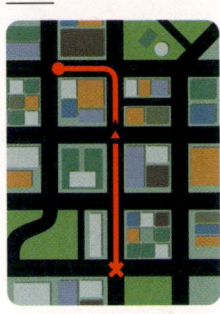

   a. Siga recto tres cuadras, doble a la derecha y siga recto una cuadra.
   b. Siga recto tres cuadras, doble a la izquierda y siga recto una cuadra.
   c. Siga recto una cuadra, doble a la derecha y siga recto tres cuadras.

PASO 2. Ahora dibuja (*draw*) una imagen para cada descripción.

1. Siga recto una cuadra, doble a la derecha y siga recto una cuadra.
2. Siga derecho cuatro cuadras.
3. Siga derecho dos cuadras, gire a la izquierda y siga derecho tres cuadras.
4. Siga derecho una cuadra, doble a la derecha y siga derecho una cuadra. Doble a la izquierda y siga derecho tres cuadras.

[a]Me… *They are watching me!*

B. De vacaciones en Ushuaia En parejas (*With a partner*), imaginen que están en Ushuaia, una ciudad en la región de Patagonia, al sur (*south*) de Argentina. Están en la X y quieren llegar a los lugares (*places*) de las listas. **Estudiante 1** debe consultar **Mapa 1** y **Estudiante 2** debe consultar **Mapa 2**. No mires el mapa de tu pareja.

MODELO: E1: Perdone, ¿dónde está la Casa de Gobierno?
E2: Siga recto cinco cuadras hasta llegar a Comodoro Augusto Lasserre. Doble a la derecha en Lasserre. Siga recto una cuadra y media y la Casa de Gobierno está a la izquierda.
E1: Muchas gracias.

Estudiante 1 (le pregunta a **Estudiante 2**)

Pregúntale a tu pareja cómo llegar a los siguientes lugares que no están en tu mapa. Luego, marca en el mapa dónde está cada lugar.

1. el Museo Marítimo
2. la oficina de correos (*post office*)
3. el Museo del Fin del Mundo
4. el Restaurante Kaupé
5. el Hotel Austral

MAPA 1

(*Continues*)

Estudiante 2 (le pregunta a **Estudiante** 1)
Pregúntale a tu pareja cómo llegar a los siguientes lugares que no están en tu mapa. Luego, marca en el mapa dónde está cada lugar.

1. la Oficina de Información Turística
2. la Antigua Legislatura
3. el Pub Restaurante Naútico

4. el Hostal Los Calafates
5. la agencia de turismo Rumbo Sur

MAPA 2

Restaurante Kaupé · Museo Marítimo · Museo del Fin del Mundo · Hotel Austral · Casa de Gobierno · La oficina de correos

C. ¿Cómo llego? En parejas, túrnense para describir un lugar en su universidad o ciudad sin mencionar el nombre. Tu pareja primero tiene que adivinar el lugar y luego darte (*give you*) direcciones. ¿Pueden decir cómo llegar a cada lugar?

MODELO: E1: ¿Cómo llego al lugar donde puedo estudiar y buscar libros?
E2: ¿A la biblioteca? ¿A la librería?
E1: A la biblioteca.
E2: De aquí gire a la derecha, siga recto hasta llegar al centro estudiantil. Luego, doble a la izquierda y la biblioteca está enfrente.

Paisajes urbanos
Urban landscapes

A. Lugares   Empareja la descripción con la mejor foto.

1. ____

2. ____

3. ____

a. Muchas personas viven en las **afueras** de la ciudad.
b. El **campo** es un lugar rural.
c. Una **ciudad** como Buenos Aires, Madrid o Nueva York es un lugar urbano.

En español...

The very American concept of *suburbs* does not exist in the Spanish-speaking world. If you are an American from the suburbs, you can use **las afueras,** which means *outside of* or *the outskirts* to give Spanish-speakers an idea of where you live.

Vivo en las afueras de Phoenix.
I live in the suburbs of Phoenix.

B. Más vocabulario: En la ciudad

PASO 1. Mira los siguientes dibujos y lee los párrafos. Escoge el párrafo que mejor (*best*) describe cada dibujo y llena (*fill in*) los espacios en blanco con la palabra apropiada de la lista, según (*according to*) el dibujo.

1. ____

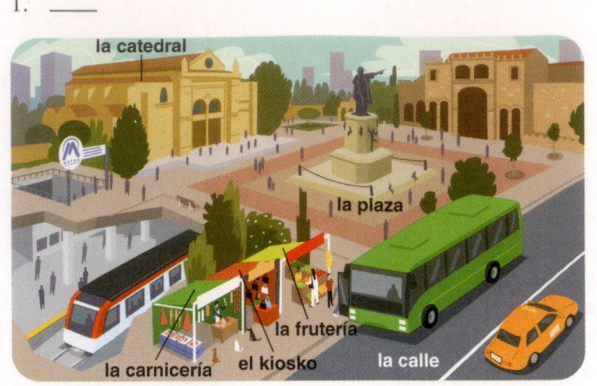

2. ____

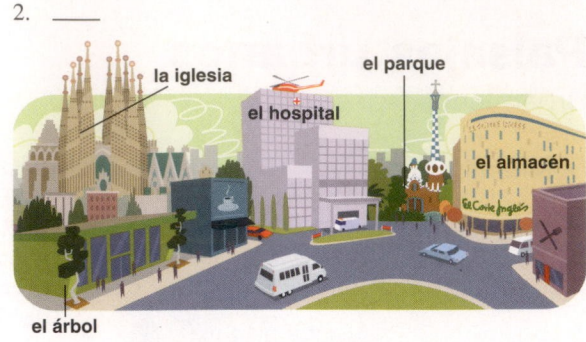

3. ____

4. ____

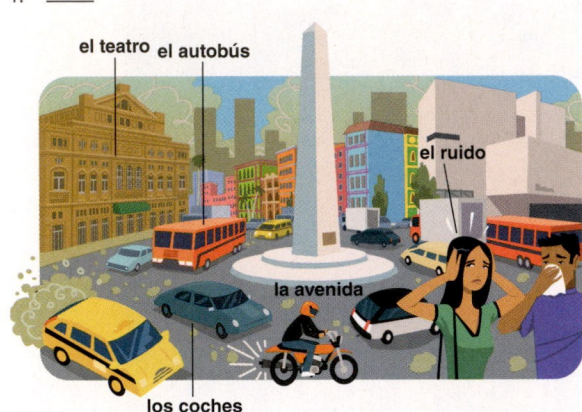

apartamentos	jardín (*garden*)	museo	tráfico
cine	mercado	restaurantes	
contaminación	metro	taxis	

a. En Barcelona, hay muchas construcciones del famoso arquitecto Antoni Gaudí, como La Sagrada Familia, una **iglesia** muy grande y **moderna** que ha estado en construcción (*has been under construction*) desde 1882. Si (*If*) quieres un poco de **tranquilidad,** puedes visitar el **parque** Güell, también diseñado por Gaudí. Aquí hay un _____ lleno de flores, **árboles** y esculturas (*sculptures*) decoradas con mosaicos coloridos. Además de (*Besides*) la arquitectura, se puede ir de compras en los grandes **almacenes** y comer en los varios _____ sofisticados de esta ciudad.

b. Buenos Aires es la **capital** de Argentina. Entre sus lugares famosos están el **Teatro** Colón (1908); el _____ de Arte Latinoamericano de Buenos Aires (MALBA), construido (*built*) en 2001; y la **avenida** 9 de Julio, nombrada por el día de independencia del país en el año 1816. Al igual que (*Just like*) muchas ciudades grandes, la cantidad (*quantity*) de **coches,** _____ y **autobuses** resulta en mucho _____, lo cual (*which*) produce _____ del aire y mucho **ruido** por los sonidos de todos los motores.

c. En el **centro moderno** de la ciudad de Panamá, hay casi todo lo que (*almost everything which*) se necesita para la vida (*life*). Muchas personas viven en **edificios** de _____ muy altos (llamados **rascacielos**) como la Torre Vitri, construida en 2012. Hay un _____ para el entretenimiento de los aficionados a las películas, **escuelas** para estudiar desde el primer grado hasta la universidad, **tiendas** para comprar todo tipo de cosas —incluso la famosa **librería** Exedra donde se venden (*sell*) libros de todo el mundo. Si cruzas (*you cross*) el Canal de Panamá por el **Puente** de las Américas, puedes viajar por la **carretera** Panamericana para visitar el **campo** (*countryside, rural area*) y otros **pueblos** del país.

d. Santo Domingo es una de las ciudades más viejas de las Américas, pero tiene una mezcla (*mixture*) de lo moderno y lo **antiguo.** Por ejemplo, el tren subterráneo (es decir, el _____) fue completado en 2009 y es uno de los principales **transportes públicos** de la ciudad; y la primera **catedral** del Nuevo Mundo (*World*), conocida como la Catedral Primada de América, fue construida en 1541. Junto a la catedral está la **plaza** central, que en 1887 cambió su nombre a Parque Colón (*Colombus*). En una de las calles centrales hay un _____ con **kioscos** (o quioscos) en los que se puede comprar de todo, además de **carnicerías** y **fruterías.**

 PASO 2.   En grupos, hagan una lista de palabras que se asocian con los siguientes temas (*topics*): el transporte, los edificios, el campo, la cultura, las compras, la ciudad, la naturaleza.

Los números del 100 al 9.999
Numbers from 100 to 9,999

100 cien/ciento	1.000 mil
200 doscientos/as	2.000 dos mil
300 trescientos/as	3.000 tres mil
400 cuatrocientos/as	4.000 cuatro mil
500 quinientos/as	5.000 cinco mil
600 seiscientos/as	6.000 seis mil
700 setecientos/as	7.000 siete mil
800 ochocientos/as	8.000 ocho mil
900 novecientos/as	9.000 nueve mil

By itself, the number 100 is **cien.** When any other number follows it, use **ciento.**

101 ciento uno
199 ciento noventa y nueve

Do not use **y** immediately after **ciento, cientos,** or **mil.**

178 ciento setenta y ocho
235 doscientos treinta y cinco
1.315 mil trescientos quince

To say the year in Spanish, say the whole four-digit number.

1492 = mil cuatrocientos noventa y dos
1988 = mil novecientos ochenta y ocho
2015 = dos mil quince

En español…

In contrast with English, in much of the Spanish-speaking world, a period is used to separate the thousands from the hundreds. Many attempts have been made to internationally standardize the representation of numbers, but in addition to the 1,000, you might see the number *one thousand* represented as any one of the following:
1.000
1 000
1000

A. ¿Cuántos años tiene?   Refiriéndote a las imágenes y las descripciones de la **Actividad B,** contesta las siguientes preguntas. **¡Atención!** Escribe el número completo.

1. ¿Cuántos años tiene el Teatro Colón?
2. ¿Cuántos años tiene el metro de Santo Domingo?
3. ¿Cuántos años tiene la iglesia La Sagrada Familia?
4. ¿Cuántos años tiene la Catedral Primada de América?
5. ¿Cuál es el día de la independencia de Argentina?
6. ¿Cuánto tiempo hace que (*How long since*) la plaza central de Santo Domingo se llama «Parque Colón»?
7. ¿Cuándo cumplió (*turned*) 100 años el Teatro Colón?
8. ¿En qué año se construyó (*was built*) la Torre Vitri?

■ The audio files for in-text listening activities are available in the eBook, within Connect Plus activities, and on the Online Learning Center.

La Plaza de la Constitución (mejor conocida como «el Zócalo») en México, D.F.

 B. ¿Qué sabemos de los paisajes urbanos y rurales? Escucha las descripciones. ¿Qué palabra de vocabulario describe cada una?

 C. ¿Dónde vive tu familia? En grupos de tres personas, hagan y contesten las siguientes preguntas. Según las respuestas de sus compañeros, adivinen (*guess*) si cada uno es de la ciudad, el campo o las afueras.

¿Tu familia…

1. vive en un apartamento?
2. viaja más de un kilómetro (0,6 millas) para ir de compras?
3. vive en un lugar donde los niños caminan (*walk*) a las escuelas?
4. viaja más de diez minutos para ir a un museo?
5. vive en un lugar donde los niños van al parque para jugar?
6. viaja en transporte público por lo menos una vez (*time*) a la semana?

Creo que eres de la ciudad / el campo / las afueras. ¿Tengo razón? (*Am I right?*)

 D. A ver: ¿Dónde estamos en este momento?

PASO 1. Mira las imágenes en el video y, según lo que ves (*you see*), decide dónde está cada persona. ¿Por qué crees que la persona está en ese lugar?

 1. _____ Abril está en…
   a. un almacén.
   b. una iglesia.
   c. un parque.

5. _____ José Manuel está en…
   a. un campo.
   b. una plaza.
   c. un parque.

 2. _____ Aníbal está en…
   a. una ciudad.
   b. un jardín.
   c. un parque.

 6. _____ María está en…
   a. un museo.
   b. una iglesia.
   c. una plaza.

 3. _____ Antonio está en…
   a. un mercado.
   b. un restaurante.
   c. una tienda.

7. _____ Roberto está en…
   a. un mercado.
   b. un restaurante.
   c. una tienda.

 4. _____ Jama está en…
   a. un mercado.
   b. una galería de arte.
   c. una plaza.

PASO 2. Mira y escucha, luego empareja la descripción con el lugar que se describe.

_____ 1. la Plaza Francia
_____ 2. la parte antigua de la ciudad
_____ 3. Buenos Aires
_____ 4. la galería de arte
_____ 5. el Jardín Borda
_____ 6. la Plaza Manuel Belgrano
_____ 7. El Mirador

a. la capital de Argentina
b. el Centro Cultural de Morelos, México
c. la ciudad de Panamá
d. la calle Ocho en Miami
e. un parque en Argentina
f. una plaza principal en Argentina
g. un restaurante en Costa Rica con vistas muy bonitas

E. ¿Dónde están ahora? Nombra por lo menos tres de tus seres queridos (*loved ones*) y di (*say*) dónde están ahora.

   MODELO: Mi novio (*boyfriend*) está en el supermercado ahora.

COMUN | VOCABUL | **ESTRUCTURA** | ATE

⟳ Reciclaje

The verbs *estar, ir, ser,* and *tener*

Escribe la forma **yo** de uno de los siguientes verbos en cada oración. Luego, indica si la persona habla de **la ciudad** o **del campo.**

estar   ir   ser   tener

	CIUDAD	CAMPO
1. «_____ de Buenos Aires.»	☐	☐
2. «_____ a la casa de mi abuelo, donde tiene muchas gallinas (*chickens*).»	☐	☐
3. «_____ de una zona rural.»	☐	☐
4. «_____ en una estación del metro.»	☐	☐
5. «_____ tres caballos (*horses*).»	☐	☐
6. «_____ en la capital del país.»	☐	☐

Mi abuelo cría (*raises*) gallinas en su finca (*farm*).

■ Answers to this activity are in Appendix 2 at the back of your book.

5.1 Traigo el mapa del metro.

Verbs with irregular *yo* forms

Para empezar...

Las siguientes oraciones (*sentences*) hablan de la vida (*life*) en el campo y en la ciudad. Selecciona de la lista para completar las oraciones de una manera lógica. Los verbos **oír** (*to hear; to listen to*), **salir** (*to leave; to go out*) y **traer** (*to bring; to carry*) son nuevos. **¡Atención!** La respuesta **d** se usa dos veces.

EN EL CAMPO

1. «Cuando **salgo** de mi casa, **oigo** _____ y _____.»
2. «Cuando camino por (*I walk through/ along*) _____, siempre **traigo** _____.»
3. «Cuando voy al campo para descansar, no **hago** _____.»

EN LA CIUDAD

4. «Cuando **salgo** de mi apartamento, **oigo** _____ y _____.»
5. «Cuando camino por _____, siempre **traigo** _____.»
6. «Cuando corro por las calles, **hago** _____.»

a. los campos
b. el mapa del metro
c. los coches
d. mucho ejercicio
e. los autobuses
f. los caballos
g. el centro
h. las gallinas
i. un bastón (*stick*) para caminar

■ Answers to these activities are in Appendix 2 at the back of your book.

Actividades analíticas

1 Use what you saw in **Para empezar** to complete this set of conjugations.

	hacer	poner	traer	salir
yo		pongo		
tú	haces	pones	traes	sales
él/ella, Ud.	hace	pone	trae	sale
nosotros/as	hacemos	ponemos	traemos	salimos
vosotros/as	hacéis	ponéis	traéis	salís
ellos/ellas, Uds.	hacen	ponen	traen	salen

In the present tense, these verbs are irregular only in the **yo** form. They are otherwise completely regular.

¿Dónde **pongo** mi tarjeta de metro?   *Where do I put my metro pass?*

Ponen sus libros en la mesa.   *They put their books on the table.*

2 Some stem-changing verbs also add **g** in the **yo** form. **Tener** and **venir** (*to come*) belong to the **e → ie** family, and **decir** belongs to **e → i** family. Complete their conjugations here.

	tener (e → ie)	venir (e → ie)	decir (e → i)
yo		vengo	
tú	tienes		dices
él/ella, Ud.		viene	
nosotros/as	tenemos		decimos
vosotros/as	tenéis	venís	decís
ellos/ellas, Uds.		vienen	

Vengo de Nicaragua.   *I come from Nicaragua.*

¿**Vienes** a la fiesta el sábado?   *Are you coming to the party on Saturday?*

3 **Oír** (*to hear; to listen to*) is another common verb with **g** in the **yo** form. It makes some spelling adjustments with **y** the **tú, el/ella,** and **Ud,** and **ellos/ellas** and **Uds.** forms (the **i** changes to **y** when between two vowels) but is otherwise regular.

	oír (y)
yo	
tú	oyes
él/ella, Ud.	
nosotros/as	oímos
vosotros/as	oís
ellos/ellas, Uds.	oyen

Oigo el tráfico de mi casa.   *I hear the traffic from my house.*

¿Ud. **oye** mucha música clásica?   *Do you listen to a lot of classical music?*

¡Anticipa!

The following verbs follow the same pattern as their root verbs (the ones you just learned). Based on that knowledge, see if you can conjugate them.

componer (*to compose; to form*)
yo _____
tú _____
él/ella, Ud. _____
nosotros/as _____
vosotros/as _____
ellos/ellas, Uds. _____

contener (*to contain*)
yo _____
tú _____
él/ella, Ud. _____
nosotros/as _____
vosotros/as _____
ellos/ellas, Uds. _____

deshacer (*to undo*)
yo _____
tú _____
él/ella, Ud. _____
nosotros/as _____
vosotros/as _____
ellos/ellas, Uds. _____

Respuestas: compongo, compones, compone, componemos, componéis, componen; contengo, contienes, contiene, contenemos, contenéis, contienen; deshago, deshaces, deshace, deshacemos, deshacéis, deshacen

4 The verbs **saber** (to know [*a fact*]) and **conocer** (*to know, be familiar with*) are two important verbs with irregular **yo** forms. With **saber,** the **yo** form is **sé,** and with **conocer,** it is **conozco.** The present tense of these verbs is completely regular otherwise.

Saber and **conocer** can both be translated as *to know,* but they are not the same. **Saber** means to know a fact or to know how to do something.

Sé que vives en el centro.	*I know that you live downtown.*
Sabemos que Miami está en Florida.	*We know that Miami is in Florida.*
—¿**Sabes** dónde está la biblioteca?	*Do you know where the library is?*
—Sí, sé dónde está la biblioteca. Está detrás del gimnasio.	*Yes, I know where the library is. It's behind the gym.*
Ella sabe nadar.	*She knows how to swim.*

Conocer, on the other hand, means to be familiar with something or someone.

Conozco muy bien mi universidad.	*I know my university very well.*
Juan **conoce** Boston.	*Juan knows (is familiar with) Boston.*
¿**Conoces** a mi hermano?	*Do you know my brother?*

Actividades prácticas

A. Preguntas y respuestas Empareja cada pregunta con la respuesta más lógica.

1. _____ ¿Tienes un lápiz?
2. _____ ¿Por qué estás cansado?
3. _____ ¿Qué tipo de música te gusta?
4. _____ ¿Qué haces los sábados?
5. _____ ¿Qué haces cuando tienes mucho sueño en el trabajo?
6. _____ ¿Conoces Chicago?
7. _____ ¿Cuál es la capital de Guinea Ecuatorial?

a. Pongo la cabeza (*head*) en el escritorio y duermo.
b. ¡Claro! Vengo de allí.
c. No, pero traigo un bolígrafo en mi mochila.
d. Salgo a bailar con mis amigos.
e. No sé.
f. Oigo mucho rock en español.
g. Vengo del gimnasio.

B. ¿Saber o conocer? Para cada uno de los siguientes lugares, actividades, cosas o personas, indica si sería (*it would be*) apropiado usar **saber** o **conocer** para expresar *to know.*

1. cuál es la capital de México
2. México, D.F.
3. quién es Beto Cuevas
4. cantar
5. la comida italiana
6. preparar una pizza
7. mi abuela
8. cómo se llama mi abuela

¿Por qué?

Why is the **yo** form of the verb often irregular, and why is **g** so often added? The reason is that many verbs' **yo** forms have changed over time to make them easier to pronounce. The vowel **o** is pronounced with the tongue positioned in the back of the mouth. The **g,** which is also pronounced with the tongue in the back of the mouth, makes the word flow more easily.

■ For more on **saber** and **conocer,** as well as more irregular verbs ending in **-zco,** see **Para saber más 5.1** at the back of your book.

C. Una conversación entre dos estudiantes Las siguientes oraciones vienen de una conversación entre dos estudiantes que se encuentran (*who meet*) en la calle. Ponlas en orden (*Put them in order*).

___1___ —¡Hola! ¿Por qué no contestas el teléfono?

_____ —No, no conozco ese lugar, pero dicen que es muy bueno. Oye, ¿pongo mi mochila aquí en tu coche?

_____ —¡Sí, puedo! ¿Adónde quieren ir? ¿Conoces un lugar bueno?

___7___ —Sí, está bien. ¿Viene Silvia también?

_____ —Sí traigo, pero no mucho.

_____ —Pues, te llamo para saber si puedes salir a comer con mi compañero de cuarto y yo.

_____ —Sí. ¿Conoces el restaurante La Buena Vida? Cuando salgo con mis compañeros del trabajo, vamos allí, y me gusta mucho.

_____ —No sé. Sé que tiene un examen mañana y tiene que estudiar. Oye, ¿traes dinero?

_____ —¡Ay, perdón! Vengo de mi clase de historia, y tengo el teléfono apagado (*turned off*).

D. Los extranjeros en la ciudad En las grandes ciudades de España y Latinoamérica, hay muchos extranjeros (*foreigners*) de muchos países diferentes. Estos son algunos ejemplos.

	Benjamín	**Elena**	**Miguel**
PAÍS	Bélgica	Rumania	Portugal
TRABAJO	turismo	camarera (*waitress*)	promoción de eventos de surf y eventos rastafari
CIUDAD DONDE VIVE Y TRABAJA	México, D.F.	Madrid	Panamá

Completa cada una de las siguientes oraciones con uno de estos verbos. **¡Atención!** Tienes que cambiar (*change*) el verbo a la forma **yo**. Luego, usa la tabla para escribir en la segunda (*second*) columna el nombre de la persona que probablemente dice la oración.

conocer   oír   saber   salir   tener   venir

1. «_____ de mi casa para ir al restaurante.»   _____
2. «_____ una agencia de viajes.»   _____
3. «_____ del trabajo a las tres de la mañana.»   _____
4. «_____ de Lisboa.»   _____
5. «_____ música reggae cuando estoy en el trabajo.»   _____
6. «_____ muchas partes de México. Es un país fascinante.»   _____
7. «_____ que hay muchas películas belgas muy buenas.»   _____
8. «_____ de Rumania.»   _____
9. «_____ muchas playas de muchas partes del mundo, y puedo decir que las playas de Panamá son excelentes.»   _____

E. ¿Sales los sábados?

PASO 1. En general, ¿sales los sábados por la noche? Si sales, ¿a qué hora? ¿Con quién? ¿Adónde van? Entrevista (*Interview*) a un compañero / una compañera y completa las primeras dos líneas de la tabla.

¿Quién?	¿Sale(n) los sábados?	¿A qué hora?	¿Con quién?	¿Adónde?
yo				
mi compañero/a: _____				
Estudiantes de <u>aquí</u>				
Estudiantes de <u>Madrid</u>				

PASO 2. Con tu compañero/a, decide qué hace la mayoría de los estudiantes en su universidad. Luego, lee la información sobre los estudiantes de Madrid y completa el resto de la tabla.

En general en España, los estudiantes salen a las diez o a las once de la noche. Álvaro, un estudiante de Madrid, dice: «Todo el mundo (*Everybody*) sale… con sus amigos, con la gente de clase».

Andrea, también estudiante en Madrid, dice: «Salen a bailar y van a los bares».

F. ¿Qué hace tu compañero/a?

PASO 1. En parejas, pregúntense si hacen estas actividades **siempre, casi** (*almost*) **siempre, a veces, casi nunca** o **nunca.**

escuchar música en español

poner la computadora en la mochila

traer una mochila a clase

venir a clase tarde (*late*) / temprano (*early*)

venir a la universidad a pie (*on foot*)

MODELO: E1: ¿Vienes a la universidad a pie?
E2: Sí, a veces vengo a pie. ¿Y tú?
E1: No, casi nunca vengo a pie. Siempre vengo en autobús/bicicleta/coche/taxi.

PASO 2. En grupos de dos miren las actividades del **Paso 1** y escriban cuatro oraciones que resumen (*summarize*) lo que (*what*) hacen Uds. Si los/las dos hacen lo mismo (*the same thing*), usen **los/las dos** (*the two of us*) y la forma **nosotros/as.** Si hay una diferencia, describan qué hace cada uno/a. Luego, compartan (*share*) las respuestas con la clase para ver qué cosas tienen en común.

MODELOS: Los dos escuchamos música en español a veces.
Yo nunca traigo una mochila, pero Kevin casi siempre trae una mochila.

CONÉCTATE AL MUNDO HISPANO

Los **bares** en España no son iguales a los *bars* en Estados Unidos y Canadá. En España, los bares son el centro de la vida (*life*) social para mucha gente y no abren solo por la noche. Además de (*In addition to*) bebidas (*beverages*) alcohólicas, sirven las famosas tapas y comidas (*meals*). Muchas personas van al bar por la mañana para charlar (*chat*) con los amigos y tomar café y pan tostado (*toast*).

Reciclaje

The verb *llamarse*

En la siguiente conversación, escribe las formas apropiadas del verbo **llamarse**.

ELENA: Hola! ¿Cómo _____¹?

RAFAEL: _____² Rafael.

ELENA: ¿Conozco a tu hermano? ¿Cómo _____³?

RAFAEL: _____⁴ Jorge. Y tú, ¿cómo _____⁵?

ELENA: _____⁶ Elena.

■ Answers to this activity are in Appendix 2 at the back of your book.

5.2 Me ducho en el gimnasio.

Reflexive verbs

Para empezar...

Usa la siguiente lista para escribir algunas (*some*) actividades que son comunes en cada lugar.

despertar**se**   maquillar**se**   duchar**se**/bañar**se**   peinar**se**   afeitar**se**

vestir**se**   sentar**se**   bañar**se**   acostar**se**   dormir**se**

■ Answers to these activities are in Appendix 2 at the back of your book.

LUGARES	EJEMPLOS DE ACTIVIDADES COMUNES			
En una biblioteca	_____	_____		
En un gimnasio	_____	_____	_____	_____
En un hotel	_____	_____	_____	_____

Actividades analíticas

■ For additional reflexive verbs, see **Para saber más 5.2** at the back of your book.

1 The verbs in **Para empezar** are all infinitives, but they have an ending that other infinitives don't have. What is this ending? _____

This ending is a *reflexive pronoun* (**pronombre reflexivo**) and verbs that have it are called *reflexive verbs* (**verbos reflexivos**). Reflexive verbs often, but not always, indicate an action that one does to oneself: **afeitarse** (*to shave* [*oneself*]), **bañarse** (*to bathe* [*oneself*]).

2 Reflexive verbs are conjugated just like other verbs, but when fully conjugated, the reflexive pronoun is placed *before* the verb. The form of the reflexive pronoun depends on the subject.

SUJETO	PRONOMBRE REFLEXIVO	EJEMPLO
yo	**me**	Yo **me peino** después de hacer ejercicio. *I comb my hair after exercising.*
tú	**te**	¿A qué hora **te duermes**? *At what time do you fall asleep?*
él/ella, Ud.	**se**	Marisa **se baña** por la mañana. *Marisa bathes in the morning.*

SUJETO	PRONOMBRE REFLEXIVO	EJEMPLO
nosotros/as	**nos**	Julieta y yo **nos acostamos** temprano. *Julieta and I go to bed early.*
vosotros/as	**os**	¿**Os afeitáis** cada día? *Do you shave every day?*
ellos/ellas, Uds.	**se**	Esos estudiantes **se duchan** en el gimnasio. *Those students shower at the gym.*

Now complete the conjugations of these reflexive verbs.

	afeitarse	bañarse	peinarse
yo	me afeito		
tú		te bañas	
él/ella, Ud.	se afeita		se peina
nosotros/as	nos afeitamos		
vosotros/as	os afeitáis	os bañáis	
ellos/ellas, Uds.		se bañan	se peinan

3 Some reflexive verbs have stem changes.

FAMILIA	VERBO		
o → ue	acostarse	**Me acuesto** a las once.	*I go to bed at 11:00.*
	dormirse	A veces **me duermo** en el autobús.	*Sometimes I fall asleep on the bus.*
e → ie	despertarse	**Me despierto** a las siete.	*I wake up at 7:00.*
	sentarse	**Me siento** para cenar con mi familia.	*I sit down to eat dinner with my family.*
e → i	vestirse	**Me visto** en tres minutos.	*I get dressed in three minutes.*

Mi hermano mayor y yo nos cepillamos los dientes.

4 Reflexive verbs are very common in Spanish. In fact, one of the first verbs you learned is a reflexive verb. **Me llamo Miguel** literally means *I call myself Miguel.* Here are some other common reflexive verbs.

acordarse (de) (*to remember*)

    Me acuerdo muy bien **de** mis abuelos.   *I remember my grandparents very well.*

cepillarse los dientes (*to brush one's teeth*)

    Me cepillo los dientes cada noche antes de dormir.   *I brush my teeth every night before bed.*

irse (*to go away, to depart*)

    ¿A qué hora **te vas**?   *At what time are you leaving?*

lavarse (las manos / la cara) (*to wash one's hands / face*)

    Me lavo la cara antes de salir para el trabajo.   *I wash my face before leaving for work.*

levantarse (*to get up, to stand up*)

    Me levanto muy tarde.   *I get up very late.*

ponerse (los lentes / los lentes de contacto) *to put on* (*glasses / contact lenses*)

    Me pongo los lentes cuando me levanto.   *I put on my glasses when I get up.*

quedarse (*to stay*)

    Siempre **se queda** con su tía en Miami.   *He always stays with his aunt in Miami.*

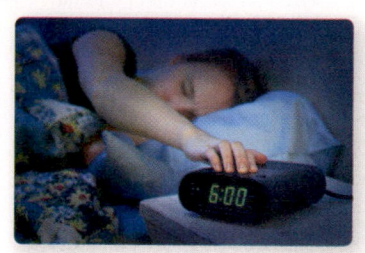

Amaya se despierta todos los días a las seis en punto.

5 When reflexive verbs are in their infinitive form, the reflexive pronoun may be attached to the end of the infinitive.

¿A qué hora **vas a acostarte**? / ¿A qué hora **te vas a acostar**?
What time are you going to sleep?

No tengo que ducharme antes de ir a la fiesta. / **Me tengo que duchar** antes de ir a la fiesta.
I don't have to shower before going to the party.

Actividades prácticas

A. Tu rutina   Usa números para indicar el orden (*order*) en que haces las siguientes actividades. Si hay una actividad que no haces, marca una equis («X»).

_____ Me acuesto.   _____ Me baño.   _____ Me duermo.   _____ Me maquillo.

_____ Me afeito.   _____ Me despierto.   _____ Me levanto.   _____ Me peino.

B. Preguntas y respuestas   Empareja cada pregunta con la respuesta apropiada.

1. _____ ¿Te acuerdas dónde queda la oficina de correo?
2. _____ ¿Nos vamos inmediatamente después de la clase?
3. _____ ¿A qué hora se despiertan los niños?
4. _____ ¿Te maquillas todos los días?
5. _____ ¿Te quedas o te vas con nosotros?
6. _____ ¿Me pongo estos zapatos (*shoes*) negros?
7. _____ ¿A qué hora se acuesta Abril?

a. Mejor no. Vamos al gimnasio, ¿por qué no te pones los tenis (*tennis shoes*)?
b. Sé que está en esta calle.
c. Sí, por supuesto (*of course*). No me pongo maquillaje solo cuando hago ejercicio.
d. Me quedo. No puedo salir todavía (*yet*), y ya conozco ese museo.
e. Sí, está bien. Tengo que llegar a casa temprano.
f. Ella dice que se acuesta a las doce.
g. Normalmente, a las siete.

C. Tus hábitos   Usa la imagen para completar cada pregunta. Luego, en parejas, túrnense para hacer y contestar las preguntas.

MODELO: ¿A qué hora _____ los domingos?
E1: ¿A qué hora te acuestas los domingos?
E2: Me acuesto a las once de la noche los domingos.

1. ¿A qué hora _____ los días de entre semana? ¿Y los fines de semana?

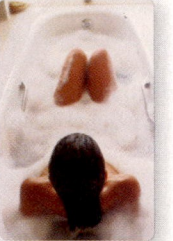

2. ¿Normalmente _____ por la mañana o por la noche?

3. ¿Cuántas veces _____ al día?

4. ¿Con qué frecuencia _____? ¿Todos los días? ¿Una vez a la semana?

D. ¿Qué hace Pudenciano?

PASO 1. Pudenciano es un maestro de secundaria (*high school*) en México. Tu profesor(a) va a leer lo que (*what*) dice Pudenciano sobre (*about*) su rutina de la mañana. Escucha y apunta take notes on lo que hace. **¡Atención!** Tienes que cambiar el verbo a la forma **él.**

¿A qué hora se levanta Pudenciano?

¿Qué hace Pudenciano?

Se levanta a las _____¹ de la mañana. _____,² _____³ y _____⁴ en su auto hacia (*toward*) su trabajo. Su trabajo es una escuela tele-secundaria.

PASO 2. En una hoja de papel, usa la oración de Pudenciano como modelo para describir lo que tú haces por la mañana. Luego, crea (*create*) una oración para decir qué tienes en común con Pudenciano, y otra oración en que dices una diferencia entre Pudenciano y tú.

> **MODELO:** **Mi rutina:** Me levanto a las ocho de la mañana. Desayuno, me baño, me visto y a las nueve y media me voy en autobús a clase.
> **Comparación:** Los dos desayunamos. Prudenciano se baña antes de desayunar, pero yo me baño después de desayunar.

E. ¡Una crisis por la mañana!

En parejas, lean la situación. Luego, usen la lista de posibles actividades para escribir qué hacen Uds. en esta situación y a qué hora. **¡Atención!** No hay tiempo para hacerlo todo. ¡Tienen que negociar!

Situación: Tú y tu compañero/a viven en la misma casa. Se despiertan. Son las siete menos un minuto. Hoy hay muchísimo tráfico y tienen que salir a las siete y cuarto para llegar a la universidad a tiempo. Solo hay un baño (*bathroom*) en la casa.

afeitarse	cepillarse los dientes	maquillarse	ponerse los lentes (de contacto)
bañarse	desayunar	peinarse	vestirse

	YO	**MI COMPAÑERO/A**
6:59	Me despierto.	Se despierta.
7:04	_____	_____
7:08	_____	_____
7:12	_____	_____
7:15	Nos vamos juntos/as.	

F. ¿Te acuerdas?

PASO 1. Pregúntales a cuatro de tus compañeros si se acuerdan de cómo se llaman los siguientes lugares o personas.

> **MODELO:** ¿Te acuerdas de cómo se llama tu escuela primaria?

1. tu escuela primaria (*elementary school*)
2. tu profesor(a) de primer año (*first grade*) en la escuela primaria
3. tu profesor(a) de tu primera clase en la universidad
4. el hospital o la clínica donde naciste (*you were born*)
5. tu mejor amigo/a en la escuela primaria

PASO 2. Crea un resumen (*summary*) de los resultados y compártelos (*share them*) con la clase.

> **MODELO:** De cuatro estudiantes, tres se acuerdan de cómo se llama su escuela primaria.

⟳ Reciclaje

The verbs *ser* and *estar*

Empareja cada sujeto con la información apropiada. Luego completa cada oración con la forma apropiada de **ser** o **estar.**

1. _____ nosotros
2. _____ Shakira
3. _____ el banco nacional y la biblioteca nacional
4. _____ Rafael Nadal y Javier Bardem
5. _____ el árbol

a. _____ de Colombia.
b. _____ en el parque.
c. _____ de España.
d. _____ estudiantes.
e. _____ en el centro de la capital.

■ Answers to this activity are in Appendix 2 at the back of your book.

5.3 ¿Cómo es? ¿Cómo está?

Ser and *estar* with adjectives

Para empezar...

en la calle

en el Banco Mundial (*World Bank*)

en un teatro

■ Answers to these activities are in Appendix 2 at the back of your book.

Shakira es una cantante de Colombia, pero también trabaja en varias organizaciones como la Fundación Pies Descalzos (*Bare Feet*) y ALAS (Fundación América Latina en Acción Solidaria [*Supportive*]), que ayudan a niños pobres. Mira las fotos y decide si las siguientes oraciones son ciertas o falsas.

	CIERTO	FALSO		CIERTO	FALSO
1. **Es** famosa.	☐	☐	6. En la foto de la calle, **está** enojada.	☐	☐
2. En la foto del teatro, **está** triste.	☐	☐	7. **Es** fea.	☐	☐
3. **Es** pobre.	☐	☐	8. En la foto del banco, **está** seria.	☐	☐
4. En la foto de la calle, **está** contenta.	☐	☐	9. **Es** delgada.	☐	☐
5. **Es** vieja.	☐	☐	10. En la foto de la calle, **está** bonita.	☐	☐

Actividades analíticas

1 In **Capítulo 4,** you saw that the verb **ser** is used to express origin or identity.

Mis padres **son** de Honduras.　　　　*My parents are from Honduras.*

Maritza **es** estudiante.　　　　*Maritza is a student.*

You also saw that the verb **estar** may express location.

Mario **está** en el parque.　　　　*Mario is at the park.*

In **Para empezar,** both **ser** and **estar** are used with adjectives to describe Shakira. Which type of description uses **ser,** and which uses **estar?**

¿SER O ESTAR?

_____ Shakira en general

_____ Shakira en la foto (en un momento específico)

■ For more comparison of **ser** and **estar,** see **Para saber más 5.3** at the back of your book.

2 The sentences in **Para empezar** are good examples of the basic difference between **ser** and **estar** when used with adjectives.

	CONCEPTO	EJEMPLOS
ser + *adjective*	intrinsic quality (unlikely to change suddenly)	Shakira **es** famosa. Estos libros **son** interesantes. Bill Gates **es** rico.
estar + *adjective*	quality subject to change or resulting from change	Shakira **está** contenta. Jorge **está** muy triste. ¿**Estás** enojado?

3 The same adjective can often be used with either **ser** or **estar,** but the overall meaning of the sentence will be different.

Shakira **es** muy bonita.	*Shakira is very pretty.*
Shakira **está** muy bonita en la foto.	*Shakira looks very pretty in the photo.*
Víctor **es** muy viejo.	*Víctor is very old.*
¡Víctor **está** muy viejo!	*Víctor is very old (compared to when I last saw him)!*
María **es** muy limpia.	*María is a very clean and tidy person.*
María **está** muy limpia.	*María is all cleaned up.*

The sentences with **ser** describe lasting qualities or properties of the people that are not likely to change suddenly. The sentences with **estar** describe qualities or properties that could change or that are the result of change: Shakira looks pretty in this particular photo, but in another less flattering photo she may not, and Víctor didn't appear old before, but now he does. María was dirty before, but now she is clean (or she looks particularly clean).

Notice that expressing the meaning of **estar** in English often involves the use of additional words, such as *look* or *appear*.

4 Here is a summary of all the uses of **ser** and **estar** that you have seen.

ser		estar	
origin	Shakira **es** de Colombia.	**location**	Shakira **está** en el parque.
identity	Shakira **es** cantante.	**subject to change** **or resulting from change**	Shakira **está** bonita en la foto.
intrinsic quality	Shakira **es** famosa.		

Which of these uses does each of the following sentences exemplify?

a. Tegucigalpa está en Honduras. _____
b. Estoy muy enojado. _____
c. Tegucigalpa es la capital de Honduras. _____
d. Jorge es muy alto. _____
e. Esther es de La Ceiba, una ciudad en el norte de Honduras. _____

La Catedral San Miguel Arcángel está en la Plaza Morazán, Tegucigalpa.

En español...

Estar may be followed by a verb form that ends in **-ndo** to indicate an action that is taking place at the moment, and therefore is subject to change or that is the result of change. This structure is easy to recognize.

Guillermo Anderson **está cantando** en este momento.
Ahora **estoy trabajando** en el museo.
Por el momento, **estamos viviendo** en un apartamento.

Guillermo Anderson is singing at this moment.
I'm working at the museum right now.
For right now, we're living in an apartment.

This use of **estar** with a verb ending in **-ndo** is known as the present progressive tense. It is less frequent than its counterpart in English (with *-ing*) and is sometimes overused by English speakers learning Spanish. It will be treated in more detail in **Estructura 11.3.**

Actividades prácticas

A. Español e inglés Gracias al uso de **ser** y **estar,** el español puede expresar ideas muy complejas (*complex*) con muy pocas (*few*) palabras. Empareja cada oración en español con la traducción apropiada.

1. _____ Eres malo.
2. _____ Estoy muy fea.
3. _____ Son bastante (*quite*) serios.
4. _____ ¡Qué delgado estás!
5. _____ Soy muy fea.
6. _____ Están muy serios.
7. _____ Estás malo.
8. _____ Eres muy delgado.

a. You've really slimmed down!
b. They look like they're in a very serious mood.
c. You are a bad person.
d. You are very thin.
e. I look like a mess.
f. They are pretty serious people.
g. I'm very ugly.
h. You are sick / not doing well.

B. Diferentes lugares en la ciudad En cada oración, primero escoge la forma correcta de **ser** o **estar.** Luego (*Then*) contesta la pregunta, usando una de estas opciones.

En un parque.   En un museo.   En un hospital.   En un banco.

1. [Soy / Estoy] una persona muy tranquila en general, pero en este momento [soy / estoy] enojada y triste porque dicen que no tengo dinero en mi cuenta (*account*).
   ¿Dónde [soy / estoy]? _____

2. [Soy / Estoy] muy aburrida porque no me gusta el arte, y este edificio tiene puro (*only*) arte. A mi amigo le gusta mucho el arte, y él [es / está] fascinado (*fascinated*).
   ¿Dónde [soy / estoy]? _____

3. [Soy / Estoy] muy contenta porque [soy / estoy] en un lugar muy tranquilo. También [es / está] un lugar muy bonito, porque hay muchos árboles y flores (*flowers*).
   ¿Dónde [soy / estoy]? _____

4. [Soy / Estoy] aquí porque [soy / estoy] malo. No [soy / estoy] médico (*doctor*), pero dicen que los médicos aquí [son / están] muy buenos.
   ¿Dónde [soy / estoy]? _____

C. Se ponen...

PASO 1. Completa cada oración en la primera columna con la terminación más lógica en la segunda columna. Usa cada terminación solo una vez (*time*).

1. Julia se pone bastante enojada cuando _____
2. Me pongo muy triste cuando _____
3. Nos ponemos muy cansados y aburridos cuando _____
4. Me pongo muy gordo cuando _____
5. Los jardines y los parques se ponen muy bonitos _____
6. Los estudiantes se ponen bastante serios cuando _____
7. Los estudiantes se ponen muy contentos cuando _____

a. hablan con el maestro.
b. tenemos que estudiar mucho.
c. como mucho.
d. no puede usar la computadora.
e. sacan buenas notas.
f. saco mala nota en una clase.
g. en primavera.

Vocabulario

Spanish has many ways of expressing the idea of *to become* but when used with adjectives that describe changeable mental or physical conditions, the most common way is with the reflexive verb **ponerse.**

Me pongo **contenta cuando estoy en el parque.**
I become/get happy when I'm at the park.

Se ponen **muy divertidos en las fiestas.**
They become lots of fun at parties.

Se pone **muy serio en el trabajo.**
He becomes/gets very serious at work.

PASO 2.   En parejas, digan cómo se ponen Uds. en las siguientes situaciones. Pueden usar las palabras de esta lista u otras.

asustado/a (*scared*)	contento/a	nervioso/a
cansado/a	enojado/a	triste

MODELO: Pierdes (*You miss*) el autobús. Cuando pierdo el autobús, me pongo frustrado/a.

1. Tienes un examen.
2. Tus amigos no dejan de enviarte (*won't stop sending you*) mensajes de texto.
3. Ves una película de terror.
4. Haces mucho ejercicio.
5. No ves a tu familia por mucho tiempo.

¿Cómo te pones cuando pierdes el autobús?

 D. ¿Estás de acuerdo? ¿Somos así?   Muchos norteamericanos viven y trabajan en las grandes ciudades de Latinoamérica y España, y muchos van de turistas también. ¿Qué fama (*reputation*) tienen? En grupos de tres o cuatro, lean las opiniones de estas personas y para cada persona, contesten las preguntas.

■ **Jorge, Panamá:** «Son muy trabajadores, y son muy buenos para la tecnología.»
■ **Lourdes, México:** «Son personas amables (*nice*). Los jóvenes que vienen a Cancún no son tan (*so*) amables, a lo mejor (*probably*), pero los que viven allá sí son amables.»
■ **María, Argentina:** «Tengo compañeros norteamericanos en el trabajo, y son muy buenas personas. Son quizá (*perhaps*) más nacionalistas que nosotros.»
■ **Eric, México:** «A lo mejor quieren ser dominantes y superiores a los otros países.»
■ **Jimena, México:** «Van mucho a fiestas y son muy divertidos.»

1. ¿Están Uds. de acuerdo con esta persona?
2. ¿Las personas de este país son así (*like that*)?
3. ¿Uds. son así?

MODELO: Estoy de acuerdo con Jorge. En general, somos muy trabajadores en este país, pero yo no soy así.

 E. La personalidad de tu compañero/a

PASO 1.   En parejas, pregúntense y contesten lo siguiente.

■ ¿Cómo eres en general?
■ ¿Cómo estás hoy?
■ ¿En qué momentos te pones muy contento/a (triste, enojado/a…)?

PASO 2.   Haz (*Make*) una oración para describir a tu compañero/a. Luego, haz otra oración que explica si Uds. dos son parecidos/as o diferentes, y por qué. Después, comparte la información con la clase.

MODELO: Mi compañero es simpático, divertido y trabajador; se pone muy contento cuando está con sus amigos. Somos parecidos porque yo soy simpática y divertida y me pongo muy contenta cuando estoy con mis amigos, pero somos diferentes porque no soy muy trabajadora.

Paraguay

F. Cultura: Asunción, la capital de Paraguay

PASO 1. Lee el texto sobre Asunción, la capital de Paraguay.

Asunción fue[a] una de las primeras ciudades en ser fundada[b] cuando los españoles llegaron[c] a Sudamérica. Es la ciudad más grande de Paraguay y está situada en la región suroeste[d] del país, cerca de la frontera con Argentina. La zona metropolitana se llama Gran Asunción.

Aunque[e] Paraguay es un país interior (no tiene acceso al mar), es un puerto[f] industrial muy importante en esta región. El río[g] Paraguay, que forma una de las fronteras naturales con Argentina, permite que los barcos entren y salgan de[h] esta ciudad portuaria.[i] La economía de Paraguay está creciendo[j] mucho en estos años y varias corporaciones tienen sus oficinas en las afueras de Asunción.

Una de las calles más antiguas y más conocidas[k] de Asunción es la calle Palma. Comienza en la Plaza de los Héroes, donde se encuentra[l] el histórico monumento llamado, el Panteón Nacional de los Héroes. La calle Palma sigue hacia el noroeste[m] y termina a unas cuadras del puerto. A lo largo de[n] la historia de Asunción, esta avenida ha sido[ñ] un importante espacio público para los habitantes, lleno de[o] tiendas, boticas (antiguas farmacias) y grandes librerías. Hoy en día las personas que visitan Asunción pueden encontrar tiendas y puestos[p] con productos locales, restaurantes con comida típica y bellas casas históricas.

[a]*was* [b]*en... to be founded* [c]*arrived* [d]*southwest* [e]*Although* [f]*port* [g]*River* [h]*barcos... ships enter and leave* [i]*port* (adj.) [j]*growing* [k]*más... most well-known* [l]*se... is located* [m]*northwest* [n]*A... Throughout* [ñ]*ha... has been* [o]*lleno... filled with* [p]*stands*

PASO 2. Ahora completa las oraciones con la forma apropiada de **ser** o **estar.**

1. Asunción _____ en Paraguay.
2. Argentina _____ al sur (*south*) del país.
3. Asunción _____ una ciudad portuaria que _____ en el río Paraguay.
4. Asunción _____ una de las ciudades en la zona metropolitana Gran Asunción.
5. Las oficinas de las grandes corporaciones _____ en las afueras de la ciudad.
6. Asunción _____ grande y antigua.
7. La calle Palma y el Panteón Nacional de los Héroes _____ sitios importantes en la historia de Asunción.
8. Últimamente (*lately*) muchos paraguayos _____ contentos porque su economía está creciendo.

PASO 3. En parejas, contesten las preguntas y explíquense (*explain to each other*) sus respuestas.

1. Muchas ciudades portuarias, como Asunción, tienen una población muy grande. ¿Por qué crees que es así?
2. ¿Hay otras ciudades grandes en el mundo hispano que son puertos? ¿Y hay ciudades grandes que no tienen puerto?
3. En tu país, ¿hay ciudades grandes que son portuarias? ¿Hay otras ciudades grandes que no tienen puerto?

↻ Reciclaje

Demonstrative adjectives

Escribe la terminación de género y número para cada adjetivo demostrativo. Luego, completa cada oración con la expresión apropiada.

est___ muchacho   est___ catedral   est___ edificios

est___ chicas   est___ tienda

1. _____ son más altos que los otros.
2. _____ tiene mejores precios que la otra.
3. _____ es más fuerte que el otro.
4. _____ son más bonitas que las otras.
5. _____ es más alta que la otra.

■ Answers to this activity are in Appendix 2 at the back of your book.

5.4   Hay algo interesante en Tegucigalpa.

Indefinite and negative expressions

Para empezar...

Mira el mapa del centro de Tegucigalpa, la capital de Honduras. Usando la información en este mapa, decide si cada oración es cierta o falsa.

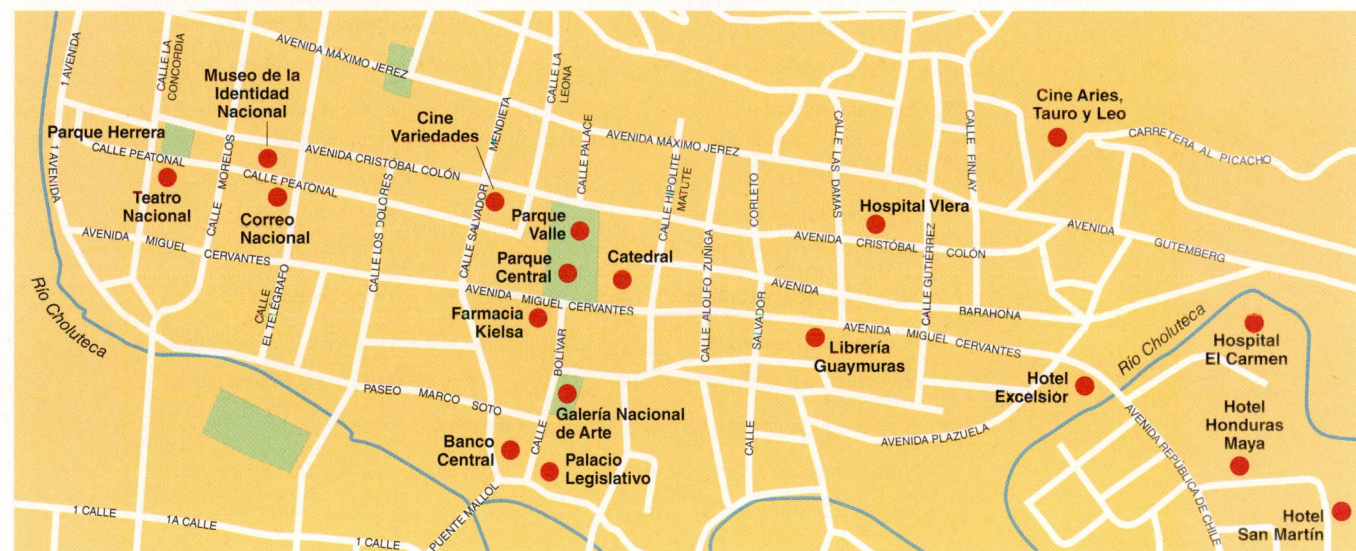

	CIERTO	FALSO

En este mapa…

1. **algunos** hoteles están cerca de (*close to*) la avenida República de Chile. ☐ ☐
2. no hay **ningún** parque en Tegucigalpa. ☐ ☐
3. hay **algo** interesante en la calle Bolívar, si te gusta el arte. ☐ ☐
4. **ninguna** librería está en la avenida Jerez. ☐ ☐
5. hay **algunas** tiendas en la avenida Cervantes. ☐ ☐
6. no hay **ningún** cine en la carretera al Picacho. ☐ ☐
7. **algunos** hospitales están en la calle Morelos. ☐ ☐
8. **ningún** museo está en la calle Los Dolores. ☐ ☐
9. hay **algunos** edificios del gobierno (*government*) en la calle Bolívar. ☐ ☐
10. no hay **nada** interesante en el centro de Tegucigalpa. ☐ ☐

■ Answers to these activities are in Appendix 2 at the back of your book.

Actividades analíticas

1 In **Para empezar,** you see some words in **boldface** type. Write those words in the appropriate position in the chart here. When there are two forms of the same word, write both next to the same English translation.

_____ *something*		_____ _____ *some*
_____ *nothing*		_____ _____ *no* (*not one/any*)

2 Given what you know about Spanish adjectives, you should not be surprised to see that **algún** and **ningún** change their form to agree with the gender and number of the noun that follows them. Circle the correct form to complete the sentences here.

a. Hay <u>algunos / algunas</u> casas en la avenida Cervantes.
b. Tengo <u>algunos / algunas</u> libros en mi mochila.
c. No hay <u>ningún / ninguna</u> parque en esta parte de la ciudad.
d. No conozco <u>ningún / ninguna</u> galería de arte en esa calle.

For **algunos/algunas**, the plural forms are the most common, though singular forms do exist (**algún/alguna**). For **ningún/ninguna**, it is the singular forms that are the most common, though plural forms also exist (**ningunos/ningunas**).

3 The verb must be preceded by **no** when negative expressions such as **ningún/ninguna** or **nada** come after the verb. Unlike English, double negatives are common in Spanish.

No hay **ningún** cine en la carretera al Picacho.	*There isn't any movie theater on the Picacho Highway.*
No tengo **nada** en mi mochila.	*I don't have anything in my backpack.*

4 **Algo** and **nada** both refer to things. To talk about people, use **alguien** (*someone*) and **nadie** (*no one*). These words are invariable; that is, there are no separate masculine/feminine or singular/plural forms.

Hay **alguien** en esa tienda.	*There is someone in that store.*
Nadie vive en esa casa.	*No one lives in that house.*

When **alguien** and **nadie** are objects of the verb, they are preceded by **a.**

¿Conoces **a alguien** en Tegucigalpa?	*Do you know anyone in Tegucigalpa?*
No conozco **a nadie** en ese banco.	*I don't know anyone in that bank.*

5 A common negative expression for time is **nunca** (*never*).

Nunca llego tarde a mi clase.	*I never arrive late to my class.*
No voy al campo **nunca.**	*I never go to the countryside.*

The opposite of **nunca** is **siempre** (*always*).

Siempre voy al parque los domingos.	*I always go to the park on Sundays.*

Actividades prácticas

A. El centro de tu ciudad ¿Cómo es el centro de tu ciudad? ¿Qué hay y qué no hay? Completa las oraciones que tienen un espacio en blanco. Luego, escoge **a** o **b** como la mejor descripción del centro de tu ciudad.

1. ____
   a. Hay algunos lugares buenos para bailar.
   b. No hay ningún lugar bueno para bailar.
2. ____
   a. Algunas veces hay conciertos buenos.
   b. Nunca hay conciertos buenos.
3. ____
   a. Hay algunos museos buenos.
   b. No hay ningún museo bueno.
4. ____
   a. Hay algunas galerías de arte.
   b. No hay _____.
5. ____
   a. Hay algunos cines.
   b. No hay _____.
6. ____
   a. Hay _____.
   b. No hay ningún parque bonito.
7. ____
   a. Hay _____.
   b. No hay ningún teatro.

B. Los miembros de Calle 13   Calle 13 es un grupo musical de Puerto Rico. Sus miembros son los hermanastros René Pérez Joglar y Eduardo José Cabra Martínez, conocidos como (*known as*) «Residente» y «Visitante», y su media hermana, Ileana Cabra Joglar, conocida como «PG-13». Completa las oraciones usando la siguiente lista. Cada palabra se usa solo una vez. **¡Atención!** Dos de las oraciones son falsas. ¿Cuáles son?

Eduardo José Cabra Martínez, Ileana Cabra Joglar
y René Pérez Joglar del grupo Calle 13

alguien   algunas   algunos   nada   nadie   ningún   nunca

	CIERTO	FALSO
1. _____ personas dicen que el estilo de su música es reggaetón, pero ellos dicen que es «música urbana».	☐	☐
2. En su música, siempre canta _____. Casi siempre son los dos hermanastros, pero a veces es su media hermana, Ileana.	☐	☐
3. Reciben (*They receive*) _____ premios (*awards*) Grammy en 2006, 2007, 2008, 2009, 2010 y 2011.	☐	☐
4. _____ compra sus discos nunca.	☐	☐
5. Como muchos músicos latinoamericanos, no tienen _____ problema (*m.*) en mezclar (*mixing*) la música con la política.	☐	☐
6. _____ pierden (*miss*) la oportunidad de colaborar con otros artistas, como Nelly Furtado o Café Tacuba.	☐	☐
7. Los miembros de este grupo musical no tienen _____ de importancia en la vida (*life*) cultural de Puerto Rico.	☐	☐

C. Algunas ciudades   Indica si conoces a alguien en cada una de las siguientes ciudades. Si no conoces a nadie en alguna ciudad, pregúntales a varios (*several*) compañeros si conocen a alguien allí. Apunta el nombre de la persona que conoce a alguien en esa ciudad.

MODELO: E1: ¿Conoces a alguien en Atlanta?
E2: No, no conozco a nadie allí. (Sí, conozco a alguien allí.)

☐ Atlanta _____   ☐ Lima _____   ☐ Panamá _____

☐ Boston _____   ☐ Madrid _____   ☐ Portland _____

☐ Buenos Aires _____   ☐ México, D.F. _____   ☐ Vancouver _____

D. ¿Qué hacen los estudiantes en la clase?

PASO 1.   ¿Qué hace un estudiante bueno en nuestra clase? ¿Hay cosas que nunca hace? Crea tres respuestas con **siempre** y tres respuestas con **nunca.**

MODELOS: Un estudiante bueno siempre habla español en la clase.
Los estudiantes buenos nunca hablan inglés en la clase.

PASO 2.   Algunos estudiantes de universidades hispanas dan las siguientes respuestas sobre los estudiantes de su país. ¿Estas respuestas también son válidas para tu clase?

	¿TAMBIÉN EN NUESTRA CLASE?
1. «Siempre nos sentamos bien.»	☐
2. «Nunca tomamos café o refrescos (*soft drinks*) en la clase.»	☐
3. «No dormimos nunca en la clase.»	☐

¡Leamos!

«¿Padre, hijo o caballo?», por don Juan Manuel

Antes de leer

PASO 1. Indica si cada palabra se refiere a la ciudad, al campo o a los dos.

1. la tranquilidad
2. los edificios
3. los caballos

4. el silencio
5. la metrópoli
6. el monumento histórico

7. el taxi
8. el estrés (*stress*)
9. la soledad (*solitude*)

10. los mercados y las tiendas

 PASO 2. En grupos de tres o cuatro personas, ¿cuántos otros lugares, cosas o personas que se asocian con la ciudad y el campo pueden apuntar (*write down*) en una lista en dos minutos? Comparen con los otros grupos.

A leer

PASO 1. Mientras (*While*) lees el cuento (*story*), empareja cada párrafo con el dibujo que mejor lo acompañe.

«¿Padre, hijo o caballo?»

por don Juan Manuel

—Hoy es día de mercado; vamos al pueblo para comprar unas cuantas[a] cosas que necesitamos.

1. Deciden llevar con ellos un caballo para transportar sus compras. Parten[b] por la mañana muy temprano para el mercado: el caballo sin carga,[c] ellos a pie.[d]

2. Por el camino[e] se topan con[f] unos hombres que regresan del pueblo. Dichos[g] señores dicen entonces que ni el padre ni[h] el hijo parecen muy cuerdos[i] pues ambos[j] van a pie cuando el caballo va sin carga. Al oír esto, el padre le pide opinión a su hijo. Este admite que los hombres tienen razón,[k] y que, como el caballo no tiene carga, uno de ellos debe montarlo. Así pues, el padre manda[l] montar a su hijo y siguen adelante.[m]

3. Un poco más tarde, topan con otro grupo de hombres que regresan del pueblo. Estos hombres declaran que el padre está loco pues, viejo y cansado, va a pie mientras que su hijo, tan joven y robusto, va montado a caballo. El padre pide consejo[n] a su hijo y este declara que, en efecto, los hombres tienen razón. Así es que el hijo baja[ñ] del caballo y el padre se monta.

4. Algunos minutos más tarde, otros hombres que regresan del mercado critican al padre: según ellos un joven tan[o] delicado no debe ir a pie. Por eso[p] el padre hace montar a su hijo en su caballo y ninguno de los dos va entonces a pie.

   Más adelante se topan con otros hombres que también regresan del pueblo y estos critican tanto al padre como al hijo. Dicen:
   —¿Cómo va a poder cargar un caballo tan flaco a dos hombres tan grandes y pesados[q]?

5. El padre le pregunta al hijo qué deben hacer para no ser reprochados[r] ya más y al fin[s] llegan a la conclusión de que lo único que les resta[t] es cargar con el caballo. Padre e hijo llegan al mercado, pues, con el caballo en sus hombros[u] pero, a pesar de[v] esto, muchos se lo critican.

[a]unas... *a few* [b]*They depart* [c]*load* [d]a... *on foot* [e]*Por... On the road* [f]*se... they run into* [g]*These* [h]ni... *neither the father nor* [i]*sane* [j]*los dos* [k]tienen... *are right* [l]*orders* [m]*ahead, forward* [n]*advice* [ñ]*gets down* [o]*so* [p]*Por... For that reason* [q]*heavy* [r]*criticized* [s]al... *in the end* [t]*lo... the only option that remains* [u]*shoulders* [v]a... *despite*

a. ____

b. ____

c. ____

d. ____

e. ____

PASO 2. Indica si cada oración es cierta o falsa. Corrige (*Correct*) las oraciones falsas.

	CIERTO	FALSO
1. El padre y su hijo viven en la ciudad.	☐	☐
2. El padre y su hijo van al pueblo para comprar un coche.	☐	☐
3. El padre y su hijo llevan el caballo para transportar sus cosas.	☐	☐
4. El padre y su hijo escuchan los consejos de los hombres que ven (*they see*) durante el viaje.	☐	☐
5. Después de mucha crítica, el padre y su hijo deciden llevar (*carry*) el caballo en sus hombros.	☐	☐

Después de leer

PASO 1. Contesta las preguntas según lo que leíste (*what you read*) en el cuento.

1. ¿Cómo es el padre? ¿Cómo es el hijo?
2. ¿Dónde están ellos? ¿Adónde van?
3. ¿Cómo se pone el padre cuando lo critican los hombres del pueblo?
4. ¿Cómo se ponen los hombres del pueblo al ver a dos hombres llevando un caballo?
5. ¿Cómo crees que se sienten (*feel*) el padre y su hijo después de llevar el caballo?

PASO 2. Escoge la mejor moraleja del cuento para ti.

☐ No debes escuchar los consejos de otras personas.
☐ Es importante explicar las razones por las que haces algo.
☐ Es importante entender por qué haces algo.
☐ Es imposible evitar (*avoid*) la crítica.
☐ Es importante pensar por uno mismo (*oneself*).

¡Escuchemos!

¿Cómo llego al Ranario?

Antes de escuchar

Empareja cada palabra con su antónimo.

1. _____ bajar
2. _____ la derecha
3. _____ doblar
4. _____ salir

a. continuar sin desviarte (seguir derecho)
b. entrar
c. la izquierda
d. subir

El Ranario en Monteverde, Costa Rica

A escuchar

PASO 1. Yenaro trabaja en el Ranario (*Frog Pond*), una atracción muy popular entre (*among*) los turistas en Monteverde, Costa Rica. Allí puedes ver más de veintiocho diferentes especies de ranas (*frogs*) y sapos (*toads*) nativos de Costa Rica. Además de servir como guía en el Ranario, a veces Yenaro tiene que ayudar a los turistas que buscan algo que comer o dónde alojarse (*to stay*). Mira y escucha mientras explica cómo se llega del Ranario a otros lugares de Monteverde. Luego completa las indicaciones (*directions*) con la información que escuchas.

1. Tomas la calle a la _____. Bajas. Llegas a la intersección. De la _____, doblas hacia la _____. Subes un poco. Después del supermercado, SuperCompro, doblas a la _____, caminas unos veinticinco metros y llegas al restaurante Tree House.

2. Al Hotel Montaña, okay, _____ esta dirección, hacia arriba. Continúas sin _____, o desviarte, como un kilómetro. Después del Hotel Establo, a mano derecha _____ perfectamente al Hotel Montaña.

PASO 2. Mira y escucha mientras otros explican cómo se llega al Ranario de sus lugares de trabajo. Luego contesta las preguntas con un compañero / una compañera.

Expresiones útiles...	
el cruce	intersection
la curva	curve

1. ¿En qué restaurante está Erick?
2. ¿Cuántos metros hay que viajar para llegar al Ranario?
3. ¿Subes o bajas para llegar al Ranario?

4. ¿Dónde está Anlluly?
5. ¿Cuántos metros hay que viajar para llegar al Ranario?
6. ¿Vas a la izquierda o a la derecha para llegar al Ranario?

Después de escuchar

Mira el mapa y escoge un punto de partida (*starting point*) y un destino final en el pueblo. Luego, dile (*tell*) a un compañero / una compañera dónde tiene que empezar (pero no su destino final) y dale (*give him/her*) instrucciones para ir de un lugar al otro.

¡Escribamos!

Un lugar que conozco

Es importante poder escribir una descripción de un lugar que conoces para el uso de un turista de visita en ese lugar.

Antes de escribir

Haz (*Make*) una lista de las ciudades que conoces bien. De esas ciudades, decide qué ciudad conoces mejor y piensa en todas las cosas que se pueden hacer allí. Dibuja una rueda (*wheel*) de todas las categorías de atracciones de la ciudad y da por lo menos un ejemplo para cada una. El modelo te puede ayudar.

MODELO: Chicago, ~~Ocean City~~, ~~Philadelphia~~

A escribir

Ahora usa la información de tu dibujo (*drawing*) para formar un párrafo sobre la ciudad que escogiste (*you chose*). Escribe oraciones completas para dar una descripción amplia de la ciudad. ¿Cuáles son los mejores lugares para visitar y por qué? ¿Qué se puede hacer en una visita de un día o un fin de semana?

Después de escribir

Revisa (*Check over*) tu ensayo. Luego, intercambia (*exchange*) ensayos con un compañero / una compañera. Lee el ensayo de tu compañero/a y determina si falta (*it lacks*) información necesaria. Lee de nuevo (*again*) el ensayo de tu compañero/a con cuidado (*carefully*) para revisar los siguientes puntos de gramática.

- usa **ser** y **estar** de manera correcta (es decir, describe dónde **están** los mejores lugares para visitar y cómo **son** los mejores lugares para visitar)

- usa comparaciones correctas (**más… que, menos… que**)

- hay concordancia entre los sustantivos (*nouns*) y verbos

- hay concordancia (*agreement*) de género (*gender*) entre los adjetivos y lo que describen

- tiene ortografía (*spelling*) correcta

Después de revisar el ensayo de tu compañero/a, devuélveselo (*return it to him/her*). Mira tu propio (*own*) ensayo para ver los cambios que tu compañero/a recomienda y haz las revisiones necesarias.

¡Hablemos!

Hagamos un viaje°   *Let's take*

Antes de hablar

Primero escoge un destino de la lista. Luego, piensa en las respuestas a las preguntas que siguen.

- el barrio (*neighborhood*) favorito de tu ciudad
- el mejor parque que conoces
- una ciudad grande de este país
- el mejor lugar para ir de compras

- la mejor atracción cultural
- tu lugar natural favorito (un lago [*lake*], una montaña, una playa, etcétera)

1. ¿Dónde está el lugar?
2. ¿Cómo es el lugar?
3. ¿Cuál es la mejor manera de viajar al destino? (¿A pie, en autobús, en avión, en coche, en metro o en taxi?) Explica cómo llegar, paso por paso (*step by step*).
4. ¿Cuál es la mejor manera de viajar una vez llegado/a (*once you've arrived*) al destino?
5. ¿Cuánto cuesta(n)…

- el viaje?
- el transporte en el destino?
- las entradas (*tickets*)?

- el alojamiento (*lodging*)?
- la comida y las bebidas?

6. ¿Cuáles son los monumentos y/o edificios famosos?

A hablar

Usa las preguntas de **Antes de hablar** para entrevistar a tres compañeros de clase para saber más sobre sus destinos y apunta sus respuestas. ¡No te olvides de agradecerles (*thank*) a tus compañeros por sus recomendaciones!

COMPAÑERO/A	DESTINO	TRANSPORTE LOCAL	PRECIOS	MONUMENTOS FAMOSOS
1.				
2.				
3.				

Después de hablar

De los lugares que han descrito (*have described*) tus compañeros, ¿adónde quieres ir? ¿Por qué? Justifica tu decisión. ¿Cuál es el lugar más popular entre tus compañeros de clase?

Un consejo…

When students travel, study, and live abroad, a lot of the culture shock (**los choques culturales**) may stem from the differences between suburban living and urban living. For example, if you aren't used to using public transportation at home, but you have to use it a lot when you study abroad, that may be because you're living in a large city for the first time. You'd probably find the same difference if you moved from a small town to New York or Chicago, where you might also feel lost and confused when you didn't understand the language of the public transportation system—even if that language were English!

Conéctate a la música

Canción: «No hay nadie como tú» (2008)
Artistas: Calle 13 con Café Tacuba

Calle 13 es un grupo puertorriqueño que consiste en los hermanastros «Residente» (René Pérez Joglar) y «Visitante» (Eduardo José Cabra Martínez), y a veces su media hermana «PG-13» (Ileana Cabra Joglar). Calle 13 hace música urbana y alternativa, con influencias fuertes de hip hop y reggaetón. En esta canción, también participa el grupo mexicano Café Tacuba.

Antes de escuchar

Esta canción habla de muchos opuestos (*opposites*) en el mundo. Para empezar, piensa en un opuesto de cada uno de los siguientes conceptos.

1. ciudad _____
2. silencio _____
3. mujer _____
4. ricos _____

A escuchar

PASO 1. Escucha y contesta las siguientes preguntas.

La primera estrofa (*verse*)

Dicen que hay micrófonos y altoparlantes (*loudspeakers*), y que el mundo tiene _____ millones de habitantes (*inhabitants*).

El estribillo (*chorus*)

El estribillo es muy sencillo (*simple*). ¿Qué dice?

_____

Según la canción, ¿cuál es la idea opuesta (*opposite*) de cada una de las siguientes cosas?

La segunda estrofa

a. vegetarianos: _____
b. enfermedades (*diseases*): _____
c. capitalismo: _____

La tercera estrofa

d. muchas preguntas: _____

PASO 2. En tu opinión, ¿cuál es el mensaje principal de esta canción?

> **MODELO:** Pienso que el mensaje principal es que…

Después de escuchar

PASO 1. Escribe por lo menos cinco oraciones para describirte. Piensa en tus intereses, tus talentos, tu familia, tu hogar (*home*), tu educación, tus esperanzas (*hopes*) y tus planes.

PASO 2. Luego, comparte tu descripción con uno/a o dos compañeros/as de clase. Tacha (*Cross out*) cualquier parte de tu descripción que también aparezca (*that also appears*) en la descripción de uno de los miembros de tu grupo, y reemplázala con algo único (*replace it with something unique*). Al terminar, comparte las cinco maneras en que no hay nadie como tú.

> **MODELO:** Me llamo Silvia Pérez y soy hija única. Vivo en Austin, pero soy de Baltimore. Me gusta jugar fútbol y soy bastante rápida: puedo correr cinco kilómetros en menos de veintidós minutos. Un día quiero participar en los Juegos Olímpicos. ~~Estudio terapia física en la universidad.~~ Me levanto todos los días a las cinco de la mañana y hago ejercicio con mi equipo.

Residente y Visitante, dos miembros del grupo Calle 13

■ For copyright reasons, the songs referenced in **Conéctate a la música** have not been provided by the publisher. The video for this song can be found on YouTube, and it is available for purchase from the iTunes store.

VOCABULARIO

Comunicación

Gracias por + *noun/verb.*	Thank you for . . .
Much(ísim)as gracias.	Thank you (very much).
Sí, gracias.	Yes, please.
Te/Le/Les agradezco por...	I appreciate that you . . . / I thank you for . . .
De nada. / No hay de qué.	You're welcome.
¿Dónde está... / queda... ?	Where is . . . ?
aquí / allí	here / there
Siga...	Go / Keep going
derecho/recto	straight
hasta llegar a	until you arrive at
(la esquina de)...	(the corner of) . . .
Doble/Gire...	Turn . . .
a la derecha/izquierda	(to the) right/left
Suba... / Baje...	Go up . . . / Go down . . .
por esta calle	this street
Está... / Queda...	It's . . .
a la derecha/izquierda	on the right/left
al lado de...	next to . . .
detrás de...	behind . . .
enfrente de...	across from . . .
en la esquina de... y...	on the corner of . . . and . . .

Los paisajes urbanos y rurales / Urban and rural landscapes

las afueras	outskirts, suburbs
el almacén	department store
el árbol	tree
el autobús	bus
la calle	street
el campo	countryside / rural area
la carnicería	butcher shop
la carretera	highway
la ciudad	city
el coche	car
la cuadra	block
el edificio	building
la escuela	school
la frutería	fruit store
la iglesia	church
el jardín	garden
la librería	bookstore
el lugar	place
el pueblo	town
el puente	bridge
el rascacielos	skyscraper
el ruido	noise
la tienda	store

Cognados: el apartamento, la avenida, el banco, la capital, la catedral, el centro, el cine, la contaminación, el hospital, el kiosko, el mercado, el metro, el museo, el parque, la plaza, el restaurante, el taxi, el teatro, el tráfico, la tranquilidad, el transporte público

Los adjetivos y los adverbios

antiguo/a	ancient; former; old
bastante	quite, enough
muy	very

Cognados: moderno/a, rural, urbano/a

Los verbos

acordarse (ue) (de)	to remember
acostarse (ue)	to go to bed
afeitarse	to shave
bañarse	to bathe (oneself)
cepillarse los dientes	to brush one's teeth
conocer (zc)	to know; to be familiar with
despertarse (ie)	to wake up
dormirse (ue)	to go to sleep
ducharse	to shower
hacer (*irreg.*)	to make; to do
irse (*irreg.*)	to leave; to go away
lavarse	to wash (oneself)
las manos	to wash one's hands
levantarse	to get up
llegar	to arrive
maquillarse	to apply make-up
oír (*irreg.*)	to hear; to listen to
peinarse	to comb (one's hair)
poner (*irreg.*)	to put
ponerse (*irreg.*)	to put on; to become
contento/a	to become happy
los lentes / los lentes de contacto	to put on glasses/ contacts
quedarse	to stay
saber (*irreg.*)	to know (*a fact*)
salir (*irreg.*)	to leave; to go out
sentarse (ie)	to sit down
traer (*irreg.*)	to bring; to carry
venir (*irreg.*)	to come
vestirse (i)	to get dressed

Las expresiones indefinidas y negativas

algo	something
alguien	someone
algunos/as	some
nada	nothing
nadie	no one
ningún/ninguna	none, not any

¡A comer!

Un camarero guatemalteco nos presenta los postres del día.

Objetivos

In this chapter you will learn how to:

- respond affirmatively to a request
- decline invitations politely
- describe meals, table settings, and foods
- talk about the past
- use pronouns to avoid repetition
- discuss meals and foods in the Spanish-speaking world

COMUNICACIÓN ~~LARIO~~ ~~UCTURA~~ ~~ATE~~

¡Cómo no!
Responding to requests

 A. A ver: ¡Cómo no! Mira y escucha, luego escoge la expresión que usa cada uno para contestar la pregunta.

		¡CLARO QUE SÍ!	¡CÓMO NO!	CON MUCHO GUSTO.	¡POR SUPUESTO!
1.	¿Quieres vivir en otro país?	☐	☐	☐	☑
2.	¿Es importante poder hablar inglés?	☑	☐	☐	☐
3.	¿Ud. tiene un sueño (*dream*) en la vida?	☐	☐	☐	☐
4.	¿Quiere mandarles un saludo (*send a greeting*) a los estudiantes de español?	☐	☐	☐	☑
5.	¿Nos hace el favor de presentarse?	☐	☐	☐	☐
6.	¿Nos hace el favor de describir el propósito (*purpose*) del viaje a Madrid?	☐	☐	☐	☐
7.	¿Quiere mandarles un saludo a los estudiantes de español?	☐	☐	☐	☐
8.	¿Nos hace el favor de presentarse?	☐	☑	☐	☐

If someone invites you to do something or offers you something, here's what you might say if you want to accept.

Sí, gracias.	Yes, please.
Si no es molestia.	If it's not a bother.

¡Atención! Remember, in Spanish, **gracias** is used in instances where North Americans might say *please*.

—¿**Quieres un café?**
—**Sí, gracias.**

You can also use any of these expressions, which convey the English *Sure!*, *No problem*, and *Of course*, to respond in the affirmative.

¡Claro que sí!	**Con mucho gusto.**
¡Cómo no!	**Por supuesto.**

—¿**Me traes un café, por favor?**
—**Sí. ¡Cómo no!**
—**Gracias.**

¡Atención! The expression **¡Cómo no!** means *Of course!*, but **como no...** followed by a verb means *since/because + negative statement*.

Como no tenemos tiempo, no vamos a tener la prueba hoy.	Since we don't have time, we're not going to have the quiz today.

B. ¡Por supuesto!

PASO 1. Para cada pregunta, escoge la respuesta más adecuada para ti y luego termina la frase para dar una explicación.

1. ¿Quieres vivir en otro país?
   ☐ No, quiero vivir aquí, porque…
   ☐ Por supuesto. Quiero vivir en…

2. ¿Es importante poder hablar español?
   ☐ No. Es útil (*useful*), pero no es importante, porque…
   ☐ ¡Claro que sí! Es importante porque…

3. ¿Tienes un sueño (*dream*) en la vida?
   ☐ No, no soy ambicioso/a.
   ☐ Por supuesto. Quiero…

4. ¿Quieres cenar en mi casa esta noche?
   ☐ No, gracias. Ya (*Already*) tengo planes. Voy a…
   ☐ ¡Claro que sí! Yo puedo llevar…

5. ¿Nos haces el favor de presentarte (*introduce yourself*) a la clase?
   ☐ Lo siento. No puedo. Soy muy introvertido/a y no me gusta…
   ☐ ¡Cómo no! ¡Hola! Me llamo…

6. Quieres ir al campo conmigo este fin de semana?
   ☐ Lo siento. No puedo. Este fin de semana…
   ☐ ¡Cómo no! Podemos…

PASO 2. En parejas, practiquen las expresiones, pidiéndole algo a su compañero/a.

MODELO: E1: ¿Puedo sentarme aquí?
E2: Por supuesto. ¿Me prestas (*Can you lend me*) el diccionario?
E1: ¡Claro que sí!

Tengo muchas ganas de vivir en Guanajuato, México, el año que viene.

—¿Quieres... ? —No, gracias.
Inviting and declining politely

To ask someone if they want something, you can use **querer.**

TÚ	UD.
¿Quieres + *noun***?**	**¿Quiere (Ud.) +** *noun***?**
¿Quieres un café?	**¿Quiere Ud. un sándwich?**

There are many ways to invite someone to do something.

TÚ	UD.
¿Quieres + *infinitive***?**	**¿Quiere (Ud.) +** *infinitive***?**
¿Quieres ir al restaurante?	**¿Quiere Ud. ir al restaurante?**
¿Tienes ganas de + *noun/infinitive***?**	**¿Tiene (Ud.) ganas de +** *noun/infinitive***?**
¿Tienes ganas de pizza?	**¿Tiene Ud. ganas de una cerveza?**
¿Tienes ganas de pedir una pizza?	**¿Tiene ganas de tomar algo?**
¿Qué te parece + *noun/infinitive***?**	**¿Qué le parece +** *noun/infinitive***?**
¿Qué te parece una hamburguesa?	**¿Qué le parece un mango?**
¿Qué te parece cenar en casa?	**¿Qué le parece pedir un café?**
¿Te apetece + *noun/infinitive***?**	**¿Le apetece +** *noun/infinitive***?**
¿Te apetece un café?	**¿Le apetece un café?**
¿Te apetece tomar un café?	**¿Le apetece salir a comer?**

In some cultures it is polite to decline an invitation to eat or drink something the first time and then accept when it's been offered for a second or third time. To politely decline say: **No, gracias.**

If you really want to decline, it's nice to add a reason the second (and maybe third) time you decline: **No puedo.** (*I can't.*)

Debo + *infinitive.*	I should . . .
Debo regresar a casa.	I should go back home.

A. ¿Por qué no?   Empareja la invitación con la justificación más apropiada.

1. _____ ¿Quieres dar un paseo (*take a walk*) después de la cena?
2. _____ ¿Quieres ir al nuevo club con nosotros?
3. _____ ¿Quieres tomar un café?
4. _____ ¿Quieres almorzar con nosotros el domingo?

a. No, gracias. Voy a viajar este fin de semana.
b. Gracias, pero no puedo. No me gusta hacer ejercicio después de comer.
c. No, gracias. No puedo tomar la cafeína.
d. Gracias, pero no puedo. No sé bailar.

B. Gracias, pero...

PASO 1.   Haz una lista de cinco actividades que normalmente haces y cuándo piensas hacerlas (*plan to do them*).

MODELO:

ACTIVIDAD	¿CUÁNDO?
correr en el parque	*mañana a las tres de la tarde*
estudiar en la biblioteca	*hoy, después de almorzar*
tomar un café en el Café Turrón	*el sábado a las diez de la mañana*

PASO 2.   Circula por la clase e invita a otros compañeros a participar en algunas de tus actividades. Responde a las invitaciones que recibes, ofreciendo una justificación si la respuesta es «no».

MODELO: E1: ¿Quieres ir al Café Turrón a tomar un café el sábado a las diez de la mañana?
E2: No, gracias. No puedo. Debo visitar a mis padres.

C. ¿Dónde quieres comer?

PASO 1.   Consulta la publicidad de estos tres restaurantes. En parejas, decidan dónde quieren ir a comer. **¡Atención!** Los precios están en dólares estadounidenses.

MODELO: E1: ¿Quieres comer en El Mirasol?
E2: No me gusta mucho la carne (*meat*). ¿Quieres comer en Las Mañanitas?
E1: Pues, es muy caro (*expensive*). ¿Vamos al restaurante cubano Versailles?
E2: ¡Cómo no!

Las Mañanitas (Cuernavaca, México)

Ambiente: terrazas y áreas de comedor (*dining room*) rodeado de (*surrounded by*) un maravilloso jardín entre aves (*birds*) exóticas y obras (*works*) de arte.

Especialidades de la casa: tradicionales platillos (*main courses*) de comida mexicana hasta exquisitos platillos de la cocina (*cuisine*) internacional.

Rango de precios: de $19 a $39

El Mirasol (Buenos Aires, Argentina)

Ambiente: un excelente salón con las mejores vistas a la ciudad, un lugar para relajarse y comer sin apuro (*without being rushed*) con vista al puerto.

Especialidades de la casa: clásica comida argentina: empanadas de carne (*pastry stuffed with beef*) y carne a la parrilla (*grill*)—bifes (*steaks*), asados (*roasts*) y lomo (*loin*).

Rango de precios: de $25 a $50

Versailles (Miami, Estados Unidos)

Ambiente: uno de los mejores restaurantes cubanos de Miami, ubicado en la Pequeña Habana, con precios moderados (*moderate*). Aquí se reúnen (*meet*) muchos cubanos a disfrutar de (*to enjoy*) un café y discutir (*discuss*) sobre la política de Cuba.

Especialidades de la casa: comida típica cubana, arroz (*rice*) con frijoles (*beans*) y ropa vieja (*shredded beef in tomato sauce*).

Rango de precios: de $6 a $12

PASO 2.   Díganle al resto de la clase adónde van a comer y por qué.

MODELO: Vamos a comer en el restaurante cubano Versailles porque tienen precios muy económicos para una comida buena.

En español...

To say *Enjoy your meal,* use: **¡Buen provecho!**

English doesn't have an exact equivalent for **¡Buen provecho!** The closest thing in English is *Bon appétit!,* borrowed from French. In the Spanish-speaking world it would be rude to come across anyone eating and not say **¡Buen provecho!**

En la mesa
Food and meals

A. De compras

Vas al supermercado para comprar toda la comida que necesitas para la semana. Haz una lista de lo que vas a comprar usando las siguientes categorías: **aperitivos** (*appetizers*), **bebidas, desayunos, ensaladas, meriendas** (*snacks*), **platos principales para la cena, postres** y **sándwiches.**

eSuper.com

[Buscar]   Mi carrito

| Comestibles | Limpieza | Hogar | Ofertas |

Las carnes y los mariscos

los calamares   los camarones   la carne de res   el chorizo   el jamón   el pescado   el pollo   la carne de puerco

Los comestibles enlatados y empaquetados

el arroz   el atún   el azúcar   la sopa / el caldo (*broth*)   los frijoles   la harina   el pan   la pasta

Los productos lácteos y los huevos   **Los postres**

los huevos   la leche   el queso   el yogur   el flan   el helado   el pastel / la torta

Las verduras

el brócoli   la cebolla   los champiñones / los hongos   los chiles   la lechuga   el maíz   las papas   el pepino   el perejil   el tomate

Las frutas

las fresas   el limón   el mango   la manzana   la naranja   la piña   el plátano

Los condimentos

el aceite   la mantequilla   la pimienta   la sal   el vinagre

Las bebidas

el agua   la cerveza   el jugo   el refresco   el vino blanco   el vino tinto

En español…

Según la región del mundo, varían las palabras que se usan para describir la misma fruta o verdura. La palabra más común aparece primero. Aquí tienes algunos ejemplos de la variación.

fresa / frutilla (*Arg.*)	strawberry
chile / pimiento (*Sp.*)	pepper
durazno / melocotón (*Sp.*)	peach
pomelo / toronja (*Mex.*)	grapefruit
plátano / banana (*Sp.*) **/ guineo** (*R.D.*)	banana
pepino / cohombro (*P.R.*)	cucumber
papa / patata (*Sp.*)	potato
tomate / jitomate (*Mex.*)	tomato

Además, hay muchas frutas tropicales que pueden ser difíciles de encontrar (*to find*) en este país. Algunos ejemplos incluyen **la chirimoya, la guanábana, la guayaba** (*guava*)**, la lúcuma, la maracuyá** (*passion fruit*)**, la papaya** y **el zapote.** Si te gusta la fruta, ¡es muy divertido probar todas las opciones!

B. Las comidas

PASO 1. ¿Cuántas veces comes al día? Apunta a qué horas comes durante el día. Luego, haz un sondeo del resto de la clase. Puedes usar las siguientes palabras para completar las descripciones. **¡Atención!** No te olvides de conjugar los verbos.

Comidas	Verbos
el desayuno	desayunar
el almuerzo	almorzar
la comida	comer
la merienda	merendar
la cena	cenar

MODELO: E1: Desayuno a las ocho de la mañana, almuerzo a la una de la tarde y ceno a las siete de la noche. ¿Y tú? ¿Cuántas veces comes al día?

E2: Dos veces. A las once de la mañana y a las siete de la noche.

	2 Veces	3 Veces	4 Veces	5 Veces
Número de estudiantes				

¡Buen provecho!

PASO 2. Ahora, usa las siguientes preguntas (o inventa otras) para saber más detalles sobre las comidas que tus compañeros de clase comen. ¿Uds. tienen algo en común?

- ¿Te sientas para desayunar o comes algo en el camino (*on the way*) a la universidad / al trabajo?
- ¿Normalmente traes tu almuerzo o compras comida en la cafetería?
- ¿Con quién cenas usualmente?
- ¿Qué comidas son tus favoritas para merendar?
- ¿Sabes cocinar? ¿Qué te gusta cocinar?
- ¿Prefieres la comida saludable (*healthy*) o la comida basura (*junk food*)?

C. A ver: Las horas de comer   Mira y escucha, luego escribe las palabras que usa cada individuo para las distintas comidas.

¿Cómo es el horario de comidas en su país?

Selene de México dice:

«En México es el _____¹ primero que nada, y es un café. Después sigue el _____² que ya es un... la comida fuerte que son huevos, cereal, algo así por el estilo. Después como a eso de la una y media, dos de la tarde, que ya es la _____³ es una comida fuerte. Después sigue la _____⁴ que es el café, un pastel o algo por el estilo, y ya por la noche la _____,⁵ que por lo tradicional son los antojitos mexicanos o tacos».

María de Argentina dice:

«Bueno, empezamos con _____⁶ que es a las siete u ocho según a la hora que uno se levanta, y después a las doce que yo les doy el _____⁷ a mis hijos, y después tiene la _____⁸ que es a las cinco de la tarde, nada más. Y después la _____⁹ a la noche».

Víctor de España dice:

«Como algo muy suave porque aquí en España se hace _____¹⁰ en casa, eh... luego _____¹¹ a las 14:30, una ensalada, un postre, un poco de pasta habitualmente y luego por la noche, _____¹² en casa más fuerte, de la comida más fuerte».

Carolina de Costa Rica dice:

«Aquí dan desayunos de seis de la mañana a las nueve de la mañana, se puede tomar el _____.¹³ Un _____¹⁴ casi siempre empieza al mediodía o a la una de la tarde. Tenemos algo muy típico que es la hora del _____¹⁵ o depende del área de la provincia que es la hora del aguadulce que es una bebida muy nacional. Y después tenemos la _____¹⁶ que ya sería como algo también como parecido a lo que se sirve en el almuerzo en algunas familias como entre las siete de la noche a las nueve de la noche».

Vocabulario

Aquí hay algunas palabras para describir la comida y su preparación.

a la plancha	grilled
al ajillo	fried with garlic
asado/a	roasted
dulce	sweet
frito/a	fried
picante	spicy
salsa	sauce
saludable	healthy

- The audio files for in-text listening activities are available in the eBook, within Connect Plus activities, and on the Online Learning Center.

D. Tus platos favoritos

En grupos, describan sus platos favoritos en casa con sus familias y sus platos favoritos de un restaurante en su ciudad. Comparen y contrasten los dos platos.

MODELO: En casa mi plato favorito es la pasta con pollo y brócoli. Aquí mi plato favorito es la pizza de Frisky's. La pasta es más saludable, pero me encanta la pizza...

E. ¡Suena (*It sounds*) delicioso!   Escucha las descripciones y escribe el número al lado del plato correspondiente.

____ el banana split   ____ el espagueti   ____ el sándwich
____ la ensalada   ____ el omelet   ____ la sopa
____ la hamburguesa   ____ la quesadilla

¡Pongamos la mesa!

Setting the table

El cubierto (*place setting*) consiste en varios elementos que se usan para comer. Estos son los más comunes.

el vaso — la taza

el bol — la cuchara

el tenedor — el cuchillo

la servilleta — el plato

A. A la mesa   ¿Qué elementos del cubierto usas para cada cosa? **¡Atención!** Las bebidas y la sopa (*soup*) requieren un verbo distinto.

MODELO: Como el brócoli con un tenedor y un plato.

1. la pasta
2. la ensalada
3. el café
4. la sopa
5. una torta de chocolate
6. el yogur
7. el agua
8. la carne

B. Vamos de compras   Mira las siguientes imágenes, identifica la comida y di adónde puedes ir para comprar cada una.

MODELO: Para comprar camarones, puedo ir a la pescadería.

1.

2.

3.

4.

5.

6.

C. ¿Para pedir o para evitar (*avoid*)? Las siguientes personas van a comer en el Restaurante Piña. En parejas, miren la carta (*menu*) y decidan qué platos y/o bebidas cada uno va a pedir y qué va a evitar.

Restaurante Piña

Aperitivos

coctel de camarón	₡2,500
empanada de jamón y queso	₡1,750
empanada de verdura	₡1,500
melón con jamón	₡3,500

Primero

ensalada mixta	₡2,750
ensalada rusa (de patatas)	₡2,500
sopa de champiñones	₡2,500
sopa de pollo con fideos (pasta)	₡2,750

Segundo

filete de carne "la Piña"	₡6,000
pescado del día	₡5,000
salmón asado	₡5,750
ravioles de queso	₡4,500
ravioles de verdura	₡4,500

Acompañamientos

arroz	₡1,000
champiñones al ajillo	₡1,500
frijoles negros	₡1,500
papas fritas	₡1,000
puré de papas	₡1,000

Postres

flan	₡750
fruta fresca	₡1,000
helado de piña	₡1,000
torta de chocolate	₡1,200

Bebidas

agua	₡750
café	₡950
cerveza	₡2,000
vino	₡2,500

Restaurante Piña 879A Paseo Colón, San José, Costa Rica

MODELO: E1: Teresa está a dieta.
E2: Ella pide una ensalada mixta y pescado a la plancha. Evita los postres.

1. Ronaldo no tiene hambre.
2. Pablo y Javier tienen hambre.
3. Sara es vegetariana.
4. Elena y Tomás van al gimnasio después de la comida.
5. Olga no toma alcohol.
6. Ricardo tiene prisa (*is in a hurry*).
7. A Margarita no le gustan los mariscos.
8. Franco no come carbohidratos.

D. Nunca como...

PASO 1. Consulta la carta del Restaurante Piña y haz una lista de cinco alimentos (*foods*) y bebidas que nunca comes o bebes.

Nunca como...	Nunca bebo...
salmón	*vino*

 PASO 2. En parejas, entrevístense para determinar si evitan las mismas (*same*) comidas y bebidas. Luego, presenten lo que tienen en común al resto de la clase.

MODELO: E1: Nunca como salmón. ¿Y tú?
E2: Me gusta el salmón. Nunca como carne. ¿Y tú?
E1: ¡Yo tampoco! (*Me neither!*)

E. ¡A pedir!

PASO 1. Usando la carta del Restaurante Piña, completa el diálogo entre el camarero (*server*) y un cliente alérgico a los productos lácteos y a quien no le gustan ni (*neither*) el pescado ni (*nor*) los mariscos. **¡Atención!** Al servir la comida, usa: **¡Buen provecho!**

EL CAMARERO: ¿Está listo/a para pedir?
EL CLIENTE: Para primero, quiero _cóctel de camarón_
EL CAMARERO: ¿Y para segundo?
EL CLIENTE: _hamburguesa_
EL CAMARERO: ¿Y para tomar?
EL CLIENTE: _el vino_
EL CAMARERO: ¿Algo más?
EL CLIENTE: _no gracias_ — _buen provecho_
EL CAMARERO: ¿Está listo para pedir postre?
EL CLIENTE: _un helado_

 PASO 2. En grupos, túrnense para ser camarero/a mientras los otros piden comida de la carta. Es importante usar el trato formal (**Ud.**).

MODELO: E1: ¿Está listo/a para pedir?
E2: Para primero, la ensalada mixta, por favor.
E1: ¿Y para segundo?

COMUN VOCABU **ESTRUCTURA** TE

Reciclaje

The present indicative

¿Eres igual a un cocinero (*chef*) profesional? Escribe cada verbo en tiempo presente y así di cómo es un cocinero profesional y cómo eres tú. ¡Usa **no** si es necesario!

Un cocinero profesional		**Yo**
cocinar	_____ muy bien.	_____ muy bien.
escribir	_____ libros de cocina.	_____ libros de cocina.
trabajar	_____ en un restaurante.	_____ en un restaurante.
aprender	_____ a cocinar cosas nuevas de vez en cuando.	_____ a cocinar cosas nuevas de vez en cuando.

Según tus respuestas, ¿qué tienes en común con un cocinero profesional? Si no tienen nada en común, escribe eso.
Los dos _____.

■ Answers to this activity are in Appendix 2 at the back of your book.

6.1 Empezó a trabajar como cocinero

The preterite: Regular verbs

Ferran Adrià, director de elBulliFoundation

Para empezar...

Según muchos, Ferran Adrià es el mejor cocinero (*chef*) del mundo y su restaurante **El Bulli,** en el noreste de España, fue (*was*) uno de los más famosos del mundo. Adrià es conocido (*known*) por el uso de nuevas técnicas (*techniques*) en la cocina que cambian la textura y el aspecto de los alimentos (*foods*) para hacer algo inesperado (*unexpected*). Por ejemplo, una de sus técnicas más conocidas es hacer espuma (*foam*) de cosas como el café, los champiñones (hongos) o la carne. Ahora Adrià es director de *elBulliFoundation,* un centro de innovación culinaria.

PASO 1. Usa la introducción y tu sentido (*sense*) común para emparejar cada evento en la vida de Ferran Adrià con el año correspondiente. Dos ya están hechos.

AÑO	EVENTO
1. ___ 1962	a. **Escribió** el libro *Cocinar en 10 minutos con Ferran Adrià.*
2. ___ 1980	b. **Empezó** a trabajar en El Bulli.
3. ___ 1981	c. **Cocinó** con espuma por primera vez (*for the first time*) en El Bulli.
4. _b_ 1984	d. **Ganó** por primera vez el premio al mejor restaurante del mundo.
5. ___ 1988	e. **Abrió** su nuevo centro culinario, elBulliFoundation.
6. _a_ 1998	f. **Trabajó** como lavaplatos (*dishwasher*) en un hotel. **Aprendió** a cocinar.
7. ___ 2002	g. **Cerró** su restaurante El Bulli para concentrarse en la gastronomía creativa.
8. ___ 2011	h. **Empezó** a trabajar como cocinero en el servicio militar.
9. ___ 2013	i. **Nació** (*He was born*) en la región de Barcelona, España.

PASO 2.   Ahora que sabes más sobre la vida de Ferran Adrià, haz tu propia (*own*) mini-biografía. Para cada pregunta, escoge la respuesta adecuada y escribe la información que falta (*is missing*). Si es necesario, puedes empezar tu respuesta con **nunca** (por ejemplo, «Nunca aprendí a cocinar»).

■ Answers to these activities are in Appendix 2 at the back of your book.

1. _____ ¿En qué año **naciste**?
2. _____ ¿Dónde **naciste**?
3. _____ ¿Dónde **estudiaste** primaria?
4. _____ ¿En qué año **empezaste** a estudiar en la universidad?
5. _____ ¿En qué año **trabajaste** como lavaplatos?
6. _____ ¿En qué año **aprendiste** a cocinar una cena completa?

a. **Empecé** a estudiar en la universidad en el año _____.
b. **Nací** en el año _____.
c. **Trabajé** como lavaplatos en el año _____.
d. **Nací** en _____.
e. **Aprendí** a cocinar una cena completa en el año _____.
f. **Estudié** primaria en _____.

En español...

To express the idea of *ago*, use the word **hace** followed by the time expression.

Trabajé en el restaurante **hace cinco años.**	*I worked in the restaurant five years ago.*
Comimos **hace dos minutos.**	*We ate two minutes ago.*

To ask how long ago something happened, use **¿cuánto tiempo hace que** + *preterite*?

¿Cuánto tiempo hace que cerró El Bulli?	*How long ago did El Bulli close?*

Some other useful time expressions are **ayer** (*yesterday*) and **anoche** (*last night*).

¿Aprendiste algo **ayer**?	*Did you learn something yesterday?*
Anoche cené a las ocho.	*I had dinner at 8:00 last night.*

Actividades analíticas

1   The verbs in **Para empezar** are in the *preterite tense* (**el tiempo pretérito**). This tense is used when you want to portray an event as happening at a specific point in the past. Use the verb forms from **Para empezar** to complete these conjugations of **trabajar, aprender,** and **escribir** in the preterite.

	trabaj**ar**	aprend**er**	escrib**ir**
yo			escrib**í**
tú			escrib**iste**
él/ella, Ud.			
nosotros/as	trabaj**amos**	aprend**imos**	escrib**imos**
vosotros/as	trabaj**asteis**	aprend**isteis**	escrib**isteis**
ellos/ellas, Uds.	trabaj**aron**	aprend**ieron**	escrib**ieron**

2   Complete this chart of endings for **-ar, -er,** and **-ir** verbs in the preterite. Note that the endings for **-er** and **-ir** verbs are the same.

	-ar		-er / -ir	
yo	_-é_ trabaj**é**		_____ aprend**í**	escrib**í**
tú	_-aste_ trabaj**aste**		_____ aprend**iste**	escrib**iste**
él/ella, Ud.	_-ó_ trabaj**ó**		_-ió_ aprend**ió**	escrib**ió**
nosotros/as	_____ trabaj**amos**		_-imos_ aprend**imos**	escrib**imos**
vosotros/as	_-asteis_ trabaj**asteis**		_____ aprend**isteis**	escrib**isteis**
ellos/ellas, Uds.	_____ trabaj**aron**		_____ aprend**ieron**	escrib**ieron**

■ For more verbs in the preterite, see **Para saber más 6.1** at the back of your book.

En español...

Some **-ar** verbs have stems that end in **g-** (such as **jugar** and **llegar**). When these verbs have an **-é** ending in the preterite, add a **-u-** to preserve the hard **g** sound. This change is not needed when the ending begins with **a** or **o.**

Llegué ayer en la tarde.	*I arrived yesterday in the evening.*
¿**Llegaste** a tiempo?	*Did you arrive on time?*

Similarly, for **-ar** verbs whose stems end in **-c-** (such as **practicar**), change the **-c-** to **-qu-** to preserve the hard [k] sound with the **-é** ending. For verbs whose stems end in **-z-** (such as **empezar**), change the **-z-** to **-c-.** These changes are not needed when the ending begins with **a** or **o.**

Empecé a estudiar matemáticas el año pasado. ¿Cuando **empezaste** tú?	*I started studying math last year. When did you start?*
Ayer no **practiqué** tenis. ¿Tú sí **practicaste**?	*I didn't practice tennis yesterday. Did you practice?*

Actividades prácticas

A. Preguntas y respuestas   Empareja cada pregunta con una respuesta adecuada.

1. _____ ¿A qué hora cenaron anoche?
2. _____ ¿Estudiaste mucho ayer?
3. _____ ¿Cuándo empezaste a bailar salsa?
4. _____ ¿Quién cocinó ayer?
5. _____ ¿A qué hora cenaste anoche?
6. _____ ¿Dónde vivieron el año pasado?
7. _____ ¿Estudiaron mucho para el examen?
8. _____ ¿Cuándo empezaron a cocinar?
9. _____ ¿Dónde vivió Ud. en 2012?

a. Cené a las nueve.
b. Viví en la casa de mi madre.
c. Cenamos a las siete.
d. Empezamos hace diez minutos.
e. Empecé el año pasado.
f. Cociné yo.
g. Vivimos en la universidad.
h. Sí, estudiamos mucho.
i. Sí, estudié mucho.

B. Entrevistas   Lee las entrevistas con Gonzalo, Isabel, María y Pilar sobre qué comieron y cuándo comieron. Usa la siguiente información para completar las entrevistas en la página 173.

- Los argentinos tienen fama (*reputation*) de comer mucha carne.
- Los argentinos y los españoles tienen fama de cenar a las diez o más tarde.
- Los mexicanos tienen fama de desayunar y comer (almorzar) mucho, pero cenar poco.

Gonzalo (Argentina)

PREGUNTA	¿CÓMO CONTESTA GONZALO?
1. —_____	—Desayuné a las seis y media.
2. —¿Y qué desayunaste?	—_____
3. —¿A qué hora cenaste ayer?	—_____
4. —¿Qué cenaste?	—_____

María y Pilar (España)

PREGUNTA	¿CÓMO CONTESTAN MARÍA Y PILAR?
5. —_____	—Cenamos anoche a las diez.
6. —¿Qué cenaron?	—_____

Isabel (México)

PREGUNTA	¿CÓMO CONTESTA ISABEL?
7. —_____	—Desayuné a las ocho.
8. —¿Y qué desayunó?	—_____
9. —¿A qué hora comió?	—_____
10. —_____	—Comí una sopa, arroz, un guisado (*stew*)
11. —¿A qué hora cenó?	y un postre.
12. —¿Qué cenó?	—_____
	—_____

a. Cené a las nueve.
b. ¿A qué hora cenaron anoche?
c. Cené muy ligero (*light*): un pan y un vaso con leche.
d. ¿A qué hora desayunaste esta mañana?
e. Cené anoche a las diez.
f. Desayuné huevo, frijoles, pan de dulce y fruta.
g. ¿Y qué comió?
h. Cené carne y una ensalada.
i. Comí a las tres.
j. Cenamos pescado.
k. ¿A qué hora desayunó Ud. esta mañana?
l. Desayuné una medialuna (*croissant*) con un café.

 C. ¿Cómo comen los estudiantes?   ¿Tus compañeros comen de una manera balanceada (*balanced*)? Escoge uno de los siguientes tipos de comida y pregúntales a tres de tus compañeros cuántas veces comieron cada comida durante las últimas (*last*) veinticuatro horas. Apunta los resultados. **¡Atención!** Para la comida sólida, usa el verbo **comer.** Para los líquidos, usa **tomar** o **beber.**

MODELO: E1: ¿Cuántas veces comiste carne en las últimas veinticuatro horas?
           E2: Comí carne dos veces.

1. agua
2. carne
3. frijoles
4. fruta
5. granos integrales (*whole grains*)
6. leche
7. pescado
8. verduras

 D. ¡A juntarse!

PASO 1.   En muchos países hispanos, es muy común juntarse (*get together*) con toda la familia los domingos para comer. ¿Es así (*like that*) para tus compañeros también? En parejas, pregúntense con quién desayunaron, con quién almorzaron y con quién cenaron el domingo pasado.

MODELO: E1: ¿Con quién desayunaste el domingo pasado?
           E2: Desayuné solo.

PASO 2.   ¿Cuándo fue (*was*) la última vez que se juntó tu familia? En parejas, túrnense para describir la reunión y den (*give*) muchos detalles. (¿Celebraron Uds. algo específico? ¿Cuántas personas asistieron [*attended*]? ¿Dónde fue el evento? ¿Quién preparó la comida? ¿Cocinaste tú alguna comida especial? ¿Qué comieron Uds.? ¿A qué hora terminó la reunión?)

La comida del domingo

⟳ Reciclaje

Verbs with irregular **yo** forms

Completa cada oración usando uno de los siguientes verbos en la forma **yo** del presente.

decir   hacer   ir   poner   ser

1. _____ una persona perfecta.
2. Cada mañana, _____ un desayuno muy rico para todos mis amigos.
3. _____ «¡Buen provecho!» antes de empezar a comer.
4. _____ al súper cada día para comprar la comida más fresca.
5. Siempre _____ las cosas en el lugar correcto.

■ Answers to this activity are in Appendix 2 at the back of your book.

6.2   ¿Hice algo mal en la cena?

The preterite: Some common irregular verbs

Para empezar...

Uno de tus amigo está en Buenos Aires, y la semana pasada lo invitaron (*they invited him*) a una cena. **Fue** (*He went*), pero ahora tiene la impresión de que **hizo** (*he did*) algo mal en la cena. Según él, estas son las cosas que **hizo**. ¿Qué **estuvo** (*was*) bien, y qué **estuvo** mal? Primero lee **Conéctate al mundo hispano,** luego haz la actividad. **Un consejo:** ¡Tu amigo solo **hizo** dos cosas bien!

CONÉCTATE AL MUNDO HISPANO

Muchos aspectos de **una cena latinoamericana** son similares a las costumbres en este país, pero hay algunas diferencias importantes.

■ Al llegar (*Upon arriving*) es normal darse la mano o darle un beso a cada persona presente.
■ En general, la cena empieza más tarde.
■ Debes tener las manos sobre (*on top of*) la mesa durante la comida, no debajo de (*under*) la mesa.
■ La conversación en la mesa (conocida como «la sobremesa») es animada y puede durar (*last*) hasta mucho después de terminar (*end*) la cena.

Puede haber diferencias en ciertos lugares, pero estas características se aplican en la mayoría de los países hispanos.

LAS COSAS QUE YO HICE (*I DID*)	ESTUVO BIEN	ESTUVO MAL
1. Primero **fui** (*I went*) a la casa equivocada (*wrong*).	☐	☐
2. Llegué a la casa de mis amigos a las seis y media.	☐	☐
3. **Fui** (*I was*) muy educado (*polite*). Les di la mano a todos los invitados.	☐	☐
4. **Hice** un brindis (*a toast*) con un vaso de agua.	☐	☐
5. Antes de empezar a comer, **dije:** «¡Qué rara comida!»	☐	☐
6. **Puse** (*I put*) las manos debajo (*under*) de la mesa.	☐	☐
7. Tomé mucho vino y **me puse** muy borracho (*drunk*).	☐	☐
8. Después de cenar, **dije:** «**Estuvo** muy rica la cena. ¡Gracias!».	☐	☐
9. Me levanté y **me fui** inmediatamente después de cenar.	☐	☐

Actividades analíticas

1 In **Para empezar** you saw some new verb forms in the preterite tense. One of these verb forms, **fui,** has two meanings. Write out the sentence from **Para empezar** that illustrates each of the meanings listed here.

EXAMPLE

fui = *I went*   _____

fui = *I was*   _____

The reason that **fui** has two meanings is that the verbs **ir** (*to go*) and **ser** (*to be*) are conjugated in exactly the same way in the preterite.

■ Answers to these activities are in Appendix 2 at the back of your book.

	ir/ser
yo	fui
tú	fuiste
él/ella, Ud.	fue
nosotros/as	fuimos
vosotros/as	fuisteis
ellos/ellas, Uds.	fueron

The context generally makes it clear which meaning (**ir** or **ser**) is intended.

¿Adónde **fueron** Uds.?	*Where did you (pl.) go?*
Fuimos al supermercado.	*We went to the supermarket.*
Alberto Fujimori **fue** presidente de Perú.	*Alberto Fujimori was president of Peru.*
La fiesta **fue** en casa de Ana.	*The party was at Ana's house.*

2 Use the other verbs forms that you saw in **Para empezar** to complete these conjugations.

	decir	estar	hacer	poner
yo		estuve		
tú	dijiste	estuviste	hiciste	pusiste
él/ella, Ud.	dijo		hizo	puso
nosotros/as	dijimos	estuvimos	hicimos	pusimos
vosotros/as	dijisteis	estuvisteis	hicisteis	pusisteis
ellos/ellas, Uds.	dijeron	estuvieron	hicieron	pusieron

«Hice sopa de tortilla para la comida. ¡Buen provecho!»

These verbs use a special stem in the preterite (**dij-, estuv-, hic-, pus-**). Despite their irregular stems, the endings of these verbs all follow the same pattern. The only exception to this pattern is **dijeron** (and other irregular preterite verbs whose stems end in **-j**, such as **traer [trajeron]**), in which **i** of the **-ieron** ending is dropped, making the ending **-eron.** Use the examples to complete the chart.

Terminaciones del pretérito: Verbos de raíz irregular			
yo	-e	No **dije** nada.	*I didn't say anything.*
tú	_____	¿**Estuviste** en la fiesta?	*Were you at the party?*
él/ella, Ud.	-o	¿Qué **hizo** Mario?	*What did Mario do?*
nosotros/as	_____	**Pusimos** la comida allí.	*We put the food there.*
vosotros/as	-isteis	¿**Estuvisteis** contentos ayer?	*Were you happy yesterday?*
ellos/ellas, Uds.	-ieron	**Hicieron** sopa para todos.	*They made soup for everyone.*

3 Here is a list of the most common verbs with irregular stems in the preterite, including the four just seen.

Verbos de raíz irregular en el pretérito		
INFINITIVO	**RAÍZ**	**EJEMPLO**
decir	dij-	¿Qué **dijo** tu amigo?	*What did your friend say?*
estar	estuv-	Eva no **estuvo** en la cena.	*Eva was not at the dinner.*
hacer	hic-	**Hicieron** una paella muy rica.	*They made a delicious paella.*
poder	pud-	**Pude** llegar a la clase a tiempo.	*I was able to arrive to class on time.*
poner	pus-	¿Dónde **pusiste** las peras?	*Where did you put the pears?*
tener	tuv-	Ayer **tuvimos** un día muy bonito.	*We had a very nice day yesterday.*
traer	traj-	¿**Trajeron** Uds. la comida?	*Did you bring the food?*

¿Por qué?

With regular verbs, the preterite endings for **yo** and **él/ella** are stressed and thus written with an accent mark (**hablé, habló**). So why are these endings not accented for verbs with special stems in the preterite (for example, **dije, dijo**)? The answer is that the stem itself is enough to signal that the verb is in the preterite in these cases, and the special stressed ending is not necessary.

Actividades prácticas

A. ¡Arepas!   Las arepas son una comida tradicional de Colombia y Venezuela hecha (*made*) de harina de maíz. Hay comidas parecidas en otros países, como **las pupusas** de El Salvador y **las gorditas** de México. Las siguientes oraciones describen lo que hicieron Bárbara y Mari para preparar arepas, pero las oraciones están desordenadas (*in the wrong order*). Ponlas (*Put them*) en orden, ¡y aprende a hacer arepas!

CÓMO HICIMOS AREPAS

a. _____ Separamos la masa en bolas (*balls*).
b. _____ Comimos las arepas.
c. _____ Pusimos la harina de maíz en agua, con un poco de sal.
d. _____ Pusimos las arepas en aceite caliente.
e. _____ Mezclamos (*We mixed*) todo, y así hicimos la masa (*dough*).
f. __1__ Tuvimos que salir a comprar harina de maíz.
g. __5__ Pusimos queso entre (*between*) dos bolas y las aplastamos (*we flattened them*) en forma de arepa.
h. _____ ¡Estuvieron muy ricas!

La preparación de arepas

B. Completar la oración

PASO 1.   Completa cada oración con el verbo apropiado. **¡Atención!** Cada palabra se puede usar solo una vez.

dijeron   estuvimos   fue   fuimos   hicieron   pudieron   trajo   tuviste

1. Araceli _____ la mejor estudiante de la clase ayer.
2. Beto y yo _____ a la biblioteca para estudiar.
3. Edgar _____ un perro a nuestra clase.
4. Los cocineros _____ una paella exquisita.
5. ¿_____ un examen de matemáticas?
6. Brenda y Gustavo no _____ hacer la tarea.
7. ¡_____ en la biblioteca por cuatro horas ayer!
8. _____ que el español es muy bonito.

PASO 2.   Cambia cada oración del **Paso 1** a la forma **yo** y contesta si hiciste eso ayer.

		¿HICISTE ESO AYER?	
		SÍ	NO
1.	Fui el/la mejor estudiante de la clase.	☐	☐
2.	_____	☐	☐
3.	_____	☐	☐
4.	_____	☐	☐
5.	_____	☐	☐
6.	_____	☐	☐
7.	_____	☐	☐
8.	_____	☐	☐

C. ¿Adónde fuiste a comer?

PASO 1.   Pregúntale a tu compañero/a cuándo fue la última vez que salió a comer. ¿Adónde fue? ¿Qué comió? ¿Cómo estuvo la comida? Apunta sus respuestas.

PASO 2.   Ahora reporta a la clase sobre las experiencias de tu compañero/a.

MODELO: Kristen salió a comer anoche. Fue a Dino's Restaurante Italiano y comió pasta con verduras. ¡La comida estuvo muy rica!

D. ¿Qué hicieron?

PASO 1.   En un grupo, pregúntense si hicieron alguna de estas acciones en los últimos doce meses, y apunten los resultados.

MODELO: E1: ¿Quién dijo «bon appétit» en una comida?
E2: Yo dije eso muchas veces.

¿Quién hizo esto?

1. decir «bon appétit» en una comida
2. hacer comida mexicana en casa
3. hacer un brindis (*a toast*) en una comida
4. ir a un restaurante peruano
5. tener una cena especial en Año Nuevo (*New Year's*)
6. traer comida para una clase

PASO 2.   Creen (*Create*) un resumen de lo que hicieron.

MODELO: Chris dijo «bon appétit» en una comida.
Kathy y Sean hicieron comida mexicana en casa.
Nadie hizo un brindis en una comida.

PASO 3.   En sus grupos, hablen de otras experiencias culinarias que han tenido Uds. (*you have had*) recientemente. Pueden ayudarlos/las (*help you*) las siguientes palabras.

cocinar   **comer**   **ir**   **probar**   **tener**

POSIBLES PREGUNTAS: ¿Probaste (*Did you try*) una comida nueva este año? ¿Cuál fue? ¿Te gustó? ¿Comiste en un restaurante nuevo este año? ¿Dónde? ¿Te gustó? ¿Cocinaste una cena especial recientemente? ¿Por qué? ¿Qué preparaste?

C Reciclaje

Definite articles

Para cada sustantivo, escribe el artículo definido (**el, la, los, las**) correcto. Cinco de estos sustantivos son cosas que no se puede comer. ¿Cuáles son?

1. _____ aceite
2. _____ carne
3. _____ cebolla
4. _____ chile
5. _____ cuchara
6. _____ cuchillo
7. _____ fresas
8. _____ frijoles
9. _____ leche
10. _____ lechuga
11. _____ maíz
12. _____ pan
13. _____ papas
14. _____ pollos
15. _____ servilleta
16. _____ tazas
17. _____ tenedor
18. _____ tomates
19. _____ vainilla
20. _____ yogur

■ Answers to this activity are in Appendix 2 at the back of your book.

6.3 Lo encontraron en México

Direct objects and direct object pronouns

Para empezar...

¿Qué tienen en común el chile, la papa, el tomate y la vainilla? Todos son originarios (*natives*) de América. En la siguiente lista de oraciones, escribe **C** si se trata (*it's about*) del chile, **P** si se trata de la papa, **T** si se trata del tomate y **V** si se trata de la vainilla. **¡Atención!** Para entender las oraciones mejor, acuérdate que **chile** y **tomate** son sustantivos masculinos, y **papa** y **vainilla** son sustantivos femeninos.

el chile (C)   **la papa (P)**   **el tomate (T)**   **la vainilla (V)**

1. _____ **La** domesticaron en la región de los Andes. Los españoles **la** llevaron a Europa y ahora **la** usan mucho en la cocina alemana e irlandesa, por ejemplo.
2. _____ En Sudamérica y en el Caribe, **lo** conocen como «ají». **Lo** usan para hacer más picante la comida.
3. _____ **La** usan mucho en los postres.
4. _____ En España, **lo** conocen como «pimiento».
5. _____ En el centro y el sur de México, **lo** conocen como «jitomate».
6. _____ Los españoles **lo** encontraron en varias partes de América y **lo** llevaron a Europa y Asia en tiempos coloniales. Ahora **lo** usan mucho en la cocina tailandesa, china y coreana.
7. _____ En España, **la** llaman «patata».
8. _____ Los españoles **lo** encontraron en México y **lo** llevaron a Europa. Desde entonces (*since then*) es un ingrediente muy importante en la cocina española e italiana (en la pizza, por ejemplo).

Actividades analíticas

1 In the examples in **Para empezar, lo** and **la** are *pronouns* (**pronombres**) like *it, him,* or *her* in English. They are used to avoid repetition and replace the full name of a person or thing. **Lo** and **la** specifically replace the *direct object* (**el objeto directo**) of the sentence. The direct object is the person or thing upon which the action of the verb is performed. Circle the direct object in each sentence, then note how it is replaced by **lo** or **la.** The first is done for you.

a. Los españoles encontraron (el chile) en México.
→ Los españoles **lo** encontraron en México.
b. Los españoles llevaron la papa a Europa.
→ Los españoles **la** llevaron a Europa.
c. Veo a mi hermano todos los días.
→ **Lo** veo todos los días.
d. Gustavo conoce muy bien a Marisela.
→ Gustavo **la** conoce muy bien.

2 Circle the direct object of each sentence, then rewrite the sentence, replacing the direct object with **lo** or **la**. The first is done for you.

a. Encontré (este libro) en la biblioteca.   →   ___Lo encontré en la biblioteca.___

b. Ana toma café por la mañana.   →   _____

c. Julián compró la fruta ayer.   →   _____

3 If the direct object is plural, the pronouns **los** or **las** are used.

Necesito **los libros.**   →   **Los** necesito.

Mi amiga conoce **a Ana y Luisa.**   →   Mi amiga **las** conoce.

The other direct object pronouns (**me, te, nos,** and **os**) are already familiar to you, because they look exactly the same as the reflexive pronouns (**Estructura 5.2**). The full set is given here.

PRONOMBRES DE OBJETO DIRECTO

singular		plural	
me	*me*	**nos**	*us*
te	*you* (inform.)	**os**	*you* (inform., Sp.)
lo	*him/it* (m.)	**los**	*them* (m.)
	you (m., form.)		*you* (m., form.)
la	*her/it* (f.)	**las**	*them* (f.)
	you (f., form.)		*you* (f., form.)

¿**Me** conoces?   *Do you know me?*

Perdón, no **te** oí.   *I'm sorry, I didn't hear you.*

Marta **nos** invitó a una fiesta.   *Marta invited us to a party.*

4 Direct object pronouns are usually placed before the conjugated verb. If the conjugated verb is immediately followed by an infinitive, the pronoun can instead be attached to the end of the infinitive.

Puedo encontrar **el libro** en la biblioteca. →   { **Lo** puedo encontrar en la biblioteca.
  Puedo encontrar**lo** en la biblioteca.

You will explore the placement of the pronoun in more detail in **Estructura 8.3.**

5 In addition to being used to mean *it* (m. and f.) and *him/her/them,* the pronouns **lo, la, los,** and **las** may be used to refer to people that you are addressing as **Ud.** or **Uds.** (*you*).

Mi madre **la** conoce.   *My mother knows you* (f. sing., form.). / *My mother knows her.*

Los invité a la cena.   *I invited you* (m. pl., form.) *to the dinner. / I invited them to the dinner.*

The following sentences are addressing the person as **tú.** Change them to address the person as **Ud.**

a. Te invito a desayunar con nosotros.   →   _____
                                                    (addressing a male)

b. Te llevamos (*take*) a la fiesta.   →   _____
                                                    (addressing a female)

¡Anticipa!

Once again, bearing in mind the importance of gender and number agreement in Spanish, what direct object pronoun would be needed if **a Ana y Luisa** were changed to **a Ana y Luis** in the sample sentence?

Mi amiga conoce a Ana y Luisa. →
Mi amiga *las* **conoce.**
Mi amiga conoce a Ana y Luis. →
Mi amiga ____ conoce.

Why?

Respuestas: los, because the direct object pronoun would represent one female and one male, and thus would default to the masculine, mixed group form.

■ Answers to these activities are in Appendix 2 at the back of your book.

Actividades prácticas

A. El maíz y las tortillas   De las siguientes oraciones, ¿cuáles se refieren (*refer*) al maíz y cuáles se refieren a las tortillas? Además (*In addition*), hay dos oraciones falsas, una sobre el maíz y una sobre las tortillas. ¿Cuáles son?

¿El maíz o las tortillas?

		CIERTO	FALSO
1. _____	Lo domesticaron en América.	☐	☐
2. _____	Los españoles las llevaron a Europa, y desde entonces las comen mucho los españoles y los italianos.	☐	☐
3. _____	Las comen en México, Guatemala y El Salvador.	☐	☐
4. _____	Lo ponen en agua con cal (*lime*) para hacer la masa para las tortillas.	☐	☐
5. _____	Lo ponen en agua con azúcar para hacer la masa para las tortillas.	☐	☐
6. _____	Tradicionalmente las hacen de maíz.	☐	☐
7. _____	Los españoles lo llevaron a Europa y al resto del mundo.	☐	☐
8. _____	En muchos países lo llaman «choclo».	☐	☐
9. _____	En el norte de México, donde tradicionalmente no hay mucho maíz, las hacen de harina.	☐	☐

CONÉCTATE AL MUNDO HISPANO

Tortillas de harina

La tortilla es importante a la gastronomía mexicana, centroamericana y española. Pero, ¿sabes que hay varios tipos de tortillas?

En el norte de México, se puede encontrar tortillas de harina. Estas suelen ser más grandes y se usan para hacer los burritos. En el centro y el sur de México y en Centroamérica se encuentran tortillas de maíz. Son hechas con harina de maíz, y normalmente son más pequeñas. Se usan para hacer los tacos o enchiladas, o para acompañar algún plato.

En España, la tortilla tradicional es totalmente distinta. Está hecha de huevo y papa y es un tipo de «omelette».

Una tortilla española

B. Preguntas y respuestas   Vas a escuchar ocho preguntas. Escoge la respuesta más apropiada para cada una.

1. ____	a.	¿No me conoces? Soy Mari, la amiga de Jorge.
2. ____	b.	La tiré (*threw out*).
3. ____	c.	Las puse en la cocina.
4. ____	d.	Porque no nos invitaron a la fiesta.
5. ____	e.	Sí, está bien. Te veo allí.
6. ____	f.	¿No lo conoces? Es el amigo de Ana.
7. ____	g.	Lo puse en la cocina.
8. ____	h.	Los tiré.

C. La comida mexicana en tu país   De toda la comida hispana, la mexicana es la más conocida en este país. Pero ¿tú la conoces bien? En esta lista de platillos (*dishes*) mexicanos, ¿cuáles conoces? ¿Cuáles tienen en restaurantes donde tú vives? En parejas, comparen sus experiencias. **¡Atención!** El número y género de cada platillo es diferente.

> **MODELO:**   E1: ¿Conoces el arroz con leche?
>   E2: No, no lo conozco, pero lo tienen en restaurantes aquí.

ALGUNOS PLATILLOS MEXICANOS

1. el arroz con leche
2. la birria (carne de chivo [*goat*])
3. las carnitas
4. los chilaquiles (trozos [*pieces*] de tortilla de maíz con huevo y salsa picante)
5. la crema de espárragos (*cream of asparagus soup*)
6. la sopa de tortilla
7. los huevos motuleños (tortilla de maíz con huevos, frijoles negros y queso)
8. los nopalitos (*cactus pads*)
9. la sopa de lima (de pollo con jugo de lima [*lime*])
10. los tamales dulces

D. El tenedor y el cuchillo   Hay dos maneras de cortar (*to cut*) la comida con el tenedor y el cuchillo en el mundo: «el estilo norteamericano» y «el estilo europeo». Lee las siguientes descripciones, y trata de identificar cuál es el estilo norteamericano y cuál es el estilo europeo. Luego, cambia la expresión subrayada (*underlined*) a un pronombre y escribe la descripción en el espacio correcto.

> **MODELO:**   Tengo el tenedor en la mano izquierda (*left hand*). →
>   Lo tengo en la mano izquierda.

El estilo A:

1. Tengo el tenedor en la mano izquierda. Después de cortar algo, cambio el tenedor de la mano izquierda a la mano derecha (*right*) para comer.
2. Tengo el cuchillo en la mano derecha. Después de cortar algo, pongo el cuchillo en el plato.

El estilo B:

1. Tengo el tenedor en la mano izquierda. Después de cortar algo, dejo (*I leave*) el tenedor en esa mano para comer.
2. Tengo el cuchillo en la mano derecha. Después de cortar algo, dejo el cuchillo en esa mano.

Estilo ____ es el estilo europeo.

> **El tenedor:** _____
> **El cuchillo:** _____

Estilo ____ es el estilo norteamericano.

> **El tenedor:** _____
> **El cuchillo:** _____

E. ¿A quién ves fuera de la clase?   Haz una lista de los compañeros de tu clase que ves fuera de la clase de vez en cuando. En parejas, explíquense dónde y cúando ven a cada persona en su lista.

> **MODELO:**   *Tú:* Te veo en mi clase de biología los martes y jueves.
>   *Steve:* Lo veo en la residencia todos los días.
>   *Alycia y Karen:* Las veo en el trabajo de vez en cuando.

Chile

El pescado es un producto económico importante de Chile.

F. Cultura: Los productos agrícolas en Chile

PASO 1. Lee el texto sobre Chile.

¿Conoces la comida chilena? Aunque no conozcas[a] todos los platillos tradicionales, sin duda[b] conoces los ingredientes. Chile produce y exporta mucha comida que llega a las mesas de familias en otros países. Por ejemplo, se cultivan muchas frutas y verduras. Chile es el primer exportador de manzanas, uvas, duraznos y ciruelas[c] en el mundo. También produce muchos aguacates, fresas, peras y espárragos.

Por tener una costa tan larga, claro que otra comida que se exporta de Chile es el pescado. Después de Noruega, Chile es el segundo exportador en todo el mundo de salmón y trucha.[d] Un dato interesante es que en los Estados Unidos y Canadá, el pez que se pesca en los océanos entre Patagonia y Antártida, y que antes se conocía como *Patagonian toothfish,* es ahora mejor conocido como *Chilean sea bass,* el nombre que inventó un vendedor de pescado.* Chile produce otros pescados y varios mariscos también, como mejillones, vieiras,[e] ostras y abulón.

Y una mesa de comida chilena no está lista hasta tener una botella (o tal vez, una caja[†]) de vino chileno. Chile es el quinto[f] exportador de vino en todo el mundo. Los vinos que más produce son los Cabernet Sauvignon y los Merlot. El valle de Maipo es una de las regiones más reconocidas por la producción de vino chileno excelente.

[a]Aunque... *Even if you aren't familiar with* [b]*doubt* [c]uvas... *grapes, peaches, and plums* [d]*trout* [e]mejillones... *mussels, scallops* [f]*fifth*

PASO 2. Ahora empareja cada producto chileno con la oración que lo describe con un pronombre de objeto directo.

_____ 1. Chile la exporta al resto del mundo.
_____ 2. Los niños de los Estados Unidos las traen en sus almuerzos.
_____ 3. Chile los exporta junto (*along*) con sus pescados.
_____ 4. Incluso los franceses y los italianos lo beben durante la cena.
_____ 5. Los sirven en los restaurantes vegetarianos en todo el mundo.
_____ 6. Los noruegos (*Norwegians*) casi no lo comen porque tienen un producto nacional similar.

a. la fruta chilena
b. el vino chileno
c. los mariscos chilenos
d. las manzanas chilenas
e. el salmón chileno
f. los espárragos chilenos

PASO 3. En parejas, contesten las preguntas y explíquense sus respuestas.

1. Chile es uno de los pocos países hispanos que exporta grandes cantidades (*quantities*) de vino al resto del mundo (los otros son Argentina y España). ¿Por qué produce tanto (*so much*) vino Chile, y no países como Colombia o Guatemala?
2. En comparación al resto de América Latina, Chile es un país relativamente rico y tiene una economía fuerte. ¿Ves una relación entre eso y la producción de vino en Chile?
3. En tu país, ¿dónde producen vino y dónde no? En general, ¿las zonas donde producen vino son más ricas que otras partes del país?

_____

*Este pez, que tiene el nombre científico de *Dissostichus eleginoides,* se conoce como «bacalao de profundidad» (*deep-water cod*) en Chile y «merluza (*hake*) negra» en Argentina.
†En Chile algunos de los vinos más sabrosos (*best-tasting*) se venden en caja.

¡Leamos!

El huitlacoche

Antes de leer

PASO 1. Indica tus gustos en cuanto (*with regards to*) la comida mexicana.

	ME GUSTA(N)	NO ME GUSTA(N)	NUNCA HE PROBADO (*HAVE TRIED*)...
1. los chiles asados	☐	☐	☐
2. la pechuga (*breast*) de pollo rellena (*stuffed*) de hongos (champiñones)	☐	☐	☐
3. las quesadillas	☐	☐	☐
4. los tamales	☐	☐	☐
5. las tortillas de harina	☐	☐	☐
6. las tortillas de maíz	☐	☐	☐

 PASO 2. Responde en oraciones completas a las siguientes preguntas.

1. ¿Eres atrevido/a (*daring*) cuando pruebas (*you try*) comida? ¿Te gusta probar comidas nuevas?

2. ¿Cuál fue la última (*last*) comida nueva que probaste? ¿Te gustó?

3. ¿Te gustan los hongos?

4. Nombra dos platos que normalmente tienen hongos.

5. ¿Conoces el huitlacoche?

A leer

PASO 1. Lee el artículo sobre el hongo huitlacoche.

El huitlacoche

¡Todas las mazorcas[a] de maíz de esta cosecha[b] están arruinadas[c]! Atacadas por hongos que crecen dentro de la chala,[d] hasta abrirla.[e] Qué desastre, ¿no?

¡No! Porque estos hongos que atacan el maíz son muy nutritivos, deliciosos y, para el agricultor[f] de maíz, no son desastrosos porque los hongos se venden en el mercado a un precio mucho más alto que el maíz.

Estos hongos se llaman huitlacoche o cuitlacoche, un nombre que viene de dos palabras indígenas: *cuitlatl* (*excremento*) y *cochi* (*dormir*).

Según los científicos de la alimentación,[g] estos parásitos del maíz ofrecen una generosa cantidad[h] de proteínas, minerales y propiedades nutritivas.

El «ataque» de estas bolitas hongosas[i] resulta en un proceso metabólico dentro de la mazorca que produce nutrientes nuevos y más robustos. Uno de los minerales derivados de este hongo es la lisina.[j] Prácticamente ausente en el maíz, la lisina abunda en el huitlacoche. La lisine es un aminoácido fundamental para nuestra salud, que el organismo no reproduce por sí mismo.[k] Combate infecciones, fortifica el esqueleto y es popular entre los

---

[a]*cobs* [b]*crops* [c]*ruined* [d]*crecen... grown inside the husk* [e]*hasta... until it opens it* [f]*farmer* [g]*científicos... nutrition scientists* [h]*quantity* [i]*bolitas... mushroom balls* [j]*lysine* [k]*por... on its own*

(*Continues*)

fisicoculturistas y los esteticistas[l] para aumentar los músculos y rejuvenecer la piel.[m]

No tienes que tomar una pastilla[n] para recibir los beneficios del huitlacoche. Pero sí tienes que cenar en restaurantes exclusivos, como James Beard House de Nueva York, donde periódicamente este hongo indígena luce[ñ] en el menú. Saboréalo[o] también en el platillo de pechuga de pollo rellena de huitlacoche en La Cocina Michoacana de Cedar Park, Texas, en las quesadillas de Tú y Yo en Boston o en los tamales de La Casita Mexicana de Los Ángeles.

Steve Sando —dueño de Rancho Gordo en el Valle de Napa—diría: «¡Olvídate del valor nutritivo[p]! El sabor[q] es espectacular». Sando viajó a México para obtener el hongo. Probó el huitlacoche en una feria culinaria con su amiga Ruth Alegría, una chef mexicana. En la feria, comieron quesadillas de maíz rellenas de huitlacoche, cebollas y granos de maíz y otros platos con el hongo. Son platos como este que inspiran su compañía, Rancho Gordo, donde cultiva[r] productos únicos y exclusivos como el huitlacoche y otros cultivos indígenas.

[l]fisicoculturistas... *bodybuilders and aestheticians*   [m]aumentar... *build muscle and rejuvenate skin*   [n]tragar... *swallow a pill*   [ñ]*is featured*   [o]*Taste it*   [p]valor... *nutritional value*   [q]*flavor*   [r]*cultivates*

 PASO 2. Ahora contesta las preguntas sobre la lectura.

1. ¿Qué es el huitlacoche?

2. Según estudios, ¿qué propiedades nutritivas tiene el huitlacoche?

3. ¿Cuál **no** es un beneficio de la lisina?
   a. ayuda a sacar músculos   b. combate infecciones   c. protege los órganos internos

4. ¿Cómo es el sabor del huitlacoche?

5. Describe el negocio de Steve Sando: ¿Qué es? ¿Dónde está? ¿Por qué visitó México?

6. ¿Qué platos hechos con huitlacoche menciona el artículo?

7. En este país se puede comer huitlacoche en…
   a. algunos de los mejores restaurantes.   c. exclusivamente en los restaurantes de baja calidad.
   b. todos los restaurantes Tex-Mex.

Después de leer

En grupos, contesten las preguntas.

1. ¿Qué comidas que te parecen raras, extrañas o asquerosas (*disgusting*)? ¿Por qué?

2. ¿Hay comidas que se comen en este país que pueden ser raras para gente de otros países? Expliquen.

3. ¿Te gustaría (*would you like*) probar el huitlacoche? ¿Por qué sí o por qué no?

En español…

Los nombres de varias comidas que tienen sus orígenes en América vienen del náhuatl, el idioma (*language*) del imperio azteca y actualmente la lengua indígena más grande de México. La influencia del náhuatl se nota en el español y aun en el inglés.

NÁHUATL	ESPAÑOL
ahuacatl	aguacate
chocolatl	chocolate
colanto	cilantro
chilli	chile
xitomatl	(ji)tomate

¡Escuchemos!

La cocina tradicional

 ### Antes de escuchar

En grupos, describan platos típicos de sus países, estados o familias. Cada estudiante debe añadir detalles. Describan por lo menos cuatro platos típicos.

MODELO: E1: La hamburguesa es como un sándwich de carne con pan.
E2: Los acompañamientos incluyen lechuga, tomate, queso y salsa de tomate.
E3: Normalmente lleva papas fritas como acompañamiento.

A escuchar

Mira y escucha las descripciones de platos tradicionales que se comen en varias partes del mundo hispano. Completa las recetas con los ingredientes que corresponden a cada plato.

El ceviche (de Perú y otros países costeros de América)

LISTA DE INGREDIENTES

las cebollas rojas	el limón
el culantro (*cilantro*)	el pescado

PREPARACIÓN

Tenemos el ceviche que es _____ crudo que lo maceramos (*marinate*) con _____ y _____ y _____.

El gallo pinto (de Costa Rica)

LISTA DE INGREDIENTES

el arroz	el chile	la mantequilla
la cebolla	los frijoles	

PREPARACIÓN

Bueno, gallo pinto son especias como _____, _____ picado, luego se le pone _____, y ya le pone _____, _____ y se mezcla. Sí, es el plato típico.

El gazpacho (de España)

LISTA DE INGREDIENTES

el aceite	el pan	el pimiento (*bell pepper*)	el tomate
la cebolla	el pepino	la sal	el vinagre

PREPARACIÓN

¿El gazpacho? Pues es _____, _____, _____ y _____, y _____ mojado (*wet*)... Se pasa por la batidora (*blender*), se le echa (*add*) _____, _____ y _____ y luego se cuela (*strain*) y se bebe líquido como si fuera, pues yo que sé... como un zumo (*jugo*).

El pico de gallo (de Nicaragua)

LISTA DE INGREDIENTES

la cebolla	la pimienta	la sal	el tomate

(*Continues*)

PREPARACIÓN

Pico de gallo es tomate picado con _____ y todo eso mezclado. Es como una salsita, pero de _____ picado en cuadritos más cebolla y _____ y _____.

El pabellón criollo (de Venezuela)

LISTA DE INGREDIENTES

el arroz   los frijoles   el huevo   el plátano

PREPARACIÓN

El pabellón criollo es un plato a base de _____ negros y _____. Luego lleva un _____ frito y _____ frito también.

Después de escuchar

En grupos, hablen de cuál(es) de los platos descritos quieren probar y por qué.

MODELO: Quiero probar el ceviche porque me gustan los mariscos. No sé si quiero probar los plátanos fritos del pabellón criollo.

¡Escribamos!

Una celebración memorable

¿Recuerdas una celebración especial en que la comida estuvo muy rica?

A. Antes de escribir

Piensa en una celebración que a la que asististe y en la que estuvo muy rica la comida que sirvieron. Puede ser una fiesta, una celebración de cumpleaños o «todos los domingos en casa de mis padres». Prepara dos listas de vocabulario: todas las palabras en español relacionadas con el tema y las palabras que necesitas en español pero que no sabes.

MODELO: *el primer cumpleaños de mi prima*

Vocabulario en español:	Vocabulario en inglés:
la ensalada	*candle*
la lechuga	*carrots*
el tomate	*gifts*
el helado	
la torta	

A escribir

Escribe un ensayo de diez frases (mínimo) para describir la celebración. Explica qué celebraron Uds., qué comida sirvieron, quiénes estuvieron y por qué la recuerdas.

Después de escribir

Revisa tu ensayo. Luego, intercambia ensayos con un compañero / una compañera. Lee el ensayo de tu compañero/a y determina si falta información necesaria. Lee de nuevo (*again*) el ensayo con cuidado para revisar los siguientes puntos de gramática.

- el ensayo está escrito en el pasado
- los verbos regulares tienen las terminaciones correctas en el pasado
- los verbos irregulares tienen las conjugaciones correctas en el pretérito
- hay concordancia de sustantivos y adjetivos
- tiene la ortografía (*spelling*) correcta

Después de revisar el ensayo de tu compañero/a, devuélveselo (*return it to him/her*). Mira tu propio (*own*) ensayo para ver los cambios que tu compañero/a recomienda y haz las revisiones necesarias.

¡Hablemos!

La fiesta de la clase

Antes de hablar

¡La clase va a hacer una fiesta! En grupos de tres o cuatro, hagan una lista de los elementos de un menú que van a incluir para la fiesta (bebidas, aperitivos, postre, etcétera).

A hablar

Cada grupo escoge un tema (comida argentina, china, cubana, española, italiana, mexicana...) para su menú y habla de lo que se va a servir para cada elemento de **Antes de hablar.** Decidan quién va a traer cada cosa. Mencionen una por una (*Go one by one*) las cosas de su lista y pidan voluntarios. **¡Atención!** Tengan cuidado (*Be careful*) con los pronombres de objeto directo.

> **MODELO:** E1: Para nuestra fiesta española, necesitamos una tortilla española.
> E2: Yo la traigo.
> E1: También necesitamos olivas.
> E3: Yo las traigo.

Después de hablar

Cada grupo presenta su menú e invita a la clase a asistir. Los otros grupos deben o aceptar o rechazar la invitación usando el vocabulario de este capítulo.

Conéctate al cine

Película: *Como agua para chocolate*
(comedia/drama, México, 1992)
Director: Alfonso Arau

Sinopsis:

Tita y sus hermanas, Gertrudis y Rosaura, viven con su madre en un rancho en México durante los años de la Revolución (1910 a 1920). El joven Pedro declara su amor por Tita, pero la madre de Tita prohíbe el matrimonio (*marriage*) porque Tita, la menor de las tres hermanas, tiene que cuidar a (*care for*) su madre el resto de su vida. Entonces Pedro se casa con (*marries*) Rosaura porque quiere vivir cerca de (*close to*) Tita. A Tita le gusta cocinar y ella prepara unos platillos tan sabrosos como (*both delicious and*) místicos para toda la familia.

Escena (Netflix, 00:15:46–00:21:38):

Tita está triste porque Pedro y Rosaura se casan y ella tiene que preparar la comida para la boda (*wedding*). Ella ayuda a Nacha, la cocinera de la familia, en la cocina y la madre de Tita las regaña (*scolds*). Luego, en la boda, pasa algo misterioso cuando los invitados (*guests*) comen lo que Tita y Nacha prepararon.

Antes de ver

Tita y Nacha preparan la comida para la boda de Rosaura y Pedro. ¿Qué tipo de comida se sirve (*is served*) en las bodas de tu familia o de tus amigos? ¿Qué beben las personas en una boda? ¿Qué tipo de postre comen?

_____

_____

A ver

Lee la lista de **Expresiones útiles** y mira el video.

Después de ver

PASO 1. Contesta las preguntas usando el pretérito.

1. ¿Qué ingrediente usaron Tita y Nacha para preparar el postre?
   _____

2. ¿Qué hizo Tita en la cocina porque estaba muy triste?
   _____

3. ¿Qué comieron los invitados en la boda? _____

4. ¿Qué bebieron los invitados en la boda? _____

5. ¿Qué hicieron los invitados después de comer? _____ y
   _____

PASO 2. Con un compañero / una compañera, responde a las siguientes preguntas.

1. Explica en tus propias palabras qué pasó en la boda. ¿Por qué pasó?

2. Nacha le dice a Tita: «Solo las ollas saben los hervores de su caldo… ». ¿Qué puede significar este refrán (*saying*)?

Expresiones útiles

solo nos faltan	we only need . . . more
apúrense	hurry up
suelta tus lágrimas	let it all out
adivino	I (can) guess
las ollas	pots
los hervores	boiling (*n.*); ardor (*fig.*)
deja de chillar	stop crying
la masa	batter
logré	I managed to
anhelaba	I was longing for
no me engañes	don't try to fool me
el llanto	weeping
añorando	yearning for
se escapó del hechizo	escaped the spell
la vomitona colectiva	group vomiting

■ For copyright reasons, the feature-film clips referenced in **Conéctate al cine** have not been provided by the publisher. Each of these films is readily available through retailers or online rental sites such as Amazon, iTunes, or Netflix.

VOCABULARIO

Comunicación

¿Quieres/Quiere + *noun/inf.*?	Do you (*inform./form.*) want . . . ?
¿Tienes/Tiene ganas de + *noun/inf.*?	Do you (*inform./form.*) feel like . . . ?
¿Qué te/le parece + *noun/inf.*?	How about (*inform./form.*) . . . ?
¿Te/Le apetece + *noun/inf.*?	How about (*inform./form.*) . . . ?
Sí, gracias.	Yes, please.
Si no es molestia.	If it's not a bother.
No, gracias.	No, thank you.
Debo + *inf.*	I have to (*do something*).
¡Cómo no! / ¡Claro que sí! / ¡Por supuesto!	Of course!
¡Con mucho gusto!	With pleasure!

La comida — Food

el aceite	oil
el acompañamiento	side dish (*food*)
el agua	water
el aperitivo	appetizer
el arroz	rice
el atún	tuna
el azúcar	sugar
la bebida	drink
los calamares	squid
el caldo	broth, clear soup
los camarones	shrimp
la carne	(red) meat
la cebolla	onion
la cerveza	beer
los champiñones/hongos	mushrooms
los chiles	chili pepper
el chorizo	sausage
los comestibles…	groceries, food
empaquetados	packaged goods
enlatados	canned goods
la ensalada	salad
el flan	custard
la fresa	strawberry
los frijoles	beans
el guisado	stew
la harina	flour
el helado	ice cream

el huevo	egg
el jamón	ham
el jugo	juice
la leche	milk
la lechuga	lettuce
el limón	lime; lemon
el maíz	corn
la mantequilla	butter
la manzana	apple
los mariscos	seafood
la merienda	snack
la naranja	orange
el pan	bread
la papa	potato
el pastel	cake
el pepino	cucumber
el perejil	parsley
el pescado	fish
la pimienta	black pepper
la piña	pineapple
el plátano	banana
el pollo	chicken
el postre	dessert
los productos lácteos	dairy products
el puerco	pork
el queso	cheese
el refresco	soda
la sal	salt
la salsa	sauce
la sopa	soup
la torta	cake
la verdura	vegetable
el vino blanco/tinto	white/red wine

Cognados: el brócoli, el condimento, el flan, la fruta, el mango, la pasta, el tomate, el vinagre, el yogur

El cubierto — Place setting

el bol	bowl
el/la camarero/a	waiter, server
la carta	menu
la cuchara	spoon
el cuchillo	knife
el plato	plate
la servilleta	napkin
la taza	coffee cup
el tenedor	fork
el vaso	(drinking) glass

Las tiendas de comida

Food stores

el hipermercado	large supermarket
el mercado	(outdoor) market
la panadería	bakery
la pescadería	fish market
el supermercado (el súper)	supermarket
la verdulería	vegetable market

Los verbos

abrir	to open
aprender	to learn
cerrar (ie)	to close
merendar (ie)	to have a snack
nacer (zc)	to be born
ver	to see

Otros términos culinarios

a la plancha	grilled
al ajillo	sauteed with garlic
asado/a	roasted
dulce	sweet
frito/a	fried
picante	spicy
saludable	healthy

Los pronombres de objeto directo

me, te, lo/la, nos, os, los/las

Los recuerdos y la nostalgia

Unos amigos celebran el Año Nuevo en Medellín, Colombia.

Objetivos

In this chapter you will learn to:

- say you had a good time
- wish someone well and congratulate them
- talk about holidays and celebrations in the Spanish-speaking world
- talk about ongoing events in the past
- express to whom or for whom an action is performed

Lo pasé bien

Expressing *to have a good time*

A. A ver: ¿Cómo lo pasan bien los estudiantes?   Mira y escucha, luego completa las frases.

1. Según (*According to*) Adrián, los estudiantes van a _____.

2. Ellos practican _____, usan _____ y salen _____.

3. Según José Antonio y David, van de _____ y juegan mucho _____.

4. En España, los jóvenes se divierten en _____ y en _____.

5. A Aline le gusta _____.

6. A William le gusta _____, _____, _____ y _____.

7. A Keylin le gusta _____.

8. A Esteban le gusta _____, _____, _____ e _____.

9. A Anlluly le gusta _____.

10. A Ignacio le gusta _____, _____ y _____.

To say you had a good time in Spanish, use **pasarlo/la bien** (*to have a good time*) or **divertirse** (*to have fun*).

—**Lo pasé muy bien de vacaciones. ¿Y tú?** *"I had a good time on vacation. And you?"*
—**Sí, me divertí mucho en las montañas.** *"Yes, I had a lot of fun in the mountains.*
 ¿Adónde fuiste tú? *Where did you go?"*
—**A la playa.** *"To the beach."*

¡Atención! There is no literal translation of the English *to have a good time*. You must use an expression like one of those presented here.

B. ¿Adónde van para divertirse? Lee la cita (*quote*) de cada persona y luego selecciona la frase que mejor la describe.

1. _____ Nuria (de Madrid, España), dice: «El fin de semana pasado, mis amigos y yo nos divertimos tomando el sol y nadando en el mar».
 a. Fueron a las montañas.
 b. Fueron a la playa.
 c. Fueron al campo.
 d. Fueron al mercado.

2. _____ Eduardo (de Panamá) dice: «Me gustan las películas de acción».
 a. Eduardo lo pasa bien en el cine.
 b. Eduardo lo pasa bien en la playa.
 c. Eduardo lo pasa bien en los mercados.
 d. Eduardo lo pasa bien en las fiestas.

3. _____ Sara (de Colombia) dice: «El año pasado fui a Buenos Aires, Río de Janeiro, Tokio, Londres y Barcelona. Siempre me divierto».
 a. Sara lo pasa bien en la cocina.
 b. Sara lo pasa bien en la clase de música.
 c. Sara lo pasa bien en la oficina.
 d. Sara lo pasa bien en los viajes.

4. _____ María (de México) dice: «Los jóvenes la pasan bien en los antros y discos».
 a. Se divierten en los clubes.
 b. Se divierten en la playa.
 c. Se divierten en la biblioteca.
 d. Se divierten en las pistas de fútbol.

5. _____ Rodrigo (de Buenos Aires) dice: «Los fines de semana me divierto en las fiestas con mis amigos de la universidad».
 a. Rodrigo lo pasa bien en la biblioteca.
 b. Rodrigo lo pasa bien en los cafés.
 c. Rodrigo lo pasa bien en las casas de sus amigos.
 d. Rodrigo lo pasa bien en los salones de clase en la universidad.

En español...

The word **antro** literally means *cave* or *cavern,* but in Mexico it's a very common term for *club*—a place to socialize, dance, and drink. **Discoteca** is the general word that is understood everywhere, but other words may be used locally. Part of the fun of meeting people from around the Spanish-speaking world is learning the local slang terms that they use.

El fin de semana pasado, me divertí con mis amigos en la costa de Alicante.

C. ¿Te divertiste?

PASO 1. Para cada actividad que hiciste alguna vez, concluye con una de las siguientes expresiones, según tu experiencia.

(no) me divertí   **(no) lo pasé bien**

MODELO: Visité a mi familia y *lo pasé bien.*

1. Bailé en un club y _____.
2. Cené en un nuevo restaurante y _____.
3. Estudié en la biblioteca y _____.
4. Fui a la playa y _____.
5. Fui de compras y _____.
6. Hice la tarea y _____.
7. Limpié mi cuarto y _____.
8. Practiqué un deporte y _____.
9. Tomé un café en el centro estudiantil y _____.
10. Visité a mis abuelos y _____.

PASO 2. Habla con tres personas para saber qué hicieron o adónde fueron el fin de semana pasado y si lo pasaron bien.

MODELOS: E1: ¿Qué hiciste el fin de semana pasado?
E2: Visité a mi familia, que vive en Chicago.
E1: ¿Lo pasaste bien?
E1: Sí, lo pasé muy bien. (No, lo pasé mal.)

E1: ¿Qué hiciste el sábado por el día?
E2: Fui a una fiesta para celebrar el cumpleaños de mi sobrina.
E1: ¿Te divertiste?
E2: Sí, me divertí mucho. (No, no me divertí nada.)

Mi sobrina celebró su
cumpleaños con una piñata.

Felicitaciones/Felicidades/ Enhorabuena

Congratulating someone

To say *Congratulations* in Spanish, use **Felicitaciones, Felicidades,** or **Enhorabuena.**

—**Voy a graduarme de la universidad en mayo.**	"I'm going to graduate from the university in May."
—**¡Felicitaciones!**	"Congratulations!"

Sometimes this is expressed with the verb **felicitar** and a direct object pronoun.

—**En agosto empiezo a trabajar de psicólogo escolar.**	"In August, I will start working as a school psychologist."
—**Te felicito. / Te felicitamos.**	"I/We congratulate you."

Note: To express your condolences for something say **Lo siento** (*I'm sorry*).

A. ¿Bueno o malo?   Para cada cita, indica si es más apropiado decir «**Felicitaciones**» o «**Lo siento**».

	FELICITACIONES.	LO SIENTO.
1. Saqué mala nota en mi examen ayer.	☐	☐
2. Mi hermana tuvo un bebé. ¡Soy tío!	☐	☐
3. Estoy comprometida (*engaged*).	☐	☐
4. Tengo malas noticias (*bad news*) de mis padres.	☐	☐
5. Conseguí un trabajo.	☐	☐
6. Recibí mi título (*degree*) de la universidad.	☐	☐
7. ¡Gané la lotería!	☐	☐
8. No lo pasé bien en la fiesta anoche.	☐	☐

B. ¡Gracias!

PASO 1.   Escoge una de las siguientes situaciones y díselo (*tell it*) a tu compañero/a. Tu compañero/a debe responder de manera lógica y ofrecer una solución si es apropiado. Luego, cambien de papeles (*roles*).

MODELO: E1: Tengo examen mañana y perdí mi libro.
E2: Lo siento mucho. ¿Quieres usar mi libro?
E1: ¡Gracias! Te lo agradezco.

1. Mi equipo de fútbol ganó el campeonato.
2. Estamos muy tristes; nuestro perro se murió (*died*).
3. Me voy a graduar de la universidad en mayo.
4. Me voy a casar (*get married*) este verano.
5. No me aceptaron en el máster (los estudios de posgrado).

PASO 2.   Siguiendo el modelo del **Paso 1**, dile a tu compañero/a tres cosas (muy buenas o muy malas) que hiciste la semana pasada o que vas a hacer pronto. Tu compañero/a tiene que responder de una manera apropiada.

¿Cómo se celebra?

Celebrations in the Spanish-speaking world

A. ¡Celebremos!

PASO 1. Empareja cada descripción en la próxima página con una de las siguientes imágenes.

En español...

The term **quinceañera** has made its way from Spanish into common usage in English, where it refers to a party for a girl turning 15 years old. However, in Spanish, **quinceañera** originally refers to the girl herself. The party is most often referred to as **la fiesta de quinceañera** or **la fiesta de quince años.**

a. **el Día de los Reyes Magos** (*Wise Men*)

b. **el Carnaval**

c. **la fiesta de quinceañera**

d. **la Semana Santa**

e. **el Día de la Independencia**

f. **el Día de los Muertos**

g. **el Jánuca**

h. **la Nochebuena y la Navidad**

i. **la Nochevieja y el Año Nuevo**

1. _____ Son dos días festivos en invierno que celebran el **nacimiento** (*birth*) del niño Jesús. Muchas familias **cristianas** tienen tradiciones especiales para **celebrar,** pero la mayoría de ellas cenan juntas e intercambian **regalos.**

2. _____ El 1 y 2 de noviembre, los mexicanos y algunos centroamericanos tienen la **costumbre** de honrar a sus parientes muertos (*dead*). Hacen altares con objetos personales de los muertos y calaveras (*skulls*) de azúcar.

3. _____ Es una fiesta **judía** que dura (*lasts*) ocho noches. Cada noche se enciende (*light*) otra vela (*candle*) de la menorá. Se celebra mucho en Argentina donde vive la población de judíos más grande del mundo hispano.

4. _____ Cuando una niña **cumple** 15 años, muchas familias hispanas dan una gran fiesta para marcar la transición de niña a mujer. La niña lleva un vestido elegante, hay mucha comida y una torta especial. Ella recibe muchos **regalos, flores** (*flowers*) y **tarjetas** (*cards*) con dinero.

5. _____ Es una celebración del establecimiento de una nación independiente. Normalmente hay **desfiles,** es decir, procesiones en que las personas caminan, llevan banderas y tocan música. En muchos países se celebra con **fuegos artificiales** por la noche.

6. _____ Esta celebración conmemora (*commemorates*) la visita de los tres reyes (*kings*) al niño Jesús. Muchos hispanos dan **regalos** en este día porque los reyes le llevaron regalos de oro (*gold*), incienso y mirra (*myrrh*) al bebé. Se celebra el 6 de enero con desfiles y reconstrucciones (*reenactments*) de la visita.

7. _____ Es una celebración del fin de un año y la esperanza de un nuevo comienzo (*beginning*). La gente come platos especiales, sale con amigos y toma **champán** cuando el reloj marca la medianoche.

8. _____ Esta es la semana más importante en la tradición cristiana. Siempre cae (*falls*) en primavera. Empieza con el Domingo de Ramos (*Palm*) que recuerda la entrada de Jesús en Jerusalén y termina en el Domingo de **Pascua Florida** que celebra su resurrección.

9. _____ Son tres días de fiesta antes de la Cuaresma (*Lent*) cristiana. La gente usa muchos **disfraces,** hay desfiles, y se come y bebe mucho antes de los cuarenta días de la Cuaresma.

PASO 2. Empareja la imagen con la mejor descripción.

Vocabulario

La mayoría de los hispanos se identifica como **católica / cristiana.** Sin embargo, hay gente de varias religiones en el mundo hispano. Por ejemplo, hay grandes comunidades **judías** en Argentina y México, y hay comunidades **musulmanes** en España, Argentina, México y Venezuela. Se encuentran **budistas** en México, Costa Rica y especialmente en Perú, gracias a las grandes inmigraciones de japoneses y chinos al país en los siglos XIX y XX.

a. acción de ofrecer buenos deseos antes de beber
b. algo que una persona le da a otra persona
c. una celebración, puede ser por cualquier (*any*) razón
d. una celebración religiosa y fiesta para un bebé
e. una celebración de un viaje o una mudanza (*move*)
f. una celebración al recibir un título académico
g. una celebración o aniversario de un nacimiento
h. la celebración del casamiento (*marriage*) de una pareja

1. _____ el brindis

2. _____ el cumpleaños

3. _____ la despedida

4. _____ la fiesta

CONÉCTATE AL MUNDO HISPANO

En algunas partes del mundo hispano, un término para un fin de semana largo es **un puente** (*bridge*). Si el día festivo que se celebra es un jueves, hacen «un puente» de viernes para crear un fin de semana de cuatro días. Es parecido a la tradición en los Estados Unidos en que el viernes después del **Día de Acción de Gracias** también es día festivo.

5. _____ el regalo

6. _____ el bautizo

7. _____ la boda

8. _____ la graduación

B. Asociaciones

PASO 1.   Indica todas las asociaciones que evoca con cada celebración.

	LAS BEBIDAS	UNA CENA	UNA CEREMONIA	UNA FIESTA	UN REGALO	UNA TARJETA
1. el Año Nuevo	☐	☐	☐	☐	☐	☐
2. la boda	☐	☐	☐	☐	☐	☐
3. el Carnaval	☐	☐	☐	☐	☐	☐
4. el cumpleaños	☐	☐	☐	☐	☐	☐
5. la graduación	☐	☐	☐	☐	☐	☐
6. el Jánuca	☐	☐	☐	☐	☐	☐
7. la Navidad	☐	☐	☐	☐	☐	☐
8. la Nochebuena	☐	☐	☐	☐	☐	☐
9. la Nochevieja	☐	☐	☐	☐	☐	☐

PASO 2.   Trabajen en grupos de dos o tres. Para cada una de las celebraciones del **Paso 1,** digan en qué mes Uds. normalmente la celebran. Si es algo que celebran sus familias, digan qué hacen Uds. para conmemorarlo.

MODELO: El Año Nuevo se celebra en enero. Siempre celebro el Año Nuevo con mi familia de una manera muy tranquila, porque la noche anterior, la Nochevieja, siempre estoy con mis amigos en una gran fiesta hasta muy tarde. Nos despertamos tarde, miramos El Desfile de las Rosas en la televisión y pedimos comida a domicilio (*we order food to be delivered*). El Año Nuevo pasado estuve en pijama todo el día.

C. Vocabulario: ¿Qué le dices?   En parejas, túrnense para dar la expresión apropiada para cada celebración o evento.

¡Buen viaje! (*Bon voyage!*)	**¡Enhorabuena!**	**¡Feliz cumpleaños!**
¡Buena suerte! (*Good luck!*)	**¡Feliz Año Nuevo!**	**¡Feliz Navidad!**

1. «Hoy cumplo 20 años.»
2. «Salgo para Hawai mañana.»
3. «Es el 25 de diciembre.»
4. «Hoy bautizan a mi ahijado (*godson*).»
5. «Hoy tengo un examen.»
6. «Es el primero de enero.»

D. ¿Para cuándo?   Consulta el calendario y empareja cada elemento de la lista de quehaceres (*chores*) con la fecha más adecuada.

1. ＿＿ Celebrar la medianoche.
2. ＿＿ Celebrar el nacimiento del niño Jesús.
3. ＿＿ Llegar a la iglesia con media hora de anticipación (*early*).
4. ＿＿ Preparar lo que voy a decir sobre los novios para el brindis.
5. ＿＿ Salir a un restaurante elegante con mi esposo.
6. ＿＿ Encender las velas (*candles*) con los vecinos.
7. ＿＿ Enviar (*Mail*) la tarjeta de cumpleaños.
8. ＿＿ Invitar a los compañeros de trabajo a la fiesta para Jaime.

a. el 3 de diciembre
b. el 7 de diciembre
c. el 9 de diciembre
d. el 12 de diciembre
e. el 13 de diciembre
f. el 15 de diciembre
g. el 25 de diciembre
h. el 31 de diciembre

E. Festividades típicas Antes de ver los videos, decide si cada afirmación describe algo típico o no.

	ES TÍPICO.	NO ES TÍPICO.
1. Se hace una fiesta con todos los amigos para celebrar el cumpleaños.	☐	☐
2. Se celebran los bautizos con fuegos artificiales.	☐	☐
3. Hay un DJ (*pronounced "DEE yay"*) en la Nochebuena en la iglesia.	☐	☐
4. Se celebra la boda en una iglesia.	☐	☐
5. En la Nochebuena y la Navidad hay mucha comida con toda la familia.	☐	☐
6. En la Nochevieja se hace un brindis con champán.	☐	☐
7. La fiesta de quinceañera celebra el paso de la niñez a la adolescencia.	☐	☐

F. A ver: Las celebraciones típicas

PASO 1. Mira y escucha las descripciones de varias celebraciones y eventos. ¿De qué celebración o celebraciones habla cada uno?

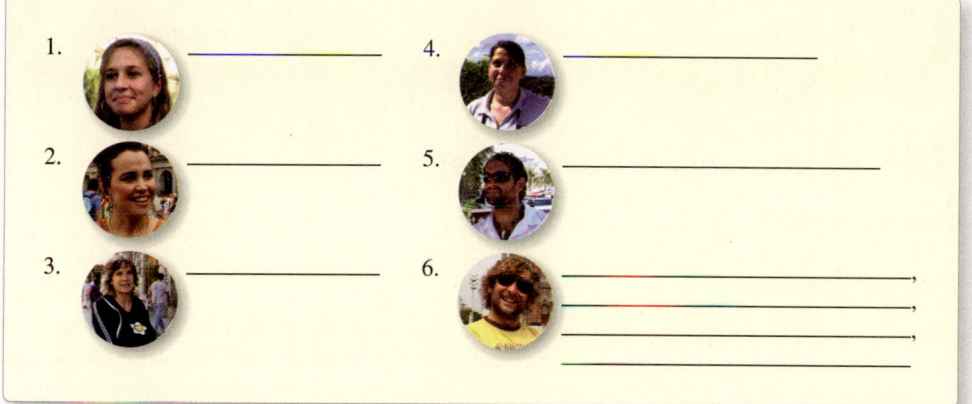

1. _____ 4. _____
2. _____ 5. _____
3. _____ 6. _____,
   _____,
   _____,
   _____

PASO 2. Mira y escucha otra vez, luego contesta las preguntas.

1. ¿Qué comida preparan en la casa de Caitlin?
2. ¿A qué hora termina la celebración que describe Isabel?
3. Según Charo, ¿quiénes eligen (*choose*) la madrina (*godmother*)?
4. Según Anlluly, ¿cómo son las fiestas de quince años?
5. ¿Cuál es el Día de la Independencia argentina?
6. ¿En qué tipo de evento *no* trabaja Rodrigo?

G. Nuestras tradiciones ¿Qué tradiciones tiene tu familia? Escoge una de las siguientes celebraciones (u otra celebración especial) y describe la tradición familiar a tu compañero/a: el Día de Acción de Gracias, el Día de la Independencia, el Día del Amor y la Amistad, la Pascua Florida, la Víspera del Día de Todos los Santos (*Halloween*).

Una procesión durante Las Posadas

El Día de los Reyes Magos representa la visita de los tres reyes al niño Jesús doce días después de su nacimiento. El 6 de enero, «los reyes» les reparten (*give out*) regalos a los niños que se portan (*behave*) bien (y los que no, reciben carbón [*coal*]). Tradicionalmente, en los países hispanos se dan regalos navideños (*Christmas*) en esta fecha, pero cada vez se hace más común el intercambio de regalos para la Nochevieja y la Navidad.

En México se celebran **Las Posadas** (*The Inns*) del 16 al 24 de diciembre. Es una actuación de la búsqueda (*search*) de alojamiento (*lodging*) que hicieron José y la Virgen María antes del nacimiento del niño Jesús. Cada noche, una procesión va pidiendo posada (*lodging at the inn*) y en la tercera casa se aceptan todos los participantes para una fiesta.

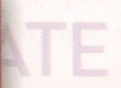

Reciclaje

Present indicative and preterite

¿Ayer fue un día típico para ti? Usa los verbos indicados para completar las oraciones sobre lo que haces **regularmente** (en tiempo presente) y lo que hiciste **ayer** (en tiempo pretérito) y agrega (*add*) la información que falta.

	regularmente	**ayer**
hablar	_____ estos idiomas (*languages*): _____.	_____ estos idiomas: _____.
comer	_____ _____ porciones de fruta.	_____ _____ porciones de fruta.
leer	Sí / No _____ las noticias (*news*) en línea.	Sí / No _____ las noticias en línea.
dormir	_____ _____ horas.	_____ _____ horas.
ir	Sí / No _____ a clases.	Sí / No _____ a clases.

■ Answers to this activity are in Appendix 2 at the back of your book.

7.1 ¿Cómo vivían los mayas?

The imperfect

Para empezar...

En muchos países latinoamericanos, tienen un gran orgullo (*pride*) y cierta nostalgia por las civilizaciones prehispánicas que existían (*existed*) antes de la llegada (*arrival*) de los españoles. Lee las siguientes oraciones y decide si son ciertas o falsas. Si no sabes alguna respuesta, adivina (*guess*). **¡Atención!** Solo tres oraciones son falsas.

Los mayas en los tiempos prehispánicos...

		CIERTO	FALSO
1.	**vivían** en el sur de México y en Centroamérica.	☐	☐
2.	**comían** maíz.	☐	☐
3.	**escribían** libros.	☐	☐
4.	**usaban** caballos y **comían** arroz.	☐	☐
5.	**sabían** mucho de astronomía.	☐	☐
6.	**tenían** una arquitectura espectacular.	☐	☐
7.	**vivían** en el Perú.	☐	☐
8.	**hablaban** español.	☐	☐

El Templo de la Serpiente en el Parque Nacional Tikal, Petén, Guatemala

■ Answers to these activities are in Appendix 2 at the back of your book.

Actividades analíticas

1 The verbs you saw in **Para empezar** are in the *imperfect* tense (**el imperfecto**). The imperfect is used when you want to portray an event as being in the past, but it is not important exactly when the event started or if it ended.

De niño, Carlos **vivía** en Honduras.	*As a child, Carlos lived in Honduras.*
Los mayas **comían** mucho maíz.	*The Mayas ate a lot of corn.*
Cuando **estaba** en Madrid, Julieta **trabajaba** con su tía.	*When she was in Madrid, Julieta worked with her aunt.*

In all of these examples, the action occurs over an extended period of time, but it is not specified when it started or stopped.

2 Use the verb forms in **Para empezar** and the patterns you see here to complete these conjugations in the imperfect.

	hablar	comer	vivir
yo	hablaba	comía	vivía
tú	hablabas	comías	
él/ella, Ud.	hablaba	comía	vivía
nosotros/as	hablábamos		vivíamos
vosotros/as	hablabais	comíais	vivíais
ellos/ellas, Uds.			

3 Complete this chart of endings for **-ar** and **-er/-ir** verbs in the imperfect.

	-ar	-er/-ir	
yo	_-aba_: hablaba	_____: comía	vivía
tú	_____: hablabas	_____: comías	vivías
él/ella, Ud.	_____: hablaba	_-ía_: comía	vivía
nosotros/as	_____: hablábamos	_-íamos_: comíamos	vivíamos
vosotros/as	_-abais_: hablabais	_____: comíais	vivíais
ellos/ellas, Uds.	_____: hablaban	_____: comían	vivían

4 The verbs **ir, ser,** and **ver** are the only irregular verbs in the imperfect. There are no verbs with stem changes or spelling changes.

	ir	ser	ver
yo	iba	era	veía
tú	ibas	eras	veías
él/ella, Ud.	iba	era	veía
nosotros/as	íbamos	éramos	veíamos
vosotros/as	ibais	erais	veíais
ellos/ellas, Uds.	iban	eran	veían

The stems of these verbs are irregular in the imperfect, but the endings show similarities with those of regular verbs.

Íbamos a muchas fiestas cuando yo **era** niño. — *We went to a lot of parties when I was a child.*

¿**Veías** ese programa de televisión todos los días? — *Did you watch that TV show every day?*

5 The verb form **hay** becomes **había** in the imperfect.

Había un edificio maya en este lugar. — *There was a Mayan building in this place.*

Había cuatro niños en la fiesta. — *There were four children at the party.*

Un estatua en las ruinas de Uxmal, antigua ciudad maya en México

Actividades prácticas

A. Las tradiciones de mi familia

Las siguientes descripciones están basadas en la imagen de la vida tradicional norteamericana que se ve en el cine y en la televisión. Indica las que son ciertas en el caso de tu familia.

1. ☐ Íbamos a la playa en verano.
2. ☐ Cenábamos con mis abuelos el Día de Acción de Gracias.
3. ☐ Íbamos a la iglesia los domingos.
4. ☐ Celebrábamos mi cumpleaños cada año.
5. ☐ Comprábamos un árbol de Navidad cada año.
6. ☐ Veíamos los fuegos artificiales el Día de la Independencia.
7. ☐ Hacíamos una fiesta de Nochevieja en casa.
8. ☐ Jugábamos béisbol en la calle.
9. ☐ Mis amigos y yo íbamos a la escuela en un autobús amarillo.
10. ☐ Comíamos de vez en cuando en casa de mi abuela.

B. España y América antes de 1492

Las siguientes oraciones describen la vida en España y en América en los siglos (*centuries*) antes de la llegada de los españoles a América.

PASO 1. Primero, escoge el verbo apropiado para cada oración y escríbelo en la forma **ellos** del imperfecto (por ejemplo, **trabajar → trabajaban**).

comer	ir	tener (x2)
hablar (x2)	ser	vivir

Antes de 1492...   **¿E, A o E/A?**

1. _____ tomates.   _____
2. _____ caballos.   _____
3. el calendario y los días festivos _____ muy importantes.   _____
4. _____ español, árabe y otros idiomas (*languages*).   _____
5. en algunas ciudades, _____ a las pirámides (*pyramids*) para hacer
   ritos religiosos.   _____
6. _____ ciudades muy grandes.   _____
7. en algunas partes, los cristianos, los judíos y los musulmanes
   _____ en armonía (*harmony*).   _____
8. _____ náhuatl, quechua y otros idiomas.   _____

PASO 2. Ahora escribe **E** si la oración describe la vida en España antes del año 1492, **A** si describe la vida en América, o **E/A** si describe los dos lugares.

La Piedra (*stone*) del Sol muestra (*shows*) los varios soles de la cosmología mexica de México.

C. El Día de los Muertos
Una de las tradiciones mexicanas más conocidas es el Día de los Muertos. Tradicionalmente, ese día la gente va a las tumbas (*graves*) de sus familiares difuntos (*deceased*), hacen altares y comen varios tipos de pan y dulces (*sweets*) especiales.

PASO 1. Los siguientes apuntes vienen de una entrevista hecha con una mujer mexicana en 1984. Ella dijo cinco de las siguientes oraciones sobre las tradiciones en su familia para el Día de los Muertos. De las ocho oraciones en total, ¿cuáles dijo y cuáles no?

	LO DIJO.	NO LO DIJO.
1. «Vamos al cementerio.»	☐	☐
2. «Limpiamos las tumbas (*graves*) y las decoramos con flores.»	☐	☐
3. «Hacemos un altar con una foto del difunto (*deceased*) y algunos de sus objetos favoritos.»	☐	☐
4. «Hacemos una fiesta y bailamos mucho.»	☐	☐
5. «Comemos pan de muerto —un pan dulce, a veces con figuras en forma de hueso (*bone*).»	☐	☐
6. «Vamos a una ceremonia especial en Buenos Aires.»	☐	☐
7. «Nos ponemos disfraces y vamos de casa en casa para pedir dulces.»	☐	☐
8. «Hacemos calaveras (*skulls*) de dulce.»	☐	☐

Una ofrenda para el Día de los Muertos

PASO 2. Ahora usa las oraciones que dijo para hacer una descripción de lo que hacía esta familia el Día de los Muertos en 1984. **¡Atención!** Usa la forma **ellos** del imperfecto.

> **MODELO:** «Vamos al cementerio.» → *Iban* al cementerio.

D. ¿Qué hacías antes?
Por razones (*reasons*) sociales, emocionales o físicas, hay muchas cosas que hacíamos de niños que ya no hacemos ahora. Pregúntales a tres de tus compañeros qué hacían antes que ya no hacen. Usa una de las siguientes ideas o pensar en otra.

correr muy rápido	jugar todo el día
dormir mucho	recibir muchos regalos
ir a muchas fiestas de cumpleaños	ver televisión todo el día

> **MODELO:** E1: ¿Qué hacías antes que no haces ahora?
> E2: Nadaba mucho, pero ya no (*no longer*) nado.

E. Tus padres cuando tenían tu edad

PASO 1. Entrevista a tu compañero/a para saber qué hace y qué hacían sus padres cuando tenían tu edad. Apunta las respuestas.

- ¿Dónde vives? ¿Dónde vivían tus padres cuando tenían tu edad (*age*)?
- ¿Qué haces? ¿Trabajas? ¿Estudias? ¿Ya tienes hijos? Y tus padres, ¿qué hacían cuando tenían tu edad? ¿Trabajaban?…

PASO 2. Crea una oración con una semejanza (*similarity*) entre tu compañero/a y sus padres, y otra oración con una diferencia.

> **MODELO:** Alex estudia. Cuando tenían su edad, sus padres también estudiaban.
> Alex tiene una hija. Cuando tenían su edad, sus padres no tenían hijos.

Uruguay

F. Cultura: El Carnaval en Uruguay

PASO 1.   Lee el texto sobre Uruguay.

En general, los uruguayos tienen vidas largas. ¿A qué se debe?[a] Quizás[b] a la belleza de su país con su larga costa y bellas playas, o quizás a su espíritu positivo y fiestero que se ve, por ejemplo, cuando celebran el Carnaval. El Carnaval uruguayo, como en el resto del mundo, se caracteriza por música, baile, disfraces y máscaras, desfiles y mucha diversión, pero en contraste con las costumbres del resto del mundo, el Carnaval en Uruguay es mucho más largo.

El Carnaval es una tradición de fiestas públicas que se observa en varios países europeos, caribeños[c] y latinoamericanos. Los orígenes del Carnaval vienen de Europa, donde las fiestas paganas del equinoccio de primavera se combinaron con tradiciones católicas. El Carnaval se celebra las semanas antes de la Cuaresma,[d] un periodo de solemnidad y ascetismo. Un elemento muy importante del Carnaval uruguayo es «la murga». Las murgas son canciones interpretadas por un coro[e] de quince a veinte personas. Tienen influencia del teatro español y así usan las canciones para contar historias.[f]

Otra cosa notable del Carnaval uruguayo es que una gran parte de su música viene de tradiciones afro-uruguayas. Estas tradiciones musicales se conocen como «candombe» y se practicaban entre[g] las comunidades de esclavos[h] en la época de la colonia. Durante el Carnaval, las comparsas[i] de candombe consisten en[j] muchos bailadores disfrazados y por lo menos cincuenta percusionistas que tocan ritmos africanos.

Un tamboril es el tipo de tambor (*drum*) usado para la música candombe.

[a]¿A... *To what is this owed?*   [b]*Perhaps*   [c]*Caribbean*   [d]*Lent*   [e]*choir, chorus*   [f]contar... *tell stories*   [g]*among*   [h]*slaves*   [i]*musical groups*   [j]consisten... *are made up of*

PASO 2.   Indica si cada oración es lógica (L) o ilógica (I) según la información que leíste.

_____ 1. Los esclavos afro-uruguayos cantaban murgas.

_____ 2. Los primeros inmigrantes españoles a Uruguay tocaban música candombe.

_____ 3. Para los primeros africanos que llegaron a Uruguay, era importante conservar sus tradiciones musicales.

_____ 4. Las fiestas paganas de Europa marcaban el fin (*end*) del invierno.

_____ 5. Los católicos creían que era importante tener un periodo festivo en las semanas antes de la Cuaresma.

PASO 3.   En parejas, contesten las preguntas y explíquense sus respuestas.

1. La cultura afro-uruguaya existe porque en la época de la colonia llegaban muchos esclavos africanos, principalmente por la capital, Montevideo. ¿Qué relación hay entre esto y la ubicación geográfica de Uruguay, y de Montevideo en particular?

2. Hoy en día, hay muchos descendientes de esclavos africanos en varios países de Latinoamérica, pero sobre todo en las islas del Caribe, en algunas zonas de Centroamérica, y en Colombia y Venezuela. ¿Por qué piensas que llegaron tantos esclavos a estos lugares en particular?

3. La cultura latinoamericana tiene mucha influencia africana. ¿La cultura de tu país es así también? ¿Hay más influencia africana en las zonas donde llegaban muchos esclavos en los tiempos de antes (*earlier*)?

↻ Reciclaje

Direct object pronouns

Cuando eras niño/niña, ¿a quién veías? Completa las siguientes oraciones usando el pronombre de objeto directo (**me, la, lo, los** o **las**) apropiado e indica si la oración es cierta o falsa para ti.

	CIERTO	FALSO
1. A mi abuela, _____ veía todos los días.	☐	☐
2. A mi abuelo, _____ veía todos los días.	☐	☐
3. A los amigos de la escuela, _____ veía todos los días.	☐	☐
4. A las amigas de mi mamá, _____ veía todos los días.	☐	☐
5. A mí, mis papás _____ veían todos los días.	☐	☐

■ Answers to this activity are in Appendix 2 at the back of your book.

7.2   Le doy un abrazo

Indirect objects and indirect object pronouns

Para empezar...

PASO 1.   Cuando es tu cumpleaños, ¿cómo te felicitan? ¿Te dan la mano? ¿un beso? ¿un abrazo? Y cuando es el cumpleaños de alguien más, ¿cómo lo/la felicitas tú? Indica tus respuestas aquí.

	LA MANO	UN BESO	UN ABRAZO
En el día de mi cumpleaños…			
mi papá **me** da:	☐	☐	☐
mi mamá **me** da:	☐	☐	☐
mis amigos **me** dan:	☐	☐	☐
mis amigas **me** dan:	☐	☐	☐
En el día de su cumpleaños…			
a mi papá **le** doy:	☐	☐	☐
a mi mamá **le** doy:	☐	☐	☐
a mis amigos **les** doy:	☐	☐	☐
a mis amigas **les** doy:	☐	☐	☐

PASO 2.   ¿Piensas que las respuestas serían (*would be*) diferentes en un país hispano? ¿Cómo?

■ Answers to these activities are in Appendix 2 at the back of your book.

Actividades analíticas

1   The words **me, le,** and **les** in **Para empezar** are *indirect object pronouns* (**pronombres de objeto indirecto**). Add these words to the chart of indirect object pronouns here.

Singular		Plural	
_____	to me	**nos**	to us
te	to you (*inform.*)	**os**	to you (*inform.*)
_____	to him/her/it; to you (*form.*)	_____	to them; to you (*form.*)

Me dio un abrazo y un beso.

2 An indirect object is the person or thing that receives something from the action of the verb. In English, it is often indicated by the preposition *to*. For instance, in the sentence *Mary gave the book to John*, the indirect object is *John*. Underline the indirect object in these sentences.

a. Bill sent a letter to his parents.

b. Diane explained the problem to her friends.

3 In Spanish, an indirect object is usually indicated by the preposition **a**. In general, an indirect object pronoun is used whenever there is an indirect object.

Le doy un abrazo **a mi papá.**	*I gave a hug to my dad.*
Mi mamá **les** da besos **a sus amigas.**	*My mom gives kisses to her friends.*

Indirect object pronouns differ in this way from direct object pronouns, which replace the direct object. Indirect object pronouns may also be used on their own, when the context makes it clear who the pronoun refers to.

Ellos son mis vecinos. **Les** doy el periódico cada mañana.	*They are my neighbors. I give the newspaper every morning.*
Mis amigos **me** dan un abrazo en mi cumpleaños.	*My friends give me a hug on my birthday.*

4 Indirect objects are very frequent with the verb **dar** and **gustar** and similar verbs. They are also common with verbs of communication such as **decir, hablar, pedir,** and **preguntar,** as well as verbs such as **enseñar** (*to show, teach*) and **regalar** (*to give* [*a present*]).

Te digo que es la verdad.	*I'm telling you that it's the truth.*
Nos habló de su viaje a Lima.	*He told us about his trip to Lima.*
Le pido un café.	*I ask him/her for a coffee.*
¿**Les preguntaste** dónde está la universidad?	*Did you ask them where the university is?*
Miguel **me enseñó** su nueva casa.	*Miguel showed me his new house.*
Nos regalaron un libro.	*They gave us a book.*

5 Just as you saw with direct object pronouns, indirect object pronouns can be placed before the main verb or they can instead be attached to the end of infinitives.

Le voy a preguntar algo.	*I am going to ask him/her/you* (form.)
Voy a preguntar**le** algo.	*something.*

You will explore the placement of object pronouns in more detail in **Estructura 8.3.**

En español…

The indirect object pronouns that you are studying here are the same as those used with the verb **gustar.**

Me gusta nadar en el mar.	*I like to swim in the ocean.* (Lit., *It is pleasing to me to swim in the ocean.*)
Le gusta ese tipo de películas.	*She likes that type of movie* (Lit., *That type of movie is pleasing to her*).
Nos gusta ir a fiestas.	*We like to go to parties.* (Lit., *Going to parties is pleasing to us.*)

Actividades prácticas

A. ¿Por qué no... ? (*Why don't you . . .*)   A veces las invitaciones y los regalos pueden causar situaciones difíciles. Pero cuando le explicas el problema a un amigo, casi siempre hay una solución. Empareja cada problema con la respuesta adecuada.

PROBLEMA	RESPUESTA
1. _c_ Quiero invitar a Silvia a la fiesta, pero no está aquí.	a. ¿Por qué no les dices que estás enfermo y que no puedes ir?
2. _d_ Ayer le compré un regalo a mi mamá, pero en realidad no me gusta.	b. ¿Por qué no le buscas otra cosa?
3. _f_ No quiero ir a la fiesta de Juan.	c. ¿Por qué no nos acompañas a la cena antes de la fiesta?
4. _b_ ¿Te compro este lápiz por tu cumpleaños?	d. ¿Por qué no me regalas algo mejor?
5. _e_ Paula y Jorge me invitaron a su casa, pero no quiero ir.	e. ¿Por qué no le hablas por teléfono?
6. _a_ No puedo ir con Uds. a la fiesta.	f. ¿Por qué no le dices que estás enfermo y que no puedes ir?

 ### B. Los padres y los hijos   Los padres a veces les dan regalos a los hijos, y los hijos a veces les dan regalos a los padres, pero ¿quién lo hace más? Completa las dos frases sobre tu familia con el pronombre apropiado.

Ejemplos: el cumpleaños, el Día de las Madres / los Padres, el Jánuca, la Navidad, la Semana Santa

1. Mis padres _____ dan regalos en las siguientes ocasiones: _____
2. Yo _____ doy regalos a mis padres en las siguientes ocasiones: _____

Ahora pregúntale a tu compañero/a sobre su familia y completa las oraciones sobre ellos.

3. ¿En qué ocasiones tus padres _____ dan regalos? _____
4. ¿En qué ocasiones tú _____ das regalos a tus padres? _____

¿Quién me dio este regalo?

C. ¿A quién le pides ayuda? Cuando tienes problemas, ¿a quién le pides ayuda (*help*)? Escoge un tipo de problema de la siguiente lista. Pregúntales a varios compañeros de clase a quién(es) le(s) piden ayuda en ese caso y apunta los resultados.

> **MODELO:** E1: Cuando tienes problemas de dinero, ¿a quién le pides ayuda?
> E2: Les pido ayuda a mis papás.

1. problemas de amor
2. problemas de dinero
3. problemas en una clase
4. problemas con tu coche

D. El problema de «Anónimo»

PASO 1. Un chico anónimo le escribe al Doctor Amor para decirle su problema y proponer (*propose*) algunas posibles soluciones. Lee la carta (*letter*) al Doctor Amor. En la lista de ideas de la carta, encierra (*circle*) cada pronombre de objeto indirecto. Luego, decide cuáles son las tres mejores ideas que tiene el chico que escribió la carta.

Doctor Amor:

Me gusta mucho una chica que trabaja en la universidad donde estudio. Me ve casi todos los días, pero parece que ni sabe que existo. ¿Qué hago? Quiero salir con ella, pero no sé qué hacer. Tengo algunas ideas, pero no sé si son buenas o no.

MIS IDEAS

1. Preguntarle directamente si quiere salir conmigo (*with me*) el día de mi cumpleaños.
2. Decirle que es muy bonita.
3. Enseñarle que traigo mucho dinero.
4. Hablarle de cosas triviales —por ejemplo, el clima, las películas, etcétera— y así puede ver que soy muy buena persona.
5. Preguntarle adónde le gusta salir. Va a ser más fácil hablar con ella en un club que en el sitio donde trabaja.
6. No prestarle atención (*pay attention*). Posiblemente así empieza a hablarme más.
7. Decirle que soy de otra ciudad, que no conozco a nadie y que me siento (*feel*) muy solo.
8. Decirle que solo me quedan (*remain*) seis meses de vida y no sé todavía qué es el amor.

¿Qué piensas? ¿Puedes ayudarme con este problema?

Gracias,

Anónimo

PASO 2. En grupos de dos o tres, piensen en otras cosas que podría hacer «Anónimo» (es decir, ideas que no están en la lista del **Paso 1**). Conversen, seleccionen las tres mejores y apúntenlas (*write them down*) para compartir con la clase. ¡Sean creativos!

Reciclaje

Subject pronouns

Los vecinos van a tener una fiesta de cumpleaños para su hija y te invitan a ti. Empareja cada persona de la lista con la oración apropiada, y completa la oración con el pronombre que le corresponde.

las abuelas   el hermano   el hermano y yo   la mamá   el papá   los papás

¿Quién(es)?

_____ 1. <u>Ellos</u> están organizando la fiesta.
_____ 2. _____ está muy contenta por el cumpleaños de su hija.
_____ 3. _____ quiere jugar con los regalos de su hermana.
_____ 4. _____ está muy contento porque le compró una bicicleta a su hija.
_____ 5. _____ le vamos a cantar una canción a la niña.
_____ 6. _____ quieren ir a la fiesta pero no pueden porque las dos (*both of them, female*) viven lejos.

■ Answers to this activity are in Appendix 2 at the back of your book.

7.3   Un buen regalo para mí

Pronouns after prepositions

Para empezar...

Cada persona tiene sus propios gustos (*tastes*), y no puedes darles el mismo regalo a todos. Compara los gustos de tu mamá, de tu papá, los tuyos y de alguien más (tu amigo/a, tu primo/a, etcétera). ¿Qué sería (*would be*) un buen regalo para cada uno?

	PARA MI MAMÁ	PARA MI PAPÁ	PARA MÍ	PARA _____
1. una bicicleta	☐	☐	☐	☐
2. una computadora	☐	☐	☐	☐
3. flores	☐	☐	☐	☐
4. un libro de historia	☐	☐	☐	☐
5. una planta	☐	☐	☐	☐
6. ropa	☐	☐	☐	☐
7. un teléfono	☐	☐	☐	☐
8. _____	☐	☐	☐	☐

Actividades analíticas

1 Based on what you saw in **Para empezar,** complete the following chart of singular pronouns after prepositions (that is, words such as **a, de, en, por,** and **para**).

■ Answers to this activity are in Appendix 2 at the back of your book.

para/de _____	*for me*
para/de ti	*for you* (sing., inform.)

2 The pronouns **mí** and **ti** may be thought of as specialized forms of **yo** and **tú.** They are only used when they are the object of a preposition such as **a, de,** and **para.**

A mí me llevaban a la playa cada verano.	*They would take me to the beach every summer.*
Vamos a hablar **de ti.**	*We're going to talk about you* (sing., inform.).
Tengo un regalo **para ti.**	*I have a gift for you.*

(*continues*)

All other pronouns (**él/ella, Ud., nosotros/as, vosotros/as, ellos/ellas, Uds.**) retain their regular form when used as the object of a preposition.

A **él** le dan un abrazo cuando lo ven.	*They give him a hug when they see him.*
¿Este libro es **de Ud.**?	*Is this book yours (sing., form.)?*
Ya escogieron un regalo **para nosotros.**	*They already chose a present for us.*
A **ellas** les gusta estudiar en la biblioteca.	*They like to study in the library.*

3 The preposition **con** has two special forms: **conmigo** (*with me*) and **contigo** (*with you* [sing., inform.]).

¿Quieres ir a la playa **conmigo**?	*Do you want to go to the beach with me?*
Vamos a comer **contigo.**	*We are going to eat with you.*

With other pronouns, **con** is used in the regular way, without any special form.

El profesor quiere hablar **con nosotros.**	*The teacher wants to speak with us.*
Vamos a comer **con Ud.**	*We are going to eat with you (sing., form.).*

4 Some other useful prepositions that are often followed by pronouns are **en** (*in, on*), **sin** (*without*), and **sobre** (*on, above; about*).

¿Crees **en** mí?	*Do you believe in me?*
¡No puedo vivir **sin** ti!	*I can't live without you!*
Van a hacer un libro **sobre** ella.	*They are going to make a book about her.*

The preposition **en** is especially common with the verb **pensar.** In English, you *think about* someone, but in Spanish, the equivalent expression is **pensar en.**

Cuando veía esa película, pensaba **en** ti.	*When I was watching that movie, I was thinking about you.*

■ For more on the use of pronouns after prepositions, and to learn about stressed possessives, see **Para saber más 7.3,** at the back of your book.

Autoprueba

Since you know how the verb **gustar** works, you also can work with verbs that function similarly. Use the present tense of the verbs in parentheses.

1. Al chico le _____ (molestar) cuando sus padres lo dejan con una niñera (*babysitter*).
2. A mí me _____ (encantar) los días festivos.
3. Nos _____ (interesar) aprender cómo se celebran los días festivos en otros países.

Respuestas: 1. molesta; **2.** encantan; **3.** interesa

Vocabulario

The verb **gustar** generally takes an indirect object, and as you saw in **Estructura 7.2,** this is expressed by using an indirect object pronoun. The preposition **a** is sometimes used as well to specify or emphasize the indirect object.

A mí me gusta trabajar de noche.	*I like to work at night.*
A Teresa le gusta el fútbol.	*Teresa likes soccer.*

Some other verbs that behave like **gustar** are: **encantar** (*to delight*), **fascinar** (*to fascinate*), **importar** (*to matter*), **interesar** (*to interest*), **molestar** (*to bother*), and **parecer** (*to seem*). They all use an indirect object pronoun, and they all allow further specification or emphasis with **a.**

A mí me encanta este libro.	*I love this book.*
A María le fascinan las películas viejas.	*María loves / is fascinated by old movies.*
¿**A ti** no **te importa**?	*Doesn't it matter to you?*

Actividades prácticas

A. Completa la oración   Completa las oraciones con una de las siguientes opciones. **¡Atención!** Cada opción se puede usar *solo una vez.*

1. ¿Quieres salir ____? ¡Yo sí quiero salir ____!
2. Magda, ¿____ te gusta correr en la calle?
3. ¿De quién hablan? ¿Hablan ____?
4. ¿Sabes que ____ me encanta salir a bailar los sábados?
5. ¿Y Marcos? ¿Ya le preguntaste ____ si puede ir a la fiesta?
6. ¿Te gustan las flores? Espero que sí, porque estas flores son ____.
7. Tus amigos van a salir a cenar este fin de semana. ¿Quieres ir ____?

a. a mí
b. a ti
c. a él
d. conmigo
e. contigo
f. con ellos
g. de mí
h. para ti

B. ¿Le gusta o le molesta?   Escucha las descripciones de algunas personas y empareja cada descripción con una de las siguientes oraciones.

a. _____ Le encantan las fiestas muy grandes.
b. _____ No le gustan las fiestas muy grandes.
c. _____ Le fascina el cine.
d. _____ Le parece muy caro ir al cine.
e. _____ Le interesa viajar a América del Sur.
f. _____ Le interesa viajar a Europa.
g. _____ Le encanta ver televisión con la familia.
h. _____ Le molesta ver televisión con la familia.

C. El Día del Amor y la Amistad   En muchos países se celebra el Día del Amor y la Amistad. Es común mandarle una tarjeta o un mensaje romántico a otra persona.

PASO 1.   En cada mensaje, escribe el pronombre más lógico: **yo, tú, mí** o **ti.**

1. ¿_____ piensas en _____ de vez en cuando?
2. _____ voy a escribir un poema sobre _____.
3. _____ no quiero pasar el día sin _____.
4. Eres horrible. Cuando pienso en _____, me siento mal.
5. _____ eres mi vida.
6. _____ soy mucho más atractivo/a que tú.
7. ¿Quieres una foto de _____?

PASO 2.   Dos de los mensajes no son apropiados para el Día del Amor. ¿Cuáles son?

 PASO 3.   En parejas, siguen el modelo del **Paso 1** y crean tres oraciones apropiadas para el Día del Amor y la Amistad y tres oraciones que no son apropiadas.

■ The audio files for in-text listening activities are available in the eBook, within Connect Plus activities, and on the Online Learning Center.

¡¿Para mí?!

 D. Los cumpleaños

PASO 1.   En un grupo, hablen de los siguientes temas.

1. A los niños, ¿qué les gusta hacer para el cumpleaños?
2. A ti, ¿qué te gustaba hacer para tu cumpleaños cuando eras niño/a?
3. ¿Qué te gusta hacer ahora para tu cumpleaños?

PASO 2.   Apunten sus conclusiones y compártanlas con la clase.

 E. Las diferencias   Pregúntale a tu compañero/a qué le gusta hacer y compara sus respuestas con tus propios (*own*) intereses. Usen las actividades de la lista o inventen sus propias ideas. ¿Qué diferencias pueden encontrar?

bailar	jugar al básquetbol	salir con mis amigos
cantar	nadar	viajar
cocinar	practicar yoga	visitar a mi familia

MODELO: A mí me gusta correr, pero a ella no. A ella le encanta ver películas viejas pero a mí no.

¡Leamos!

Los ritos y conjuros° de la Nochevieja   *spells*

Antes de leer

PASO 1. Contesta las siguientes preguntas.

1. ¿Cuáles son algunas de las costumbres que tenemos para celebrar la Nochevieja en este país? ¿Qué significado (*meaning*) tienen estas costumbres?

2. Nombra dos cosas que mucha gente espera del Año Nuevo.

3. ¿Qué haces tú para celebrar la Nochevieja?

PASO 2. Para entender mejor la lectura sobre los ritos de la Nochevieja en el mundo hispano, empareja las actividades con los resultados esperados (*desired results*).

ACTIVIDADES

1. ____ comer doce uvas (*grapes*) a medianoche

2. ____ comer las uvas apoyándose (*standing*) en la pierna (*leg*) izquierda

3. ____ barrer (*sweep*) la casa de dentro a fuera (*from inside to out*)

4. ____ quemar (*burn*) muebles (*furniture*) y ropa vieja

5. ____ correr por la ciudad con las maletas (*luggage*)

6. ____ usar ropa interior (*underwear*) de color amarillo

RESULTADOS ESPERADOS

a. atraer (*attract*) el amor
b. atraer la prosperidad y la buena suerte
c. empezar el Año Nuevo con el pie (*foot*) derecho para entrar mejor al porvenir (*future*)
d. hacer muchos viajes en el nuevo año
e. limpiar todas las impurezas (*impurities*)
f. purificarse de lo malo con el fuego (*fire*)

A leer

PASO 1. Lee el artículo de Carmen Domingo.

«Los ritos y conjuros de la Nochevieja»

escrito por Carmen Domingo

La tradición de comer una uva con cada campanada[a] a las 12 de la noche el 31 de diciembre es originaria de España.

La última noche del año tiene siempre algo de mágico y se presta[b] a toda clase de conjuros y agüeros[c] que, aunque tienen diferentes manifestaciones, persiguen[d] el objetivo común de atraer la prosperidad y la buena suerte en los 365 días siguientes.

Millones de latinoamericanos siguen la tradición española de tomar las doce uvas al compás de las campanadas[e] de la medianoche del 31 de diciembre, aunque hay multitud de supersticiones acordes con[f] la idiosincrasia popular.

El ritual de las uvas se puede complicar un poco para aumentar[g] sus efectos y tomarlas de pie,[h] apoyándose solo en la pierna izquierda para entrar en el Año Nuevo con el pie derecho, por suponérsele más hábil[i] que el izquierdo en la caminata hacia el porvenir.[j]

Los mexicanos siguen ese rito al son[k] de las campanadas de la Catedral Metropolitana de la Ciudad de México, pero antes o después de tomar las uvas, barren la casa, de dentro a fuera, para dejarla limpia[l] de impurezas de todo tipo.

Otra forma de acabar con[m] lo malo es someterlo[n] al fuego purificador. Se queman muebles y ropas viejas en el Perú, Honduras y Ecuador. […]

Pasear o correr con maletas en Nochevieja no es una prueba[ñ] de atletismo urbano. Se trata de un ritual para que el Año Nuevo traiga[o] muchos viajes, muy extendido en Colombia y seguido también por venezolanos, panameños, paraguayos, peruanos, chilenos, salvadoreños y costarricenses. […]

En Argentina todos corren también, pero a abrir sus regalos después del brindis con champán o sidra[p] en la medianoche del 31 de diciembre. […]

Comer una cucharada[q] de las lentejas[r] en Nochevieja es una tradición en Chile, donde también está muy extendido el uso de ropa interior de color amarillo para atraer el amor. […]

Todos estos rituales ayudan a franquear el umbral[s] del nuevo año y hasta aquellos que se dicen más escépticos[t] siguen alguno… por si acaso.[u]

[a]*stroke of the clock* [b]*se… lends itself* [c]*omens* [d]*follow* [e]*al… to the rhythm of the bells tolling* [f]*acordes… in keeping with* [g]*increase* [h]*de… standing up* [i]*por… because one would suppose that it is more capable* [j]*caminata… journey toward the future* [k]*sound* [l]*dejarla… leave it clean* [m]*acabar… do away with* [n]*to subject it* [ñ]*test* [o]*para… so that the New Year might bring* [p]*hard cider* [q]*spoonful* [r]*lentils* [s]*franquear… clear the way* [t]*hasta… even those said to be more skeptical* [u]*por… just in case*

PASO 2. Ahora apunta los países (*countries*) donde se hace cada actividad.

	PAÍS
1. Comen doce uvas en…	_____
2. Barren la casa en…	_____
3. Queman muebles y ropa vieja en…	_____
4. Corren con las maletas en…	_____
5. Abren regalos en…	_____
6. Comen lentejas en…	_____
7. Usan ropa interior de color amarillo en…	_____

Después de leer

En grupos de tres o cuatro estudiantes, hablen de las tradiciones del mundo hispano que quieren adoptar y expliquen por qué. ¿Cuál les parece la idea más extraña (*strange*)? ¿Por qué?

MODELO: Me gusta la tradición de correr con las maletas porque me gusta viajar. La costumbre de llevar ropa interior de color amarillo para la Nochevieja me da risa (*makes me laugh*), pero como mi vida romántica no va muy bien, necesito la suerte ¡así que la voy a probar (*try*)!

¡Escuchemos!

Nuestros recuerdos°

memories

Antes de escuchar

Indica si tienes un buen recuerdo asociado con cada uno de los siguientes eventos o celebraciones. Apunta algunos detalles sobre los recuerdos para poder compartirlos con la clase.

¿Tienes buenos recuerdos…

	SÍ	NO		SÍ	NO
1. del Año Nuevo?	☐	☐	5. de la Navidad?	☐	☐
2. del bautizo de un bebé?	☐	☐	6. de la Nochevieja?	☐	☐
3. de un juego infantil (*childhood game*)?	☐	☐	7. de un viaje para visitar a tus tíos y primos?	☐	☐
4. del nacimiento de un bebé?	☐	☐	8. de una visita de tus tíos y primos?	☐	☐

A escuchar

Mira y escucha los siguientes recuerdos felices. Luego, empareja cada persona con el recuerdo que describe.

1. _____ Guadalupe, de Costa Rica

2. _____ Henry, de Costa Rica

3. _____ Catalina, de Colombia

4. _____ Michael, de Guatemala

5. _____ Anlluly, de Costa Rica

6. _____ Olman, de Costa Rica

7. _____ Zuly, de Colombia

a. la graduación
b. el nacimiento de primas
c. el nacimiento de perritos
d. el nacimiento de sus hijos
e. el regreso a su país después de vivir fuera (*away*)
f. un viaje a Guatemala
g. una visita a la casa de una persona famosa

Después de escuchar

Escoge una de las siguientes celebraciones y cuéntale a tu compañero/a un recuerdo feliz. ¿Qué año era? ¿Quiénes estaban? ¿Cómo se sentía la gente? ¿Qué hacía la gente para prepararse?

un bautizo   un cumpleaños   una Navidad
una boda   una graduación   una Nochevieja

¡Escribamos!

Una entrada° en un blog

entry

Es muy común usar un blog para compartir información nueva y explicarle algo a un grupo que no sabe nada con respecto al tema presentado. ¿Puedes explicarle una tradición o celebración única a un grupo que no sabe nada de las costumbres asociadas con el evento?

 ### Antes de escribir

En grupos, hagan una lista de algunas celebraciones de este país o región. ¿Qué hace la gente? ¿Cuáles son las costumbres y tradiciones? ¿Saben Uds. el origen de las costumbres? De su lista de celebraciones, ¿cuáles serían (*would be*) las más interesantes para personas de otros países?

A escribir

PASO 1. Escoge una celebración de la lista que hicieron en **Antes de escribir** y escribe una entrada en un blog sobre esa celebración. Tu entrada informativa debe contestar todas las preguntas: **¿quién?, ¿qué?, ¿cuándo?, ¿dónde?, ¿por qué? y ¿cómo?**

> **MODELO:** la víspera del Día de Todos los Santos (*Halloween*)
> **¿quién?** los niños (menores de 13 años)
> **¿qué?** se ponen disfraces y van de casa en casa pidiendo dulces
> **¿cuándo?** el 31 de octubre
> **¿dónde?** en todos los estados de los Estados Unidos
> **¿por qué?** es una tradición relacionada con la cosecha (*harvest*) en otoño, los disfraces imitan y/o asustan a los espíritus malignos
> **¿cómo?** los jóvenes tocan a la puerta, dicen «*trick or treat*» y la gente (*people*) en la casa les da dulces

PASO 2. Escribe una descripción detallada para una persona que no sabe nada de la celebración. ¿Qué se celebra? ¿Qué hace la gente? ¿Cuáles son las costumbres/tradiciones? Describe la historia de la celebración. Usa oraciones completas e incluye todos los detalles del **Paso 1.**

 ### Después de escribir

Revisa tu ensayo. Luego, intercambia descripciones con un compañero / una compañera para evaluarlas. Lee el ensayo de tu compañero/a y determina si el ensayo explica la celebración para una persona que no sabe nada de ella o si falta información necesaria. Lee de nuevo (*again*) el ensayo con cuidado para revisar los siguientes puntos de gramática.

☐ usa el imperfecto para describir la historia de las costumbres
☐ hay concordancia entre sujetos y verbos
☐ hay concordancia entre sustantivos (*nouns*) y adjetivos
☐ la ortografía es correcta

Después de revisar el ensayo de tu compañero/a, devuélveselo (*return it to him/her*). Lee tu propio (*own*) ensayo para ver los cambios que tu compañero/a te recomienda y haz las revisiones necesarias.

ESTRATEGIA

Question-asking for richer narration

When you have to explain something to someone who knows nothing about it, using the 5 Ws from journalism (*Who?, What?, When?, Where?, Why?* [and *How?*]) ensures that you are covering all the details from a perspective that will be understandable to someone who is unfamiliar with the subject. To organize your piece, jot down answers for each of these questions, then make sure to work in the responses as you write.

¡Hablemos!

Un regalo terrible

Antes de hablar

Cada año recibimos regalos en varias ocasiones —para el cumpleaños, la Navidad, el Día del Amor— y la mayoría del tiempo los regalos son buenos. Pero, ¿recibiste alguna vez un regalo terrible? Haz dos listas: una de los peores regalos que recibiste en tu vida y otra de los regalos que querías recibir en su lugar (*in their place*).

Recibí… Quería recibir…

 ### A hablar

Habla con un compañero / una compañera sobre el peor regalo que recibiste. ¿Qué fue? ¿Quién te lo dio? ¿Por qué fue tan terrible? ¿Qué querías como regalo?

 ### Después de hablar

Compartan sus historias con la clase. ¿Quién de la clase recibió el peor regalo?

Conéctate a la música

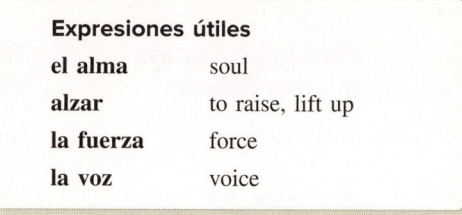

Canción: «Tu Amor» (2006)
Artista: Luis Fonsi

Luis Alfonso Rodríguez López, conocido artísticamente como Luis Fonsi, es un cantante puertorriqueño de música pop. Desde los 10 años vive en la Florida, y estudió música en Florida State University.

Expresiones útiles	
el alma	soul
alzar	to raise, lift up
la fuerza	force
la voz	voice

Un concierto de Luis Fonsi en Pasadena, California

■ For copyright reasons, the songs referenced in **Conéctate a la música** have not been provided by the publisher. The video for this song is available on YouTube or from the ITunes store.

Antes de escuchar

1. Según el título, ¿a quién le canta esta canción?
2. Generalmente, ¿de qué se tratan las canciones de amor? ¿Las canciones que hablan de un amor actual (*current*) son diferentes de las que hablan de un amor del pasado (*past*)? ¿De qué manera?

A escuchar

Esta canción tiene dos estrofas (*verses*) principales. Las dos tratan de contestar la pregunta «¿Cómo era mi vida contigo?».

PASO 1.   Primera estrofa   Empareja cada frase con lo que le sigue (*what follows it*) en la canción.

1. Contigo me sentía ____
2. ...no me acordaba ____
3. Contigo no había ____
4. Contigo no morían (*weren't dying*) ____ mis labios (*lips*)
5. Contigo una y otra vez quería ____
6. Contigo el mundo parecía ____
7. Contigo yo era ____
8. ...porque al quererte (*when I loved you*) quería ____

a. del pasado
b. un día gris ni noches frías antes de dormir
c. volver para salvarme (*save myself*)
d. bien
e. de hambre ni de sed
f. ser mejor
g. un lugar amable (*kind, nice*)
h. más que yo

PASO 2.   Segunda estrofa   En la primera parte de la segunda estrofa, el cantante usa los verbos **reírse** (*to laugh*) y **gustar** en tiempo imperfecto. Escribe la forma apropiada de los verbos aquí.

Contigo _____ (reírse) más porque la vida me _____ (gustar).

Después de escuchar

Televisión Española invitó a Luis Fonsi a presentar esta canción en su programa de Año Nuevo. ¿Por qué crees que a la gente le gusta este tipo de canciones (o esta canción en particular) para Año Nuevo?

VOCABULARIO

Comunicación

¡Felicitaciones!/¡Felicidades!/ ¡Enhorabuena!	Congratulations!
Lo pasé bien/mal.	I had a good/bad time.
pasarlo/la bien/mal	to have a good/ bad time
Lo siento.	I'm sorry. / Condolences.
Me divertí mucho.	I had a lot of fun.
Te felicito/felicitamos.	I/We congratulate you.

Los días festivos — Holidays

el Año Nuevo	New Year's
el bautizo	baptism
la boda	wedding
el brindis	toast (*to a person*)
el Carnaval	Carnival (*the festivities in the days preceding Lent*)
el champán	champagne
la costumbre	custom, habit
el cumpleaños	birthday
el desfile	parade
la despedida	farewell, good-bye
el Día de Acción de Gracias	Thanksgiving
el Día de la Independencia	Independence Day
el Día de los Muertos	Day of the Dead
el Día de los Reyes Magos	Three Kings' Day (Epiphany)
el disfraz (*pl.* los disfraces)	costume
la fiesta	party
la flor	flower
los fuegos artificiales	fireworks
la graduación	graduation
el Jánuca	Hanukkah
el nacimiento	birth
la Navidad	Christmas
la Nochebuena	Christmas Eve
la Nochevieja	New Year's Eve
la Pascua (Florida / de Resurrección)	Easter
la fiesta de quinceañera	*15th birthday celebration for girls*
el regalo	gift
la Semana Santa	Holy Week (*from Palm Sunday to Holy Saturday before Easter*)
la tarjeta	card

Los adjetivos

budista	Buddhist
cristiano/a	Christian
judío/a	Jewish
musulmán/musulmana	Muslim

Para expresar los buenos deseos — To express good wishes

¡Buen viaje!	Bon voyage! / Have a good trip!
¡Buena suerte!	Good luck!
¡Feliz Año Nuevo!	Happy New Year!
¡Feliz cumpleaños!	Happy Birthday!
¡Feliz Navidad!	Merry Christmas!

Los verbos

celebrar	to celebrate
cumplir ___ años	to turn ___ years old
divertirse (ie, i)	to have fun
encantar	to delight
enseñar	to show; to teach
escoger (j)	to choose
escribir	to write
fascinar	to fascinate
felicitar	to congratulate
importar	to matter
interesar	to interest
invitar	to invite
molestar	to bother
parecer (zc)	to seem
preguntar	to ask
regalar	to give

Los pronombres de objeto indirecto

me, te, le, nos, os, les

Las preposiciones y los pronombres

a	to
con	with
conmigo	with me
contigo	with you
de	of, from
en	in, on
para	for
para mí	for me
para ti	for you
sin	without
sobre	on, above; about

La ropa y la moda

En un desfile de moda en México, una modelo lleva un vestido de la diseñadora Lydia Lavin.

Objetivos

In this chapter, you will learn how to:

- say how great something is
- use polite expressions in appropriate contexts
- talk about clothing and fashion
- talk about the human body
- express how clothing fits
- express events in the past
- discuss the fashion world and industry

8

¡Qué padre!

Talking about how great something is

A. A ver: ¿Cómo se dice «¡qué bueno!» en su país? Mira y escucha. Luego, empareja cada persona con la expresión que usa.

1. Edgardo, de Venezuela, dice… _____
2. Olga, de España, dice… _____
3.  Mirelle, de México, dice… _____
4.  Jordi, de España, dice… _____
5. Nadia Angélica, de México, dice… _____
6.  Víctor, de México, dice… _____
7.  Luis, de Nicaragua, dice… _____
8. Daniela, Ana Marcela y Estela, de Costa Rica, dicen… _____

a. Qué bien, qué chulo, qué guay…
b. Qué chido, está muy padre…
c. Qué bueno, ¡qué chévere!
d. ¡Qué bárbaro!
e. ¡Qué bien! ¡Estupendo! ¡Fenomenal!
f. ¡Pura vida!
g. ¡Está padre!
h. Qué padre, qué chido…

En español…

En Costa Rica, se usa la expresión «**pura vida**» para todo: puede significar **hola, adiós, ¿qué pasa?, perfecto, estoy satisfecho, la vida es bella** y más. La expresión existe en otros países hispanos, pero se ha convertido en (*it has become*) el lema (*motto*) nacional de Costa Rica gracias a su uso tan (*so*) común.

To express *cool!* or *awesome!* in Spanish, use one of the following words.

bárbaro/a (*Arg., Chile, C.A.*)	**estupendo/a**
bien	**fenomenal**
chévere (*Carib., Andes*)	**guay** (*Spain*)
chido/a (*Mex.*)	**padre** (*Mex.*)
chulo/a (*Spain, D.R.*)	**pura vida** (*C.R.*)

Many of these are often used as exclamations with **¡Qué… !**

—**Mira, compré un teléfono nuevo.**   *"Look, I bought a new phone."*
—**¡Qué chévere/chido/chulo/padre!**   *"Cool!"*

To say something is *not* cool or great, use one of these expressions.

¡Qué aburrido/a (*boring*)!   **¡Qué pesado/a** (*annoying*)!
¡Qué malo!   **¡Qué pésimo/a** (*awful*)!

B. ¿Chévere o pesado?   Indica tu reacción a cada actividad de la lista.

	¡QUÉ CHÉVERE!	¡QUÉ PESADO!
1. estudiar en la biblioteca	☐	☐
2. acampar (*go camping*) en las montañas	☐	☐
3. ir a la ópera	☐	☐
4. ir a la playa	☐	☐
5. ir a una entrevista de trabajo	☐	☐
6. ir de compras	☐	☐
7. jugar los videojuegos	☐	☐
8. preparar la cena	☐	☐
9. hacer una presentación en una clase	☐	☐
10. salir con los amigos	☐	☐

C. Las marcas (*brands*) más chéveres

 PASO 1.   En grupos, decidan si cada cosa es **chévere, pesado/a** o **pésimo/a. ¡Atención!** Usen también los sinónimos que ya saben.

MODELO: E1: ¿Qué piensas de la consola Wii?
E2: ¡Qué aburrida!

1. un teléfono Droid
2. el iPad
3. la ropa de H&M
4. la marca Hollister
5. la marca Óscar de la Renta
6. los zapatos Nike

PASO 2.   Ahora, apunta tus cosas favoritas en cada una de las siguientes categorías: **marca de ropa, sitio web, marca de teléfono celular, videojuego.**

 PASO 3.   Habla con tres compañeros de clase para saber si están de acuerdo contigo o no. ¿Qué piensan ellos de tus cosas favoritas? ¿Cuáles son sus cosas favoritas? Usa las expresiones de la página 220 para reaccionar.

MODELO: E1: Me gusta la marca Gap.
E2: ¡Qué padre! ¡A mí también! ¿Qué piensas de… ?

El diseñador de modas Óscar de la Renta

Disculpe...
Using polite expressions in appropriate contexts

There are many ways to say *Excuse me,* most of which depend on the situation. (You've already seen some of these in **Capítulo 3.**)

Con permiso.	Excuse me.
Disculpa. / Disculpe. / Disculpen.	Excuse me. (*sing. inform./form.; pl. form.*)
Perdón.	Sorry. / Excuse me. / Pardon me.
Perdona. / Perdone. / Perdonen.	Sorry. / Excuse me. / Pardon me. (*sing. inform./ form.; pl. form.*)
¿Puedo pasar?	Excuse me. (*Literally,* May I pass by? *or* May I enter?)

While any of these phrases can mean *Excuse me,* **Con permiso** is generally used when entering or leaving a room, to leave the table, or to get past someone. **Perdón** and the forms of the verbs **disculpar** and **perdonar** are usually used as apologies for an interruption or inconvenience.

To apologize for something, you can also say **Lo siento.** (*I'm sorry.*)

To respond politely to a request, use one of these expressions.

¡Claro (que sí)!	Of course!
¡Cómo no!	Sure!
Con mucho gusto.	With pleasure.
Gracias.	Thank you.
Gracias por...	Thank you for . . .
No, gracias.	No, thank you.
No puedo.	I can't.
Pasa. / Pase.	Come in. / Go on. (*inform./form.*)
Por supuesto.	Of course.
Sí, gracias.	Yes, please.

A. ¿Puedo pasar?   Escoge la mejor expresión para cada situación.

1. Estás en una cena y quieres ir al baño (*restroom*).
   - ☐ Con permiso.
   - ☐ Lo siento.
   - ☐ Con mucho gusto.

2. Estás en el transporte público con mucha gente y quieres bajar en la próxima parada (*get off at the next stop*).
   - ☐ ¡Claro que sí!
   - ☐ Sí, gracias.
   - ☐ ¿Puedo pasar?

3. Chocas con (*bump into*) otra persona sin querer (*unintentionally*).
   ☐ Con permiso.
   ☐ Lo siento.
   ☐ ¡Cómo no!

4. Das una fiesta y tienes que dejar (*leave*) una conversación para darle la bienvenida a la persona que llega.
   ☐ Con permiso.
   ☐ ¿Puedo pasar?
   ☐ Pase.

5. Tienes que preguntarle algo a alguien, pero esta persona ya está hablando con otra persona. Decides interrumpir.
   ☐ Con mucho gusto.
   ☐ Disculpen.
   ☐ Por supuesto.

6. Quieres pedirle la hora a alguien en la calle.
   ☐ Con mucho gusto. ¿Qué hora es?
   ☐ Perdón. ¿Qué hora es?
   ☐ ¿Puedo pasar? ¿Qué hora es?

B. ¡Sí, gracias!

PASO 1.   En parejas, den una reacción de aceptación o una de negación para cada oración.

MODELO: E1: ¿Te apetece estudiar conmigo esta noche?
        E2: Sí, como no. ¿A qué hora? / Lo siento, pero no puedo. Tengo que trabajar esta noche. ¿Tal vez (*perhaps*) mañana?

1. ¿Quieres un chicle (*gum*)?
2. Tengo coche, así que te puedo llevar a la casa de tus padres este fin de semana.
3. Vamos al cine hoy a las diez. ¿Quieres ir?
4. ¿Me puedes ayudar con la tarea?
5. ¿Me puedes prestar (*lend*) cien dólares?
6. Vamos a tomar un café después de clase. ¿Quieres ir?

PASO 2.   Escoge un lugar o una actividad e invita a tu compañero/a a ir contigo. Responde a las invitaciones que recibes con una expresión apropiada.

MODELO: E1: Después de clase, voy de compras en La Bella. ¿Quieres ir?
        E2: No, gracias. No puedo. Tengo otra clase.

C. Perdón, ¿puedo usar el teléfono?
Circula por la clase y pídeles algo prestado (*ask to borrow*) a tus compañeros: el libro, el teléfono, el bolígrafo, etcétera. **¡Atención!** Usa expresiones como **Con permiso** y **¿Puedo pasar?** mientras circulas por la clase.

MODELO: E1: Perdón, ¿puedo usar tu teléfono?
        E2: Lo siento. No tengo teléfono. / ¡Cómo no!
        E1: Gracias.
        E2: De nada.

¿Quieres un chicle?

¿Qué llevas?
Describing clothing

A. ¿Cierto o falso? Escucha las frases sobre las prendas (*articles*) de ropa que aparecen en el anuncio en la página 224. Indica si cada frase es **cierta** o falsa y corrige las oraciones falsas.

	CIERTO	FALSO		CIERTO	FALSO		CIERTO	FALSO
1.	☐	☐	4.	☐	☐	7.	☐	☐
2.	☐	☐	5.	☐	☐	8.	☐	☐
3.	☐	☐	6.	☐	☐	9.	☐	☐

■ The audio files for in-text listening activities are available in the eBook, within Connect Plus activities, and on the Online Learning Center.

B. ¿De qué color es la ropa?

PASO 1. En parejas, creen una tabla con los siguientes colores para categorizar las prendas de ropa del anuncio. Túrnense para hacerse preguntas sobre los colores y describir el color de cada prenda. No se olviden de que los colores son adjetivos y concuerdan con las palabras que modifican.

MODELO: E1: ¿Hay alguna prenda rosada?
E2: El traje de baño de la niña es rosado. También el calzón de mujer es rosado.

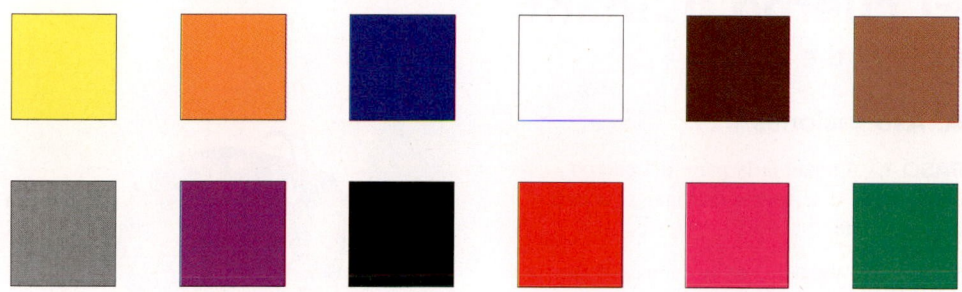

PASO 2. Luego, túrnense para describir su propia ropa y añadan cada prenda a la lista debajo del (*below the*) color apropiado.

MODELO: E1: Hoy llevo una camiseta roja y azul y unos pantalones cortos color caqui (*khaki*). También llevo calcetines blancos, los zapatos marrones y una gorra de los Red Sox.

C. A ver: ¿Qué llevas hoy?

PASO 1. Mira las fotos e indica todas las prendas que llevan Alexander, Carolina y David.

1.

☐ el anillo   ☐ el cinturón   ☐ los calcetines   ☐ el reloj
☐ la camisa   ☐ la gorra   ☐ los jeans   ☐ los zapatos
☐ la camiseta   ☐ la falda

2.

☐ la pulsera   ☐ la camisa   ☐ el cinturón   ☐ el pantalón
☐ la blusa   ☐ la camiseta   ☐ la falda   ☐ el paraguas
☐ los lentes   ☐ el collar   ☐ el bolso

(*Continues*)

En español...

The verb **llevar** has several meanings in Spanish. Two of the most common uses are *to wear* (**La niña lleva un vestido rosado.**) and *to bring* or *to carry* (**Llevo refrescos a la fiesta.**)

The verb **usar** can also be used to mean *to wear*: **Yo no uso lentes, pero mis padres sí los usan.**

3.

☐ la gorra ☐ la camiseta	☐ los calcetines ☐ la pulsera
☐ el anillo ☐ el cinturón	☐ el pantalón ☐ los tenis

PASO 2. Mira y escucha. Apunta cada prenda y accesorio que mencionan Alexander, Carolina y David.

PASO 3. Escucha otra vez y apunta una descripción más detallada (*detailed*) de la ropa que describe cada una.

MODELO: Alexander lleva una camiseta gris.

El cuerpo humano
Parts of the body

A. Asociaciones

PASO 1. Empareja la parte del cuerpo con la ropa o accesorio que más se asocia con esa parte.

1. _____ el torso   a. la camisa
2. _____ la cabeza   b. la corbata
3. _____ las manos   c. la gorra
4. _____ las orejas   d. los guantes
5. _____ el cuello   e. los calcetines
6. _____ los pies   f. el pantalón
7. _____ las piernas   g. los pendientes

PASO 2. Di qué parte del cuerpo se asocia más con cada verbo. **¡Atención!** A veces hay más de una posibilidad.

1. comer   5. pensar   9. ver
2. escribir   6. correr   10. hablar
3. saludar   7. escuchar
4. abrazar   8. sentarse

B. ¿Qué es... ? En grupos, túrnense para describir la ropa y las partes del cuerpo mientras los otros miembros del grupo adivinan qué palabra describes.

MODELOS: E1: Llevamos estas prendas de ropa en los pies, sobre los calcetines.
E2: ¿Son los zapatos?
E1: ¡Exacto!

E3: Es la parte del cuerpo que usas para besar (*to kiss*).
E1: ¿Es la cabeza?
E3: No exactamente. Pero sí están en la cabeza.
E2: ¿Son los labios?
E3: ¡Correcto!

C. ¿Qué debo llevar?   Tu amigo/a no tiene sentido para la moda (*fashion sense*) y necesita tu ayuda para escoger varios conjuntos. En parejas, túrnense para decirle a tu amigo/a qué debe llevar en cada ocasión.

MODELO: E1: ¿Qué debo llevar para conocer (*meet*) a los padres de mi novia en un restaurante?

E2: Tienes que llevar un traje azul, con camisa y corbata. Y necesitas zapatos negros o marrones; no puedes usar tenis.

1. un concierto de música rock
2. una entrevista de trabajo
3. una cita a ciegas (*blind date*) en un restaurante elegante
4. un partido (*game*) de fútbol americano
5. la playa
6. las montañas de Colorado en enero
7. una fiesta con amigos
8. la boda de un buen amigo

¿Cómo te queda?
Expressing how clothing fits

Vocabulario

The verb for *to try* (*something*) *on* is **probarse (ue).** To talk about how clothing fits, use the verb **quedar. Quedar** is conjugated in the same manner as **gustar.**

Me probé este vestido. Me queda bien.   I tried on this dress. It fits me well.
Los pantalones de mi hermano le   My brother's pants fit him poorly.
quedan mal. Están demasiado   They're too tight.
apretados.

Here are other words to describe how clothing fits.

ancho/a	loose
apretado/a	tight
corto/a	short
grande	loose, big
largo/a	long
pequeño/a	small

¡Atención! Note that **largo** means *long*; use **grande** to say that something is *large*.

To talk about a particular size of clothing, use **el número** to refer to shoe size and **la talla** for clothing size.

Disculpe, señor. ¿Tiene este zapato   Excuse me, sir. Do you have this shoe
en el número 9?   in a size 9?
Perdone, señorita, pero quisiera   Excuse me, miss, but I would like to try
probarme la camisa en una talla   on the shirt in a larger size.
más grande.

Here are some words you can use to talk about fashion in general.

el desfile de moda	fashion show
el/la diseñador(a)	designer
estar de moda	to be in fashion
la marca; de marca	brand; brand-name
estar pasado/a de moda	to be out of fashion

A. En una tienda de zapatos   Completa el diálogo con las palabras adecuadas.

apretados   moda   diseñadores   marca   número   probarme

XOCHITL: Normalmente uso zapatos de _____ nueve. Estos son de ocho y me quedan muy _____. Quiero _____ los de nueve.

SUSANA: Esos zapatos no me gustan. Prefiero los zapatos de _____, por ejemplo, los de _____ como Manolo Blahnik y Jimmy Choo. No me gusta estar pasada de _____.

B. Nada me queda bien

PASO 1.   En parejas, identifiquen toda la ropa que no les queda bien a las personas de la ilustración. ¿Qué tienen que cambiar?

MODELO: E1: Los pantalones grises que lleva el hombre calvo (*bald*) le quedan grandes.
E2: Sí. Necesita una talla más pequeña.

PASO 2.   Imagina la escena: Un(a) cliente entra en una tienda de ropa y se prueba varias prendas de ropa; nada le queda bien. En parejas, inventen un diálogo entre el/la cliente y el/la dependiente (*salesclerk*) que le ayuda al / a la cliente a encontrar un conjunto apropiado.

COMUN VOCABUL **ESTRUCTURA** ATE

Reciclaje

The preterite

PASO 1. Estos cinco panameños dicen qué hicieron el fin de semana pasado. Subraya todos los verbos que están en el tiempo pretérito.

 Kathyuska, 19 años, estudiante: «Pasé el fin de semana en la casa de una amiga. Después, regresé a la casa y terminé de hacer mis quehaceres (*chores*)».

 Graciela, 47 años, ingeniera (*engineer*) y gerente de una empresa (*business manager*): «Estuve en la playa con mi familia».

 Marco Antonio, 48 años, trabaja en el sistema de bibliotecas de la Universidad de Panamá: «Les ayudé a unos muchachos de la escuela secundaria a estudiar».

 Mauricio, 20 años, estudiante: «Fui a una fiesta en la playa. La pasamos muy bien. Hicimos una fogata (*bonfire*), comimos y bailamos».

 Ricardo, 32 años, gerente de una cadena (*chain*) de tiendas: «Trabajé».

PASO 2. Da un ejemplo de dos personas que hicieron cosas parecidas.

Nombres: _____ y _____
¿Qué hicieron?_____

Ahora da un ejemplo de dos personas que hicieron cosas distintas.

Nombre: _____ ¿Qué hizo? _____
Nombre: _____ ¿Qué hizo? _____

¿Y tú? ¿Hiciste lo mismo que una de estas personas?
El fin de semana pasado, _____ y yo _____.

 PASO 3. En grupos de tres, hablen de lo que hicieron Uds. el fin de semana pasado. Cada persona debe nombrar por lo menos tres cosas. Mientras conversan, apunten las actividades para poder compartir la información con la clase.

■ Answers to this activity are in Appendix 2 at the back of your book.

8.1 Balenciaga vistió a la familia real española

More irregular preterite forms

Para empezar...

Cristóbal Balenciaga y Carolina Herrera son grandes figuras en el mundo de la moda. Tres de las siguientes oraciones describen a Balenciaga y cuatro a Carolina Herrera. Indica cuáles se refieren a Balenciaga con **B** y cuáles a Herrera con **H**.

Cristóbal Balenciaga,
español, 1895–1972

Carolina Herrera,
venezolana, 1939–

1. _____ **Nació** en el País Vasco (*Basque Country*).
2. _____ **Vistió** (*He/She dressed*) a Jacqueline Kennedy Onassis en los últimos años de su vida. Ahora viste a Oprah Winfrey y a Hillary Clinton.
3. _____ **Asistió** a un desfile de moda de Balenciaga a los trece años (*at age thirteen*).
4. _____ **Murió** en 1972.
5. _____ Le **pidió** ayuda a su hija Carolina Adriana para crear una línea de perfumes.
6. _____ **Nació** en Caracas.
7. _____ Una exposición (*exhibition*) en el Metropolitan Museum of Art en 1973 **sirvió** como reconocimiento (*recognition*) de su importancia después de su muerte.

Actividades analíticas

1 Complete these conjugations in the preterite using the verbs you saw in **Para empezar** and following the pattern that you see here. **¡Atención!** Pay close attention to the stems of these verbs and note where they do and do not change. They share a pattern!

	pedir (i, i)	seguir (i, i)	servir (i, i)	vestir (i, i)
yo	pedí	seguí		
tú	pediste			vestiste
él/ella, Ud.			sirvió	
nosotros/as			servimos	
vosotros/as	pedisteis	seguisteis	servisteis	vestisteis
ellos/ellas, Uds.		siguieron		

Remember that the verb **vestir** is often used in its reflexive form (**vestirse**) with the sense of *to dress oneself* or *to get dressed.*

Carlos **se vistió** bien para la entrevista.   *Carlos dressed well for the interview.*

Ayer **me vestí** después de desayunar.   *Yesterday I got dressed after having breakfast.*

■ Answers to these activities are in Appendix 2 at the back of your book.

■ **NOTE:** The letters in parentheses following stem-changing verbs such as **dormir (ue, u)** and **pedir (i, i)** will help you know what type of change(s) to expect when those verbs appear in different tenses. When there is one set of vowels in parentheses (such as for **despertar [ie]** and **probar [ue])**, it refers to the stem change that occurs in the present tense in all forms but **nosotros/as** and **vosotros/as: despiert-, prueb-.** When there are two sets of vowels in parentheses (such as for **dormir [ue, u]** and **pedir [i, i]),** the first item in parentheses refers to the stem change that occurs in the present tense and the second is the change that occurs in the preterite: **durmió, durmieron; pidió, pidieron.**

2 The verbs **pedir, seguir, servir,** and **vestir** are all **-ir** verbs with an **e** in the stem. In the **él/ella/ Ud.** and **ellos/ellas/Uds.** forms of this type of verb, the stem vowel **e** becomes **i.** Circle these verb forms in the conjugation.

¡Atención! Recall that these verbs also change their stem vowel in the present tense: **pedir, seguir, servir** and **vestir** all belong to the **e → i** family in the present tense, though the pattern of stem changes there is slightly different.

3 Use the verbs in **Para empezar** once again, as well as the general pattern that you see here, to complete the conjugations of these verbs.

	dormir (ue, u)	morir (ue, u)
yo	dormí	
tú		moriste
él/ella, Ud.	durmió	
nosotros/as	dormimos	
vosotros/as		moristeis
ellos/ellas, Uds.		murieron

4 With the verbs **dormir** and **morir,** the stem vowel **o** becomes **u** in the **él/ella/Ud.** and **ellos/ ellas/Uds.** forms of the conjugation. Circle the verb forms in the chart where this vowel change occurs.

¡Atención! Recall that these verbs also change their stem vowel in the present tense: **dormir** and **morir** both belong to the **o → ue** family in the present tense.

Actividades prácticas

A. Completa las oraciones   Usa los verbos para completar las siguientes oraciones. **¡Atención!** Debes usar uno de los verbos dos veces.

durmió   murió   pidió   siguió   sirvió   vistió

1. ¿A quién le _____ dinero Jorge?
2. A causa del examen que tiene ahora, Marisela _____ muy poco anoche.
3. Parece que Santiago se levantó y se _____ en treinta segundos.
4. Eva _____ el mismo camino.
5. Paco _____ una cena exquisita. Él lo preparó todo.
6. Iván está triste porque su perro _____ hace unos días.
7. María Elena tenía mucho sueño y _____ por mucho tiempo.

B. Preguntas y respuestas   Empareja cada pregunta con la respuesta apropiada.

1. _____ ¿Quién durmió más anoche? ¿Guillermo o Pedro?
2. _____ ¿Ya se vistieron los niños?
3. _____ Después de las elecciones, ¿Villegas siguió como presidente?
4. _____ ¿Por qué te pidieron cinco dólares?
5. _____ ¿Sirvió ese teléfono desechable (*disposable*) que compraste?
6. _____ ¿Seguiste las instrucciones?
7. _____ ¿En qué año murió tu abuelo?

a. No, perdió las elecciones presidenciales.
b. Yo sí, pero no las siguió Elena.
c. No, no muy bien.
d. Pedro. Durmió diez horas.
e. En 2011.
f. Sí. Ya salieron a jugar.
g. Porque quieren comprar algo.

■ For additional irregular verbs in the preterite, see **Para saber más 8.1** at the back of your book.

¡Anticipa!

In the preterite, several other stem-changing **-ir** verbs, such as **preferir (ie, i)** (*to prefer*) and **sugerir (ie, i)** (*to suggest*), follow the same basic pattern you see with **morir (ue, u)**, **pedir (i, i)**, and **vestir (i, i)**.

Once again, you can see how understanding a pattern can help you work with words you haven't even studied yet. Try it! Bearing in mind the particular stem change for **preferir** and **sugerir**, follow the pattern to conjugate these two verbs in the preterite.

preferir:
yo _____
tú _____
él/ella, Ud. _____
nosotros/as _____
vosotros/as _____
ellos/ellas, Uds. _____

sugerir:
yo _____
tú _____
él/ella, Ud. _____
nosotros/as _____
vosotros/as _____
ellos/ellas, Uds. _____

Respuestas: preferí, preferiste, prefirió, preferimos, preferisteis, prefirieron; sugerí, sugeriste, sugirió, sugerimos, sugeristeis, sugirieron

C. Poner las acciones en orden

PASO 1. Mira la lista de las cosas que hizo Angélica esta mañana. Pon las oraciones en el orden más lógico.

a. ____ «Antes de ir al trabajo, fui a un café.»
b. ____ «Me levanté temprano.»
c. ____ «Tomé el café solo.»
d. ____ «Me puse los zapatos.»
e. ____ «Me sirvieron un café solo (*black*) por equivocación (*by mistake*).»
f. __1__ «Dormí.»
g. ____ «Fui al trabajo.»
h. ____ «Pedí un café con leche.»
i. ____ «Me vestí.»

 PASO 2. Ahora, con un compañero / una compañera, usa la lista de lo que hizo Angélica esta mañana para crear una narración del día de ella. ¡**Atención!** Para una narración más natural, usa expresiones de tiempo: **primero, entonces** (*then*), **luego** (*later, then*), **después** (*next, afterwards*), **al final** (*in the end*), **finalmente** (*finally, at last*) / **por fin** (*finally, at last*).

MODELO: E1: Primero, Angélica durmió.
E2: Luego…

 PASO 3. En parejas, túrnense para explicar cuáles de las actividades del **Paso 1** hicieron Uds. esta mañana. ¿Alguien hizo todas las cosas? ¿Alguien no hizo ninguna?

MODELO: Dormí, …

 ## D. Cuatro preguntas

PASO 1. Pregúntales a cuatro compañeros una de las siguientes preguntas y apunta las respuestas.

1. ¿En qué año murió el presidente venezolano Hugo Chávez? (Si no lo sabes, ¡adivina [*guess*]!)
2. La última vez que comiste en un restaurante, ¿qué pediste de tomar?
3. ¿Cuántas horas dormiste anoche?
4. ¿En cuánto tiempo te vestiste esta mañana?

PASO 2. Presenta tus resultados del **Paso 1** a la clase.

MODELO: Dos personas dicen que Hugo Chavez murió en el año ____, una persona dice…

Hugo Rafael Chávez Frías, presidente venezolano

C Reciclaje

The imperfect

¿Cómo te vestías de niño o de niña? Usa el verbo indicado para completar las preguntas en el imperfecto. Luego, contesta cada pregunta.

1. ¿Qué tipo de ropa _____ (llevar)? _____
2. ¿Qué tipo de zapatos _____ (tener)? _____
3. ¿Quién te _____ (escoger) la ropa? _____
4. ¿Te _____ (gustar) la ropa que te escogían? _____
5. ¿Quién te _____ (lavar) la ropa? _____

■ Answers to this activity are in Appendix 2 at the back of your book.

8.2   Él modelaba y ella lo vio

The preterite and imperfect together

Para empezar...

Las carreras (*careers*) artísticas de los actores españoles Penélope Cruz y Javier Bardem se han cruzado (*have crossed*) en más de una ocasión. Basándote en la información de la tabla, indica cuáles de las siguientes oraciones son ciertas y cuáles son falsas.

	PENÉLOPE CRUZ	**JAVIER BARDEM**
1969		Nace el primero de marzo en las Islas Canarias.
1974	Nace el 28 de abril en Madrid.	
1975		Empieza a trabajar como actor.
1989	Empieza a trabajar como actriz.	
1992	Tiene su primer gran éxito con *Jamón, jamón,* una película sobre un modelo de ropa interior masculina.	Tiene su primer gran éxito con *Jamón, jamón,* una película sobre un modelo de ropa interior masculina.
2001	Empieza a salir con Tom Cruise.	
2004	Termina su relación con Tom Cruise.	Sale (*Appears*) en *Mar Adentro.*
2006	Sale en *Volver.*	
2007	Empieza una relación con Javier Bardem. Recibe la nominación para el Premio Óscar a la mejor actriz para *Volver.*	Empieza una relación con Penélope Cruz. Sale en *No Country for Old Men.* Gana un Premio Óscar.
2008	Sale en *Vicky Cristina Barcelona.* Gana un Premio Óscar.	Sale en *Vicky Cristina Barcelona.*
2010	Se casa con Javier Bardem.	Se casa con Penélope Cruz.
2011	Da a luz (*Gives birth*) a su hijo, Leonardo.	Nace su hijo, Leonardo.
2012		Sale en *Skyfall.*
2013	Da a luz a su hija, Luna.	Nace su hija, Luna.

Javier Bardem y Penélope Cruz

■ For more comparisons of preterite and imperfect, see **Para saber más 8.2** at the back of your book.

(*continues*)

	CIERTO	FALSO
1. Cuando **nació** Penélope, Javier ya **tenía** cinco años.	☐	☐
2. En 1982, Javier **trabajaba** como actor y Penélope como actriz.	☐	☐
3. En 1992, los dos **tuvieron** su primer gran éxito, en la película *Jamón, jamón.*	☐	☐
4. De 2001 a 2004, Penélope **tuvo** una relación romántica con Tom Cruise.	☐	☐
5. Mientras **tenía** la relación con Tom Cruise, Penélope **salió** en *Volver.*	☐	☐
6. Javier ya **tenía** una relación romántica con Penélope cuando **salió** en *No Country for Old Men.*	☐	☐
7. Penélope y Javier **empezaron** a tener una relación en 2007 y **salieron** juntos en *Vicky Cristina Barcelona* en 2008.	☐	☐
8. Penélope y Javier ya **estaban** casados (*were already married*) cuando ella **ganó** el Premio Óscar.	☐	☐
9. Penélope y Javier **se casaron** en 2010 y su hijo Leo **nació** dos años después.	☐	☐
10. Javier solo **tenía** un hijo cuando **salió** en *Skyfall.*	☐	☐

■ Answers to these activities are in Appendix 2 at the back of your book.

Actividades analíticas

1 You have seen the imperfect tense used to portray an event as happening over a period of time, where the exact starting and ending points don't matter.

Javier **tenía** una relación con Penélope.   *Javier was in a relationship with Penelope.*

You have seen that the preterite tense, in contrast, is used to portray an event as being completed at a specific point in time.

Javier **salió** en esa película en 2007.   *Javier appeared in that movie in 2007.*

These same basic principles apply when the two tenses are in the same sentence.

Javier ya **tenía** una relación con Penélope cuando **salió** en esa película.   *Javier was already in a relationship with Penelope when he appeared in that movie.*

The verb **tenía** is in the imperfect because it refers to the time period when they are already in the relationship. It is not important here when it started or if it ever ended. The verb **salió** is in the preterite because it portrays that action as being completed. The implication is that Javier was in the relationship first, and then while still in it, he appeared in the movie.

2 Here is one way the use of the preterite and imperfect tenses together can be visualized.

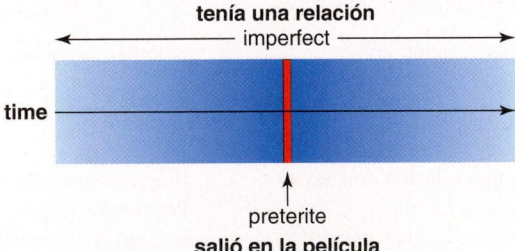

The imperfect verb portrays an ongoing action happening in the background, while the preterite verb portrays an action that "interrupts" it, something that happens and is completed while the background action is still going on. Here are some examples of this type.

Enrique **buscaba** una camisa en la tienda cuando María Elena lo **vio.**   *Enrique was looking for a shirt at the store when María Elena saw him.*

Cuando Pilar **vivía** en Caracas, consiguió su primer trabajo en Zara.   *When Pilar was living in Caracas, she got her first job at Zara.*

Fuimos a la playa porque **hacía** mucho calor.   *We went to the beach because it was really hot.*

Which sentences in **Para empezar** are also of this type, containing one verb in the imperfect and another in the preterite? _____

3 When both verbs in a sentence are in the imperfect, it means that the two events happened at the same time, or at least overlapped.

Enrique **buscaba** una camisa en la tienda y **hablaba** con María Elena.

Enrique was looking for a shirt at the store and talking with María Elena (at the same time).

Cuando Pilar **vivía** en Caracas, **trabajaba** en Zara.

When Pilar was living in Caracas, she worked at Zara. (Whether she continued working for the company afterwards is not relevant.)

This can be visualized in the following way.

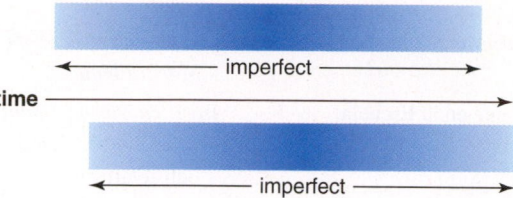

4 When both verbs in a sentence are preterite, it means that both events were completed, usually one after the other.

Enrique **buscó** una camisa y luego **habló** con María Elena.

Enrique looked for a shirt and then spoke with María Elena.

Pilar **fue** a Caracas y **trabajó** en Zara.

Pilar went to Caracas and worked at Zara.

Sequential actions in the past can be visualized like this.

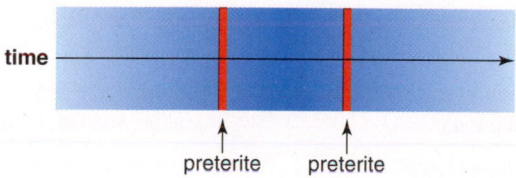

Which sentences in **Para empezar** are an example of this? _____

Dana encontró los zapatos perfectos para la fiesta mientras paseaba por la avenida con sus amigas.

El pretérito versus el imperfecto

THE PRETERITE: To show that an action was completed

Enrique **habló** con María Elena ayer en la tienda.	*Enrique spoke with María Elena yesterday at the store.*
Angélica **fue** estudiante en la Escuela Argentina de Moda en 2009.	*Angélica was a student at the Argentina School of Design in 2009 (but not after).*

THE IMPERFECT: To show that an action was ongoing (when beginning and end points are not important)

De niño, Enrique **hablaba** mucho con María Elena.	*As a child, Enrique spoke a lot with María Elena.*
Angélica **era** estudiante en la Escuela Argentina de Moda en 2009.	*Angélica was a student at the Argentina School of Design in 2009 (and possibly before/after).*

¿Encontró la camisa que buscaba?

Para expresar dos acciones en el pasado

IMPERFECT AND PRETERITE TOGETHER: Imperfect shows ongoing action occurring in background. Preterite shows "interruption," something that happened while background was going on.

Enrique **buscaba** una camisa en la tienda cuando María Elena **lo vio.**	*Enrique was looking for a shirt at the store when María Elena saw him.*
Cuando Pilar **vivía** en Caracas, **consiguió** su primer trabajo en Zara.	*When Pilar was living in Caracas, she got her first job at Zara.*
Fuimos a la playa porque **hacía** mucho calor.	*We went to the beach because it was really hot.*

BOTH IMPERFECT: The actions are simultaneous (or overlapping).

Enrique **buscaba** una camisa mientras (*while*) **hablaba** con María Elena.	*Enrique was looking for a shirt while he was talking with María Elena. (at the same time)*
Angélica **era** estudiante y **trabajaba** en la universidad.	*Angélica was a student and worked at the university.*

BOTH PRETERITE: Two actions occur one after another.

Enrique **buscó** una camisa y luego **habló** con María Elena.	*Enrique looked for a shirt and then spoke with María Elena.*
Angélica primero **fue** estudiante y después **trabajó** en la misma universidad.	*Angélica first was a student and then she worked at the same university.*

Actividades prácticas

A. La historia y la moda Para cada año, escribe las letras que corresponden a lo que pasó y pasaba en el mundo hispano en ese año. **¡Atención!** Las imágenes te pueden ayudar.

AÑO	¿QUÉ PASÓ EN LA HISTORIA?	¿QUÉ PASABA EN EL MUNDO DE LA MODA?
1. 1492	b	g e
2. 1821	f	g
3. 1939	h	c
4. 1973	d	a

a. Las mujeres usaban minifaldas (*miniskirts*). Los hombres (y también las mujeres) usaban pantalones de campana (*bell*). Los dos sexos llevaban zapatos de plataforma.

b. Los primeros españoles llegaron a América.

c. Las mujeres usaban faldas que iban hasta debajo (*below*) de las rodillas. También era muy común usar guantes. Los hombres llevaban trajes con corbatas anchas y sombreros Fedora.

d. El comandante Augusto Pinochet derrocó (*overthrew*) al gobierno de Salvador Allende en Chile.

e. Las mujeres usaban vestidos largos con mangas (*sleeves*). Los hombres usaban camisas, pero no usaban pantalones. Llevaban medias (*stockings*) que llegaban hasta la cadera.

f. Simón Bolívar ganó la Batalla de Carabobo. Venezuela se independizó (*became independent*) de España.

g. Las mujeres llevaban corsés (*corsets*) con sus vestidos cónicos (*conical*) con mangas muy voluminosas (*bulky*). Los hombres usaban corsés con pantalón y chaqueta.

h. Terminó la Guerra (*War*) Civil Española.

B. Más sobre Penélope Basándote en la información de la tabla, escoge el tiempo del verbo más adecuado en cada caso.

ALGUNOS EVENTOS EN LA VIDA DE PENÉLOPE CRUZ

1974	Nace en Madrid.
1980	Empieza a estudiar danza.
1989	Deja (*leaves*) la danza; empieza a trabajar como actriz.
1999	Sale en *Todo sobre mi madre,* su primera película con el director Pedro Almodóvar.
2000	Se hace vegetariana.
2005	Empieza una relación con Matthew McConaughey.
2006	Sale en *Volver;* termina la relación con Matthew McConaughey.
2007	Empieza una relación con Javier Bardem.
2008	Gana un Premio Óscar por su interpretación en *Vicky Cristina Barcelona.*
2010	Se casa con Javier Bardem.
2011	Nace su primer hijo, Leo.

1. En 1974, Penélope nació / nacía en Madrid.
2. En 1981, cuando Javier salió / salía en una película, Penélope estudió / estudiaba danza.
3. Estudió / estudiaba danza por nueve años, y después empezó / empezaba a trabajar como actriz.
4. Primero salió / salía en *Todo sobre mi madre,* y luego se hizo / se hacía vegetariana.
5. Mientras estuvo / estaba en una relación con McConaughey, salió / salía en *Volver.*
6. Tuvo / Tenía una relación con Javier Bardem cuando ganó / ganaba el Premio Óscar.

C. La clase de actuación

PASO 1. En las siguientes oraciones, subraya los verbos que aparecen en el pretérito y encierra (*circle*) los verbos que aparecen en el imperfecto.

SITUACIÓN 1

a. Una persona se ponía los zapatos y la otra escribía una carta.
b. Mientras (*While*) una persona se ponía los zapatos, la otra escribió una carta.
c. Una persona se puso los zapatos mientras la otra escribía una carta.
d. Una persona se puso los zapatos y luego la otra escribió una carta.

SITUACIÓN 2

a. Una persona se ponía la corbata mientras la otra cantaba una canción.
b. Mientras una persona se ponía la corbata, la otra cantó una canción.
c. Una persona se puso la corbata mientas la otra cantaba una canción.
d. Una persona se puso la corbata y luego la otra cantó una canción.

SITUACIÓN 3

a. Una persona se probaba la chaqueta y la otra se lavaba los dientes.
b. Mientras una persona se probaba la chaqueta, la otra se lavó los dientes.
c. Una persona se probó la chaqueta mientras la otra se lavaba los dientes.
d. Una persona se probó la chaqueta y luego la otra se lavó los dientes.

PASO 2. En parejas, escojan una oración y actúen lo que dice que pasó. Sus compañeros de clase tienen que adivinar qué oración escogieron y decidir si las acciones eran (1) simultáneas, (2) consecutivas o (3) si una acción interrumpió a la otra.

PASO 3. En parejas, usen el modelo del **Paso 1** para crear cuatro oraciones nuevas. Las oraciones deben (*should*) tener los mismos (*same*) dos verbos en diferentes combinaciones del pretérito y el imperfecto.

D. Amancio Ortega y Zara

Amancio Ortega es el presidente de Zara, una compañía española que tiene más de 1800 tiendas de ropa en más de 70 países del mundo. Ortega vive en A Coruña, una ciudad en el noroeste de España. En cada una de las siguientes oraciones, conjuga los verbos en el tiempo (pretérito o imperfecto) más apropiado. Además, una oración es falsa. ¿Cuál piensas que es?

1. Amancio Ortega _____ (llegar) a A Coruña cuando _____ (tener) 14 años y su padre _____ (trabajar) en los ferrocarriles.
2. En 1975, _____ (abrir) en A Coruña su primera tienda, Zara. Esta tienda _____ (hacerse) muy popular porque _____ (tener) versiones más económicas de ropa de diseñador.
3. A finales (*At the end*) de los años 80, la compañía Zara ya _____ (tener) más de ochenta tiendas en España.
4. En 1988, Ortega _____ (abrir) la primera tienda en el extranjero (*abroad*), en Portugal.
5. Ortega _____ (crear) un sistema en que pueden diseñar un producto nuevo y tenerlo en las tiendas en menos de quince días.
6. En 1989, _____ (entrar) al mercado norteamericano, pero su presencia en Europa y Latinoamérica sigue siendo (*continues to be*) mucho más fuerte.
7. En 2010, Amancio Ortega _____ (comprar) una de las casas más grandes de Madrid.
8. En 2013, la revista Forbes _____ (anunciar) que Amancio Ortega _____ (ser) el tercer (*third*) hombre más rico del mundo, después de Carlos Slim Helu y Bill Gates.

Amancio Ortega con la reina Letizia

 E. Una excusa ¿Te gusta inventar excusas? Haz varias excusas para explicar por qué no pudiste terminar las siguientes actividades y compártelas con un compañero / una compañera. Tu excusa no tiene que ser verdadera (*truthful*), ¡pero sí tiene que ser creativa!

estudiar para el examen   hacer la tarea   lavar los platos   limpiar la casa

MODELO: Hacía mi tarea anoche, pero perdí mi lápiz y mientras lo buscaba, mi perro comió todas las hojas de tarea, entonces no pude terminar.

 F. Un cuento de cuando era niño/a Cuéntale a tu compañero/a algún evento verdadero o falso de cuando eras niño o niña, y luego pregúntale si piensa que es cierto o no. Usa la siguiente estructura en tu cuento.

■ ¿Cuántos años tenías?
■ ¿Dónde vivías?
■ ¿Dónde estabas y qué ropa llevabas?
■ ¿Qué pasó?

MODELO: Tenía 10 años y vivía en Nueva York con mis papás. Estaba en el parque y llevaba una camiseta y pantalones cortos porque era verano y hacía calor. Entonces vi que Rihanna caminaba cerca de mí. ¿Cierto o falso?

la República
Dominicana   Cuba

G. Cultura: Los modistas (*fashion designers*) de la República Dominicana y Cuba

PASO 1. Lee el texto sobre la República Dominicana y Cuba.

Cuando piensas en la ropa del Caribe, sin duda[a] viene a la mente la guayabera, una camisa tradicional para hombres, generalmente con cuatro bolsillos[b] y muchos pliegues[c] verticales. Pero los países caribeños como Cuba y República Dominicana han contribuido[d] mucho más al mundo de la moda. Un gran número de influyentes diseñadores de alta costura[e] son de esta región y ahora trabajan en los centros urbanos de moda en los Estados Unidos, Canadá, Europa, Asia y Latinoamérica. Adolfo Sardina y Óscar de la Renta son dos ejemplos.

Adolfo Sardina nació en la provincia de Matanzas, Cuba, en 1933. Su madre murió en el parto[f] y por eso, durante su niñez Adolfo vivía con una tía. Ellos solían viajar[g] juntos y en un viaje a Europa, Adolfo conoció a la famosa diseñadora Coco Chanel. Inspirado por ese encuentro, Adolfo salió de Cuba y se fue a vivir a Nueva York, donde trabajaba como sombrerero.[h] En 1955, empezó a trabajar con telas[i] para diseñar vestidos elegantes. Entre sus clientes estaban la diseñadora Gloria Vanderbilt y la Duquesa de Windsor. Luego, conoció a la primera dama Nancy Reagan y durante muchos años la vistió con sus trajes.

El diseñador Adolfo Sardina

Óscar de la Renta nació en Santo Domingo en 1932. Cuando tenía 18 años, decidió ir a estudiar arte en Madrid. Allí se dio cuenta de[j] su interés en la moda y empezó a trabajar con varios diseñadores conocidos. En 1963, fue a Nueva York para colaborar con Elizabeth Arden y dos años después creó una empresa[k] de moda con su propio nombre. A lo largo de[l] su carrera, recibió muchos premios[m] por sus diseños. En 1977, lanzó[n] un perfume para mujeres, «Óscar». En los años 80 y 90, lanzó varias otras fragancias, incluso para hombres.

[a]sin... *without doubt* [b]*pockets* [c]*pleats* [d]han... *have contributed* [e]alta... *haute couture* [f]*childbirth* [g]solían... *usually traveled* [h]*hat maker* [i]*fabrics* [j]se... *became aware of* [k]*company* [l]A... *Throughout* [m]*awards* [n]*launched*

PASO 2. Completa las oraciones con la forma apropiada del verbo en el pretérito o el imperfecto.

1. Cuando Adolfo _____ (nacer) en Cuba, Óscar _____ (tener) 7 meses de edad y su familia _____ (vivir) en Santo Domingo.
2. Cuando _____ (estar) en Nueva York, Adolfo _____ (conseguir* [*to get*]) su primer trabajo como sombrerero.
3. _____ (Ser) el año 1955 cuando Adolfo _____ (decidir) diseñar vestidos.
4. Óscar _____ (ir) a estudiar en España cuando _____ (tener) 18 años.
5. La Duquesa de Windsor y Gloria Vanderbilt ya (*already*) _____ (ser) clientes de Adolfo cuando Nancy Reagan le _____ (pedir) diseñar un vestido para ella.
6. Mientras Adolfo _____ (trabajar) como sombrerero en Nueva York, Óscar y varios diseñadores _____ (colaborar) en Europa.
7. Ya _____ (existir) el perfume «Óscar» para mujeres cuando el diseñador _____ (lanzar) la colonia para hombres.

PASO 3. En parejas, contesten las preguntas y explíquense las respuestas.

1. Cuando gente talentosa como Alfono Sardina y Óscar de la Renta se va de su país para vivir en otro, se llama «fuga de cerebros» (*brain drain*) y es un fenómeno muy común en muchos países. En el caso de Sardina y de la Renta, ¿por qué crees que se fueron?
2. ¿Qué piensas que siente la gente que se ha ido (*have left*) de su país natal (*native*)?
3. La fuga de cerebros no es siempre hacia (*toward*) Estados Unidos, Canadá o Europa. En los últimos años, mucha gente joven de todas partes del mundo se ha ido a vivir a la Ciudad de México, por las oportunidades económicas y culturales que ofrece (*offers*). ¿A ti te interesa vivir en otro país por razones (*reasons*) profesionales o económicas? ¿Por qué sí o por qué no?

---

*__Conseguir__ follows the same pattern as __seguir__.

↻ Reciclaje

Direct and indirect object pronouns

Empareja cada palabra con la definición adecuada, luego completa la definición con el pronombre **lo, la, los, le** o **les.**

1. _____ el abrigo
2. _____ el anillo
3. _____ la camisa
4. _____ los guantes
5. _____ el pantalón
6. _____ el sombrero
7. _____ los zapatos

a. _____ usas en la parte inferior del cuerpo.
   _____ pones un cinturón.
b. _____ usas para proteger (*protect*) las manos.
c. _____ pones en la cabeza.
d. _____ usas para proteger los pies.
e. _____ usas para protegerte contra (*against*) el frío.
f. _____ das esto a tu novio/a cuando te casas.
g. _____ usas para tapar la parte superior del cuerpo.

■ Answers to this activity are in Appendix 2 at the back of your book.

8.3   ¡Lo voy a comprar!

Object pronoun placement with infinitives

Para empezar...

Empareja a cada persona con su reacción al ver (*after seeing*) la ropa mencionada.

■ For additional uses and placement of object pronouns, see **Para saber más 8.3** at the back of your book.

■ Answers to these activities are in Appendix 2 at the back of your book.

PERSONA Y ROPA

1. _____ Un muchacho de 15 años: una corbata muy seria, pero barata
2. _____ Un joven de 25 años en su primer trabajo profesional: un traje
3. _____ Una muchacha de 17 años: un anillo y un collar
4. _____ Una estudiante de 20 años: unas sandalias
5. _____ Un estudiante de 22 años: unos zapatos de Zara

REACCIONES

a. «No **los** necesito, pero **los** voy a comprar.»
b. «No **lo** quiero, pero **lo** tengo que comprar.»
c. «**Los** quiero y **los** voy a comprar. Como (*Since*) son negros, ahora necesito calcetines negros también.»
d. «**Las** tengo que comprar, porque voy a la playa y allí no quiero usar zapatos.»
e. «**La** puedo comprar, pero ¿para qué **la** quiero?»

Actividades analíticas

1 As you saw in **Estructura 6.3** and **7.2,** object pronouns generally appear before verbs that are conjugated, whether they are in the present, preterite, or imperfect tense.

Lo quiero.   *I want it.*
Le di el libro ayer.   *I gave the book to him/her yesterday.*

The object pronoun in these cases is written as a separate word.

2 Object pronouns can appear after infinitive verb forms; in this case, the infinitive and the object pronoun are written as a single word.

Es importante leer**lo**.   *It's important to read it.*
Es necesario dar**le** el libro mañana. *It's necessary to give the book to him/her tomorrow.*

3 You've seen that when a conjugated verb is followed by an infinitive, the object pronoun can appear after and be attached to the infinitive: **¿Las camisas? Queremos compararlas** (*compare them*). Alternatively, in many cases it may be placed before the conjugated verb: **Las queremos comparar.** Use the sentences in **Para empezar** to find examples of the following expressions, and write the sentences here.

a. **voy a** + *infinitive*   _____
b. **quiero** + *infinitive*   Los quiero comprar.
c. **tengo que** + *infinitive*   _____
d. **puedo** + *infinitive*   _____

Autoprueba

Using what you now know about the placement of direct and indirect object pronouns with infinitives, determine what object pronoun would be used for the following sentences, then express each sentence using the two possible placements of the object pronoun.

1. Quiero comprar estas botas.
2. Necesitamos ver los guantes de cerca (*up close*).
3. ¿Vas a llevar tu chaqueta nueva?

Respuestas: 1. Las quiero comprar. Quiero comprarlas. **2.** Los necesitamos ver de cerca. Necesitamos verlos de cerca. **3.** ¿La vas a llevar? ¿Vas a llevarla?

4 Now write these same sentences, but with the pronoun placed after and attached to the infinitive verb.

a. **voy a** + *infinitive* _____
b. **quiero** + *infinitive* _____
c. **tengo que** + *infinitive* _____
d. **puedo** + *infinitive* _____

Actividades prácticas

A. Corbatas, sombreros y zapatos Para cada oración, escribe **C** si se trata de (*it has to do with*) corbatas, **S** si se trata de sombreros y **Z** si se trata de zapatos. Hay dos oraciones que no se tratan de ninguno de estos objetos. En esos casos, escribe **N**. **¡Atención!** Presta (*Pay*) atención a los pronombres de objeto directo e indirecto.

1. _____ En los restaurantes, casi siempre los tienes que usar.
2. _____ No es común usarlas cuando haces deporte.
3. _____ Es común comprarlos en tiendas especializadas que se llaman zapaterías.
4. _____ Es muy común usarlas cuando vas a la playa.
5. _____ No los puedes comprar en muchas tiendas de ropa, porque mucha gente no los usa.
6. _____ Los tienes que usar para hacer casi cualquier (*any*) tipo de deporte. En ese caso, se llaman «tenis» o «zapatillas».
7. _____ Los hombres las tienen que usar en muchos tipos de eventos formales.
8. _____ Es común comprarlas en los grandes almacenes.
9. _____ Tradicionalmente, los caballeros (*gentlemen*) no pueden llevarlos puestos (*put on*) dentro (*inside*) de un edificio.
10. _____ Los puedes comprar en las bibliotecas.

Tengo muchas corbatas. Me las pongo para ir al trabajo.

■ The audio files for in-text listening activities are available in the eBook, within Connect Plus activities, and on the Online Learning Center.

B. Preguntas y respuestas Escucha las preguntas y escoge la respuesta más adecuada para cada una.

a. _____ No, pero me van a regalar algo mañana.
b. _____ No, pero lo tengo que comprar para mañana.
c. _____ No, pero la tenemos que comprar para mañana.
d. _____ Las voy a poner en el coche.
e. _____ No. La puedo hacer mañana.
f. _____ No, pero voy a regalarle un collar esta noche.
g. _____ Están en el coche todavía, pero los vamos a poner en la habitación (*room*).

C. Pregúntales a tus compañeros ¿Qué haces con tus cosas cuando ya no las necesitas o cuando ya no te sirven? Por ejemplo, ¿qué vas a hacer después con estos objetos? ¿Venderlos (*Sell them*)? ¿Guardarlos (*Save them*)? ¿Donarlos (*Donate them*)? ¿Tirarlos (*Throw them away*)? ¿Reciclarlos? ¿Algo más? Escoge uno de estos objetos, pregúntales a varios compañeros sobre el objeto y apunta los resultados.

■ este libro
■ tu teléfono
■ tus zapatos

■ tus lentes, si usas lentes
■ tu computadora
■ tu cepillo de dientes

> **MODELO:** E1: ¿Qué vas a hacer con este libro?
> E2: Voy a guardarlo.

D. ¿Cómo puedes usar este libro? Es obvio que puedes usar este libro para estudiar, pero, ¿para qué más? ¿Y cómo puedes usar tu mochila y tus zapatos? En parejas, piensen en otras maneras de usarlos.

> **MODELO:** Este libro: Puedo usarlo para protegerme (*protect myself*) contra los criminales.
> Mi mochila: Puedo usarla como sombrero.

Este libro: _____

Mi mochila: _____

Mis zapatos: _____

¡Leamos!

Conceptos que cautivan°   *captivate*

 Antes de leer

En grupos de dos o tres, conversen sobre las siguientes preguntas.

1. Describe tu estilo de vestirte. ¿Es un estilo formal o informal? ¿Es profesional o relajado? ¿cómodo (*comfortable*) o lujoso (*luxurious*)? ¿de moda? ¿diseñador? ¿único (*unique*)?

2. ¿Cuáles factores consideras al comprar (*when buying*) ropa? ¿Consideras la talla / el número? ¿Piensas en cómo te queda? ¿en la marca? ¿el color? ¿la tela (*fabric*)? ¿el precio? ¿otros factores? De ellos, ¿cuáles son los tres factores que te importan más?

3. ¿Cuáles diseñadores de ropa puedes nombrar?

4. ¿Qué factores crees que les importan más a los diseñadores al crear ropa para el público?

5. ¿Dónde crees que encuentran la inspiración los diseñadores?

A leer

PASO 1. Lee el artículo sobre Ángel Sánchez, un diseñador venezolano.

Conceptos que cautivan

¿Moda arquitectónica[a]? ¿Vestidos construidos? ¿Prendas conceptualizadas? ¿Conceptos a medida[b]? Pues, claro.

La energía y el brío[c] de los diseños[d] de Ángel Sánchez fascinan a las más famosas, como Taylor Swift, Eva Longoria, Beyonce, Brooke Shields y Sandra Bullock.

Estas y muchas más estrellas empezaron a cautivarse por las creaciones del modista venezolano cuando se estableció en Nueva York en 1997. El ingenio de sus diseños brota[e] de sus experiencias en la casa de su niñez, de sus estudios y carrera en la arquitectura y de una cierta chispa creativa regalada del cielo.[f]

Sánchez nació en Valera, Venezuela, donde se crió en la modistería[g] de su madre. Desde muy temprano, el mundo del diseño impregnó[h] su mundo e imaginación, pero siguió una carrera en arquitectura. En los años 90, volvió al mundo de su juventud, el diseño. Pero no dejó atrás[i] su formación y sus destrezas[j] arquitectónicas.

Como la conceptualización de los edificios[k] de una comunidad, las colecciones de Sánchez se estructuran alrededor[l] de un concepto unificador.[m] «Concepto es la palabra más clara que define cómo yo asumo[n] mi trabajo. A mí me gusta no solo hacer el vestido bonito, sino que[ñ] el vestido te diga[o] algo. Todo tiene su explicación, su concepto, técnicamente y creativamente hablando.» Cada prenda de sus colecciones tiene un principio y un final,[p] y se relaciona con las otras prendas de la colección.

Pero el diseñador no se limita a sus colecciones. Sandra Bullock lo buscó para diseñar su vestido de boda y otras lo han buscado con el deseo de lucir[q] una de sus creaciones en la alfombra[r]

Eva Longoria en un diseño de Sánchez en los premios ALMA

[a]*architectural* [b]*a... custom-made* [c]*spirit* [d]*designs* [e]*springs, flows*
[f]*chispa... God-sent creative spark* [g]*dress shop* [h]*impregnated, imbued*
[i]*behind* [j]*skills* [k]*buildings* [l]*around* [m]*unifying* [n]*take on, approach*
[ñ]*sino... but rather* [o]*te... tell you* [p]*principio... beginning and an end*
[q]*to dress up* [r]*carpet*

(Continues)

Ángel Sánchez

roja u otra ocasión especial, ¿De dónde vienen los conceptos para estos vestidos a medida? De las clientas mismas.[s] Sánchez primero escucha a sus clientas para entender su personalidad y sus gustos.[t]

El concepto de su última colección se inspiró en la arena[u] y en el desierto. En muchos aspectos, el diseñador salió de su elemento.

Sánchez es famoso por sus elegantes y suntuosos trajes de noche y vestidos de novia, pero esta colección es más casual, «prendas que no necesiten una ocasión para ser usadas, que puedan estar en el clóset listas[v] para salir». Además, la arquitectura de esta colección se basó en una tela más ruda:[w] el lino. Sánchez quiso retarse,[x] explorar materiales desconocidos[y] y crecer como artista.

[s]*themselves* [t]*taste* [u]*sand* [v]*ready* [w]*tela... course cloth* [x]*challenge himself* [y]*unfamiliar*

PASO 2. Decide si cada frase se refiere a Ángel Sánchez, o a la actriz y activista, Eva Longoria.

	Ángel Sánchez	Eva Longoria
1. Luce (*wears, shows off*) un elegante vestido en los Emmys.	☐	☐
2. Es de Venezuela, pero vive en Nueva York.	☐	☐
3. Crea vestidos y otra ropa.	☐	☐
4. Quiere llevar ropa única en eventos especiales.	☐	☐
5. Su preparación en la arquitectura forma la base de su trabajo actual (*current*).	☐	☐
6. Cada traje de su colección tiene algo en común con los otros trajes de la misma colección.	☐	☐
7. Le inspiran el desierto, la playa y la arena.	☐	☐

Después de leer

Contesta las siguientes preguntas según lo que leíste en la lectura.

1. _____ Las creaciones de Ángel Sánchez son resultado de:
   a. su formación académica
   b. su niñez en la modistería de su madre
   c. su talento creativo
   d. todas las respuestas son correctas

2. _____ ¿Cuál es la mejor descripción de las colecciones de Ángel Sánchez?
   a. Las colecciones son como los planes arquitectónicos para una ciudad entera.
   b. Todos los elementos de una colección se relacionan.
   c. Primero que nada, los vestidos son bonitos.
   d. Todas las colecciones tienen un principio y un final.

3. Según Sánchez, ¿cuál es la palabra que mejor describe sus colecciones? ¿Por qué usa esa palabra?

4. Además de sus colecciones, ¿qué tipo de ropa diseña?

5. Si Sánchez diseña algo especial para una de sus clientas famosas, ¿de dónde vienen las ideas para sus vestidos? ¿por qué?

6. ¿Cómo es diferente su nueva colección de lo típico de Sánchez?

7. ¿Cuáles son los elementos inspiradores de la nueva colección?

¡Escuchemos!

Lo tradicional y lo moderno de los indios kuna

Antes de escuchar

PASO 1. Vas a escuchar a Marlina hablar de las molas, una artesanía (*handicraft*) típica de Panamá. Primero, empareja lo que dice Marlina con su explicación más adecuada.

MARLINA DICE

1. _____ «Nosotros tenemos tres tipos de molas.»

2. _____ «Las antiguas son de dos telas (*fabrics*) y son puras figuras geométricas.»

3. _____ «Las tradicionales vienen de diferentes capas (*layers*). Pueden tener hasta cinco capas: se van cortando (*cutting*) para que la otra capa vaya saliendo y saliendo…»

4. _____ «La nueva mola comercial que ha salido (*has come out*) es cosida (*sewed*) a mano, pero no se corta la capa: uno le pone la figura para ir cosiéndola encima (*on top*) de la tela negra.»

5. _____ «Mi mamá no puede usar esta clase de mola para su vestuario (ropa) porque no tienen los diseños ni los colores tradicionales.»

EXPLICACIÓN

a. Marlina dice que el vestuario tradicional Kuna usa la mola con colores y diseños (*designs*) tradicionales; las molas que venden a los turistas son diferentes.

b. Marlina explica cómo se hace la mola tradicional de varias capas.

c. Marlina dice que la mola comercial no tiene varias capas.

d. Marlina va a describir diferentes tipos de molas.

e. Marlina dice que no hay animales ni flores en las molas antiguas.

CONÉCTATE AL MUNDO HISPANO

Marlina es de la Comarca (región) **Kuna Yala,** también conocida como San Blas, una comunidad indígena (*indigenous*) de Panamá. La gente Kuna Yala tiene sus propias costumbres, tradiciones, cultura e idioma, pero también tiene éxito comercializando sus productos. Uno de los productos es la **mola,** un textil tradicional que se usa para la ropa femenina. Cada mola tiene varias capas (*layers*) de tela (*fabric*) colorida cosida (*sewn*) y cortada (*cut*) para revelar muchos colores y figuras.

PASO 2. Ahora lee las citas (*quotes*) de Marlina y decide si cada cita se refiere a una **tradición** cultural o a la **comercialización** de sus productos.

1. «Estas [molas] son tradicionales, ellas vienen de diferentes capas. Tienen… pueden tener hasta cinco capas, se van cortando y se van, para que la otra capa vaya saliendo y saliendo… »

   ☐ tradición ☐ comercialización

2. «[La nueva mola comercial] es cosida a mano, pero no es elaborada por corte: […] uno le va poniendo la figura para ir cosiéndola encima de la tela negra.»

   ☐ tradición ☐ comercialización

3. «Siempre son estos y estos colores que representan más el vestuario Kuna.»

   ☐ tradición ☐ comercialización

A escuchar

Mira y escucha. Luego, contesta las preguntas.

1. _____ Las molas antiguas son…
   a. de diferentes capas —hasta cinco capas en total.
   b. dos telas con figuras geométricas.
   c. una tela negra con una figura cosida a mano encima.

2. _____ Las molas tradicionales para los vestuarios son…
   a. de diferentes capas —hasta cinco capas en total.
   b. dos telas con figuras geométricas.
   c. una tela negra con una figura cosida a mano encima.

3. _____ ¿Cuáles son los colores principales de la mola tradicional que muestra Marlina?
   a. negro, morado, rosado y verde
   b. negro, rojo oscuro y anaranjado
   c. rojo oscuro, anaranjado y verde
   d. rojo oscuro, morado y rosado

4. _____ Las nuevas molas comerciales son…
   a. de diferentes capas —hasta cinco capas en total.
   b. dos telas con figuras geométricas.
   c. una tela negra con una figura cosida a mano encima.

5. _____ ¿Cuáles son los colores principales de la mola comercial que muestra Marlina?
   a. negro, morado, rosado y verde
   b. negro, rojo oscuro y anaranjado
   c. rojo oscuro, anaranjado y verde
   d. rojo oscuro, morado y rosado

6. De los tres tipos de molas, ¿cuáles son hechas a mano?

7. ¿Qué tipo de mola *no* muestra Marlina: la antigua, la tradicional, o la comercial?

Después de escuchar

En grupos, hagan un plan para popularizar la mola (u otro producto cultural que conocen) en su país. ¿Qué hacen con la mola? ¿Cómo la van a presentar al público? ¿Cómo la van a explicar?¿Dónde la van a vender? Compartan sus ideas con el resto de la clase para ver quiénes tienen el mejor plan.

MODELO: Vamos a poner la mola en la pared de nuestros dormitorios y así se populariza la mola entre los estudiantes universitarios.

¡Escribamos!

Ser testigo°

witness

En la vida diaria, especialmente al leer y escribir, es importante ser buen observador / buena observadora. Para ayudarte a practicar esta habilidad, en esta actividad vas a ser testigo de un robo imaginario. Vas a observar todos los detalles que puedas sobre «los sospechosos» (*suspects*) y luego usar esa información para formar una descripción detallada para las autoridades.

Antes de escribir

Primero, a escondidas (*secretly*), observa la ropa que llevan tres compañeros de clase. Luego, inventa una descripción de lo que hacía cada uno antes de que empezara la clase (*before class started*). **¡Atención!** Incluye detalles sobre el color de la ropa y los accesorios que llevan.

Nombre	Ropa que lleva	¿Qué hacía? / ¿Qué pasaba en el salón de clase?
Gladys	*los jeans azules; una camiseta verde; un suéter gris; los pendientes verdes…*	*Ponía su mochila debajo del escritorio mientras escribía un text a una amiga…*

A escribir

Imagínate que alguien le robó un diccionario de español del salón de clase antes de clase. Inventa una historia: describe «el lugar del crimen» y los estudiantes que observaste cerca del diccionario. Usando la información de **Antes de escribir,** escribe dos párrafos. En el primer párrafo describe el escenario.

- ¿Qué pasaba en el salón de clase?
- ¿Qué ropa llevaban los sospechosos?

En el segundo párrafo, describe las acciones que viste.

- ¿Qué hizo cada uno de los sospechosos y cuándo?

Termina tu historia con una conclusión. Por ejemplo: **Creo que _____ robó el diccionario porque…**

Después de escribir

Revisa tu ensayo. Luego, intercambia ensayos con un compañero / una compañera para evaluarlos. Lee el ensayo de tu compañero/a y determina si falta información necesaria. Lee de nuevo (*again*) el ensayo con cuidado, subrayando todos los verbos conjugados en el imperfecto y encerrando todos los verbos conjugados en el pretérito. Verifica que…

☐ usa el imperfecto para describir en el pasado.

☐ usa el pretérito para hablar de las acciones que ocurrieron en el pasado.

☐ hay concordancia entre sujetos y verbos.

☐ se puede entender qué ropa se describe en el ensayo.

☐ usa adjetivos descriptivos para describir la ropa.

☐ hay concordancia entre sustantivos y adjetivos (género y número).

Después de revisar el ensayo de tu compañero/a, devuélveselo. Mira tu propio ensayo para ver los cambios que tu compañero/a te recomienda y haz las revisiones necesarias.

 **¡Hablemos!**

Un pase de modelos° *fashion runway*

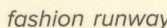

Antes de hablar

En grupos, practiquen como si presentaran (*as if you were presenting*) un desfile de moda. Cada persona debe describir la ropa de otro miembro del grupo. Cambien de papeles (*Change roles*) hasta que todos hayan sido (*have been*) modelos y presentadores.

A hablar

Ahora, escojan a una persona de cada grupo para ser el/la modelo y otra para ser el presentador / la presentadora en un pase de modelos de la clase. El/La modelo debe tener ropa variada y complementos.

Los modelos salen del salón de clase y esperan en el pasillo. Un(a) modelo entra a la vez. Cada presentador(a) presenta el/la modelo de **otro** equipo. Los otros estudiantes deben tomar apuntes.

- ¿Qué describe el presentador / la presentadora?
- ¿Falta algo (*Is something missing*)? ¿Qué?
- ¿Incluye detalles además de nombrar las prendas de ropa?

Después de hablar

De toda la clase, ¿quién fue el/la mejor modelo? ¿el mejor presentador / la mejor presentadora? Defiende tu opinión con detalles de los apuntes que tomaste para la sección de **A hablar.**

Conéctate al cine

Película: *Volver* (drama, España, 2006)
Director: Pedro Almodóvar

Sinopsis:

Sisters Raimunda (Penélope Cruz) and Sole (Lola Dueñas) have a strained relationship, but they are united by grief over their mother's death a few years earlier, and now they must deal with the death of their Aunt Paula. To make matters worse, Raimunda has a corpse in the freezer that she must somehow dispose of. These circumstances result in a film that is an unlikely mix of comedy, mystery, and touching drama. Penélope Cruz was nominated for an Academy Award for her performance as Raimunda.

Escena (54:10–58:54):

Raimunda and her daughter stop by Sole's apartment to use the bathroom. Sole's odd behavior and an unexpected smell make Raimunda suspicious, and she begins snooping around the apartment. She is surprised by what she finds and accuses Sole of taking their late aunt's possessions for her own use.

Antes de ver

La ropa que usamos es algo tan ligado (*bound*) a nuestra identidad que es difícil saber qué hacer con esa ropa cuando ya no nos queda. ¿Qué haces tú con la ropa que ya no necesitas?

A ver

Mira esta escena, luego contesta las siguientes preguntas.

1. El cinturón y los zapatos de la hija, y la bolsa de Raimunda son todos del mismo color. ¿De qué color son? _____

2. ¿Qué le dice Sole a la hija de Raimunda?

   Dice: «Te voy a cortar un poquito _____».

3. Raimunda encuentra ropa de su madre sobre la cama. ¿Qué tipo de ropa dice que es?

   a. una bata   b. una falda   c. un vestido

4. Según Raimunda, ¿qué hay que hacer con la ropa de los muertos?

   Raimunda dijo: «Hay que _____».

5. Cuando Raimunda ve el joyero, ¿qué le pregunta a Sole? _____

6. Según Sole, ¿ella trajo la maleta de la tía a la casa? _____

7. Sole empieza a dar una explicación (*explanation*), pero no termina. ¿Qué dice?

   «Cuando _____.»

Expresiones útiles

lavabo	bathroom
me meo	I've gotta pee!
olor a pedo	the smell of passed gas
peyéndose a culo lleno	passing a huge amount of gas
la bata	bathrobe
maleta/maletilla	suitcase / small suitcase
joyero	jewelry box
¡Qué poca vergüenza!	What little shame (you have)!
¡No pienses mal!	Don't think badly (of me)!
¡No te vayas así!	Don't go like that!

■ For copyright reasons, the feature film clips referenced in **Conéctate al cine** have have not been provided by the publisher. Each of these films is readily available through retailers or online rental sites such as Amazon, iTunes, or Netflix.

Después de ver

Esta escena de la película trata (*treats*) varios temas un poco delicados: el funcionamiento (*functioning*) del cuerpo humano, las pertenencias (*belongings*) de los muertos y los conflictos entre dos hermanas. En tu país, ¿las películas tratan estos temas de la misma manera? Explica tu respuesta y da ejemplos.

VOCABULARIO

Comunicación

¡Claro (que sí)!	Of course!
¡Cómo no!	Sure!
Con mucho gusto.	With pleasure.
Por supuesto.	Of course.
Sí, gracias.	Yes, please.
Disculpa/Disculpe/ Disculpen	Excuse me . . .
Con permiso.	Excuse me.
Perdón/Perdona/ Perdone/Perdonen.	Pardon./ Excuse me.
¿Puedo pasar?	Excuse me. (May I pass by/enter?)
¡Está padre!	That's cool!
Gracias (por + noun/verb).	Thank you (for . . .).
No, gracias.	No, thank you.
No puedo.	I can't.
Lo siento.	I'm sorry.
Pasa/Pase/Pasen.	Come in.; Go ahead.
¡Pura vida!	Cool!
¡Qué bárbaro/bien/ chévere/chido/chulo/ estupendo/fenomenal/ guay/padre!	How cool/awesome!
¡Qué... !	How . . . !
aburrido	How boring!
malo	That's terrible!
pesado	How annoying!
pésimo	That's awful!

¿Qué llevas? — What are you wearing?

el abrigo	coat
el anillo	ring
la bolsa	bag
el bolso	purse
los calcetines	socks
el calzón / los calzones	underwear
la camisa	shirt
la camiseta	t-shirt
el cinturón	belt
el collar	necklace
el conjunto	outfit
la corbata	tie
el desfile de moda	fashion show
el/la diseñador(a)	designer
la falda	skirt
la gorra	(baseball) cap
el gorro	knitted hat
los guantes	gloves
los lentes	(eye) glasses
la marca; de marca	brand; brand-name

el número	number; shoe size
el pantalón	pants
los pantalones cortos	shorts
el paraguas	umbrella
los pendientes	earrings
la pulsera	bracelet
la rebaja	sale
el reloj	watch
la ropa interior	undergarments
las sandalias	sandals
el sombrero	hat
el sujetador	bra
los tacones (altos)	high-heeled shoes
la talla	clothing size
la tendencia	trend
los tenis	tennis shoes
el traje	suit; formal gown
el traje de baño	bathing suit
el vestido	dress
los zapatos	shoes

Cognados: los accesorios, la chaqueta, los jeans, el pijama, el suéter

El cuerpo humano — The human body

la boca	mouth
el brazo	arm
la cabeza	head
la cadera	hip
la cara	face
el codo	elbow
el cuello	neck
el dedo	finger
los dientes	teeth
el hombro	shoulder
los labios	lips
la mano	hand
la nariz	nose
el ojo	eye
la oreja	ear
el pecho	chest; breast
el pelo	hair
el pie	foot
la pierna	leg
la rodilla	knee

¿Cómo te queda? — How does it fit?

ancho/a	loose
apretado/a	tight
corto/a	short
largo/a	long

Los verbos

buscar (q)	to look for
estar (pasado) de moda	to be (un)fashionable
guardar	to save
llevar	to wear; to bring; to carry

lucir (zc)	to wear; to shine
morir (ue, u)	to die
probarse (ue)	to try on
quedarle + *adj./adv.*	to fit
tirar	to throw (away)

¿Adónde te gustaría viajar?

 M0-M1-M2-M3 ↓  Portes / Gates / Puertas 01 to a 3

Sortida / Way out / **Salida**    ↓  **Informació Trànsits** / Transits Information / **Información Tránsit**

 **Recollida d'equipatges** / Baggage claim / **Recogida equipajes**

Viajeros caminan por el aeropuerto en Barcelona, España.

Objetivos

In this chapter you will learn how to:

- say what you would like to do
- use infinitives to express rules
- talk about travel and the weather
- talk about destinations, travel routes, and modes of transportation
- talk about what people do customarily
- talk about travel in the Spanish-speaking world

9

COMUNICACIÓN LARIO UCTURA ATE

¿Te gustaría... ? / ¿Le gustaría... ?

Asking what people would like to do

 **A. A ver: ¿Qué le gustaría hacer algún día?** Mira y escucha, luego empareja la persona con la actividad apropiada.

1. A Charo... ___

4.  A Isabel... ___

2. A Juan... ___

5. A Israel... ___

3. A Mirelle... ___

6. A Daniel... ___

  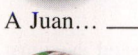  

a. le gustaría estudiar administración de restaurantes.
b. le gustaría participar en el ciclismo.
c. le gustaría tener una casa lejos (*far*) de la ciudad.
d. le gustaría vivir en otro país europeo.
e. le gustaría ver canguros y koalas en su hábitat.
f. le gustaría visitar todos los países del mundo.

To ask someone if he or she would like to do something, use **¿Te/Le gustaría +** *infinitive*?

TÚ	UD.
—¿Te gustaría ir a la playa?	—¿Le gustaría viajar (*travel*) a Costa Rica?
—¡Claro que sí!	—Sí, y me gustaría ir a Panamá también.

B. ¿Cuáles son tus preferencias?

PASO 1. Indica si te gustaría hacer las siguientes actividades.

ME GUSTARÍA	NO ME GUSTARÍA	NO SÉ SI ME GUSTARÍA	
☐	☐	☐	1. pasar las vacaciones de primavera (*spring break*) en la playa
☐	☐	☐	2. viajar por toda Europa
☐	☐	☐	3. trabajar en otro país
☐	☐	☐	4. vivir en Alemania (*Germany*)
☐	☐	☐	5. viajar por toda Sudamérica
☐	☐	☐	6. ver las pirámides en Egipto
☐	☐	☐	7. ir al Caribe
☐	☐	☐	8. mudarme (*move*) a Costa Rica
☐	☐	☐	9. viajar por el mundo en un crucero (*cruise ship*)
☐	☐	☐	10. ver el Tour de France

(*Continues*)

PASO 2.   Pon tus preferencias en orden de más (1) a menos (5).

a. _____ Me gustaría mudarme a otro país para estudiar.
b. _____ Me gustaría mudarme a otro país para vivir y trabajar.
c. _____ Me gustaría viajar a un destino y pasar dos o tres semanas allí.
d. _____ Me gustaría viajar para un acontecimiento (*event*) especial (como una boda, una feria, etcétera).
e. _____ Me gustaría viajar a muchos lugares diferentes durante las vacaciones.

PASO 3.   Ahora pregúntale a tu compañero/a si le gustaría hacer las actividades del video (u otras actividades) y por qué sí (o por qué no). Puedes usar las opciones de los **Pasos 1** y **2** u otras actividades para crear las preguntas.

MODELO: E1: ¿Te gustaría trabajar en el extranjero?
E2: ¡Sí, claro! (No, creo que no.)
E1: ¿Por qué? (¿Por qué no?)
E2: Porque me gusta aprender sobre otras culturas. (Porque no me gusta viajar en avión.)

Favor de no fumar.

Expressing rules with infinitives

The infinitive can be used to express rules and regulations that are often posted as signs. You may see them on buses, trains and taxis and in streets, parks and restaurants as you travel.

Empujar.	Push.
Jalar.	Pull.
No beber y conducir.	Don't drink and drive.
No dar de comer.	Don't feed (the animals).
No doblar. / No girar.	Do not turn.
No entrar. / No pasar.	Do not enter.
No estacionar.	No parking.
No fumar.	No smoking.
No pisar.	Stay off. (*Lit.*, Do not step on.)
No tirar basura.	No littering. (*Lit.*, Do not throw trash.)

A. No...   Empareja la regla (*rule*) con la señal más apropiada

1. _____ No estacionar.
2. _____ No pisar el césped (*grass*).
3. _____ No beber y conducir.
4. _____ No entrar.
5. _____ No dar de comer.
6. _____ No tirar basura.
7. _____ No doblar.
8. _____ No fumar.

a.    d.   g.

b.   e.    h.

c.    f.

B. Las reglas de la universidad   En grupos, usen el infinitivo para inventar cinco reglas para la universidad donde estudian o para otro lugar de la comunidad.

MODELO: No andar en bicicleta en la plaza central de la universidad.

VOCABULARIO

Los mejores lugares turísticos

Travel, tourism, and weather

En el pico de la montaña Huayna Potosí siempre hay nieve.

✏️ Blog de viajes: Aventuras en La Paz
La Paz, Bolivia

Si viajas a La Paz en **avión**, prepárate para un **viaje** largo —tuvimos que **hacer escala** (cambiar a otro avión) en los **aeropuertos** de Miami y Lima. Al llegar, encontramos muchas oportunidades para el **turismo de aventura**. Por ejemplo, hicimos **kayak** en los cañones y bajamos en **bicicleta de montaña** por el Camino de la Muerte —la carretera más peligrosa (*dangerous*) del mundo. ¡Fue muy divertido! Como nos gusta pasar tiempo en las **montañas**, también contratamos a (*hired*) un **guía** para ir a la cumbre (*peak*) de Chacaltaya (5.421msnm*) y para **escalar** las paredes (*walls*) de la montaña Huayna Potosí. ¡Si lo quieres hacer, lleva ropa de abrigo (*warm clothing*) porque **nieva** durante todo el año en las montañas. Me encantó ver todo cubierto (*covered*) en blanco, pero por supuesto **hace frío** en **la nieve**! Después de tanta (*so much*) aventura, comimos bien y vimos una presentación de baile **folclórico** en una peña† tradicional. Compré unos **recuerdos** muy bonitos —**artesanías** como aguayos (tejidos [*textiles*] coloridos), gorros y otros productos hechos de lana (*wool*) de alpaca.

A Mario le gusta escalar.

Paisaje con volcán

✏️ Blog de viajes: ¡Costa Rica es un paraíso!
Volcán Arenal, Costa Rica

Fui a Costa Rica con unos amigos durante las vacaciones de primavera. ¡Si te interesa el **ecoturismo**, tienes que ir! En Costa Rica, hay alta humedad (*humidity*) en los **bosques tropicales** (*rain forests*) y a veces **llueve** mucho, pero por suerte (*luckily*) llegamos durante la estación seca (*dry*) y no **llovió**. La **naturaleza** —los volcanes, plantas y animales exóticos— crea un **paisaje** increíble. En la reserva de Monteverde vimos perezosos (*sloths*), mariposas (*butterflies*), quetzales‡ y árboles grandísimos. Pero lo mejor del viaje fue **bajar en tirolina** en el parque nacional Volcán Arenal. ¡Qué divertido volar por el follaje (*canopy*) de los árboles! Una cosa más: Puede ser difícil navegar las carreteras de Costa Rica; por eso, recomiendo hacer un **recorrido** —un viaje en autobús o en auto, planeado por un guía turístico con un chofer local. Nosotros lo hicimos en un autobús. Como todos los ticos (costarricenses), nuestro chofer era muy amable y sabía mucho sobre el país y las **atracciones** más interesantes.

Bajar en tirolina es muy divertido.

En las playas, hay palmas.

✏️ Blog de viajes: Las hermosas playas dominicanas
Puerto Plata, República Dominicana

Acabo de (*I just*) pasar unas vacaciones relajadas en la República Dominicana—no hay mejor lugar que las playas de Puerto Plata. En los **hoteles** de lujo (*luxury*) se ofrece el mejor **servicio** —¡hay bares y meseros en la playa y la piscina a todas horas! Si te gusta tomar el **sol** (*sun*) como a mí, ¡ten cuidado! **Hace calor** y **hace mucho sol** así que es importante beber agua y llevar **bloqueador solar**. Se me olvidó ponérmelo un día y me quedé con una **quemadura de sol** terrible. ¡Estaba completamente roja! Puerto Plata también es un lugar perfecto para **hacer snorkel** o **bucear** para ver los bonitos peces tropicales y tortugas marinas (*sea turtles*). Y si no te gusta mucho la playa, puedes **visitar** las **cataratas** Damajaqua. Allí puedes saltar (*jump*) y deslizarte (*slide*) por una serie de veintisiete caídas (*falls*) de agua.

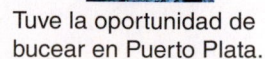

Tuve la oportunidad de bucear en Puerto Plata.

(Continues)

---

*Metros sobre el nivel del mar = *Meters above sea level*
†Un lugar en donde se escucha música tradicional en vivo
‡Una especie de pájaro que se encuentra en Centroamérica

La catedral se Sevilla es muy grande.

Blog de viajes: De viaje en España
Sevilla, España

Si quieres hacer una **visita** al **extranjero** (otro país), agarra (*grab*) tu **pasaporte** y ve a Sevilla, una ciudad encantadora (*enchanting*). No está muy **lejos** (una larga distancia) de Madrid, y puedes tomar el **tren** conocido como el AVE (Alta Velocidad Española). En el otoño, **hace buen tiempo** —no **hace viento,** pero sí hay brisas suaves. Si te gusta caminar, puedes **dar un paseo** para explorar los callejones (calles pequeñas) del famoso Barrio de Santa Cruz. Descansa (*rest*) un rato en una bodeguita y toma un poco de sangría y algunas tapas riquísimas. Y si te interesa la historia, debes visitar el Alcázar, un palacio árabe impresionante. No debes **perderte** (*miss*) la catedral —la tercera más grande del mundo— y la Giralda, una torre (*tower*) **cerca** de la catedral con vistas preciosas de la ciudad. ¡Compra un **boleto** de avión, **haz las maletas** y vete para Sevilla ahora!

Hice las maletas un día antes de viajar.

A. De vacaciones

PASO 1. Para cada viaje en **Vocabulario,** organiza las palabras **en negrita** en tres categorías: **el clima, los preparativos y el transporte** y **las atracciones.** Puedes crear otra(s) columna(s) y nombrarla(s) apropiadamente.

	EL CLIMA	LOS PREPARATIVOS Y EL TRANSPORTE	LAS ATRACCIONES
Bolivia			
Costa Rica			
República Dominicana			
España			

Mira la tabla que creaste. Según esa información, ¿qué vacaciones prefieres?

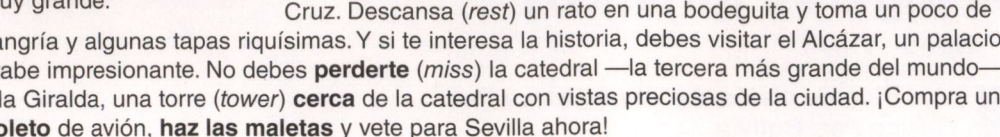

PASO 2. Formen grupos según el viaje que escogieron en el **Paso 1**. ¿Por qué les interesa viajar a ese lugar? (¿Es más por el clima, por los preparativos y el transporte, por las atracciones o por otra razón?) Hagan una lista de sus razones y compártanla con la clase.

B. Viajes a lugares turísticos

Empareja el lugar turístico con la actividad más apropiada.

1. ____ Un hotel de lujo en Cancún o Puerto Vallarta con vista al mar
2. ____ Madrid, Barcelona u otra ciudad grande
3. ____ El parque nacional Torres del Paine en Patagonia, Chile
4. ____ La reserva natural Tambopata en la Amazonia del Perú
5. ____ El mercado de Chichicastenango, Guatemala, con sus muchos productos hechos a mano
6. ____ San Carlos de Bariloche, Argentina, u otro lugar frío con montañas

a. comprar artesanías
b. acampar en la naturaleza
c. aprender sobre la flora y fauna de la selva (*jungle*)
d. esquiar
e. ir a la playa
f. tomar taxi para visitar museos famosos

C. El sitio ideal

En parejas, pregúntense adónde van (por ejemplo, a la playa, a las montañas, al bosque tropical) para hacer las siguientes actividades.

bajar en tirolina	escalar	hacer snorkel / bucear
disfrutar del calor	esquiar	participar en el ecoturismo
disfrutar del paisaje tropical	hacer bicicleta de montaña	tomar el sol

En español...

La palabra **autobús** se entiende por todas partes, pero en muchos lugares cada tipo de autobús tiene su propio término. Aquí tienes algunos ejemplos.

camión	México (también se usa para decir truck)
colectivo	Argentina
guagua	Caribe, Islas Canarias
micro	varios países
pesero	México (*small city bus*)

Palabras de este tipo son fáciles de aprender si vas de viaje y ¡te van a ayudar mucho a comunicarte!

D. A ver: ¿Adónde les gustaría viajar?

PASO 1. Mira y escucha, luego contesta las preguntas.

1. _____ A Olman le gustaría viajar a…
   a. Alemania   b. Chile   c. Italia   d. Nicaragua

2. _____ A Mariana le gustaría viajar a los países…
   a. balcánicos   b. centroamericanos   c. del Cono Sur   d. medio orientales (*Middle Eastern*) y europeos

3. _____ A Henry le gustaría viajar a…
   a. África   b. Alemania   c. Antártida   d. Asia

4. _____ A Aline le gustaría viajar a…
   a. África o el Medio Oriente (*Middle East*)   b. Sudamérica   c. Australia y Nueva Zelanda   d. España

5. _____ A Yenaro le gustaría viajar a…
   a. Asia   b. España   c. Europa   d. Inglaterra

6. _____ A Selene le gustaría viajar a…
   a. Asia   b. España   c. Europa   d. Inglaterra

PASO 2. Mira y escucha otra vez, luego contesta las preguntas.

1. ¿A quiénes les gustaría viajar a Europa?
2. ¿A quiénes les gustaría viajar a África?
3. ¿A quién le gustaría ir de safari?
4. ¿A quién le gustaría viajar a Italia?
5. ¿A quién le gustaría conocer culturas diferentes?
6. ¿A quién le gustaría viajar a España?

E. ¿Adónde van Uds.?

PASO 1. Circula por el salón de clase para preguntarles a tus compañeros adónde les gustaría viajar y qué les gustaría hacer allí.

MODELO: E1: ¿Adónde te gustaría viajar?
E2: Me gustaría viajar a Canadá y esquiar en las Montañas Rocosas canadienses. ¿Y a ti?
E1: Me gustaría viajar a Argentina. Allí me gustaría visitar las cataratas del Iguazú.

PASO 2. Después de hablar con los compañeros, organícense según las regiones geográficas del mundo adonde les gustaría viajar. ¿Qué región representa cada grupo? ¿Por qué quieren ir a ese lugar? Hagan un informe (*report*) para decir adónde quieren ir los miembros del grupo y por qué. ¿Cuál es la región más popular? ¿el país más popular? ¿la actividad más popular? ¿Cuál es el grupo con los planes más aventureros? ¿más relajantes? ¿más caros (*expensive*)? ¿más baratos (*cheap*)?

MODELO: A todos nosotros nos gustaría ir a África porque queremos ir de safari. A Lisa y a James les gustaría visitar Sudáfrica para ver pingüinos, a Karen le gustaría ir a Egipto para caminar por las pirámides y a mí me gustaría ir a Kenia para ver leones y jirafas. El viaje más popular en nuestro grupo es visitar Sudáfrica para ver pingüinos.

F. El mejor transporte En parejas, decidan los criterios para usar cada modo de transporte. Luego, comparen con otra pareja. ¿Tienen los mismos criterios?

MODELO: Viajas en avión si…
- es un viaje largo
- el viaje cruza el mar
- tienes suficiente dinero (porque es caro viajar en avión)
- tienes un modo de transporte al llegar (*upon arrival*)

1. Viajas en taxi si…
2. Viajas en tren si…
3. Viajas en autobús si…
4. Viajas en bicicleta si…
5. Viajas a pie (*on foot*) si…
6. Viajas en coche alquilado (*rented*) si…

Vocabulario

The verb **hacer** is used to ask about the weather in Spanish.

¿Qué tiempo hace? *What's the weather like?*

To answer, use the verb form **hace.**

 **Hace (muy) buen tiempo.** The weather's (very) good.

 **Hace (muy) mal tiempo.** The weather's (very) bad.

 **Hace (mucho) calor.** It's (very) hot.

 **Hace (mucho) frío.** It's (very) cold.

 **Hace (mucho) sol.** It's (very) sunny.

 **Hace (mucho) viento.** It's (very) windy.

You can use the verb **estar** for some answers.

Está despejado. The skies are clear.
Está (muy) nublado. It's (very) cloudy.

To talk about precipitation, use the verb **llover (o → ue)** (*to rain*) or **nevar (e → ie)** (*to snow*).

 **Llueve. / Está lloviendo.** It's raining.

 **Nieva. / Está nevando.** It's snowing.

G. ¿Qué tiempo hace? Para cada situación que escuchas, indica el tiempo más típico donde vives.

■ The audio files for in-text listening activities are available in the eBook, within Connect Plus activities, and on the Online Learning Center.

1. ☑ Hace calor. ☐ Hace frío. ☐ Llueve.
2. ☐ Hace calor. ☑ Hace frío. ☐ Llueve.
3. ☑ Hace buen tiempo. ☐ Hace mal tiempo. ☐ Nieva.
4. ☐ Hace calor. ☑ Hace viento. ☐ Nieva.– *otoño*
5. ☐ Hace calor. ☑ Hace frío. ☑ Llueve.
6. ☑ Hace calor. ☑ Hace frío. ☑ Hace viento.
7. ☐ Hace calor. ☐ Hace frío. ☑ Llueve.

H. ¿Qué estación es? ¿Qué tiempo hace? Mira las siguientes fotos y di lo más que puedas (*as much as you can*) sobre cada una. ¿Qué estación es? ¿Qué tiempo hace? ¿Qué ropa debes llevar cuando hace este tiempo? ¿Cuáles son algunas actividades que puedes hacer en esta estación? ¿Qué te gusta hacer cuando hace este tiempo?

MODELO:

Hace viento. Tal vez es el otoño, pero puede hacer viento en todas las estaciones. Cuando hace viento y también frío, es necesario llevar una chaqueta. No debes usar un paraguas (*umbrella*) ni (*nor*) un sombrero cuando hace viento. Es divertido volar una cometa (*kite*) en el parque o en la playa cuando hace viento. A mucha gente le gusta navegar en bote de vela (*sailboat*). A mí me gusta leer un libro.

1.

2.

3.

4.

 I. ¿Qué tiempo hace en el destino ideal? En grupos, escojan uno de los siguientes sitios. Deben nombrar una ciudad o lugar en particular y decidir qué tiempo hace en el viaje al destino ideal. Luego, decidan qué actividades quieren hacer allí y qué deben empacar para el viaje.

1. una ciudad grande
2. las montañas
3. la playa
4. un pueblo pequeño sin electricidad

⟳ Reciclaje

The prepositions *de* and *a*

El aeropuerto internacional de la Ciudad de México, conocido oficialmente como el Aeropuerto Internacional Benito Juárez, ofrece vuelos a más de cien destinos en todo el mundo y es el aeropuerto más grande de Latinoamérica. ¿Cuánto crees que duran los vuelos de México a otras ciudades? Empareja cada ciudad con la duración del vuelo, describiendo el vuelo con las preposiciones **de** y **a.** Usa los mapas al final del libro si necesitas ayuda.

Bogotá   Guatemala   Madrid   Nueva York   Santiago   Guadalajara

Duración del vuelo

1. 1 hora 20 minutos
2. 2 horas
3. 4 horas 30 minutos
4. 5 horas
5. 8 horas 25 minutos
6. 10 horas 50 minutos

¿De México a qué otra ciudad?

_____

De México a Bogotá
_____

_____

_____

_____

■ Answers to this activity are in Appendix 2 at the back of your book.

9.1   Salimos para Machu Picchu

The prepositions *por* and *para*

Para empezar...

¿Te gustaría ir al Perú? Las ciudades de Lima y Cusco tienen mucho que ofrecer, pero la atracción turística número uno del país es la zona arqueológica de Machu Picchu. Cada día visitan las ruinas 1.800 personas, o casi 700.000 por año. Las ruinas quedan a cuatro horas de Cusco. Usando el mapa y tu sentido (*sense*) común, escoge la respuesta apropiada para cada oración. Si no estás seguro/a, ¡adivina (*guess*)!

En las ruinas de Machu Picchu

1. _____ **Para** ir a Machu Picchu, primero tienes que llegar a…
   a. Bogotá
   b. Cusco
2. _____ De allí a Machu Picchu, puedes ir…
   a. **por** avión
   b. **por** tren
3. _____ Hay salidas **para** Machu Picchu…
   a. cuatro veces al día
   b. veinte veces al día
4. _____ Cuando vas, pasas…
   a. **por** Quito
   b. **por** el Valle Sagrado (*Sacred Valley*)
5. _____ Si quieres prepararte **para** tu viaje, es recomendable leer un libro como…
   a. *La vida de los incas*
   b. *La vida de los mayas*
6. _____ **Para** evitar (*avoid*) los grandes grupos de turistas, es aconsejable (*advisable*) ya estar en la zona de las ruinas…
   a. **para** las ocho
   b. **para** la una
7. _____ Si quieres comprar recuerdos **para** tus amigos o **para** tu familia, es más barato hacerlo…
   a. en Cusco
   b. en Machu Picchu
8. _____ Algunos piensan que el futuro de Machu Picchu está en peligro (*danger*)…
   a. **por** los animales que llegan de noche
   b. **por** la gran cantidad de turistas que llegan todos los días

Actividades analíticas

1 The core meaning of the preposition **para** is *aiming toward*. You may aim toward a place, a time (as in a deadline), or an outcome that you desire, or your action may be intended for, or benefiting, someone or something.

■ Answers to this activity are in Appendix 2 at the back of your book.

PARA	IDEA CENTRAL: *AIMING TOWARD*
A PLACE	Mañana salimos **para** España. *Tomorrow we're departing for (toward) Spain.*
A DEADLINE	Tenemos que estar en el aeropuerto **para** las seis. *We have to be at the airport by 6:00.*
A DESIRED OUTCOME **(with infinitive verb)**	Vamos a España **para** ver a mi tía. *We are going to Spain (in order) to see my aunt.*
A PERSON OR THING **THAT BENEFITS**	¡Compré este regalo **para** ti! *I bought this present for you (intended for you)!* Esta tarea es **para** mi clase de química. *This homework is for (intended for) my chemistry class.*

2 Find one example of each of these uses of **para** in the numbered items of **Para empezar** and write each example beside its corresponding **para** usage listed below. In some cases, more than one example is available.

Aiming toward . . .

a. a place   _____
b. a time deadline   _____
c. a desired outcome   _____
d. a person/thing that will benefit _____

3 The core meaning of the preposition **por** is *passing through*. You may pass through a place or a time period, or **por** may indicate the means that you used ("passed through") in order to achieve an end. This core meaning of *passing through* may also be extended to include what *caused* you to undergo ("pass through") some experience.

(Continues)

POR	IDEA CENTRAL: *PASSING THROUGH*
A PLACE	Cuando vamos a España tenemos que pasar **por** Francia. *When we go to Spain we have to pass through France.* El año pasado viajamos **por** todo Chile. *We traveled throughout all of Chile last year.*
A TIME PERIOD	Siempre estudio **por** la noche. *I always study at night (during the night).*
A MEANS (noun) TO DO SOMETHING	Llegué **por** avión. *I arrived by plane.* Vamos a hablar **por** teléfono. *We're going to speak by phone.*
A CAUSE	**Por** el calor, me siento muy cansado. *Because of the heat, I feel very tired.* Decidí vivir en Honduras **por** las playas. *I decided to live in Honduras because of the beaches.*

Autoprueba

Now that you've read about the different uses of **para** and **por,** see if you can identify which would be used in each of the following sentences. Notice how you cannot consistently substitute a particular Spanish word for a particular English word, but rather you have to think about the "aiming toward" versus "passing through" meaning of each sentence.

1. On Saturday we leave <u>for</u> Panama.
2. We picked Panama <u>because</u> of its interesting history.
3. Tomorrow I'm staying home <u>to</u> pack.
4. <u>Throughout</u> the morning I'll be getting ready, but you can reach me <u>by</u> phone.
5. I don't need to go to the bank <u>to</u> change currency, because they use both the Panamanian balboa and the U.S. dollar there.
6. We're going to the airport <u>by</u> bus, so I have to be ready <u>by</u> 9 o'clock.
7. Don't worry, I'll buy a souvenir <u>for</u> you!

Respuestas: 1. para; **2.** por; **3.** para; **4.** por, por; **5.** para; **6.** por, para; **7.** para

■ For more on the uses of **por** and **para,** see **Para saber más 9.1** at the back of your book.

4 Now find one example of each of these uses of **por** in the numbered items of **Para empezar** and write each example beside its corresponding **por** usage listed below.

Passing through . . .

a. a place   _____
b. a time period   _____
c. a means to an end   _____
d. What caused you to have an experience   _____

En español...

Although both **para** or **por** can be translated as *for,* there are many additional meanings and English equivalents. Rather than learning the meanings by translation, focus on the simple core meaning of each word. Visualizing this meaning may help. Since **para** can be thought of as *aiming towards,* think of an arrow pointing at the object of **para.**

Vamos al hotel **para** dormir.
We're going to the hotel (in order) to sleep.

No me gusta estudiar **para** los exámenes.
I don't like to study for exams.

Since **por,** on the other hand, often can be thought of as *passing through,* think of the arrow as passing through the object of **por.**

Vamos al hotel **por autobús**.
We're going to the hotel by (means of) bus.

No me gusta estudiar **por la mañana**.
I don't like to study in/during the morning.

Actividades prácticas

A. La agenda

PASO 1. Mira la agenda de Susana, una estudiante universitaria. Luego, lee las oraciones y decide cuáles son ciertas y cuáles son falsas.

	lunes	martes	miércoles	jueves	viernes
9:00	sociología	ciencias políticas	sociología: examen	ciencias políticas	
10:00					
11:00	economía	historia	economía	historia	
12:00					
13:00					13:15 salir al aeropuerto
14:00		trabajo		trabajo	
15:00	hacer ejercicio		hacer ejercicio		15:30 vuelo
16:00			tarea: ciencias políticas		
17:00		tarea: historia			

	CIERTO	FALSO
1. Asiste a clase todos los días por la mañana.	☐	☐
2. Trabaja el martes y jueves por la tarde.	☐	☐
3. El martes, tiene que entregar la tarea de historia para las diez.	☐	☐
4. Probablemente va a revisar el libro de sociología el martes por la noche.	☐	☐
5. Para el jueves tiene que estar lista para el examen de sociología.	☐	☐
6. Para el miércoles a las diez, tiene que entregar la tarea de ciencias políticas.	☐	☐
7. El viernes, tiene que hacer la maleta para las nueve.	☐	☐
8. El viernes por la tarde, va a salir de la ciudad.	☐	☐
9. Tiene que salir para el aeropuerto para la una y cuarto.	☐	☐
10. Tiene que estar en el aeropuerto para las tres cuarenta y cinco.	☐	☐

PASO 2. En general, ¿qué hace Susana por la mañana? ¿Y qué hace por la tarde? ¿Crees que ella tiene una vida equilibrada (*balanced*)?

La lista de salidas en el Aeropuerto de Madrid-Barajas

B. Itinerarios

PASO 1. En los viajes largos, es común hacer escala en otra ciudad. Empareja cada itinerario con la mejor descripción. Usa los mapas al final del libro si necesitas ayuda.

ITINERARIO	DESCRIPCIÓN
1. _f_ París → Madrid → Lisboa	a. Van para Uruguay.
2. _d_ Londres → París → Madrid	b. Van para Puerto Rico.
3. _e_ Nueva York → Montreal → La Habana	c. Van por Colombia.
4. _c_ Cartagena → Medellín → Bogotá → Cali	d. Van para España.
5. _b_ Dallas → Miami → San Juan	e. Van por Canadá.
6. _a_ Bogotá → Caracas → Buenos Aires → Montevideo	f. Van por España.

PASO 2. Ahora completa la descripción de cada itinerario con **por** o **para**.

ITINERARIO	DESCRIPCIÓN
1. Oaxaca → México, D.F. → Durango → El Paso	Van _para_ los Estados Unidos.
2. Guatemala → San Salvador → Tegucigalpa → Managua	Van _por_ Centroamérica.
3. Los Ángeles → México, D.F. → Managua	Van _por_ Centroamérica.
4. Caracas → Miami → Lisboa	Van _por_ los Estados Unidos.
5. Lima → San Salvador → Santo Domingo	Van _por_ Centroamérica.

C. Los viajes

PASO 1. En parejas, háganse las preguntas usando **por** o **para** y las palabras de la lista para completar cada oración.

> **MODELO:** E1: ¿Se quedan muchos estudiantes en albergues (*hostels*)? (los precios bajos)
> E2: Sí, muchos estudiantes se quedan en albergues por los precios bajos.

avión	mi madre	tomar el sol
comprar un boleto	la mañana	ver el Canal
la lluvia	las oportunidades de hacer escalada	

1. ¿Cómo se llega a Argentina?
2. ¿Por qué te gusta pasar tiempo en las montañas?
3. ¿Para qué tienes dinero?
4. ¿Por qué cancelaron el vuelo?
5. ¿Compras recuerdos cuando estás de viaje?
6. ¿Cuándo tienes clases?
7. ¿Por qué quieres ir a Panamá?
8. ¿Por qué vas a la playa?

PASO 2. Ahora, indiquen por qué se usa **por** o **para** en cada circunstancia. Compartan sus respuestas con el resto de la clase. ¿Tienen todos las mismas respuestas?

D. Tu agenda ¿Cuáles son las fechas límites (*deadlines*) que tienes en las próximas (*upcoming*) semanas? Escribe una lista, usando la agenda de Susana en la **Actividad A** como modelo. En parejas, compárenlas y decidan entre los dos quién tiene el horario más difícil.

> **MODELO:** Para mañana, tengo que estar listo para el examen de historia. Para el próximo lunes, tengo que terminar un proyecto para mi clase de inglés.

E. Tu itinerario Usando el mapa y siguiendo el ejemplo de la **Actividad C,** escribe un itinerario de vuelos de múltiples <u>ciudades</u> y dáselo a un compañero / una compañera. Tu compañero/a va a describir tu viaje en términos (*terms*) de <u>países</u> usando **por** y **para**.

MODELO: E1: Los Ángeles a México, y de México a Managua.

E2: ¡Vas para Nicaragua y vas por México!

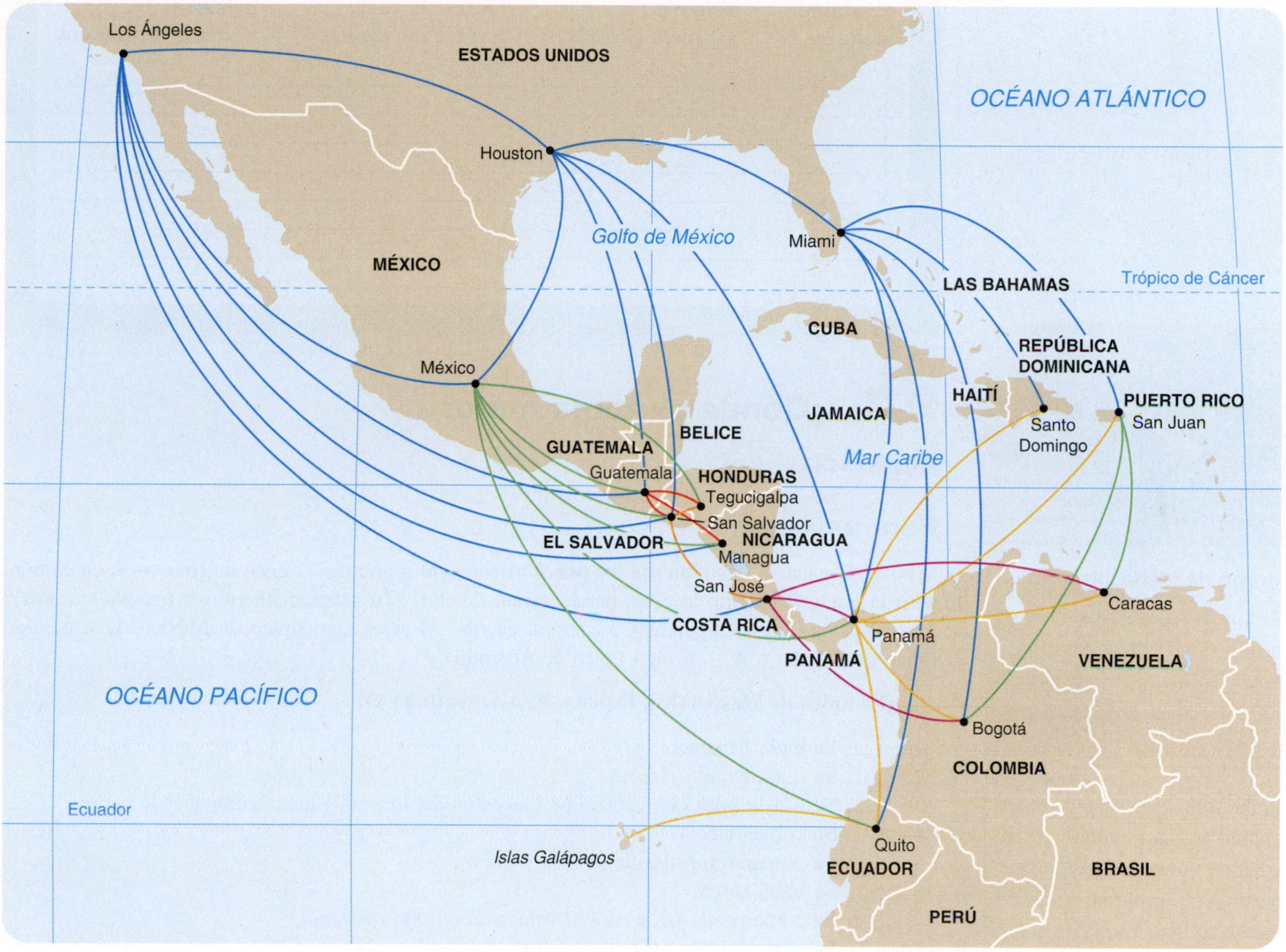

⟳ Reciclaje

Reflexive verbs

Cuando pasas toda la noche viajando por autobús o avión, ¿qué haces primero cuando llegas a tu destino? Pon las siguientes actividades en orden de prioridad. **¡Atención!** Hay que conjugar cada verbo en la forma **yo** del tiempo presente.

acostarse   bañarse   lavarse la cara   peinarse
afeitarse   estirarse (*stretch*)   lavarse los dientes   quitarse los zapatos

1. _____
2. _____
3. _____
4. _____
5. _____
6. _____
7. _____
8. _____

Un grupo de mariachis, México

■ Answers to these activities are in Appendix 2 at the back of your book.

Autoprueba

In the following sentences about Peru, determine whether the verb should be singular or plural, and then conjugate each one accordingly.

En el Perú…

1. se _____ (comer) papas a la huancaína, un plato de papas, crema y huevos.
2. también se _____ (comer) ají de gallina, un plato picante de pollo.
3. se _____ (tomar) pisco, una bebida alcohólica hecha de uvas.
4. se _____ (escuchar) música andina.
5. se _____ (masticar [*to chew*]) hojas de coca para aliviar el soroche (*altitude sickness*).

Respuestas: 1. comen; **2.** come; **3.** toma; **4.** escucha; **5.** mastican

9.2   ¿Dónde se toma mate?

Impersonal *se*

Para empezar…

México, España y Argentina son los países hispanos más grandes. Tienen muchas cosas en común, pero la gente y cultura de estos países varían mucho. ¿Tú sabes distinguirlos (*tell them apart*)? Para cada una de las siguientes oraciones, escribe **M** si es algo típico de México, **E** si es algo típico de España o **A** si es algo típico de Argentina.

¿Es típico de México (M), España (E) o Argentina (A)?

1. _____ **Se** baila flamenco.
2. _____ **Se** toma tequila.
3. _____ **Se** usa la salsa chimichurri (*a sauce similar to pesto*) para acompañar la carne.
4. _____ **Se** comen tacos.
5. _____ **Se** preparan tortillas de patatas y huevo.
6. _____ **Se** baila tango.
7. _____ **Se** come paella (*rice cooked with seafood and sausage*).
8. _____ **Se** toma sangría (*wine mixed with fruit and juice*).
9. _____ **Se** hacen tortillas de maíz.
10. _____ **Se** come más carne que en ningún otro país del mundo.
11. _____ **Se** escucha música mariachi.
12. _____ **Se** toma mate (*a hot herbal drink*).

Actividades analíticas

1 You have seen **se** used for reflexive verbs (see **Estructura 5.2**), but the sentences in **Para empezar** show a different use of **se**, often referred to as *impersonal se* (**el se impersonal**). This usage means that the action indicated is something that people do in general.

En España **se** baila flamenco.   *People dance flamenco in Spain.*

Impersonal **se** is often used to avoid referring to a specific person or to avoid saying that everyone does the action.

Aquí **se** habla español.   *Spanish is spoken here.*

This is often used as a sign in stores or other businesses, with the meaning that there are Spanish speakers at that location, without specifying who or how many.

2 In most sentences with impersonal **se,** the verb is in the third-person singular (**él/ella/Ud.**) form, but sometimes it is in the third-person plural (**ellos/ellas/Uds.**) form. Which three sentences in **Para empezar** use this plural form? _____, _____, _____

Why do you think the verb is plural in these sentences but not in the others? _____

Las cosas típicas de un país muchas veces vienen de una sola región del país. Por ejemplo, **el flamenco** viene de Andalucía en el sur de España, **el mariachi** es de Jalisco en el oeste de México y **el tango** tiene su origen en Buenos Aires, la capital de Argentina. ¿Hay cosas que se consideran típicas de tu país, pero que en realidad son de una región en particular?

Actividades prácticas

A. Tres países chicos

En **Para empezar,** aprendiste información sobre tres países muy grandes. Aquí vas a leer algo sobre tres países chicos: Nicaragua, Paraguay y Uruguay. Lee la descripción de cada país y luego escribe **N** para Nicaragua, **P** para Paraguay o **U** para Uruguay.

Raul, de Uruguay, muestra su mate.

- **Nicaragua** es un país centroamericano que tiene volcanes, lagos y playas. Todavía (*Still*) hay mucha influencia de las antiguas civilizaciones mesoamericanas (las culturas indígenas de la región).
- **Paraguay** tiene fronteras con Brasil, Argentina y Bolivia pero no tiene costa. Hay mucha influencia indígena.
- **Uruguay** está ubicado entre Brasil y Argentina. Tuvo mucha inmigración europea a principios (*beginning*) del siglo (*century*) XX, sobre todo de Italia.

¿Se refiere a Nicaragua (N), Paraguay (P) o Uruguay (U)?

1. _____ En los volcanes, se puede esquiar sobre arena (*sand*).
2. _____ Se comen muchos tipos de pasta y de pizza.
3. _____ Se hablan español y guaraní (una lengua indígena de Sudamérica).
4. _____ En la costa del Caribe, se habla inglés criollo (*creole*).
5. _____ Se hace «sopa paraguaya», pero no es una sopa normal. Es sólida, y se hace con huevos, queso y harina de maíz.
6. _____ Se toma «grappamiel», un licor con miel (*honey*) que trajeron los inmigrantes europeos.
7. _____ En las playas del Pacífico, se hace muchísimo surf.
8. _____ Se come «gallo pinto», un plato de arroz y frijoles que se come con tortillas de maíz.
9. _____ No hay mar y no hay mucho turismo, pero sí se hace «turismo rural». Los turistas se quedan en estancias (*ranches*) y disfrutan del campo y de la naturaleza.
10. _____ Se toma mate.

¿Por qué?

You have seen that **se** is sometimes used to indicate a reflexive verb and sometimes used to indicate an impersonal action (i.e., performed by people in general).

Reflexive verb:

Marta **se** despierta a las siete.   *Marta wakes up at 7:00*

Impersonal:

Se habla portugués en Brasil.   *Portuguese is spoken in Brazil.*

Why is this same pronoun used for such different functions? The answer is that **se** is a kind of "catch-all" pronoun, used in a variety of situations where no other pronoun can do the job. If Spanish did not have **se,** it would have to have a much larger collection of pronouns, each specialized for a very particular function. Spanish avoids this situation by allowing the single pronoun **se** to perform many functions in the language.

B. El turismo sostenible Cuando viajas, ¿piensas en los efectos de tu viaje en el medio ambiente (*environment*) y en la gente del lugar? El «turismo sostenible (*sustainable*)» tiene el propósito de evitar los efectos negativos y de crear así una alternativa al turismo tradicional.

PASO 1. Para cada oración, cambia el verbo a la forma correcta del **se** impersonal.

1. **aprender:** Se aprende mucho sobre la vida de la gente del lugar.
2. **usar:** _____ muchísimos recursos (*resources*) naturales, como el agua y la electricidad.
3. **gastar** (*to spend*)**:** _____ dinero en pequeñas empresas (*enterprises*) locales.
4. **aprender:** _____ muy poco sobre la vida de la gente del lugar.
5. **hacer:** No _____ nada a beneficio de (*to benefit*) la gente del lugar.
6. **minimizar:** _____ el uso de recursos naturales.
7. **donar:** _____ cosas que la gente de la comunidad necesita.
8. **gastar:** _____ mucho dinero en los grandes hoteles y otros negocios grandes.

Se ven papagayos y otros pájaros en los bosques tropicales.

PASO 2. En parejas, decidan si cada oración del **Paso 1** tiene que ver con (*has to do with*) el turismo tradicional o el turismo sostenible. Escriban el número de la oración en la posición correcta en la tabla según la categoría.

CATEGORÍA	EL TURISMO TRADICIONAL	EL TURISMO SOSTENIBLE
el bienestar (*well-being*) **de la gente del lugar**	_____	_____
el dinero	_____	_____
la educación	_____	_____
los recursos naturales	_____	_____

PASO 3. En parejas, contesten las preguntas.

1. ¿Cómo se puede gastar dinero en pequeñas empresas locales?
2. ¿Cómo se puede aprender algo sobre la vida de la gente del lugar?
3. ¿Cómo se puede minimizar el uso de recursos naturales?
4. ¿Cómo se puede saber qué necesita la gente del lugar?

C. Tu ciudad o tu región

PASO 1. En parejas, creen tres oraciones ciertas y una falsa para explicarle a un turista extranjero lo que se hace en la ciudad o región de Uds. Usen la **Actividad A** como modelo. **¡Atención!** Acuérdense que una de sus oraciones tiene que ser falsa.

PASO 2. Ahora compartan sus oraciones con la clase. ¿Sus compañeros pueden decir cuál oración es falsa?

D. ¡Adivinanzas!

Piensa en un lugar en tu universidad o en tu ciudad, y dile a tu compañero/a qué se hace en ese lugar sin decirle el nombre. ¿Tu compañero/a puede adivinar en qué lugar estás pensando?

> **MODELO:** E1: Aquí se come, se habla con amigos y se estudia.
> E2: ¿Es el centro estudiantil?
> E1: No, es otro lugar.
> E2: ¿La cafetería?
> E1: ¡Sí!

Costa Rica

E. Cultura: El ecoturismo en Costa Rica

PASO 1.   Lee el texto sobre Costa Rica.

Costa Rica es uno de los grandes destinos en el mundo para el ecoturismo. Fue uno de los primeros países en desarrollar[a] esa industria. ¿Cómo es diferente el ecoturismo del turismo convencional? El ecoturismo tiene como objetivo dejar[b] un impacto mínimo sobre los lugares que se visitan y sobre el planeta en general. Además, una parte del dinero que se genera en el ecoturismo se dirige hacia[c] la conservación de la naturaleza. Los ecoturistas pueden hacer actividades muy divertidas y emocionantes,[d] disfrutar de[e] la flora y la fauna del país y a la vez[f] ayudar a conservarlas.

La geografía de Costa Rica es ideal para el ecoturismo porque ya se ofrecen muchas actividades distintas. Se puede ir a la playa para nadar en las aguas tibias[g] del Caribe o rentar una tabla[h] para surfear en el Pacífico. Para observar animales como monos, pájaros y perezosos,[i] se puede viajar por los canales del Parque Nacional Tortuguero. En el Parque Nacional Arenal, donde se encuentra el gran volcán Arenal, los turistas más tranquilos pueden simplemente dar un paseo mientras que los más aventureros pueden hacer una visita al bosque y bajar en tirolina.

Los turistas son bienvenidos[j] en Costa Rica y muchas de las personas que trabajan en el turismo son bilingües o trilingües para poder hablar con los extranjeros. El ecoturismo es importante para los costarricenses no solo porque genera ingresos[k] y crea empleos, sino también porque a ellos les da la oportunidad de compartir[l] la espectacular naturaleza y biodiversidad con el resto del mundo. Estas cosas se consideran importantes y la actitud de Costa Rica frente a[m] la conservación sirve como ejemplo para otros países.

[a]en... *to develop* [b]*to leave* [c]se... *is directed toward* [d]*exciting* [e]disfrutar... *enjoy* [f]a... *at the same time* [g]*tepid*
[h]*board* [i]monos... *monkeys, birds, and sloths* [j]*welcome* [k]*income* [l]*share* [m]frente... *toward*

PASO 2.   Completa las oraciones con los verbos de la lista usando el **se** impersonal. **¡Atención!** Cada verbo se usa solo una vez.

alquilar (*to rent*)	**hablar**	**poder**	**valorar** (*to value*)
dar	**ofrecer**	**usar**	**ver**

1. En las playas de Costa Rica _____ tablas de surf.
2. Durante el día _____ mucho bloqueador solar.
3. En todo el país, _____ la naturaleza y la biodiversidad.
4. _____ paseos en los volcanes.
5. Para ver monos, _____ viajes en kayak por los canales de Tortuguero.
6. _____ una variedad de pájaros en los bosques tropicales.
7. _____ bajar en tirolina en lo alto del bosque.
8. En muchos hoteles y tiendas _____ inglés.

PASO 3.   En parejas, contesten las preguntas y explíquense las respuestas.

1. Costa Rica tiene un nivel (*level*) de desigualdad (*inequality*) económica relativamente baja y un sistema político estable. ¿Piensas que hay una relación entre estos dos factores? ¿Y piensas que estos factores ayudan a crear un ambiente (*atmosphere*) atractivo para los turistas?
2. Además del turismo, la economía de Costa Rica depende de la agricultura (principalmente los plátanos y el café) y la manufactura de componentes electrónicos. ¿Piensas que es mejor tener una economía variada de este tipo o especializarse en una sola cosa?
3. ¿Hay mucho turismo donde tú vives? ¿Por qué sí o por qué no? Si lo hay, ¿puedes ver efectos positivos y negativos?

Un ecoturista escala un árbol en una reserva natural de Costa Rica.

Reciclaje

Verbs like **gustar**

Usa uno de estos verbos para describir tu reacción a las siguientes actividades. ¿Te encantan, te fascinan, te gustan o te molestan?

encantar   fascinar   gustar   molestar

1. los viajes en autobús: _____
2. llevar una maleta muy pesada: _____
3. los viajes en avión: _____
4. hacer nuevos amigos en los aviones o autobuses: _____
5. la playa: _____
6. los trenes: _____

9.3   Se me olvidó el nombre del hotel

Se for unplanned events

Para empezar...

Las oraciones en la página 271 describen un día horrible en el aeropuerto, pero están desordenadas. Usa los dibujos (*drawings*) para poner las oraciones en el orden más adecuado.

1.

2.

3.

4.

5.

6.

7.

8.

9.

Mi día horrible

_____ …**se me cayó** (*I dropped*) el teléfono y…

_____ Luego iba a registrarme para el vuelo, pero **se me olvidó** (*I forgot*) mi tarjeta de identificación.

_____ Llegué muy temprano, y **se me antojó** (*I felt like*) un café.

__1__ Fui al aeropuerto para ir a San Salvador.

_____ Cancelaron mi vuelo, y por eso regresé a casa.

_____ …**se me rompió** (*I accidentally broke it*).

_____ Iba a llamar a mi amigo para traérmela (*bring it to me*), pero…

_____ **Se me mancharon** (*I accidentally stained*) el chaleco (*vest*) y los pantalones.

_____ Compré un café, pero **se me cayó.**

■ Answers to these activities are in Appendix 2 at the back of your book.

Actividades analíticas

1 What nouns agree with the verbs in the bold-faced expressions in **Para empezar**?

se me cayó   el teléfono; _____

se me olvidó   _____

se me antojó   _____

se me rompió   _____

se me mancharon   _____

All these verbs use **se** because they are reflexive (see **Estructura 5.2**). Like many reflexive verbs, these indicate an action that occurs without anyone intentionally doing it. **Caerse**, for instance, means *to fall down,* an action that does not occur intentionally. The indirect object pronoun **me** indicates who is affected by this unintentional action (see **Estructura 7.2**). This can be the person who owns the object that underwent the action, such as the owner of the phone in **Se me cayó el teléfono** or the person who is experiencing the mental state, such as the person who experienced a craving in **Se me antojó un café.**

2 Most of these verbs may be used with or without the indirect object pronoun. The meaning of each verb is constant in Spanish, but adding the indirect object pronoun sometimes requires a different way of expressing the idea in English. In the following chart, use the pattern that you see to add the two missing sentences.

VERBO	SIN OBJETO INDIRECTO	CON OBJETO INDIRECTO
caerse *to fall down*	**Se cayó** el teléfono. *The phone fell down.*	**Se me cayó** el teléfono. *I dropped the phone. /* *My phone fell down.*
mancharse *to get stained*	**Se manchó** la camisa. *The shirt got stained.*	**Se me manchó** la camisa. *I (accidentally) stained the shirt. /* *My shirt got stained.*
romperse *to break* *(get broken)*	**Se rompió** el lápiz. *The pencil broke.*	**Se me rompió** el lápiz. *I (accidentally) broke the pencil. /* *My pencil broke.*
acabarse *to end, run out*	**Se acabó** el dinero. *The money ran out.*	_____ *I ran out of money.*
perderse *to get lost*	**Se perdió** el pasaporte. *The passport got lost.*	_____ *I lost my passport.*

With **antojarse** (*to feel like, have a craving for, be in the mood for*) the indirect object pronoun is almost always included.

—¿**Se te antoja** un helado?   *"Are you in the mood for (Do you feel like) an ice cream?"*

—No, gracias. Pero sí **se me antojan** estos caramelos.   *"No, thank you. But I do have a craving for these candies."*

■ For more on **se** for unplanned events, see **Para saber más 9.3** at the back of your book.

3 Any of the indirect object pronouns may be used with these verbs in order to express who is affected by the action. To clarify further who this person is, use the preposition **a.**

Se **te** cayó el café.	*You dropped the coffee.*
Se **le** rompió el teléfono.	*His/Her/Your (form.) telephone broke.*
Se **nos** antojó un café.	*We felt like a coffee.*
A mis amigos se **les** olvidó la fecha.	*My friends forgot the date.*

Actividades prácticas

A. ¿Qué pasó? Completa cada oración con la expresión apropiada. **¡Atención!** Tienes que usar cada expresión dos veces.

se me antoja   se me cayeron   se me cayó   se me olvidó   se me rompió

1. _olvidó_ tu número de teléfono.
2. _antoja_ ir al cine esta noche contigo. ¿A qué hora vamos?
3. La computadora _se cayó_, pero por suerte (*luckily*) no _se me rompió_
4. No _se me antoja_ salir a bailar hoy. Tengo que limpiar el apartamento.
5. ¡ _olvidó_ de mi bolso los pases de abordar! ¿Dónde están?
6. _se me rompió_ el plato y _se me rompió_ en pedacitos (*little pieces*).
7. _se me olvidó_ cómo se llama nuestro libro. ¿Recuerdas tú el nombre?
8. ¡Perdón! _se me cayeron_ los libros en el piso.

B. Reacciones Completa cada oración o pregunta usando la persona indicada entre paréntesis. Luego, empareja la oración o pregunta con la respuesta más lógica.

_a_ 1. ¿Qué se _te_ antoja hacer? (tú)
_f_ 2. Se _me_ olvidó decirte que tuviste una A en el examen. (yo)
_c_ 3. A tu primo, ¿qué se _le_ antoja comer? (él)
_b_ 4. ¡Se _te_ olvidó nuestro aniversario! (tú)
_g_ 5. ¿Se _te_ cayó algo? (tú)
_a_ 6. ¿A quién se _le_ cayó este lápiz? (él/ella)
_h_ 7. ¿Se _te_ olvidaron las llaves? (tú)
_e_ 8. ¿Cuándo se _le_ rompió el brazo a tu hermano? (él)

a. ¡A mí!
b. ¿Que no es mañana?
c. Le gustan las hamburguesas.
d. No quiero hacer nada.
e. El martes, cuando fue a esquiar (*ski*).
f. ¡Qué bueno! ¡Gracias!
g. Sí, mi teléfono, pero no le pasó nada.
h. No, no las necesito.

  C. ¿Qué se te olvida llevar? En grupos de tres o cuatro compañeros, túrnense para saber qué es lo que a sus compañeros más se les olvida llevar cuando van de viaje. ¿El cargador (*charger*) del teléfono? ¿El pasaporte? ¿El traje de baño? Apunten los resultados y repórtenlos a la clase.

MODELO: E1: ¿Qué se les olvida llevar cuando van de viaje?
E2: A mí siempre se me olvida llevar el cargador del teléfono.
E3: ¡A mí no! Pero a mí sí se me olvida el cepillo de dientes con frecuencia.

Autoprueba

For each of the following situations, select the most logical verb and form an appropriate expression with **se** and an indirect object pronoun, based on the context clues.

acabarse
caerse
olvidarse
perderse

1. _____ los lentes. No los puedo encontrar.
2. ¿Estás en el aeropuerto y _____ el pasaporte? No te preocupes, te lo traigo en seguida.
3. Creo que _____ las tarjetas de embarque (*boarding passes*) en el baño (*restroom*). Regreso para ver si todavía están en el suelo (*floor*).
4. ¿Estuviste en la playa y _____ el bloqueador solar (*sunscreen*)? ¿Fuiste a comprar más?

Respuestas: 1. Se me perdieron; **2.** se te olvidó; **3.** se me cayeron; **4.** se te acabó / se te perdió

D. Historias En parejas, escojan tres de las siguientes imágenes e inventen historias para explicar qué pasó. Creen situaciones lógicas y creativas. Para cada una, escriban por lo menos tres frases.

Los siguientes verbos les pueden ayudar.

acabarse   caerse   olvidarse   romperse

MODELO:

Tenía mucha prisa esta mañana porque me desperté tarde y tenía que estar en la estación de tren a las diez. Estaba muy nerviosa porque no quería llegar tarde. Hice mi maleta y salí de la casa con prisa, pero mientras corría, se me rompió el zapato, me caí y se me cayó el contenido de mi bolso en el suelo.

1.

2.

3.

4.

5.

E. ¿Adónde se te antoja ir?

PASO 1. En parejas, túrnense para entrevistarse, preguntándole a su compañero/a adónde se le antoja ir para sus próximas vacaciones, qué se le antoja hacer y qué se le antoja ver. Apunten las respuestas en la tabla. **¡Atención!** Para hacer las preguntas en forma de **tú**, tienen que cambiar el pronombre **le** a **te** y el adjetivo posesivo **sus** a **tus.**

> **MODELO:** E1: ¿Adónde se te antoja ir para tus próximas vacaciones?
> E2: Se me antoja ir a una playa. ¿Y a ti?
> E1: Se me antoja ir a una ciudad vieja e histórica.

A tu compañero/a,…

¿adónde se le antoja ir para sus próximas vacaciones?

☐ a una ciudad grande   ☐ a una playa
☐ a un lugar histórico o antiguo   ☐ a un rancho o una granja (*farm*)
☐ a las montañas   ☐ a otro lugar: _____

¿qué se le antoja hacer?

☐ dormir, leer libros y pensar   ☐ hacer turismo de aventura
☐ escuchar música y bailar   ☐ observar animales
☐ hacer deportes de invierno   ☐ otra cosa: _____

¿qué se le antoja ver?

☐ artesanías típicas   ☐ el mar
☐ una cultura indígena   ☐ montañas o volcanes
☐ edificios coloniales   ☐ otra cosa: _____

PASO 2. Lee la siguiente información sobre cuatro destinos turísticos muy populares y piensa en las respuestas de tu compañero/a a las preguntas del **Paso 1.** ¿Qué lugar recomiendas tú para tu compañero/a? Dile tu recomendación y pregúntale si está de acuerdo (*if he or she agrees*).

Antigua, Guatemala: Una ciudad fundada (*founded*) por los españoles en el siglo (*century*) dieciséis, con calles muy bonitas, edificios hermosos y mucha artesanía indígena. Está rodeada de (*surrounded by*) volcanes activos.

Bariloche, Argentina: También conocida como San Carlos de Bariloche, es una ciudad a un lado de la cordillera (*mountain range*) de los Andes. Tiene lagos, bosques y montañas, y es un centro importante de esquí.

Islas Galápagos, Ecuador: En las famosas islas que le encantaron a Carlos Darwin, hay mucho que ver a pie (*by foot*) —como las famosas tortugas gigantes— pero también se puede bucear, hacer snorkel o explorar en kayak.

Samaná, República Dominicana: En esta península, hay hermosas playas y lugares para ver ballenas (*whales*). Como en toda la República Dominicana, la música es buenísima y hay muchos lugares para bailar si te gustan la salsa y el merengue.

¡Leamos!

Vacaciones en Tequila

Antes de leer

PASO 1. Para cada actividad a continuación, escribe una **A** si le gustaría (*would like*) a una persona **aventurera** o una **C** si le gustaría a una persona **cautelosa** (*cautious*). **¡Atención!** Hay algunas actividades que les interesarían a ambos.

_____ 1. aprender cómo se hace el tequila
_____ 2. conocer del folclor
_____ 3. aprender de la historia
_____ 4. explorar cavernas
_____ 5. hacer camping
_____ 6. montar en bicicleta

_____ 7. hacer una escalada
_____ 8. hacer turismo de aventura
_____ 9. nadar debajo de cascadas (*waterfalls*)
_____ 10. montar a caballo
_____ 11. hacer caminatas
_____ 12. visitar ruinas arqueológicas

PASO 2. Ahora haz una lista de las actividades del **Paso 1** que te gustaría hacer y otra de las actividades que no te gustaría hacer. ¿Eres una persona aventurera o cautelosa?

A leer

PASO 1. Lee el artículo.

Vacaciones en Tequila

En 2006, UNESCO designó como Patrimonio de la Humanidad el paisaje entre el volcán Tequila y el Valle del Río Grande. La «Ruta del Tequila», un programa establecido al final del siglo XX,[a] promociona el turismo en esa zona tequilera. No se limita al pueblo Santiago de Tequila, sino que[b] el tren Tequila Express hace giras[c] por todo el valle. El turista puede degustar[d] tequila en las destilerías y haciendas de todo el valle.

Agave tequilana en Guadalajara, Jalisco, México

El inmenso valle azul-esmeralda[e] de las plantaciones de agave —la planta que nos brinda el «vino de mezcal[f]»— por sí solo proporciona[g] oportunidades de recorridos[h] hermosos de mucha historia, pero más allá de las enormes plantaciones, Ruta del Tequila ofrece una variedad seductora[i] de turismos.

Unas vacaciones en Tequila pueden saciar a diversos gustos[j] e intereses. Los *agroturistas* van a estar muy a gusto[k] con una estadía[l] en una de las grandes haciendas tequileras. En las haciendas el turista puede visitar destilerías, presenciar muestras[m] de los procesos, visitar museos y probar[n] las especialidades (tequilas y comidas) de la casa.

Los *histoturistas* y *arqueoturistas* disfrutarán[ñ] de una visita a las ruinas de las pirámides circulares en Guachimontones. Las ruinas quedan al oeste de Guadalajara en el estado de Jalisco, y datan de 300 aC.[o]

[a]siglo... *twentieth century* [b]sino... *but rather* [c]*tours, excursions* [d]*taste* [e]*emerald-blue* [f]*mescal* [g]por... *in and of itself provides* [h]*tours, excursions* [i]*alluring* [j]saciar... *satiate a variety of tastes (preferences)* [k]estar... *feel very comfortable* [l]*stay (n.)* [m]presenciar... *witness demonstrations* [n]*taste, try* [ñ]*will enjoy* [o]datan... *date from 300 B.C.*

La Ruta del Tequila también complace[p] todos los turistas que prefieren pasar sus vacaciones al aire libre.[q] Los *excurturistas* pueden dar caminatas en las faldas[r] del Volcán Tequila, o hacer ciclismo o montar a caballo por los senderos[s] que serpentean[t] la rica vegetación hasta la Barranca de Tequila y la Cascada de los Azules. En la barranca,[u] los *ecoturistas* pueden acampar cerca de las cascadas y relajarse en las aguas azul-turquesas de los estanques.[v] Los *aventuristas* pueden practicar el rápel en los precipicios o la espeleología[w] en las cavernas cerca de las cascadas.

En Tequila, todos pueden degustar los mejores tequilas del mundo, la excelente cocina de la región y una variedad de platos especiales preparados con tequila.

¿Vacaciones en Tequila? ¡Cómo no!

[p]*pleases* [q]*al... outdoors* [r]*foothills* [s]*trails, paths* [t]*wind* [u]*ravine* [v]*pools* [w]*spelunking*

PASO 2. Contesta las siguientes preguntas.

1. _____ ¿Cuál **no** es un lugar que se puede visitar en la Ruta del Tequila?
   a. las cascadas
   b. las destilerías que fabrican el tequila
   c. las playas tropicales
   d. las ruinas arqueológicas

2. _____ ¿Cuál es el enfoque de los atractivos turísticos en el Valle del Río Grande?
   a. el aventurismo
   b. la cerveza
   c. la naturaleza
   d. el tequila

3. _____ ¿Cuál **no** es un campo profesional relacionado con los atractivos que se mencionan?
   a. la arqueología
   b. la astronomía
   c. la destilería
   d. la historia

4. _____ ¿Cuántas destilerías hay en Jalisco?
   a. cero
   b. una
   c. dos
   d. varias

5. _____ ¿Cómo se puede hacer un recorrido de la Ruta del Tequila?
   a. a caballo
   b. a pie
   c. en bicicleta
   d. todas las anteriores

6. _____ ¿Cuál es la actividad que **no** menciona el artículo?
   a. el camping
   b. la tirolina
   c. las degustaciones
   d. la exploración de cavernas

7. _____ ¿Qué se ofrece en todos los restaurantes de la región?
   a. la comida hecha de las hojas de la planta agave
   b. degustaciones de diferentes tequilas
   c. degustaciones de diferentes vinos
   d. los postres más ricos de México

8. _____ ¿Cuál **no** es una atracción además del tequila?
   a. el rápel
   b. el ciclismo
   c. el vino
   d. la historia

Después de leer

PASO 1. En grupos, usen la información de la lectura para planear un fin de semana largo en Tequila. ¿Qué actividades les gustan? ¿Qué actividades no les gustan? ¿Por qué? ¿Cuándo van a participar todos en grupo y cuándo se van a separar? Hagan un itinerario para mostrar qué van a hacer cada día por la mañana, por la tarde y por la noche.

PASO 2. En grupos, repasen todas las actividades que se pueden hacer en estas excursiones y piensen en por lo menos cinco reglas que los organizadores de las excursiones Ruta del Tequila probablemente tienen para los turistas.

MODELOS: Tener cuidado al subirse y bajarse de sus caballos.
No pisar las plantas de agave.

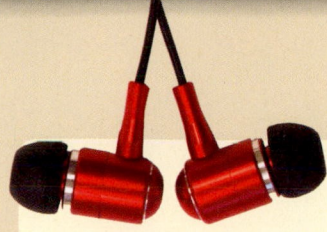

¡Escuchemos!

Los viajes ideales

🦻 Antes de escuchar

Vas a escuchar las opiniones de varias personas sobre sus vacaciones. Decide si esa persona describe vacaciones buenas o malas.

	VACACIONES BUENAS	VACACIONES MALAS
1.	☐	☐
2.	☐	☐
3.	☐	☐
4.	☐	☐
5.	☐	☐
6.	☐	☐
7.	☐	☐

▶ A escuchar

PASO 1. Mira y escucha las descripciones de las vacaciones. Mientras ves el video, empareja la persona con los lugares que menciona.

1. _____ Adrián, de México

2. _____ Juan Andrés, de Costa Rica

3. _____ Magdalena, de Argentina

4. _____ Erick, de Nicaragua

5. _____ Olman, de Costa Rica

6. _____ Natalia, de Argentina

7. _____ Víctor, de México

a. Cancún y Puerto Vallarta
b. Colombia y Miami
c. Europa, los Estados Unidos y Canadá
d. las playas del Pacífico, como Guanacaste
e. Ushuaia, Argentina
f. varios ciudades grandes y estados de los Estados Unidos
g. varios países en varios continentes

(*Continues*)

PASO 2. Mira y escucha otra vez, indicando las tres atracciones que menciona cada uno.

	ADRIÁN	ERICK	NATALIA	VÍCTOR
1. un clima cálido	☐	☐	☐	☐
2. hoteles excelentes	☐	☐	☐	☐
3. un intercambio cultural	☐	☐	☐	☐
4. un lugar agradable	☐	☐	☐	☐
5. playas muy buenas	☐	☐	☐	☐
6. viajar a los Estados Unidos	☐	☐	☐	☐
7. viajar a Europa	☐	☐	☐	☐
8. visitar pueblos chicos con mucha cultura	☐	☐	☐	☐

Después de escuchar

PASO 1. En grupos, decidan si a cada persona del video le gustan o no las siguientes cosas y expliquen por qué.

MODELO: A Víctor le gustan los museos porque va a las ciudades más grandes de Europa, pero no le gustan las playas.

las ciudades grandes	la naturaleza	los pueblos chicos
los hoteles excelentes	el paisaje	los viajes internacionales
los museos	las playas	

PASO 2. Comparen sus propios (*your own*) gustos con los de las personas del video.

MODELO: Me gustan las playas más que a Víctor porque prefiero pasar las vacaciones en las playas más que en las ciudades grandes. No me gustan mucho los museos.

¡Escribamos!

Las mejores y peores vacaciones

Algunas vacaciones son mejores que otras. ¿Puedes describir dos vacaciones muy diferentes? Si no tienes la experiencia de haber tenido (*having had*) unas vacaciones excelentes y otras desastrosas, describe viajes de amigos o familiares.

Antes de escribir

Piensa en el peor viaje y el mejor viaje de tu vida y llena la tabla. (Y claro, puedes inventar tus respuestas si quieres.)

	EL MEJOR VIAJE	EL PEOR VIAJE
¿Adónde fuiste?		
¿Cuándo fuiste?		
¿Con quién(es) fuiste?		
¿Por qué fuiste?		
¿Qué hiciste?		
¿Se te olvidó algo?		

A escribir

Usando la información de **Antes de escribir,** escribe dos párrafos —el primero para describir el peor viaje de tu vida y el segundo para describir el mejor.

> **MODELO:** Esta es la historia de dos viajes… El año pasado, fui a Chile con mis padres. Fue mi primer viaje fuera del país y por eso se me olvidó el pasaporte. Regresé a casa para recogerlo, pero luego perdí (*I missed*) el vuelo. El próximo vuelo no salió hasta el próximo día y por eso…

Después de escribir

Revisa tu ensayo. Luego, intercambia ensayos con un compañero / una compañera para evaluarlos. Lee el ensayo de tu compañero/a y determina si cuenta una historia completa sobre el mejor y el peor viaje o si falta información necesaria. Lee de nuevo (*again*) el ensayo con cuidado para revisar los siguientes puntos de gramática.

- ☐ usa el imperfecto para describir el pasado
- ☐ usa el pretérito para hablar de las acciones que ocurrieron en el pasado
- ☐ usa **se + me/te/le(s)/nos** correctamente
- ☐ hay concordancia entre sustantivos (*nouns*) y adjetivos
- ☐ tiene la ortografía correcta

Después de revisar el ensayo de tu compañero/a, devuélveselo (*return it to him/her*). Mira tu propio (*own*) ensayo para ver los cambios que tu compañero/a recomienda y haz las revisiones necesarias.

ESTRATEGIA

Cause and effect

With the benefit of hindsight, it is almost always possible to trace a chain reaction that makes an extreme experience either a very positive one or a very negative one. When describing the best and worst travel experiences, for example, think of one event or piece of background information that set the cause-and-effect chain in motion and then describe what came of each action. Was it forgetting something? An illness? (Not) Making a list? (Not) Packing ahead of time? Then, use these sequences to carry the narrative thread throughout your descriptive paragraphs logically.

¡Hablemos!

¿Adónde vamos?

Antes de hablar

Haz una lista de por lo menos cinco criterios para tus vacaciones ideales. Por ejemplo, ¿prefieres vacaciones activas o prefieres relajarte? ¿Prefieres el calor o el frío? ¿Quieres comer en los mejores restaurantes? ¿Quieres ir a muchos museos?

MODELO: Me encanta la playa, pero no quiero gastar mucho dinero…

A hablar

En parejas, túrnense para hacer el papel de agente de viajes (*travel agent*) y el/la cliente que quiere ir de vacaciones pero no sabe adónde ir. El/La agente de viajes tiene que hacerle por lo menos siete preguntas al / a la cliente y luego recomendarle un lugar para sus vacaciones ideales. Pueden usar los lugares del capítulo u otros destinos que conocen.

MODELO: E1: ¿Te gustaría ir de vacaciones durante el invierno o el verano?
E2: Me gustaría ir de vacaciones durante el verano.
E1: Bueno, y ¿te gustaría estar en la playa o en las montañas?
E2: …

Después de hablar

¿Quiénes están de acuerdo con las recomendaciones del / de la «agente de viajes» con quien hablaron en la sección **A hablar**? ¿Quiénes no están de acuerdo? Expliquen al resto de la clase por qué sí o por qué no.

Conéctate a la música

Canción: «Me voy» (2006)
Artista: Julieta Venegas

Julieta Venegas es una cantante mexicana, de Tijuana, Baja California. Es una de las más reconocidas cantantes de pop de los últimos años y ha tenido (*has had*) muchísimo éxito (*success*) en Latinoamérica, Norteamérica y Europa.

Antes de escuchar

Cuando uno sale de viaje, es muy común usar expresiones como **me voy, adiós** y **me despido** (*I say good-bye*). Pero además de lo que se dice, ¿qué es lo que se hace en estas circunstancias? ¿Qué tipo de acción o gesto es común?

A escuchar

Escucha la canción, luego contesta las siguientes preguntas.

1. ¿Por qué se va? (Escoge cuatro respuestas.)
   a. Porque su pareja (*partner*) no sabe entender a su corazón.
   b. Porque ella quiere viajar por muchos países del mundo.
   c. Porque su pareja no tiene el valor (*courage*) de ver quién es ella.
   d. Porque su pareja no escucha lo que está tan cerca de él.
   e. Porque ella tiene que estar en Canadá para la próxima semana.
   f. Porque ella sabe que le espera (*awaits*) algo mejor.

2. ¿Va a llorar la cantante?

3. Según la cantante, ¿es probable que merezca (*she deserves*) esta situación?

4. ¿La cantante quiere quedarse con su pareja? ¿Qué hace?

 ## Después de escuchar

Cuando una persona termina una relación romántica, ¿qué hace típicamente? ¿Se queda en casa a llorar? ¿Sale de viaje? ¿Qué más se puede hacer? En grupos, hagan una lista de por lo menos cinco cosas que se puede hacer al terminar una relación romántica.

La cantante mexicana Julieta Venegas toca el acordeón durante un concierto.

■ For copyright reasons, the songs referenced in **Conéctate a la música** have not been provided by the publisher. The video for this song can be found on YouTube, and it is available for purchase from the iTunes store.

Expresiones útiles	
merezco (merecer)	I deserve
qué lástima	what a pity

VOCABULARIO

Comunicación

Me gustaría + *inf.*	I would like (*to do something*).
¿Te/Le gustaría + *inf.*?	Would you (*inform./form.*) like (*to do something*)?
Favor de no fumar.	Please don't smoke.
Empujar.	Push.
Jalar.	Pull.
No beber y conducir.	Don't drink and drive.
No dar de comer.	Don't feed (the animals).
No doblar. / No girar.	Do not turn.
No entrar. / No pasar.	Do not enter.
No estacionar.	No parking.
No fumar.	No smoking.
No pisar (el césped).	Stay off / Do not walk on (the grass).
No tirar basura.	Don't litter (*lit.* throw trash).

Las vacaciones

el aeropuerto	airport
la artesanía	crafts
la atracción	attraction
el avión	airplane
la bicicleta de montaña	mountain bike
el bloqueador solar	sunscreen
el boleto	ticket
el bosque tropical	rainforest
la catarata	waterfall
el equipaje	baggage
la escala	layover
la escalada	rock/mountain climbing
el extranjero	abroad
el/la guía	guide (*person*)
la maleta	suitcase
la naturaleza	nature
el paisaje	scenery, landscape
un paseo	a walk/trip
la quemadura de sol	sunburn
el recorrido	trip/tour
el recuerdo	souvenir
la regla	rule
el sol	sun
el tren	train
el turismo de aventura	adventure tourism
el viaje	trip

Cognados: el ecoturismo, el hotel, el kayak, la montaña, el pasaporte, el servicio, el snorkel, el turismo, la visita

El tiempo / Weather

¿Qué tiempo hace?	What's the weather like?
Está despejado/nublado.	It's clear/cloudy.
Hace buen/mal tiempo.	It's good/bad weather.
Hace (mucho) calor/frío/ sol/viento.	It's (very) hot/cold/ sunny/windy.
llover (ue)	to rain
Llueve. / Está lloviendo.	It rains. / It's raining.
nevar (ie)	to snow
Nieva. / Está nevando.	It snows. / It's snowing.

Los adjetivos

agradable	pleasant
cálido/a	warm, hot
folclórico/a	folk
próximo/a	next; upcoming

Los adverbios

| cerca (de) | close, near (to) |
| lejos (de) | far (from) |

Los verbos

antojarse + *inf.*	to feel like (*doing something*)
antojarse + *n.*	have a craving for (*something*)
bajar en tirolina	to go ziplining
bucear	to scuba dive
caerse (*irreg.*)	to fall down
dar un paseo	go for a walk
disfrutar de + *n.*	to enjoy (*something*)
escalar	to go rock climbing
gastar	to spend
hacer...	
escala	to have a layover
la maleta	to pack a suitcase
un recorrido	to take a trip / go on a tour
snorkel	to go snorkeling
mancharse	to stain
olvidarse	to forget
perder (ie)	to miss (*a bus/flight/ event*); to lose
perderse (ie)	to get lost
romperse	to break
tomar el sol	to sunbathe
visitar	to visit

La vida profesional

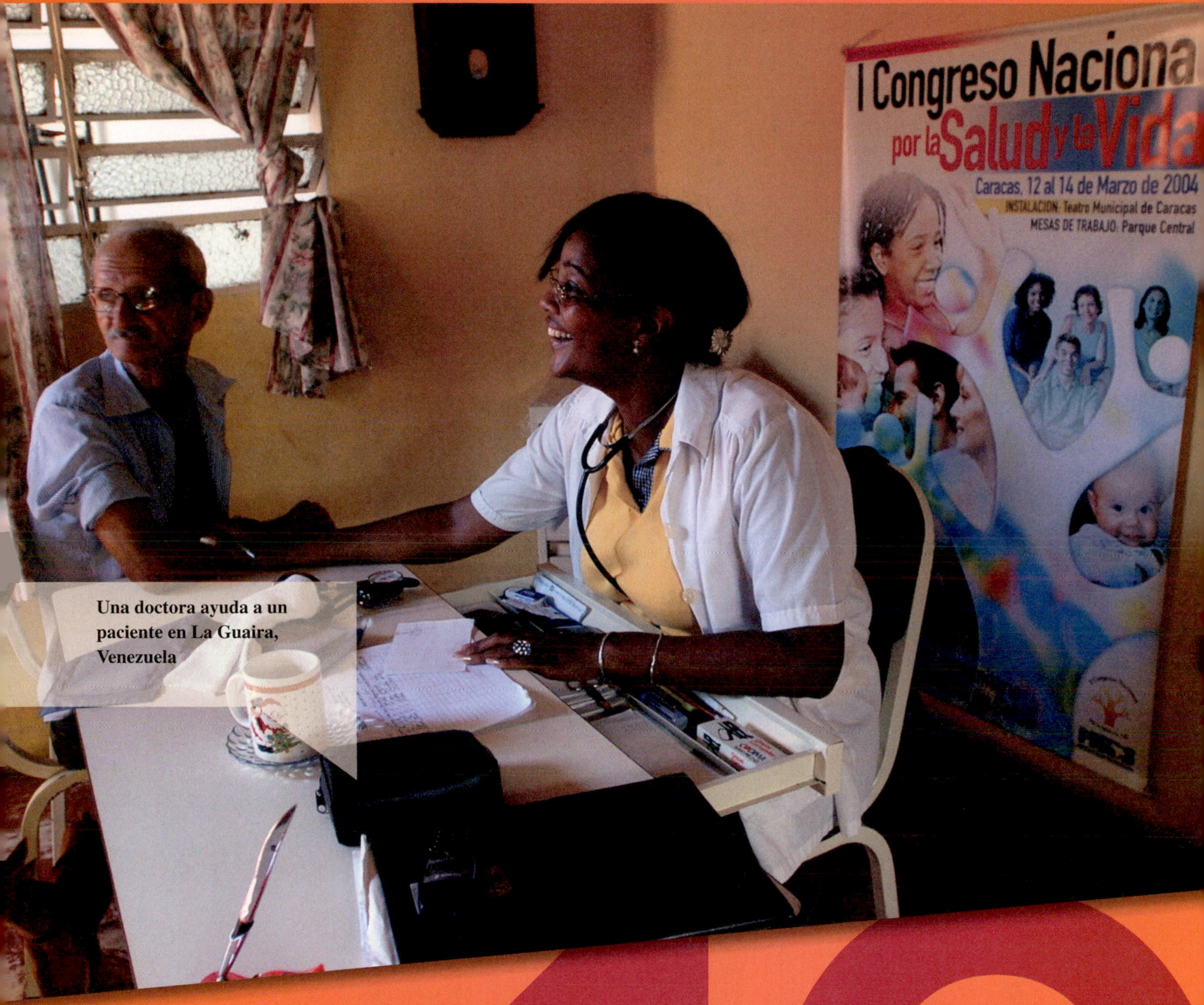

Una doctora ayuda a un paciente en La Guaira, Venezuela

I Congreso Naciona
por la Salud y la Vida
Caracas, 12 al 14 de Marzo de 2004
INSTALACION: Teatro Municipal de Caracas
MESAS DE TRABAJO: Parque Central

Objetivos

In this chapter you will learn how to:

- conduct yourself professionally on the phone
- introduce people to each other
- talk about professions and technology used in the workplace
- give more detailed descriptions of a person, place, or thing
- make requests, invitations, and commands
- talk about work and professions in the Spanish-speaking world

COMUNICACIÓN LARIO UCTURA ATE

A sus órdenes
Expressions for professional contexts

 A. A ver: A sus órdenes Mira y escucha, luego apunta la expresión que usa cada persona.

1. _____ Angélica

2. _____ Alexis

3. _____ Eva

4. _____ Guadalupe

5. _____ Seiji

6. _____ Felicitas

7. _____ Ana

8. _____ Mayra

9. _____ Eduardo

10. _____ Olman

a. Con mucho gusto.
b. Es un placer.
c. Estoy a sus órdenes.
d. Fue un placer.
e. Ha sido un placer.
f. Para servirle(s).

To ask politely to do something, use: **Quisiera** + *infinitive.*

> **Quisiera hablar con la directora.**

To ask *How can I help you?,* say: **¿En qué puedo servirle?**
When someone thanks you for your assistance, respond with one of the following expressions.

Para servirle. **A sus órdenes.**	*At your service.*
Es / Fue / Ha sido un placer.	*It's / It was / It has been a pleasure.*
Con mucho gusto.	*My pleasure. / With pleasure.*

B. ¿En qué puedo servirle? Escoge la frase apropiada para cada situación.

1. _____ En el banco
   a. La cuenta (*bill*), por favor.
   b. Quisiera cambiar (*cash*) un cheque.
   c. Perdone. Busco las manzanas.
   d. Quisiera enviar (*send*) estas cartas (*letters*).

2. _____ En la librería
   a. Dos entradas (*tickets*), por favor.
   b. Perdone. ¿Dónde están los diccionarios?
   c. Quisiera cambiar un cheque.
   d. Quisiera hablar con el director.

3. ____ En el mercado
   a. Quisiera hablar con el director.
   b. ¿Me trae un tenedor, por favor?
   c. Perdone. Busco las manzanas.
   d. Quisiera enviar estas cartas.

4. ____ En el museo
   a. Dos entradas, por favor.
   b. Quisiera comprar estampillas (*stamps*).
   c. Quisiera cambiar el cheque.
   d. Perdone. Busco los tomates.

5. ____ En la oficina de correos
   a. ¿Me trae un refresco, por favor?
   b. Perdone, ¿dónde están las novelas de detectives?
   c. ¿Me trae un tenedor, por favor?
   d. Quisiera enviar estas cartas.

6. ____ En el restaurante
   a. Dos entradas, por favor.
   b. La cuenta, por favor.
   c. Disculpe. ¿Me puede decir dónde están los diccionarios?
   d. Quisiera hablar con el director.

C. ¿Qué se hace?

 PASO 1. En parejas, hagan una lista de dos o tres actividades que se hacen en cada lugar.

MODELO: en el banco: se depositan cheques, se cobran (*cash*) cheques, se saca dinero

1. en la librería
2. en el mercado
3. en el museo
4. en la oficina de correos
5. en el restaurante

 PASO 2. Ahora pónganse en dos filas, cara a cara. Los estudiantes de una fila son los clientes; los estudiantes de la otra son los empleados (*employees*) de los lugares de la lista. Hay que tener una conversación completa con la persona delante de (*in front of*) ti. Luego, todos los estudiantes de una fila deben tomar un pasito (*small step*) a la izquierda para empezar de nuevo con otra pareja en una situación nueva.

MODELO: E1: Buenas tardes. ¿En qué puedo servirle?
E2: Quisiera depositar un cheque y cambiar (*exchange*) dinero.
E1: ¡Cómo no!
E2: Gracias.
E1: Para servirle.

1. el banco
2. la librería
3. el mercado
4. el museo
5. la oficina de correos
6. el restaurante

Quisera cambiar dinero.

En español…

Telephone interactions are more challenging than face-to-face interactions, in part because there are no visual cues. Often it is important to be able to get just the most basic information, such as a name and telephone number, so that a fluent speaker can return the call. Here are a few sentences that can help you take control of the conversation and successfully acquire the most basic information.

MAKING THE CALL

Buenos días. / Buenas tardes. Habla ____, **de la compañía** ____.	Good morning/afternoon. This is ____, from ____ (*company*) speaking.
¿Puedo hablar / Me puede comunicar con + *name of person?*	May I speak / Can you connect me with ____?
¿Está / Se encuentra + *name of person?*	Is ____ there?
¿Puedo dejarle un mensaje?	May I leave him/her a message?
Más despacio, por favor.	Slower, please.
Gracias, muy amable. Adiós.	Thank you, you've been very kind. Good-bye.

ANSWERING THE TELEPHONE

Buenos días. / Buenas tardes. + *name of company*	
¿De parte de quién?	Who's calling?
Un momento, por favor.	Just a moment, please.
No está en este momento. **¿Le quiere dejar un mensaje?**	He's/She's not here right now. Would you like to leave a message for him/her?
¿Cuál es su nombre y su número de teléfono?	What is your name and telephone number?
Le voy a repetir la información…	I am going to repeat back the information to you . . .
Alguien lo/la volverá a llamar.	Someone will call you back.
Gracias por llamar. Adiós.	Thank you for calling. Good-bye.

These simple phrases can lead to a clear and successful telephone interaction that will be a lot less frustrating for both parties than a conversation full of requests for general repetitions such as **¿Cómo?** or **¿Qué?**

■ The audio files for in-text listening activities are available in the eBook, within Connect Plus activities, and on the Online Learning Center.

D. «No está. ¿Le quiere dejar un mensaje?»   Imagínate que contestas el teléfono para una compañía. Escucha los mensajes que dejan los clientes y apunta con quién quieren hablar, los nombres y apellidos de las personas que llaman y sus números de teléfono.

	MENSAJE PARA…	NOMBRE(S)	APELLIDO(S)	NÚMERO DE TELÉFONO
1.	Daniel Castro	Miguel	Antoni Marcos	918-304-5720
2.	Alberto Sinas	Deborah Maldonado		673-916-4593
3.	President Elizabeth	Arzaseta		971-726-8429
4.	Representante Publico	maria	Lucia Garcia Mendez	426-372-1644
5.		Ignas O Ennes		0011643290278
6.	Flores	Elina Amadir		823-746-3493

E. ¡Rin, rin!

PASO 1. En parejas, pónganse espalda con espalda (*back to back*) y túrnense para apuntar un mensaje telefónico. Empiecen con el «¡rin, rin!» del teléfono. Cada mensaje debe incluir: la fecha y la hora de la llamada, el nombre de quien recibe la llamada, el nombre de la persona que llama y su número de teléfono.

MODELO: E1: ¡Rin, rin!

E2: Buenos días, oficina de Suzy.

E1: ¿Está Suzy?

E2: No está en este momento. ¿Le quiere dejar un mensaje?

E1: Sí, gracias.

E2: ¿Cuál es su nombre, apellido y número de teléfono?

E1: Mi nombre es…

PASO 2. Ahora, verifiquen los mensajes usando la siguiente lista.

- ¿El mensaje tiene correcto el nombre de quien recibe el mensaje?
- ¿El mensaje tiene correctas la fecha y hora de la llamada?
- ¿Tiene el nombre completo (nombre y apellido) de la persona que llama?
- ¿Tiene el número correcto?

Quiero presentarle a...

Introducing people to each other

To introduce people to each other, address by name the person with the highest status or whom you know less well and say: **Quiero presentarte/le a...**

—**Sara, quiero presentarte a mi hermano, Juan.**

—**Señor Olivares, quiero presentarle a mi amiga Sara.**

To introduce someone to more than one person, you can say: **Quiero presentarles a...**

—**Niños, quiero presentarles al nuevo estudiante, Antonio.**

To reply with something along the lines of *Nice to meet you* or *It's a pleasure,* use one of these expressions.

Mucho gusto.
Encantado/a.
Es un placer.

As you learned in **Capítulo 1,** if someone says *Nice to meet you* first, you can respond with **Igualmente,** which means *Likewise.*

—**Mario, quiero presentarte a mi amiga Anita.**

—**Mucho gusto, Anita.**

—**Igualmente, Mario.**

—**Profesora Alemán, quiero presentarle a mi madre, Magda Ordóñez Gil.**

—**Encantada, señora Ordóñez.**

—**Igualmente, profesora Alemán.**

A. A presentar Pon la siguiente conversación en orden (de 1 al 5).

_____ Adiós.

_____ Buenas tardes, Juan Andrés. Quiero presentarte a mi novia, Elena.

_____ Igualmente.

_____ Mucho gusto, Elena.

_____ Tengo clase en cinco minutos. Hasta luego.

Fernando, quiero presentarte a mi amiga Maribel.

B. Quiero presentar...

PASO 1. Indica la mejor manera de presentar a las personas.

1. _____ A tu amigo y tu profesor de inglés
   a. Efra, quiero presentarte a mi profesor de inglés, Adam White.
   b. Profesor White, quiero presentarle a mi amigo Efra.
   c. Los dos están bien.
   d. Ninguno de los dos está bien.

2. _____ A una amiga de la universidad y tus padres
   a. Mariela, te presento a mis padres, Ernesto y Liliana.
   b. Mamá, papá, quiero presentarles a mi amiga Mariela.
   c. Los dos están bien.
   d. Ninguno de los dos está bien.

3. _____ A dos amigos tuyos
   a. Héctor, quiero presentarte a Juan.
   b. Juan, quiero presentarte a Héctor.
   c. Los dos están bien.
   d. Ninguno de los dos está bien.

4. _____ A la nueva gerente (*manager*) y el presidente de la compañía
   a. Estefanía Guzmán Torres, quiero presentarte al presidente, José Antonio López Gómez.
   b. Presidente López, quiero presentarte a la nueva gerente, Estefanía Guzmán.
   c. Los dos están bien.
   d. Ninguno de los dos está bien.

5. _____ Al nuevo estudiante y la maestra
   a. Diego, quiero presentarte a la maestra, señora Maldonado.
   b. Señora Maldonado, quiero presentarle al nuevo estudiante, Diego.
   c. Los dos están bien.
   d. Ninguno de los dos está bien.

PASO 2. En parejas, túrnense para presentarles a su amiga Elena a las siguientes personas. Hagan la presentación de dos maneras si se puede.

MODELO: tus hermanos (Esteban y Manolo) → Esteban, Manolo, quiero presentarles a mi amiga Elena.
o Elena, quiero presentarte a mis hermanos, Esteban y Manolo.

1. tu mejor amigo/a
2. el profesor de inglés
3. los miembros de tu equipo (*team*)
4. el gerente de una compañía
5. la directora de marketing de una compañía
6. el vecino
7. tus padres

C. A conocernos...

En grupos de cuatro o cinco, túrnense para presentarle un(a) estudiante a otro/a.

MODELO: E1: Chelsea, quiero presentarte a mi amiga Leslie.
E2: Encantada, Leslie.
E3: Igualmente. Chelsea, ¿conoces a... ?

COMUN **VOCABULARIO** UCTURA ATE

Las profesiones y los oficios

Professions and careers

el fotógrafo

el jefe

la ingeniera

la directora de marketing

la programadora

el bloguero

la diseñadora gráfica

la ejecutiva

la dueña

el empleado

la arquitecta

la agente de seguros

el gerente

el asistente administrativo / secretario

el agente de bienes raíces

el cajero

la jueza

la maestra /profesora

el bombero

la cosmetóloga

la abogada

la mujer policía

el estudiante

la trabajadora social

el dentista

el enfermero

el cirujano

la médica

A. Somos profesionales   ¿Dónde se practica cada profesión? Escribe la profesión que corresponde a cada descripción.

1. _____ saca fotos en bodas y otras celebraciones.
2. _____ organiza reuniones, toma mensajes y ayuda a los empleados de un negocio.
3. _____ diseña edificios, pero solo supervisa la construcción de ellos.
4. _____ ayuda a gente que quiere vender o comprar una casa.
5. _____ trabaja en la comunidad para asegurar la seguridad pública.
6. _____ trabaja en una escuela donde enseña a los estudiantes.
7. _____ ofrece su argumento delante del juez / de la jueza en un tribunal.
8. _____ toma decisiones importantes dentro de una sala de justicia.
9. _____ trabaja en una peluquería o salón de belleza.
10. _____ trabaja en el quirófano (*operating room*) operando a los pacientes.
11. _____ trabaja en una clínica médica u hospital.
12. _____ trabaja en una clínica dental.

Vocabulario

Here are some useful verbs that have to do with work.

conseguir (un puesto de trabajo)	to get (a job)
contratar	to hire
entrevistar	to interview
estar dispuesto/a	to be ready/willing
preparar un currículum	to prepare a resumé
solicitar empleo/trabajo	to apply for a job

B. La jerarquía (*hierarchy*) en el lugar de trabajo

PASO 1. Para cada grupo, pon los profesionales en orden de la persona más alta en la jerarquía (1) a la menos alta (3).

1. ____ el/la gerente
   ____ el/la ejecutivo/a
   ____ el/la secretario/a

2. ____ el/la asistente médico/a
   ____ el/la cirujano/a
   ____ el/la enfermero/a

3. ____ el/la cajero/a
   ____ el/la dueño/a
   ____ el jefe / la jefa

 PASO 2. En parejas, decidan cuál de las profesiones del **Paso 1** es la que más se aplica a cada palabra y cuál es la que menos se aplica. Compartan sus decisiones con la clase y expliquen sus razones.

1. prestigioso
2. peligroso
3. interesante
4. divertido
5. lucrativo
6. fácil

El empleado le muestra el informe (*report*) a su gerente.

C. ¿Qué hacen para el trabajo? Indica si cada frase es lógica o no para la persona de la profesión que se menciona.

	ES LÓGICA.	NO ES LÓGICA.
1. Un agente de seguros usa un libro de texto.	☐	☐
2. Una asistente administrativa usa mucho el teléfono.	☐	☐
3. Los estudiantes y profesores crean las leyes (*laws*).	☐	☐
4. Un fotógrafo usa una cámara.	☐	☐
5. Un ingeniero usa un bisturí (*scalpel*).	☐	☐
6. Los estudiantes y profesores usan los libros de texto.	☐	☐
7. Una cosmetóloga usa una cámara.	☐	☐
8. Un cirujano usa un bisturí.	☐	☐
9. Una diseñadora de multimedia y un escritor usan las computadoras.	☐	☐
10. Una cosmetóloga usa las tijeras (*scissors*).	☐	☐
11. Un abogado usa las leyes.	☐	☐

D. A ver: Las profesiones Mira y escucha, luego apunta la profesión de cada persona.

NOMBRE	PROFESIÓN
1. Catalina Haayen	profesor de college J you
2. Juan Asconapé	abogado
3. Lourdes Díaz	cosmo?
4. Zuly Viera	asiguraln
5. Pedro Vera	el pticía
6. Mario Lageire	agente seguros
7. Néstor Olivera	ingeniero computción
8. María Jesús Madrigal	profesor de Esp
9. Juan Francisco Funer Rodríguez	medico
10. Vanessa Anaya Loera	administración
11. Juan Sol	estudiante
12. Andrea Suárez	marketing

E. ¿Quién es? En grupos, túrnense para describir una profesión de la lista de vocabulario sin mencionar el nombre de la profesión. Los otros miembros del grupo deben hacer preguntas sobre la profesión hasta adivinar qué es.

> **MODELO:** E1: Esta persona enseña a otras personas.
> E2: ¿Es un juez?
> E1: No, esta persona tiene una clase de estudiantes.
> E3: ¿Es un profesor o una profesora?
> E1: ¡Acertaste (*You guessed correctly*)!

F. ¿Qué profesiones te interesan? Mira de nuevo la lista de profesiones y decide cuáles son las tres que más te interesan. Nómbralas y explícale a un compañero / una compañera de clase por qué te interesan estas tres profesiones. ¿Qué destrezas (*skills*) requieren? ¿Las tienes tú? ¿Qué profesión de la lista te interesa menos? ¿Por qué?

La tecnología en el lugar de trabajo
Technology in the workplace

A. La tecnología Usando la siguiente lista de vocabulario, identifica cada elemento del dibujo.

los archivos
los audífonos
el blog
la computadora /
  el disco duro
la (computadora)
  láptop / portátil

el email / correo
  electrónico
el enlace
el escáner /
  la impresora
la memoria USB
el micrófono

el módem
la página web
la pantalla / el
  monitor
el ratón
la red social
la tableta

el teclado
el (teléfono)
  celular / móvil
el WiFi

el enlace

los archivos

el teclado

Vocabulario

Here are some useful verbs that have to do with technology.

cargar	to upload
copiar	to copy
cortar	to cut
descargar	to download
deshacer	to undo
guardar	to save
hacer clic / pinchar (*Sp.*)	to click (*with a mouse or trackpad*)
mandar un email/mensaje/texto	to send an email/message/text
pegar	to paste
recibir un email/mensaje/texto	to receive an email/message/text
textear	to text

B. ¿Para qué lo usas?

PASO 1. En parejas, túrnense para decir qué se usa para hacer estas actividades.

1. Para mover el cursor o hacer clic, se usa…
2. Para reproducir un documento en papel para uso en la computadora, se usa…
3. Para imprimir un documento electrónico en una hoja de papel, se usa…
4. Para pasar de un sitio web a otro, se entra la dirección o se hace clic en…
5. Para compartir información con varios lectores (*readers*) y leer comentarios de ellos, se puede escribir…
6. Para trabajar en computadora fuera de la oficina, se usa…
7. Para conectarse al Internet, se usa…
8. Para ver el trabajo en computadora, se usa…
9. Para guardar los archivos, se usa…
10. Para escribir rápidamente, es importante poner los dedos en la posición correcta en…

PASO 2. Ahora, hagan una lista de los sistemas y aparatos (*gadgets*) tecnológicos que usan cada día y digan para qué los usan. ¿Pueden pensar en otros usos que no están incluidos en la lista del **Paso 1**?

C. Los beneficios y riesgos de la tecnología

PASO 1. Indica la frase que mejor describa el beneficio y el riesgo de cada tipo de tecnología. **¡Atención!** En algunos casos hay más de una respuesta posible.

	BENEFICIO (+)	RIESGO (−)
1. la tableta	____	____
2. los archivos electrónicos	____	____
3. el email	____	____
4. el escáner	____	____
5. las redes sociales	____	____

a. Ahorra papel y espacio porque no tienes que imprimir todo y guardar los documentos impresos (*printed*).
b. Facilita la comunicación escrita (*written*).
c. Facilita el intercambio electrónico de documentos impresos.
d. La puedes llevar a cualquier parte y siempre «estar conectado».
e. No tiene teclado ni ratón y cuesta más tiempo y trabajo escribir un email.
f. No pueden controlar todo el contenido; por ejemplo, los amigos pueden cargar fotos vergonzosas (*embarrassing*) o no muy apropiadas.
g. Facilita el plagio (*plagiarism*) u otra violación de los derechos (*rights*) de autor.
h. Se puede comunicar directamente con los clientes sin tener que gastar mucho dinero en el marketing.
i. Si hay algún fallo (*failure*) técnico en el disco duro, es posible perderlo todo.
j. Es fácil e informal, y por eso existe la posibilidad de escribir un mensaje sin pensar en las consecuencias negativas.

PASO 2. En grupos pequeños, compartan sus respuestas del **Paso 1.** ¿Están todos de acuerdo con los beneficios y riesgos de cada innovación tecnológica? Piensen en por lo menos un beneficio adicional y un riesgo para cada innovación. Luego, hagan una lista de beneficios y riesgos para otro objeto tecnológico popular y compártanla con la clase.

CONÉCTATE AL MUNDO HISPANO

En zona rurales en todas partes del mundo, la tecnología ha aportado (*provided*) **la conectividad** donde antes no existía. Por ejemplo, los teléfonos celulares proveían acceso a muchos lugares donde no llegaban los cables de los teléfonos tradicionales. Lo mismo es cierto de la educación a larga distancia. Por ejemplo, en México existía **Telesecundaria** mucho antes de que surgió cualquier forma de educación a distancia en los Estados Unidos. Telesecundaria es un programa mexicano muy completo (*comprehensive*) que empezó en 1968 con televisiones que transmitían en blanco y negro. Tras (*Over*) los años, siguió el desarrollo (*development*) de Telesecundaria y hoy en día el programa utiliza los avances tecnológicos tales como satélites, libros digitales, computadoras y láptops, videos y la interactividad integral.

COMUN VOCABUL **ESTRUCTURA** ATE

◯ Reciclaje

Adjectives

Empareja cada profesión con la frase que describe su especialización más común, modificando el número y género de los adjetivos cuando sea necesario. Luego, escribe cada término (*term*) bajo el nombre del sector de la economía donde pertenece (*it belongs*).

los arquitectos	civil y estructural
una profesora	especializado en cardiología
los ingenieros	universitario
un médico	clínico
un policía	de bienes raíces
las psicólogas	comercial y residencial
una agente	motorizado (*mobile, on a motorcycle*)

EDIFICIOS / INFRAESTRUCTURA	**EDUCACIÓN**	**SALUD** (*HEALTH*)	**SEGURIDAD**
_____	_____	_____	_____
_____		_____	
_____			

■ Answers to this activity are in **Appendix 2** at the back of your book.

10.1 El arquitecto que diseñó este puente

The relative pronoun *que*

Para empezar...

Santiago Calatrava y Carlos Slim son dos de los profesionales más destacados (*noteworthy*) y los dos son de países hispanos. Lee las oraciones e indica con una **C** las que describen a Calatrava y con una **S** las que describen a Slim. **¡Atención!** Hay dos oraciones que no tienen que ver ni con Calatrava ni con Slim. Usa **X** para estas oraciones.

1. _____ Muchos lo comparan con Antoni Gaudí, un arquitecto español **que** hizo muchos edificios muy famosos en Barcelona.
2. _____ Tiene varias compañías **que** administran sus hijos Carlos, Marco Antonio y Patrick.
3. _____ Es el dueño de Telmex, una compañía **que** tiene el noventa por ciento de las líneas telefónicas en México.
4. _____ Es uno de los dueños de un periódico **que** se llama el *New York Times*.
5. _____ Diseñó la Ciudad de las Artes y las Ciencias, un complejo (*complex*) de museos **que** se encuentra en Valencia, España.
6. _____ Es cocinero en un restaurante mexicano **que** está en Los Angeles.
7. _____ Uno de sus puentes nuevos es el Puente Margaret Hunt Hill, **que** se abrió en 2012 en Dallas, Texas.
8. _____ Es el dueño de Telcel y de América Móvil, las dos compañías **que** dominan el mercado de teléfonos celulares en México y el resto de Latinoamérica.
9. _____ Su novela *El enlace,* **que** escribió en 1971, es de ciencia ficción.
10. _____ Es un hombre **que** aparece en las listas de las personas más ricas del mundo.

Santiago Calatrava: Arquitecto de edificios y puentes; nació en Valencia, España, en 1951.

Carlos Slim Helú: Dueño de compañías e inversionista (*investor*) en telecomunicaciones y otras industrias; nació en México, D.F., en 1940.

Actividades analíticas

1 The relative pronoun **que** is used to give additional information about a noun. You can easily make your sentences more informative by adding a clause with **que.**

La señora vive en esa casa.	*The woman lives in that house.*
La señora **que trabaja en el banco** vive en esa casa.	*The woman who works at the bank lives in that house.*

The additional information (here, **que trabaja en el banco**) is called a *relative clause* (**una cláusula relativa**). The relative pronoun **que** introduces the relative clause. Its equivalent in English is *that, which,* or *who,* depending on the context.

In sentence 1 in **Para empezar,** what is the relative clause that describes **un arquitecto español?** _____

2 If a relative clause has an expressed subject, this subject may appear either before or after the verb.

El libro $\begin{Bmatrix} \textbf{que Ana leyó} \\ \textbf{que leyó Ana} \end{Bmatrix}$ es muy bueno. *The book that Ana read is very good.*

In this case, **Ana** may appear either before or after the verb **leyó** and the basic meaning is the same. With this in mind, who manages the companies described in sentence 2 of **Para empezar?** _____

Actividades prácticas

A. Beto Cuevas Lee el párrafo sobre Beto Cuevas, un músico, cantante y compositor chileno. Luego, empareja cada oración con la terminación apropiada. **¡Atención!** Hay una terminación que no se usa. ¿Cuál es?

La Ley, con su premio gramófono de los Grammy Latino 2001

Beto Cuevas nació en Santiago de Chile en 1967. Su familia se mudó a Montreal, Canadá, en los años setenta para escapar de la dictadura de Augusto Pinochet. Es allí donde Beto empezó su carrera musical. En 1987, se hizo cantante de La Ley, un grupo de rock muy popular en Latinoamérica. El grupo ganó un Grammy Latino por su álbum *La Ley MTV Unplugged* en 2001. En 2008, Beto lanzó (*released*) su primer álbum solista. El cantante tiene dos hijos, Martina y Diego, y vive ahora en Los Ángeles.

1. _____ Nació en Chile, pero se crió (*was raised*) en Canadá, un país…
2. _____ Su familia es de Chile, un país…
3. _____ Su familia salió de Chile por la dictadura de Pinochet, un militar…
4. _____ Fue vocalista en la banda chilena La Ley, un grupo…
5. _____ Además del español, habla francés e inglés,…
6. _____ Ahora vive en Los Ángeles, una ciudad…
7. _____ Empezó como solista en 2008 e hizo una gira (*tour*)…
8. _____ Tiene dos hijos…

a. que se llaman Martina y Diego.
b. que estuvo veintisiete años en el poder (*power*).
c. que es conocida como el centro de la industria musical.
d. que está en el suroeste (*southwest*) de Sudamérica.
e. que está en el suroeste de Centroamérica.
f. que son los dos idiomas que se hablan más en Montreal, donde creció (*grew up*).
g. que fue uno de los más importantes en el mundo del rock en español entre 1987 y 2005.
h. que lo llevó a muchas ciudades de los Estados Unidos y Latinoamérica.
i. que recibió a miles de exiliados (*exiles*) chilenos después del golpe de estado (*coup d'état*) dirigido (*directed*) por Augusto Pinochet en 1973.

■ Answers to these activities are in Appendix 2 at the back of your book.

■ For more on the relative pronoun **que,** see **Para saber más 10.1,** at the back of your book.

Autoprueba

Let's see how much you remember about some of the people, places, and things we've read about thus far. For each of the following phrases, think of an appropriate relative clause you could add to provide further description for your listener or reader. The **que** has been provided for you. If you need to refresh your memory, refer to the chapters that are given.

1. En el **Capítulo 5,** leímos sobre la vida de Shakira, una cantante que _____.
2. En el **Capítulo 6,** aprendimos sobre El Bulli, un restaurante catalán que _____.
3. También leímos sobre el huitlacoche, un hongo que _____.
4. En el **Capítulo 8,** leímos sobre las molas, una artesanía que _____.
5. En el **Capítulo 9,** aprendimos sobre la Ruta del Tequila, unas excursiones mexicanas que _____.

B. Los profesionales

PASO 1.   La educación y el trabajo de los profesionales son parecidos en los distintos países, pero no son siempre idénticos. En parejas, usen lo que ya saben de este tema para encontrar una terminación adecuada para cada oración. **¡Atención!** Hay una terminación que tienen que usar dos veces.

LOS ABOGADOS

1. _____ Los abogados son las personas…
2. _____ Para ser abogado en en este país, primero tienes que graduarte de una escuela de derecho (*law*), una escuela especializada…
3. _____ Para ser abogado en la mayoría de los demás países, tienes que graduarte de una facultad (*school*) de derecho, una escuela especializada…
4. _____ En algunos países, «licenciado» es una palabra…

LOS MÉDICOS

5. _____ Un médico es un profesional…
6. _____ Los médicos son profesionales…
7. _____ Para ser médico en este país, primero tienes que graduarte de una escuela de medicina, una escuela especializada…
8. _____ Para ser médico en muchos otros países, primero tienes que graduarte de una facultad de medicina, una escuela especializada…

LOS TRABAJADORES SOCIALES

9. _____ Un trabajador social es un profesional…
10. _____ Los trabajadores sociales son profesionales…

TERMINACIONES

a. que trabajan en hospitales, clínicas y otros lugares.
b. que usan también para decir «abogado».
c. que sigue después de la escuela secundaria y que también ofrece carreras en enfermería (*nursing*), nutrición y tecnología médica.
d. que ayudan a encontrar soluciones a los problemas sociales.
e. que ofrece la licenciatura (*bachelor's degree*) en Derecho.
f. que tiene la licenciatura en Trabajo Social.
g. que sigue después de la licenciatura.
h. que defienden los intereses del cliente en cuestiones jurídicas (*legal*).
i. que se dedica al tratamiento (*treatment*) y prevención de las enfermedades.

PASO 2.   Como ya vieron, en muchos países es común obtener una licenciatura en Medicina o en Derecho, mientras en este país, normalmente se requiere estudios de posgrado (*postgraduate*). En parejas, hagan una comparación entre el sistema que usan en este país y el sistema que usan en otros países. ¿Cuáles son las ventajas y desventajas de cada sistema?

C. Una encuesta sobre la tecnología

PASO 1.   Circula por tu salón de clase para hacerles a tus compañeros dos de las siguientes preguntas. **¡Atención!** Todos deben responder con oraciones completas que usen el pronombre relativo **que.**

MODELO: E1: ¿Cuál es el tipo de blog que te gusta más?
            E2: Los blogs que me gustan más son los blogs culinarios.

1. ¿Cuál es la página web que usas más?
2. ¿Cuál es la marca de teléfono que te parece mejor?
3. ¿Cuál es el navegador web (*browser*) que usas más?
4. ¿Cuál es el aparato que usas más: el teléfono, la portátil, la tableta u otra cosa?
5. ¿Cuál es el tipo de computadora que te gusta más: las PC o las Mac?
6. ¿Cuál es la aplicación o programa que te gusta más?

(Continues)

PASO 2. Ahora, en parejas, creen oraciones para resumir la información que Uds. juntaron (*gathered*) y compartan los resultados con la clase. ¿Qué diferencias de opiniones ven entre los estudiantes?

> **MODELO:** Para nosotros, la página web que usamos más es Facebook.

D. ¿Cómo se llama? ¿Sabes bien cómo se llaman los demás estudiantes en tu clase? Pregúntale a un compañero / una compañera cómo se llaman varias personas de la clase, sin mirarlas directamente ni señalar (*nor pointing*).

> **MODELO:** ¿Cómo se llama la persona que está a la izquierda de Erica y que tiene el pelo negro?

el Perú

E. Cultura: El empleo en el Perú

PASO 1. Lee el texto sobre el Perú.

Si un país quiere que su economía crezca,[a] es importante tener trabajadores talentosos y bien formados[b] en las industrias que más van a expandirse. Los expertos dicen que en el Perú en los próximos años va a subir[c] la inversión,[d] en particular en la infraestructura (calles y carreteras, puentes, edificios, servicios públicos, etcétera) y en la minería.[e] En estos dos campos[f] se requieren personas con experiencia en ingeniería y en construcción.

Igual que el resto del mundo, los campos tecnológicos también necesitan más gente calificada, como por ejemplo personas que sepan[g] crear páginas web o manejar bases de datos. Hay un gran número de trabajos que emplean la tecnología en el sector financiero, que también está expandiéndose mucho. Y en esta época de la globalización, es cada vez más[h] importante saber hablar varios idiomas para tratar con[i] empresas internacionales.

A pesar de la expansión, la tasa[j] de desempleo y el porcentaje de personas en el Perú que trabajan sin beneficios siguen siendo altos. Una de las razones[k] es que no hay suficientes personas con experiencia y formación adecuada para ocupar los puestos.[l] En ese sentido, es importante poner énfasis en la educación. Además, es necesario que los estudiantes que se especializan en las áreas de ingeniería, minería, tecnología, administración de negocios y relaciones internacionales se mantengan al tanto de[m] los avances recientes de sus disciplinas. Y por esa razón, siempre va a haber vacantes[n] en el sector de la educación, particularmente para profesores con un buen conocimiento de estos campos laborales.

[a]quiere... *wants its economy to grow* [b]*trained* [c]*increase* [d]*investment* [e]*mining* [f]*fields* [g]*know how* [h]cada... *increasingly* [i]tratar... *deal with* [j]*rate* [k]*reasons* [l]*positions* [m]se... *keep themselves up-to-date on* [n]*vacancies*

PASO 2. Ahora empareja las frases para crear oraciones completas.

1. Las personas _____ no reciben beneficios.
2. Los alumnos peruanos _____ encuentran trabajos en empresas internacionales.
3. En una facultad de informática hay mucha gente _____.
4. Los trabajadores _____ consiguen empleo en la construcción de puentes y carreteras.
5. El Perú es un país _____.
6. El sector financiero es un campo _____.

a. que sabe manejar bases de datos
b. que está creciendo (*growing*) mucho
c. que estudian inglés o chino
d. que trabajan en el sector informal
e. que quiere expandir su economía
f. que tienen experiencia en ingeniería

PASO 3. En parejas, contesten las preguntas y explíquense las respuestas.

1. El Perú no es un país muy pobre, pero no tiene los recursos (*resources*) de un país rico como Canadá o los Estados Unidos. ¿Cómo piensas que debería gastar su dinero para crecer? ¿En qué orden de prioridad pones la educación, el ejército (*army*), la salud, el sistema judicial y el transporte, por ejemplo?
2. Las universidades son necesarias para el desarrollo económico, pero implican muchos gastos (*expenses*): las bibliotecas, las computadoras, los edificios, el mantenimiento (*maintenance*), los profesores, otros servicios para los estudiantes, etcétera. Para un país sin muchos recursos, ¿en qué orden de prioridad pones estos gastos?
3. En tu país, ¿ves una relación entre las universidades y el desarrollo económico? ¿En las regiones donde hay buenas universidades, también hay un alto nivel económico?

↻ Reciclaje

Present indicative: *tú* forms

Empareja la profesión con la actividad que se hace en esa profesión, usando uno de los siguientes verbos. Conjuga el verbo en la forma **tú** del tiempo presente.

aceptar	arreglar	cuidar	escribir	llevar
apagar (*put out*)	cortar	dar	hacer	tomar

Si eres…   **¿Qué haces?**

1. ____ bombero
2. ____ cajero
3. ____ cirujano
4. ____ enfermero
5. ____ escritor

6. ____ estilista
7. ____ fotógrafo
8. ____ taxista

a. _____ artículos o libros.
b. _____ operaciones para curar las enfermedades.
c. _____ fotos de personas u objetos.
d. _____ y _____ el pelo de tus clientes.
e. _____ el dinero de los clientes y les _____ cambio.
f. _____ la salud de la gente.
g. _____ incendios.
h. _____ a la gente de un lugar a otro en tu coche.

■ Answers to this activity are in **Appendix 2** at the back of your book.

10.2 Pide ayuda para revisar tu currículum

Informal (*tú*) commands

Para empezar…

Alguna vez en la vida, casi todos tenemos que buscar trabajo. Aquí hay doce consejos (*pieces of advice*) que te pueden ayudar en ese proceso, ¡pero uno no es un buen consejo! Decide cuál es y táchalo (*cross it out*).

1. **Busca** el tipo de trabajo que quieres.
2. **Pide** ayuda para revisar tu currículum.
3. **Evita** cualquier tipo de error ortográfico en tu currículum.
4. **Piensa** bien si estás dispuesto/a (*willing*) a cambiarte de ciudad.
5. **Usa** todos los medios (*media*) posibles para buscar trabajo: el Internet, los contactos personales, tu universidad, etcétera.
6. **Vístete** bien para la entrevista. ¡Las primeras impresiones sí cuentan!
7. **No te bañes** el día de tu entrevista. ¡Eso te da buena suerte (*luck*)!
8. **No hables demasiado,** pero **no te quedes** callado/a (*silent*) tampoco.
9. **Aprende** los nombres de las personas que te entrevistan.
10. **No hables** mal de los lugares donde trabajaste antes.
11. **No comas** durante la entrevista.
12. **Escribe** una nota de agradecimiento (*thank-you note*) después de la entrevista.

■ Answers to these activities are in **Appendix 2** at the back of your book.

CONÉCTATE AL MUNDO HISPANO

Al presentarse para puestos de trabajo en los países hispanohablantes, es común incluir varios **elementos demográficos** en el currículum, como por ejemplo, la fecha de nacimiento, el estado civil y una foto. Muchos consideran que estos datos ayudan a dar una imagen más completa del candidato como ser humano. En los Estados Unidos, en cambio, no es común incluir este tipo de información, por temor (*fear*) a que fomente (*encourages*) la discriminación laboral.

Actividades analíticas

1 The command form of the verb (**el mandato**) expresses what you want another person to do. Commands are used to give advice, to offer invitations, and to give orders. The verb forms in bold in **Para empezar** are *informal commands* (**los mandatos informales**), used when you address the person you're speaking to as **tú.** You will see other types of commands in **Estructura 10.3.**

Using as examples the boldfaced words in **Para empezar,** determine the informal command form of each of the following verbs.

	MANDATOS INFORMALES (TÚ)		
	pensar	**aprender**	**pedir**
POSITIVE	_____	_____	_____

This form is exactly the same as which form of the verb in the present tense? _____
_____

2 The examples in **Actividades analíticas 1** are all *positive commands,* which means that they invite the other person *to do* something. When you want the other person *not* to do something, you use a *negative command.*

Complete the following chart using examples that you find in **Para empezar.**

	MANDATOS INFORMALES (TÚ)		
	hablar	**comer**	**escribir**
POSITIVE	habl**a**	com**e**	escrib**e**
NEGATIVE	_____	_____	no escrib**as**

The negative informal command is the same as the **tú** form of the present tense, but with the "opposite" vowel in the ending: **-es** for **-ar** verbs and **-as** for **-er** and **-ir** verbs.

3 As expected, verbs with stem changes in the present tense will also show this change in negative informal commands.

e → ie   pensar → p**ie**nsas → no p**ie**nses
o → ue   dormir → d**ue**rmes → no d**ue**rmas
e → i   pedir → p**i**des → no p**i**das

Verbs ending in **-car, -gar,** and **-zar** have a spelling change to preserve the **-c-, -g-,** and **-z-** sounds.

c → qu   buscar → no bus**qu**es
g → gu   pagar (*to pay*) → no pa**gu**es
z → c   empezar → no empie**c**es

Autoprueba

Use the pattern you just learned to give the positive (+) and negative (−) informal commands for the following verbs.

1. **trabajar**
   + _____
   − no _____

2. **correr**
   + _____
   − no _____

3. **dormir**
   + _____
   − no _____

Respuestas: 1. trabaja, trabajes **2.** corre, corras **3.** duerme, duermas

4 Some common irregular verbs have a special positive informal command form.

VERBO	MANDATO POSITIVO INFORMAL (TÚ)	EJEMPLO	
decir	**di**	**Di** «por favor».	*Say "please."*
hacer	**haz**	¡**Haz** la tarea!	*Do your homework!*
ir	**ve**	**Ve** a la biblioteca.	*Go to the library.*
poner	**pon**	**Pon** los libros aquí.	*Put the books here.*
salir	**sal**	¡**Sal** a la calle!	*Go out on the street!*
ser	**sé**	**Sé** buen niño.	*Be a good boy.*
tener	**ten**	**Ten** esto.	*Have (Take) this.*
venir	**ven**	**Ven** a mi casa.	*Come to my house.*

Many of these positive command forms are easy to remember, because they are simply the stem of the verb (the part that precedes the final **-ar, -er,** or **-ir**) without any ending. Circle those forms that are of this type.

Note that **ve** is the positive command form of both **ir** and verb **ver.** The context makes it clear which is intended.

Ve a tu casa.   *Go to your house.*

Ve la dirección de esa casa.   *Look at / See the address of that house.*

5 For verbs that use a **-g-** in their stem in the **yo** form of the present tense, such as **decir** (**digo**) and **hacer** (**hago**) (see **Estructura 5.1**), they use this same stem with **-g-** in the negative informal command.

VERBO	MANDATO NEGATIVO INFORMAL (TÚ)	EJEMPLO	
decir	no **digas**	No **digas** nada.	*Don't say anything.*
hacer	no **hagas**	No **hagas** eso.	*Don't do that.*
poner	no **pongas**	No **pongas** los pies allí.	*Don't put your feet there.*
salir	no **salgas**	No **salgas** a la calle.	*Don't go out on the street.*
tener	no **tengas**	No **tengas** miedo.	*Don't be afraid (lit., have fear).*
venir	no **vengas**	No **vengas** tan temprano.	*Don't come so early.*

All of these are **-er** and **-ir** verbs, so they all take the ending with the "opposite" vowel (**-as**).

6 The verbs **ir, ser,** and **ver** have irregular forms when they are negative informal commands.

VERBO	MANDATO NEGATIVO INFORMAL (TÚ)	EJEMPLO	
ir	no vayas	No vayas a la playa.	*Don't go to the beach.*
ser	no seas	No seas así.	*Don't be like that.*
ver	no veas	No veas la película.	*Don't watch the movie.*

7 Object pronouns are attached to the *end* of positive commands, where they are written as a single word together with the verb. After the object pronouns are attached, a written accent mark is added if needed in order to keep the stress on the original stressed syllable.

| ¡Haz**lo**! | *Do it!* |
| ¡Levánta**te**! | *Get up!* |

Find one example of a positive command with an object pronoun in **Para empezar.** _____
With negative commands, object pronouns are always written before the verb.

| ¡No **lo** hagas! | *Don't do it!* |
| ¡No **te** levantes! | *Don't get up!* |

Find at least one other example of this in **Para empezar.** _____

¡Siéntate!

En español...

All of the commands shown here are used when you are addressing people as **tú.** Because **tú** is strictly singular, these commands are only used for addressing one person. To give a command to more than one person, you must use an **Uds.** command, which you will learn more about in **Estructura 10.3.**

In Spain, you would likely use **vosotros** commands to a group of people you would address as **tú.** Positive **vosotros** commands are just like the infinitive form, but with the final **-r** replaced by a **-d.**

hablar → ¡Hablad (vosotros)!
comer → Comed ahora.
escribir → Escribid la tarea.

Negative **vosotros** commands are like the negative **tú** commands except that the final vowel of the **tú** command is accented, then the vowel **-i-** is added before the final **-s.**

no hables → ¡No habléis!
no comas → ¡No comáis!
no escribas → ¡No escribáis!

Autoprueba

Using what you now know about informal command formation and the different positions of object pronouns, write the positive (+) and negative (−) commands for the following reflexive verbs. **¡Atención!** One of the verbs has a stem change.

1. **bañarse**
   + _____ − _____

2. **ducharse**
   + _____ − _____

3. **dormirse**
   + _____ − _____

The verb **apurarse** (*to hurry*) is a new verb to you, but since it is regular and you know the pattern to form informal commands, you have the tools to form its positive and negative commands. Try it!

4. **apurarse**
   + _____ − _____

Actividades prácticas

A. Organiza tu día   ¿Cómo podemos usar el tiempo mejor? Las siguientes oraciones te dicen, paso por paso, cómo organizar un día de trabajo, pero están desordenadas. Ponlas en orden: la primera y la tercera ya están hechas.

a. _____ Al final del día, revisa tu lista y tacha (*cross out*) todo lo que ya hiciste. Usa las cosas que quedan pendientes (*pending*) para empezar una nueva lista para mañana.

b. _____ Haz una lista de todo lo que tienes que hacer.

c. _____ Empieza a hacer las cosas que aparecen en tu lista. Ten en mente (*Keep in mind*) el orden de prioridad que hiciste y el tiempo en que trabajas mejor.

d. _____ Revisa (*Review*) tu lista y pon las cosas en orden de prioridad.

e. _____ ¡Vete a la casa!

f. __1__ Al llegar al trabajo, siéntate en tu escritorio.

g. _____ Divide tu día en segmentos. Cada persona es distinta, así que si trabajas mejor por la mañana, usa ese tiempo para hacer los proyectos más difíciles de tu lista.

h. __3__ Pon absolutamente todo en la lista: desde las cosas más triviales hasta las cosas más importantes. ¡No tengas miedo! Si quieres, ¡puedes poner «haz una lista» en tu lista!

 B. Consejos buenos y consejos malos   Como probablemente ya sabes, no todos los consejos son buenos. Escucha los consejos sobre la preparación para una entrevista profesional e indica si son buenos o malos.

	UN CONSEJO BUENO	UN CONSEJO MALO
1.	☑	☐
2.	☐	☑
3.	☑	☐
4.	☑	☐
5.	☐	☑
6.	☑	☐
7.	☑	☐
8.	☑	☐
9.	☐	☑
10.	☑	☐

Vístete con ropa profesional.

 C. ¿Qué hacer con tantos emails?   En muchos trabajos, la cantidad de correos electrónicos es increíble y no es posible dejarlo a un lado. En parejas, creen consejos sobre qué hacer con este problema tan común. Usen las ideas de abajo o hagan sus propios consejos. Luego, compártanlos con la clase. **¡Atención!** Usen mandatos para crear los consejos.

IDEAS

contestar inmediatamente

indicar los mensajes que tienes que contestar todavía

borrar (*delete*) sin leer los mensajes que son correo basura (*junk*)

no dejar nada para otro día

no leer el correo electrónico antes de acostarte

no leer el correo electrónico si no tienes tiempo para contestar en ese momento

MODELO: IDEA: leer los emails
      CONSEJO: Lee solamente los emails que tienen que ver (*have something to do*) con el trabajo.

 D. ¡Hazme caso!   Crea cinco mandatos y léelos uno por uno a un compañero / una compañera para que los haga. ¡Entre más creativo, mejor! Si quieres, puedes usar expresiones como **al mismo tiempo,** o **primero… , después… .**

MODELO: Levántate.
      Baila y canta al mismo tiempo.

¿Por qué?

Why does Spanish switch to the "opposite" vowel in many command forms? If the language has to signal that the verb is a command, changing the vowel in the ending is a very simple and efficient way to do this. Spanish only has five vowels to choose from, though, and of these, **i** and **u** are generally not used in unstressed syllables at the end of the word. This leaves **a, e,** and **o.** For **-ar** verbs, switching to a new vowel would mean **e** or **o,** but **o** is already used for the **yo** form. This is why **-ar** verbs use the vowel **e** when they switch to a new vowel (**hablas → no hables**). For the same reason, **-er** and **-ir** verbs switch to a (**comes → no comas, duermes → no duermas**). We see, then, that what initially looks strange is actually a very simple and straightforward way for Spanish to signal commands.

Reciclaje

Present indicative: *Ud.* forms

En las oficinas y otros lugares de trabajo, es común usar las formas correspondientes a **Ud.** cuando hablas. Practícalo con estas oraciones, cambiándolas de **tú** a **Ud.**

TÚ	UD.
1. ¿Necesitas ayuda?	_____
2. Eres el nuevo gerente de la tienda.	_____
3. ¿Sabes cómo hacer esto?	_____
4. ¿Dónde pones los documentos?	_____
5. ¿Me puedes ayudar en algo, por favor?	_____
6. ¿En qué te puedo ayudar?	_____
7. Te voy a dejar el archivo en tu escritorio.	_____
8. ¿Te vas después de la reunión (*meeting*)?	_____

■ Answers to this activity are in **Appendix 2** at the back of your book.

10.3 Ponga el documento sobre el cristal.

Formal (*Ud./Uds.*) commands

Para empezar...

Las siguientes oraciones vienen de instrucciones para el uso de diferentes aparatos. Empareja cada oración con el aparato apropiado.

INSTRUCCIONES

1. _____ **No lo use** dentro del restaurante.
2. _____ **Ponga** el documento sobre el cristal (*glass*).
3. _____ **Ponga** más tinta (*ink*) negra.
4. _____ **Conecte** el ratón antes de usarla.
5. _____ **Use** «control c» para copiar y «control v» para pegar (*paste*).
6. _____ **Oprima** (*Press*) este botón para tomar una foto de sus amigos.
7. _____ **Indique** el tamaño del papel que va a usar: A4 o 8½ × 11.
8. _____ Si la va a usar mucho, **cómprela** con una pantalla grande.

APARATOS

a. una computadora
b. un escáner
c. una impresora
d. un teléfono móvil

■ Answers to these activities are in **Appendix 2** at the back of your book.

Actividades analíticas

1 *Formal commands* (**los mandatos formales**) are used with people that you address as **Ud.** or **Uds.*** Unlike singular informal commands, the form of the verb is the same for both positive and negative formal commands (**compre Ud., no compre Ud.**). Use the examples that you saw in **Para empezar** to complete the following chart of formal command forms for **Ud.**

	MANDATOS FORMALES (UD.)		
	usar	comer	oprimir
POSITIVE (AND NEGATIVE)	_____	(no) coma	_____

*Remember that you use formal **Ud.** with strangers, people who are considerably older than you, and anyone you treat with respect (such as your professor, doctor, or boss). In most places outside of Spain you'd use **Uds.** as plural *you,* so it's the plural of both **tú** and **Ud.**

As you saw with informal negative commands in **Estructura 10.2,** formal commands consist of the verb stem plus the "opposite" vowel, that is **-ar** verbs use the **-e** ending, and **-er** and **-ir** verbs use the **-a** ending. Verbs that use a special stem with **-g-** in the **yo** form of the present tense, such as **poner** (**pongo**) use this same stem in formal commands (**ponga**).

Write the verbs from **Para empezar** in their infinitive forms and put them in the correct column below. Don't repeat any verbs.

-ar VERBS   **-er VERBS**   **-ir VERBS**

_____ _____   _____   _____

_____ _____

As with negative informal commands, the verbs **ir, ser,** and **ver** have special forms: **vaya, sea,** and **vea.**

2 When addressing a group of people as **Uds.,** the command form of the verb is just like the **Ud.** command form except that **-n** is added to the end. Use this information to complete this chart.

MANDATOS FORMALES (UDS.)		
usar	**comer**	**oprimir**
POSITIVE (AND NEGATIVE) _____	_____	_____

3 As you saw with informal commands, the placement of object pronouns changes depending on whether the formal command is positive or negative. Complete the chart by writing whether the object pronouns for the formal commands appear *before the verb* or *after and attached to the verb,* then give an example of each case from **Para empezar.**

TIPO DE MANDATO	LOS PRONOMBRES DE OBJETO SE COLOCAN...	EJEMPLO
POSITIVE FORMAL (UD./UDS.)	_____	_____
NEGATIVE FORMAL (UD./UDS.)	_____	_____

En español…

The forms for the formal commands (**Ud.** and **Uds.**) should remind you of the negative informal (**tú**) commands seen in **Estructura 10.2.**

INFORMAL (**TÚ**) COMMAND, NEGATIVE:	¡No **pongas** el documento allí!	*Don't put* (inform. sing.) *the document there!*
FORMAL COMMAND (**UD.**):	¡**Ponga** el documento allí!	*Put* (form. sing.) *the document there!*
FORMAL COMMAND (**UDS.**):	¡**Pongan** el documento allí!	*Put* (pl.) *the document there!*

Because positive and negative formal (**Ud./Uds.**) commands and negative informal (**tú**) commands use the stem from the **yo** form of the present tense, when the negative informal command has an irregular form, so does the formal command. You will notice the same sound-preserving spelling changes here, too (for example, for **-car** verbs, **c → qu**). The formal commands and the negative informal commands look the same as the *present subjunctive* forms. You will begin to explore the subjunctive in **Capítulo 12.**

Actividades prácticas

A. Problemas y soluciones Empareja cada problema con una posible solución para ofrecerles consejos a varios estudiantes universitarios.

1. _____ No tenemos el libro.
2. _____ Siempre estamos cansados.
3. _____ No tenemos suficiente dinero.
4. _____ Llegamos tarde a la primera clase.
5. _____ Tenemos hambre.
6. _____ Tenemos un examen.
7. _____ Tenemos sed.
8. _____ Es viernes y ya no tenemos nada que hacer aquí.

a. Tomen un vaso de agua fría.
b. Coman algo. ¿Desean unos sándwiches?
c. Estudien mucho.
d. Pues, vayan a la librería a comprarlo.
e. ¡Duerman más!
f. ¡Váyanse a la casa!
g. ¡Levántense más temprano!
h. Pidan más horas en el trabajo.

B. Deseos El arquitecto español Santiago Calatrava, el inversionista mexicano Carlos Slim (ejecutivo de Telcel y América Móvil) y el empresario español Amancio Ortega (dueño de Zara) son personas de mucha influencia en el mundo de los negocios. Por cierto (*Indeed*), Slim y Ortega están entre las personas más ricas del mundo.

PASO 1. Las siguientes oraciones son deseos (*wishes*) que podrías (*you could*) pedir de estos tres hombres. Completa cada deseo (si es necesario) para hacerlo más a tu gusto (*to your taste*) e indica a quién le corresponde.

SANTIAGO CALATRAVA	CARLOS SLIM	AMANCIO ORTEGA	
☐	☐	☐	1. Haga más ropa de color _____.
☐	☐	☐	2. Invíteme a su casa en México.
☐	☐	☐	3. Diseñe un edificio para la ciudad de _____.
☐	☐	☐	4. Deme un trabajo como _____ en Telcel o América Móvil.
☐	☐	☐	5. Haga un puente en el río _____ (o entre _____ y _____).
☐	☐	☐	6. Ponga una tienda Zara en _____.
☐	☐	☐	7. Regáleme un plan de servicio telefónico.
☐	☐	☐	8. Déme un trabajo como _____ en Zara.
☐	☐	☐	9. Diseñe un(a) _____ para el campus de mi universidad.

PASO 2. ¿Qué industria te interesa más: la de la moda, de las telecomunicaciones o de la arquitectura? Formen grupos según sus intereses y hagan por lo menos tres recomendaciones (en forma de mandato) para el hombre del **Paso 1** (Calatrava, Slim o Ortega) que corresponde al interés del grupo.

> **MODELO:** Haga faldas largas para la colección del otoño.

C. Descripciones y consejos Para cada uno de las profesiones en la tabla, escoge **una descripción** de lo que hace una persona con mucha experiencia. Luego escoge el mandato formal para darle **un consejo** a una persona que apenas (*barely*) empieza en ese trabajo.

	UNA DESCRIPCIÓN	UN CONSEJO
1. una abogada	_____	_____
2. una enfermera	_____	_____
3. un policía	_____	_____
4. un profesor de yoga	_____	_____

a. Piensa en la seguridad (*security*) del público.
b. Cuide a sus pacientes.
c. Defienda los derechos (*rights*) de su cliente.
d. Tiene mucha paciencia cuando da la clase.

e. Defiende los derechos (*rights*) de su cliente.
f. Piense en la seguridad del público.
g. Cuida a sus pacientes.
h. Tenga mucha paciencia cuando da la clase.

D. Amor en la oficina

PASO 1. Lee la carta al Doctor Amor. Luego, en grupos decidan cuáles son las tres mejores y las tres peores sugerencias (*suggestions*). ¿Hay alguno en la lista de las mejores respuestas de un grupo y también en la lista de las peores respuestas de otro grupo?

Para: Doctor@amor.com
De: Anónimo
Asunto: Problemas del amor

Doctor Amor:

Somos amigos de muchos años, y desde hace un mes, trabajamos en la misma compañía. El problema que tenemos es que estamos enamorados (*in love*) de la misma mujer. Los tres somos arquitectos y trabajamos juntos en la misma oficina, pero ella lleva mucho más tiempo en este trabajo que nosotros y tiene un puesto (*position*) más alto. ¡Ayúdenos! ¿Qué hacemos? Ella no sabe nada de esto.

—Dos amigos anónimos

---

1. **Hablen** con ella y **explíquenle** cómo es la situación. **Pídanle** su opinión.
2. **Regresen** al trabajo y ya no **piensen** en eso.
3. **Salgan** juntos a cenar y a bailar con ella, y a ver qué pasa.
4. **Olvídenla** y **busquen** trabajo en otra compañía.
5. **Busquen** novias en otra parte, fuera del trabajo.
6. **Túrnense.** Si ella está de acuerdo, uno de Uds. puede salir con ella un fin de semana y el otro el siguiente fin de semana.
7. **Explíquenles** la situación a todos sus compañeros del trabajo y **pídanles** su opinión.
8. **Cálmense** (*Calm down*) y **esperen** un mes. Si para ese entonces todavía tienen el mismo problema, **escríbanme** de nuevo.
9. **Pónganse** a pelear (*fight*) allí en la oficina. El ganador (*winner*) puede preguntarle a ella si quiere salir con él.
10. No le **digan** nada. **Pongan** todo su tiempo y energía en el trabajo, y van a ver que este problema va a desaparecer (*disappear*).

PASO 2. Ahora creen dos consejos más, uno bueno y uno malo y compártanlos con la clase.

E. ¿Qué les dices a los nuevos?

A los nuevos estudiantes que llegan a tu universidad por primera vez, ¿qué les puedes aconsejar sobre dónde comer, dónde estudiar, dónde vivir y qué clases tomar? En un grupo, creen una lista de tres o cuatro consejos para cada una de estas categorías. Pongan su mejor sugerencia para cada categoría en la pizarra.

dónde comer   dónde estudiar   dónde vivir   qué clases tomar

MODELO: Coman (Uds.) en el restaurante Mi Rancho Grande. Allí tienen la mejor comida de la ciudad a los mejores precios.

¡Leamos!

Puestos y placeres

Antes de leer

PASO 1. En parejas, definan el trabajo «ideal». ¿En qué consiste? ¿Qué beneficios (*benefits*) les ofrece el trabajo ideal a sus trabajadores? ¿Cómo es el sueldo (*salary*)? ¿Dónde trabaja la persona que ocupa este puesto ideal? (¿Trabaja en una ciudad grande? ¿en la playa?) Describan los aspectos del trabajo ideal y prepárense para compartir sus ideas con la clase. ¿Están de acuerdo Uds. o tienen ideas muy distintas?

PASO 2. Todos sabemos de los puestos «normales» que hay en el mundo profesional, pero también hay muchos trabajos raros, y alguien los tiene que hacer. Empareja cada puesto de trabajo con la descripción apropiada. Luego, indica cuáles de los trabajos te gustaría hacer y cuáles no.

	ME GUSTARÍA	NO ME GUSTARÍA
1. _____ catador (*taster*) de helados	☐	☐
2. _____ cuidador (*caretaker*) de isla paradisíaca	☐	☐
3. _____ diseñador de los vestidos de Barbie	☐	☐
4. _____ diseñador de nuevos videojuegos	☐	☐
5. _____ enfermo imaginario	☐	☐
6. _____ probador (*tester*) / crítico de aire	☐	☐

a. cuidar de la isla de Hamilton, situada en la Gran Barrera de Coral (*Great Barrier Reef*) de Australia
b. probar los sabores (*flavors*) hasta encontrar el resultado más satisfactorio para ser lanzado (*launched*) al mercado
c. viajar en los vuelos de los competidores para saber qué ofrecen
d. desarrollar (*develop*) ropa para la compañía Mattel
e. fingir (*pretend*) que tiene una enfermedad para que los alumnos de medicina se entrenen haciendo diagnósticos
f. desarrollar ideas o conceptos y crear niveles (*levels*) para los juegos en desarrollo

A leer

PASO 1. Lee el artículo sobre los puestos ideales.

Puestos y placeres

por Soraya Almendros

Entrevistamos sobre su futuro a más de cien alumnos recién graduados de la universidad. Un tema que salió en todas las entrevistas fue querer conseguir un puesto divertido, bien remunerado[a]... ideal. Le pedimos a los entrevistados que describieran[b] el puesto de sus sueños, pero las respuestas nos decepcionaron.[c] ¡Qué aburridas!

[a]*well paid* [b]*que... to describe* [c]*disappointed*

Este resultado nos hizo preguntarnos: «¿Cuál es el puesto ideal? ¿Existe?» A partir de esto, realizamos más entrevistas y este artículo.

LUCILA: Soy crítica de aire. Estudié idiomas porque me gustaba viajar. Después de tres puestos agobiadores,[d] conseguí este con la aerolínea. No soy pilota o azafata.[e] Hago viajes todo el año, en primera clase, en vuelos de la competencia,[f] a ciudades grandes y a algunos destinos exóticos.

TOMÁS: Bueno, en la universidad era muy quejón[g] y me hacía el enfermo[h] para no ir a clase. Ahora tengo el puesto de enfermo imaginario. Trabajo en un hospital docente[i] donde me quejo[j] de mis síntomas. Hoy tengo la gripe.

ALBERTO: Cuando mi esposa y yo nos casamos, fuimos de luna de miel[k] a Australia. Allí supimos que se solicitaba un cuidador para la isla Hamilton. La visitamos y, como mi esposa es escritora y puede trabajar dondequiera,[l] solicité el puesto.

MONA: Hay algo de revancha[m] en mí, por todos esos años que mis padres me regañaban[n]: «Basta ya[ñ] de los videojuegos» o mi favorito: «¡Te pierdes la vida jugando esa basura!» Sigo perdiéndome la vida jugando videojuegos, pero ahora los diseño.

RAÚL: Me gradué en moda y diseño. Trabajé con dos compañías antes de conseguir este puesto, el más divertido y gratificante. En este puesto —mis amigos se divierten con esto— diseño ropa para la muñeca[o] Barbie.

LOLA: Soy catadora de helados. Mi puesto en dos palabras: ¡Como helado!

Para los que piensan que estos puestos pagan poco, a ver si estos datos desvanecen[p] sus dudas. Al volver de sus viajes, el jefe de Lucila le paga 2,400 dólares al mes por sus informes sobre la competencia. Por cada mes que pasa haciéndose el enfermo, le pagan a Tomás 1,440 dólares. Alberto y Susan no solo viven en un paraíso donde pasan los días buceando y disfrutando de[q] las playas, sino que Alberto también recibe 16,000 dólares al mes por cuidar la isla. Por cada juego que Mona diseña, le pagan 2,000 dólares. Raúl gana 5,000 dólares mensuales[r] por diseñar vestidos chiquititos[s] para Barbie. Y finalmente, Lola gana 4,600 al mes por degustar[t] helados y determinar el sabor más satisfactorio.

Dedicamos este informe a los alumnos recién graduados en busca del puesto ideal.

[d]*exhausting*   [e]*flight attendant*   [f]*competition*   [g]*muy... a big complainer*   [h]*me... I pretended to be sick*   [i]*teaching (adj.)*   [j]*me... I complain*   [k]*luna... honeymoon*   [l]*wherever*   [m]*vengeance*   [n]*scolded*   [ñ]*Basta... Enough already*   [o]*doll*   [p]*dispell*   [q]*disfrutando... enjoying*   [r]*monthly*   [s]*tiny*   [t]*tasting*

PASO 2. Ahora escribe el puesto de trabajo que corresponde a cada sueldo.

1. _____
   1.440 dólares al mes

2. _____
   2 mil dólares mensuales

3. _____
   2.400 dólares al mes

4. _____
   4.600 dólares mensuales

5. _____
   5 mil dólares al mes

6. _____
   16 mil dólares al mes

De los seis, ¿cuál es el trabajo que paga mejor?

Después de leer

PASO 1. Contesta las siguientes preguntas.

1. Según el título, ¿por qué son ideales los empleos que describe el autor?

2. ¿Cuál puesto de trabajo requiere los talentos de un actor? ¿Por qué?

3. De los trabajos descritos en el artículo, ¿cuál es el mejor pagado? ¿Y el peor pagado?

4. Si trabajas como crítico de aire para Southwest, ¿vas a viajar mucho en vuelos de Southwest como parte de tu trabajo? Explica por qué.

PASO 2. De los trabajos mencionados en el artículo, ¿cuál prefieres tú? Explica tu decisión.

PASO 3. En grupos, escojan uno de los trabajos del artículo y preparen una descripción para presentar al resto de la clase. Usen la información del artículo y sus propias ideas o busquen en Internet para hablar de:

- los requisitos del puesto de trabajo
- las ventajas del puesto de trabajo
- las desventajas del puesto de trabajo

¡Escuchemos!

La tecnología en el lugar
de trabajo

Antes de escuchar

En parejas, túrnense para describir en español algunas de las palabras tecnológicas sin mencionar
el nombre.

MODELO: E1: Se usan para escuchar música o un video en la computadora.
              E2: ¿Hablas de los audífonos?
              E1: ¡Sí!

la computadora	la láptop
el correo electrónico / email	el micrófono
el escáner	la pantalla
la impresora	

A escuchar

Mira y escucha a Esteban, que describe algunos términos tecnológicos en español. Mientras ves
el video, rellena los espacios en blanco con la forma correcta de las palabras de **Antes de
escuchar** para completar la descripción.

Básicamente en una oficina hay… o en una oficina generalmente los elementos que más se utilizan son…
el teléfono, ¿verdad?, algunas todavía tienen fax, aunque el fax es algo que se está perdiendo porque
ya la gente prefiere usar Internet y entonces tiene un _____.[1] Entonces escanean las
facturas (*bills*) o los recibos (*receipts*) y las mandan a través de (*by*) Internet por _____.[2]
Entonces, también hay escáner y hay _____,[3] que muchas de las veces es el mismo…
la misma consola, la misma máquina que hace ambas (*both*) cosas y también a veces le añaden la
función de fotocopias. Entonces, después está el monitor, que es el monitor de la computadora… la
_____,[4] siempre hay una _____,[5] que es la torre, digamos (*let's
say*), donde se conecta ahí todos los demás dispositivos (*devices*) que son los parlantes (*speakers*),
el _____,[6] el mouse es como lo decimos, ¿verdad? Y también tiene los accesos
para conectar dispositivos de almacenamiento (*storage*) masivo como USBs, las tarjetas de
_____,[7] o si quiere conectar la impresora se conecta ahí, también tiene la unidad de
DVD y de CD, entonces también eso es parte de la computadora. Y también tiene algunas aliadas como
para sacar a veces videos por ahí a través de… digamos, de cables o a través de también como
conectores de audífonos o _____[8]… Eso se usa más también como para hacer
videollamadas por Internet. Entonces uno conecta la cámara de video allí a la computadora y el
micrófono y el _____[9] y puede, digamos, usar Skype y hablar con alguien más.

Después de escuchar

En grupos, comparen las aplicaciones tecnológicas que usan con frecuencia: los audífonos, el
email, el escáner, la impresora, la láptop, el ratón, la memoria USB, el teléfono inteligente
(*smart phone*), televisión/videojuegos en 3D. ¿Uds. las usan todas? ¿Cuándo y para qué las
usan? Si no usan algunas, ¿por qué no las usan?

MODELO: Uso el correo electrónico para la comunicación profesional y uso la impresora para
              imprimir los correos electrónicos. No uso un escáner porque no tengo uno.

¡Escribamos!

La carrera de mis sueños

Para conseguir un puesto de trabajo, tienes que explicar por qué eres el/la mejor candidato/a, ofreciendo justificaciones y ejemplos de tu experiencia. ¿Puedes describir la carrera profesional ideal para ti?

Antes de escribir

Escribe la información apropiada para la carrera de tus sueños.

- el campo (*field*)
- el puesto de trabajo
- las responsabilidades
- experiencia necesaria para el puesto
- la tecnología necesaria (para todos los aspectos del trabajo: la comunicación, la publicidad, etcétera)
- otras destrezas (*skills*) necesarias para el puesto

A escribir

En tres párrafos, describe la carrera de tus sueños. En la primera frase, describe la carrera ideal. En el resto del primer párrafo, explica por qué te interesa el campo (o cómo te interesó). En el segundo párrafo describe con más detalle el puesto ideal para ti, qué experiencia requiere el puesto y luego explica si tienes esa experiencia o si la vas a tener en el futuro. Termina el ensayo con un párrafo sobre qué tipo de tecnología se requiere, cómo tiene que usarse y si hay otras destrezas necesarias que tienes que te pueden ayudar en este campo.

MODELO: La carrera de mis sueños es la medicina. Mis padres son doctores en una zona rural del estado. Desde una edad joven, entendí la importancia del cuidado médico básico para toda la gente de mi pueblo. En el colegio, disfruté de mis cursos de ciencia y siempre sacaba buenas notas (*grades*) en química, biología y física. El verano pasado hice una práctica en una clínica en mi pueblo.

El puesto ideal para mí es ser doctor familiar. En los Estados Unidos hay muchos especialistas, pero no hay muchos doctores familiares (o doctores de atención primaria)…

Después de escribir

Revisa tu ensayo. Luego, intercambia ensayos con un compañero / una compañera para evaluarlos. Lee el ensayo de tu compañero/a y determina si el ensayo tiene sentido (*makes sense*). Lee de nuevo el ensayo con cuidado para revisar los siguientes puntos.

☐ empieza con una descripción breve y clara de la carrera ideal
☐ explica la historia de su interés en el campo
☐ usa detalles para describir el puesto ideal
☐ describe la experiencia necesaria para el puesto
☐ explica el papel de la tecnología en su trabajo futuro
☐ usa el imperfecto para describir en el pasado
☐ usa el pretérito para hablar de las acciones que ocurrieron en el pasado
☐ hay concordancia entre sujetos y verbos
☐ hay concordancia entre sustantivos y adjetivos
☐ tiene la ortografía correcta

Después de revisar el ensayo de tu compañero/a, devuélveselo. Mira tu propio ensayo para ver los cambios que tu compañero/a te recomienda y haz las revisiones necesarias.

ESTRATEGIA

Supporting details

A solid thesis statement to open a paragraph should assert something, then the rest of the paragraph should explicitly support that assertion. Good supporting details include facts, statistics, examples, background information, descriptive adjectives, and brief anecdotes.

¡Hablemos!

¿Le puedo dar un mensaje?

Antes de hablar

En parejas, hablen de las llamadas telefónicas más profesionales que han hecho (*made*) o recibido (*received*). Pueden ser llamadas para hablar del producto o servicio de una compañía, un mensaje recordatorio sobre una cita médica, llamadas en el lugar de trabajo, entrevistas por teléfono —cualquier contexto que no sea personal (entre amigos).

■ ¿Cuándo fue?

■ ¿Llamaste tú o te llamaron?

■ ¿Con quién(es) hablaste?

■ ¿Por qué?

A hablar

En parejas, túrnense para hacer las llamadas telefónicas en que le pides a tu compañero/a la información específica que tu profesor(a) le dará (*will give*).

MODELO: *Instrucciones para E1: Quieres el número de servicio al cliente.*
E1: ¡Rin, rin!
E2: ¿Aló? (¿Bueno?, ¿Diga?, ¿Dígame?)
E1: Buenas tardes. Soy _____. Busco el número de teléfono de servicio al cliente.
E2: Claro. Es 3-52-60-70.
E1: Gracias.
E2: De nada.

Después de hablar

En grupos, hablen de las llamadas telefónicas. ¿Entendieron lo que querían las personas que llamaron? ¿Consiguieron lo que querían? ¿Cuáles fueron los retos (*challenges*) y los triunfos? Presenten los resultados al resto de la clase.

Conéctate al cine

Película: *Los lunes al sol* (drama, España, 2002)
Director: Fernando León de Aranoa

Sinopsis:

Santa, José y Lino son amigos. Ninguno de ellos tiene empleo desde que la fábrica donde trabajaban eliminó muchos trabajos en el proceso de industrializarse. Pasan tiempo juntos hablando y tomando alcohol, muchas veces en el bar de otro amigo, Rico. Cada uno de ellos tiene una actitud diferente frente a estos tiempos difíciles.

Escena (DVD, 00:02:30 to 0:05:50):

José y Lino están en el transbordador (*ferry*) cuando sube Santa, sin boleto (*ticket*). Lino tiene un periódico con un anuncio de empleo. Santa y José le hacen preguntas sobre el trabajo.

Antes de ver

Lino va a una entrevista de trabajo. ¿Qué debe tener un candidato para tener éxito (*success*) en una entrevista profesional? Pon estos en orden del 1 al 6, de más importante (1) a menos importante (6).

_____ un buen aspecto   _____ una edad apropiada (*appropriate*)

_____ una buena actitud   _____ mucha experiencia previa

_____ un conocimiento de la industria   _____ un vehículo propio

A ver

PASO 1. Lee las **Expresiones útiles** y ve el video. No trates de entender cada palabra, pero escucha con atención cuando los amigos hablan del anuncio de trabajo.

PASO 2. Lee las preguntas y posibles respuestas. Luego, ve el video otra vez y escucha con atención para encontrar las respuestas correctas.

1. _____ ¿A qué hora es la entrevista?

   a. a las doce   b. a las dos   c. a las diez

2. _____ Según el anuncio, ¿qué ofrece el trabajo?

   a. 14 pagas   b. 40 pagas   c. 120 pagas

3. _____ ¿Qué límite de edad tiene el trabajo?

   a. 25 años   b. 35 años   c. 45 años

4. _____ ¿Cómo va a conseguir Lino un vehículo propio?

   a. Su esposa se lo compra.   b. Su hijo se lo compra.   c. Él mismo (*himself*) se lo compra.

5. _____ Según Santa, ¿qué debe tener el candidato?

   a. una buena actitud   b. un buen aspecto   c. un buen vehículo

6. _____ ¿De qué se preocupa Lino?

   a. sus canas   b. su ropa   c. su vehículo

7. _____ ¿Cómo va a aprender Lino las cosas necesarias para el trabajo?

   a. Su hijo le va a enseñar.   b. Va a tomar un curso.   c. Va a comprar libros.

Expresiones útiles

tiene buena pinta	it looks promising
pagas	payments
vehículo propio	one's own vehicle
conocimientos de informática	knowledge of computers
posibilidades de ascenso	opportunities for promotion
edad	age
me echa a mí la culpa	puts the blame on me
canas	gray hair(s)
tener buen aspecto	to look presentable
ya veremos	we'll see
ni idea	(I have) no idea

■ For copyright reasons, the feature-film clips referenced in **Conéctate al cine** have not been provided by the publisher. Each of these films is readily available through retailers or online rental sites such as Amazon, iTunes, or Netflix.

Después de ver

En parejas, contesten las siguientes preguntas.

¿Alguna vez hiciste una entrevista de empleo? ¿Estabas nervioso/a? ¿Qué te preguntaron durante la entrevista? ¿Cómo respondiste a las preguntas? Después de la entrevista, ¿te contrataron (*hire*)? ¿Por qué crees que (no) te contrataron?

VOCABULARIO

Comunicación

Quiero presentarle(s) a...	I'd like you (*form. s./pl.*) to meet . . .
Quiero presentarte a...	I'd like you (*inform. s.*) to meet . . .
Encantado/a.	Nice to meet you. (*Lit.,* Enchanted.)
Es un placer.	Nice to meet you. (*Lit.,* It's a pleasure.)
¿En qué puedo servirle(s)?	How may I help you (*form. s./pl.*)?
Quisiera + *inf.*	I'd like to . . .
A sus órdenes.	At your (*form.*) service. (*Lit.,* At your orders.)
Es / Fue / Ha sido un placer.	It's / It was / It has been a pleasure.
Para servirle.	At your (*form.*) service. (*Lit.,* [I'm here] To serve you.)

Las profesiones y los oficios / Professions and Trades

el/la agente de bienes raíces	real estate agent
el/la agente de seguros	insurance agent
el/la arquitecto/a	architect
el/la asistente administrativo/a	administrative assistant
el/la bloguero/a	blogger
el bombero / la mujer bombero	firefighter
el/la cajero/a	cashier
el/la cirujano/a	surgeon
el/la cosmetólogo/a	cosmetologist
el currículum	resumé, curriculum vitae (CV)
el/la dentista	dentist
el/la director(a) de marketing	director of marketing
el/la diseñador(a) gráfico/a	graphic designer
el/la dueño/a	owner
el/la ejecutivo/a	executive
el/la empleado/a	employee
el/la empresario/a	business person
el/la enfermero/a	nurse
el/la escritor(a)	writer
el/la fotógrafo/a	photographer
el/la gerente	manager
el jefe / la jefa	boss
el/la juez(a)	judge
el/la programador(a)	programmer

la sala de justicia	court room
el/la secretario/a	secretary
el/la trabajador(a) social	social worker
el tribunal	court

Reciclaje: el/la abogado/a, el ama de casa, el/la camarero/a, el/la chofer, el/la doctor(a), el/la guía (naturalista), el/la ingeniero/a, el/la médico/a, el/la periodista, el/la pintor(a), el policía / la mujer policía, el/la profesor(a), el/la psicólogo/a, el/la sociólogo/a

La tecnología

el archivo	file
los audífonos	headphones
el correo electrónico	e-mail
el disco duro	hard drive
el enlace	link
la impresora	printer
la página web	web page
la pantalla	monitor, screen
la (computadora) portátil	laptop computer
el ratón	mouse
la red social	social network
la memoria USB	memory card/stick
el teclado	keyboard

Cognados: el blog, la computadora, el email, el escáner, el Internet, la (computadora) láptop, el micrófono, el módem, la tableta, el (teléfono) celular/móvil, el WiFi

Los verbos

cargar (gu)	to load; to upload
conseguir (i, i) (un puesto de trabajo)	to get (a job/position)
contratar	to hire
copiar	to copy
cortar	to cut
descargar (gu)	to download
deshacer (like **hacer**)	to undo
entrevistar	to interview
estar (*irreg.*) dispuesto/a	to be ready/willing
guardar	to save
hacer (*irreg.*) **clic / pinchar**	to click (on something)
pegar (gu)	to paste
preparar un currículum	to prepare a resumé/CV
solicitar (empleo / un trabajo)	to apply for (work / a job)
textear	to text

¡Estás en tu casa!

En Quechualla, Perú, una mujer regresa a casa.

Objetivos

In this chapter you will learn how to:

- welcome people to your home or country
- make polite invitations
- describe homes and furnishings
- talk about what you have done
- talk about what you are currently doing
- discuss housing in the Spanish-speaking world and its cost

11

COMUNICACIÓN LARIO JCTURA ATE

¡Bienvenido!
Welcoming people

 A. A ver: ¡Bienvenidos! ¿Qué les dicen estos hispanos a los estudiantes que piensan visitar sus países? Mira y escucha, luego escoge la mejor respuesta.

1. Aníbal, de Panamá
   a. Le damos la bienvenida siempre.
   b. Os doy la bienvenida.
   c. Siempre van a ser bienvenidos.
   d. Son bienvenidos.

2. Guillermo, de España
   a. Le damos la bienvenida.
   b. Os doy la bienvenida.
   c. Siempre van a ser bienvenidos.
   d. Son bienvenidos.

3. Pedro, de México
   a. Si pueden venir, ¡bienvenidos!
   b. Siempre van a ser bienvenidos.
   c. Son bienvenidos.
   d. Todo el mundo es bienvenido.

4. Allan, de Costa Rica
   a. Si pueden venir, ¡bienvenidos!
   b. Siempre van a ser bienvenidos.
   c. Son bienvenidos.
   d. Todo el mundo es bienvenido.

5. Vilma, de Colombia
   a. Bienvenidos siempre.
   b. Le damos la bienvenida.
   c. Son bienvenidos.
   d. Todo el mundo es bienvenido.

6. Alexis, de Costa Rica
   a. Le damos la bienvenida.
   b. Os doy la bienvenida.
   c. Siempre son bienvenidos.
   d. Todo el mundo es bienvenido.

7. Sylvia, de Argentina
   a. Si pueden venir, ¡bienvenidos!
   b. Siempre van a ser bienvenidos.
   c. Son bienvenidos.
   d. Todo el mundo es bienvenido.

8. Víctor, de México
   a. Bienvenidos siempre.
   b. Le damos la bienvenida.
   c. Son bienvenidos.
   d. Todo el mundo es bienvenido.

9. Mauricio, de Costa Rica
   a. Si pueden venir, ¡bienvenidos!
   b. Bienvenidos siempre.
   c. Siempre van a ser bienvenidos.
   d. Todo el mundo es bienvenido.

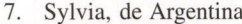

To say *Welcome!,* use **¡Bienvenido(s)!** or **¡Bienvenida(s)!**

To specify who is welcome, use this construction: *subject* + **ser** + **bienvenido/a/os/as.**

Los estudiantes siempre son bienvenidos aquí.	Students are always welcome here.

To use the equivalent of the verb *to welcome,* use this construction: *indirect object pronoun* + **dar** + **la bienvenida a** + *noun.*

Les damos la bienvenida a los estudiantes.	We welcome students. (*Lit.,* We give welcome to the students.)

B. ¡Bienvenidos!   Mira las imágenes y decide qué saludo de bienvenida debes usar para cada una.

MODELO:

¡Bienvenida, señora!

1.

Bienvenido

2.

Bienvenidos

3.

Bienvenidas

4.

Bienvenida

Pasa.

Making polite invitations

Here are some commands that can be used as polite invitations. Adding **por favor** to these commands will soften them even more, ensuring that your audience receives them as friendly, not bossy.

TÚ	UD.	UDS.	
Come más.	**Coma más.**	**Coman más.**	Have some more (food).
¡Diviértete!	**¡Diviértase!**	**¡Diviértanse!**	Have fun!
Pasa.	**Pase.**	**Pasen.**	Come in.
¡Sírvete!	**¡Sírvase!**	**¡Sírvanse!**	Help yourself!
Siéntate.	**Siéntese.**	**Siéntense.**	Have a seat.

A. Pase Ud.

PASO 1. Empareja cada imagen con la mejor invitación. **¡Atención!** Usa cada invitación solo una vez.

1. _____

2. _____

   a. Diviértanse.
   b. Pase.
   c. Pasen.
   d. Siéntese.
   e. Sírvanse.

3. _____

4. _____

5. _____

PASO 2. Para cada imagen, indica qué mandato debes usar.

1.

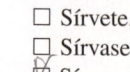

- ☑ Siéntate.
- ☐ Siéntese.
- ☐ Siéntense.

2.

- ☐ Pasa.
- ☐ Pase.
- ☑ Pasen.

3.

- ☑ Pasa.
- ☐ Pase.
- ☐ Pasen.

4.

- ☐ Siéntate.
- ☐ Siéntese.
- ☑ Siéntense.

5.

- ☐ Sírvete.
- ☐ Sírvase.
- ☑ Sírvanse.

6.

- ☐ Come más.
- ☐ Coma más.
- ☑ Coman más.

PASO 3. En parejas, inventen por lo menos dos mandatos apropiados más para cada imagen en el **Paso 2**. **¡Atención!** No se olviden de mantener el nivel de formalidad apropiado.

MODELO: (imagen 1) ¡Juega un videojuego conmigo! Cuéntame de tu día. No te olvides de llamar a tu mamá.

B. Las invitaciones en la clase En parejas, practiquen «las visitas». Un(a) estudiante llega, toca a (*knocks on*) la puerta y el otro/la otra lo/la invita a entrar, a sentarse y a comer algo. Luego, practiquen con otra pareja para usar la forma de **Uds.**

MODELO: E1: (Toca a la puerta.)
E2: ¡Hola! Pasa. Bienvenido/a.
E1: ¿Qué pasa?
E2: Tenemos pizza. Sírvete, por favor.

COMUN **VOCABULARIO** UCTURA ATE

La casa y los muebles
Rooms and other parts of a home

A. Un piso en Madrid

PASO 1. Usa el vocabulario de los dibujos para completar la descripción de un apartamento en Madrid.

apartamento **ascensor** **escalera** **jardín** **pasillo** **tendedero**

Vivo en un ___apartamento___ (o «piso», como decimos aquí en España) en un **edificio** moderno en Madrid. Para subir a **la tercera planta,** tienes que usar el ___ascensor___ o, si prefieres hacer más ejercicio, la ___escalera___. Al entrar en nuestro piso, hay dos **dormitorios.** Luego si pasas por el ___pasillo___, llegas al **cuarto de baño.** Hay un **salón** a la izquierda y **la cocina** a la derecha. Si cruzas el salón, vas a ver **la terraza** con plantas, hierbas y flores. ¡Tenemos nuestro propio ___jardín___ en la terraza! Tenemos una mesa para comer y relajarnos allí. La vista es bellísima. Además, tenemos el ___tendedero___ allí para colgar la ropa limpia para secarse al aire.

PASO 2. Contesta las siguientes preguntas sobre el lugar donde vives.

1. El edificio tiene cuatro plantas. ¿Cuántas plantas tiene tu casa o apartamento?
2. ¿Hay ascensor en tu edificio? No
3. ¿Tienes tu propio dormitorio o lo compartes con otra(s) persona(s)? Si, una persona
4. ¿Cuántas personas comparten el cuarto de baño donde vives? ¿Quién normalmente lo limpia? approx ocho chicas, una persona de limpia
5. Si hay una cocina donde vives, ¿cómo es? ¿Es grande? ¿moderna? Si no hay cocina, ¿echas de menos (*miss*) tener una cocina? es grande y moderna

Los muebles y los electrodomésticos
Furniture and appliances

A. ¿Cúal no se encuentra (*isn't found*) en... ?   Lee las siguientes preguntas y para cada una, selecciona la respuesta más lógica.

1. ¿Cuál de las siguientes cosas no se encuentra en una cocina normalmente?

   a. **un sofá**   b. **un fregadero**   c. **un horno**   d. **un refrigerador**

2. ¿Cuál de las siguientes cosas no se encuentra en un cuarto de baño?

  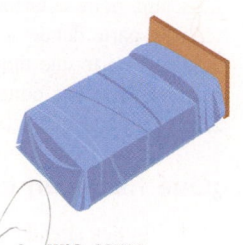 

   a. **una bañera**   b. **un lavabo**   c. **una cama**   d. **un espejo**

3. ¿Cuál de las siguientes cosas no se encuentra en un dormitorio / una habitación?

   a. **un armario**   b. **una mesita de noche**   c. **una lámpara**   d. **un lavaplatos**

4. ¿Cuál de las siguientes cosas no se encuentra en el salón?

   a. **un sillón**   b. **un estante**   c. **una ducha**   d. **un televisor**

5. ¿Cuál de las siguientes cosas no requiere la electricidad para funcionar?

   a. **la aspiradora**   b. **el inodoro**   c. **la lavadora**   d. **el microondas**

Vocabulario

To talk about household chores (**los quehaceres domésticos**) in Spanish, the following vocabulary is useful.

barrer (el piso)	to sweep (the floor)
hacer la cama	to make the bed
lavar (los platos, el suelo)	to wash/clean (the dishes, the floor)
limpiar	to clean
pasar la aspiradora	to vacuum
sacar la basura	to take out the trash
sacudir	to dust

B. ¿Cómo son las partes de la casa?   Empareja las partes de la casa con su mejor descripción.

1. ____ la parte subterránea
2. ____ el cuarto (*room*) que se usa para dormir durante la noche
3. ____ una parte exterior con plantas y flores
4. ____ la parte donde se aparca el coche
5. ____ el cuarto que tiene mesa y sillas y que se usa para cenar
6. ____ la parte que conecta un cuarto a otro
7. ____ el cuarto que se usa para ducharse

a. el comedor
b. el cuarto de baño
c. el dormitorio
d. el garaje
e. el jardín
f. el pasillo
g. el sótano

C. ¿Qué haces en cada cuarto?

PASO 1.   Indica si cada oración describe una acción lógica o no.

	LÓGICA	NO ES LÓGICA
1. Me afeito en el garaje.	☐	☑
2. Me baño en la cocina.	☐	☑
3. Me lavo los dientes en el cuarto de baño.	☑	☐
4. Cocino en el dormitorio.	☐	☑
5. Como en el comedor.	☑	☐
6. Descanso (*I rest*) en la terraza.	☐	☑
7. Duermo en el cuarto de baño.	☐	☑
8. Me ducho en el pasillo.	☐	☑
9. Escucho música en el salón.	☑	☐
10. Lavo la ropa en el sótano.	☐	☑
11. Me lavo las manos en el salón.	☑	☐
12. Leo en el dormitorio.	☑	☐
13. Tomo el sol en el jardín.	☑	☐
14. Veo la televisión en el salón.	☑	☐

PASO 2.   Ahora, en parejas, túrnense para cambiar todas las acciones ilógicas a acciones lógicas para Uds.

CONÉCTATE AL MUNDO HISPANO

Antoni Gaudí i Cornet fue un famoso arquitecto español que nació en Cataluña en 1852 y murió en 1926. Cuando diseñaba casas y otras estructuras, prefería trabajar con modelos tridimensionales en vez de con modelos planos (*flat*), y siempre improvisaba e incorporaba otros trabajos artesanales hechos de madera, cerámica, metal, vidrio y otros materiales. Su estilo, orgánico e innovador para esa época, ha sido reconocido mundialmente. A Gaudí le gustaba mucho la naturaleza y sus obras fueron inspiradas por ella. Entre sus mejores obras destacan (*stand out*) tres que están en Barcelona: la Casa Milà (en la página 117 de este libro), de paredes ondulantes (*wavy*); el Parque Güell, cubierto de mosaicos multicolores; y el Templo de la Sagrada Familia, una catedral que todavía está en construcción.

D. A ver: En casa de Jordi y Elena

PASO 1.   Mientras miras el video, indica las partes de la casa mencionadas por Jordi.

☒ la cocina ☐ el dormitorio ☒ el salón
☐ el cuarto de baño ☐ el garaje ☐ el sótano
☒ la despensa (*pantry*) ☐ el jardín ☒ la terraza

¿Qué electrodoméstico *no* menciona Jordi?

☒ la batidora (*mixer*) ☒ el lavavajillas ☐ la nevera
☐ el horno (*oven*) ☐ el microondas ☒ la placa (*cooktop*)

PASO 2.   Mientras miras el video otra vez, indica tres verbos que usa Jordi en cada parte de su apartamento. Luego, contesta la pregunta.

1. EN EL SALÓN
   ☐ comer ☐ dormir
   ☐ descansar ☐ lavar

2. EN LA TERRAZA
   ☐ comer ☐ estar
   ☐ descansar ☐ preparar

3. EN LA COCINA
   ☐ cocinar ☐ lavar
   ☐ descansar ☐ preparar

Según Jordi, ¿cuál es la cosa que no puede faltar en ninguna cocina española? _____

E. El juego de las veinte preguntas   Formen grupos de por lo menos tres personas. Un miembro del grupo debe seleccionar un cuarto, un mueble o un aparato electrodoméstico. Los otros miembros deben hacerle preguntas de sí o no hasta adivinar la palabra correcta.

MODELO: (E1 selecciona la palabra «fregadero» sin decirla a los otros estudiantes)
E2: ¿Es un mueble?
E1: No.
E2: ¿Está en el salón?
E1: No.
E3: ¿Está en la cocina?
E1: ¡Sí!
E2: ¿Se usa para cocinar? …

F. ¿Cómo son nuestras casas?

PASO 1.   Piensa en un cuarto de tu casa, residencia o apartamento. Apunta todos los detalles que puedes recordar sobre el cuarto. (Puedes usar estas preguntas para ayudar tu memoria: ¿Qué cuarto es? ¿Qué muebles y otras cosas hay en el cuarto? ¿Dónde se encuentran (*are they located*)? ¿Qué haces en el cuarto?) Para explicar bien la ubicación (*location*) de cada mueble, usa estas expresiones.

a la derecha/izquierda de	detrás de
al lado de	en medio de (*in the middle of*)
cerca/lejos de	encima de (*on top of*)
debajo de (*below*)	enfrente de

PASO 2.   En grupos de dos, túrnense para describir sus cuartos. Mientras una persona describe el cuarto, la otra debe dibujar el plano (*floor plan*) con todas las cosas que escucha y hacer preguntas cuando no comprende bien. Luego, intercambien (*exchange*) dibujos. ¿Es parecido el dibujo de tu pareja al cuarto que describiste?

G. ¿Cómo viven los estudiantes?

PASO 1.   En grupos, túrnense para contestar las preguntas sobre el lugar donde vive cada uno ahora. Un miembro del grupo debe apuntar las respuestas de los otros miembros del grupo.

¿Cómo es el edificio? ¿Cúantos pisos hay? ¿Hay ascensor en el edificio? ¿Hay cocina compartida (*shared*)?

¿Cuántos dormitorios hay? ¿Cuántos cuartos de baño?

Si hay cocina, ¿es moderna o anticuada? ¿Cuáles son los electrodomésticos en la cocina?

¿Cuántos televisores hay? ¿Dónde están? ¿Hay equipo de música? ¿Dónde?

¿Hay lavadora y secadora? ¿Dónde están?

¿Hay garaje? ¿sótano? ¿escaleras? ¿jardín?

PASO 2.   Basándote en la información del **Paso 1,** ¿quiénes viven en un apartamento, quiénes en una residencia estudiantil y quiénes en una casa? ¿Cuáles son algunas otras diferencias en los lugares donde viven tus compañeros?

¿Cuál dormitorio es más similar al tuyo?

COMUN VOCABUL **ESTRUCTURA** ATE

↻ Reciclaje

Present, preterite, and imperfect tenses

¿Quién hace los siguientes quehaceres en tu casa regularmente? ¿Quién los hizo ayer? ¿Y quién los hacía cuando eras niño/a? Dibuja la siguiente tabla y complétala con esta información, usando los verbos indicados. Y si la respuesta es **nadie,** escribe eso, pero con el verbo.

	Regularmente...	Ayer...	Cuando era niño/a...
1. preparar el desayuno			
2. pasar la aspiradora			
3. limpiar la casa			
4. hacer la cama			
5. lavar la ropa			
6. sacudir los muebles			

11.1 He limpiado mi cuarto cinco veces.

The present perfect

Para empezar...

Muchos profesionales en los países hispanos dicen que se vive mejor en su país que en los Estados Unidos o Canadá. Una razón es que es relativamente barato (*inexpensive*) contratar a alguien para hacer los quehaceres domésticos y ayudar con los niños. Esto les deja mucho tiempo que pueden pasar (*spend*) con los amigos y con la familia, y por eso la vida en general es más relajada.

¿Y para ti, cómo es la vida? ¿Tienes que hacer muchos quehaceres domésticos? ¿Tienes tiempo para relajarte con los amigos y la familia? Para explorar este tema, completa las siguientes oraciones con un número (usa el cero si es necesario). Marca **vez** o **veces** según sea necesario.

Los quehaceres domésticos

En la última semana,...

1. **he preparado** (*I have prepared*) la cena ____0____ vez / veces.
2. **he lavado** los platos ____0____ vez / veces.
3. **he pasado** la aspiradora ____0____ vez / veces.
4. **he sacudido** los muebles ____0____ vez / veces.
5. **he limpiado** mi cuarto ____1____ vez / veces.
6. **he hecho** (*made*) la cama ____5____ vez / veces.

He lavado los platos.

(Continues.)

■ Answers to these activities are in Appendix 2 at the back of your book.

El tiempo con los amigos y la familia

En la última semana,…

1. mis amigos y yo **hemos comido** juntos _____ vez / veces.
2. mis amigos y yo **hemos tomado** un café o un refresco juntos _____ vez / veces.
3. **he visto** (*seen*) una película en el cine _____ vez / veces.
4. **he salido** a bailar _____ vez / veces.

Ahora, ¿cuáles son tus conclusiones?

1. En general, hago _____ quehaceres domésticos.
   a. muchos   b. algunos   c. pocos
2. En general, paso _____ tiempo con mis amigos y mi familia.
   a. mucho   b. algún   c. poco

Actividades analíticas

1 The verbs in first two sections of the **Para empezar** questionnaire are in the *present perfect* (**el presente perfecto**). The use of this verb form is similar in both Spanish and English.

He preparado la cena cinco veces.   *I have prepared dinner five times.*

The present perfect consists of two words: the *auxiliary verb* (**el verbo auxiliar**) **haber** in the present tense and the *past participle* (**el participio pasado**). To make a statement negative, just add **no** in front of the auxiliary verb.

No he preparado la cena todavía.   *I haven't prepared dinner yet.*

Based on what you saw in **Para empezar,** complete the following conjugation of the auxiliary verb **haber** and provide an example of its use.

EL VERBO AUXILIAR *haber*			
yo	he		
tú	has	¿**Has hecho** la cama?	*Have you made the bed?*
él/ella, Ud.	ha	Javier **ha lavado** los platos.	*Javier has washed the dishes.*
nosotros/as	hemos		
vosotros/as	habéis	¿**Habéis comido**?	*Have you eaten?*
ellos/ellas, Uds.	han	Ya **han salido.**	*They have already left.*

2 Use the forms in **Para empezar** to complete this chart of past participles.

	INFINITIVO	PARTICIPIO PASADO
-ar VERBS	lavar	lavado
-er VERBS	comer	comido
-ir VERBS	salir	salido

The rule for forming regular past participles is very simple. For **-ar** verbs, add **-ado** to the stem (for example, **preparar → prepar- + -ado**), and for **-er** and **-ir** verbs, add **-ido** to the stem (for example, **sacudir → sacud- + -ido**). Note that regular past participles can only end in **-ado** or **-ido**; they do not change to agree with the subject. Form the past participle for these verbs.

INFINITIVO	PARTICIPIO PASADO
trabajar	trabajado
aprender	aprendido
vivir	vivido

Autoprueba

Use the pattern you just learned to form the past participles of these regular verbs.

lavar: _____

barrer: _____

sacudir: _____

Respuestas: lavado, barrido, sacudido

3   A few verbs have irregular past participles. Use what you saw in **Para empezar** to complete this table of the most common past participles and examples of how they are used.

INFINITIVO	PARTICIPIO PASADO		
decir	dicho	**He dicho** eso muchas veces.	*I have said that many times.*
escribir	escrito	Ella **ha escrito** cinco libros.	*She has written five books.*
hacer	hecho		
morir	muerto	El rey **ha muerto.**	*The king has died.*
poner	puesto	¿Dónde **has puesto** la llave?	*Where have you put the key?*
ver	visto		

■ For more on past participles in Spanish, see **Para saber más 11.1** at the back of your book.

4   You know that **hay,** from the verb **haber,** expresses the idea of *there is* or *there are* in the present tense.

Hay un cambio en nuestros planes.   *There is a change in our plans.*

Hay muchos rumores sobre el nuevo celular.   *There are many rumors about the new cell phone.*

To express this idea in the present perfect (*there has been* or *there have been*), use the auxiliary **ha** and the past participle **habido.**

Ha habido un cambio en el horario.   *There has been a change in the schedule.*

Ha habido muchos rumores sobre la nueva láptop.   *There have been a lot of rumors about the new laptop.*

Notice that just as you saw with **hay,** which has one form for *there is* and *there are,* the singular form **ha habido** is used even when you are talking about something plural, such as **rumores.**

En español...

In general, the use of the present perfect in Spanish parallels its use in English. In both languages, the present perfect describes events that happened in the past but that are still relevant to the current moment.

Han cancelado el vuelo. ¿Ahora qué hago?	*They've canceled the flight. Now what do I do?*

For many speakers from Spain, however, the present perfect is also used to describe events that happened very recently.

He comido a la una.	*I ate at 1:00.*

For Latin American speakers, and for some from Spain as well, the simple preterite is used in these cases.

Comí a la una.	*I ate at 1:00.*

Actividades prácticas

A. Preguntas y respuestas   Empareja cada pregunta con la respuesta apropiada.

1. __f__ ¿Qué han dicho los médicos?
2. __d__ ¿Dónde has puesto la aspiradora?
3. __b__ ¿Qué has hecho últimamente (*lately*)?
4. __e__ No me acuerdo. ¿Hemos visto esa película?
5. __h__ ¿Ya ha muerto el arquitecto que diseñó ese hotel?
6. __a__ ¿Ya has escrito la composición para mañana?
7. __g__ ¿Han ido a Ecuador?
8. __c__ ¿Les ha gustado esa casa?

a. No, pero me voy a levantar mañana muy temprano para escribirla.
b. Ayer fui al cine y hoy en la mañana ayudé a mi abuela a sacudir la casa.
c. Sí, más o menos. Es pequeña, pero tiene muy bonita terraza.
d. Creo que la dejé en el pasillo.
e. ¡Claro que sí! El DVD está allí (*over there*) en el salón.
f. Dicen que tu abuelo está muy bien.
g. No, pero tenemos muchas ganas de ir a conocerlo.
h. Sí. Se murió hace tres años.

B. Los quehaceres que hemos hecho esta semana   Lee la lista de quehaceres domésticos y marca los que has hecho esta semana. Luego, forma oraciones completas para decir cuáles has hecho y cuáles no.

> **MODELO:** lavar la ropa → He lavado la ropa esta semana.
> barrer el piso → No he barrido el piso.

1. ☐ pasar la aspiradora *No he pasado la aspiradora*
2. ☒ hacer la cama *Le hizo la cama*
3. ☒ pagar una cuenta (*bill*)
4. ☐ lavar los platos
5. ☐ limpiar el baño
6. ☐ sacudir los muebles
7. ☐ sacar la basura
8. ☐ sacar el reciclaje (*recycling*)

C. De África y Asia a América

¿Te has cambiado de casa alguna vez en tu vida? ¿Te has mudado de continente? En la historia de la humanidad, muchos sí lo han hecho, y la población actual de Latinoamérica es prueba (*proof*) de eso. La mayoría es de origen indígena y europeo, pero muchos también tienen sangre (*blood*) africana o asiática. ¿Cómo es eso? Las siguientes oraciones lo explican. Primero, indica si la información tiene que ver con los inmigrantes africanos o asiáticos. Luego, completa la oración con el verbo apropiado en el espacio en blanco. **¡Atención!** Cada verbo se usa dos veces.

Epsy Campbell Barr es una política costarricense. Su abuela era jamaicana.

Jorge Miyagui es un artista peruano, de ascendencia japonesa.

han emigrado (*emigrated*)   **ha habido**   **ha sido**   **han tenido**   **han vivido**

AFRICANOS	ASIÁTICOS	
☐	☒	1. Los filipinos _han tenido_ una presencia en Latinoamérica desde los primeros años de la colonia, cuando llegaron a México marineros (*sailors*) de Manila en barcos (*ships*) españoles.
☐	☐	2. Los chinos y los japoneses _____ en Latinoamérica desde las últimas décadas (*decades*) del siglo (*century*) XIX. Sus descendientes viven ahora en todos los países de Latinoamérica, pero sobre todo en Argentina, México y el Perú.
☐	☐	3. Desde los primeros años de la colonia, la influencia africana en Latinoamérica _____ muy importante. Algunos africanos llegaron con los españoles como marineros y exploradores, y muchos otros llegaron después como esclavos (*slaves*).
☐	☐	4. _____ muchos que son famosos: el astronauta costarricense Franklin Chang-Díaz, la actriz mexicana/uruguaya Bárbara Mori y el ex presidente peruano Alberto Fujimori.
☐	☐	5. Muchos inmigrantes de Jamaica y otras islas del Caribe _____ en Panamá desde los tiempos de la construcción del Canal de Panamá, cuando muchos llegaron para buscar trabajo.
☐	☐	6. Por siglos, la presencia africana _____ muy notable en el Caribe, Centroamérica, Colombia y Venezuela, pero los afrolatinos _____ influencia en todos los países latinoamericanos, desde México hasta Chile.
☐	☐	7. _____ muchísimos que son muy famosos: la cantante cubana Celia Cruz, el beisbolista dominicano Robinson Canó y el futbolista mexicano Giovani Dos Santos.
☐	☐	8. Muchos _____ a los Estados Unidos y a Canadá por razones económicas, y algunos de origen japonés _____ a Japón.

D. Los cambios en la vida

PASO 1. En parejas, entrevístense sobre los cambios importantes en sus vidas. Pregúntale a tu compañero/a en cuántos países, en cuántas ciudades y en cuántas casas ha vivido. ¿En cuántas universidades ha estudiado? En la casa donde vive su familia ahora, ¿siempre ha dormido en la misma habitación? Apunta los resultados.

MODELO: E1: ¿En cuántos países has vivido?
E2: He vivido en dos países: en Canadá y en los Estados Unidos.

PASO 2. Según los resultados, ¿crees que tu compañero/a ha llevado una vida relativamente estable (*stable*) o una con muchos cambios? ¿Piensas que este caso es típico de tu país? Está preparado/a para compartir los resultados con la clase.

E. Una encuesta

PASO 1. ¿Quién en tu clase ha hecho las siguientes actividades? Pregúntales a tus compañeros y, en una hoja de papel, apunta por lo menos una persona que ha hecho cada actividad. Si nadie ha hecho una, escribe «nadie». **¡Atención!** Los verbos **hacer** y **ver** tienen participios pasados irregulares.

MODELO: E1: ¿Has bailado tango?
E2: No, nunca he bailado tango.
E1: Yo tampoco. ¿Has probado (*tried, tasted*) comida española?

ACTIVIDAD   NOMBRE

1. bailar tango
2. probar comida española
3. probar comida salvadoreña
4. escuchar la música de Aleks Syntek
5. hablar en español con alguien fuera de la clase
6. hacer surf
7. tomar horchata (*rice drink*)
8. tomar mate (un té que se bebe en Argentina, Uruguay y Paraguay)
9. ver en persona a un actor famoso / una actriz famosa
10. viajar a México

PASO 2. En grupos, hagan oraciones para decir lo que han hecho todos del grupo, lo que no ha hecho nadie y lo que han hecho solo algunos.

MODELO: Todos hemos bailado tango y todos hemos tomado horchata.
Nadie ha hecho surf, nadie ha tomado mate y nadie ha viajado a México.
Chris y Mary han probado comida española.

PASO 3. Inventa por lo menos tres preguntas originales para saber qué más han hecho los otros miembros de tu grupo. ¡Sé creativo/a! Luego, haz las preguntas a tus compañeros y contesta las suyas (*theirs*).

MODELO: ¿Han visto una película española? ¿Han ido a un partido (*game*) de fútbol? ¿Han estudiado otro idioma?

F. ¿Qué has hecho? ¿Qué quieres hacer todavía (*still*)?

PASO 1. Haz una lista de cuatro cosas significativas (*significant*) que has hecho en tu vida y cuatro cosas que quieres hacer todavía.

MODELOS: He terminado la escuela secundaria y todavía quiero terminar la universidad.
He viajado a siete estados. Todavía quiero viajar a Alaska.

PASO 2. Entrevista a un compañero o una compañera para saber qué cosas significativas ha hecho y qué quiere hacer en la vida. ¿Uds. dos han hecho cosas parecidas o diferentes? ¿Tienen metas (*goals*) parecidas o diferentes?

G. Cultura: Mario Pani y la arquitectura moderna en México

PASO 1.   Lee el texto sobre México.

México

México es un país tan cosmopolita como rico[a] en cultura propia,[b] una característica que le ofrece complejidad a su expresión artística. En todo el mundo es conocido por sus grandes artistas, como los muralistas Diego Rivera y José Clemente Orozco. En paralelo a los movimientos artísticos del siglo XX, México produjo varias generaciones de arquitectos que también se han hecho famosos en todo el mundo. Por ejemplo, María Luisa Dehesa fue la primera mujer latinoamericana en recibir su título[c] en arquitectura. El modernista Luis Barragán es conocido por las casas que construyó, por pintar las paredes con colores vibrantes que eran autóctonos[d] de México y por usar ventanas y tragaluces[e] para controlar de manera muy creativa el movimiento de la luz y la sombra. El arquitecto Juan O'Gorman, quien diseñó la casa-estudio de Diego Rivera y Frida Kahlo, también era pintor y tenía vínculos[f] fuertes con los otros artistas de su época. Y la hija de Rivera, Ruth Rivera Marín, es una arquitecta reconocida por su colaboración en la construcción del Museo de Arte Moderno en México.

Para los mexicanos, y sobre todo para los de la capital, el arquitecto Mario Pani es quizás[g] el más emblemático del urbanismo y la arquitectura moderna en México. La gran tarea[h] de Pani fue aplicar los conceptos del funcionalismo del famoso arquitecto suizo Le Corbusier a los aspectos particulares de la vida urbana en México. Logró[i] integrar los estilos de la arquitectura internacional con los detalles coloniales y precolombinos[j] que ya eran intrínsecos a los espacios domésticos en México.

Uno de los edificios más destacados de Pani es el multifamiliar[k] Presidente Alemán, la primera residencia multifamiliar de América Latina, construida en 1948. Este complejo cuenta con nueve edificios de trece pisos y seis edificios de tres pisos, con un total de 1.080 departamentos.[l] A pesar[m] de tener un terreno bastante grande, estos edificios altos solo ocupan un 25 por ciento del espacio y el otro 75 por ciento queda para áreas verdes, como parques y jardines. Era importante para Pani que el multifamiliar fuera[n] no solo una residencia grande, sino una comunidad, como un pueblo chico dentro de una ciudad monstruosa. Por eso el diseño incorporó espacios para los servicios que los habitantes necesitaban todos los días: tiendas, una guardería,[ñ] una oficina de correos, una lavandería y lugares para deportes, como una piscina semiolímpica.

[a]tanto... *both cosmopolitan and rich*   [b]*(its) own*   [c]*degree*   [d]*native*   [e]*skylights*   [f]*ties, connections*   [g]*perhaps*   [h]*task*
[i]*He succeeded in*   [j]*pre-Columbian*   [k]*multifamily apartment complex*   [l]*apartments (Méx.)*   [m]*A... In spite*   [n]*be*
[ñ]*daycare center*

PASO 2.   Completa las oraciones con los participios pasados de los verbos de la lista.
¡Atención! Cada verbo se usa solo una vez.

decir   haber   producir   seguir   ser   tener

1. México ha _____ habido _____ varios artistas importantes.
2. Las culturas precolombinas siempre han _____ seguido _____ una influencia sobre la arquitectura mexicana.
3. Las familias de los multifamiliares han _____ tener _____ participantes en un gran experimento social.
4. Desde que se construyó, siempre ha _____ producir _____ muchos espacios verdes en el Multifamiliar Presidente Alemán.
5. Muchas personas han _____ ser _____ que la arquitectura es lo más fascinante de la historia de México.
6. Los arquitectos de hoy han _____ decir _____ con el estilo moderno que Mario Pani estableció en México en el siglo XX.

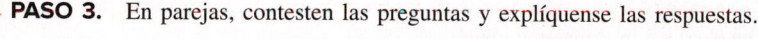

PASO 3.   En parejas, contesten las preguntas y explíquense las respuestas.

1. México tiene una población muy grande y en comparación con otros países, su economía es fuerte. ¿Ves una relación entre eso y la gran tradición de arquitectura que tiene?
2. En las zonas residenciales más elegantes de las ciudades grandes en México, muchas de las casas tienen un estilo muy contemporáneo. ¿Por qué crees que es así? ¿Piensas que los habitantes son conscientes de la tradición de arquitectura moderna en el país?
3. ¿En tu país, cómo son las casas? ¿En su mayoría, tienen un estilo contemporáneo o un estilo más tradicional (por ejemplo, un estilo colonial o «*ranch*»)? ¿Por qué crees que es así?

↻ Reciclaje

Direct objects and direct object pronouns

¿Tus hábitos en la casa son comunes o son diferentes a los de otras personas? Completa las siguientes oraciones con el pronombre de objeto directo apropiado, y luego indica si la oración es cierta para ti.

¿CIERTO PARA TI?

1. La televisión: _____ veo en la cocina. Es más común ver_____ en el salón. ☐
2. Los libros: _____ leo en la cama. Es más común leer_____ en el sofá. ☐
3. Las sábanas (*sheets*): _____ lavo cada dos meses. Es más común lavar_____ cada dos semanas. ☐
4. El comedor: _____ uso para estudiar. Es más común usar _____ para cenar. ☐
5. La habitación: _____ uso para hacer ejercicio. Es más común usar_____ para dormir. ☐

■ Answers to this activity are in **Appendix 2** at the back of your book.

11.2 ¡No te sientes allí!

Commands with object pronouns

Para empezar...

Los siguientes mandatos son comunes en casi cualquier casa, pero ¿en qué cuarto se oyen, generalmente? Para cada mandato, indica el lugar donde típicamente se escucharía (*you would hear it*): el cuarto de baño (B), la cocina o el comedor (C) o el dormitorio (D). Algunos mandatos pueden tener más de una respuesta.

1. _____ **Duérmete,** hijo. Ya es tarde.
2. _____ **Sírvele** el cereal a tu hermanito. **No le pongas** demasiado (*too much*) azúcar.
3. _____ **No te sirvas** mucho, papi. Ya sabes que no puedes comer todo.
4. _____ **Lávate** las manos. Están sucias.
5. _____ **¡No te sientes** allí! Es para nuestro invitado.
6. _____ **Báñate.** La fiesta es en dos horas.
7. _____ **¡Despiértate!**
8. _____ **Levántate.** Vas a llegar tarde a la escuela.
9. _____ Si te quitas los zapatos, **no los dejes** aquí. **Ponlos** en tu dormitorio.
10. _____ **Mírate** en el espejo, porque me parece que no te peinaste.
11. _____ **Ponte** el pijama verde; el rojo está sucio.
12. _____ Si los platos están sucios, **lávalos.**

Actividades analíticas

■ Answers to these activities are in Appendix 2 at the back of your book.

1 As you saw in **Capítulo 10,** object pronouns are attached to the end of positive informal and formal commands. Find examples with the verb **poner** in **Para empezar** to complete the following chart for informal commands.

	EJEMPLO CON MANDATO POSITIVO INFORMAL
Direct Object Pronoun	
Indirect Object Pronoun	Ponle más azúcar al café.
Reflexive Pronoun	

When needed, a written accent mark is added to keep the stress on the same syllable after the pronoun is attached. Can you find examples of this in **Para empezar?**

2 With negative commands, whether informal or formal, object pronouns are written as a separate word before the verb. With this in mind, take the examples from the chart in **Actividades analíticas 1** and convert them to negative commands in the chart below.

	EJEMPLO CON MANDATO NEGATIVO INFORMAL
Direct Object Pronoun	No los pongas en tu dormitorio.
Indirect Object Pronoun	
Reflexive Pronoun	

3 The general rule seen here is that object pronouns appear after and are attached to positive commands and come before negative commands. This holds true for all command forms. Use this rule to complete this chart of commands with **limpiar** and the direct object pronoun **lo.**

	POSITIVO	NEGATIVO
tú		no lo limpies
Ud.	límpielo	
vosotros/as	limpiadlo	no lo limpiéis
Uds.		

Actividades prácticas

A. Objetos y mandatos

PASO 1. Empareja cada objeto con el mandato apropiado. **¡Atención!** Cada mandato solo se puede usar una vez.

1. ___ la aspiradora
2. ___ la cama
3. ___ el equipo de música
4. ___ el fregadero
5. ___ el lavaplatos
6. ___ la mesa
7. ___ el horno y el microondas
8. ___ el refrigerador

a. Sacúdela.
b. Límpialo por dentro (*inside*).
c. Límpialos por dentro.
d. Pásala.
e. Sacúdelo.
f. Hazla.
g. Llénalo (*Fill it*) con agua y lava bien las papas.
h. Ponle los platos sucios.

PASO 2. Ahora, en parejas, túrnense para cambiar los mandatos informales del **Paso 1** a mandatos formales.

¡Ponte los tenis!

Autoprueba

Create positive and negative informal (**tú**) commands for these verbs by following the pattern you just learned for object pronoun placement.

1. sacudir los muebles
   + _____
   − _____

2. barrer el piso
   + _____
   − _____

3. lavar la camisa
   + _____
   − _____

Respuestas: 1. Sacúdelos., No los sacudas. **2.** Bárrelo., No lo barras. **3.** Lávala, No la laves.

■ To learn how to say *Let's do something!* in Spanish, see **Para saber más 11.2** at the back of your book.

B. ¡Limpia tu cuarto!   Cuando limpias un cuarto, una de las cosas más difíciles es decidir qué tirar (*throw out*) y qué guardar (*keep*). ¿Qué consejos darías (*would you give*) en cuanto a los siguientes objetos?

> **Consejos:**   Tíralo/la/los/las.
> No lo/la/los/las tires.

1. _____Tírala_____ una pizza de hace un mes
2. _____Tíralas_____ unas revistas del año pasado
3. _____No los tires_____ unos cupones para comprar pizza con un descuento de setenta y cinco por ciento (*percent*)
4. _____No tíralo_____ el libro de tu clase de español
5. _____Tíralos_____ los exámenes de tus clases del año pasado
6. _____No las tires_____ las llaves de tu coche
7. _____Tírelo_____ un periódico del mes pasado
8. _____No las tires_____ los DVDs de las películas en que salen juntos Penélope Cruz y Javier Bardem
9. _____No la tires_____ una foto de tu abuelo cuando era niño
10. _____Tírala_____ una foto de tu exnovio/a

C. Tu «ángel» y tu «demonio»   Cuando tienes que tomar una decisión, ¿qué dicen tu «ángel» (tu lado bueno) y tu «demonio» (tu lado malo)? Con un compañero o una compañera, creen por lo menos un consejo de tu «ángel» y otro de tu «demonio» para cada situación. **¡Atención!** Usa mandatos informales para dar los consejos.

> **MODELO:**   **Situación:** Sabes que tu amigo tiene un examen a las nueve. Son las ocho y media y está dormido todavía.
> «Ángel»: Despiértalo y dile qué hora es.
> «Demonio»: Déjalo dormir. No es tu problema.

SITUACIONES

1. Son las seis y media de la mañana y estás en la cama. Tu primera clase empieza a las ocho.
2. Son las once de la noche. Estás en una fiesta con unos amigos y estás muy contento. Mañana tienes un examen a las ocho.
3. A un compañero en tu clase se le cae un billete de veinte dólares. Tú lo ves pero él no.
4. Un compañero de clase se va al cuarto de baño y deja un sándwich en su escritorio. Tienes mucha hambre.

D. Actuación en la casa y en el jardín

PASO 1.   En grupos de tres o cuatro estudiantes, usen los verbos de la lista para decir cosas que se pueden hacer en la casa o en el jardín y exprésenlas en forma del mandato de **Uds.**

> **MODELO:**   Bárranlo! (apuntando [*pointing*] al piso)
>
> bañarse
>
> despertarse
>
> lavar (apuntando a los platos)
>
> levantarse
>
> planchar (apuntando a la ropa)
>
> preparar (apuntando a la comida)

PASO 2.   Lean sus mandatos a otro grupo. El otro grupo tiene que decir en qué parte de la casa (o en el jardín) se hace cada uno y luego actuarlo.

> **MODELO:**   ¡Báñense! → Se hace en el cuarto de baño. (*El grupo actúa el mandato.*)

⟲ Reciclaje

Ser and estar

¿Cómo es el lugar donde vives? ¿Y en qué condiciones está en este momento? Completa las oraciones con **es** o **está**, e indica si son ciertas o falsas para ti.

		CIERTO	FALSO
1.	_____ una casa.	☐	☐
2.	_____ una habitación en una residencia estudiantil.	☐	☐
3.	La ropa limpia _____ guardada (*put away*).	☐	☐
4.	La ropa sucia _____ en el piso.	☐	☐
5.	_____ en la universidad.	☐	☐
6.	La cama _____ grande.	☐	☐
7.	_____ buen lugar para estudiar.	☐	☐
8.	_____ muy limpio hoy.	☐	☐
9.	_____ un apartamento.	☐	☐
10.	El coche en el garaje _____ de Japón.	☐	☐

■ Answers to this activity are in **Appendix 2** at the back of your book.

11.3 Estoy ayudando a mi mamá en la casa

The present progressive

Para empezar...

Alicia, una estudiante mexicana, tuitea (*tweets*) varias veces durante el día. Mira las fotos de su día y luego empareja cada una con el tuit que mandó a esa hora.

1. _____ 5:45   2. _____ 6:10   3. _____ 9:22   4. _____ 13:12   5. _____ 14:03

6. _____ 14:54   7. _____ 16:12   8. _____ 18:26   9. _____ 20:10   10. _____ 20:45

Los tuits de Alicia

a. «Mi mamá y yo **estamos comiendo.**»
b. **«Estoy haciendo** la tarea.»
c. **«Estoy desayunando.»**
d. **«Estoy ayudando** a mi mamá en la casa.»
e. **«Estoy regresando** (*returning*) a casa.»
f. **«Estoy cenando.»**
g. «Mis amigos y yo nos **estamos tomando** una foto en la universidad.
h. **«Estoy bebiendo** refrescos con mis amigos. ¡Jorge **está bailando** en el pasillo!»
i. «Mi mamá y yo **estamos viendo** televisión.»
j. **«Estoy esperando** el autobús para ir a la universidad.»

■ Answers to these activities are in **Appendix 2** at the back of your book.

Actividades analíticas

1 The verb forms in **Para empezar** are in the *present progressive* (**el presente progresivo**). The present progressive consists of the *auxiliary verb* (**el verbo auxiliar**) **estar** in the present tense, followed by the *present participle* (**el participio presente**), a verb with an **-ndo** ending. Find the present participles in the following sentences and write their infinitives in the column on the right.

		INFINITIVE
Estoy cenando.	*I am having dinner.*	
Están estudiando.	*They are studying.*	
Mari **está escribiendo** una carta.	*Mari is writing a letter.*	

As you saw in **Estructura 5.3**, **-ar** verbs add **-ando** to the stem, and **-er** and **-ir** verbs add **-iendo**. Given this information, what is the present participle (**-ndo** form) of each of these verbs?

EL PARTICIPIO PRESENTE (-ndo)	
comer	
salir	
ayudar	
ver	

2 Verbs from the **e → i** stem-changing family (such as **decir, pedir, seguir,** and **servir**) change their vowel in the present tense (see **Estructura 4.2**), in the preterite (see **Estructura 8.1**), and here in the present participle: **diciendo, pidiendo, siguiendo, sirviendo.** Verbs that undergo a **o → u** change in the preterite (only **dormir** and **morir**) do the same here: **durmiendo, muriendo.**

¿Qué estás d**i**ciendo?	*What are you saying?*
Estamos p**i**diendo tu ayuda.	*We are asking for your help.*
Estoy s**i**guiendo tu ejemplo.	*I am following your example.*
¡Ya están s**i**rviendo la cena!	*They're already serving dinner!*
morir (ue, u): Las plantas están muriéndo porque no ha llovido.	*The plants are dying because it hasn't rained.*
Los niños están d**u**rmiendo.	*The children are sleeping.*

The verbs **leer, oír,** and **traer** (and other **-er** and **-ir** verbs whose stem ends in a vowel) have a spelling change in the present participle form. The ending for these verbs is **-yendo** rather than **-iendo.**

¿Estás le**y**endo?	*Are you reading?*
Estamos o**y**endo la música.	*We're listening to the music.*

3 The present progressive describes an action in progress and is very similar in meaning to its counterpart in English with *-ing*. The present progressive is used less frequently in Spanish than it is in English, however. This is partly because the simple present in Spanish is often used for actions that are currently underway, whereas English has to use *-ing* in these cases.

Voy a la biblioteca.	*I am going to the library.*

In addition, *-ing* is often used in English to refer to future events, but the Spanish present progressive is not used in this way. The present indicative is used instead.

Mañana **hablo** con ella.	*I am speaking with her tomorrow.*

4 The **–ndo** form may also be used with **ir, andar** (*to walk*) or **seguir** (*to continue*) in place of **estar. Andar** gives the sense of doing the action while moving around, and **seguir** gives the sense of continuing the action.

Manuel **va/anda buscando** una casa.	*Manuel is looking for a house.*
¿Qué **andas haciendo** aquí?	*What are you doing here?*
¿**Sigues barriendo** el pasillo?	*Are you still sweeping the hallway?*

■ To learn how to say in Spanish what you were doing in a past moment, see **Para saber más 11.3** at the back of your book.

¿Por qué?

Why is the verb **estar** used in the present progressive instead of **ser?** You saw in **Estructura 5.3** that **estar** is used with adjectives to describe a state that is subject to change or is the result of a change.

Estamos contentos.   We are happy.

In the present progressive, the verb **estar** plays the same role with respect to verbs. It shows that the action described by the verb is subject to change or is the result of change.

Estamos trabajando.   We are working.

Just as **estamos contentos** conveys the idea that we haven't necessarily always been happy, **estamos trabajando** suggests that we are working right at the moment, but that this wasn't necessarily true in the past and might not be in the future either.

Actividades prácticas

A. ¿Qué estás haciendo?   Empareja cada pregunta con la respuesta apropiada.

1. ___ ¿Qué estás comiendo?
2. ___ ¿Sigues buscando un coche?
3. ___ ¿Qué están leyendo en esa clase?
4. ___ ¿Qué andas diciendo de mí?
5. ___ ¿Están pidiendo mi consejo?
6. ___ ¿Por qué hay tanto ruido?
7. ___ ¿Dónde está tu hermano?
8. ___ ¿Estás haciendo la cama cada mañana como te dije?

a. Está en la cocina lavando platos.
b. Sí. No sabemos qué hacer.
c. No. Sí quiero, pero se me olvida.
d. Una novela de detectives.
e. ¡Que eres muy inteligente!
f. Pan con chocolate. ¿Quieres?
g. Están pasando la aspiradora.
h. Sí, todavía necesito uno.

B. ¿Dónde estoy?   Escucha las oraciones e indica en qué lugar normalmente pasa ese tipo de acción.

	LA COCINA	EL COMEDOR	EL DORMITORIO	EL JARDÍN
1.	☐	☑	☐	☐
2.	☑	☐	☐	☐
3.	☑	☐	☑	☐
4.	☐	☐	☐	☑
5.	☑	☐	☐	☐
6.	☐	☐	☐	☑
7.	☐	☑	☐	☐
8.	☑	☐	☐	☐

Estoy trabajando en el jardín.

■ The audio files for in-text listening activities are available in the eBook, within Connect Plus activities, and on the Online Learning Center.

C. Un día típico para un estudiante típico

PASO 1.   Si un estudiante típico de tu universidad tuiteara (*tweeted*) en cada uno de los siguientes momentos, ¿qué diría que está haciendo? Escribe el tuit más probable, según tu criterio.

MODELO: 7:00 Estoy desayunando.

	Mensaje
7:00	_____
9:00	_____
12:00	_____
16:00	_____
18:00	_____
22:00	_____

PASO 2.   Compara tus respuestas con las de un compañero o una compañera. ¿Pueden llegar a un acuerdo entre los dos sobre los tuits más probables?

D. ¿Qué están haciendo?

PASO 1.   Piensa en por lo menos tres de tus seres queridos (*loved ones*) y en qué están haciendo probablemente en este momento. Comparte tus ideas con un compañero / una compañera de clase.

MODELOS: Mi perro probablemente está durmiendo en el sofá.
Mis padres probablemente están trabajando en su restaurante.

PASO 2.   Ahora, túrnense para nombrar a por lo menos cuatro personas famosas (por ejemplo, el papa, el presidente, tu estrella de cine favorita, tu atleta favorito) e imaginar qué es lo que probablemente están haciendo en este momento.

E. ¡Actúen!   Escoge una acción de la lista o inventa tu propia acción. En grupos pequeños, actúala para tus compañeros. ¿Pueden adivinar qué estás haciendo?

barrer

sacar la basura

hacer la cama

lavar (la ropa, el coche, los platos, el suelo)

pasar la aspiradora

sacudir

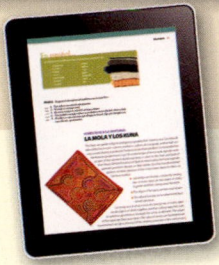

¡Leamos!

La casa en Mango Street, por Sandra Cisneros

Antes de leer

Contesta las preguntas sobre tu casa ideal y el lugar en que vives ahora.

	LA CASA IDEAL	EL LUGAR EN QUE VIVES
1. ¿Es casa propia (*own*)?		
2. ¿Cómo es el jardín? ¿Hay flores? ¿árboles? ¿bancos (*benches*)?		
3. ¿Tiene sótano? ¿desván (*attic*)?		
4. ¿Es grande o pequeña?		
5. ¿De qué color es?		
6. ¿Cuántos cuartos de baño tiene? ¿Cuántos dormitorios?		

A leer

PASO 1. En la novela *La casa en Mango Street,* Esperanza, la narradora, habla de la pequena y vieja casa en que vive con su familia en un barrio pobre de Chicago. También habla de su casa ideal. Presta atención a las descripciones de las dos casas y enfócate en las diferencias.

La casa en Mango Street

Siempre decían que algún día nos mudaríamos[a] a una casa, una casa de verdad, que fuera[b] nuestra para siempre, de la que no tuviéramos que[c] salir cada año, y nuestra casa tendría[d] agua corriente y tubos[e] que sirvieran.[f] Y escaleras interiores propias, como las casas de la tele. Y tendríamos[g] un sótano, y por lo menos[h] tres baños para no tener que avisarle a todo mundo cada vez que nos bañáramos. Nuestra casa sería[i] blanca, rodeada de[j] árboles, un jardín enorme y el pasto creciendo sin cerca. Esa es la casa de la que hablaba Papá cuando tenía un billete de lotería y esa es la casa que Mamá soñaba[k] en los cuentos que nos contaba[l] antes de dormir.

Pero la casa de Mango Street no es de ningún modo como ellos la contaron. Es pequeña y roja, con escalones apretados[m] al frente y unas ventanitas tan chicas que parecen guardar su respiración. Los ladrillos[n] se hacen pedazos[ñ] en algunas partes y la puerta del frente se ha hinchado tanto que uno tiene que empujar fuerte para entrar. No hay jardín al frente sino cuatro olmos chiquitos[o] que la ciudad plantó en la banqueta.[p] Afuera, atrás hay un garaje chiquito para el carro que no tenemos todavía, y un patiecito[q] que luce[r] todavía más chiquito entre los edificios de los lados. Nuestra casa tiene escaleras pero son ordinarias, de pasillo, y tiene solamente un baño. Todos compartimos recámaras,[s] Mamá y Papá, Carlos y Kiki, yo y Nenny.

[a]nos... *we would move* [b]*was* [c]*no... we wouldn't have to* [d]*would have*
[e]*agua... running water and plumbing* [f]*worked* [g]*we would have* [h]*por...
at least* [i]*would be* [j]*rodeada... surrounded by* [k]*was dreaming about*
[l]*nos... she told us* [m]*escalones... narrow steps* [n]*bricks* [ñ]*se... are falling apart*
[o]*olmos... little elm trees* [p]*sidewalk* [q]*little patio* [r]*appears* [s]dormitorios

(*Continues*)

PASO 2. Según el fragmento que has leído de *La casa en Mango Street,* indica si cada afirmación se refiere a la casa ideal (**I**) o la casa verdadera en que vive la narradora (**V**).

I   V   1. Una casa con agua corriente (*running*).

I   V   2. Tiene la puerta tan hinchada (*swollen*) que uno tiene que empujar fuerte para entrar.

I   V   3. Tiene un sótano.

I   V   4. Tiene escaleras ordinarias (*bad quality*).

I   V   5. Tiene un jardín enorme lleno de pasto (*grass*).

I   V   6. Tiene las ventanitas muy chicas.

I   V   7. Tiene olmos (*elm trees*) chiquitos al frente que la ciudad plantó en la banqueta.

I   V   8. Tiene por lo menos tres cuartos de baño.

Después de leer

PASO 1. Contesta las siguientes preguntas.

1. Según la lectura, ¿qué quiere la narradora? ¿Por qué?

2. ¿Dónde ha visto la narradora escaleras interiores propias?

3. Según la narradora, ¿cuál es el problema con compartir un cuarto de baño con muchas personas?

4. Nombra tres detalles que menciona la narradora sobre la casa que desea.

5. Nombra tres detalles que menciona la narradora sobre la casa en que vive ahora.

6. ¿Cuántos dormitorios hay en la casa de Mango Street?

 PASO 2. En parejas, entrevístense sobre sus casas ideales. ¿Cómo son? ¿Tienen sus casas ideales algo en común con la casa ideal que describe Esperanza? ¿Dónde están? ¿Cuántos cuartos hay? ¿Qué hay dentro de cada cuarto? ¿Cómo es el jardín? Apunten las respuestas.

¡Escuchemos!

¿Cuánto cuesta vivir aquí?

Antes de escuchar

En grupos, hagan una lista de los lugares en que pueden vivir los estudiantes de su universidad. Luego, pongan los lugares en orden de más barato a más caro. **¡Atención!** Recuerda que la palabra para *dorm* en español es **residencia estudiantil.**

Así se dice

Las personas del video son de México, España, Panamá y Argentina, y las palabras que usan varían bastante.

	el apartamento	**la comunidad**	**el dinero**	**el pago**
Abigaíl y Óscar (México)	el departamento	la colonia	pesos (mexicanos)	la renta
Armando (España)	el piso	el barrio	euros	el alquiler
Liliana (Panamá)	el apartamento	el barrio	dólares	el alquiler
Eugenia y Carina (Argentina)	el departamento	el barrio	pesos (argentinos)	el alquiler

A escuchar

Mira y escucha. Mientras escuchas, indica las respuestas a las preguntas.

1.  Según Abigaíl, ¿cuánto cuesta un departamento en una zona residencial del D.F. (la Ciudad de México) que tenga electricidad y servicios sanitarios?
   a. 2.000 pesos
   b. 4.000 pesos
   c. 6.000 pesos
   d. 8.000 pesos

2.  Según Óscar, ¿cuánto cuesta un departamento en una colonia cultural en México?
   a. de 3.000 a 4.000 pesos
   b. de 5.000 a 6.000 pesos
   c. de 7.000 a 8.000 pesos
   d. de 10.000 a 12.000 pesos

3. Según Óscar, ¿dónde en México pagas entre 5.000 y 6.000 pesos mensuales?
   a. en una colonia cultural
   b. en el centro de la ciudad
   c. en colonias no tan buenas
   d. en apartamentos exclusivos

4. Según Armon, ¿cuánto es el alquiler en el centro de Madrid?
   a. entre 200 y 300 euros
   b. entre 300 y 400 euros
   c. entre 400 y 500 euros
   d. entre 500 y 600 euros

5. Según Armon, ¿cuánto es el alquiler en las afueras de Madrid?
   a. entre 200 y 300 euros
   b. entre 300 y 400 euros
   c. entre 400 y 500 euros
   d. entre 500 y 600 euros

6.  Según Liliana, ¿cuánto es un alquiler económico (*affordable*) en Panamá?
   a. 500
   b. 1.000
   c. 1.500
   d. 2.000

(Continues)

7. Según Liliana, ¿cuánto es un alquiler caro en Panamá?
   a. 500
   b. 1.000
   c. 1.500
   d. 2.000

8.  Según Eugenia y Carina, ¿cuánto cuesta un departamento con un dormitorio en el centro de Buenos Aires?
   a. entre 600 y 700 pesos
   b. entre 700 y 800 pesos
   c. entre 800 y 900 pesos
   d. entre 900 y 1.000 pesos

 ### Después de escuchar

En grupos, hablen de las ventajas y desventajas de vivir en diferentes comunidades (las comunidades urbanas, rurales, en las afueras, ciudades grandes / de tamaño medio / pequeñas). Sin hablar de los costos específicos, hablen de sus propias experiencias. ¿Dónde prefiere vivir la mayoría? ¿Por qué?

¡Escribamos!

Un día típico en casa

Cuando compartimos con otras personas nuestras experiencias de la infancia (*childhood*), muchas veces tenemos más en común de lo que pensábamos. En esta actividad vas a describir tu rutina diaria cuando eras más joven (o niño/a o adolescente). Antes de escribir, vas a comparar tus ideas con un compañero / una compañera.

 ### Antes de escribir

Vas a describir los fines de semana cuando eras niño/a o adolescente. Primero, rellena las primeras dos columnas de la tabla con los miembros de tu familia y las actividades (los quehaceres tanto como las actividades divertidas) en que participaba cada uno. Luego, intercambia tablas con un compañero / una compañera de clase. Lee su tabla y dale comentarios o hazle preguntas a tu compañero/a. Apunta los comentarios de la otra persona en la tercera columna.

los miembros de mi familia	lo que hacían estas personas	comentarios y preguntas
yo		

MODELO: E1: Veo que todos los sábados por la mañana ibas a un café con tu padre y él leía el periódico. Luego Uds. iban al parque. ¿Qué hacían Uds. en el parque? ¿Jugaban algún deporte?

E2: Eso es lo más interesante. Mi padre es biólogo y me enseñaba los nombres científicos de diferentes plantas, animales, insectos y cosas así. Luego jugábamos para ver si yo podía recordar los nombres.

A escribir

Ahora escribe tres párrafos para describir tu rutina y trata de incorporar las sugerencias de tu compañero/a de clase para fortalecer (*strengthen*) tu descripción. En el primer párrafo, escribe una introducción en la que presentes el tema de la composición y la información que vas a detallar en los siguientes párrafos. En el segundo párrafo, describe el lugar donde vivías cuando eras niño/a. Luego, describe qué hacían los miembros de tu familia allí.

Después de escribir

Revisa tu ensayo. Luego, intercambia ensayos con un compañero / una compañera para evaluarlos.

1. Lee la introducción. ¿Sabes qué esperar (*to expect*) en el resto del ensayo?
2. Subraya todos los verbos en el segundo párrafo.
   a. ¿Tienen concordancia los sujetos y los verbos subrayados?
   b. ¿Controla el pretérito e imperfecto?
3. Después de leer toda la composición, lee de nuevo la introducción. ¿Describe lo que va a presentar en los siguientes párrafos en el orden en que se presenta en el resto del ensayo?

Después de revisar el ensayo de tu compañero/a, devuélveselo (*return it to him/her*). Mira tu propio (*own*) ensayo para ver los cambios que tu compañero/a recomienda y haz las revisiones necesarias.

¡Hablemos!

Andamos buscando un apartamento

Antes de hablar

1. ¿Has alquilado un apartamento o comprado una casa? ¿Cómo fue la experiencia? ¿Qué aprendiste?
2. ¿Qué hacen los agentes de bienes raíces? ¿Has trabajado con uno/a? ¿Para qué?
3. ¿Cuáles son las preguntas que normalmente le hacen los clientes al / a la agente de bienes raíces?
4. ¿Cuáles son las cosas más importantes para investigar al ver un apartamento por primera vez?

A hablar

En grupos de tres, creen un diálogo en el que uno o una de Uds. va a hacer el papel de agente de bienes raíces que debe darles un tour de un apartamento disponible a los otros miembros del grupo, que andan buscando un apartamento para alquilar. Primero, el/la agente debe darles la bienvenida a los clientes (los otros estudiantes). Luego, debe invitarlos a entrar y darles un tour de un apartamento. El apartamento puede ser perfecto para ellos o absolutamente terrible. Lo importante es que el/la agente mantenga (*maintains*) un tono cortés (*polite*) y una actitud profesional.

Después de hablar

Ahora ensayen (*rehearse*) su diálogo y prepárense a presentarlo al resto de la clase.

Conéctate a la música

Canción: «Loca» (2009)
Artista: Aleks Syntek

Aleks Syntek (Raúl Alejandro Escajadillo Peña) es cantante y compositor de música pop, a veces conocido como «el rey (*king*) del pop mexicano».

Antes de escuchar

En general, decir que una persona está loca es un comentario bastante negativo, pero a veces sí tiene un significado más positivo. ¿Cuáles de la siguientes palabras podrían ser equivalentes de «loco» en su sentido positivo?

☐ aburrido   ☐ divertido   ☐ serio

☐ alegre   ☐ espontáneo   ☐ trabajador

Expresiones útiles...

me encanta cuando provocas   I love it when you provoke (me)

voy a sacarte el instinto animal   I'm going to bring out your animal instinct

---

Aleks Syntek, cantante mexicano

A escuchar

PASO 1. El cantante usa los siguientes verbos en forma de mandato. Escribe la forma exacta que él usa, incluyendo los pronombres y **no,** cuando los usa.

acercarse (*to approach*): _____

besar: _____

ser: _____

PASO 2. El cantante usa el participio presente de cuatro verbos. Apúntalos aquí y escribe el infinitivo de cada verbo.

PARTICIPIO PRESENTE	INFINITIVO
	bailar
	(*to dream*)
	(*to fight*)

■ For copyright reasons, the songs referenced in **Conéctate a la música** have not been provided by the publisher. The video for this song can be found on YouTube, and it is available for purchase from the iTunes store.

Después de escuchar

Todos tenemos un lado (*side*) loco de nuestra personalidad. En general, ¿piensas que en tu vida diaria deberías (*you should be*) ser un poco más serio/a o un poco más loco/a? ¿Por qué?

VOCABULARIO

Comunicación

¡Bienvenido/a/os/as!	Welcome!
subject + ser + bienvenido/a (bienvenidos/as).	____ is/are welcome.
Ud. es (siempre) bienvenido/a.	You are (always) welcome.
indirect object pronoun + dar + la bienvenida.	*subject* + welcome + *direct object.*
¡Le damos la bienvenida a Ud.!	We welcome you!
¡Come/Coma(n) más!	Have some more!
¡Diviértete!/¡Diviérta(n)se!	Have fun!
¡Siéntate!/¡Siénte(n)se!	Have a seat!
¡Sírvete!/¡Sírva(n)se!	Help yourself!

La casa y los muebles / House and furniture

el armario	armoire, closet
el ascensor	elevator
la aspiradora	vacuum cleaner
el balcón	balcony
la bañera	bathtub
la cama	bed
la cocina	kitchen
el comedor	dining room
el (cuarto de) baño	bathroom
la despensa	pantry
el dormitorio / la habitación	bedroom
la ducha	shower
el edificio (de apartamentos)	(apartment) building
la escalera	stairs
el espejo	mirror
el estante	bookshelf
la estufa	stove
el fregadero	kitchen sink
el horno	oven
el inodoro	toilet

el jardín	yard; garden
la lámpara	lamp
el lavabo	bathroom sink
la lavadora	washing machine
el lavaplatos	dishwasher
la mesa	table
la mesita de noche	nightstand
el microondas	microwave
el pasillo	hallway
la piscina	pool
el piso	floor, story; apartment (*Sp.*)
la (primera, segunda, tercera) planta	(second, third, fourth) floor
los quehaceres (domésticos)	(household) chores
el salón	living room
la silla	chair
el sillón	armchair
el sofá	sofa
el sótano	basement
el techo	roof
el televisor	television (set)
el tendedero	clothesline
la terraza	terrace

Cognados: el apartamento, el garaje, el refrigerador

Los verbos

barrer	to sweep
hacer (*irreg.*) la cama	to make the bed
descansar	to rest
lavar (los platos, el suelo)	to wash/clean (the dishes, the floor)
limpiar	to clean
pasar la aspiradora	to vacuum
sacar (qu) la basura	to take out the trash
sacudir	to dust

El deporte y el bienestar

El equipo de la República Dominicana celebra después de ganar el Clásico Mundial de Béisbol en 2013.

Objetivos

In this chapter you will learn how to:

- wish someone well
- say what needs to be done
- talk about sports, wellness, and injuries
- say what you would like to happen
- talk about sports and wellness in the Spanish-speaking world

12

COMUNICACIÓN LARIO JCTURA ATE

¡Suerte!

Wishing someone good luck

 A. A ver: ¿Qué dicen?   ¿Qué les dice a las personas que se preparan para correr un maratón? Mira y escucha, luego escoge la respuesta que corresponde a lo que dice cada persona.

1. Rogelio, de México
   a. Ánimo.
   b. Que les vaya bien.
   c. Suerte.
   d. Las respuestas **b** y **c** están bien.

2. Sonia, de España
   a. Ánimo.
   b. Que les vaya bien.
   c. Suerte.
   d. Las respuestas **b** y **c** están bien.

3. Olman, de Costa Rica
   a. Adelante.
   b. Ánimo.
   c. Suerte.
   d. Las respuestas **b** y **c** están bien.

4. Delano, de Argentina
   a. Les deseo mucha suerte.
   b. Mucha suerte.
   c. Que les vaya bien.
   d. Suerte.

5. Marta, de Argentina
   a. Ánimo.
   b. Buena suerte.
   c. Les deseo muchísima suerte.
   d. Las respuestas **a** y **b** están bien.

6. Erick, de Nicaragua
   a. Espero que les vaya muy bien.
   b. Les deseo mucha suerte.
   c. Sí, se puede.
   d. Suerte.

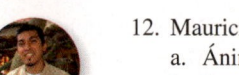

7. Anlluly, de Costa Rica
   a. Espero que les vaya muy bien.
   b. Les deseo mucha suerte.
   c. Suerte.
   d. Sí, se puede.

8. Ramón, de Argentina
   a. Ánimo.
   b. Les deseo mucha suerte.
   c. Mucha suerte.
   d. Que les vaya bien.

9. Darío, de Argentina
   a. Les deseo mucha suerte.
   b. Buena suerte.
   c. Que les vaya bien.
   d. Suerte.

10. Juan, de Argentina
    a. Ánimo.
    b. Muchísima suerte.
    c. Que les vaya bien.
    d. Que sigan adelante.

11. Francisco, de Colombia
    a. Les deseo muchísima suerte.
    b. Mucha suerte.
    c. Que les vaya bien.
    d. Suerte.

12. Mauricio, de Panamá
    a. Ánimo.
    b. Les deseo muchísima suerte.
    c. Que les vaya bien.
    d. Las respuestas **b** y **c** están bien.

To wish someone good luck in Spanish, you can use one of these expressions.

Buena suerte.	Good luck.
Suerte (con todo).	Good luck (with everything).
Mucha suerte.	Best of luck.
Le(s) deseo mucha suerte.	I wish you well. / I wish you lots of luck.

To give someone extra encouragement with something difficult (such as during a competition or before an exam or interview), you can use one of these.

¡Ánimo!	Best of luck! / Keep your spirits high! / Give it all you've got! / You can do it!
¡Adelante!	Come on! / Go, go, go! / Let's go! / You can do it!
¡Sí se puede!	Yes you/we can! (*Lit.,* Yes, it can be done!)

To wish someone well in Spanish when you are saying good-bye, use one of these expressions.

Que te/le(s) vaya bien.	Have a good one. / I hope things go well for you.
Que tenga(s) un(a) buen(a) + *period of time*	Have a good . . .
Que tenga(s) un buen día / fin de semana / verano.	Have a good day/weekend/summer.
Que tenga(s) una buena tarde.	Have a good afternoon.

B. Que te vaya bien.   Imagínate que un amigo o una amiga te dice las siguientes cosas. ¿Qué le contestas? Indica la mejor expresión para responder.

1. —Me voy al médico a hacerme unas pruebas (*tests*). No sé qué me van a decir.
   a. —Adiós.   b. —Que tengas una buena tarde.   c. —Suerte.

2. —Mi equipo perdió ayer y estoy destrozado (*devastated*).
   a. —¡Ánimo!   b. —¡Que te vaya bien!   c. —¡Suerte!

3. —Me voy al gimnasio a hacer ejercicio. Nos vemos más tarde.
   a. —Adiós.   b. —Ánimo.   c. —Mucha suerte con todo.

4. —Me voy a la biblioteca; tengo un examen de biología mañana. Hasta luego.
   a. —Adiós.   b. —Buena suerte.   c. —Que tengas un buen fin de semana.

5. —Hace semanas que estoy entrenando, pero no estoy lista (*ready*) para correr el maratón el sábado.
   a. —Adiós.   b. —Ánimo.   c. —Que tengas una buena tarde.

6. —Y con esto terminamos la tarea para hoy. Hasta el lunes.
   a. —Ánimo.   b. —Muy buena suerte.   c. —Que tengas un buen fin de semana.

 C. Después de clase   Pregúntale a un compañero / una compañera qué va a hacer hoy después de clase, hoy por la noche y este fin de semana. Luego despídete de él/ella usando una de las expresiones que acabas de aprender (*you just learned*).

MODELO: E1: ¿Qué vas a hacer después de clase?
E2: Voy a estudiar para mi examen de biología.
E1: ¿Y esta noche?
E2: Voy a acostarme temprano. El examen es a las 8 de la mañana.
E1: ¡Suerte en tu examen!

Para mantenerse sano/a,° hay que...
Giving advice on healthy living

stay healthy

> To say *You (don't) have to* (do something) using the impersonal or generic *you* (where *one, a person,* or *people* might be used instead as the subject), use: **(No) Hay que +** *infinitive*. This can also be translated as *It's (not) necessary to* (do something).
>
> | | |
> |---|---|
> | **Para mantenerse sano/a, hay que comer bien. Para bajar de peso, hay que hacer ejercicio.** | To stay healthy, one has to (it's necessary to) eat well. To lose weight, one has to exercise. |
> | No hay **que levantar pesas para mantenerse en forma.** | People/You don't have to lift weights to stay in shape. |

A. Para llevar una vida más sana...

PASO 1. Indica si estás de acuerdo o no con cada afirmación que escuchas.

	ESTOY DE ACUERDO	NO ESTOY DE ACUERDO
1.	☑	☐
2.	☐	☐
3.	☑	☐
4.	☐	☐
5.	☐	☑
6.	☐	☑
7.	☐	☐
8.	☑	☐

PASO 2. En parejas, completen cada frase de dos maneras: con algo que hay que hacer y también con algo que *no* hay que hacer. No repitan la información del **Paso 1.**

MODELO: Para participar en deportes, no hay que tener talento. Hay que querer jugar.

1. Para llevar una vida más activa... *hay que / no hay que*
2. Para comer mejor...
3. Para bajar de peso...
4. Para conocer a otras personas sanas...
5. Para participar en deportes...

B. ¿Qué hay que hacer para mantenerse o ponerse más sano/a?

PASO 1. Escribe tres oraciones sobre lo que debes hacer tú para ponerte más sano/a.

MODELO: Para vivir una vida más sana, debo inscribirme (*sign myself up*) en un gimnasio. También debo comer más verduras y menos azúcar. Debo preparar la comida en casa en vez de ir a restaurantes y comer comida rápida.

PASO 2. En grupos, compartan lo que quieren hacer para vivir más sano. Decidan cuáles son los dos puntos más importantes y preséntenlos a la clase. Empiecen su resumen (*summary*) con: **Según nuestro grupo...**

MODELO: Según nuestro grupo, para vivir una vida sana hay que comer muchas verduras y dormir ocho horas cada noche.

En español...

> **Mantenerse** contains the verb **tener** and therefore is conjugated the same way.
>
> | | |
> |---|---|
> | **Ella se mantiene en forma usando una combinación de ejercicio y dieta.** | She stays in shape using a combination of exercise and diet. |
>
> You'll find the same pattern with other verbs you will come across that contain the verb **tener,** such as **contener** (*to contain*), **detener** (*to stop; to detain*), **obtener** (*to get, obtain*), **retener** (*to retain*), and **sostener** (*to sustain; to hold, support*).

■ The audio files for in-text listening activities are available in the eBook, within Connect Plus activities, and on the Online Learning Center.

Los deportes y cómo mantenerse en forma

Sports, health, and fitness

A. ¿Eres sedentario/a o activo/a?   Haz la encuesta para saber si eres una persona sedentaria o activa.

PASO 1.   ¿Con qué frecuencia haces las siguientes actividades?

1. ____ Miro la televisión…
   a. menos de una hora al día.
   b. de una a tres horas al día.
   c. más de tres horas al día.

2. ____ Viajo en coche o transporte público…
   a. menos de 30 minutos al día.
   b. de 30 a 90 minutos al día.
   c. más de 90 minutos al día.

3. ____ Camino… (Hago caminatas… / Voy a la universidad a pie…)
   a. más de 45 minutos al día.
   b. de 20 a 45 minutos al día.
   c. menos de 20 minutos al día.

4. ____ Practico un deporte o hago una actividad física…
   a. más de cuatro horas a la semana.
   b. de dos a cuatro horas a la semana.
   c. menos de dos horas a la semana.

5. ____ Tomo siestas largas…
   a. muy raras veces.
   b. de vez en cuando.
   c. todos los días.

6. ____ Uso la computadora…
   a. menos de dos horas al día.
   b. de dos a cuatro horas al día.
   c. más de cuatro horas al día.

NÚMERO TOTAL DE CADA RESPUESTA

   a. _____
   b. _____
   c. _____

PASO 2. Ahora, indica todos los deportes y otras actividades físicas que haces con frecuencia.

☐ **andar en bicicleta**   ☐ **hacer alpinismo**   ☐ **jugar voleibol**

☐ **andar en patineta**   ☐ **jugar béisbol**   ☐ **levantar pesas**

☐ **boxear,** el boxeo   ☐ **jugar fútbol americano**   ☐ **patinar sobre hielo,** el patinaje

☐ **esquiar,** el esquí   ☐ **jugar tenis**   ☐ **surfear,** el surf

☐ bailar   ☐ hacer ejercicio aeróbico   ☐ montar a caballo   ☐ otro: _____
☐ correr   ☐ jugar básquetbol   ☐ nadar, **la natación**
☐ dar paseos largos   ☐ jugar fútbol   ☐ practicar yoga

¿Cuántas actividades físicas marcaste? _____

PASO 3. Ahora, calcula los resultados.

En el **Paso 1,** todas las respuestas **a** valen 10 puntos; las **b** valen 5 puntos y las **c** valen 0 puntos. Para calcular los resultados de la encuesta, suma los resultados de tus respuestas al **Paso 1** (máximo: 60). Luego suma el número total de deportes y actividades del **Paso 2** (máximo: 18) y agrega (*add*) el total al primer número.

0–25: Tienes una vida muy sedentaria. No te gusta mucho la actividad física o no tienes tiempo en tu horario para hacerlo. Piensa en maneras en que puedes incorporar más actividad en tu vida. El trabajo es importante, pero mantenerte en buena salud también es importante.

26–45: Participas con frecuencia en actividades físicas y tal vez has encontrado un buen equilibrio entre el trabajo y el ejercicio. ¡Felicidades! Si también comes bien y duermes lo suficiente, vas hacia una vida muy sana.

46+: Eres una persona muy activa. Te gusta moverte y te molesta quedarte tranquilo/a. ¡Lo que puedes hacer ahora es explorar y probar otras actividades físicas para buscar aún (*even*) más aventuras!

B. ¿Para qué se usa?

PASO 1. En parejas, túrnense para decidir para qué deporte(s) puede servir cada uno de los siguientes elementos.

1. la bicicleta

4. **la raqueta**

5. **la patineta**

8. los pies

9. **la piscina**

2. **el casco**

6. **la pelota**

10. los tenis

7. **las pesas**

3. las manos

PASO 2. En parejas, túrnense para pensar en un deporte y —sin decir el nombre del deporte— nombrar todo el equipo que se necesita para jugarlo. Tu compañero/a debe adivinarlo.

MODELO: E1: Este deporte requiere una piscina, un traje de baño, un gorro…
E2: ¡Es la natación!

C. A ver: El deporte en los países hispanos

PASO 1. Mira y escucha. Mientras miras, contesta las siguientes preguntas.

1. ¿Qué deporte(s) menciona cada persona?

Adrián, de México

Eduardo, de México

Isabel, de España

Zaryn, de la República Dominicana

Marco Antonio, de México

Juan, de Argentina

2. ¿Qué deporte(s) les gusta ver en la televisión?

Moravia y Gisela,
de México
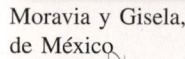

Paula, de México

Henry, de Costa Rica
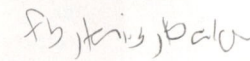

Adrián, de España

PASO 2.   Mira y escucha otra vez. Luego, contesta las preguntas en oraciones completas.

1. Según Zaryn, ¿cuál es el deporte nacional de la República Dominicana?
2. ¿Qué tipo de patinaje sobre hielo practica Eduardo?
3. ¿Es atlética Isabel? ¿Qué hace ella para mantenerse en forma?
4. ¿A Juan le gustaría hacer ejercicio en un gimnasio? ¿Por qué sí o por qué no?
5. ¿Cuáles son los dos equipos de la NFL que mencionan Moravia y Gisela?
6. ¿Cuál es el deporte que a Adrián (de España) no le gusta ver en la televisión?

 PASO 3.   En parejas, contesten las preguntas del video (¿Qué deportes practican?, ¿Qué deporte les gusta ver en la televisión?) según sus propios (*own*) intereses. ¿Tienen algo en común las respuestas de Uds. con las respuestas de las personas del video?

D. Los mejores atletas

PASO 1.   Lee sobre estos tres atletas hispanos. Mientras lees, subraya (*underline*) el país de origen de cada atleta, el año en que nació y el deporte (o los deportes) en que compite.

Kilian Jornet Burgada

1. **Kilian Jornet Burgada,** atleta de élite nacido en 1987 en el norte de España, es corredor de montaña (*ultrarunner*), esquiador, alpinista (*mountaineer*) y ciclista de montaña. En la corrida de montaña, los participantes corren mientras aguantan (*put up with*) cambios de terreno y de temperatura y falta de acceso a las «necesidades básicas» como comida, agua y cama. Durante sus carreras (*races*), Jornet sube a las cumbres (*peaks*) más altas y cubre distancias que a la mayoría de la gente no le interesa viajar en coche, y lo hace en tiempo récord. En los meses fríos del invierno, cambia sus zapatos por los esquís Jornet ha ganado más de ochenta carreras y competencias de esquí.
2. **Fernanda González** es una nadadora mexicana. Después de ganar tres bronces en los Juegos Panamericanos de 2011 en Guadalajara y competir en los Juegos Olímpicos de verano en Londres en 2012, se prepara para los Juegos Olímpicos de Río de Janeiro en 2016. Nacida en 1990, González es la mejor nadadora de dorso (*backstroker*) de México y una de las mejores del mundo.
3. **Gastón Ramírez:** Este joven futbolista juega en dos equipos: Southampton en Inglaterra y su equipo nacional de Uruguay, con el que participó en los Juegos Olímpicos de verano en Londres en 2012. Ramírez nació en 1990, empezó a jugar profesionalmente en 2009 y en ese mismo año participó en la Copa Mundial Sub-20 de la FIFA en Egipto. Su posición es volante ofensivo (*attacking central midfielder*): juega en el mediocampo recuperando pelotas con facilidad, creando jugadas (*plays*) y contribuyendo a la anotación de goles. Ha jugado en varios equipos y ganó su fama en Italia como parte del equipo de Boloña.

 PASO 2.   En parejas, hagan una lista de tres actividades que hay que hacer y tres hábitos que hay que tener para mantenerse en forma y tener éxito (*success*) como atleta de élite en cada uno de estos deportes: la carrera de montaña, el esquí, el alpinismo, la natación, el fútbol. **¡Atención!** No repitan actividades ni hábitos.

 PASO 3.   Formen un grupo de cuatro con otra pareja y pongan en orden los elementos de las dos listas, de lo más importante a lo menos importante para mantenerse en forma para cada deporte. ¿Qué deporte les parece más difícil? ¿Por qué les parece tan difícil?

Vocabulario

Para hablar de **las heridas** (*wounds, injuries*), **las enfermedades** (*illnesses*) y **los síntomas** (*symptoms*), puedes usar las siguientes palabras.

desmayarse	to faint	**el dolor**	pain
doler (ue)	to hurt, ache	**el estornudo**	sneeze
estornudar	to sneeze	**la fiebre**	fever
lastimarse	to injure oneself	**la gripe**	flu
pegar	to hit; to paste	**la hinchazón**	swelling
romperse	to break	**el moretón**	bruise
sufrir (de)	to suffer (from)	**el resfriado**	cold (the illness)
torcerse (ue)	to sprain (one's	**la torcedura**	sprain
(el tobillo)	ankle)	**la tos**	cough
constipado/a	congested		

Cognados: vomitar; las alergias, el asma (*f.*), **la depresión, la fractura, la infección, el insomnio, las náuseas.**

El verbo **doler** funciona como **gustar.**

—**¿Te duele la cabeza?** Does your head hurt?
—**No, pero me duele mucho el estómago.** No, but my stomach hurts a lot.

—**¿Le duelen a Ud. los pies?** Do your feet hurt?
—**No, no me duelen los pies; pero ayer** No, my feet don't hurt; but yesterday
  me torcí el tobillo. I sprained my ankle.

E. ¿De qué sufren? Empareja la oración con la imagen más apropiada.

1. _____ Tiene el insomnio y no quiere comer. Sufre de **depresión.**
2. _____ Está constipado y tiene fiebre y nauseas. Sufre de **gripe.**
3. _____ Se ha roto el brazo. Sufre de **una fractura.**
4. _____ Se ha torcido el tobillo. Sufre de **una torcedura.**

a.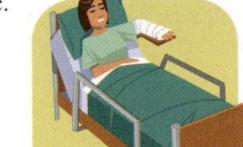

b.

c.

d.

F. ¿Herida, enfermedad o síntoma?

PASO 1. Estudia el vocabulario sobre las heridas, las enfermedades y los síntomas. Luego, organiza las palabras en categorías: **heridas, enfermedades** o **síntomas.**

PASO 2. En grupos de tres o cuatro estudiantes, túrnense para actuar las palabras. ¿Pueden adivinar (*guess*) qué herida, enfermedad o síntoma tiene cada persona?

G. ¡Cuidado!

PASO 1.   Con un compañero / una compañera, di cuáles son las heridas más comunes para los atletas que practican los siguientes deportes.

MODELO: el tenis → torcerse el tobillo, lastimarse la muñeca (*wrist*), romperse el brazo…

1. el boxeo
2. la carrera por montaña
3. el esquí
4. el alpinismo
5. la natación
6. el fútbol americano

PASO 2.   ¿Qué pueden hacer los atletas que participan en los deportes mencionados en el **Paso 1** para protegerse mejor y no sufrir de las heridas? Usa las palabras de la lista para contestar.

estirarse (*stretch*)	usar casco
hacer calentamientos (*warm-ups*)	usar rodilleras (*knee pads*) y coderas (*elbow pads*)
tomar mucha agua	

H. La historia médica

PASO 1.   ¿Has experimentado (*Have you experienced*) estas condiciones o síntomas alguna vez? Marca tu historia médica.

SÍ   **NO**

☐ ☐   1. ¿Te has desmayado alguna vez?
☐ ☐   2. ¿Has sufrido de insomnio?
☐ ☐   3. ¿Has tenido una fiebre alta?
☐ ☐   4. ¿Te has torcido alguna parte del cuerpo? (¿Cuál?)
☐ ☐   5. ¿Te has fracturado algo? (¿Qué?)
☐ ☐   6. ¿Has sufrido de una quemadura (*burn*)?
☐ ☐   7. ¿Has sufrido de una hinchazón? (¿De qué?)
☐ ☐   8. ¿Has tenido escalofríos (*chill*)?
☐ ☐   9. ¿Has tenido la gripe?
☐ ☐ 10. ¿Has sufrido de alergias? (¿A qué?)

PASO 2.   Ahora entrevista a un compañero o una compañera para saber más detalles de su historia médica y anota sus respuestas.

MODELO: E1: ¿Qué pasó cuando te desmayaste? ¿Dónde estuviste?
                E2: Fue terrible. Me desmayé en la escuela cuando tenía 14 años. Cuando me caí, me pegué la cabeza en un estante y me lastimé. Tuve una hinchazón grave (*serious*) que luego se convirtió en un moretón muy feo.

PASO 3.   ¿Cuántas diferencias y semejanzas hay entre tu historia médica y la de tu compañero/a? ¿Han experimentado algunas de las mismas condiciones? ¿Hay alguna condición que ninguno/a de Uds. haya experimentado? Compartan los resultados con la clase.

MODELO: Teresa y yo sufrimos de hinchazones, por diferentes razones: ella se torció el tobillo y yo sufrí una reacción alérgica a algo que comí.

I. ¿Qué deben hacer?

PASO 1. En parejas, túrnense para explicar la situación médica y ofrecer consejos.

> **MODELO:** E1: Necesito hacer más ejercicio pero me duelen las rodillas.
> E2: Debes practicar la natación. Y no uses tenis viejos para hacer ejercicio.

1. Me duele la cabeza.
2. Creo que tengo gripe.
3. Mi doctor me dijo que tengo que perder diez libras (*pounds*).
4. Quiero mantenerme en forma, pero no soy muy bueno/a en deportes.
5. Sufro de insomnio.
6. Necesito hacer más ejercicio y prefiero jugar en un equipo.
7. Me siento muy débil (*weak*) y quiero tener músculos más grandes.
8. Hace tres semanas que tengo tos.
9. Mi tobillo está hinchado.
10. Tengo náuseas.

PASO 2. En parejas, representen el papel de un entrenador (*trainer*) personal y su cliente. Usen mandatos para preparar un plan de entrenamiento (*training*) para mejorar la salud de los siguientes clientes y para mantenerse en forma para siempre. No se olviden de pensar en la edad y la habilidad física de cada cliente al crear su plan.

1.

Un hombre de 45 años que trabaja en una oficina de cincuenta a setenta horas a la semana. Come comida rápida por lo menos una vez al día, toma algunas cervezas después del trabajo todos los días y fuma veinte cigarrillos cada día.

2.

Un ama de casa (*housewife*) de 37 años que pesa (*weighs*) 175 libras, pasa dos o tres horas diarias llevando a sus dos hijos a sus varias actividades; camina dos millas (*miles*) tres veces cada semana con otras señoras de su comunidad. En su tiempo libre limpia la casa, cultiva el jardín y mira la televisión.

3.

Un estudiante universitario que no duerme lo suficiente, no tiene tiempo para comer bien y toma muchas bebidas con cafeína cada día. Pasa todo su tiempo estudiando y trabajando en una tienda.

4.

Una señora de 70 años con artritis que come mucha comida grasosa (*greasy*) y no hace ningún tipo de ejercicio.

Reciclaje

The present perfect

PASO 1. Dicen que es bueno para la salud hacer las siguientes actividades todos los días. Para cada actividad, crea una oración para decir cuántas veces has hecho esa actividad en las últimas cuarenta y ocho horas. Si no has hecho la actividad, dilo.

1. caminar por más de veinte minutos
2. comer frutas o verduras
3. meditar o practicar yoga
4. dormir una noche completa (de ocho horas)
5. hacer media hora de ejercicio aeróbico
6. tomar agua

En las últimas cuarenta y ocho horas…

1. _____
2. _____
3. _____
4. _____
5. _____
6. _____

PASO 2. Haz dos comparaciones entre lo que tú has hecho en las últimas cuarenta y ocho horas y lo que ha hecho una persona muy saludable (*healthy*). ¿A qué conclusión llegas? ¿Llevas una vida relativamente sana?

MODELO: En las últimas cuarenta y ocho horas, una persona muy saludable ha hecho ejercicio aeróbico pero yo no he hecho nada de ejercicio.

En las últimas cuarenta y ocho horas…

1. _____
2. _____

Conclusión: _____

■ Answers to this activity are in Appendix 2 at the back of your book.

12.1 Sofía lo ha ganado

The present perfect with object pronouns

Para empezar...

Sofía Mulánovich es una surfista peruana que ha ganado muchos premios (*awards*), incluyendo el título de Campeona Mundial (*World Champion*) de Surf de la Asociación de Surfistas Profesionales. En las siguientes oraciones, vas a aprender un poco más sobre su carrera como deportista. Empareja cada oración con el objeto apropiado.

Sofía Mulánovich se desliza sobre (*rides*) una ola.

1. _____ **Lo ha practicado** desde que tenía 9 años, porque vivía cerca de la playa.
2. _____ **Lo han considerado** desde hace tiempo como uno de los mejores lugares para surfear en Latinoamérica.
3. _____ Sofía es la primera latinoamericana que **lo ha ganado.**
4. _____ **Los han tomado** más en serio desde que Sofía Mulánovich empezó a tener tanto éxito.
5. _____ **Las ha tenido** desde muy chica.
6. _____ **La han introducido** al Salón de la Fama (*Hall of Fame*) del Surf.
7. _____ **Los ha usado** para estar en contacto con los aficionados (*fans*).
8. _____ **Lo ha sabido** hacer desde que tenía 3 años, cuando empezó a tomar clases.

a. el surf
b. el Campeonato Mundial de Surf
c. Sofía Mulánovich
d. nadar
e. ganas de ganar
f. el Perú
g. los surfistas latinoamericanos
h. su página web y su blog

■ Answers to these activities are in Appendix 2 at the back of your book.

Actividades analíticas

1 As you saw in **Estructura 6.3**, object pronouns (**pronombres de objeto**) appear before conjugated verbs.

Sofía **lo ganó.**   *Sofía won it.*

It's no different in the present perfect tense, where object pronouns appear before the auxiliary verb **haber,** because it is the conjugated verb.

Sofía **lo ha** ganado.   *Sofía has won it.*

In this example, the object pronoun (**lo**) is a direct object pronoun. What type of pronoun do you see in the following sentences: direct object, indirect object, or reflexive?

_____   Sofía **se** ha despertado temprano.   *Sofía has woken up early.*

_____   Sofía **le** ha escrito una carta.   *Sofía has written a letter to him/her/you* (form.).

2 You also saw in **Estructura 6.3** that when a conjugated verb is followed by an infinitive, the object pronoun may appear either before the conjugated verb or after and attached to the infinitive.

Sofía **lo quiere** ganar.
Sofía quiere **ganarlo.** } *Sofía wants to win it.*

The same is true when a present perfect verb form is followed by an infinitive. The object pronoun may appear either before the conjugated form of **haber** or after and attached to the infinitive. The meaning is the same regardless of the placement of the object pronoun.

Sofía **lo ha** querido ganar.
Sofía ha querido **ganarlo.** } *Sofía has wanted to win it.*

The present perfect follows the same pattern of object pronoun placement as other verb tenses, but English speakers sometimes find these sentences difficult to understand. Check your comprehension by translating the following sentences into English.

Lo he tenido que hacer. _____

¿Le has podido contestar su pregunta? _____

La hemos querido comprar por mucho tiempo. _____

Actividades prácticas

A. Los deportes y el mundo hispano   Empareja cada oración con el deporte o premio que le corresponde. **¡Atención!** Dos respuestas se usan más de una vez.

1. ____ Los puertorriqueños Roberto Clemente y Orlando Cepeda **se han considerado** desde los años 60 como figuras muy importantes en la historia de este deporte tan popular en el Caribe.

2. ____ Argentina, España y Uruguay son los únicos países hispanos que **la han ganado** (¡y Argentina y Uruguay **la han ganado** dos veces!).

3. ____ El panameño Roberto Durán **lo ha practicado** desde 1968 y es reconocido (*recognized*) como uno de los mejores en toda la historia de este «deporte de los guantes».

4. ____ El español Ricky Rubio **lo ha practicado** a nivel (*level*) profesional desde los 14 años. Ahora lo juega en la NBA de los Estados Unidos.

5. ____ Los futbolistas de Chile nunca **la han ganado,** pero sí han llegado a las semifinales.

6. ____ Cuba **la ha ganado** más de setenta veces, más que cualquier otro país hispano. (Nunca ha participado en los Juegos Olímpicos de invierno.)

7. ____ España es el único país hispano que **la ha ganado** en esquí alpino.

8. ____ La República Dominicana **les ha mandado** a más de 400 jugadores a las Grandes Ligas (*Leagues*) de este deporte, entre ellos el lanzador Juan Marichal y el segunda base Robinson Canó.

a. la Copa Mundial de Fútbol
b. la medalla de oro (*gold medal*) en los Juegos Olímpicos de verano
c. la medalla de oro en los Juegos Olímpicos de invierno
d. el béisbol
e. el boxeo
f. el básquetbol

B. El deporte en tu país

PASO 1. Para cada deporte en la tabla, escribe cuántas veces lo has visto (en televisión o en persona) y cuántas veces lo has practicado este año.

Número de veces que...	LO/LA HE VISTO	LO/LA HE PRACTICADO
1. el básquetbol	_____	_____
2. el béisbol	_____	_____
3. la escalada	_____	_____
4. el esquí (esquiar)	_____	_____
5. el fútbol	_____	_____
6. el fútbol americano	_____	_____
7. la natación (nadar)	_____	_____
8. el tenis	_____	_____
9. el voleibol	_____	_____
10. el yoga	_____	_____

 PASO 2. En grupos, comparen sus respuestas. Para cada deporte, ¿quién lo ha visto más y quién lo ha practicado más? ¿Hay algún deporte que todos han visto o han practicado?

C. Compras para el deporte

Escoge una de las cuatro respuestas posibles para responder a las siguientes preguntas. Completa cada respuesta con el pronombre de objeto directo o indirecto apropiado y escríbela en el espacio indicado.

Respuestas posibles: Sí, _____ he comprado.
Sí, _____ hemos comprado.
Sí, _____ he comprado una raqueta.
Sí, _____ hemos comprado una raqueta.

PREGUNTAS

1. ¿Has comprado el casco?
2. ¿Han comprado las revistas de deporte que les recomendé?
3. ¿Has comprado las bicicletas?
4. ¿Le han comprado algo a Victoria?
5. ¿Han comprado los boletos para el partido?
6. ¿Has comprado la raqueta de tenis que querías?
7. ¿Le has comprado algo a Gerardo?

RESPUESTAS

1. Sí, lo he comprado
2. Sí, las he comprado
3. Sí, las he comprado
4. Sí, hemos comprado zapatos. Sí, los hemos comprado.
5. Sí, los hemos comprado.
6. Sí, lo he comprado
7. Sí, le he comprado algo.

D. ¿Qué te ha funcionado?

PASO 1. Todos hemos empezado algún hábito bueno y después no lo continuamos. ¿A ti te ha pasado lo contrario (*the opposite*)? ¿Has podido empezar algo bueno para tu salud (hacer algún tipo de ejercicio, por ejemplo, o cambiar tu manera de comer) y lo has podido continuar? En parejas, hablen de este tema y creen una lista de cosas que han funcionado para Uds. Un ejemplo ya está hecho.

HÁBITO/ACTIVIDAD	¿POR CUÁNTO TIEMPO LO HAS HECHO?
Correr por la mañana	Lo he hecho por dos años.
_____	_____
_____	_____

PASO 2. Ahora, crea dos mandatos informales para tu compañero/a y justifica tus recomendaciones con tu propia experiencia.

MODELO: Corre. Lo he hecho por dos años ya y me siento más fuerte y he bajado de peso.

Colombia

Venezuela

E. Cultura: Los deportes en Colombia y Venezuela

PASO 1. Lee el texto sobre Colombia y Venezuela.

Si preguntas a los sudamericanos cuál es el deporte más importante para su país, muchos van a mencionar el fútbol. Este es el caso de Colombia, donde la selección nacional ha participado cuatro veces en la Copa Mundial de fútbol y en 2001 ganó la Copa América. Por otro lado, su nación vecina Venezuela no ha podido generar tanto entusiasmo alrededor del fútbol y, de hecho,[a] es el único país sudamericano que nunca ha participado en la Copa Mundial. Sin embargo, los venezolanos sí tienen mucho orgullo y mucho éxito en su deporte nacional: el béisbol. Se ve evidencia de esto en el gran número de beisbolistas —¡más de 300!— que participaron en las Grandes Ligas desde la primera edición en 1939.

Entonces, ¿el fútbol es el deporte nacional de Colombia? Para nada. El deporte nacional se llama «el tejo», un juego que se originó en la época prehispánica. El jugador tiene que lanzar un disco de metal a una distancia de dieciocho metros al centro de una cancha de arcilla.[b] Lo divertido es que cuando el disco cae exactamente en el centro, hace ruido y saca chispas[c] porque allí hay unos pequeños paquetes de pólvora.[d] Y aparte del fútbol y el tejo, los colombianos son ciclistas excelentes. El ciclista Víctor Hugo Peña llevó el maillot[e] amarillo durante tres días en el Tour de France de 2003.

En Venezuela, no todos los deportistas están satisfechos con el ritmo lento de un partido de béisbol. De hecho, el país es conocido por la naturaleza espectacular que ofrece lugares tanto bellos como peligrosos, ideales para los deportes extremos. En la zona alrededor de Mérida, se puede hacer alpinismo en varios picos, los dos más altos de casi 5.000 metros. Los más atrevidos[f] pueden bajar volando, haciendo parapente,[g] un deporte muy popular. ¿Y en qué deporte participan los más atrevidos (o los más locos)? Hacen salto[h] B.A.S.E. de la catarata[i] más alta del mundo, el Salto Ángel, ubicada en el Parque Nacional Canaima.

[a]de... *in fact* [b]*clay* [c]saca... *makes sparks* [d]*gunpowder* [e]*jersey* [f]*daring* [g]*paragliding* [h]*jumping* [i]*waterfall*

PASO 2. Usa la lectura para identificar a lo que se refieren los siguientes objetos directos.

1. La selección nacional de fútbol de Colombia la ha ganado. _América_
2. Venezuela los ha mandado a las Grandes Ligas más de 300 veces. _beisbolistas_
3. Los colombianos lo han jugado desde los tiempos prehispánicos. _el tejo_
4. Las genera el disco de tejo cuando cae en el centro de la cancha. _chispas_
5. Lo ha llevado el ciclista Víctor Hugo Peña en el Tour de France. _maillot_
6. Los que hacen parapente en Venezuela la pueden admirar porque es espectacular. _deportes extremos_
7. Los deportistas más atrevidos de Venezuela lo han hecho. _béisbol_

PASO 3. En parejas, contesten las preguntas y explíquense las respuestas.

1. El béisbol empezó en los Estados Unidos en el siglo XIX y ganó mucha popularidad en países que tenían mucho contacto con los Estados Unidos. Considerando la ubicación geográfica de Colombia y de Venezuela, ¿por qué crees que el béisbol se hizo mucho más popular en Venezuela que en Colombia?
2. Basándote de nuevo en la geografía, ¿en qué otros países hispanos piensas que es muy popular el béisbol?
3. ¿Cómo se comparan el béisbol y el fútbol en tu país? ¿Cuál se juega más? ¿Cuál es más popular en la televisión?

↻ Reciclaje

The present progressive

¿Qué están haciendo en los siguientes dibujos? **¡Atención!** Usa el presente progresivo para formar tus respuestas.

1. _____

2. _____

3. _____

4. _____

5. _____

6. _____

7. _____

8. _____

■ Answers to this activity are in Appendix 2 at the back of your book.

Rafael Nadal en el
Abierto de Francia

12.2 Lo está ganando

The present progressive with object pronouns

Para empezar...

Estos son algunos momentos clave (*key*) en la vida del tenista español Rafael Nadal. Él es de Mallorca, una isla en el Mediterráneo, y se considera uno de los mejores jugadores de la historia del tenis. Empareja cada hora, fecha y tema con lo que está haciendo Nadal en ese momento.

HORA	FECHA	TEMA
a. 16:32	23 de mayo, 2005	El Abierto (*Open*) de Francia
b. 11:08	13 de febrero, 2008	La Fundación Rafa Nadal
c. 19:28	6 de julio, 2008	Roger Federer
d. 10:35	12 de julio, 2008	El asteroide 128036
e. 14:42	16 de agosto, 2008	La medalla de oro en los Juegos Olímpicos
f. 20:35	24 de octubre, 2008	El premio Príncipe de Asturias
g. 10:48	8 de enero, 2010	Un video con Shakira, la cantante colombiana
h. 17:47	8 de junio, 2014	El Abierto de Francia

1. _____ **La está recibiendo** en Pekín (*Beijing*).
2. _____ **La está anunciando** como una fundación de asistencia social.
3. _____ **Lo está ganando** por primera vez, y con eso **se está haciendo** muy famoso en todo el mundo.
4. _____ **Lo está filmando** en Barcelona.
5. _____ **Lo está ganando** por novena (*ninth*) vez —más que cualquier otro tenista.
6. _____ La Unión Astronómica Internacional **le está dando** el nombre «Rafaelnadal» en honor a «uno de los mejores tenistas de todos los tiempos».
7. _____ **Lo está recibiendo** del Príncipe Felipe en una ceremonia en Oviedo.
8. _____ **Lo está venciendo** (*beating*) en Wimbledon. Según muchos, es el mejor partido en la historia del tenis.

■ Answers to these activities are in Appendix 2 at the back of your book.

Actividades analíticas

1 As you saw in **Estructura 11.3,** the present progressive consists of the auxiliary verb **estar** followed by the present participle of the main verb. Object pronouns can appear before **estar,** since it is the conjugated verb of the form.

Nadal **lo está** ganando.   *Nadal is winning it.*

In this example, the pronoun **lo** is a direct object pronoun. In **Para empezar,** find one example each of an indirect object pronoun and a reflexive pronoun, and write the pronoun and complete verb form here.

With indirect object pronoun: _____

With reflexive pronoun: _____

2 Object pronouns may instead appear after and attached to the present participle of the verb, just as you've seen with infinitives (see **Estructura 8.3**).

Nadal está **ganándolo.**   *Nadal is winning it.*

If you attach the object pronoun to the end of a present participle, you will need to write an accent mark in order to keep the stress on the right vowel: on the **a** of **-ando** for **-ar** verbs, and over the **e** of the **-iendo** of **-er** and **-ir** verbs. Whether you place the object pronoun before the conjugated verb or attach it to the end of the present participle, the meaning is the same.

Take the sentences that you wrote in **Actividad analítica 1** and move the object pronoun to the end of the present participle. Don't forget the accent marks!

Indirect object: _____

Reflexive: _____

■ For more on the use of object pronouns with the present progressive, see **Para saber más 12.2** at the back of your book.

Actividades prácticas

A. ¡Qué mala excusa!

PASO 1. Si invitas a un amigo o una amiga a hacer ejercicio contigo y te da una de las siguientes excusas, ¿cuáles son buenas y cuáles son ridículas?

No puedo hacer ejercicio contigo porque…	BUENA	RIDÍCULA
1. ya me estoy acostando. Tengo que levantarme muy temprano mañana.	☐	☐
2. me interesa más la televisión. La estoy viendo y cuando cambio el canal (*channel*), eso es muy buen ejercicio.	☐	☐
3. me estoy acordando de que mi abuela me decía que el ejercicio era malo.	☐	☐
4. me estoy sintiendo mal y creo que me estoy enfermando.	☐	☐
5. me estoy lavando los dientes.	☐	☐
6. encontré un libro en la basura y lo estoy leyendo.	☐	☐
7. tengo que presentar este libro mañana en mi clase de literatura y apenas (*barely*) lo estoy empezando a leer.	☐	☐
8. no encuentro mi computadora y la ando buscando.	☐	☐

PASO 2. Ahora, en parejas, creen dos excusas buenas y dos excusas ridículas para decir por qué no pueden hacer ejercicio en este momento. ¿Qué están haciendo que no les permite hacer ejercicio?

B. ¿Qué está haciendo? En parejas, para cada foto, túrnense para contestar la pregunta «¿Qué está(n) haciendo?»

   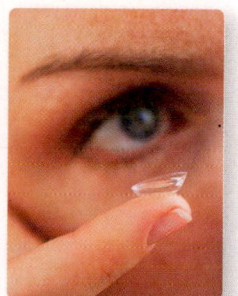

1. Mónica   2. Luis   3. El padre y su hija   4. Yo

  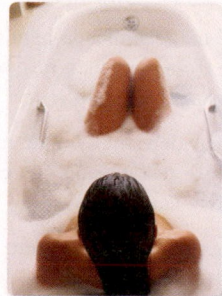 

5. Gloria   6. Francisco   7. Elena   8. Amaya y Marlén

C. Dos contra dos En parejas, túrnense para actuar para otra pareja algunas de las siguientes acciones, pero sin hablar. ¿La otra pareja puede adivinar qué están haciendo?

MODELO: ¿Lo/La estás ayudando a practicar yoga? (¿Estás ayudándolo/la a practicar yoga?)

ayudarla/la a ponerse un casco	hablarle en francés
ayudarlo/la a practicar yoga	invitarlo/la a nadar
darle una raqueta	pasarle la pelota en un partido de fútbol
decirle que es muy buen(a) futbolista	saludarlo/la
decirle que tiene que comer más frutas y verduras	seguirlo/la

⟳ Reciclaje

Commands

Usando las recomendaciones de la lista, crea consejos en forma de mandatos para tus compañeros que tienen los problemas mencionados. Cada recomendación se puede usar solo una vez. **¡Atención!** Algunos de los mandatos tienen que estar en forma singular (**tú**) y otros en plural (**Uds.**).

comer menos y hacer más ejercicio   dormir más   practicar yoga
correr   levantar pesas   tomar agua

PROBLEMA	CONSEJO
1. Tenemos sed.	_____
2. Quiero tener más flexibilidad.	_____
3. Queremos tener más músculo.	_____
4. Siempre tengo sueño.	_____
5. Quiero bajar de peso.	_____
6. Queremos tener mejor condición cardiovascular.	_____

■ Answers to this activity are in Appendix 2 at the back of your book.

12.3 Te recomiendo que comas chocolate

The subjunctive: Volition with regular verbs

Para empezar...

Lee las siguientes preguntas sobre la salud y las respuestas del Doctor América. Él te recomienda (*recommends*) puros productos autóctonos (*native*) de América para ayudarte con los problemas de salud. Pero, ¡cuidado! Una de sus recomendaciones es falsa.

1. Quiero bajar (*lower*) mi colesterol. ¿Qué hago?
   Doctor América dice: «Yo te recomiendo que **comas** mucho aguacate».

2. ¿Qué me recomienda para aumentar (*increase*) mi consumo (*consumption*) de antioxidantes?
   Doctor América dice: «Te recomiendo que **comas** o **tomes** mucho chocolate. El chocolate tiene un nivel muy alto de antioxidantes».

3. No me gusta el jugo de naranja. ¿Qué puedo hacer para tener suficiente vitamina C?
   Doctor América dice: «Te recomiendo que **comas** chiles. Los chiles contienen muchísima vitamina C».

4. Soy vegetariano. ¿Qué me recomienda para comer suficiente proteína?
   Doctor América dice: «Te recomiendo que **busques** quinua. Es de los Andes (sobre todo Bolivia) y tiene muchísima proteína. Se usa en forma de harina para hacer pan».

5. A veces tengo problemas digestivos. ¿Qué me recomienda?
   Doctor América dice: «Te recomiendo que **compres** papaya. Ayuda mucho a la digestión y tiene muchas vitaminas y antioxidantes».

6. Sé que tengo que comer más verduras, pero no me gustan. ¿Qué hago?
   Doctor América dice: «Te recomiendo que le **des** una oportunidad al maíz. ¿Lo has probado (*tried*) en verano? Con sal y mantequilla (o chile, ¿por qué no?), es muy rico».

7. Me estoy quedando calvo (*bald*) y no sé qué hacer. ¿Ud. me puede recomendar algo?
   Doctor América dice: «Te recomiendo que **vivas** una vida muy tranquila y que **tomes** agua con vainilla todas las noches antes de acostarte. En poco tiempo vas a tener mucho pelo de nuevo (*once again*)».

8. ¿Ud. me puede recomendar alguna fruta o verdura para ayudar a prevenir (*prevent*) el cáncer?
   Doctor América dice: «Yo te recomiendo que **comas** mucho tomate. Su color rojo es por la presencia de licopeno (*lycopene*), un antioxidante importante».

La recomendación falsa es la del número _____.

Una planta de quinua roja

■ Answers to these activities are in Appendix 2 at the back of your book.

Actividades analíticas

1 The verbs in bold in **Para empezar** are all in the **tú** form of the *present subjunctive* (**el presente de subjuntivo**). The subjunctive is used in a variety of situations, and here it is used to express a recommendation, a piece of advice, or a desire.

Write the subjunctive forms in bold from **Para empezar** in the right-hand column of this chart. Then write the **tú** form for the *present indicative* (**el presente de indicativo**), the grammatical name for the simple present tense.

INFINITIVO	PRESENTE DE INDICATIVO	PRESENTE DE SUBJUNTIVO
	tú	tú
buscar	buscas	
comer		
comprar	compras	
dar	das	
tomar		
vivir		

2 You can identify subjunctive forms by the vowel in the ending. Just as in the formal commands and negative informal commands, both **-ar** and **-er/-ir** verbs use the "opposite" vowel (**vocal**). Use the examples given to complete the following chart.

	La vocal en el presente de indicativo	La vocal en el presente de subjuntivo
-ar verbs	-a-	
Example	Tom**a**s chocolate.	...que tom**e**s chocolate.
-er/-ir verbs	-e-	
Example	Com**e**s chocolate.	...que com**a**s chocolate.

3 Apart from the change in vowel that you just saw in **Actividades analíticas 2,** the endings in the present subjunctive are similar to those of the present indicative. Complete the following chart to see the entire conjugation.

	tomar	comer	vivir
yo	tome	coma	viva
tú			
él/ella, Ud.	tome		viva
nosotros/as		comamos	
vosotros/as	toméis		viváis
ellos/ellas, Uds.			vivan

Note that the **yo** form and the **él/ella, Ud.** form are identical in the subjunctive. Context will help to determine which subject is intended, or the subject pronoun may be used.

4 You saw in **Para empezar** that the verb **recomendar** is followed by the subjunctive. Here are some other expressions that do the same.

Se usa el subjuntivo después de...	Ejemplo
esperar (to hope)	**Espero** que **puedas** venir a la fiesta. *I hope that you can come to the party.*
ojalá (I hope)	**Ojalá** que **puedas** venir a la fiesta. *I hope that you can come to the party.*
pedir	**Están pidiendo** que **trabajemos** en Bolivia. *They're asking us to work in Bolivia.*
querer	**Quiero** que **lleguen** temprano mañana. *I want them to arrive early tomorrow.*
ser necesario	**Es necesario** que tu papá **coma** más fruta. *It's necessary for your father to eat more fruit.*

These expressions trigger the use of subjunctive after **que** because they convey a recommendation, a piece of advice, or a desire.

5 The verb **decir** sometimes expresses a recommendation, in which case it is followed by the subjunctive. When it simply describes a situation, it is followed by the indicative.

decir CON EL SUBJUNTIVO Y EL INDICATIVO	
Subjunctive (Recommendation)	Los médicos **dicen** que **tomes** mucho chocolate. *The doctors say that you should / tell you to drink a lot of hot chocolate.*
Indicative (Description)	Los médicos **dicen** que **tomas** mucho chocolate. *The doctors say that you drink a lot of hot chocolate.*

Verbs such as **pensar** and **creer** never express a recommendation, so they are followed by the indicative.

Pienso que mi hijo **toma** mucho chocolate.   *I think my son drinks a lot of hot chocolate.*

■ For more expressions of volition, see **Para saber más 12.3** at the back of your book.

¡Anticipa!

As you have seen, the present indicative and the present subjunctive are conjugated very similarly, apart from the change in vowel. With this in mind, how do you think stem-changing verbs like **poder** and **cerrar** are conjugated in the subjunctive?

1. poder (ue)	2. cerrar (ie)
yo _____	yo _____
tú _____	tú _____
él / ella, Ud. _____	él / ella, Ud. _____
nosotros/as _____	nosotros/as _____
vosotros/as _____	vosotros/as _____
ellos/as, Uds. _____	ellos/as, Uds. _____

¡Anticipa! 1. pueda, puedas, pueda, podamos, podáis, puedan. **2.** cierre, cierres, cierre, cerremos, cerréis, cierren

Actividades prácticas

A. ¿Pensar o querer?   Escoge **pensar** o **querer** para completar cada oración. **¡Atención!**
Presta atención al verbo que sigue después de **que.** ¿Está en el indicativo o el subjuntivo?

1. **Pienso / Quiero** que Pepe está en el gimnasio.
2. **Pienso / Quiero** que Martina trabaja en San José.
3. **Pienso / Quiero** que gane Nadal.
4. **Pienso / Quiero** que van a limpiar la piscina al mediodía.
5. **Pienso / Quiero** que llueva mañana.
6. **Pienso / Quiero** que va a ganar Nadal.
7. **Pienso / Quiero** que esté muy limpia la casa.
8. **Pienso / Quiero** que corramos todos juntos en el parque mañana.

B. En otras palabras   En el español, como en el inglés, a veces hay más de una manera
de decir las cosas. Empareja cada oración con la oración en el subjuntivo con el mismo sentido
(*meaning*).

1. _____ Llámame antes del partido, por
favor.
2. _____ ¿Por qué no hablan tus padres con
el entrenador? Creo que sería buena
idea.
3. _____ Diles a tus padres que tienen que
hablar con el entrenador.
4. _____ ¡Por favor! ¡Come más fruta!
5. _____ Los atletas tienen que practicar.
Es obligatorio.
6. _____ Tienes que cooperar (*cooperate*)
con el resto del equipo. No hay otra
opción.
7. _____ Si trabajas bien con el resto del
equipo, voy a estar muy contento.
8. _____ Si ganas en la competencia
(*competition*), voy a estar muy
contento.

a. Es necesario que trabajes bien con ellos.
b. Recomiendo que tus padres hablen con el
entrenador.
c. Espero que ganes en la competencia.
d. Ojalá que trabajes bien con ellos.
e. Te estoy pidiendo que me llames antes del
partido.
f. Quiero que tus padres hablen con el
entrenador.
g. Te estoy pidiendo que comas más
manzanas, naranjas, plátanos, etcétera.
h. Es necesario que los atletas practiquen.

¿Por qué?

Why does the subjunctive look so similar to formal commands (and negative **tú**
commands)? The reason is that their meaning is almost the same. Commands express
what you want to happen, and the subjunctive does something similar: it expresses what
the subject of the main verb wants to happen. These commands and the subjunctive
both use the "opposite" vowel in their endings, and as you saw in **10.3**, this makes
sense. Spanish only uses **a**, **e**, and **o** in unstressed endings, and since **o** is reserved for
the **yo** ending of the present indicative, the simplest way to distinguish the subjunctive
from the indicative is to "switch" the vowels **a** and **e**.

C. Lo que dice la gente   Indica el verbo más lógico en cada oración. **¡Atención!** Presta
atención al sentido de la oración. ¿Está expresando una recomendación o una descripción?

1. Mi mamá siempre me está diciendo que **come / coma** más frutas y verduras para estar
más sana.
2. Este artículo en el Internet dice que Nadal **juega / juegue** tenis.
3. Gloria dice que muchos estudiantes en su universidad **nadan / naden** todos los días.
4. La maestra dice que **escribimos / escribamos** una carta en español como tarea para
mañana.
5. Las instrucciones dicen que **nos acostamos / nos acostemos** después de tomar la
pastilla (*pill*).
6. Marcos dice que sus papás **viven / vivan** en el Perú.
7. La televisión dice que el presidente **está / esté** viajando esta semana.
8. Para poder ganar la competencia, dicen que **estamos / estemos** presentes en todos los
entrenamientos.

D. ¿Qué nos recomiendan los médicos?

PASO 1. En cada una de las siguientes oraciones, usa el verbo entre paréntesis en su forma **nosotros/as.** Luego, indica si la oración es **cierta** o **falsa.**

Los médicos nos recomiendan...

	CIERTO	FALSO
1. que (consultar) _____ con un doctor antes de empezar un programa de ejercicio fuerte.	☐	☐
2. que (comer) _____ mucho azúcar para tener los dientes muy bonitos.	☐	☐
3. que (tomar) _____ jugo de papaya para poder nadar más rápido.	☐	☐
4. que (usar) _____ bloqueador solar cuando estamos expuestos (*exposed*) al sol.	☐	☐
5. que (escuchar) _____ música en español una hora al día.	☐	☐
6. que (evitar) _____ el estrés si es posible.	☐	☐
7. que (lavarse) _____ los dientes por lo menos dos veces al día.	☐	☐
8. que le (dar) _____ muchos regalos a nuestro médico favorito.	☐	☐

PASO 2. Ahora Uds. son los doctores. En grupos, creen seis recomendaciones para sus pacientes que tienen gripe. Usen las sugerencias de la lista o inventen otras.

> beber muchos líquidos
>
> comer caldo de pollo
>
> comprar jarabe (*syrup*) para la tos
>
> descansar
>
> sonarse (ue) (*to blow*) la nariz
>
> tomar unas aspirinas

MODELO: Les recomendamos que Uds. se queden en casa.

E. El espíritu deportivo (*Good sportsmanship*)

En parejas, creen tres recomendaciones para un atleta que quiere ser un(a) ganador(a) cortés y no un perdedor resentido / una perdedora resentida (*sore loser*).

> Te recomiendo que...   Ojalá que...   Es necesario que...

MODELO: Te recomiendo que no insultes a nadie.

¡Leamos!

Trancos° de gratitud en la 21K   *strides*

Antes de leer

Contesta las siguientes preguntas sobre un deporte popular: carreras de fondo (*long-distance running*).

1. Para cada distancia, rellena la tabla con el nombre de la carrera y los tiempos típicos para completar cada una.

maratón	**ultramaratón**	**2–8 horas**
medio maratón	**1–3 horas**	**24 horas o más**

DISTANCIA	NOMBRE DE LA CARRERA	TIEMPO TÍPICO
21 kilómetros		
42 kilómetros		
100 kilómetros		

2. En general, ¿qué pisan (*step on*) los corredores?
   a. asfalto   b. flores   c. agua

3. En tu opinión, ¿para qué participan los mejores atletas?
   a. el espíritu de la competencia   b. el viaje   c. los premios

4. ¿Qué tipo de zapatos llevan la mayoría de los participantes en las carreras de fondo?
   a. Corren descalzos.   b. Llevan tenis.   c. Llevan sandalias.

5. ¿Qué tipo de ropa llevan los participantes?
   a. cómoda y ligera   b. fuerte y tradicional   c. larga y elegante

6. ¿Cuál no es un requisito para participar en una carrera de fondo?
   a. el entrenamiento   b. la predisposición genética   c. la resistencia (*endurance*) física

A leer

PASO 1.   Hay varias distancias de carrera, algunas cortas y otras muy largas, pero cada una requiere habilidad y disciplina. La siguiente lectura trata de un grupo de corredores indígenas que tienen una profunda apreciación por las carreras y una manera bastante única de correrlas.

Trancos de gratitud en la 21K

por Santino Ayala

Saltillo, Coahuila, México — Mañana, nuestras calles se atestarán de[a] participantes en la Gran Carrera de México, la 21K de Coahuila. ¡A correr!

Las motivaciones para correr son tan variadas como las personas que corren: el buen estado físico, los beneficios cardíacos y aeróbicos, el alivio[b] del estrés y el deseo de competir. Y claro, a veces corremos por el peligro[c] o el miedo.

[a]se... *will be filled with*   [b]*relief*   [c]*danger*

(Continues)

En la Sierra[d] Tarahumara del estado de Chihuahua, los tarahumaras corren por motivaciones muy disímiles[e] de las que típicamente influyen en que nosotros salgamos con tenis a correr unos kilómetros por el vecindario[f] o el parque.

Correr es la tradición más antigua de los tarahumaras. Históricamente, corrían, descalzos[g] o con huaraches,[h] para cazar,[i] para comunicarse y para expresar su devoción y agradecimiento[j] a dios por su existencia. Rarámuri, el nombre de los tarahumaras en su idioma, significa *pie corredor.*[k]

Una de las carreras más importantes de su comunidad es el *rarajípari* o carrera de bolas.[l] Es una carrera que puede durar[m] unas horas o un par[n] de días. En esta carrera comunitaria, dos equipos de corredores lanzan[ñ] una bola entre sí hasta llegar a la meta,[o] que puede ser de unos metros o hasta 200 kilómetros. Para las carreras más largas, la comunidad corre con los equipos. Las mujeres participan con aros y palitos[p] y otros miembros corren al lado de los equipos, proveyéndoles[q] comida y bebida y, durante la noche, luz para iluminar el paso.

Un rarámuri expresa su devoción

Según un miembro de la comunidad tarahumara, los rarámuris corren «para alegrar[r] al corazón de la Madre Tierra, al mismo Sol que es nuestro dios y nuestra Madre Luna[s]».

Aunque por muchas décadas esta comunidad vivía muy aislada del mundo moderno, ahora participan en carreras más allá de[t] la Sierra. Corren en maratones en las ciudades más grandes de México y también en maratones en el extranjero, en lugares como Colorado, Nevada y California.

Este año, un grupo de diez tarahumaras de Tatahuichi vuelve a Saltillo para participar en la Gran Carrera de México, la 21K de Coahuila. Entre ellos, Martín Roberto Ramírez dice que ha participado en esta carrera por cuatro años seguidos.[u] ¿Le será difícil? Dudable.[v] Más de una vez, Martín se puso los huaraches y corrió 100 millas seguidas en ultramaratones de los Estados Unidos.

Mientras Martín y sus compañeros expresan su gratitud y devoción durante la carrera, nosotros también queremos expresar nuestro agradecimiento a su comunidad y a esta gran comunidad de corredores que llega a nuestro estado todos los veranos —¡algunos por veinte años seguidos!— para correr. A todos les deseamos suerte y una buena carrera.

[d]*Mountains* [e]*unlike* [f]*neighborhood* [g]*barefoot* [h]*sandals* [i]*hunt* [j]*thankfulness* [k]*running* [l]*balls* [m]*last* [n]*couple* [ñ]*equipos… running teams throw* [o]*finish line* [p]*aros… hoops and sticks* [q]*providing them with* [r]*fill with joy* [s]*Moon* [t]*más… beyond* [u]*in a row* [v]*Doubtful*

PASO 2. Ahora lee las siguientes preguntas y, según lo que leíste en la lectura, responde con oraciones completas.

1. ¿Cuántos kilómetros corren los participantes en la carrera de Saltillo, en México?

2. ¿Por qué tienen un significado especial las carreras para los tarahumaras?

3. ¿Cómo corren los hombres y las mujeres tarahumaras en la sierra? ¿Qué cosas llevan?

4. ¿En qué tipo de carrera han participado los tarahumaras en los Estados Unidos?

5. ¿Qué llevan en los pies para correr los tarahumaras?

6. ¿Cómo son los tarahumaras como (*like*) los corredores / las corredoras de maratones de tu país? ¿Cómo son diferentes? Explica.

Después de leer

En parejas, lean las siguientes situaciones y den una felicitación, una reacción o una sugerencia apropiada para cada una. **¡Atención!** Pueden usar las expresiones en la página 348 y en **Estructura 12.3.**

1. tu amigo está por correr su primera carrera 5K

2. tu amiga ha corrido la mitad de (*half of*) su carrera y está cansada, pero quiere seguir

3. a tus amigos solo les queda una milla más (*only one mile left*) por correr en el maratón

4. tu amiga no sabe qué llevar para correr una carrera de larga distancia

5. un corredor tarahumara está por correr por veinticuatro horas seguidas y te pide consejos (*advice*)

¡Escuchemos!

El sueño° de ser deportista   *dream*

Antes de escuchar

PASO 1.   Completa cada una de las siguientes oraciones con tres posibilidades.

   MODELO: De niña, quería trabajar como guía naturalista, periodista o veterinaria.

1. De niño/a, esperaba trabajar como…

2. Soy aficionado/a (*fan*) de los siguientes equipos deportistas: …

3. Los miembros de mi familia son aficionados de los siguientes equipos deportistas: …

4. Según mi opinión, los deportes más populares en el mundo hispano son…

 PASO 2.   En grupos pequeños, comparen sus respuestas al **Paso 1** y luego contesten las siguientes preguntas.

1. ¿Quiénes del grupo aún (*still*) quieren hacer el mismo trabajo que querían hacer en su niñez?

2. ¿Qué hacen los aficionados de los varios equipos deportistas que apuntaron en el **Paso 1?** ¿Cuál es la tradición más extraña?

3. ¿Quién(es) conoce(n) a alguien que haya tenido éxito como atleta profesional?

4. Según la mayoría, ¿cuál es el deporte más popular en el mundo hispano?

CONÉCTATE AL MUNDO HISPANO

Los buenos **comentaristas del fútbol** tienen un estilo de narrar los partidos para que cada patada (*kick*) de la pelota parezca emocionante (*seems exciting*). Tienen fama de gritar (*yell*) y cantar el «GOOOOOOOOOOOOOLLLLLL!» como en ningún otro deporte. Imagínate la siguiente escena emocionante en un partido entre dos gran rivales.

COMENTARISTA: ¡La reconocida pelota blanca y negra pasa con rapidez entre los jugadores de los dos equipos: Barcelona y Manchester United! El entrenador Vilanova grita, pero nadie lo oye porque los aficionados en el estadio hacen un ruido tremendo. Ninguno de los dos equipos ha marcado (*scored*) un gol y ahora —en los últimos segundos del partido— el nuevo jugador joven está por meter un gol: patea (*he kicks*) la pelota hacia el hombro izquierdo del portero (*goalkeeper*) inglés, pero el portero salta y agarra (*jumps and grabs*) la pelota con las manos. ¡Y así el partido termina en un empate (*tie*): 0–0!

A escuchar

PASO 1. Mira y escucha el video. Mientras escuchas, marca los trabajos que mencionan los entrevistados.

bailador(a)   corredor(a)   guitarrista   tenista

beisbolista   futbolista   nadador(a)   torero/a (*bullfighter*)

PASO 2. Según lo que escuchaste, empareja cada equipo con su mejor descripción.

1. _____ un equipo profesional de fútbol de Madrid
2. _____ un equipo profesional de fútbol de la capital de México, el Distrito Federal
3. _____ el equipo representativo del país en los partidos nacionales

a. Real Madrid
b. La selección de fútbol de Paraguay
c. Cruz Azul

Después de escuchar

PASO 1. Mira y escucha otra vez. Luego, contesta las preguntas.

El futbolista portugués Cristiano Ronaldo, del Real Madrid Club de Fútbol

LOS AFICIONADOS

1. Según Laura, ¿cuál es el deporte nacional de España?
2. Según Ludmila y Paula, ¿cuál es el deporte nacional de Argentina?
3. ¿Qué hizo Víctor el sábado por la tarde?
4. ¿Qué término usan Mariano, David y William para decir «jugador de fútbol»?

EL SUEÑO DE MUCHOS NIÑOS

1. Describe el sueño de Mariano.
2. Describe el sueño de Pedro. ¿Por cuánto tiempo entrenó profesionalmente? ¿Por qué dejó de entrenar profesionalmente?
3. ¿Qué carrera quiere seguir Dávid?
4. ¿Qué sueño tiene William?

 PASO 2. En parejas, contesten las siguientes preguntas sobre lo que escucharon.

1. Laura dice que el fútbol es «el deporte Rey (*King*)». ¿Qué significa? ¿Cuál es «el deporte Rey» donde viven Uds.?
2. ¿Por qué puede costar mucho dinero cumplir el sueño de ser atleta profesional? ¿No ganan mucho dinero los atletas profesionales?

¡Escribamos!

Cómo nos mantenemos en forma

Cada persona tiene su propia perspectiva en cuanto a la salud, la dieta y el ejercicio. Pero a veces es difícil mantener esa perspectiva. En esta actividad, le vas a ofrecer consejos a alguien que, debido (*due*) a un cambio de circunstancias, busca nuevo equilibrio.

Antes de escribir

Lee las descripciones de la salud y los hábitos de Mila, Félix y Elena e indica las partes tal vez problemáticas. Para cada descripción, apunta algunas cosas que debe hacer esta persona para mejorar su salud.

MILA: Estoy en clase toda la mañana de lunes a viernes. Luego por las tardes estudio y trabajo en la oficina de seguridad pública de la universidad. Como en la cafetería tres veces al día y no he subido de (*gained*) peso, pero siempre me siento cansada y sé que soy más débil que hace un año cuando hacía mucho más ejercicio con los equipos deportivos de mi colegio. Tengo que mantenerme en forma. ¿Qué hago?

FÉLIX: Recientemente me hice socio del nuevo gimnasio al lado de mi oficina. Voy los cinco días de la semana, pero no he perdido ni un kilo. Con todo el ejercicio, tengo ganas de comer más de lo normal para mí. Además de las comidas normales, como un sándwich y unas papas fritas en la tarde y algún postre después de la cena.

ELENA: Antes iba al gimnasio cinco veces a la semana pero ahora con un trabajo de tiempo completo y dos hijos no tengo tiempo. Seguir una dieta equilibrada es muy importante para mí y más o menos sigo comiendo lo que siempre he comido.

ESTRATEGIA

Persuasive paragraph

Words can be powerful, even when up against strong convictions, tightly held beliefs, or deeply engrained habits. Being able to write a persuasive paragraph is therefore an invaluable skill to have. This involves being able to argue a point and strengthen your case by bringing in supporting statements, using solid reasoning, and anticipating the counterpoints to your argument and preemptively responding to them.

A escribir

Escoge una de las tres personas de **Antes de escribir** y escribe una composición para ayudarla a mejorar su salud. Escribe dos párrafos: un párrafo de introducción en el que describes lo que está haciendo mal la persona y un párrafo en que le ofreces recomendaciones de lo que debe hacer para mejorar su salud. Para convencer a la persona de que debe cambiar sus hábitos, explica por qué cada acción sugerida (*suggested*) es beneficiosa. Trata de anticipar las respuestas de la persona y responde también a ellas.

MODELO: No coma el sándwich y las papas fritas extras.

(Reacción anticipada: ¡Pero tengo hambre por hacer tanto ejercicio!)
En vez de comer el sándwich y las papas fritas, coma fruta y un puñado (*handful*) de nueces; así no tendrá hambre, pero podrá bajar de peso. Estas comidas son mejores que su merienda típica porque la fruta tiene muchas vitaminas y poca grasa (*fat*), y las nueces son altas en proteína.

Después de escribir

Revisa tu composición. Luego, intercambia composiciones con un compañero / una compañera para evaluarlas.

☐ Lee la introducción. ¿Explica lo que está haciendo la persona mal?

☐ ¿Tiene un párrafo en el que le ofrece consejos usando el subjuntivo?

☐ Subraya todos los adjetivos en el ensayo. ¿Tienen concordancia los adjetivos y los sustantivos que describen?

☐ Hazle una recomendación a tu compañero/a: *Recomiendo / Es necesario que...*

☐ Dile a tu compañero/a qué hay que hacer para recibir una A en la composición: *Para recibir una A, hay que...*

Después de revisar la composición de tu compañero/a, devuélvesela. Revisa tu propia composición para ver los cambios que tu compañero/a recomienda y haz las revisiones necesarias.

¡Hablemos!

Somos entrenadores

Antes de hablar

Haz una lista de seis o más pasos básicos que hay que seguir para practicar un aspecto de tu deporte favorito o actividad física favorita.

MODELO: dar un paseo → ponerse los calcetines y los tenis, levantarse, levantar el pie derecho, dar un paso, levantar el pie izquierdo, dar un paso, repetir más rápidamente…

 ### A hablar

En grupos de tres o cuatro estudiantes, túrnense en el papel de entrenador/a para enseñarles a los otros estudiantes cómo hacer el deporte o la actividad que explicaron en su lista. Los otros miembros del grupo deben intentar seguir las instrucciones del entrenador o la entrenadora. Presten atención y anoten si a los líderes se les olvida algún paso importante. **¡Atención!** Usen mandatos de **Uds.** para dar instrucciones a más de una persona.

MODELO: dar un paseo → Pónganse los calcetines y los tenis. Ahora levántense. Levanten el pie derecho y den un paso. Levanten el pie izquierdo y den otro paso. Repitan más rápidamente…

Expresiones útiles	
coger	to catch
doblar	to bend
lanzar	to throw
mover	to move
patear	to kick
pegar	to hit
rebotar	to bounce
saltar	to jump
usar rodilleras y coderas	to wear knee pads and elbow pads

 ### Después de hablar

En parejas, comenten las siguientes preguntas.

1. ¿Hay alguna instrucción importante que los otros entrenadores / las otras entrenadoras en tu grupo hayan olvidado (*have forgotten*) incluir? Añadan por lo menos una instrucción más a cada una de sus presentaciones.

2. ¿Cuáles son las instrucciones más comunes que dieron los entrenadores / las entrenadoras?

Conéctate al cine

Película: *Hermano* (drama, Venezuela, 2010)
Director: Marcel Rasquín

Sinopsis:

Julio, un niño, y su madre encuentran a un bebé abandonado en la calle, llorando como un gato. La madre lo adopta y Julio y Daniel crecen como hermanos. Julio le da a Daniel el apodo (*nickname*) «gato». A los dos hermanos les encanta jugar fútbol y son muy competitivos entre sí. Llega la oportunidad de ir a las pruebas (*tryouts*) de un equipo profesional, el Caracas Fútbol Club. Sin embargo, sucede una tragedia que les complica la vida.

Escena (Netflix, 00:03:40 to 00:08:52):

Julio y Daniel/Gato están jugando en un partido importante. Después del partido, un cazatalentos (*talent scout*) del Caracas Fútbol Club quiere hablar con ellos.

Antes de ver

Julio y Daniel son hermanos que juegan en el mismo equipo. ¿Puedes imaginar cómo sería (*would be like*) la interacción entre dos hermanos en un campo de fútbol? Indica qué se dirían (*they would say to each other*). Luego explica tu respuesta.

_____ ¡Ánimo!   _____ ¡Lo hiciste mal!

_____ ¡Bien hecho!   _____ ¡No hagas eso!

_____ ¡Corre más rápido!

A ver

PASO 1. Lee las **Expresiones útiles** y ve el video. No trates de entender cada palabra, pero escucha con atención.

PASO 2. Indica si cada declaración es cierta (**C**) o falsa (**F**).

Expresiones útiles

la (tarjeta) roja	red card
quieto	quiet, calm
canchita	small, neighborhood field
el pase	pass
¡Qué golazo!	What a great goal!
licorería	liquor store
¡Qué juegazo!	What a great game!
la generación de relevo	incoming team/players
unos mesecitos	just a few short months
el más chamo (*Ven.*)	the youngest
humillar	humiliate

	C	F
1. Julio le sugiere al portero que se quede quieto.	☐	☐
2. El entrenador les dice a los jugadores que metan (*score*) dos goles más.	☐	☐
3. Daniel (Gato) le dice a Julio que suba y espere el pase.	☐	☐
4. La mamá desea que el equipo vaya a las finales.	☐	☐
5. Daniel le pide a su amiga que deje a su novio por él.	☐	☐
6. El entrenador aconseja a los hermanos que no hablen con el cazatalentos.	☐	☐
7. El cazatalentos recomienda a los hermanos que vayan a las pruebas.	☐	☐
8. Daniel no quiere que Julio juegue en Caracas Fútbol Club con él.	☐	☐

Después de ver

En parejas, túrnense para hacerse las siguientes preguntas y contestarlas.

¿Has practicado algún deporte? ¿Lo sigues haciendo? ¿Eres/Eras competitivo/a o juegas/jugabas para divertirte? ¿Tienes/Tenías sueños de ser deportista profesional? ¿Qué es lo más importante que has aprendido de practicar ese deporte?

■ For copyright reasons, the feature-film clips referenced in **Conéctate al cine** have not been provided by the publisher. Each of these films is readily available through retailers or online rental sites such as Amazon, iTunes, or Netflix.

VOCABULARIO

Comunicación

¡Adelante!	Come on! / Let's go! / Cheer up!
¡Ánimo!	Come on! / Let's go! / Cheer up!
(No) Hay que + *inf.*	You (don't) have to / It's (not) necessary to (*do something*)
Que le(s) vaya bien.	May things go well for you (*sing./pl.*)
Que tenga(s) un(a) buen(a)...	Have a good . . .
¡Que tengas un buen día!	Have a good day!
Sí, se puede.	Yes, we can! (It can be done!)
¡Suerte!	Good luck!
¡(Buena/Mucha) suerte!	Good luck!
Le(s) deseo mucha suerte.	I wish you (*sing./pl.*) luck.

Los deportes — Sports

el/la atleta	athlete
el béisbol	baseball
la carrera	race
el casco	helmet
la competencia	competition
el/la entrenador(a)	coach, trainer
el equipo	team
el estadio	the stadium
el fútbol americano	(American) football
los Juegos Olímpicos	Olympic Games
el/la jugador(a)	player
la natación	swimming
el partido	game, match
los patines	skates
la patineta	skateboard
la pelota	ball
las pesas	weights
las piscina	pool
la raqueta	raquet
el tenis	tennis
el voleibol	volleyball

La salud — Health

el dolor	pain
la enfermedad	illness
el estornudo	sneeze
la fiebre	fever
la gripe	flu
la herida	wound; injury
la hinchazón	swelling
el moretón	bruise
el peso	weight
el resfriado	cold
el síntoma	symptom
la torcedura	sprain
la tos	cough
bajar/subir de peso	to lose/gain weight
desmayarse	to faint
doler (ue)	to hurt, to ache
estornudar	to sneeze
lastimarse	to injure oneself
sufrir de	to suffer (from)
tener alergia a	to be allergic to
torcerse (ue) (el tobillo)	to sprain (one's ankle)
constipado/a	congested

Cognados: las alergias, el asma (*f.*), la depresión, la fractura, la infección, el insomnio, las náuseas; vomitar

Los verbos

andar...	
en bicicleta	to ride a bike
en patineta	to skateboard
boxear	to box
esperar	to hope; to wait (for)
esquiar	to ski
ganar	to win
hacer alpinismo	to do/go mountaineering (mountain climbing)
jugar...	to play . . .
béisbol	baseball
fútbol americano	football
tenis	tennis
voleibol	volleyball
levantar pesas	to lift weights
mantenerse/ponerse en forma	to stay/get in shape
mantenerse sano	to stay healthy
patinar sobre hielo	to ice skate
recomendar (ie)	to recommend
surfear	to surf

La naturaleza y el medio ambiente

Un tour de la Reserva Nacional Tambopata en la selva amazónica del Perú

13

Objetivos

In this chapter you will learn how to:

- say what you think should happen
- say how long something has been going on
- talk about nature and the environment
- express what someone wants to happen
- express what someone thinks may not be true
- discuss nature and the environment in the Spanish-speaking world

connect SPANISH

http://www.connectspanish.com

COMUNICACIÓN ~~LARIO~~ ~~UCTURA~~ ~~ATE~~

Debería...

Talking about what you think someone should do

A. A ver: ¿Qué deberíamos hacer para mejorar el mundo?

PASO 1. Empareja cada frase con la palabra que describe.

1. _a_ Todos deberíamos cuidar (*take care of*) el planeta.   a. el ecologismo
2. _c_ Todos deberían ayudarse y entenderse.   b. el ecoturismo
3. _b_ Deberían visitar la naturaleza bonita.   c. el humanitarismo

PASO 2. Mira y escucha. Luego, indica si cada persona habla del **ecologismo,** del **ecoturismo** o del **humanitarismo.**

		ECOLOGISMO	ECOTURISMO	HUMANITARISMO
1.	Nelly habla del…	☐	☐	☐
2.	Yenaro habla del…	☐	☐	☐
3.	Juan Andrés habla del…	☐	☐	☐
4.	María Emilia habla del…	☐	☐	☐
5.	Enrique habla del…	☐	☐	☐
6.	Mayra habla del…	☐	☐	☐

PASO 3. Mira y escucha otra vez y luego indica qué sugiere cada uno.

1. _____ Nelly dice que todos deberíamos…
2. _____ Yenaro dice que todos deberíamos…
3. _____ Juan Andrés dice que todos deberíamos…
4. _____ Maria Emilia dice que todos deberíamos…
5. _____ Enrique dice que todos deberíamos…
6. _____ Mayra dice que todos deberíamos…

a. ayudarnos los unos a los otros.
b. cuidar el agua y poner la basura en el lugar apropiado.
c. cuidar el planeta.
d. hacer el turismo sin dañar el medio ambiente (*environment*).
e. servirle a la humanidad y servirles a las personas.
f. tratar de no contaminar más el medio ambiente.

To talk about what you think you or someone else should or should not do, use a form of **(no) debería** + *infinitive.*

Debería ir en bicicleta en vez de coche.	I should ride my bike instead of driving.
Deberíamos reciclar.	We ought to recycle.
No deberías contaminar.	You shouldn't pollute.
Deberían cuidar el planeta.	They should take care of the planet.

B. ¿Qué deberíamos hacer?   Empareja la imagen con la cita (*quote*) más adecuada.

1. _____ «Deberíamos ahorrar (*save*) agua.»
2. _____ «Deberíamos evitar (*avoid*) el uso excesivo de electricidad.»
3. _____ «Deberíamos hacer abono (*fertilizer*) con los desechos (*waste*) orgánicos.»
4. _____ «Deberíamos proteger (*protect*) el mar (*sea*).»
5. _____ «Deberíamos reciclar.»
6. _____ «Deberíamos usar menos los coches.»

a.   c.   e.

b.   d.   f.

 C. ¿Qué deberían hacer los nuevos estudiantes?   En parejas, decidan qué deberían hacer los nuevos estudiantes que quieren participar en diversas actividades. Luego, compartan sus respuestas con la clase.

¿Qué debería hacer un nuevo estudiante o una nueva estudiante que quiere…

1. comprar productos de bajo impacto medio ambiental (*environmental*)?
2. ahorrar agua?
3. hacer abono con los desechos orgánicos de la cafetería y los restaurantes de la universidad?
4. reciclar el papel y los plásticos del campus?

¿Cuánto tiempo hace que... ?

Expressing how long you've been doing something

To ask someone how long they have been doing something, use one of these expressions. Recall that you learned the present participle (the **-ndo** forms) with the present progressive in **Estructura 11.3.**

¿Cuánto tiempo lleva(s) + *present participle*?
¿Cuánto tiempo hace que + *present tense*?

¿Cuánto tiempo llevas reciclando?
¿Cuánto tiempo hace que reciclas? } How long have you been recycling?

To respond, you can use one of these expressions.

Llevo + *time expression* + *present participle*.
Hace + *time expression* + *present tense*.

Llevo tres años reciclando.
Hace tres años que reciclo. } I've been recycling for three years.

To express that something *hasn't* happened for a certain period of time, you can use one of these.

Llevo + *time expression* + **sin** + *infinitive*.
Hace + *time expression* + **que no** + *present tense*.

Llevo tres años sin usar bolsas de plástico.
Hace tres años que no uso bolsas de plástico. } I haven't used plastic bags for three years. / It's been three years since I've used plastic bags.

Here are some useful time expressions.

toda la vida	all my (your/his/her) life; all our (your/their/our) lives
mucho tiempo	a long time
number + **días/semanas/meses/años**	*number* + days/weeks/months/years

A. La historia de la ecología

Lee las siguientes oraciones con fechas importantes en la historia de la ecología. Luego, completa las oraciones para decir cuántos años hace (*how many years it's been*) que pasan estas cosas. **¡Atención!** ¡Vas a tener que hacer un poco de matemática!

1. En 1962, la Fundación Charles Darwin estableció una estación de investigación (*research*) en las islas Galápagos.
   Hace _____ **años que** los científicos (*scientists*) de la Fundación Charles Darwin estudian los animales de las islas Galápagos.

2. En 1977, el presidente Jimmy Carter instaló los primeros paneles solares en la Casa Blanca de los Estados Unidos.
   Hace _____ **años que** se usan paneles solares en la Casa Blanca.

3. En 1996, se fundó la organización Amazon Watch para proteger los bosques tropicales (*rainforests*) de Colombia, Ecuador, el Perú y Brasil.
   La organización Amazon Watch **lleva** _____ **años trabajando** para proteger los bosques tropicales.

4. En 2005, la Universidad de Puerto Rico en Humacao empezó su programa de reciclaje (*recycling*).
   Los estudiantes de la Universidad de Puerto Rico en Humacao **llevan** _____ **años reciclando.**

5. En 2011, la energía eólica (*wind*) se convirtió en la principal industria enérgica en España.
   Hace _____ **años que** la energía eólica es la fuente (*source*) de energía más usada en España.

B. Actividades a favor del medio ambiente

PASO 1.   Indica todas las actividades ambientales en que participas.

☐ comer comidas orgánicas
☐ comprar productos de bajo impacto ambiental
☐ conducir un auto eléctrico o híbrido
☐ ahorrar agua
☐ evitar el uso excesivo de electricidad
☐ hacer abono de los desechos orgánicos de la cocina

☐ llevar bolsas reusables al supermercado
☐ reciclar (el papel, las botellas, el cartón [*cardboard*], las latas [*cans*], etcétera)
☐ trabajar con organizaciones ecologistas
☐ transportarse en bicicleta en lugar de en coche

PASO 2.   Para cada actividad del **Paso 1** en que participas, di cuánto tiempo llevas haciéndola.

1. ¿Cuánto tiempo hace que comes comidas orgánicas? *un año*
2. ¿Cuánto tiempo llevas comprando productos de bajo impacto ambiental? *3 años*
3. ¿Cuánto tiempo hace que intentas ahorrar agua? *8 años*
4. ¿Cuánto tiempo llevas ahorrando (*saving*) electricidad? *todos los años*
5. ¿Cuánto tiempo llevas guardando los desechos orgánicos en el jardín? *mu*
6. ¿Cuánto tiempo hace que vas y vienes en bicicleta? *un año*
7. ¿Cuánto tiempo hace que reciclas? *muchos años*
8. ¿Cuánto tiempo llevas trabajando con una organización ecologista? *much*

PASO 3.   En parejas, túrnense para hacer y contestar preguntas sobre su participación en las actividades del **Paso 1**. Si no participas en una actividad, debes decirlo.

MODELO: E1: ¿Cuánto tiempo hace que comes comidas orgánicas? / ¿Cuánto tiempo llevas comiendo comidas orgánicas?
E2: Hace cinco años que como comidas orgánicas. / Llevo cinco años comiendo comidas orgánicas. (Nunca como comidas orgánicas.)

C. Todos somos ecologistas   Contesta las preguntas para decir cuántos años estas personas llevan haciendo cosas que benefician al medio ambiente.

MODELO: ¿La ciudad tiene un programa de reciclaje? (1990)
Hace _____ años que la ciudad tiene un programa de reciclaje.

1. ¿Cuántos años lleva Teresa usando transporte público en vez de conducir? (2013)
    _____ *lleva odro años que cudsarde*

2. ¿Cuánto tiempo hace que tu tío conduce un auto híbrido? (2003)
    _____ *hace dieyodro años que conduce.*

3. ¿Cuánto tiempo llevan participando en el club de ecologistas? (2009)
    Sí, _____ *lleva doce años que participado*

4. ¿Hace mucho tiempo que tu familia usa abono natural en su jardín? (1998: tener un compostador para desechos orgánicos)
    Sí, _____ *Hace vintres años que usangas*

5. ¿Las tiendas de tu barrio todavía ofrecen bolsas de plástico a sus clientes? (2012: no ofrecer)
    No, _____ .

CONÉCTATE AL MUNDO HISPANO

El lago Enriquillo en la República Dominicana siempre ha sido el lago más grande del Caribe. Pero últimamente le pasa algo muy raro: se está haciendo más grande todavía. En 2004, el lago cubría (*covered*) 164 kilómetros cuadrados (102 millas cuadradas), pero diez años después, se había duplicado el tamaño: hasta 350 kilómetros cuadrados (217 millas cuadradas). El lago tenía tres islas, pero dos de ellas ya desaparecieron bajo el agua. Nadie sabe cuál es la causa, pero parece que el cambio climático es uno de los factores. El agua del mar Caribe se ha calentado (*gotten warmer*), y eso ha provocado un aumento (*increase*) en la cantidad de lluvia. Muchos campos (*fields*) agrícolas se han inundado (*flooded*) y un pueblo entero está en peligro (*danger*). El gobierno dominicano está construyendo un pueblo nuevo para que la gente afectada tenga dónde vivir.

La naturaleza y el medio ambiente
Nature and the environment

A. Nuestro medio ambiente Lee las siguientes descripciones y emparéjalas con la imagen que mejor corresponde a cada una.

1. Hay varias causas de la **deforestación.**

_b_ El descuido (*carelessness*) de una persona con un cigarrillo puede resultar en la quema (*burning*) de **bosques** enteros, matando (*killing*) muchos **árboles** y animales en muy poco tiempo.

_a_ La agricultura y la ganadería (*ranching*) requieren mucha **tierra** y resultan en la masiva **tala de árboles.** Esto pone a los bosques, como la **selva** amazónica, en **peligro** (*danger*).

_c_ Con la muerte de tantos árboles, la cadena alimenticia (*food chain*) sufre porque muchos animales dependen de los árboles para comer.

_d_ El **daño** (*damage*) a los árboles puede causar gran efecto sobre todo tipo de **fauna y flora** que puede llegar hasta la **extinción** de las **especies.**

2. El **planeta Tierra** está en peligro.

_c_ La **contaminación** del aire lleva al **calentamiento global;** o sea, la temperatura del planeta sube.

_c_ Las temperaturas del agua del **mar** van calentando también, causando el derretimiento (*melting*) de los casquetes polares (*polar ice caps*) y los icebergs y la subida (*rise*) del nivel (*level*) del mar.

_b_ El cambio climático puede causar otros problemas graves, como la **sequía** (cuando no llueve por mucho tiempo).

_a_ También puede causar los **huracanes*** que muchas veces causan **inundaciones*** (un exceso de agua que pone calles, coches y casas bajo el agua).

3. Hay que **cuidar** la Tierra.

_b_ Varios grupos de **activistas** luchan para **proteger** el medio ambiente.

_d_ Algunos activistas quieren **conservar** las plantas y animales que viven en el mar, que sufren a causa de los productos químicos y la basura que ponemos en el agua.

_a_ La **ecología** del mar es compleja: un mundo entero existe dentro de un **arrecife** (*reef*): corales, plantas y peces.

_d_ Si mueren muchos de estos animales **marinos,** la cadena alimenticia puede deteriorar rápidamente hasta afectarnos a todos los seres humanos.

---

*La forma singular de **huracanes** es **huracán** y la forma singular de **inundaciones** es **inundación.**

4. A mucha gente le gusta visitar los parques nacionales y reservas naturales.

_____ Allí pueden ver vistas panorámicas de las montañas, el mar o el desierto.

_____ Sin embargo, la **disminución** de importantes **recursos naturales** como el agua, la madera y el petróleo pone en peligro estos **paisajes** bonitos y el planeta entero.

_____ Si los grandes países y sus industrias **explotan** los recursos naturales, vamos a ver el **agotamiento** de los bosques y el agua dulce, y sin árboles y agua no podemos vivir.

_____ Dependemos de la naturaleza, la tierra y el agua del planeta. Por eso, deberíamos buscar soluciones **sostenibles** para mantener el planeta verde y saludable.

a.

b.

c.

d.

Vocabulario

Algunas especies en peligro de extinción incluyen animales terrestres (*land*) como, por ejemplo,...

el loro

el mono

el oso

el perezoso

el sapo

la tortuga

y animales **marinos** como, por ejemplo,...

la ballena

el delfín

el león marino

el pingüino

B. A ver: Los temas más importantes

PASO 1. Algunas personas van a presentar sus ideas sobre los problemas medioambientales más graves. Mira el video y luego completa cada frase con la mejor expresión.

1. _____ Para Óscar, de Costa Rica, la causa medioambiental más importante es…

   a. la conservación de los arrecifes.
   b. la conservación del ecosistema.
   c. la protección del mar y la playa.

2. _____ Para Cinthya, de Costa Rica, es importante…

   a. la conservación de los bosques.
   b. la protección de las especies en peligro de extinción.
   c. el reciclaje.

3. _____ Para Yenaro, de Costa Rica, es importante…

   a. la conservación de los bosques.
   b. la protección de las especies en peligro de extinción.
   c. el reciclaje.

4. _____ Para Andrea, de México, la causa medioambiental más importante es…

   a. el calentamiento global.
   b. la explotación de los recursos naturales.
   c. la protección del medio ambiente.

5. _____ Luis, de Panamá, está preocupado por…

   a. el calentamiento global.
   b. la enseñanza sobre el medio ambiente.
   c. la explotación de un recurso natural en particular: la naturaleza.

6. _____ Para Magdalena, de Argentina, es importante…

   a. la conservación de los arrecifes.
   b. la conservación de la naturaleza y el paisaje.
   c. la protección del mar y la playa.

7. _____ Para Victorino, de Costa Rica, es importante…

   a. la conservación de los bosques.
   b. la protección del medio ambiente.
   c. el reciclaje.

8. _____ Para Henry, de Costa Rica, es importante…

   a. el calentamiento global.
   b. la enseñanza sobre el medio ambiente.
   c. la explotación de los recursos naturales.

PASO 2. Según sus intereses, ¿qué debería hacer cada persona del video?

1. _____ Óscar debería…
2. _____ Cinthya debería…
3. _____ Yenaro debería…
4. _____ Andrea debería…
5. _____ Luis debería…
6. _____ Magdalena debería…
7. _____ Victorino debería…
8. _____ Henry debería…

a. empezar un programa sobre la diversidad de los bosques y la protección del medio ambiente.
b. fundar una compañía que proteja el mundo ecológico.
c. participar en el turismo ecológico de alguna manera.
d. participar en un programa que promueva el reciclaje para contaminar menos con basura.
e. promover (*promote*) el uso de menos plástico.
f. sembrar (*plant*) árboles.
g. trabajar en un lugar que proteja las especies en peligro de extinción.
h. trabajar para el sistema de parques nacionales.

PASO 3. Explícale a un compañero o una compañera con quién del video tienes más en común y por qué. Usa la información del **Paso 1** para formar tus respuestas.

MODELO: Tengo más en común con _____ porque los/las dos (ninguno de los/las dos)…

C. A cuidar y disfrutar del planeta

PASO 1. De las siguientes actividades, ¿cuáles te gustaría hacer?

Me gustaría…

☐ cuidar las playas y el mar
☐ disfrutar de la naturaleza
☐ participar en el turismo ecológico
☐ pasar tiempo al aire libre

☐ proteger la flora y fauna
☐ trabajar en una compañía que proteja el medio ambiente
☐ trabajar de voluntario/a para cuidar el planeta
☐ ver el paisaje de un parque nacional

PASO 2. En grupos, dense consejos sobre qué deberían hacer para impulsar sus metas medioambientales personales. Usen la estructura **debería** + *infinitivo.*

MODELO: Si a ti te gustaría trabajar de voluntaria para cuidar el planeta, entonces *deberías ponerte* en contacto con un grupo medioambiental como Greenpeace. También *deberías trabajar* con una organización local para limpiar parques en tu comunidad.

D. El medio ambiente en las noticias

PASO 1. Lee los siguientes titulares (*headlines*) de varios periódicos y revistas. En grupos, hagan una lista de por lo menos diez palabras del **Vocabulario** que esperarían (*you would expect*) leer en cada artículo. Luego, comparen sus listas con otro grupo.

1. **Huracanes amenazan° la costa**   *threaten*

2. **La tala masiva de árboles sigue en las selvas**

3. **Grupo estudiantil recauda fondos° para la protección de las especies**   *raises funds*

4. **Nueva ley protege la fauna y flora del país**

5. **El turismo: ¿ayuda o daña al medio ambiente?**

6. **¿Estamos reciclando? Nuevo estudio pone en duda la mayoría de los programas de reciclaje**

7. La explotación de recursos naturales a nivel mundial sigue en aumento

8. Nuevo estudio científico dice que están muriendo los arrecifes a un ritmo alarmante

PASO 2. En parejas, escojan uno de los titulares del **Paso 1** y escriban el primer párrafo del artículo. Intenten usar todas las palabras de la lista que su grupo formó para ese titular. Cuando leen el artículo a los otros estudiantes, ¿pueden identificar el titular del **Paso 1**?

PASO 3. En parejas, piensen en un tema medioambiental que les importe mucho y escriban un titular para un artículo sobre el tema. Luego, consideren las siguientes preguntas y escriban el primer párrafo del artículo.

¿Por qué se considera «noticia» este tema? ¿Por qué es un problema esta situación? ¿Cuáles son los datos (*pieces of information*) más importantes que deben incluir? ¿Cuáles son los factores que contribuyen al problema?

COMUN VOCABU **ESTRUCTURA** TE

Reciclaje

Present indicative: Verbs with irregular **yo** forms

Usa la forma **yo** del presente indicativo del verbo más lógico para completar cada oración. Luego, indica si es algo que diría (*would say*) un **jaguar**, un **pájaro** o una **tortuga** si pudiera hablar (*if it could talk*). Cada verbo se puede usar solo una vez. El primer verbo ya está hecho.

decir	ir	ser
estar	poner	tener
hacer	salir	traer

	JAGUAR	PÁJARO	TORTUGA
1. «A veces <u>voy</u> a los lagos y a los ríos a cazar (*hunt*) animales que están tomando agua.»	☐	☐	☐
2. «_____ nidos (*nests*) en los árboles.»	☐	☐	☐
3. «_____ una concha (*shell*) muy dura.»	☐	☐	☐
4. «_____ reptil.»	☐	☐	☐
5. «_____ de noche a cazar animales grandes y chicos.»	☐	☐	☐
6. «_____ comida al nido para los bebés.»	☐	☐	☐
7. «En la selva, _____ en el punto más alto de la cadena alimenticia.»	☐	☐	☐
8. «_____ pío, pío, pío.»	☐	☐	☐
9. «_____ los huevos en la arena (*sand*).»	☐	☐	☐

■ Answers to this activity are in Appendix 2 at the back of your book.

Las ruinas del Parque Nacional Tikal, Guatemala

13.1 Le pedimos que no salga de los senderos° *paths*

The subjunctive: Irregular verbs

Para empezar...

El Parque Nacional Tikal es la reserva natural y cultural más famosa de Guatemala y la zona arqueológica más importante de la antigua civilización maya. Aquí hay una lista de reglas (*rules*) para los visitantes del parque, pero ¡no todas son de verdad! Indica si cada regla es **cierta** o **falsa.**

Durante su estancia (stay) *en el Parque Nacional Tikal, le pedimos que...*

	CIERTO	FALSO
1. no **haga** ningún tipo de fuego.	☐	☐
2. no **salga** de los senderos.	☐	☐
3. **sea** respetuoso con las reglas del parque.	☐	☐
4. **se vaya** inmediatamente y nunca **vuelva**.	☐	☐
5. **tenga** mucho cuidado al momento de escalar (*climb*) los monumentos.	☐	☐
6. **ponga** comida para los animales en los senderos.	☐	☐
7. no **haga** fotos o videos con propósitos (*purposes*) comerciales sin la autorización adecuada.	☐	☐
8. **traiga** basura de su casa y que la **deje** en el parque.	☐	☐
9. **ponga** atención a la hora. Se apaga (*turn off*) la energía eléctrica a las 21:30. Por eso, pedimos que **esté** en su hotel antes de esa hora.	☐	☐

Actividades analíticas

1 The verbs in bold in **Para empezar** are in the present subjunctive form. Use this information, as well as what you know about how the present subjunctive is formed, to conjugate these verbs:

	hacer	poner	salir	tener	traer
yo	haga			tenga	
tú		pongas			traigas
él/ella, Ud.					
nosotros/as	hagamos		salgamos		
vosotros/as		pongáis		tengáis	
ellos/ellas, Uds.			salgan		traigan

2 For all of these verbs, the stem in the subjunctive contains a **-g-** that is not present in the infinitive: **hag-, pong-, salg-, teng-** and **traig-**. This stem is the same as that used in the **yo** form of the present indicative: **hago, pongo, salgo, tengo** and **traigo**. The verb **decir** (**digo** in the **yo** form of the present indicative) also forms its subjunctive in this way.

Quiero que me **digas** la verdad.   *I want you to tell me the truth.*

Es necesario que **digan** si van a pasar la   *It's necessary for you (plur.) to say if you are*
   noche en el parque.   *going to spend the night in the park.*

3 Two other common irregular verbs in the subjunctive are **ir** and **ser**. Use the forms that you saw in **Para empezar** to complete these conjugations.

	ir	ser
yo	vaya	
tú		seas
él/ella, Ud.		
nosotros/as	vayamos	
vosotros/as		seáis
ellos/ellas, Uds.		

Actividades prácticas

A. Voluntarios en las islas Galápagos

Cientos de voluntarios van a las islas Galápagos cada año para ayudar en el trabajo de conservación e investigación (*research*). Pon en orden los elementos de la siguiente conversación entre María, una coordinadora de voluntarios en la conservación, y Alicia, una voluntaria que acaba de llegar (*has just arrived*).

a. __1__ MARÍA: ¡Qué bueno que estás aquí en las islas Galápagos! ¿Estás contenta?

b. ____ MARÍA: ¡Ah, sí! Les voy a pedir también que hagan un conteo (*count*) de las iguanas marinas que se encuentran en la isla Genovesa. Parece que ahora hay menos y estamos un poco preocupados.

c. ____ ALICIA: Está bien. Vamos a la isla Genovesa, entonces. Ayer mencionaste algo de las iguanas en esa isla, ¿no?

d. ____ ALICIA: Bueno, vamos a hacer el conteo. El viernes viene otro grupo de voluntarios de Quito. ¿Quieres que traigan algo en especial?

e. ____ MARÍA: Quiero que salgan a inspeccionar los senderos en la isla Genovesa. Ha habido muchísimos turistas allí últimamente y hacen mucho daño.

f. ____ ALICIA: ¡Muy contenta! Mañana empezamos a trabajar todos los voluntarios de mi grupo. ¿Qué quieres que hagamos?

g. ____ MARÍA: Sí. ¿Pueden traer más folletos (*brochures*) para los turistas sobre los problemas medioambientales que tenemos aquí?

h. ____ ALICIA: ¡Claro! Les voy a decir que los traigan.

■ Answers to these activities are in Appendix 2 at the back of your book.

¿Por qué?

Why are there so many verbs that add a **-g-** both to the **yo** form of the present indicative (**pongo, salgo, tengo,** etc.) and to all of the subjunctive forms (**ponga, salga, tenga,** etc.)? These verb endings add either **-o** or **-a** to the stem, and these two vowels are both pronounced with the tongue in the back of the mouth. The consonant **-g-** is pronounced in this area too, and inserting it makes the transition between the stem (**pon-, sal-, ten-**) and the vowel easier. The vowels **-e** and **-i** are pronounced in the front of the mouth, so the **-g-** is not inserted when these vowels are added to the stem (e.g. **pone, salimos,** etc.).

■ For more verbs in the subjunctive, see **Para saber más 13.1** at the back of your book.

Una iguana en las islas Galápagos

El Salto Ángel en el Parque
Nacional de Canaima

El Parque Nacional Rapa Nui en
la isla de Pascua

B. Los parques nacionales

PASO 1. Primero, indica con un círculo el verbo apropiado para completar cada oración.

1. _____ Muchos dicen que este parque (es / sea) uno de los lugares más impresionantes del mundo. Las cataratas (*waterfalls*) son enormes y se encuentran cerca de la triple frontera (*border*) entre Paraguay, Brasil y Argentina.

2. _____ Para ir a este lugar, al norte de Brasil, te recomiendan que (vas / vayas) en un coche que está en muy buena condición, que (traes / traigas) una cámara y que (sacas / saques) fotos del famoso Salto Ángel.

3. _____ En este lugar, es necesario que (se ponen / se pongan) ropa caliente en algunos meses, por el intenso frío que hace. Hay cientos de glaciares en este parque en los Andes, a ocho horas al norte de Lima.

4. _____ (Dicen / Digan) que los jaguares en este lugar, en la costa caribeña de este país centro-americano, solo (salen / salgan) de noche.

5. _____ Si (tienes / tengas) ganas de ver muchos loros y colibríes (*hummingbirds*), puedes ir a este parque, en el extremo este de la isla.

6. _____ Si te gustan las cataratas, los jaguares y las orquídeas, te recomiendo que (vas / vayas) aquí. Por su ubicación entre los Andes y la zona amazónica, tiene una gran diversidad de hábitats, desde selvas hasta sabanas (*savannahs*).

7. _____ Si quieres que tus próximas vacaciones (son / sean) muy interesantes, considera un viaje a este parque en la Isla de Pascua, donde puedes encontrar cráteres volcánicos y estatuas creadas por los antiguos habitantes (*inhabitants*).

PASO 2. Ahora, escoge el parque nacional que corresponde a cada descripción en el **Paso 1**. Las pistas (*clues*) geográficas y los mapas al fin del libro te pueden ayudar.

Parques Nacionales

a. Parque Nacional Rapa Nui (Chile)
b. Parque Nacional de Canaima (Venezuela)
c. Parque Nacional Huascarán (el Perú)
d. Parque Nacional de Iguazú (Argentina)
e. Parque Nacional Noel Kempff Mercado (Bolivia)

f. Reserva de la Biosfera de Río Plátano (Honduras)
g. Parque Nacional Alejandro de Humboldt (Cuba)

C. El medio ambiente

Empareja cada oración con la terminación apropiada. **¡Atención!** Hay que prestar atención al verbo en cada terminación. ¿Está en el indicativo o el subjuntivo?

1. _____ Me gusta andar en bicicleta. Voy a estar muy contento si…
2. _____ Me gusta andar en bicicleta. Quiero que…
3. _____ Si vives en la ciudad, yo te recomiendo que…
4. _____ Si vives en la ciudad, probablemente no…
5. _____ Es importante que todos nosotros…
6. _____ No todos nosotros…
7. _____ A tus papás les gustan las montañas y por eso…
8. _____ Si a tus papás les gustan las montañas, yo les recomiendo que…

a. salgas a la naturaleza de vez en cuando.
b. vayan al Parque Torres del Paine en el sur de Chile.
c. ponen un sistema de carriles (*lanes*) para bicicletas en mi ciudad.
d. somos conscientes (*conscious*) del impacto que tenemos en el medio ambiente.
e. pongan un sistema de carriles para bicicletas en mi ciudad.
f. deberían ir al Parque Torres del Paine en el sur de Chile.
g. sales a la naturaleza mucho.
h. seamos conscientes del impacto que tenemos en el medio ambiente.

D. Tus prioridades para tu comunidad

PASO 1. ¿Qué quieres que haga la gente de tu comunidad para mejorar el medio ambiente? Escoge las tres ideas más importantes para ti y crea tres oraciones que expresen lo que tú quieres.

> **MODELO:** hacer más esfuerzo (*effort*) para usar el transporte público →
> Quiero que la gente haga más esfuerzo para usar el transporte público.

1. decirles a los niños que es importante cuidar el medio ambiente
2. ir al trabajo o a la escuela a pie cuando es posible
3. poner más atención al reciclaje
4. salir más a la naturaleza

5. ser más conscientes del impacto que tienen sobre el medio ambiente
6. tener más conocimiento sobre el turismo sostenible
7. traer botellas de agua de metal, y no de plástico

PASO 2. Ahora, en parejas, comparen sus prioridades. ¿Pueden llegar a un acuerdo sobre cuál es la máxima (*top*) prioridad para mejorar el medio ambiente?

C Reciclaje

Meanings of **creer, esperar, pensar,** and **saber**

Empareja cada expresión con su sinónimo.

1. ____ Creo que sí.
2. ____ No sé.
3. ____ Espero que no.
4. ____ Sé que sí.
5. ____ Espero que sí.
6. ____ Pienso que no.

a. No tengo idea.
b. Estoy muy seguro que sí.
c. No sé si es así, pero quiero que sea así.
d. Pienso que sí.
e. No creo.
f. No sé si es así, pero no quiero que sea así.

■ Answers to this activity are in Appendix 2 at the back of your book.

13.2   No creen que exista ya el sapo dorado°   *golden*

The subjunctive: Disbelief and uncertainty

Para empezar...

El sapo dorado vivió en el bosque de Monteverde en Costa Rica. Lo descubrieron por primera vez en 1966, pero no lo han visto desde 1989 y lo declararon extinto (*extinct*) en 2004. ¿Qué dicen los expertos de esto? Lee las siguientes oraciones: ocho son ciertas y dos son falsas. Indica cuáles son **ciertas** y cuáles son **falsas. ¡Atención!** Solo hay dos oraciones falsas.

Un **sapo dorado**

Los expertos...

	CIERTO	FALSO
1. creen que los machos (*males*) tenían un color dorado fluorescente.	☐	☐
2. creen que las hembras (*females*) eran de un color verde oliva con manchas (*spots*) rojas.	☐	☐
3. no creen que nadie **pueda** encontrar un sapo dorado hoy día.	☐	☐
4. piensan que vivían bajo tierra la mayor parte del año.	☐	☐
5. no piensan que las demás especies de sapos y ranas (*frogs*) **estén** fuera de peligro (*out of danger*).	☐	☐
6. esperan que no **pase** lo mismo a las otras especies de ranas y sapos.	☐	☐
7. dicen que es posible que el cambio climático **sea** un factor en la extinción de los sapos y ranas.	☐	☐
8. saben que hay sapos dorados en Wyoming.	☐	☐
9. esperan que **aprendamos** algo de esta triste historia.	☐	☐
10. esperan que otras especies **tengan** el mismo futuro que el sapo dorado.	☐	☐

■ Answers to these activities are in Appendix 2 at the back of your book.

CONÉCTATE AL MUNDO HISPANO

El lobo (*wolf*) **mexicano** es uno de los animales del hemisferio occidental (*western*) en más peligro de extinción. Su hábitat original se extendía del norte de México hasta Arizona, Nuevo México y Texas en los Estados Unidos. Sin embargo, el lobo fue casi totalmente exterminado en el siglo veinte. En las últimas décadas, los científicos han tratado de salvar al lobo mexicano y establecerlo de nuevo en las zonas donde vivía antes. Poco a poco, lo están logrando (*achieving*). Ahora hay lobos salvajes (*wild*) en Arizona y Nuevo México, y en 2014, anunciaron dos grandes eventos: nació la primera camada (*litter*) de lobos en libertad en México y nació la primera camada por inseminación artificial en el Zoológico de Chapultepec, en la Ciudad de México.

Actividades analíticas

1 As you saw in **Estructura 12.3** with expressions of volition, certain verbs and expressions require the verb that follows to be in the subjunctive form. Based on what you saw in **Para empezar,** indicate which of the following expressions require the subjunctive.

☐ creer que…   ☐ esperar que…   ☐ saber que…
☐ no creer que…   ☐ pensar que…
☐ es posible que…   ☐ no pensar que…

2 What do the expressions that you selected in **Actividades analíticas 1** all have in common?

☐ They all express the idea that what follows is (at least in the mind of the speaker) likely true.
☐ They all express the idea that what follows may not be true.

There are many more expressions that indicate uncertainty in Spanish, including **No es obvio** (*obvious*) **que…** and **Es improbable que…**

3 Similarly, expressions such as **Es imposible que…** , **No es cierto que…** , and **No es verdad que…** also require the subjunctive because what follows them is (at least in the mind of the speaker) not true.

No es cierto que puedas ver el sapo dorado en Costa Rica.

It is not true that you can see the golden toad in Costa Rica.

Antonio piensa que **no es verdad que seas** estudiante.

Antonio thinks that it's not true that you're a student.

The expressions **Es cierto que…** , **Es verdad que…** , and **Es obvio que…** are followed by an indicative form, since they express something thought to be true.

Es cierto que eres muy buen estudiante.

It is true that you are a very good student.

Actividades prácticas

A. ¿De acuerdo?

PASO 1. Escucha las oraciones e indica si estás de acuerdo (**DA**) o no (**NDA**) con lo que dice.

1. ____   2. ____   3. ____   4. ____
5. ____   6. ____   7. ____   8. ____

PASO 2. Ahora explica a la clase por qué no estás de acuerdo con ciertas declaraciones.

B. El oso hormiguero (*anteater*)

¿Cuánto sabes del oso hormiguero? Indica si cada oración debe comenzar con «**Es cierto que…** » o «**No es cierto que…** ». ¡**Atención**! Presta atención a la forma del verbo. ¿Es indicativo o subjuntivo?

ES CIERTO QUE…	NO ES CIERTO QUE…	
☑	☐	1. come hormigas (*ants*) y termitas.
☑	☐	2. tiene una lengua muy larga.
☐	☑	3. sea un tipo de oso.
☐	☑	4. viva en África.
☑	☐	5. es pariente de los perezosos.
☐	☑	6. use su cola (*tail*) para matar (*kill*) hormigas.
☐	☐	7. duerma bajo el agua.
☐	☐	8. varias especies del oso hormiguero están amenazadas (*threatened*) por la destrucción de su hábitat.
☐	☐	9. coma pájaros.
☑	☐	10. vive solo en América.

El oso hormiguero

- To learn how to use the subjunctive to describe things that don't exist, or to express how you feel about something, see **Para saber más 13.2** at the back of your book.

- The audio files for in-text listening activities are available in the eBook, within Connect Plus activities, and on the Online Learning Center.

Autoprueba

When you come across a new expression, consider if it implies that what follows is true or thought to be true (+), is uncertain or doubtful (?), or is not true or thought to be not true (–). This will help you know whether it is followed by the indicative (+) or the subjunctive (? and –). Try it here with these expressions. Does each one trigger the indicative or the subjunctive?

1. Estoy seguro/a de que…
2. No estoy seguro/a de que…
3. Es una mentira (*a lie*) que…
4. Creemos que…
5. No pensamos que…
6. Es imposible que…
7. No es probable que…

Respuestas: 1. indicative, **2.** subjunctive, **3.** subjunctive, **4.** indicative, **5.** subjunctive, **6.** subjunctive, **7.** subjunctive

C. Cuatro especies

PASO 1. Las siguientes cuatro especies son muy interesantes, pero no son muy conocidas fuera de su región. En parejas, crean oraciones usando **Creo que** y **No creo que** y las seis frases que siguen para comentar sobre los animales.

El cóndor andino
Distribución: Cordillera de los Andes
Estado de conservación: No amenazado

El quetzal
Distribución: México, Centroamérica
Estado de conservación: Amenazado

El lince (*lynx*) **ibérico**
Distribución: España
Estado de conservación: En peligro de extinción

El tapir
Distribución: Centroamérica, Sudamérica
Estado de conservación: Amenazado

MODELO: vuela / vuele →
E1: No creo que el tapir vuele.
E2: Yo tampoco, pero creo que el quetzal vuela.

1. pasa / pase mucho tiempo en el agua
2. come / coma carne
3. vive / viva en Europa
4. pone / ponga huevos
5. tiene / tenga pelo
6. vuela / vuele

PASO 2. Piensa en un animal del que sabes mucho. Dile a un compañero / una compañera dos oraciones ciertas y dos oraciones falsas sobre el animal. Tu compañero/a debe decir **Es cierto que…** o **No es cierto que…** para cada oración. Si no está seguro/a, puede decir **Es posible que…**

MODELO: E1: Los conejos (*rabbits*) comen carne.
E2: No es cierto que los conejos coman carne.
E1: Los conejos tienen el pelo muy suave.
E2: Es cierto que los conejos tienen el pelo muy suave.

D. Los pingüinos
Crea ocho oraciones sobre los pingüinos usando las siguientes expresiones y las oraciones que siguen. **¡Atención!** En algunos casos, tienes que cambiar el verbo al subjuntivo.

Sé que… **Creo que…** **Espero que…** **No creo que…**

MODELO: Los pingüinos son pájaros. → Sé que los pingüinos son pájaros.

1. Hay pingüinos azules y rojos.
2. Viven en Argentina, Chile, el Perú y las islas Galápagos.
3. Viven en Bolivia y en el Polo Norte.
4. Van a México durante el verano.
5. Trabajan en restaurantes como camareros.
6. Tienen una vida muy feliz.
7. Comen mucho pescado.
8. Tienen un futuro seguro.

Creo que los pingüinos son lindos.

Ecuador   **Bolivia**

El lago Titicaca, Bolivia

E. Cultura: Las luchas (*struggles*) ecológicas en Ecuador y Bolivia

PASO 1.   Lee el texto sobre Ecuador y Bolivia.

Los países de Ecuador y Bolivia tienen mucho en común. Los dos tienen sitios naturales espectaculares y diversos, como las islas Galápagos y los altiplanos[a] en Ecuador, y en Bolivia el lago Titicaca, la Laguna Verde y el salar[b] de Uyuni. En los dos países hay selvas amazónicas. Los dos países también cuentan con[c] grandes poblaciones indígenas que hablan una variedad de lenguas. Pero lamentablemente, desde la época de la Conquista española hasta hoy en día, los habitantes de los dos países han tenido que luchar en contra del imperialismo. El imperialismo del último siglo no solo es una conquista de la cultura autóctona,[d] sino[e] también del medio ambiente y los recursos naturales.

Desde 1971 hasta 1992, la gran empresa petrolera[f] transnacional Texaco se juntó[g] con el gobierno de Ecuador para extraer petróleo de la región amazónica y construir el Oleoducto[h] Transecuatoriano. Ahora este proyecto es conocido por muchos como «el peor desastre petrolero del mundo». Según algunas fuentes,[i] la empresa contaminó las aguas de la zona con casi 20 mil millones[j] de galones de residuo[k] tóxico. Además, del oleoducto se derramaron[l] casi 17 millones de galones de petróleo crudo. Como resultado, en las comunidades afectadas por la contaminación se aumentó drásticamente el número de casos de cáncer, enfermedades dermatológicas, problemas reproductivos y defectos de nacimiento.[m] En 2011, después de ocho años de lucha, las comunidades ganaron un juicio[n] en contra de Texaco (que ahora es Chevron).

Los problemas medioambientales en Bolivia también se conectan con el agua, pero de otra forma. A finales de los años 90, el gobierno boliviano (siguiendo los requisitos[ñ] del Banco Mundial[o]) firmó dos tratos[p] para privatizar el suministro y saneamiento[q] del agua. Les vendió a corporaciones transnacionales los sistemas de agua municipales de La Paz y de Cochabamba. Como resultado, el precio del agua subió[r] bastante y la gente pobre perdió el acceso natural que tenían a diferentes fuentes de agua potable. En 2000, hubo protestas violentas en la ciudad de Cochabamba.* En 2006, el nuevo presidente Evo Morales declaró que «El agua no puede ser un negocio privado porque […] se estaría[s] violando los derechos[t] humanos».

[a]*high plateaus* [b]*salt flat* [c]*cuentan… have* [d]*native* [e]*but* [f]*empresa… oil company* [g]*se… joined up with* [h]*pipeline* [i]*sources* [j]*mil… billions* [k]*waste* [l]*se… spilled* [m]*birth* [n]*lawsuit* [ñ]*requirements* [o]*World* [p]*firmó… signed two accords* [q]*suministro… supply and sanitation* [r]*went up* [s]*se… it would be* [t]*rights*

PASO 2.   Ahora lee cada declaración y selecciona la frase apropiada para indicar si estás de acuerdo o no. Luego, completa la oración con la forma correcta del indicativo o el subjuntivo del verbo entre paréntesis.

1. (Creo / No creo) que las empresas petroleras _____ (deber) extraer petróleo de las zonas amazónicas.
2. (Pienso / No pienso) que Texaco-Chevron _____ (ser) el responsable del desastre petrolero.
3. (Es cierto / No es cierto) que la contaminación del agua con residuo tóxico _____ (causar) problemas de la salud entre los habitantes.
4. (Es verdad / No es verdad) que las corporaciones transnacionales _____ (querer) explotar la mano de obra (*workforce*) y los recursos naturales de los países más pobres.
5. (Estoy seguro/a / No estoy seguro/a) que limitar el acceso que una comunidad tiene al agua _____ (violar) los derechos humanos de esa comunidad.
6. (Es verdad / No es verdad) que Ecuador y Bolivia _____ (tener) que luchar para proteger su naturaleza y su herencia (*heritage*) cultural.

PASO 3.   En parejas, contesten las preguntas y explíquense las respuestas.

1. Muchas veces, los países que aceptan que las grandes empresas transnacionales trabajen en zonas ecológicamente delicadas son países de pocos recursos (*resources*) económicos, como Bolivia y Ecuador. ¿Por qué crees que es así?
2. Los residentes de Bolivia y Ecuador causan mucho menos daño al planeta que los residentes de países como los Estados Unidos o Canadá. Por ejemplo, tienen una huella (*footprint*) de carbono muy baja. ¿Por qué crees que es así?
3. En tu país, ¿los grandes proyectos que pueden hacer daño al medio ambiente, como las minas o la extracción petrolera, también ocurren frecuentemente en zonas relativamente pobres?

_____

*Estas protestas son el trasfondo (*background*) de la película *También la lluvia,* que vas a ver en la sección **Conéctate al cine** del **Capítulo 14.**

⟳ Reciclaje

Para and *por*

Empareja las frases para hacer oraciones completas lógicas, completándolas con **para** o **por.**

_____ 1. Reciclamos papel …
_____ 2. Ahorramos agua …
_____ 3. Mantenemos los parques …
_____ 4. Va a haber cambios climáticos …
_____ 5. El huracán Mitch pasó …
_____ 6. La contaminación causa muchos problemas …

a. _____ Honduras en 1998.
b. _____ los bosques.
c. _____ no tener que cortar tantos árboles.
d. _____ conservar la diversidad de zonas ecológicas.
e. _____ la sequía en los últimos años.
f. _____ el calentamiento global.

■ Answers to this activity are in Appendix 2 at the back of your book.

13.3   Para que las tortugas puedan sobrevivir° *survive*

The subjunctive: Purpose and contingency

Para empezar…

Todas las especies de tortugas marinas están en peligro de extinción. Un grupo de biólogos (*biologists*) en Costa Rica ha tomado varias medidas (*measures*) para tratar de prevenir (*prevent*) la extinción de estas tortugas. Empareja cada medida con el objetivo más lógico. **¡Atención!** Cada objetivo solo se puede usar una vez.

1. __b__ No usan luz en la playa de noche…
2. _____ Cuando las tortugas ponen huevos en la arena (*sand*), los conservacionistas los sacan…
3. _____ Guardan los huevos en un lugar de temperatura controlada…
4. _____ Cuando los bebés salen del huevo, los ponen en la playa…
5. _____ Tratan de limitar el desarrollo (*development*) turístico de la costa…
6. _____ Tratan de educar a la población local…
7. _____ Hacen todo esto…

a. para que **entren** al mar.
b. para que las tortugas **lleguen** a la playa sin miedo (*without fear*) a poner los huevos en la arena.
c. para que las tortugas **tengan** playas limpias y sin gente para poner sus huevos.
d. para que los perros no los **coman.**
e. para que no **usen** los huevos de las tortugas como alimento.
f. para que las tortugas **puedan** sobrevivir en el futuro.
g. para que **se desarrollen** (*develop*) bien.

Una tortuga marina en Costa Rica

Actividades analíticas

1 Based on what you saw in **Para empezar,** which form of the verb is used after **para que** (*so that*)?

☐ indicative   ☐ subjunctive

Para que expresses what you want to happen as a result of your action.

Voy a hablar muy despacio **para que** me **entiendas.**

I'm going to speak very slowly so that you understand me.

In this example, you speak slowly because you want the other person to understand you. The meaning of **para que** is thus similar to that of **querer:** both express what you want to happen. As you saw in **12.3, querer que…** is always followed by the subjunctive, so it is not surprising that **para que** behaves the same.

Quiero que me **entiendas.**

I want you to understand me.

■ Answers to these activities are in Appendix 2 at the back of your book.

2 Another common expression that is followed by the subjunctive is **en caso de que** (*in case, in the event that*).

En caso de que llueva mañana, llámame.	*In the event that it rains tomorrow, call me.*
En caso de que no encuentres el parque, búscalo en el mapa.	*In case you don't find the park, look for it on the map.*

En caso de que expresses what might happen, when it is not at all certain that it will. Its meaning is thus similar to expressions like **Es posible que...** , and both are typically followed by the subjunctive.

Es posible que llueva mañana.	*It's possible that it will rain tomorrow (but I don't know for sure).*

3 Expressions that simply introduce a fact (rather than something that you *want* to happen or something that *might* happen) are followed by an indicative verb form. For example, **porque** is generally followed by the indicative.

Voy a hablar muy despacio, **porque** a veces no me **entiendes.**	*I'm going to speak very slowly, because sometimes you don't understand me.*
Llámame, **porque va** a llover mañana.	*Call me, because it's going to rain tomorrow.*

To see how to use the subjunctive to express situations that haven't happened yet or that will only happen under certain conditions, see **Para saber más 13.3** at the back of your book.

■ To see how to use the subjunctive to express situations that haven't happened yet or that will only happen under certain conditions, see **Para saber más 13.3** at the back of your book.

Resumen (*Summary*) de los usos del indicativo y del subjuntivo	
Indicativo	**Subjuntivo**
To indicate a fact, something thought to be true (Estructura 13.2)	**To indicate a desire, something that you want to be true (Estructura 12.3, 13.3)**
Sé que las tortugas **están** bien. *I know that the turtles are fine.*	Quiero que las tortugas **estén** bien. *I want the turtles to be fine.*
Pienso que **ahorras** agua. *I think that you save water.*	Te recomiendo que **ahorres** agua. *I recommend that you save water.*
Te voy a invitar a la playa porque **eres** mi amigo. *I'm going to invite you to the beach because you are my friend.*	Te voy a invitar a la playa para que **seas** mi amigo. *I'm going to invite you to the beach so that you'll be my friend.*
	To indicate something that may not be true (Estructura 13.2, 13.3)
	No creo que los bosques **estén** en buenas condiciones. *I don't think that the forests are in good condition.*
	Es posible que ese pájaro **sea** un cóndor. *It's possible that that bird is a condor.*
	En caso de que **veas** un oso, dime. *In the event that you see a bear, tell me.*

¿Por qué?

Actividades prácticas

A. ¿Qué hacemos para ayudar? Empareja la primera parte de cada oración con la terminación apropiada. **¡Atención!** Presta atención a los verbos en las terminaciones. ¿Están en subjuntivo o indicativo?

1. _____ Uso bicicleta para moverme por la ciudad para que…
2. _____ Uso bicicleta para moverme por la ciudad porque…
3. _____ Pongo los productos reciclables en los contenedores de reciclaje para que…
4. _____ No pido una bolsa cuando compro algo en una tienda porque…
5. _____ Trato de usar muy poca agua para que…
6. _____ Compro frutas y verduras orgánicas porque…
7. _____ Compro frutas y verduras orgánicas para que…
8. _____ Trato de minimizar el uso del papel para que…

a. no quiero que mi comida tenga pesticidas.
b. me gusta saber que no uso tanta gasolina.
c. no hagamos más daño a los bosques.
d. tengan suficiente en el futuro.
e. no esté tan sucio el aire de nuestra ciudad.
f. no la necesito y no quiero generar más basura.
g. no usen tanto pesticida en el campo.
h. puedan usarlos para producir otros productos.

B. Una casa ecológica Imagínate que planeas la construcción de una casa ecológica. Completa cada oración con una conclusión lógica, usando las frases de la lista y conjugando el verbo en su forma más adecuada.

darme dinero	poder trabajar	visitarme en la nueva casa
no molestarse	ser totalmente ecológica	ya estar viviendo allí en verano
no tener ningún defecto		

1. Primero, debo conseguir el permiso de la ciudad para que los obreros (*workers*) _____.
2. Tengo que pedir un préstamo (*loan*) para que el banco _____.
3. Voy a avisar a los vecinos (*let the neighbors know*) para que _____.
4. Luego, voy a escoger puros materiales reciclados para la casa para que _____.
5. Les voy a pedir a los obreros que trabajen con mucho cuidado para que la casa _____.
6. Quiero que la casa esté lista para julio para que mi familia _____.
7. Voy a invitar a todos mis amigos para que _____.

C. ¡Está preparado/a!   Dile a un compañero / una compañera qué hay que llevar **en caso de que** pase una de las siguientes situaciones. Tu compañero/a debe decidir si lo que dices es lógico o no.

> **MODELO:**   E1: En caso de que llueva, hay que llevar un bolígrafo.
> E2: ¡No es lógico!

En caso de que...

1. poder andar en las montañas
2. hacer mucho calor
3. ir a la playa
4. tener tiempo para relajarse
5. querer explorar el río
6. hacer mucho frío

[handwritten: En caso de que hace mucho calor, hay que llevar mucho]

[handwritten: un libro]

[handwritten: 3. En caso de ir a la playa, hay que llevar traje de baño.]

[handwritten: 4 En caso de que tener tiempo para relajarse, hay que un libro.]

[handwritten: 5.) En caso de que querer explorar el río, hay que llevar una balsa]

[handwritten: 6.) En caso de que hace mucho frío, hay que llevar un abrigo]

Hay que llevar...

un abrigo

mucha agua

una balsa (*raft*)

botas de montaña

una gorra

un libro

un traje de baño

[handwritten in margin: un balsa]

D. ¿Qué hacer en el peor de los casos?   Pasar tiempo en la naturaleza puede ser una experiencia muy bonita, pero también puede ser un poco peligroso. Pregúntale a un compañero / una compañera qué haces en caso de que te pase uno de los siguientes problemas. Tu compañero/a debe escoger la solución más lógica de la lista.

> **MODELO:**   picar (*to sting*) los mosquitos / ¡Aplástalos (*squash them*) y ponte más repelente!
> E1: ¿Qué hago en caso de que me piquen los mosquitos?
> E2: ¡Aplástalos y ponte más repelente!

PROBLEMAS (EN CASO DE QUE...)

1. atacar un oso
2. picar una viuda (*widow*) negra
3. querer morder (*bite*) un jaguar
4. picar una medusa (*jellyfish*)
5. cagar (*poop*) un pájaro
6. ir a comer las pirañas

SOLUCIONES

a. ¡Grita, mueve los brazos y trata de asustarlo!
b. ¡Usa agua y una servilleta para limpiarte!
c. ¡Salte (*Get out*) del río inmediatamente!
d. ¡Vete al hospital, porque el veneno (*poison*) de este animal es muy peligroso!
e. ¡Salte del mar y lávate la zona afectada con vinagre o agua salada (*salt water*)!
f. ¡Ponte en posición fetal, cubre la cabeza con los brazos y no te muevas!

¡Leamos!

La aventura y el ecoturismo en el Perú

Antes de leer

PASO 1. Decide si cada actividad es **sostenible** (S) o **no sostenible** (NS).

1. _____ acampar
2. _____ viajar en vehículo motorizado
3. _____ una caminata
4. _____ viajar en avión

5. _____ viajar en bote de remos (*row boat*)
6. _____ observar flora y fauna
7. _____ un proyecto ecológico
8. _____ un centro etnobotánico

PASO 2. Escoge dos actividades del **Paso 1** y escribe una oración completa para explicar tus respuestas.

    MODELO: Acampar es sostenible porque no usa muchos recursos naturales y no destruye la naturaleza.

1. _____
2. _____

A leer

PASO 1. Lee el itinerario «Aventura y ecoturismo en el Perú» y trata de imaginar cómo sería (*would be*) este viaje.

La aventura y el ecoturismo en el Perú

PAÍS:	el Perú
LOCALIZACIÓN:	Recorrido por el Perú: Cusco, Camino Inca,[a] Parque de Tambopata
MODALIDAD DE VIAJE:	Viaje de ecoturismo y aventura, turismo de naturaleza

¿Qué viaje vas a vivir?

Un viaje sostenible especialmente diseñado[b] para los amantes[c] del ecoturismo y la aventura. Conoceremos[d] algunos de los principales atractivos del Perú, pero, sobre todo, disfrutaremos del Camino Inca, de una impresionante estancia[e] en la Posada[f] Amazonas y de un espectacular recorrido en rafting. Una oportunidad sin igual para avistar[g] nutrias[h] gigantes, guacamayos,[i] monos, etcétera. Un viaje para conocer un mundo muy distinto al nuestro.

[...]

DÍA 2: Lima / Paracas / Ica / islas Ballestas

Las islas Ballestas son formaciones rocosas[j] las cuales albergan[k] a leones marinos, pingüinos de Humboldt, gatos marinos,[l] delfines y una gran variedad de aves[m] residentes y migratorias... Navegando hacia[n] las islas Ballestas, en el camino se puede apreciar El Candelabro, que es un geoglifo[ñ] de grandes dimensiones que sirve de faro[o] a los navegantes.

El Candelabro de Paracas

[a]Camino... *Inca Trail* [b]*designed* [c]*lovers* [d]*We'll get to know* [e]*stay* [f]*Lodge* [g]*view* [h]*a large freshwater mammal* [i]*macaws* [j]*rocky* [k]*house* [l]gatos... *sea otters* [m]*pájaros* [n]*toward* [ñ]*large rock art; drawings on the ground designed to be seen from above* [o]*lighthouse*

(*Continues*)

DÍA 5: Camino Inca: Cusco / Huayllabamba

Nuestro vehículo nos llevará hasta el punto de inicio de nuestra caminata. El camino sigue [el banco oeste] del río Urubamba, donde apreciamos hermosas vistas de la montaña Verónica (5850m); después del almuerzo continuaremos nuestra caminata al valle de Huayllabamba para acampar cerca de la comunidad del mismo nombre.

[...]

DÍA 11: Cusco / Puerto Maldonado

A hora oportuna traslado[p] al aeropuerto para tomar el vuelo con destino a Puerto Maldonado. Recepción en el aeropuerto y traslado al puerto de donde seguimos en bote hacia la Posada Amazonas. Durante nuestro viaje podemos observar diferente flora y fauna en las orillas.[q] Si nos queda tiempo, visitamos una granja[r] de los nativos. Después de la cena se mostrará[s] un video sobre el parque nacional de Tambopata.

El río Urubamba con vista de la montaña Verónica

[...]

DÍA 13: Posada Amazonas

Después del desayuno visitamos una pequeña collpa.[t] Desde una plataforma escondida[u] cerca de la collpa podemos observar como decenas[v] de loros y guacamayos congregan aquí para alimentarse. En días soleados[w] se juntan[x] en este lugar decenas hasta a veces centenares[y] de loros para comer arcilla.[z] Después del almuerzo visitamos el Centro EtnoBotánico de una comunidad nativa, aprendiendo más sobre la cultura local y su interacción con la selva. Regresamos [a la posada] para la cena.

Una collpa con loros y guacamayos

[p]*transportation* [q]*shorelines* [r]*farm* [s]*se... will be shown* [t]*clay lick used by birds to neutralize toxins in their diet* [u]*hidden* [v]*scores* [w]con mucho sol [x]*se... gather* [y]*hundreds* [z]*clay*

PASO 2. Ahora contesta las preguntas.

1. ¿Qué tipo de viaje describe el artículo?
2. ¿Cuáles son cuatro atractivos del viaje?
3. ¿Qué atractivos ofrecen las islas Ballestas?
4. ¿Qué ven los turistas en la caminata del Camino Inca?
5. ¿Dónde pasan la noche los turistas en el Camino Inca?
6. ¿Cómo llegan los turistas a la Posada Amazonas el día once?
7. ¿Qué tipo de información reciben los turistas en la Posada Amazonas?
8. El último día, ¿qué hacen los turistas por la mañana? ¿Y por la tarde?
9. ¿Te gustaría participar en este viaje? Explica por qué sí o por qué no. ¿En cuáles actividades te gustaría participar y en cuáles no?

Después de leer

 En grupos pequeños, diseñen un viaje ecológico en su comunidad. Para organizar el viaje, primero contesten las siguientes preguntas. Luego, organicen la presentación del viaje en la forma de un anuncio en la televisión y preséntenlo al resto de la clase.

1. ¿Adónde van a ir los turistas?
2. ¿Qué lugares de interés van a conocer? Describe cada uno.
3. ¿Cómo van a llegar los turistas a cada lugar?
4. ¿Qué van a hacer en cada lugar?
5. ¿Dónde se van a quedar?
6. ¿Qué van a aprender?

¡Escuchemos!

Algunas amenazas a nuestro planeta

Antes de escuchar

Vas a escuchar una serie de frases. Para cada una, indica a qué tema ecológico se refiere.

	EL CALENTAMIENTO GLOBAL	LA CONTAMINACIÓN DEL MAR	LA DEFORESTACIÓN	LA ESCASEZ (*shortage*) DE AGUA
1.	☐	☐	☑	☐
2.	☑	☐	☐	☐
3.	☐	☐	☐	☐
4.	☐	☐	☐	☐
5.	☐	☐	☐	☐
6.	☐	☐	☐	☐
7.	☐	☑	☐	☐

A escuchar

Mira y escucha mientras los participantes hablan sobre algunos problemas medioambientales. Mientras escuchas, indica cada expresión que oyes. **¡Atención!** En cada caso, hay tres respuestas.

1. Eduardo, de Panamá
   - ☑ cambios en el clima
   - ☑ la contaminación
   - ☑ desequilibrios en estaciones
   - ☐ medios de transporte
   - ☐ problemas ecológicos
   - ☑ las selvas tropicales

2. Anlluly, de Costa Rica
   - ☑ el cambio de clima
   - ☑ gente que corta muchos árboles
   - ☐ problemas ambientales
   - ☐ el pulmón (*lung*) del país
   - ☐ recursos naturales
   - ☑ tirar la basura en el bosque

3. Víctor, de México
   - ☑ el calentamiento global
   - ☐ el cambio climático
   - ☐ la contaminación
   - ☐ el deterioro de nuestro planeta
   - ☐ se inundan ciudades, se inundan pueblos
   - ☐ reciclar las bolsas plásticas

4. Guadalupe, de Costa Rica
   - ☑ el cambio climático
   - ☑ cortando árboles
   - ☐ el deterioro de nuestro planeta
   - ☑ se inundan ciudades, se inundan pueblos
   - ☑ mucha gente está conservando
   - ☐ protegiendo los bosques

5. Diego, de Argentina
   - ☐ el cambio climático
   - ☑ deforestación
   - ☐ problemas ambientales
   - ☑ el pulmón (*lung*) del país
   - ☐ recursos naturales
   - ☑ la selva

6. Andrea, de México
   - ☐ el cambio climático
   - ☑ cuánto daño le estamos haciendo
   - ☐ el deterioro de nuestro planeta
   - ☑ le echan todo al mar
   - ☑ el mar va a estar todo contaminado
   - ☐ el pulmón del país

7. Juan Andrés, de Costa Rica
   - ☑ la contaminación
   - ☐ desequilibrios en estaciones
   - ☑ medios de transporte
   - ☑ problemas ecológicos
   - ☑ reciclar las bolsas plásticas
   - ☐ las selvas tropicales

Después de escuchar

Lee las siguientes preguntas y luego mira el video de nuevo. En parejas, contesten las preguntas usando oraciones completas.

1. Según Eduardo, ¿qué pasa con los bosques?

2. Según Eduardo, ¿qué pasa con el clima?

3. Según Anlluly, ¿qué hace la gente que es malo para el medio ambiente?

4. Según Víctor, ¿cuáles son algunos problemas que trae el cambio climático?

5. Según Guadalupe, ¿para qué están cortando árboles muchas personas?

6. ¿De qué habla Diego?

7. Según Diego, ¿cuáles son dos ventajas de mantener los bosques?

8. Según Andrea, ¿a qué deberíamos prestar más atención?

9. Si no le prestamos más atención, ¿qué pasará?

10. ¿Qué sugerencias ofrece Juan Andrés para mejor cuidar el medio ambiente?

¡Escribamos!

El problema medioambiental más grave°   *serious*

En esta actividad, vas a describir un problema medioambiental, explicar tu opinión en cuanto al asunto (*concerning the matter*) y luego ofrecer sugerencias para una posible solución.

Antes de escribir

Escoge uno de los temas presentados en **¡Escuchemos!** y toma apuntes siguiendo el modelo.

> **MODELO:** I. El problema: *la contaminación del mar*
>
> A. la tesis del video: *no prestamos atención al mar*
>   1. detalle: *echamos basura al mar*
>   2. detalle: *dañamos los animales marinos*
>   3. detalle: *enfocamos en otros problemas (el aire, los bosques)*
>
> B. Mi opinión: _____
>   1. detalle: _____
>   2. detalle: _____
>   3. detalle: _____
>
> C. Posible solución: _____
>   1. sugerencia: _____
>   2. sugerencia: _____
>   3. sugerencia: _____

A escribir

Usa tu bosquejo (*outline*) para ayudarte a escribir un ensayo de tres párrafos. Primero, describe el problema y resume lo que dice la persona en el video. Luego, añade tu propia opinión y más detalles. Escribe una conclusión en la cual ofreces algunas sugerencias para una solución.

ESTRATEGIA

Outlining

Preparing an outline can help you to include more details than you might otherwise, which is especially important in a situation in which you are trying to urge others to action. Outlines also ensure that you organize your writing in the most logical way possible without proceeding out of order. The visual nature of the outline allows you to see where your assignment may be lacking in details, helping you address each key point equally.

Después de escribir

Revisa tu ensayo. Luego, intercambia ensayos con un compañero / una compañera para evaluarlos. Lee el ensayo de tu compañero/a y decide si falta información necesaria. ¿Se ha desarrollado (*developed*) bien cada párrafo?

¿Hay sugerencias apropiadas para una solución en la conclusión? Lee de nuevo (*again*) el ensayo con cuidado para revisar los siguientes puntos de gramática.

☐ hay concordancia entre los sujetos y los verbos

☐ hay concordancia entre los sustantivos y los adjetivos

☐ hay uso apropiado del subjuntivo

Después de revisar el ensayo de tu compañero/a, devuélveselo. Mira tu propio ensayo para ver los cambios que tu compañero/a recomienda y haz las revisiones necesarias.

¡Hablemos!

¿A quién le gusta más la naturaleza?

Antes de hablar

Mira los dibujos y di a qué actividad se refiere. Si no sabes la palabra exacta para cada actividad, usa las palabras que sí sabes para explicársela.

MODELO:

hacer camping *or* dormir fuera de la casa, en el bosque o en las montañas

1.

3.

5.

2.

4.

6.

A hablar

En parejas, túrnense para decir qué tienen que llevar o cómo tienen que preparar para hacer las actividades que identificaron en **Antes de hablar.** Expliquen para qué lo tienen que hacer o en qué situatión va a ser necesario.

MODELOS: Deberíamos comprar un colchón inflable (*air mattress*) *para que* no tengamos que dormir en el suelo.

Debería llevar un traje de baño *en caso de que* haya un buen lugar para tomar el sol.

Después de hablar

Ahora, júntense con otra pareja y decidan cuál de las actividades prefieren hacer para este fin de semana.

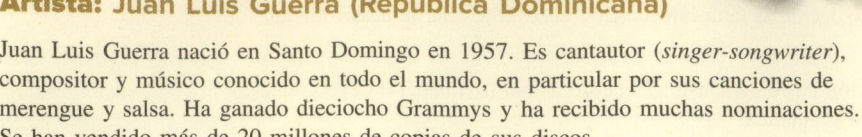

Conéctate a la música

Canción: «Ojalá que llueva café» (1989)
Artista: Juan Luis Guerra (República Dominicana)

Juan Luis Guerra nació en Santo Domingo en 1957. Es cantautor (*singer-songwriter*), compositor y músico conocido en todo el mundo, en particular por sus canciones de merengue y salsa. Ha ganado dieciocho Grammys y ha recibido muchas nominaciones. Se han vendido más de 20 millones de copias de sus discos.

Antes de escuchar

En la canción «Ojalá que llueva café», el cantante quiere que varias cosas caigan (*fall*) del cielo. ¿Cuáles son otras cosas que probablemente muchas personas esperan que caigan del cielo? ¿Por qué?

A escuchar

Lee las **Expresiones útiles** y las siguientes frases. Luego escucha la canción «Ojalá que llueva café». Mientras escucha, escribe los números 1 a 7 al lado de las frases según el orden en que las escuches.

_____ en vez de hojas secas, […] una cosecha de pitisalé.*

_____ la colina de arroz graneado

_____ un aguacero de yuca y té

_____ un alto cerro de trigo y mapuey

_____ una jarina de queso blanco

_____ una llanura de batata y fresas

_____ una montaña de berro y miel†

Después de escuchar

Lee de nuevo la lista de cosas que el cantante pide. ¿Qué tipo de cosas son? ¿Por qué crees tú que él quiere que caigan del cielo? ¿De qué se trata (*is [it] about*) esta canción? Busca pistas (*clues*) en la canción para apoyar (*support*) tus ideas.

Juan Luis Guerra inició su gira (*tour*) de 2008 con un concierto en Miami.

■ For copyright reasons, the songs referenced in **Conéctate a la música** have not been provided by the publisher. The video for this song can be found on YouTube, and it is available for purchase from the iTunes store.

Expresiones útiles

aguacero	downpour
batata	sweet potato
berro	watercress
cerro	hill
colina	hill
cosecha	harvest
en vez	instead
hojas secas	dry leaves
jarina	sprinkling
llanura	prairie
mapuey	yam
miel	honey
trigo	wheat

---

*petit-salé, un tipo de tocino (*bacon*)
†El berro y la miel se combinan en muchos remedios caseros (*home*) para curar una tos o gripe.

VOCABULARIO

Comunicación

¿Cuánto tiempo lleva(s) + -ndo *form?*	How long have you (*inform./form.*) (*done / been doing something*)?
Llevo + *time expression* + -ndo *form.*	I've been (*doing something*) for + *time.*
¿Cuánto tiempo hace que + *present tense?*	How long have you (*done / been doing something*)?
Hace + *time expression* + *present tense.*	I've been (*doing something*) for + *time.*
(no) debería + *inf.*	should (*do something*)
mucho tiempo	a long time
toda la vida	all my (your/his/her) life, all our (your/their) lives

El medio ambiente — The environment

el agotamiento	depletion, exhaustion
el árbol	tree
el arrecife	reef
el bosque	forest
el calentamiento global	global warming
el clima	climate
la contaminación	pollution
el daño	damage
el desequilibrio	imbalance
el deterioro	deterioration
la disminución	decrease
la especie	species, kind
el huracán (*pl.* huracanes)	hurricane
la inundación (*pl.* inundaciones)	flood
el mar	sea
el medio ambiente	environment
el peligro	danger
el planeta (Tierra)	planet (Earth)
el reciclaje	recycling
los recursos naturales	natural resources

la selva	jungle
la sequía	drought
la tala de árboles	tree cutting
la tierra	earth, soil

Cognados: el/la activista, la deforestación, la ecología, el ecologismo, el ecoturismo, la extinción, la fauna, la flora, el humanitarismo

Los animales

el pájaro	bird
la ballena	whale
el delfín	dolphin
el león marino	sea lion
el loro	parrot
el mono	monkey
el oso	bear
el perezoso	sloth
el pingüino	penguin
el sapo	toad
la tortuga	turtle

Los verbos

ahorrar agua	to save water
ayudar	to help
conservar	to preserve; to conserve; to keep
cuidar	to take care of
explotar	to exploit; to develop
proteger (j)	to protect
reciclar	to recycle

Los adjetivos

consciente	conscious
ecológico/a	ecological
marino/a	marine, sea
medioambiental	environmental
sostenible	sustainable

La cultura y la diversión

El taller (*studio*) de un pintor
en La Habana, Cuba

Objetivos

In this chapter you will learn how to:

- express uncertainty
- say what you and others would like or hope to do
- talk about what cultural activities you enjoy
- express desires in the past
- express future plans
- express speculation
- discuss cultural activities and entertainment in the Spanish-speaking world

14

COMUNICACIÓN ~~LARIO~~ ~~UCTURA~~ ~~ATE~~

Quizás. No sé. Tal vez...

Expressing uncertainty

A. A ver: ¿Cuáles son sus preferencias?

PASO 1. Mira y escucha, luego indica los géneros (*genres*) de cine de que habla cada persona. **¡Atención!** Algunas personas hablan de más de un género de cine. Indícalos todos.

1. _____ Mariana, de Costa Rica

2. _____ Brenda, de México

3. _____ Víctor, de España

4. _____ Denise, de Argentina

5. _____ Cinthya, de Costa Rica

a. acción
b. comedia
c. comedia musical
d. drama
e. infantil
f. romance
g. suspenso/misterio
h. terror

PASO 2. Mira y escucha otra vez. ¿Qué expresión usa cada persona para expresar certeza (*certainty*) o duda?

		SÍ	CREO	TAL VEZ	QUIZÁ(S)	NO SÉ
1.	MARIANA: «____ que me gusta la comedia... »	☐	☐	☐	☐	☐
2.	BRENDA: «...bueno de género así de terror, ____... »	☐	☐	☐	☐	☐
3.	VÍCTOR: «...que tengan algún valor y sobre todo ____ también... »	☐	☐	☐	☐	☐
4.	DENISE: «...con Julio Bocca que, ____ lo conocen... »	☐	☐	☐	☐	☐
5.	CINTHYA: «Me gusta el suspenso, pero ____... »	☐	☐	☐	☐	☐

PASO 3. Contesta las preguntas sobre lo que dijo la gente del video.

1. ¿Qué género no le gusta a Mariana? ¿Por qué no?
2. ¿Cuáles películas le gustan a Brenda?
3. ¿Qué tipo de películas le gustan a Víctor más que las otras?
4. ¿Quién es Julio Bocca?
5. ¿Ha visto Cinthya la película de suspenso, *Infección*?
6. ¿Qué género de película del **Paso 1** no menciona nadie? ¿A ti te gusta este género?

> To say *maybe* or *perhaps,* you can use **quizá/quizás** or **tal vez.**
>
> —**¿Cuál es tu película favorita?**   "What's your favorite movie?"
> —**No sé, tal vez** *Casablanca.*   "I don't know. Maybe *Casablanca.*
>   **O quizá(s)** *El padrino.*   Or perhaps *The Godfather.*"
>
> To say that you're sure of how you feel about something, you can say: **Sin duda (alguna).**
>
> —**¿Cuál es tu película favorita?**   "What's your favorite movie?"
> —**Sin duda alguna, mi película favorita**   "Without a doubt, my favorite movie is
>   es *El ciudadano Kane.*   *Citizen Kane.*"

B. ¿Cuáles son tus preferencias?

PASO 1. Apunta por lo menos dos nombres para cada categoría. Puedes mencionar obras (*works*) y personas en cada categoría.

> **MODELO:** literatura: el autor Gabriel García Márquez; *Cien años de soledad*
>
> arte
> baile (*dance*)
> cine
> literatura
> música
> ópera
> teatro

PASO 2. En parejas, túrnense para hacer preguntas sobre cada categoría para aprender sus preferencias.

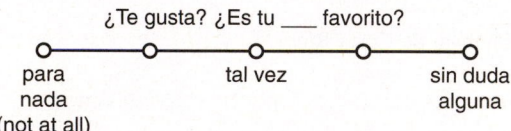

¿Te gusta? ¿Es tu ___ favorito?

para nada (not at all) — tal vez — sin duda alguna

> **MODELO:** E1: ¿*Cien años de soledad* es tu libro favorito?
>   E2: Sin duda alguna es mi libro favorito. ¿Es el tuyo?
>   E1: No sé. Tal vez. Pero también me gusta *El amor en los tiempos del cólera.*

CONÉCTATE AL MUNDO HISPANO

Durante décadas, las películas más famosas de Hollywood han entretenido a los públicos (*audiences*) en todo el mundo. En algunos países hispanohablantes, **el doblaje** (*dubbing*) es una parte importante de la industria de cine. Antes de que una película se estrene (*premieres*), doblan (*they dub*) los diálogos al español. En otras partes del mundo ponen **subtítulos.** El uso ubicuo de subtítulos hace que inglés goce de (*enjoys*) una presencia cultural incluso en los países donde no es un idioma oficial. Preocupadas por la preservación de la cultura hispana, algunas personas prefieren el doblaje, porque así los públicos escuchan la película en su propia lengua. Sin embargo, en países con su propia producción cinematográfica (*film*), muchas personas prefieren que las películas de los Estados Unidos tengan subtítulos porque las películas subtituladas presentan menos competencia (*competition*) para las películas locales.

Quisiera...

Talking about what you would like

El actor peruano Bernie Paz

A. ¿Qué quisieran hacer estas personas famosas?

Empareja cada persona famosa con la cita más apropiada.

1. ____ Bernie Paz es un actor peruano que trabaja en telenovelas (*soap operas*).
2. ____ Pilar Bustos es una pintora de Ecuador.
3. ____ Giovanna Rivero es una escritora boliviana de libros de ficción.
4. ____ José Carreras es un cantante de ópera español.
5. ____ Los Pájaros es un grupo de rock argentino.
6. ____ Zoe Saldana es una actriz dominicana.

a. «Quisiera cantar en el Teatro Colón en Buenos Aires.»
b. «Quisiera ganar otro premio para uno de mis libros.»
c. «Quisiera presentar una exposición en el Museo de Arte Moderno.»
d. «Quisiera ser directora de cine.»
e. «Quisiéramos hacer una gira mundial (*world tour*) de conciertos.»
f. «Quisiera trabajar en una película de arte.»

To talk about what you or someone else would like or hope to do, use a form of **quisiera** + *infinitive:* **(yo) quisiera, (tú) quisieras, (él/ella, Ud.) quisiera, (nosotros/as) quisiéramos, (vosotros/as) quisierais, (ellos/ellas, Uds.) quisieran.**

Quisiera ser una actriz famosa.   I would like to be a famous actress.
Quisieran asistir a clases de baile.   They would like to attend dance classes.

 B. ¿Qué quisieran estas personas?   En grupos, digan una cosa que las siguientes personas probablemente quisieran hacer. Usen la estructura **quisiera(n)** + *verb* o **quisiera(n)** + *noun*. ¡Sean lógicos y creativos!

MODELO: una persona a quien le gusta la ópera →
   E1: Esta persona quisiera asistir a una ópera famosa.
   E2: Tal vez quisiera ver *Carmen* o *La flauta mágica*.
   E3: Sin duda alguna, quisiera ver algunas óperas en el Teatro alla Scala en Milán.

1. un aficionado al ballet
2. una estudiante de arte
3. alguien a quien le gusta escuchar música clásica
4. una profesora de la historia del arte
5. una persona a quien le gusta el cine
6. una joven a quien le encantan las obras (*works*) de Cervantes y Shakespeare
7. una persona que quiere ser actor
8. una chica que quiere aprender a tocar música rock

C. ¿Qué quisieras hacer tú?

PASO 1.   Escribe por lo menos tres frases con **quisiera** y expresiones de la lista para decir qué quisieras hacer en el mundo del arte.

actuar	dibujar	pintar
bailar	escribir un guion (*screenplay*) / una novela	ser fotógrafo/a
cantar	escribir un poema / poesía	tocar la guitarra / el piano

MODELO: Quisiera aprender a tocar el piano.

 PASO 2.   Ahora, hazles preguntas a otras personas en tu clase sobre sus aspiraciones. ¿Qué tienen en común las aspiraciones de Uds.? ¿Cómo son diferentes?

MODELO: E1: Quisiera tocar la guitarra acústica. ¿Y tú?
   E2: Yo quisiera tocar la guitarra eléctrica en una banda de rock.
   E1: Yo no, para nada; prefiero la música folclórica.

El cine, el teatro, el museo
Movies, theater, and museums

A. El nuevo centro cultural   El nuevo centro cultural en tu ciudad quiere saber cómo atraer al público. Responde al siguiente sondeo (*survey*).

ACTIVIDADES PARA ESPECTADORES (*spectators*) EN EL NUEVO CENTRO CULTURAL.

	1–2 VECES AL MES	1–2 VECES AL AÑO	NUNCA
En general, me gusta ver…			
bailes	☑	☐	☐
conciertos (música en vivo)	☐	☑	☐
obras de arte	☐	☐	☑
películas	☑	☐	☐
teatro	☐	☑	☐
Me gustaría ver conciertos de música…			
alternativa	☐	☐	☐
clásica	☐	☐	☑
electrónica	☐	☐	☐
folclórica	☐	☐	☐
de ópera	☐	☐	☐
pop	☐	☐	☐
rock	☐	☐	☐

En mi opinión, tres de los mejores **cantantes** son:

_____

En mi opinión, tres de los mejores grupos/**bandas** son:

_____

	1–2 VECES AL MES	1–2 VECES AL AÑO	NUNCA
Me gustaría ver espectáculos de baile…			
clásico/ballet	☐	☐	☐
cumbia	☐	☐	☐
flamenco	☐	☐	☐
folclórico	☐	☐	☐
merengue	☐	☐	☐
salsa	☐	☐	☐
tango	☐	☐	☐
Me gustaría ver exposiciones en la galería de…			
escultura	☐	☐	☐
pintura	☐	☐	☐
Me gustaría oír/ver presentaciones de…			
literatura	☐	☐	☐
obras de **artistas, pintores,** o cineastas (*filmmakers*) famosos	☐	☐	☐
poesía	☐	☐	☐

Me interesa participar en un taller (*workshop*) de…

☐ **arte**   ☐ **dirección (dirigir)**
☐ **danza**   ☐ escritura de novelas
☐ actuación (**actuar**)   ☐ producción de cine **alternativo**

Vocabulario

Here are some common words used to talk about artists and the arts in Spanish.

el/la escritor(a)	writer
la estrella (de cine)	(movie) star
interpretar (un papel)	to play (a role or part)
el personaje	character; celebrity, well-known person
el/la pintor(a)	painter
el/la protagonista	main character, protagonist

La estrella de cine Salma Hayek fue nominada a Mejor Actriz en los Premios Óscar por su actuación en *Frida*. En esta película, Hayek **interpretó el papel** de **la protagonista**, la artista Frida Kahlo, uno de **los personajes** que Hayek más admira.

B. ¿Qué hace cada uno?

PASO 1. Empareja cada verbo con su mejor descripción.

1. ___ actuar o interpretar un papel
2. ___ dirigir
3. ___ producir
4. ___ pintar
5. ___ tocar música
6. ___ componer (*compose*) música
7. ___ esculpir (*sculpt*)
8. ___ dibujar (*draw*)

a. hacer los preparativos y arreglarlo todo
b. arreglar (*arrange*) y producir obras musicales originales
c. aplicar pintura a un lienzo (*canvas*)
d. interpretar una canción con un instrumento musical
e. trazar algo en una superficie con líneas y colores
f. es lo que hace la persona que da instrucciones a los actores
g. es lo que hacen los actores para hacer verosímil (*realistic*) el personaje
h. hacer una obra en piedra, madera o metal

 PASO 2. En parejas, describan las siguientes artes. Pueden usar el **Paso 1** como modelo. Para más ayuda, vean también la lista de **Expresiones útiles.**

1. cantar   2. bailar   3. escribir

Expresiones útiles

el cuerpo

una historia (*story*)

la voz (*voice*)

contar (*to tell*)

explicar

interpretar

C. Las estrellas y sus papeles

PASO 1. Haz una lista de tres o cuatro estrellas de cine y un personaje que ha interpretado cada uno.

MODELO:

ESTRELLA	PERSONAJE
Adrian Brody	Salvador Dalí
Salma Hayek	Frida Kahlo
Joaquin Phoenix	Johnny Cash
Daniel Radcliffe	Harry Potter

 PASO 2. Ahora, en parejas, túrnense para compartir los pares de nombres de tu lista. Digan cuál es el **personaje** y cuál es la **estrella.** Digan también si la estrella es **actor** o **actriz** y cómo se llama la película.

MODELO: E1: Will Ferrell y Ron Burgundy
E2: El personaje es Ron Burgundy. La estrella es el actor Will Ferrell. ¡La película es *El reportero*!

D. A ver: ¿Qué actividades culturales prefieren?

PASO 1. Mira y escucha, luego indica todos los elementos culturales que menciona cada persona.

	ARTE	BAILE	LITERATURA	MUSEOS	MÚSICA	PINTURA	TEATRO
¿Qué tipo de actividades culturales hay aquí?							
1. Andrea, de México	☑	☑	☐	☑	☐	☐	☑
2. Carlos, de México	☑	☐	☑	☐	☐	☑	☑
3. Ángela, de España	☐	☐	☑	☐	☑	☑	☐
4. Alejandro, de Argentina	☑	☐	☐	☑	☑	☐	☑

PASO 2. Apunta el género (o los géneros) de música que menciona cada persona.

GÉNEROS DE MÚSICA

1. _____ Rodrigo, de Argentina

2. _____ Federico, de Nicaragua

3. _____ Agustina, de Argentina

4. _____ Carlos, del Perú

5. _____ Isabel, de España

a. flamenco
b. música alternativa
c. música clásica
d. música disco
e. música hip hop
f. música latina
g. música moderna
h. música pop
i. música rap
j. música reggae
k. música rock

PASO 3. En parejas, contesten las siguientes preguntas sobre sus preferencias en música.

1. ¿Qué género de música te gusta a ti? ¿Qué género de música no te gusta para nada?
2. ¿Qué instrumentos musicales son populares en la música que te gusta?
3. ¿Te gusta la música electrónica o prefieres la música acústica?
4. ¿Bailas o cantas cuando escuchas música? ¿A qué género de música prefieres bailar? ¿A qué género te gusta cantar?
5. ¿Qué género de música escuchan las personas mayores donde vives tú? ¿Te gusta esa música también? ¿Qué instrumentos musicales son populares en esa música?

En español...

Here are names of some additional musical instruments in Spanish. As you see, many of them are cognates.

el bajo (*bass*)	la harmónica	el sintetizador
la batería (*drum set*)	el órgano	la trompeta
el clarinete	el piano	el violín
la flauta		

E. Entrevistas: Preferencias culturales

 PASO 1.   Primero, apunta tus respuestas a estas preguntas. Luego, en parejas, túrnense para entrevistarse con las mismas preguntas.

1. En tu universidad, ¿qué hacen los estudiantes para divertirse?
2. ¿Te gustaría hacer algo en tu carrera profesional relacionado con la cultura e identidad de una región o nación? ¿Por qué sí o no?
3. ¿Qué hay en la cultura norteamericana que les interesaría a los estudiantes de otros países? ¿Qué aspecto de la cultura de otro país te interesa a ti?
4. ¿De qué tipo de música u otra forma de arte de otro país (como, por ejemplo, la música salsa, la arquitectura de Gaudí, las novelas de Gabriel García Márquez, el baile folclórico o las películas de Guillermo del Toro) te gustaría aprender más?

 PASO 2.   En grupos pequeños, hablen de sus preferencias en cuanto a la música. Pueden usar las siguientes preguntas como guía.

- ¿Te gusta asistir a conciertos de música? ¿Cuál fue el primer concierto al que asististe? ¿Y cuál fue el último? ¿Qué género de música prefieres ver en vivo?
- ¿Has bajado música del Internet? ¿Cuál fue la última canción que bajaste? ¿Qué sitio usas para bajar música? Si no bajas música del Internet, ¿dónde consigues la música que escuchas?
- ¿Has asistido a una ópera o has visto una en la televisión? ¿Qué ópera viste? ¿Te gustó? Si no has visto una ópera, ¿te gustaría ver una? ¿Por qué sí o no?
- ¿Has asistido a un ballet? ¿Qué ballet viste? ¿Dónde lo viste? Si no has visto un ballet, ¿te gustaría ver uno? ¿Por qué sí o no?

F. ¿Qué quisieras hacer?

PASO 1.   Haz una lista de por lo menos tres actividades culturales en que no participas, pero en que quisieras participar algún día.

> **MODELO:**   Quisiera ir a más museos de arte.

 PASO 2.   En parejas, túrnense para expresar qué quisieran hacer. Luego, cada uno debe decirle a su compañero/a qué debería hacer él o ella para realizar sus deseos.

> **MODELO:**   E1: Quisiera ir a más museos de arte.
> E2: Deberías viajar a Washington, DC, para ver el Museo Nacional.

COMUN VOCABUL **ESTRUCTURA** ATE

Reciclaje

The subjunctive to express what may not be true

En cada ciudad, hay personas que están a favor de fomentar (*promote*) el arte y personas que están en contra de usar dinero de los contribuyentes (*taxpayers*) para esta razón. Primero, completa cada oración con la forma apropiada del verbo. Luego, indica qué oraciones diría (*would say*) una persona a favor del arte. **¡Atención!** Algunos verbos tienen que estar en el subjuntivo y otros en el indicativo.

¿A FAVOR DEL ARTE?

☐ 1. «Espero que los músicos no _____ (hacer) muchos conciertos este año.»
☐ 2. «Creo que la cultura _____ (ser) importante para nuestra ciudad.»
☐ 3. «Quiero que los dueños _____ (cerrar) las galerías de arte.»
☐ 4. «Tenemos que hacer algo para que la ciudad _____ (tener) una vida cultural más activa.»
☐ 5. «Es muy importante que todos los ciudadanos (*citizens*) _____ (participar) en la vida cultural del país.»
☐ 6. «Siempre digo que para mí, la cultura no _____ (tener) mucha importancia.»

■ Answers to this activity are in **Appendix 2** at the back of your book.

14.1 Querían que la música fuera para todos

The past subjunctive

Para empezar...

La Sinfónica de la Juventud Venezolana Simón Bolívar

El Sistema Nacional de las Orquestas Juveniles (*Youth*) e Infantiles (*Children's*) de Venezuela, conocido simplemente como «El Sistema», es un programa de educación musical y desarrollo (*development*) social que lleva la música a todos los sectores de la sociedad en todo el país. Desde su creación en 1975, ha sido un modelo para programas de música en muchos otros países, incluyendo los Estados Unidos y Canadá. La orquesta más conocida de El Sistema, la Sinfónica de la Juventud Venezolana Simón Bolívar, ha realizado giras (*tours*) en Europa, Asia y los Estados Unidos.

¿Qué querían los organizadores de El Sistema cuando lo crearon? Indica si cada una de las siguientes oraciones es cierta o falsa. **¡Atención!** Solo hay dos oraciones falsas.

	CIERTO	FALSO
1. Querían que los jóvenes músicos venezolanos **tuvieran** la oportunidad de tocar en grupo.	☐	☐
2. Querían que la música **estuviera** al alcance (*reach*) de todas las clases sociales.	☐	☐
3. Recomendaban que **pusieran** orquestas juveniles solo en Caracas.	☐	☐
4. Era muy importante que los jóvenes de todo el país **pudieran** estudiar música.	☐	☐
5. Pedían en que los profesores **pusieran** mucha pasión en sus clases.	☐	☐
6. Era necesario que el gobierno venezolano **diera** dinero para apoyar (*support*) El Sistema.	☐	☐
7. Pidieron que los profesores **hablaran** con los padres sobre la importancia de la educación musical.	☐	☐
8. Querían que los jóvenes **aprendieran** algo sobre la música clásica y la música tradicional venezolana.	☐	☐
9. Querían que los jóvenes **pudieran** estudiar música en un lugar seguro, alegre y divertido.	☐	☐
10. Esperaban que la música clásica **fuera** solo para los ricos.	☐	☐

Actividades analíticas

1 The verbs in bold in **Para empezar** are in the *past subjunctive* (**el imperfecto de subjuntivo**). Use what you saw there and what you know about Spanish verbs to complete the following conjugations.

	hablar	aprender	vivir
yo	habl**ara**	aprend**iera**	
tú	habl**aras**		viv**ieras**
él/ella, Ud.	habl**ara**	aprend**iera**	viv**iera**
nosotros/as	habl**áramos**	aprend**iéramos**	
vosotros/as	habl**arais**	aprend**ierais**	viv**ierais**
ellos/ellas, Uds.			viv**ieran**

■ Answers to these activities are in **Appendix 2** at the back of your book.

2 The past subjunctive is formed with the stem of the verb (**habl-, aprend-, viv-**) plus one of the endings from the following chart. Use what you saw in **Actividades analíticas 1** to complete this chart.

TERMINACIONES DEL IMPERFECTO DE SUBJUNTIVO		
	-ar verbs	**-er / -ir** verbs
yo	-ara	-iera
tú		-ieras
él/ella, Ud.	-ara	
nosotros/as		-iéramos
vosotros/as	-arais	-ierais
ellos/ellas, Uds.		

Autoprueba

Give the past subjunctive forms of the following verbs.

1. actuar (nosotros/as) _____

2. salir (yo) _____

3. comer (tú) _____

Respuestas: 1. actuáramos **2.** saliera **3.** comieras

3 Verbs that have an irregular stem in the preterite use this same stem in the past subjunctive, together with the endings for **-er / -ir** verbs.

verbo	raíz irregular	pretérito (yo)	imperfecto de subjuntivo (yo)
estar	estuv-	estuve	estuviera
poder	pud-	pude	pudiera
poner	pus-	puse	pusiera
tener	tuv-	tuve	tuviera

As in the preterite, **dar** is conjugated with the endings for **-er / -ir** verbs.

Yo quería que me **dieras** un libro.   *I wanted you to give me a book.*

The verbs **ir** and **ser** share the same irregular form, **fuera.** As with the preterite, the context will help you know whether **ir** or **ser** is intended.

Te recomendé que **fueras** al cine.   *I recommended that you go to the movies.*

No creían que **fuéramos** músicos.   *They didn't believe that we were musicians.*

■ For more information and examples of irregular past subjunctive forms, as well as the past perfect subjunctive, see **Para saber más 14.1** at the back of your book.

4 The past subjunctive is used in the same environments as the present subjunctive when the main verb is in the past (whether preterite or imperfect), as seen in these examples.

PRESENTE DE SUBJUNTIVO	IMPERFECTO DE SUBJUNTIVO
To indicate a desire, something that you want to be true	
Piden que **hablemos** en la reunión. *They ask that we speak at the meeting.*	**Pidieron** que **habláramos** en la reunión. *They asked that we speak at the meeting.*
Quiero que **estudies** conmigo esta noche. *I want you to study with me tonight.*	**Quería** que **estudiaras** conmigo esta noche. *I wanted you to study with me tonight.*
To indicate something that may not be true	
No **creo** que **sea** muy buena idea. *I don't think it is a good idea.*	No **creía** que **fuera** muy buena idea. *I didn't think it was a good idea.*
Es imposible que **gane** el premio este año. *It's impossible for him/her to win the prize this year.*	**Era imposible** que **ganara** el premio este año. *It was impossible for him/her to win the prize this year.*

Actividades prácticas

A. Dos cineastas importantes   Dos de las grandes figuras del cine mundial son Luis Buñuel (España/México, 1900–1983) y Pedro Almodóvar (España, 1949–). Completa la descripción de cada uno con las terminaciones más lógicas. Hay dos terminaciones que no son válidas para ninguno de los cineastas. **¡Atención!** Nota el tiempo del verbo (presente o imperfecto de subjuntivo) para ayudarte a contestar.

1. Luis Buñuel quería que sus películas _____, _____ y _____.
2. Pedro Almodóvar quiere que sus películas _____, _____ y _____.
3. No son válidas las terminaciones _____ y _____.

a. **mostraran** una visión surrealista del mundo
b. **sean** a veces humorísticas (*humorous*)
c. **fueran** fáciles de editar
d. **estén** en blanco y negro
e. **criticaran** la religión en algunos casos
f. **tengan** colores muy vivos y contrastantes (*contrasting*)
g. **tuvieran** muchos elementos de la cultura norteamericana
h. **muestren** la realidad de la sociedad contemporánea

Pedro Almodóvar

Luis Buñuel

B. Gustavo Dudamel   Gustavo Dudamel es un joven director de orquesta y un ex alumno de El Sistema en Venezuela. Empezó a dirigir orquestas en Venezuela en 1996, y en 2004 ganó el premio Gustav Mahler en Alemania. En 2009 lo designaron director de la Orquesta Filarmónica de Los Ángeles, cuando tenía solo 28 años. En octubre de ese año, hizo su primer concierto como director de la orquesta.

Escucha cada oración. Luego, escribe **D** si se trata de lo que **Dudamel** quería durante su primera noche como director de la Filarmónica y **O** si se trata de lo que la **orquesta** quería. Escribe **X** si es **falsa** para los dos. Hay dos oraciones falsas.

1. ___   3. ___   5. ___   7. ___
2. ___   4. ___   6. ___   8. ___

C. Diego Rivera y los deseos de los demás

PASO 1.   Diego Rivera fue uno de los artistas más famosos en la historia de Latinoamérica. Nació en México en 1886 y vivió en Europa entre 1907 y 1921. Desde su regreso a México hasta su muerte en 1957, fue una figura muy importante en el movimiento muralista mexicano. También es muy conocido por su matrimonio (*marriage*) con la artista mexicana Frida Kahlo.

Completa cada oración con un verbo de la lista en su forma correcta. Luego, adivina si Diego Rivera hizo lo que las personas mencionadas querían. **¡Atención!** Rivera hizo lo que querían en solo cinco de los ocho casos.

cambiar   ir   recrear (*to recreate*)
divorciarse pintar   regresar
estudiar   quedarse

Gustavo Dudamel, el director de la Orquesta Filarmónica de Los Ángeles

■ The audio files for in-text listening activities are available in the eBook, within Connect Plus activities, and on the Online Learning Center.

¿Y LO HIZO?

SÍ   NO

1. 1899: Su papá quería que _____ en una escuela militar por muchos años. □ □
2. 1906: Su maestro de arte en México quería que _____ a Europa a estudiar. □ □
3. 1921: Sus amigos europeos querían que _____ en Europa para siempre. □ □
4. 1921: El gobierno mexicano quería que _____ a su tierra natal (*home country*) a pintar murales. □ □
5. 1932: La familia Rockefeller le pidió que _____ un mural en el Rockefeller Center de Nueva York. □ □
6. 1933: La familia Rockefeller le pidió que _____ el mural porque tenía un retrato (*portrait*) de Lenin, el revolucionario ruso (*Russian*). □ □
7. 1940: El gobierno mexicano le pidió que _____ el mismo mural con el retrato de Lenin en el Palacio de Bellas Artes en México. □ □
8. 1940: Frida Kahlo le pidió que _____ pero volvieron a casarse unos meses después. □ □

Diego Rivera, muralista mexicano

PASO 2.   Siguiendo el modelo del **Paso 1,** completa las siguientes frases con lo que querían los demás que tú hicieras. Luego, di si lo hiciste o no.

¿Y LO HICISTE?

SÍ   NO

1. Cuando me gradué de la escuela secundaria, mis padres querían que yo…. □ □
2. Cuando me gradué de la escuela secundaria, mis amigos esperaban que yo…. □ □
3. Cuando empecé a estudiar en la universidad, mi familia quería que…. □ □
4. Cuando empecé a estudiar en la universidad, mis profesores me recomendaron que…. □ □

D. Antes y ahora

PASO 1. En el pasado, ¿qué tenía uno que hacer para empezar una carrera artística? En parejas, completen las oraciones con uno de los consejos de la lista. **¡Atención!** Tienen que conjugar el verbo del consejo.

> **MODELO:** Si querías ser un buen director de cine, era necesario que tuvieras experiencia con la actuación para entender el proceso de hacer cine.

CONSEJOS:

tomar clases de guitarra clásica para entender mejor su instrumento
poder bailar y cantar al mismo tiempo
cantar otro tipo de música de vez en cuando para relajar la voz
tocar algún instrumento para entender la orquesta mejor
estudiar danza clásica para entender mejor la historia del baile
aprender a dibujar para poder pintar mejor
ir a una escuela de fotografía para entender mejor la técnica de la fotografía

1. Si querías ser una buena guitarrista de rock, era necesario que…
2. Si querías ser un buen cantante de ópera, era recomendable que…
3. Si querías ser una buena directora de orquesta, era importante que…
4. Si querías ser un actor famoso, era fundamental que…
5. Si querías ser una buena bailarina, era esencial que…
6. Si querías ser un buen fotógrafo, era vital que…
7. Si querías ser una buena pintora, era primordial (*fundamental*) que…

PASO 2. Hoy en día, ¿siguen siendo válidos estos consejos? En parejas, cambien las oraciones que escribieron en el **Paso 1** al tiempo presente y decidan si cada consejo es válido todavía.

> **MODELO:** Si quieres ser un buen director de cine, es necesario que tengas experiencia con la actuación para entender el proceso de hacer cine.
> Sí, es válido todavía.

CONÉCTATE AL MUNDO HISPANO

La Escuela Internacional de Cine y TV (EICTV) empezó en 1986 en una zona rural de Cuba llamada San Antonio de los Baños con el propósito de preparar cineastas (*filmmakers*) de todas partes del mundo en estilos *no* hollywoodenses. Cuando la EICTV se estableció, era estrictamente para alumnos de Asia, África y América Latina y ofrecían becas (*scholarships*) a los alumnos. La diversidad multinacional forma una parte integral de la escuela. Los profesores son cineastas internacionales con muchísima experiencia y éxito y a la vez los estudiantes tienen muchas oportunidades de participar en todos los papeles clave (*key*) del proceso creativo: actor, camarógrafo, director, editor, guionista o productor.

⟳ Reciclaje

The infinitive

Aquí hay una conversación entre dos amigos, pero las oraciones están desordenadas. Primero, escribe la terminación correcta para cada infinitivo (**-ar, -er, -ir**). Luego, pon las oraciones en un orden lógico. La primera y la última ya están hechas.

_____ a. ¡Me encantan Los Amigos Invisibles! ¿Por qué no vamos a compr__ ropa nueva para llevar al concierto?

_____ b. ¡Perfecto! A ver si podemos com__ algo rápido antes de lleg__ también. No me gusta asist__ a los conciertos con hambre.

__1__ c. ¿Va a hab__ un concierto en el Teatro Nacional esta noche?

__7__ d. Me parece muy bien. ¡Va a s__ una noche de maravilla!

_____ e. Sí, no te preocupes. El concierto va a empez__ a las nueve.

_____ f. ¡Qué buena idea! Pero si vamos primero a las tiendas, ¿vamos a lleg__ al teatro a tiempo?

_____ g. ¡Sí! Van a toc__ Los Amigos Invisibles y quiero ir, pero no sé qué ropa us__.

■ Answers to this activity are in **Appendix 2** at the back of your book.

14.2   ¿Qué será el «arte cinético»?

The future

Para empezar...

El arte cinético es un movimiento artístico que ha tenido una importancia especial en Sudamérica. El artista Carlos Cruz-Díez es uno de sus exponentes más distinguidos. Para aprender más sobre este arte y este artista, escoge la respuesta más apropiada para cada pregunta en la lista.

■ Answers to these activities are in **Appendix 2** at the back of your book.

PREGUNTAS	RESPUESTAS
1. _____ ¿Qué **será** el «arte cinético»?	a. Vive en París.
2. _____ ¿Quién **será** Carlos Cruz-Díez?	b. Está en Caracas.
3. _____ ¿De dónde **será**?	c. Porque hay varios artistas cinéticos importantes que son de Venezuela.
4. _____ ¿Dónde **vivirá**?	d. Hace pintura, escultura y arquitectura en que el color cambia según la posición del espectador.
5. _____ ¿Qué tipo de arte **hará**?	e. Se refiere al arte que tiene movimiento o que parece tener movimiento.
6. _____ ¿Qué ciudades **tendrán** obras de él?	f. Algunas de las ciudades que tienen obras de él son Caracas, Houston, Londres, Madrid y París.
7. _____ ¿Dónde **estará** el Museo Carlos Cruz-Díez?	g. Es de Venezuela.
8. _____ ¿Por qué **será** tan importante Venezuela en el mundo del arte cinético?	h. Es un artista venezolano que hace arte cinético

Actividades analíticas

1 The verbs in bold in **Para empezar** are in the *future* tense (**el futuro**). Despite its name, this tense is commonly used to express conjectures about what might be true in the present.

| Jaime no ha llegado. **Estará** dormido. | *Jaime hasn't arrived. He might be asleep.* |

The future is particularly common in questions, when one has little idea what the answer is.

¿Dónde **estarán**?	*Where could they be?*
¿Cómo **se llamará** ese hombre?	*What is that man's name? (I really have no idea.)*
¿De dónde **será** Pedro Almodóvar?	*Where on earth is Pedro Almodóvar from?*

The future is also used to express future actions, especially in the written language.

| Mañana **tendrán** el nuevo libro de Isabel Allende. | *They will have the new book by Isabel Allende tomorrow.* |

El director del museo **hablará** en la universidad el próximo año.

The director of the museum will speak at the university next year.

As you saw in **2.4**, the future is also expressed with **ir + a +** *infinitive*.

Vamos a visitar el museo.

We're going to visit the museum.

2 Use the forms you saw in **Para empezar** and the patterns you see here to complete the following conjugations.

	estar	ser	vivir
yo		seré	viviré
tú	estarás		vivirás
él/ella, Ud.		será	vivirá
nosotros/as	estaremos	seremos	
vosotros/as	estaréis	seréis	viviréis
ellos/ellas, Uds.	estarán		vivirán

¿Por qué?

Why is the future tense used to express conjectures? Since future meaning may be expressed so easily in Spanish with **ir + a +** *infinitive*, the future tense itself is left with little purpose to fulfill and as a result, it has taken on the job of expressing conjecture and speculation. This is typical of what happens in languages: As two forms compete for the same meaning, each begins to take on a more specialized usage. **Ir + a +** *infinitive* has become the main way to express the future, and the future tense has come to mean conjecture.

3 The stem for the future consists of the entire infinitive form (in the above chart, **estar-, ser-** and **vivir-**), to which one of the following endings is added.

TERMINACIONES DEL FUTURO	
yo	-é
tú	-ás
él/ella, Ud.	-á
nosotros/as	-emos
vosotros/as	-éis
ellos/ellas, Uds.	-án

4 Several verbs have an irregular stem in the future, but they continue to use the above endings.

VERBO	RAÍZ	EJEMPLO	
decir	**dir-**	¿Qué **dirá** tu mamá?	*What will your mom say?*
haber	**habr-**	¿**Habrá** un museo en la universidad?	*Do you suppose there's a museum at the university?*
hacer	**har-**	**Haré** lo que te prometí.	*I will do what I promised you.*
poder	**podr-**	¿El guitarrista **podrá** cantar también?	*Do you think the guitarist might be able to sing too?*
poner	**pondr-**	Claro que puedes tomar prestado mi libro. Lo **pondré** en tu escritorio.	*Sure you can borrow my book. I'll put it on your desk.*
salir	**saldr-**	¿Cuándo **saldrá** el nuevo disco?	*When will the new record come out?*
tener	**tendr-**	¿**Tendrán** escultura en ese museo?	*Might they have sculpture art at that museum?*
venir	**vendr-**	¿**Vendrá** el pianista también?	*Will the pianist come too?*

■ For more examples of irregular future forms and a look at the future perfect tense, see **Para saber más 14.2** at the back of your book.

Actividades prácticas

A. ¿Qué pasará? Empareja cada pregunta con la respuesta más lógica.

1. _____ ¿Llegaré al concierto?
2. _____ ¿Cuándo saldrá la nueva película de Almodóvar?
3. _____ ¿A tus papás les gustará la pintura que hice?
4. _____ ¿Cantarán los niños en el concierto?
5. _____ ¿Tendrán algo interesante en la galería del centro?
6. _____ ¿Visitaremos el museo de arte moderno mañana?
7. _____ ¿No habrá otra obra de teatro? Esa no me gusta.
8. _____ ¿Podremos pasar un día en Cuzco?

a. ¡Sí, lo vamos a visitar!
b. No, es la única que hay esta noche.
c. Me imagino que sí, porque siempre tienen cosas interesantes.
d. ¡Claro que sí! Vamos a estar un mes en el Perú. ¡Será fabuloso!
e. Me parece que sale en noviembre.
f. Lo siento, pero sinceramente no creo que les guste.
g. Van a estar allí pero no van a cantar.
h. Sí, no hay tráfico.

B. Los países y la cultura En grupos, emparejen cada pregunta con un país o países de la lista.

Argentina	Cuba	México	la República Dominicana
Bolivia/Chile	España	el Perú	

1. ¿En qué país estará el Museo Larco (un museo de arte prehispánico andino)? _____
2. ¿De qué país vendrá el «mambo» (una forma musical que se hizo popular en La Habana en los años treinta)? _____
3. ¿De qué país será la actriz Salma Hayek? _____
4. ¿De dónde vendrá la música merengue? _____
5. ¿En qué país estará el Teatro Colón (un teatro de ópera)? _____
6. ¿Qué país hispano tendrá más películas ganadoras (*winners*) en toda la historia de los premios Óscar? _____
7. ¿En qué países bailarán «la cueca»? _____

C. La cultura en el año 2025

PASO 1. ¿Cómo será el mundo en 2025? En grupos, lean la siguiente lista de oraciones e indiquen si piensan que es **cierta** o **falsa** cada una. **¡Atención!** No hay respuestas correctas o incorrectas. Todo depende de la opinión del grupo.

	CIERTO	FALSO
1. Podremos ir al cine para ver, sentir y oler (*smell*) una película.	☐	☐
2. Comeremos en restaurantes siempre. No comeremos en casa nunca.	☐	☐
3. Solo leeremos libros electrónicos.	☐	☐
4. Iremos a museos y galerías de arte con más frecuencia.	☐	☐
5. Los músicos ya no usarán instrumentos. La música será electrónica.	☐	☐
6. Toda la música estará en inglés.	☐	☐
7. Todas las películas serán de los Estados Unidos.	☐	☐
8. Todavía habrá clases de historia de arte en las universidades.	☐	☐
9. Ya no habrá pinturas tradicionales. Los artistas harán todo en la computadora.	☐	☐
10. Iremos al teatro con más frecuencia.	☐	☐

PASO 2. ¿Cómo será el mundo según tu grupo? Cambien las oraciones falsas para que sean ciertas.

PASO 3. ¿Qué otras predicciones tienen Uds. para las artes en el futuro? Consideren la música, las artes plásticas, el baile, el teatro, el cine, la literatura, la poesía, etcétera. En sus grupos, hagan por lo menos cuatro predicciones más.

D. El futuro de tu país En grupos, creen una predicción sobre la vida en este país en 2050 relacionada con cada categoría de la lista. Según tu grupo, ¿cómo será el futuro de este país?

la cultura   la educación   el medio ambiente   la política   la sociedad   la tecnología

Argentina

E. Cultura: El cine de Argentina

PASO 1. Lee el texto sobre Argentina.

Junto con México y Brasil, Argentina ha tenido una de las industrias cinematográficas[a] más fuertes de Latinoamérica desde finales del siglo XIX. De allí se lanzaron[b] las carreras de algunas de las estrellas más glamurosas del cine hispanohablante. Pero la turbulenta historia política de Argentina tuvo un impacto sobre el cine en varios momentos, no solo en la producción sino en las historias que las películas contaban.

A partir de la década de los 30, cuando empezó la producción de cine sonoro,[c] se produjeron en Argentina grandes películas musicales, comedias y dramas. Libertad Lamarque es, quizás, la actriz más conocida de esta época. En los años 40, bajo la presidencia de Juan Perón, se incrementó bastante la censura.[d] Esto, combinado con la importación de las películas de Hollywood, tuvo un impacto negativo sobre la industria de cine. A partir de los años 1960, se empezó un movimiento de cine de fuerte compromiso[e] político, el que luego se conoció como «el Tercer Cine». Los directores de este movimiento declaraban que en Latinoamérica se debía de reconocer sus condiciones de «tercer mundo» y hacer películas que reflejaban su propia realidad. La película emblemática del movimiento es *La hora de los hornos*[f] (1968), dirigida por Octavio Getino y Fernando Solanas, y funcionaba como un manifiesto audiovisual en contra del imperialismo cultural de los Estados Unidos y Europa.

Después de que terminó la dictadura militar y se disminuyó[g] la censura, se produjo un gran número de películas que contaba las historias traumáticas de aquellos años. Películas como *La historia oficial* (1985) y *La noche de los lápices* (1986) hicieron que los eventos políticos de los años 70 se conocieran en todo el mundo. A partir de los años 90, el cine argentino se transformó, en cierta manera rechazando[h] tantos años de cine político. Los jóvenes cineastas querían contar historias sobre la vida cotidiana,[i] con una cámara que observaba a sus personajes en vez de juzgarlos.[j] Esta nueva tradición, conocida como «el Nuevo Cine Argentino», ha atraído la atención de públicos[k] en todo el mundo, en particular en festivales internacionales. Directores como Lucrecia Martel (*La niña santa, La mujer sin cabeza*) y Pablo Trapero (*El bonaerense, Elefante blanco*) están entre los más representativos de esta generación. Sus películas se caracterizan por su realismo, con observaciones agudas[l] sobre el estado de la sociedad argentina en los tiempos actuales.[m]

[a]*film (adj.)* [b]*se… were launched* [c]*sound (adj.)* [d]*censorship* [e]*engagement, commitment* [f]*furnaces* [g]*decreased* [h]*rejecting* [i]*daily* [j]*en… instead of judging them* [k]*audiences* [l]*sharp, acute* [m]*current, present-day*

PASO 2. Completa las oraciones con la forma correcta del futuro simple usando los verbos de la lista. Luego, indica las oraciones lógicas según la lectura y lo que sabes.

haber   ir   obtener   poder   poner   tener   ver   volver

Durante los próximos diez años…   **¿ES LÓGICO?**

1. los argentinos _____ más películas chinas que norteamericanas. ☐
2. los directores argentinos _____ muchos premios (*awards*) más en los festivales internacionales. ☐
3. la censura _____ a controlar los medios de comunicación del país. ☐
4. cualquier argentino _____ hacer una película, sin mucho dinero, con solo un teléfono celular y una computadora portátil. ☐
5. las películas _____ más énfasis en los efectos especiales que en sus historias. ☐
6. los actores argentinos _____ los salarios más altos de todo el mundo. ☐
7. mis amigos y yo _____ al cine para ver una película del Nuevo Cine Argentino. ☐
8. _____ un homenaje a Libertad Lamarque durante la presentación de los Premios Óscar en los Estados Unidos. ☐

PASO 3. En parejas, contesten las preguntas y explíquense las respuestas.

1. Entre los países hispanos, Argentina, España y México son de los más ricos. ¿Qué relación ves entre eso y el hecho de que también son los países hispanos que tienen la industria cinematográfica más fuerte?
2. Para los países hispanos que son chicos y no tienen muchos recursos, es difícil crear una industria cinematográfica y competir contra países como Argentina. ¿Qué países piensas que están en esa situación?
3. La industria cinematográfica en Estados Unidos es grandísima y es difícil que películas de otros países penetren el mercado norteamericano. Sin embargo, ¿hay películas de países hispanos que lo han podido hacer?

¡Leamos!

«La princesa azul» por Juan Luis Sánchez

Antes de leer

La actriz Zoe Saldana

PASO 1. Zoe Saldana es una estrella de cine bilingüe que nació en Nueva Jersey de un padre dominicano y una madre puertorriqueña. Es conocida por su sus papeles en películas como *Star Trek, Avatar* y *Piratas del Caribe*. Vas a leer un artículo sobre Saldana, pero primero, trata de poner los datos de su vida en orden cronológico (del 1 a 5).

a. _____ A los nueve años, se mudó a la República Dominicana.

b. _____ La reclutó (*recruited*) una agencia de talentos.

c. _____ Nació en Nueva Jersey en 1978.

d. _____ Participó en un programa para jóvenes interesados por la interpretación.

e. _____ Se hizo estrella con el papel de Na'vi Neytiri en *Avatar*.

PASO 2. A veces las traducciones (*translations*) de los títulos de las películas parecen mucho a los títulos originales, pero otras veces usan juegos de palabras (*plays on words*) que no se traducen bien a otro idioma. Por eso, tienen que cambiarlos un poco (o por completo) para presentar la película en otro país. Empareja el título de cada película de Zoe Saldana en español con el título correspondiente en inglés.

1. _____ *Adivina quién*
2. _____ *Guardianes de la galaxia*
3. _____ *Un funeral de muerte*
4. _____ *Ladrones*
5. _____ *El ladrón de palabras*
6. _____ *Piratas del Caribe: La maldición de la Perla Negra*
7. _____ *El ritmo del éxito*
8. _____ *La terminal*

a. *Center Stage*
b. *Death at a Funeral*
c. *Guess Who*
d. *The Words*
e. *Pirates of the Caribbean: The Curse of the Black Pearl*
f. *Takers*
g. *The Terminal*
h. *Guardians of the Galaxy*

 PASO 3. En grupos, describan qué pasa en una o más de las películas de Zoe Saldana y expliquen el papel de la actriz. Luego, compartan la información con el resto de la clase.

Adivina quién	*En el punto de mira*	*Piratas del Caribe*
Avatar	*Un funeral de muerte*	*El ritmo del éxito*
Burning Palms	*Ladrones*	*Star Trek*
Crossroads	*Los perdedores*	*La terminal*

A leer

PASO 1.   Lee el artículo sobre la actriz Zoe Saldana.

La princesa azul

No deja de[a] resultar paradójico que la protagonista de la película más taquillera[b] de la historia no se haya convertido en la gran megaestrella del momento. Pero nadie pudo ver en *Avatar* su rostro[c] porque su interpretación de la princesa azul Na'vi Neytiri fue digitalizada y retocada[d] por ordenador.[e] Aun así, Zoe Saldana empieza a ser reconocida, y se perfila[f] como una de las grandes para los próximos años. Extremadamente atractiva, transmite sencillez y simpatía.

Zoe Yadira Saldaña Nazario nació el 19 de junio de 1978, en Nueva Jersey (Estados Unidos), pero su madre era puertorriqueña y su padre dominicano. Cuando tenía 9 años, su progenitor[g] falleció[h] en accidente de tráfico, y su madre decidió trasladarse a la República Dominicana con Zoe y sus hermanas. […]

En la República Dominicana, Zoe Saldaña se apuntó[i] a clases de danza. Al regresar a los Estados Unidos a los 17 años, decidió participar en un programa llamado *Face Theater,* para jóvenes interesados por la interpretación, y descubrió que no se le daba nada mal.[j] Junto con sus compañeros, representaba obras para concienciar[k] a los adolescentes de los riesgos del uso de las drogas y otros temas de interés, pero ella demostraba un talento fuera de lo común. De hecho, antes de acabar fue reclutada por una agencia de talentos, que le consiguió un pequeño papel en un episodio de *Ley y orden.*

Poco después, aprovechó sus dotes[l] para la danza para hacerse con el papel de la talentosa bailarina Eva, una de las protagonistas de *El ritmo del éxito.* Desde entonces no le ha faltado trabajo en títulos como *Crossroads (hasta el final),* protagonizada por Britney Spears, aunque llamó especialmente la atención como la pirata Anamaría, en *Piratas del Caribe: La maldición de la Perla Negra,* donde le daba una bofetada[m] a Jack Sparrow, el personaje interpretado por Johnny Depp. Su apellido artístico es Saldana, no Saldaña, para no confundir a los angloparlantes.[n]

«Mi madre y yo éramos muy aficionadas al cine cuando yo era pequeña. Siempre veíamos películas de grandes directores como Spielberg, que para mí era muy lejano. Nunca soñé que trabajaría con él», me confesaba en la entrevista Saldana. La actriz aún no acaba de creerse los elogios[ñ] que le dedicó Steven Spielberg, muy satisfecho con su trabajo, tras reclutarla para interpretar a la agente de aduanas Dolores Torres, que le niega continuamente el permiso para pasar al personaje de Tom Hanks, en *La terminal.*

Tras sus trabajos en la comedia *Adivina quién* y el thriller *En el punto de mira,* a Saldana le llegó una gran oportunidad de la mano de J.J. Abrams, que necesitaba a una joven actriz para interpretar a Uhura, una de las protagonistas de *Star Trek* […].

El film fue un gran éxito, pero no tanto como *Avatar,* de James Cameron, un auténtico fenómeno de masas en el que Saldana interpretaba a la protagonista, la Na'vi que encandilaba[o] al personaje de Sam Worthington. Aunque preparó su papel durante seis meses, y la voz es la suya, sus movimientos fueron digitalizados, y su personaje recreado por ordenador.

Ahora que empieza a convertirse en una estrella, el futuro de Zoe Saldana no puede ser más prometedor.[p] Tras interpretar a la chica que le da una droga a su novio por error, en el remake americano de *Un funeral de muerte,* ha protagonizado la cinta de acción *Los perdedores,* la comedia dramática *Burning Palms,* y el thriller *Ladrones.* No tardarán en caer también las secuelas[q] de *Avatar* y *Star Trek.*

[a]*deja... to stop* [b]*box office success* [c]*face* [d]*retouched* [e]*computer* [f]*se... is shaping up* [g]*father* [h]*died* [i]*se... enrolled* [j]*no... she didn't find it at all bad* [k]*to make aware* [l]*talents* [m]*a slap* [n]*English-speakers* [ñ]*praises* [o]*dazzled* [p]*promising* [q]*sequels*

PASO 2.   Según lo que leíste sobre la vida de Zoe Saldana, contesta las siguientes preguntas.

1. ¿Por qué no vio nadie la cara de Zoe Saldana en la película *Avatar*?
2. ¿De dónde son los padres de Zoe Saldana?
3. ¿Por qué se mudó (*move*) a la República Dominicana?
4. ¿Cuál fue la primera pasión artística de Zoe Saldana?
5. ¿En qué año volvió a vivir en los Estados Unidos?
6. ¿Cuál fue su primer papel después de ser reclutada por una agencia de talentos?
7. ¿Por qué usa el apellido artístico «Saldana» en vez de su apellido verdadero, «Saldaña»?
8. Describe la relación entre Zoe Saldana y Stephen Spielberg.
9. Además de Stephen Spielberg, ¿con quiénes ha trabajado Zoe Saldana?

Después de leer

En parejas, hagan predicciones sobre el futuro de Zoe Saldana. ¿Cuál es la mejor predicción?

MODELO: Será la estrella de *Avatar 3, 4* y *5.* Tendrá mucho éxito y ganará un Premio Óscar.

¡Escuchemos!

La cultura que nos rodea°

nos... *surrounds us*

Antes de escuchar

Haz una lista de cuatro o cinco lugares culturales destacados (*renowned*) de tu ciudad o país. Luego, escoge uno de los lugares de la lista y prepara una descripción del lugar para un turista de habla hispana. Describe el lugar, lo que lo hace famoso y una recomendación para el turista.

> **MODELO:** El museo Smithsonian es un museo de historia natural grande y famoso. Está en una zona de muchos museos en la ciudad capital de los Estados Unidos, Wáshington, D.C. Recomiendo que visites la colección de joyería (*jewelry*) y, en especial, el diamante Hope.

A escuchar

PASO 1. Mira y escucha mientras las personas describen algunos lugares famosos de sus países. Empareja cada persona con el lugar que describe.

1. _____

Benedicto, de Costa Rica

2. _____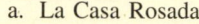

Paul, de Panamá

a. La Casa Rosada
b. El Centro Cultural de Morelos
c. El Centro de Visitantes del Canal de Panamá
d. El Museo del Prado
e. El Parque Zarcero

3. _____

Jorge, de Argentina

4. _____

Almudena, de España

5. _____

José Manuel, de México

PASO 2. Contesta las preguntas.

1. ¿Qué era el Parque Zarcero antes de ser parque?
2. ¿Cuándo fue inaugurado el Centro de Visitantes del Canal de Panamá?
3. ¿Cuál es la función de la Casa Rosada en Buenos Aires?
4. ¿Qué tipo de museo es el Museo del Prado?
5. ¿Cómo se llama el Centro Cultural de Morelos?

Después de escuchar

En grupos pequeños, escojan un lugar del video que quisieran visitar y expliquen por qué. Luego, describan el lugar que escogieron al resto de la clase.

¡Escribamos!

Dos lugares famosos

Una manera excelente de entender un lugar que no conoces es por medio de una comparación con un lugar que ya conoces bien. Para describir un lugar que conoces bien en tu propio país vas a necesitar nuevo vocabulario en español.

Antes de escribir

Escoge un lugar mencionado en **¡Escuchemos!** (u otro lugar del cual has leído hasta ahora en *Conéctate*) y un lugar de tu país. Toma apuntes de los dos lugares en la tabla. Haz una lista del vocabulario que vas a buscar en un diccionario.

	Un lugar de ¡Escuchemos!	**Un lugar de mi país**
¿Qué es?	*La Casa Rosada, casa de gobierno*	*la Casa Blanca, casa de _____*
¿Dónde está?		
¿Cómo es?		
¿Qué se puede hacer allí?		
Una recomendación/ sugerencia		
Vocabulario nuevo que necesito		*president, obelisk, diplomats*

A escribir

Usando la información de la tabla, escribe tres párrafos. En el primero, describe los dos lugares; luego, describe lo que tienen en común y las diferencias entre los dos lugares; termina con un párrafo que describe la visita que hará un turista que va a un lugar de tu país.

 ### Después de escribir

Revisa tu ensayo. Luego, intercambia ensayos con un compañero / una compañera para evaluarlos.

☐ ¿Ha usado tu compañero/a el diccionario bien para buscar e incorporar palabras? (Busca en un diccionario español cualquier palabra que te sea nueva. ¿Se entiende la palabra que ha escrito tu compañero/a?)

☐ ¿Hay concordancia de género y de número entre sustantivos y adjetivos?

☐ ¿Están bien escritas las comparaciones?

☐ ¿Hay concordancia entre sujetos y verbos?

☐ ¿Están bien escritos los usos del futuro? ¿Usa bien los verbos regulares y también los irregulares?

Después de revisar el ensayo de tu compañero/a, devuélveselo. Mira tu propio ensayo para ver los cambios que tu compañero/a te recomienda y haz las revisiones necesarias.

¡Hablemos!

Nuestros gustos musicales

Antes de hablar

PASO 1.   Nombra todos los géneros de música que puedas. Luego, toma unos minutos para pensar en un(a) artista o una banda que representa cada tipo de música que nombraste.

PASO 2.   En grupos pequeños, compartan sus ejemplos de música y músicos conocidos. ¿Pensaron Uds. en los mismos géneros y artistas? **¡Atención!** Si resulta que el resto del grupo no reconoce uno de los artistas que nombraste, explícale quién es, dándole todos los detalles que puedas.

A hablar

En sus grupos, respondan a las siguientes preguntas.

1. De todos los géneros de música, ¿cuáles son los que más les gustan a Uds.? ¿Por qué? ¿Qué tipo de música no les gusta? ¿Por qué? ¿Cuáles son sus grupos preferidos? ¿Y sus cantantes o músicos preferidos?

2. ¿Han cambiado sus preferencias musicales desde cuando eran más jóvenes? ¿Cuáles eran los grupos de música que más escuchaban Uds. de niños? Cuando eran adolescentes, ¿permitían sus padres que Uds. compraran la música que les gustaba? ¿O insistían ellos en que Uds. la escucharan gratis (*free*) en la radio o en Internet?

3. ¿Cómo escuchan Uds. su música preferida hoy en día? ¿La compran? Si usan un sitio web para escuchar la música, ¿qué sitio es? ¿Por qué prefieren ese sitio?

4. ¿Tienen Uds. discos compactos? ¿Tienen discos (*records*)? ¿casetes? ¿canciones digitales que descargaron del Internet? ¿Qué formato prefieren y por qué?

Después de hablar

Ahora que han hablado de cómo la venta (*sales*) de música y las preferencias de Uds. han cambiado durante su vida, compartan sus predicciones para el futuro. ¿Todavía se venderán los discos compactos en el año 2025? ¿Cómo compraremos la música? ¿Qué tipos de música serán populares? ¿Cómo escucharemos la música?

CONÉCTATE AL MUNDO HISPANO

La música salsa tiene una larga tradición, pero el término «salsa» es de origen relativamente reciente. Se empezó a usar en Nueva York en los años setenta para referirse a la música afrocubana, un género que incorpora el mambo, el chachachá, la rumba y otros estilos. Se caracteriza por un ritmo muy bailable y el uso de instrumentos como el piano, el bajo (*bass*), la trompeta, la conga, las claves y las maracas. La música salsa se ha hecho famosa en el mundo entero, gracias a la cubana Celia Cruz, el panameño Rubén Blades y los norteamericanos Tito Puente y Marc Anthony (los dos de padres puertorriqueños), entre muchos otros. En general, se distingue entre la salsa, con sus raíces afrocubanas, y otros estilos bailables, como el merengue, de origen dominicano, y la cumbia, de origen colombiano. Aunque cada estilo es asociado a una región en particular, todos son populares en todo el mundo hispano.

Conéctate al cine

Película: *También la lluvia* (drama, Bolivia/España/México/Francia 2010)
Directora: Icíar Bollaín

Sinopsis:

Sebastián es un director de cine mexicano y Costa es su productor español. Los dos van a Cochabamba, Bolivia, acompañados por un equipo técnico (*production crew*), para filmar una película sobre la llegada (*arrival*) de Cristóbal Colón a América y el inicio (*beginning*) de la Conquista española de las civilizaciones prehispánicas. Sin embargo, su rodaje (*film shoot*) se complica cuando se encuentran en medio de unas violentas protestas políticas en contra de (*against*) la privatización del agua en Bolivia.

Escena (Netflix, 00:40:50 to 00:47:42):

Mientras que el equipo técnico va en camino (*is on its way*) al lugar del rodaje, Sebastián lee el guion e imagina la escena que van a rodar. Luego, Sebastián y el actor Daniel, cuyo (*whose*) personaje se llama Hatuey, tratan de (*try to*) explicar una escena difícil a las actrices.

Antes de ver

Sebastián está muy serio cuando va en camino al rodaje. Para ti, ¿qué sería (*would be*) lo más difícil de hacer una película? Indica las tres cosas más difíciles y explica por qué.

_____ construir la escenografía (*set*)   _____ encontrar el financiamiento

_____ dirigir a los actores   _____ encontrar un buen equipo técnico

_____ editar la película   _____ escribir la historia

_____

A ver

PASO 1.   Lee las **Expresiones útiles** y luego lee las oraciones del **Paso 2** para que sepas a qué información debes prestar más atención. Cuando estés listo/a, ve el video.

PASO 2.   Completa las oraciones con las palabras de la lista. Conjuga los verbos cuando sea necesario y usa el artículo definido cuando sea necesario.

equipo técnico	género	interpretar	protagonista
filmar	guion	papel	tener

1. Daniel _____ el papel de Hatuey, el líder de la rebeldía en contra de los conquistadores en la isla Española.

2. _____ que escribió Sebastián está basado en hechos reales.

3. Se puede describir _____ de la película de Sebastián como un drama de ficción histórica.

4. _____ espera mientras que Daniel y Sebastián les explican la escena a las actrices.

5. En esta escena se entiende que no es fácil dirigir una película; es necesario que _____ mucha paciencia y que puedas comunicarte bien con los actores.

6. Aunque Cristóbal Colón es _____ de la película, la gente indígena que resistió la Conquista tiene un _____ igual de importante en la historia.

7. Sebastián no puede _____ la toma que planeó porque las madres bolivianas no quieren simular el acto de ahogar a sus hijos.

Después de ver

En parejas, túrnense para hacerse y responder a las siguientes preguntas.

1. ¿Cómo es que sentimos emociones al ver una película aunque sabemos que no es real?

2. ¿Qué género de películas te provoca más emoción? ¿Qué tipo de emoción te provoca? ¿Por qué crees que te afecta tanto ese género de película?

3. ¿Crees que las emociones que un buen actor o una buena actriz siente durante su actuación son iguales o similares a lo que una persona de la vida real siente en las mismas circunstancias? ¿Por qué sí o no?

Expresiones útiles

desgarradora	heartbreaking
soportar	to stand; to bear
todas juntas	all together
justamente	precisely
sumergen	(you, *pl.*) submerge
ahogan	(you, *pl.*) drown
la primera toma	the first shot
la cintura	waist
paramos	we stop
los muñecos	dolls
intercambiamos	we switch
seguro	safe
mojar	to get wet
lograr que lo hagan	get them to do it

■ For copyright reasons, the feature-film clips referenced in **Conéctate al cine** have not been provided by the publisher. Each of these films is readily available through retailers or online rental sites such as Amazon, iTunes, or Netflix.

VOCABULARIO

Comunicación

para nada	not at all
Quisiera...	I would like . . .
Quisiera + *inf.*	I would like (*to do something*)
quizá(s)	maybe, perhaps
sin duda (alguna)	without (any) doubt
tal vez	maybe, perhaps

Los sustantivos

el actor / la actriz	actor/actress
el arte (*but* las artes)	art
el/la artista	artist
el bailarín / la bailarina	dancer
el baile	dance
el/la cantante	singer
la danza	dance
el/la escritor(a)	writer
la escultura	sculpture
la estrella	star
el género	genre, type
la obra	piece; work
la obra de arte	piece/work of art
la obra de teatro	play

el papel	role, part (*in a movie or play*)
el personaje	character (*in a movie, play or novel*); celebrity, well-known person
el/la pintor(a)	painter
la pintura	painting
la poesía	poetry
el/la protagonista	main character, protagonist
el teatro	theater

Cognados: la banda, el concierto, el/la fotógrafo/a, la literatura, la ópera, la orquesta

Los adjetivos

Cognados: alternativo/a, clásico/a, folclórico/a, histórico/a, pop, rock

Los verbos

actuar (actúo)	to act
componer (like poner)	to compose
dirigir (dirijo)	to direct
interpretar (un papel)	to play (a role/part)

Si la vida fuera diferente...

Los miembros del Tribunal (*Court*) Supremo Electoral en El Salvador empiezan a recontar los votos en una elección federal.

TSE TRIBUNAL SUPREMO ELECTORAL
PAPELETAS
ELECCIÓN PRESIDENCIAL 2014

Objetivos

In this chapter you will learn how to:

- express your opinions and beliefs
- talk about what you and others know and don't know
- discuss important social issues
- describe hypothetical situations
- explore social issues from Latin American and Spanish perspectives

15

En mi opinión...

Expressing opinions

A. A ver: Los problemas más graves

PASO 1. Pon los siguientes temas en orden de más importante (1) a menos importante (7), según tus opiniones.

_____ los conflictos y la seguridad internacionales

_____ la contaminación del medio ambiente

_____ la corrupción de los políticos

_____ la educación

_____ la falta (*lack*) de recursos naturales

_____ la pobreza (*poverty*) y el hambre (*hunger*)

_____ el terrorismo

PASO 2. Mira y escucha las respuestas a la pregunta «"¿Cuál sería el problema más fuerte que enfrenta su país?» Luego, empareja cada frase con la persona que la diría (*would say*).

1. _____ Marlén, de México

2. _____ Felicitas, de Argentina

3. _____ Juan Andrés, de Costa Rica

4. _____ Pamela, de Argentina

5. _____ Bertha, de Miami

6. _____ Daniel, del Perú

7. _____ Mariana, de Costa Rica

a. «Para mí, sin educación universal, la sociedad no puede progresar.»

b. «En mi opinión, con los políticos corruptos, es difícil tener un gobierno funcional.»

c. «Para mí, el terrorismo es el problema más grave al que nos enfrentamos porque es un problema internacional.»

d. «Creo que la falta de recursos naturales es el problema más fuerte porque afecta a todos los humanos.»

e. «Estoy de acuerdo con los activistas ecológicos. Ellos dicen que si no tenemos conciencia del medio ambiente, vamos a destruir nuestro planeta.»

f. «Para mí, si no hay seguridad, siempre se tiene que andar con precaución y no se puede estar tranquilo en su propia casa.»

g. «Creo que lo peor (*the worst thing*) es ver a la gente que sufre del hambre a causa de la pobreza.»

PASO 3. Mira y escucha otra vez. Según las opiniones de las personas que hablan, ¿por qué es importante resolver los problemas que describen?

1. _____ Sin resolver el problema de la corrupción política,...

2. _____ Sin mejorar (*improving*) la educación,...

3. _____ Sin programas de ecoturismo y reciclaje,...

4. _____ Sin resolver el problema de la pobreza,...

5. _____ Sin resolver el problema del terrorismo,...

6. _____ Sin resolver el problema del uso excesivo del agua,...

7. _____ Sin resolver el problema de la seguridad,...

a. las futuras generaciones no podrán aprender a mejorar su situación.

b. la gente siempre estará muy preocupada.

c. habrá muchísima contaminación del medio ambiente.

d. habrá muchísima más hambre.

e. los niños no podrán salir a jugar tranquilos.

f. el país no va a poder salir adelante.

g. va a costar más el agua que la gasolina.

To express your beliefs and opinions, you can use the following phrases.

Para mí…	For me (personally) . . .
En mi opinión…	In my opinion . . .
Creo que…	I believe (that) . . .
Para mí, el medio ambiente es importante.	For me, the environment is important.
En mi opinión, el terrorismo es el problema más grave del mundo actual.	In my opinion, terrorism is the most serious problem in the world today.
Creo que muchos políticos son corruptos.	I think many politicians are corrupt.

Un basurero (*dump*) típico

 B. Algunos problemas sociales y nuestras predicciones Completa las siguientes oraciones con tus propias predicciones si las siguientes cosas (no) ocurren. Luego, comparte tus respuestas con un compañero / una compañera de clase y comparen sus predicciones.

MODELO: Creo que si no nos dedicamos a reciclar más,… → será terrible porque los basureros se llenarán de tanta basura

1. En mi opinión, si no reducimos nuestra dependencia de los combustibles (*fuels*) fósiles,…
2. Para mí, si no paramos (*stop*) la tala (*felling*) de árboles en las selvas y en el campo,…
3. Creo que si el seguro (*insurance*) médico no está disponible (*available*) para todos,…
4. En mi opinión, si no exploramos maneras diferentes de cultivar y producir la comida,…
5. Pienso que si todos continuamos a conducir nuestros coches en vez de usar el transporte público,…

C. Entrevistas: El problema más grave de este país

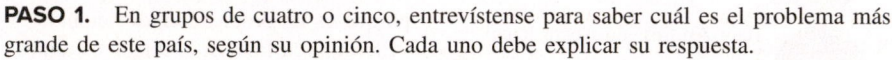

PASO 1. En grupos de cuatro o cinco, entrevístense para saber cuál es el problema más grande de este país, según su opinión. Cada uno debe explicar su respuesta.

MODELO: E1: Para ti, ¿cuál es el problema más grave que nos enfrentamos?
E2: Creo que la pobreza es el problema más grave. Hay muchos problemas económicos.

PASO 2. Responde a las siguientes preguntas basándote en las respuestas que dieron tus compañeros de clase en el **Paso 1.**

Según la mayoría, ¿cuál es el problema más grave hoy en día? ¿Estás de acuerdo con ellos? ¿Por qué sí o no? ¿Te sorprenden las ideas de tus compañeros de clase?

D. ¿Cuál es tu opinión en cuanto a las noticias?

PASO 1. ¿Lees o ves las noticias en Internet, en el periódico de la universidad, en la radio, en la televisión o en otras fuentes (*sources*)? ¿Cuáles son los eventos más importantes y comentados últimamente? Lee la lista de noticias típicas y luego apunta un ejemplo específico que has escuchado o leído de dos a cinco de ellas.

- un escándalo entre políticos
- un debate sobre el presupuesto (*budget*) en el Congreso
- una celebridad o un(a) atleta con problemas personales
- una nueva ley de tu ciudad, estado o país
- protestas contra el gobierno en otro país
- un nuevo descubrimiento científico
- un desastre natural que ocurrió o va a ocurrir

 PASO 2. En grupos, túrnense para describir una noticia que apuntaron en el **Paso 1.** Soliciten las opiniones de los otros miembros del grupo.

MODELO: E1: ¿Sabes que hay un nuevo escándalo político en Washington? ¿Cuál es tu opinión del escándalo?
E2: ¡Qué difícil! Creo que ese político debe renunciara (*resign from*) su puesto.
E3: No creo que sea nada grave. Para mí, es importante que tengamos confianza en nuestros representantes elegidos.

¿Qué sé yo?

Expressing what you know and don't know

To talk about what you and others know and what you don't know, you can use one of the following expressions.

Dejarle saber...	To let someone know . . .
¿Qué sé yo? / ¿Yo qué sé?	What do I know?, Beats me!
Que yo sepa...	That I know of . . . / As far as I know . . .
¿Quién sabe?	Who knows?
sin saber	without knowing/realizing (*that is, by coincidence or by accident*)
el/la sabelotodo	know-it-all
Ve tú / Vaya Ud. a saber.	Your guess is as good as mine.
¡Ay, lo siento! Lo hice **sin saber** lo que hacía.	*I'm so sorry! I did it without knowing/ realizing what I was doing.*
Que yo sepa Miguel no ha regresado de su viaje.	*As far as I know Miguel returned from his trip.*
Déjame saber si te puedo ayudar en algo.	*Let me know if I can help you with something.*

A. ¿Quién sabe?

PASO 1. Para cada tema, indica si es algo que ocurre **sin saber** o **a propósito** (*on purpose*).

OCURRE(N)...	SIN SABER	A PROPÓSITO
1. los conflictos armados internacionales	☐	☐
2. la contaminación del medio ambiente	☐	☐
3. la educación universal	☐	☐
4. las elecciones democráticas	☐	☐
5. la falta de agua limpia	☐	☐
6. el hambre	☐	☐
7. el precio de la gasolina	☐	☐
8. el terrorismo	☐	☐

PASO 2. Con una pareja, para cada tema del **Paso 1,** indica tu nivel de conocimiento (*level of knowledge*), de un conocimiento mínimo (**¿Qué sé yo? / ¿Yo qué sé?**) a uno amplio (**¡Soy un(a) sabelotodo!**).

```
3 ── ¡Soy un(a) sabelotodo!

2 ── Sé bastante.

1 ── ¿Qué sé yo? / ¿Yo qué sé? / No tengo el menor interés.
```

PASO 3. En parejas, entrevístense para saber cuánto saben Uds. de cinco temas globales. Pueden escoger entre los temas del **Paso 1** y los de la lista que sigue. ¿Quién es el sabelotodo del tema? ¿Quién(es) no tiene(n) el menor interés?

TEMAS ADICIONALES: el analfabetismo (*illiteracy*), la corrupción política, la crisis económica, la deuda (*debt*) externa, la pobreza, los problemas sociales relacionados con el racismo, el sistema penal (de prisiones), las violaciones de los derechos (*rights*) humanos

MODELO: E1: ¿Cuánto sabes de la participación de este país en los conflictos armados internacionales?

E2: **Que yo sepa**, el país participa menos y menos en conflictos armados internacionales.

Los problemas sociales, económicos y políticos

Social, economic, and political issues

A. Qué quieren hacer las organizaciones sin fines de lucro (*nonprofit*)?

PASO 1.   Empareja las citas (*quotes*) de los directores de varias organizaciones con las misiones correspondientes.

1. ⟨⟩

> Queremos pasar de **la corrupción** política del pasado a **la democracia.** La gente tiene que participar en **el proceso político.** Es importante tener la oportunidad de **votar** en **las elecciones** democráticas y tener elecciones **justas** (*fair*).

2.

> Para ayudar a la gente más pobre y sin trabajo, podemos alcanzar (*reach*) mucho al **nivel** (*level*) «micro». Estamos hablando no solo de microfinanzas sino también de microempresas y microproductos. Así vamos a **cambiar** (*change*) la base del sistema económico para que no dependamos del dinero de otros países.

3.

> Las organizaciones tradicionales como la Cruz Roja le dan provisiones a la gente necesitada; nosotros queremos colaborar con la gente en las zonas afectadas para que use los materiales donados para **desarrollar** (*develop*) **la infraestructura** sostenible a largo plazo (*over the long-term*).

4.

> La falta de educación es el mayor factor en **la violencia** a nivel mundial. Tenemos que trabajar con las comunidades locales para construir escuelas y educar a los niños en vez de (*instead of*) dejar que participen en **el crimen** (como, por ejemplo, **el narcotráfico**). Queremos ver la educación universal —tanto para niñas como niños— en todos los países del mundo.

5.

> Debemos combatir **los problemas sociales** relacionados con **el racismo.** Lo vemos con las poblaciones indígenas en casi todos los países. También es común en cuanto a los obreros mal pagados que salen de su propio país para hacer los trabajos más **peligrosos** (*dangerous*) en otro país.

6.

> Queremos acabar con **la guerra** (conflicto armado) entre estados y entre grupos dentro del mismo país, pero también vemos la necesidad de proteger los **derechos humanos** más básicos.

La misión es:

a. **Acabar con** (*Put an end to*) **la discriminación** contra **los indígenas** e **inmigrantes** que cruzan **las fronteras** (*borders*) internacionales para trabajar.

b. Acabar con **la tiranía** y **la dictadura** (*dictatorship*) a través de un proceso democrático.

c. Combatir **el analfabetismo, la esclavitud infantil** (*child slavery*) y **la violencia** a través de **la alfabetización** universal para que todos los niños del mundo sepan leer y escribir.

d. **Mejorar** (*Improve*) la situación internacional de **la pobreza, el desempleo** (*unemployment*) y **la desigualdad** (*inequality*) **económica** a través de programas de microfinanzas y al hacer esto evitar **la deuda externa** y **una crisis económica.**

e. Promover (*Promote*) **la paz** (*peace*) en todas sus formas.

f. Proveer (*Provide*) ayuda sostenible que desarrolle infraestructuras para que no haya tanta necesidad en el momento de **un desastre natural** como, por ejemplo, **una inundación** de agua como resultado de un huracán.

PASO 2. Ahora, empareja cada término con su antónimo.

1. _____ la alfabetización
2. _____ el hambre
3. _____ la igualdad
4. _____ **la libertad**
5. _____ **la oferta**
6. _____ la paz
7. _____ la riqueza
8. _____ **la seguridad**
9. _____ la solución

   a. la pobreza
   b. comer en exceso
   c. la demanda
   d. la desigualdad
   e. la esclavitud
   f. la guerra
   g. el peligro (*danger*)
   h. el analfabetismo
   i. el problema

B. A ver: Cada país tiene sus problemas

PASO 1. ¿De qué problemas hablan? Mira y escucha el video, luego indica todos los tipos de problemas que le preocupan a cada persona.

		PROBLEMAS POLÍTICOS	PROBLEMAS ECONÓMICOS	PROBLEMAS SOCIALES
1.	 Jama, de Cuba	☐	☑	☑
2.	 Perla, de Argentina	☐	☑	☐
3.	 Juan, de Argentina	☑	☑	☐
4.	 Mayra, de Costa Rica	☐	☐	☑
5.	 Gabriel, de Argentina	☑	☐	☑
6.	 Eduardo, de España	☑	☑	☐
7.	 Benedicto, de Costa Rica	☐	☐	☑

PASO 2. Mira y escucha otra vez. Luego, basándote en lo que dice cada persona, escoge el término al que **no** se refiere ni se puede inferir.

1. Jama
   ☐ la pobreza   ☐ la esclavitud infantil   ☐ la crisis económica   ☐ los problemas sociales

2. Perla
   ☐ la crisis económica   ☐ la desigualdad económica   ☐ la deuda externa   ☐ la inundación

3. Juan
   ☐ el analfabetismo   ☐ la crisis económica   ☐ la desigualdad económica
   ☐ la situación política

4. Mayra
   ☐ la contaminación   ☐ la delincuencia   ☐ la paz   ☐ la seguridad

5. Gabriel
   ☐ la deuda externa   ☐ la pobreza infantil   ☐ el hambre   ☐ la pobreza

6. Eduardo
   ☐ el analfabetismo   ☐ los problemas económicos   ☐ los problemas políticos
   ☐ los problemas sociales

7. Benedicto
   ☐ la contaminación   ☐ el hambre   ☐ la inseguridad   ☐ todo el mundo

C. ¿Cuál sería (*would be*) el problema?

PASO 1. En parejas, indiquen cuáles serían los problemas que llevan a las siguientes conclusiones. Luego, comparen sus respuestas con otra pareja. ¿Están de acuerdo?

> **MODELO:** «En nuestra comunidad, necesitamos más escuelas y maestros cualificados.»
> El problema sería el analfabetismo. (Los problemas serían el analfabetismo y la falta de educación.)

1. «En nuestra comunidad necesitamos atraer o desarrollar una industria que nos provea de puestos de trabajo.»
2. «En mi opinión, es muy importante tener elecciones justas.»
3. «Para mí, hay que mejorar las relaciones entre los habitantes locales y los recién llegados (*newcomers*).»
4. «En este país necesitamos renovar el sistema bancario.»
5. «Nos gustaría ver menos armas y más paz.»

PASO 2. Escoge uno de los problemas mencionados en el **Paso 1** y describe los detalles específicos en el contexto de tu universidad, tu ciudad o pueblo o el estado donde vives. Luego, en parejas, intercambien ideas y ofrezcan por lo menos una posible solución al problema.

D. Los problemas sociales

PASO 1. En grupos de tres, hagan una lista de por lo menos tres problemas (en orden de importancia) a los que cada uno de los siguientes grupos sociales se enfrenta.

> **MODELO:** Muchos ancianos (*elderly people*) no pueden conducir su propio coche.

1. los ancianos
2. los estudiantes
3. los inmigrantes
4. las mujeres
5. los padres
6. los recién titulados/graduados

PASO 2. En sus grupos, escojan uno de los grupos sociales del **Paso 1** y elaboren un mínimo de tres soluciones para empezar a resolver uno de los problemas al que se enfrenta ese grupo.

> **MODELO:** Muchos ancianos no pueden conducir su propio coche.
>
> 1. Debemos asegurar (*ensure*) que haya transporte público disponible.
> 2. Es importante tener transporte especial para llevar a los ancianos a sus citas médicas.
> 3. Hay que construir comunidades para ancianos cerca del centro de las ciudades.

¿Cuáles son los problemas a los que los ancianos se enfrentan? ¿Y las soluciones?

La alfabetización es la enseñanza (*teaching*) de la lectura y la escritura.

⟳ Reciclaje

The future

Aquí hay una lista de metas (*goals*) de diferentes organizaciones. Complétalas usando uno de los siguientes verbos en la forma **nosotros** del tiempo futuro, y luego empareja la meta con el campo de actividad que le corresponde.

acabar   conseguir   erradicar   hacer   mejorar   resolver

METAS	CAMPOS
____ 1. _____ el analfabetismo.	a. desarrollo económico
____ 2. _____ un esfuerzo para parar la violencia en la frontera.	b. educación
	c. medicina
____ 3. _____ los conflictos entre los dos países.	d. derechos de los indígenas
	e. derechos de los inmigrantes
____ 4. _____ con la pobreza.	f. diplomacia internacional
____ 5. _____ las condiciones de las mujeres indígenas.	
____ 6. _____ una solución al problema de la malaria.	

■ Answers to this activity are in **Appendix 2** at the back of your book.

15.1   Hablaría con los indígenas en Chihuahua

The conditional

Para empezar...

En muchas partes de Latinoamérica, la población indígena tiene una presencia muy notable. A veces hay relaciones muy buenas entre el grupo indígena y el resto de la población y a veces no. Si hicieras un viaje de norte a sur (¡sin retroceder [*doubling back*]!) para conocer mejor la situación de los indígenas en Latinoamérica, ¿en qué orden harías (*would you do*) las siguientes actividades? Escribe la letra de la actividad en el lugar correcto en el mapa. **¡Atención!** Dos de las siguientes actividades serían (*would be*) físicamente imposibles. Indica cuáles son.

a. **Pasaría** unos días en la ciudad de Oaxaca, hacia el oeste del istmo (*isthmus*) de Tehuantepec, la parte estrecha (*narrow*) de México, para conocer mejor a los mixtecos y los zapotecos.

b. **Haría** la última parte del viaje en el sur de Chile, donde viven los mapuches.

c. De allí **tendría** que ir a las islas donde viven los kunas en Panamá.

d. De Ecuador **saldría** para el Perú y Bolivia, donde muchas personas hablan quechua.

e. Después me **encantaría** ir a Guatemala para saber más del pueblo quiché, otro grupo maya.

f. De allí **caminaría** a la Isla de Pascua, donde muchos habitantes son de origen polinesio y hablan rapanui.

g. Primero, me **iría** a Chihuahua en el norte de México para hablar con los rarámuri, también conocidos como tarahumaras.

h. De allí, **nadaría** al estado de Chiapas en el sur de México porque allí viven los tzotziles, uno de los grupos mayas más grandes del país.

i. **Podría** conocer después a los quichuas en los Andes ecuatorianos.

Un consejo...

Relating a tense (**un tiempo verbal**) in Spanish to how you would say it in English can be helpful, but be cautious. The conditional, for instance, is almost always translated into English with *would*, as in the examples in **Actividades analíticas 1.** The reverse, however, is not always true: When *would* is used to describe a repeated past state or event (meaning *used to*), the imperfect is used in Spanish.

De niño, Mario **caminaba** a la escuela.
As a child, Mario would (used to) walk to school.

Mario **caminaría** a la escuela contigo pero no tiene suficiente tiempo.
Mario would walk to school with you but he doesn't have enough time

■ Answers to these activities are in **Appendix 2** at the back of your book.

Actividades analíticas

1 The verbs in bold in **Para empezar** are in the *conditional tense* (**el condicional**). The conditional is used to express what one *would* do under certain circumstances.

Para ayudar a esos niños, yo **donaría** dinero.   *To help those children, I would donate money.*

En un mundo ideal, todos **trabajaríamos** juntos.   *In an ideal world, we all would work together.*

2 Use the forms you saw in **Para empezar** and the patterns you see here to complete the chart.

	pasar	ser	ir
yo		ser**ía**	
tú	pasar**ías**		ir**ías**
él/ella, Ud.	pasar**ía**	ser**ía**	
nosotros/as	pasar**íamos**		ir**íamos**
vosotros/as	pasar**íais**	ser**íais**	
ellos/ellas, Uds.	pasar**ían**		ir**ían**

3 Just as you saw for the future tense in **Estructura 14.2,** the stem for the conditional consists of the entire infinitive form, to which one of the following endings is added.

TERMINACIONES DEL CONDICIONAL	
yo	-ía
tú	-ías
él/ella, Ud.	-ía
nosotros/as	-íamos
vosotros/as	-íais
ellos/ellas, Uds.	-ían

4 Those verbs that have irregular stems in the future tense use this same stem in the conditional. As with the future, there are no irregular endings in the conditional tense.

VERBO	RAÍZ	EJEMPLO	
decir	**dir-**	Yo **diría** que la situación está mejor ahora.	*I would say that the situation is now better.*
haber	**habr-**	Con el plan que tienen, **habría** menos pobreza.	*With the plan that they have, there would be less poverty.*
hacer	**har-**	**Haría** un gran esfuerzo para ayudarte.	*I would make a great effort to help you.*
poder	**podr-**	¿**Podría** hablar con Ud.?	*Could I speak with you?*
poner	**pondr-**	**Pondríamos** fin al problema, pero no tenemos suficientes recursos.	*We would put an end to the problem, but we don't have enough resources.*
salir	**saldr-**	**Saldrían** del país, pero no está permitido.	*They would leave the country, but it's not permitted.*
tener	**tendr-**	Para entendernos mejor, **tendríamos** que hablar más.	*To understand each other better, we would have to talk more.*
venir	**vendr-**	Mi hermano **vendría** también, pero no puede.	*My brother would come too, but he can't.*

■ For more conditional forms, see **Para saber más 15.1** at the back of your book.

Note that **habría** here is the conditional of **hay** (**haber**). As with **hay**, **habría** is always used in the singular to express existence.

Habría un problema   *There would be a problem.*

Habría muchos problemas.   *There would be many problems.*

Actividades prácticas

A. ¿Qué harías?

PASO 1. ¿Qué harías tú para solucionar los siguientes problemas? Empareja cada problema con una solución razonable. **¡Atención!** Los problemas indicados con (*) tienen más de una solución.

PROBLEMAS	¿QUÉ HARÍAS?
1. Hay mucha pobreza.*	a. Haría un esfuerzo para tener más policías.
2. Hay mucho analfabetismo.	b. Viajaría a España o a Latinoamérica.
3. Hay mucha corrupción.	c. Leería más artículos sobre la situación en los países hispanos.
4. Hay mucha violencia en las calles.	d. Les daría salarios decentes a los empleados del gobierno.
5. No hay suficiente comunicación entre mi país y Latinoamérica.	e. Ayudaría a crear microempresas en las comunidades pobres.
6. No conozco bien la realidad del mundo hispano.*	f. Crearía más trabajos.
	g. Tendría más escuelas para toda la población.
	h. Crearía clases de español para todos en mi país.

PASO 2. En parejas, escojan las tres soluciones de máxima prioridad para Uds. del **Paso 1** y supongan que tienen dinero ilimitado para implementarlas. ¿Qué harían Uds. bajo estas condiciones? ¿Por qué?

MODELO: Haríamos un esfuerzo para tener más policías porque si la gente no se siente segura, no puede vivir feliz.

B. ¿Cómo somos y qué haríamos?

En muchos países, existe la percepción de los norteamericanos de que no son bien informados sobre los asuntos internacionales y que tampoco son **conscientes** (*aware*) del impacto de sus acciones sobre el resto del mundo. ¿Estás de acuerdo? Escucha las oraciones y decide si es algo que haría una persona consciente y bien informado/a (**C**) o si es algo que haría una persona poco consciente (**PC**), **irrespetuosa** (*disrespectful*) y/o de **mente cerrada** (*closed-minded*).

1. _____   3. _____   5. _____   7. _____
2. _____   4. _____   6. _____

C. Prioridades para la comunidad global y local

PASO 1. En grupos pequeños, usen el vocabulario que ya aprendieron para crear una lista de tres cosas que harían Uds. para mejorar su propia comunidad o su universidad. Pueden usar la lista de abajo o hacer sus propias sugerencias.

bajar las cuotas de la matrícula (*registration fees*) para los estudiantes
comprar más libros para la biblioteca
crear más lugares de estacionamiento (*parking spaces*)
construir edificios nuevos
mejorar los salarios de los maestros/profesores
tener más actividades divertidas para los estudiantes
tener más computadoras accesibles a los estudiantes
tener mejores opciones de transporte público para llegar a la universidad

PASO 2. Ahora creen una lista de tres cosas que harían Uds. para mejorar la comunidad global.

MODELO: Ayudaríamos a otras personas a conservar el agua.

D. Tu vida ideal

PASO 1. En tu vida ideal, ¿qué harías? ¿Y qué *no* harías? Crea una lista de lo que harías y una lista de lo que no harías. **¡Atención!** Debes tener diez oraciones en total entre las dos listas.

MODELO: En mi vida ideal, estaría casado, tendría muchos hijos, nadaría en el mar todos los días y vería muchas películas. No trabajaría, no haría ejercicio en el gimnasio, no estudiaría, no me bañaría, no cocinaría y no tendría un coche.

PASO 2. Compara tus listas con las de un compañero / una compañera. ¿Tienen algo en común?

■ The audio files for in-text listening activities are available in the eBook, within Connect Plus activities, and on the Online Learning Center.

⟳ Reciclaje

The past subjunctive

Siempre ha habido gente que quiere mejorar la sociedad en la que vive. Mira la siguiente lista de afirmaciones sobre nuestra sociedad. ¿Qué crees que la gente de antes quería y qué no quería? Escribe cada afirmación bajo la categoría **Querían que…** o **No querían que…** ¡Atención! Hay que cambiar el verbo al imperfecto (pasado) de subjuntivo.

Querían que…	No querían que…
_____	_____
_____	_____
_____	_____
_____	

Crece la desigualdad económica.
Los niños pueden asistir a la escuela sin pagar.
Hay guerras.
La esclavitud ya no existe.
Las mujeres tienen el derecho de votar.

La corrupción está presente en el sistema jurídico (*judicial*).
Los trabajadores descansan dos días a la semana.
Toda la gente tiene la libertad de practicar su religión.

■ Answers to this activity are in **Appendix 2** at the back of your book.

15.2 Si nadie usara drogas, la vida sería más tranquila

Si clauses

Para empezar…

PASO 1. Dicen que cada acción tiene sus consecuencias, que esas consecuencias tienen otras consecuencias, etcétera. Usa números para poner las siguientes oraciones en orden según una «cadena (*chain*) de consecuencias». La primera ya está hecha.

a. _____ Si los narcotraficantes (*drug traffickers*) no **ganaran** tanto dinero, no **podrían** «comprar» a los políticos y a los jueces latinoamericanos.

b. _____ Si no **fuera** un buen negocio vender drogas en los Estados Unidos, los narcotraficantes no las **importarían** al país.

c. _____ Si el sistema político y judicial **funcionara** mejor, los latinoamericanos **tendrían** una vida mejor.

d. _____ Si los narcotraficantes no **pudieran** «comprar» a los políticos y a los jueces, el sistema político y judicial **funcionaría** mejor en los países latinoamericanos.

e. __1__ Si nadie **usara** drogas en los Estados Unidos, no **sería** un buen negocio venderlas.

f. _____ Si no **importara** drogas a los Estados Unidos, el crimen organizado en los países latinoamericanos no **ganaría** tanto dinero.

PASO 2. Según esta cadena de consecuencias, ¿es cierta o falsa la siguiente oración?

_____ Si nadie **usara** drogas en los Estados Unidos, muchos latinoamericanos **tendrían** una vida mejor.

■ Answers to these activities are in **Appendix 2** at the back of your book.

Actividades analíticas

1 Each of the sentences in **Para empezar** consists of an *if* (**si**) clause and a consequence (**consecuencia**). Write the verb form that appears in each part of these sentences here:

	SI...	CONSECUENCIA
a.	ganaran	podrían
b.	_____	_____
c.	_____	_____
d.	_____	_____
e.	_____	_____
f.	_____	_____

2 What is the name of the verb tense that appears in each of these two parts?

Si... : _____

Consecuencia: _____

The past subjunctive forms were presented in **Estructura 14.1.**

As in English, the **si** clause and the consequence may come in either order.

Si tuviera un millón de dólares, lo **donaría** a una organización sin fines de lucro.

If I had a million dollars, I would donate it to a non-profit organization.

Donaría un millón de dólares a una organización sin fines de lucro **si** lo **tuviera.**

I would donate a million dollars to a non-profit organization if I had it.

3 The pattern seen here with **si** + *past subjunctive,* + *conditional* is used only when the *if* (**si**) clause describes a situation that is contrary to fact.

Si Guatemala **estuviera** en Europa, no **tendría** selvas tan bonitas.	*If Guatemala were in Europe (which it is not), it would not have such beautiful jungles.*
Compraría una casa si yo **tuviera** mucho dinero.	*I would buy a house if I had a lot of money (which I do not).*

In these cases, the speaker knows that Guatemala is actually not in Europe and that he or she does not have a lot of money. The past subjunctive signals this contrary-to-fact status of the **si** clause.

If the **si** clause describes a situation that is not contrary to fact (that is, it could be true or could happen), use an indicative tense such as present, preterite, or imperfect.

Si mañana **tengo** tiempo, **voy a pasar** por tu casa.	*If I have time tomorrow, I'll stop by your house.*
Si no **estudiaste**, no te **va a ir** bien en el examen.	*If you didn't study, it's not going to go well for you on the test.*
En esos tiempos, si **había** un conflicto entre dos países, **se convertía** en guerra.	*In those days, if there was a conflict between two countries, it would turn into a war.*

> ■ To find out how to use **si** clauses to express contrary-to-fact situations on the past, see **Para saber más 15.2** at the back of your book.

To summarize, the **si** clause can be in the past subjunctive or an indicative tense. It is never in the present subjunctive.

PAST SUBJUNCTIVE

The *past subjunctive* in the **si** clause signals a situation that is contrary to fact (that is, a situation that the speaker knows is not true). The consequence is expressed with the *conditional.*

INDICATIVE

If the **si** clause is not describing a contrary-to-fact situation, then use an *indicative* tense. The consequence may also be in any indicative tense.

4 The word **hay** is **hubiera** in the past subjunctive, and it is very common in **si** clauses that express contrary-to-fact situations.

Yo estaría contento si **hubiera** menos pobreza en el mundo.	*I would be happy if there were less poverty in the world.*
Si **hubiera** un centro de la comunidad en este barrio, podríamos organizarnos allí.	*If there were a community center in this neighborhood, we could organize there.*

Complete the hypothetical statements with the appropriate form of the conditional (to indicate the consequence) or the past subjunctive (to indicate the contrary-to-fact situation).

1. Si alguien _____ (querer) ayudar a eliminar el analfabetismo, _____ (poder) hacerse voluntario en la biblioteca.
2. Nosotros _____ (construir) un nuevo refugio (*shelter*) para las mujeres en nuestra comunidad si _____ (ganar) la lotería.
3. Si a ella le _____ (interesar) la política, _____ (buscar) oportunidades para trabajar en las elecciones.
4. Yo _____ (trabajar) en el comedor de beneficencia (*soup kitchen*) todos los días si _____ (tener) más tiempo libre.

Respuestas: 1. quisiera, podría **2.** construiríamos, ganáramos **3.** interesara, buscaría **4.** trabajaría, tuviera

En español…

The standard way of expressing contrary-to-fact situations in the written language is the pattern you've just seen: **si** + *past subjunctive*. It is common in the spoken language too, but you may also hear variants in some regions. For example, it is common to hear **yo que tú** with the meaning **si yo fuera tú.**

Si yo fuera tú, no lo haría.
Yo que tú, no lo haría. } *If I were you, I wouldn't do it.*

Actividades prácticas

A. El desarrollo (*development*) **y la felicidad** El Índice (*Index*) de Desarrollo Humano clasifica a los países según el nivel económico, el nivel de educación y la esperanza de vida (*life expectancy*). El Índice de Satisfacción con la Vida muestra la felicidad (*happiness*), que se calcula según las respuestas a una encuesta. Basándote en la información en la tabla, indica si cada oración que sigue es cierta (**C**) o falsa (**F**).

	DESARROLLO HUMANO (%)	SATISFACCIÓN CON LA VIDA
Argentina	muy alto (*high*) (81)	alto (66)
Canadá	muy alto (91)	muy alto (75)
Chile	muy alto (82)	alto (66)
Costa Rica	alto (77)	muy alto (73)
España	muy alto (89)	alto (63)
los Estados Unidos	muy alto (94)	muy alto (71)
México	alto (78)	muy alto (71)
Nicaragua	medio (60)	medio (55)
la República Dominicana	medio (70)	medio (50)
Venezuela	alto (75)	muy alto (70)

1. ____ Si hubiera menos analfabetismo y más progreso económico en México, podrían tener un nivel de desarrollo más alto.
2. ____ Si fuéramos de Argentina, podríamos decir que nuestro país tiene un nivel de satisfacción con la vida «muy alto».
3. ____ Si los países tuvieran un nivel de educación más alto, tendrían un nivel de desarrollo más alto también.
4. ____ Si la República Dominicana tuviera más desarrollo económico, podría estar en la lista de países con un nivel de desarrollo «alto».
5. ____ Si yo fuera de Nicaragua, podría decir que mi país tiene el mismo nivel de desarrollo que Venezuela.
6. ____ Si la República Dominicana tuviera el mismo nivel de desarrollo que Argentina, sería uno de los países con un nivel de desarrollo «medio».
7. ____ Si hubiera más satisfacción con la vida en los Estados Unidos, los estadounidenses podrían tener un nivel de satisfacción más alto que en México.
8. ____ Si todos los países pudieran tener como mínimo el mismo nivel de desarrollo que Venezuela, el mundo sería mejor.

B. Nuestras preferencias

PASO 1.   Completa cada una de las siguientes oraciones, basándote en tus preferencias personales.

1. Si tuviera el dinero, viajaría a _____ por el fin de semana.
2. Si pudiera resolver solo un problema en mi país, sería el problema de _____.
3. Si pudiera resolver solo un problema en el mundo, sería el problema de _____.
4. Me iría a _____ si me dieran la oportunidad de vivir en otro país durante un año.
5. Cenaría con _____ si pudiera salir a cenar con cualquier persona del mundo hispano.
6. Me gustaría ser de _____ si yo pudiera ser de un país hispano.

PASO 2.   Escoge una de las oraciones del **Paso 1,** cámbiala a una pregunta y pregúntasela a tres de tus compañeros. Apunta los resultados.

MODELO: Si tuvieras el dinero, ¿adónde viajarías?

C. Si el mundo fuera diferente   Escoge la forma apropiada de los verbos en cada oración y decide si la situación es cierta o no.

1. Si Ecuador [está / estuviera] en Centroamérica, [es / sería] un país centroamericano.
2. Si la pobreza extrema [existe / existiera] en el mundo, [tenemos / tendríamos] que erradicarla.
3. Si [hay / hubiera] grandes diferencias económicas entre unos países y otros, [va a haber / habría] mucha inmigración de los países más pobres a los países más ricos.
4. Si Cristóbal Colón (*Christopher Columbus*) [está / estuviera] vivo, ¿qué [piensa / pensaría] de las Américas de hoy?
5. Si [hablan / hablaran] español en muchos países de Latinoamérica, eso no [significa / significaría] que las lenguas indígenas ya no existan.
6. Si no [hay / hubiera] ningún problema de desigualdad económica en el mundo, [podemos / podríamos] estar tranquilos.

D. Unas situaciones difíciles   En grupos de tres, creen una respuesta (una oración completa) a cada una de las siguientes preguntas.

1. Si vivieran en este país y no hablaran inglés, ¿qué trabajo podrían hacer?
2. Si fueran del norte de África y no pudieran encontrar trabajo allí, ¿a qué país se irían? ¿Por qué?
3. Si fueran líderes de un país y hubiera mucha desigualdad económica, ¿qué harían?
4. Si vivieran en un país no muy democrático, ¿qué podrían hacer para cambiar esta situación?

CONÉCTATE AL MUNDO HISPANO

En el mundo entero, la gente busca lugares donde haya mucha oferta de trabajo y los salarios sean altos. Por eso, es común ver **flujos** (*flows*) **de migración laboral,** dentro de un solo país (de las áreas rurales hacia las grandes ciudades, por ejemplo) o de un país más pobre a otro país más rico. En el mundo hispano, por ejemplo, muchos africanos buscan trabajo en España, y por la misma razón, muchos guatemaltecos y hondureños se van a México y muchos bolivianos y paraguayos se van a Argentina o Chile. Todo este movimiento ocurre porque España, México, Argentina y Chile tienen economías relativamente grandes y fuertes.

De la misma manera (*way*), muchos salen del Caribe, de México o de Centroamérica a buscar trabajo en los Estados Unidos, un país con una de las economías más fuertes del mundo. Sin embargo (*however*), aún (*even*) este fenómeno tan conocido cambia según el estado de la economía. De 2005 a 2010, por ejemplo, el flujo migratorio entre los Estados Unidos y México se equilibró: la cantidad (*quantity*) de migrantes de México a los Estados Unidos era más o menos igual a la cantidad de los que iban de los Estados Unidos a México. Esto pasó por muchas razones, pero la recesión en los Estados Unidos y el crecimiento (*growth*) económico en México eran factores importantes. La mejoría (*improvement*) en la economía mexicana tuvo otro resultado interesante: la llegada de un gran número de inmigrantes de países lejanos (*distant*), como Argentina, Corea, España, Francia y Japón, todos buscando su futuro en México.

Honduras

E. Cultura: La crisis constitucional en Honduras

PASO 1. Lee el texto sobre Honduras.

Honduras es una república constitucional y, según el censo de 2010, tiene una población de 8,2 millones de personas. Es uno de los países latinoamericanos con más desigualdad socioeconómica: el 10 por ciento más rico de la población controla un 42 por ciento de la riqueza del país.

A finales de 2008, el entonces presidente de Honduras, Manuel Zelaya, anunció su plan de hacer un referéndum en las próximas elecciones para determinar si había apoyo[a] popular para reescribir partes de la constitución federal. Dentro de los posibles cambios[b] se incluía la posibilidad de reelegir[c] un presidente, lo cual estaba prohibido en la constitución. En marzo de 2009, la Corte Suprema hondureña determinó que el referéndum no era legal, pero Zelaya siguió con su plan. El 28 de junio de 2009, el día del referéndum, un grupo de aproximadamente cien soldados[d] entraron a la fuerza en la casa del presidente y lo llevaron en avión a Costa Rica.

Este acto de quitar de su cargo[e] a un presidente democráticamente elegido usando fuerzas militares es considerado por muchos un golpe de estado[f]; el acto de llevarlo fuera del país es considerado un exilio forzado. Y el evento está rodeado de[g] mucha controversia. Por un lado, muchos piensan que Zelaya había violado la ley[h] cuando no reconoció la decisión de la Corte Suprema. Por otro lado, otros piensan que la decisión de la corte y el exilio de Zelaya eran estrategias de los grupos políticos conservadores de Honduras. Ellos temían[i] que la política de Zelaya fuera cada vez más para la izquierda, basándose en el apoyo que Zelaya tenía de los presidentes de Venezuela (Hugo Chávez), Cuba (Fidel Castro) y Nicaragua (Daniel Ortega). Además, Zelaya había hecho actos como subir el salario mínimo para tratar de mejorar[j] la situación de la pobreza extrema en Honduras y proteger a los trabajadores.

En los días después del exilio de Zelaya, el gobierno suspendió varias garantías constitucionales de los hondureños. En los primeros días, pusieron un toque de queda.[k] Cuando Zelaya regresó a Honduras el 22 de septiembre, el gobierno suspendió durante casi un mes la libertad personal, la libertad de expresión, la de tránsito,* de habeas corpus y de asamblea y asociación. El gobierno no dejó que Zelaya volviera a la presidencia y en las elecciones de enero de 2010, los hondureños eligieron a Porfirio Lobo como el nuevo presidente.

[a]*support* [b]*changes* [c]*re-elect* [d]*soldiers* [e]*position* [f]*golpe… coup de etat* [g]*rodeado… surrounded by* [h]*law* [i]*feared* [j]*tratar… try to improve* [k]*toque… curfew*

PASO 2. Completa las oraciones con tus propias opiniones.

1. Si yo fuera presidente/a de Honduras, _____.
2. Si la Corte Suprema no hubiera tomado su decisión en contra del referéndum, _____.
3. Sería justo hacer cambios a la constitución federal para permitir la reelección si _____.
4. Si Zelaya no tuviera el apoyo de otros presidentes latinoamericanos, _____.
5. Honduras sería un país más estable y próspero si _____.
6. Si el gobierno de este país suspendiera las libertades constitucionales de mis amigos y yo, _____.

PASO 3. En parejas, contesten las preguntas y explíquense las respuestas.

1. En Honduras, como en muchos países tropicales, ha sido difícil establecer una economía fuerte, por el bajo (*low*) nivel de recursos naturales y terrenos cultivables, entre otros factores. Como resultado, hay mucho desempleo y mucha desigualdad económica. ¿Piensas que este tipo de dificultad económica puede causar la inestabilidad política?
2. ¿Piensas que la inestabilidad política puede causar problemas económicos?
3. Si vives en un país como Canadá o los Estados Unidos, ¿piensas que la economía fuerte ha contribuido a la estabilidad política? ¿Piensas que el sistema político podría entrar en peligro si hubiera problemas económicos muy fuertes?

---

*la libertad de viajar dentro y fuera del país

¡Leamos!

«Malas y buenas noticias» por José Antonio Millán

Antes de leer

PASO 1. Vas a leer un texto sobre los libros digitales. Anticipando este tema, ¿a qué probablemente se refieren los siguientes términos?

_____ 1. sagas vampíricas

_____ 2. los aparatos/dispositivos (*devices*) lectores

_____ 3. un buscador

_____ 4. P2P

_____ 5. la fórmula de negocio

a. Google o Bing

b. Kindle o iPad

c. la serie *Twilight*

d. el modelo que usa una empresa para ganar dinero

e. la conexión entre varias computadoras que se usa para compartir archivos

PASO 2. Indica si cada frase a continuación se consideraría **buena noticia** o **mala noticia** para las empresas que producen libros digitales.

	BUENA NOTICIA	MALA NOTICIA
1. Hay mucha demanda de libros digitales.	☐	☐
2. Hay pocos libros digitales disponibles (*available*).	☐	☐
3. Hay muchos dispositivos lectores como iPad y Kindle.	☐	☐
4. El contenido digital más popular está en sitios ilegales.	☐	☐
5. Es difícil comprar los libros digitales legalmente.	☐	☐
6. Es fácil conseguir libros digitales sin autorización.	☐	☐
7. Los jóvenes leen más que nunca.	☐	☐
8. Los jóvenes leen libros digitales descargados (*downloaded*) ilegalmente.	☐	☐

¿Cómo lees? ¿Dónde lees? ¿Leer es diferente con un libro digital?

A leer

PASO 1. Lee el artículo sobre los libros digitales.

Malas y buenas noticias

Hagan una prueba: dejen a un puñado[a] de buenos lectores adolescentes un e-book y denles la oportunidad de bajarse[b] obras legalmente de los sitios web donde se comercializan. Al cabo[c] de unos meses comprobarán[d] que han leído vorazmente,[e] pero que las obras no provenían de descargas[f] autorizadas. Sencillamente, han buscado en las fuentes legales los libros que querían leer y no los han encontrado. Y los han localizado «en Internet». Hay muchos libros en la red. Quien quiera[g] probarlo solo tiene que escribir en un buscador el título de una obra. Y no se piense que para descargarla hay que entrar en las procelosas[h] aguas de los P2P. Basta llegar a una página web, y hacer clic en un enlace.

Pues bien: en muchos casos estos archivos para e-book no están disponibles[i] si uno trata de comprarlos legalmente. Y en Internet los encontramos: libros torpemente[j] escaneados, o archivos creados ad hoc, ¡a veces con la traducción de obras aún no aparecidas en el mercado hispanohablante! Sí: los fans seguidores[k] de sagas vampíricas no se caracterizan por su paciencia.

La oferta de libros digitales es muy inferior a la demanda que existe. Y esta seguirá creciendo, porque los dispositivos lectores han ido bajando de precio y han aparecido alternativas como el iPad. Estos son los hechos[l]: acceso a Internet muy extendido; buscadores que encuentran cualquier cosa y un montón de aparatos lectores para los que falta[m] contenido.

¿Y esta situación puede cambiar? Por ejemplo: Supongamos que los editores se apresuran[n] a sacar en versión electrónica los libros más codiciados,[ñ] ¿dejarían de descargarse ilegalmente? Pero un momento, un momento: ¿a qué precio me han dicho que pondrían la descarga?

Precios bajos, o nuevas fórmulas de negocio: no parece haber otra solución. El año que viene, la empresa madrileña 24 symbols intentará suministrar[o] libros electrónicos en dos modalidades[p]: gratis con anuncios o pagando una suscripción que permitirá leer los que se quiera. Es la fórmula que en música ha seguido Spotify, pero ¿querrán unirse a ella los editores de las obras que la gente realmente quiere leer? Se pueden pensar otras modalidades: hay empresas que patrocinan[q] ligas de fútbol o ciclos de conciertos: ¿no se animarían a patrocinar líneas editoriales[r] digitales?

¿No será que fallan[s] las alternativas de negocio? Cada vez que hay nuevos cálculos del acceso a obras sin autorización se habla de la «merma de negocio»,[t] y no es así (como se ha visto en el caso de la música): no toda obra descargada ilegalmente habría sido comprada, y menos a esos precios…

[a]*handful* [b]*to download* [c]*Al… At the end* [d]*they will confirm* [e]*voraciously* [f]*downloads* [g]*Quien… Whoever wants* [h]*stormy* [i]*available* [j]*clumsily* [k]*followers* [l]*facts* [m]*lack* [n]*se… hurry* [ñ]*coveted* [o]*deliver* [p]*ways* [q]*sponsor* [r]*publishing* [s]*are failing* [t]*merma… lost business*

PASO 2. Según el artículo escrito por José Antonio Millán, «Malas y buenas noticias», que apareció en el periódico español *El País,* indica si cada frase es cierta (C) o falsa (F).

1. _____ Los jóvenes parecen preferir los libros digitales disponibles legalmente en los sitios web que venden e-books.

2. _____ Los libros que les interesan a los jóvenes están en Internet, pero muchos de ellos no están en sitios autorizados.

3. _____ Las descargas ilegales de libros en Internet son fáciles de encontrar.

4. _____ Las descargas ilegales de libros en Internet siempre son de muy buena calidad.

5. _____ En cuanto a los libros digitales, la demanda es más alta que la oferta (*supply*).

6. _____ Con más variedad de dispositivos lectores, los precios han bajado.

7. _____ Según el autor, el precio de las descargas autorizadas de libros digitales no será muy importante.

8. _____ Según el autor, hay dos soluciones posibles: precios bajos o nuevas fórmulas de negocio.

9. _____ A los editores de los libros más populares no les van a gustar las nuevas fórmulas de negocio.

10. _____ Todas las personas que descargan libros digitales ilegalmente pagarían si estuvieran disponibles legalmente las mismas obras.

 PASO 3. En grupos, hagan una lista de ejemplos de cada una de las tres fórmulas de negocio que menciona el texto.

gratis con anuncios:

pagando una suscripción:

empresas patrocinadoras:

Después de leer

PASO 1. Contesta las preguntas sobre tus hábitos como lector(a).

1. ¿Qué tipo de textos lees?

   ☐ biografías   ☐ literatura

   ☐ cómics   ☐ noticias (*news*)

   ☐ libros de texto   ☐ reseñas (*reviews*) de películas y música

   ☐ libros de autoayuda (*self-help*)   ☐ revistas de moda

2. ¿Cuándo lees? ¿Dónde? En las situaciones en que tú lees, ¿cuál es el mejor formato para leer tus textos?

3. ¿Han cambiado en los últimos cinco o seis años tus prácticas como lector(a)? ¿Han cambiado los aparatos que usas para leer? ¿Cómo cambiaron y por qué?

4. ¿Tienes un aparato lector? ¿A ti te gusta leer con el aparato? (¿Por qué sí o no?) ¿Conoces a alguien que use uno? ¿A esa persona le gusta leer con el aparato? (¿Por qué sí o no?)

PASO 2. Ahora entrevista a un compañero / una compañera para saber sus criterios para comprar libros digitales. Luego, escoge la conclusión que mejor describa la fórmula de negocio ideal para tu compañero/a y explícala.

MODELO: E1: ¿Comprarías libros digitales si tuvieras que pagar más de diez dólares cada uno?
E2: No. Sería demasiado caro para mí. Solo compraría libros digitales si costaran menos de $3.

¿Comprarías libros digitales si…

1. …primero tuvieras que mirar veinticinco segundos de anuncios de una empresa que patrocina a la editorial?

2. …tuvieras que mirar anuncios en el margen de la pantalla?

3. …tuvieras que pagar una suscripción de $15 al mes?

4. …fuera necesario pagar una suscripción de $10 al mes?

5. …fuera necesario pagar una suscripción de $5 al mes?

En conclusión:

Para mi compañero/a, la fórmula de negocio ideal es…

☐ gratis con anuncios porque _____.
☐ pagando una suscripción porque _____.
☐ empresas patrocinadoras porque _____.

¡Escuchemos!

¿Cómo cambiarían el mundo?

Antes de escuchar

PASO 1. Marlén, Javier, Enrique y Mariana van a hablar sobre cómo cambiarían el mundo si pudieran. Antes de escuchar la conversación, conversen en grupos pequeños sobre la siguiente pregunta: si Uds. pudieran cambiar algo en el mundo, ¿qué harían?

PASO 2. Ahora, empareja cada cita que vas a escuchar en el video con dos explicaciones lógicas.

1. _____ _____ «Me gustaría darles a los niños pobres las herramientas (*tools*) necesarias con las cuales ellos, en algún momento de su vida, se puedan independizar por completo.»

2. _____ _____ «Creo que debemos establecer un organismo global para defender los derechos humanos.»

3. _____ _____ «En mi opinión, hay que participar si luego quieres tener voz (*a voice*).»

4. _____ _____ «Hay falta de vivienda barata y asequible (*cheap and affordable housing*).»

a. La ayuda para los niños pobres no solo mejora la calidad de vida en el momento actual, sino también lleva a la independencia en el futuro.
b. Es un comentario sobre las atrocidades cometidas en muchos países del mundo.
c. Es un comentario sobre la gente que no participa y luego protesta.
d. Gente de todos los estatus sociales con diversos niveles de educación no tiene dónde vivir.
e. Hay gente tirada (*thrown*) en las calles de muchas ciudades grandes.
f. Si quieres tener voz, tienes que ir a votar.
g. Si un grupo sufre en un país, no se puede recurrir a (*turn to*) ninguna entidad internacional para ayuda.
h. Tenemos que mejorar la vida de los ciudadanos más jóvenes para hacer los cambios sociales necesarios.

A escuchar

Mira y escucha las respuestas que dieron Marlén, Javier, Enrique y Mariana a la pregunta, «Si pudiera cambiar algo en el mundo, ¿qué haría Ud.?» Luego, escoge la mejor conclusión para cada frase a continuación.

1. _____ Cuando Marlén dice, «niños pobres», está hablando específicamente de…
   a. niños que no tienen acceso a las escuelas públicas.
   b. niños que viven por debajo del nivel de pobreza federal.
   c. niños de la calle.
   d. todos los niños.

2. _____ Para Marlén, el cambio clave para realizar (*achieve*) un mundo mejor es…
   a. acabar con todos los conflictos armados internacionales.
   b. sacar a los niños de la pobreza de manera que se puedan independizar como adultos.
   c. proveer la educación universal a todos los niños entre los cinco y dieciséis años de edad.
   d. darles de comer a todos los niños que viven en la calle.

3. _____ Para Javier si quieres tener voz,…
   a. debes protestar.
   b. no tienes el derecho de participar.
   c. tienes que hablar en voz alta.
   d. tienes la obligación de votar.

4. _____ Según Javier, si no vas a votar,…
   a. no puedes matricularte en los cursos universitarios.
   b. no tienes el derecho de protestar.
   c. no vas a tener éxito (*success*) profesional.
   d. no vas a ganar la elección.

5. _____ Para Enrique, el sueño (*dream, ideal*) es…
   a. un organismo internacional que defiende los derechos humanos.
   b. la vivienda asequible a todo el mundo.
   c. menos basura en las calles de las ciudades europeas.
   d. más gente tirada (*strewn about*) en las calles de las ciudades europeas.

6. ____ En Madrid, ¿cuántas personas están viviendo en la calle?
   a. 1.400
   b. 4.000
   c. 14.000
   d. 40.000

7. ____ Según Enrique, ¿qué tipo de persona está viviendo en la calle?
   a. gente de todos los estatus sociales
   b. gente con vivienda asequible
   c. gente con bajo nivel de educación
   d. gente pobre

8. ____ ¿Qué país **no** menciona Enrique?
   a. Francia
   b. Italia
   c. Portugal
   d. Bélgica

9. ____ Según Mariana, ¿qué es lo que genera la inseguridad?
   a. las elecciones
   b. el analfabetismo
   c. las leyes
   d. la pobreza

10. ____ Cuando Mariana dice «mejor educación», se refiere a programas que…
    a. animan a los niños a que sigan con sus estudios para tener mejores oportunidades.
    b. acaban con el narcotráfico.
    c. acaban con todos los conflictos armados internacionales.
    d. sacar los niños de la pobreza de manera que se puedan independizar como adultos.

Después de escuchar

PASO 1. Lee otra vez las declaraciones de **Antes de escuchar, Paso 2.** Luego, di si estás de acuerdo o no y por qué.

1. _____
2. _____
3. _____
4. _____

PASO 2. Busca a alguien que haya hecho cada una de las siguientes actividades. **¡Atención!** Para hacer las preguntas, tienes que cambiar los infinitivos al presente perfecto.

MODELO: E1: ¿Le has dado dinero, comida o ropa a una persona viviendo en la calle?
E2: Sí, una vez en Denver le di mi bufanda a una señora sin hogar. Hacía mucho frío y ella no tenía ni una chaqueta.

1. …llamar a un(a) representante del gobierno para hablar de un tema social que te importa mucho.
2. …organizar un grupo estudiantil o comunitario para mejorar la comunidad.
3. …participar en una manifestación para protestar por una injusticia.
4. …ganarte la vida (*to earn a living*) sin el apoyo (*support*) de tus padres.
5. …votar.
6. …formular un plan para lo que vas a hacer después de graduarte.
7. …votar en una elección de mitad de período (*midterm* [*not presidential*] *elections*).
8. …escribir una carta a un político / una política de Washington para protestar por algo.
9. …empezar a ahorrar dinero para tu jubilación (*retirement*).
10. …trabajar en un banco de alimentos (*food bank*) o participar un programa parecido (como, por ejemplo, Meals on Wheels).

PASO 3. Según los resultados del **Paso 2,** ¿quiénes son las personas más activistas de la clase? ¿Quiénes son las más independientes? Explica tus respuestas.

¡Escribamos!

Si tuviera un millón de dólares…

Al ganar la lotería se dice que es una bendición (*blessing*) y una maldición (*curse*). En esta actividad, vas a escribir sobre lo bueno y lo malo de tener mucho dinero, qué harías para ti y tu familia, tus amigos y tu comunidad, y qué responsabilidades o problemas tendrías a causa de haber ganado la lotería.

Antes de escribir

PASO 1. ¿Qué harías si tuvieras un millón de dólares? ¿Qué problemas tendrías? Considerando las siguientes preguntas, crea una lluvia de ideas y luego pon las ideas en orden lógico.

Si tuvieras un millón de dólares, ¿qué harías para ti, tu familia y tus amigos? (viajaría a… , me compraría… , viviría en… , tendría… , no tendría…) ¿Qué harías para la comunidad? ¿Qué responsabilidades o problemas tendrías?

> **MODELO:** viajaría mucho __2__
> necesitaría ayuda para manejar (*manage*) todo mi dinero __4__
> me compraría una casa en la playa de Costa Rica y otra casa para mi familia __1__
> viviría en la playa durante tres meses del año y en mi yate (*yacht*) el resto del año __3__
> ayudaría a los demás también __6__
> empezaría una fundación para ayudar a los niños enfermos __7__
> contrataría a un contador / una contadora (*accountant*) __5__

A escribir

En un ensayo de cuatro párrafos, explica lo que harías con un millón de dólares. En el primer párrafo, di si crees que ganar la lotería sería una bendición o una maldición para ti y explica por qué. En el segundo párrafo, describe lo que harías para ti, tu familia y tus amigos si ganaras la lotería y explica por qué. En el tercer párrafo, habla de lo que harías para tu comunidad y explica por qué. Concluye con un párrafo sobre «las maldiciones» de tener tanto dinero, es decir, los nuevos problemas y responsabilidades que tendrías, y explica por qué. El primer párrafo debe incluir un breve resumen de lo que vas a decir en el resto de tu ensayo.

Después de escribir

Revisa tu ensayo. Luego, intercambia ensayos con un compañero / una compañera para evaluarlos. Lee el ensayo de tu compañero/a y determina si el ensayo tiene sentido. ¿Se ha desarrollado (*developed*) bien cada párrafo? Lee de nuevo el ensayo con cuidado para revisar los siguientes puntos.

☐ ¿Ha escrito tu compañero/a cuatro párrafos? (uno de introducción, uno sobre sobre sí mismo y sus seres queridos, uno sobre su comunidad y el último sobre las dificultades y obligaciones asociadas con ganar la lotería)

☐ ¿Siguen los párrafos el orden que nombró tu compañero/a en su introducción?

☐ Además de escribir una lista de lo que haría, ¿hay una explicación clara en cada párrafo?

☐ ¿Concuerdan los sujetos y los verbos?

☐ ¿Concuerdan los sustantivos y los adjetivos?

☐ ¿Ha usado bien el condicional?

☐ ¿Ha usado bien las cláusulas **si**?

Después de revisar el ensayo de tu compañero/a, devuélveselo. Mira tu propio ensayo para ver los cambios que tu compañero/a recomienda y haz las revisiones necesarias.

ESTRATEGIA

Flow

In a first draft, you will almost always write the ideas as they come to you, but that doesn't necessarily result in the most logical order. And sometimes you find that some back story is required to make sense of a particular action. It's important to edit your work so that if you say in your introduction you are going to talk about A, B, and C, you truly do write about those three things in that same order in the body of your writing. To help you do this, list all of your initial ideas first, then order them, and find the strongest, most logical flow. Eliminate anything that does not flow well.

¡Hablemos!

¿Crees que es buena idea o mala idea?

Antes de hablar

¿Crees que serían buena idea o mala idea los siguientes cambios en la política de tu universidad?

	BUENA IDEA	MALA IDEA
1. abolir (*abolish*) las notas (*grades*)	☐	☐
2. solo tener clases virtuales	☐	☐
3. requerir que los estudiantes que se especializan en idiomas estudien en el extranjero (*abroad*)	☐	☐
4. usar solo libros de texto electrónicos (en vez de impresos [*printed*])	☐	☐
5. tener el voluntariado (*volunteerism*) como requisito para la graduación	☐	☐
6. subir la matrícula para tener mejores profesores y programas	☐	☐
7. Otro: _____	☐	☐

A hablar

En grupos de cuatro, escojan uno de los temas de **Antes de hablar** y hagan un debate. Dos estudiantes tienen que estar a favor del asunto y dos en contra de ello. Presenten el debate al resto de la clase.

MODELO: ¿Es buena idea abolir las notas?
E1: Creo que no, porque sin notas, los estudiantes no participarían en las clases.
E2: Yo creo que sí, porque así (*that way*) los estudiantes más interesados asistirían a las clases y la participación sería mayor.

Después de hablar

¿Quién crees que gana cada debate? Voten para saber quiénes son los ganadores de cada debate.

Conéctate a la música

Canción: «Volver a comenzar» (2007)
Artistas: Café Tacuba

Café Tacuba (o Café Tacvba) es una banda mexicana conocida por sus combinaciones muy creativas del rock con elementos de la música folclórica. Fue uno de los grupos más importantes del boom de rock alternativo en el mundo hispano en los años 90 y siguen teniendo un gran renombre internacional.

Los miembros de Café Tacuba

Antes de escuchar

En esta canción, hablan de los errores que cometemos (*we commit*) en la vida. En tu opinión, ¿cuál es el error más grande que muchos cometemos en la vida *como individuos*? ¿Cuál es el error más grande que hemos cometido *como sociedad*?

A escuchar

En la canción hay oraciones hipotéticas que usan cláusulas con **si**. Mientras escuchas, completa las oraciones a partir de lo que dice la canción. Puedes usar la lista de verbos si la necesitas. Luego, empareja cada cláusula con **si** con su consecuencia. **¡Atención!** Una de las cláusulas no tiene consecuencia.

hacer   pedir   sobrevivir (*to survive, outlive*)   tener   volver

SI…	CONSECUENCIA
1. Si _____ una lista de mis errores, _____	a. no _____ tiempo de reparar (*to make amends*).
2. Si _____ a comenzar (*to begin*), _____	b. _____ fuerzas (*ability*) para decir cuánto lo siento.
3. Si _____ un viaje a mis adentros (*insides*) y _____ a los lamentos (*laments*), _____	

Después de escuchar

¿Qué significan estas oraciones de la última parte de la canción? Empareja cada una con el significado más lógico. **¡Atención!** Hay cuatro opciones, pero solo se necesitan dos.

1. _____ «El agua derramada (*spilled*) está.»
2. _____ «La sed que siento me sanará.»

a. Ya no puedo tomar agua.
b. He cometido muchos errores.
c. Cuando tengo sed, no me siento enfermo.
d. Lamento esos errores y eso es bueno.

■ For copyright reasons, the songs referenced in **Conéctate a la música** have not been provided by the publisher. The video for this song can be found on YouTube, and it is available for purchase from the iTunes store.

VOCABULARIO

Comunicación

Creo que...	I think . . .
dejarle saber	to let someone know
En mi opinión...	In my opinion . . .
Para mí...	For me (personally) . . .
¿Qué sé yo? / ¿Yo qué sé?	What do I know?, Beats me!
Que yo sepa...	That I know of . . . / As far as I know . . .
¿Quién sabe?	Who knows?
sin saber	without knowing/ realizing (*by coincidence or by accident*)
el/la sabelotodo	know-it-all
Ve tú / Vaya Ud. a saber.	Your guess is as good as mine

Los sustantivos

la alfabetización	literacy; teaching of literacy
el analfabetismo	illiteracy
la corrupción	corruption
el crimen	serious crime
la crisis económica	economic crisis
la demanda	demand
la democracia	democracy
el derecho humano	human right
el desarrollo	development
el desastre natural	natural disaster
el desempleo	unemployment
la (des)igualdad	(in)equality
la deuda externa	foreign debt
la dictadura	dictatorship
la discriminación	discrimination
la elección	election
la esclavitud infantil	child slavery
la frontera	border
la guerra	war
el hambre (*f.*)	hunger

el/la indígena	native (indigenous) person
la infraestructura	infrastructure
el inmigrante	immigrant
la inundación	flood
la libertad	freedom
el narcotráfico	drug trafficking
el nivel	level
la oferta	supply; offer
la organización sin fines de lucro	nonprofit organization
la paz	peace
el peligro	danger
la pobreza	poverty
el/la político/a	politician
el problema social	social problem
el proceso político	political process
el racismo	racismo
la seguridad	safety; security
la tiranía	tyranny
la violencia	violence

Los verbos

acabar con	to put an end to (*a problem*)
cambiar	to change
conseguir (i, i) (g)	to achieve, obtain
desarrollar	to develop
erradicar (qu)	to eradicate
mejorar	to improve
poner (*irreg.*) fin a	to put an end to
resolver (ue)	to resolve
votar	to vote

Los adjetivos

justo/a	fair
peligroso/a	dangerous

La amistad y el amor

En La Paz, Bolivia, la familia
de los novios los felicita
después de la boda.

Objetivos

In this chapter you will learn how to:

- discuss your marital status
- express sympathy and regret
- talk about personal relationships
- discuss personal relationships in the Spanish-speaking world

In this chapter you will review how to:

- talk about activities you do
- talk about activities you used to do
- use pronouns to avoid repetition
- express things that you want to happen

16

COMUNICACIÓN ~~LARIO~~ ~~UCTURA~~ ~~ATE~~

¿Eres soltero/a? ¿Casado/a... ?

Describing your relationship status

A. A ver: Los estados civiles

PASO 1. Mira y escucha, luego indica el estado civil de cada persona que habla.

1. Gerardo, de España

☐ casado/a
☐ comprometido/a
☐ divorciado/a
☐ soltero/a
☐ viudo/a

3. Jordi, de España

☐ casado/a
☐ comprometido/a
☐ divorciado/a
☐ soltero/a
☐ viudo/a

2. Óscar, de Costa Rica

☐ casado/a
☐ comprometido/a
☐ divorciado/a
☐ soltero/a
☐ viudo/a

4. Juan Andrés, de Costa Rica

☐ casado/a
☐ comprometido/a
☐ divorciado/a
☐ soltero/a
☐ viudo/a

PASO 2. Ahora con una pareja, contesten las preguntas.

1. ¿Qué significa **estado civil**? ¿A qué se refiere?
2. ¿Cuál es la diferencia entre **ser casado/a** y **estar en una relación**?
3. ¿Cuál es la diferencia entre **ser soltero/a** y **ser divorciado/a**?

To describe your relationship status, you can use the following expressions.

casado/a	married	**en una relación**	in a relationship
comprometido/a	engaged; committed	**soltero/a**	single
divorciado/a	divorced	**viudo/a**	widowed

B. El estado civil de las personas famosas

PASO 1. Apunta una lista de personas famosas y el estado civil de cada una.

PERSONA FAMOSA	ESTADO CIVIL
_____	_____
_____	_____
_____	_____
_____	_____
_____	_____

PASO 2. Formen grupos y hablen de los cambios en el estado civil de las personas famosas que apuntaron en el **Paso 1.**

MODELO: Arnold Schwarzenegger cambió su estado civil de casado a divorciado en 2011. Dicen que había tenido relaciones extramaritales con otras mujeres.

Cuánto lo siento

Expressing sympathy and regret

To express sympathy for a loss, especially the death of a loved one, you can use these expressions.

Lo siento mucho. / Cuánto lo siento.	I'm very sorry.
Mi/Nuestro más sentido pésame.	My/Our deepest condolences.
Te/Le/Les doy/damos el pésame.	My/Our condolences.
Te/Lo/La/Los/Las acompaño en el sentimiento/dolor.	You're in my thoughts. / I'm with you in your time of pain.
Te/Lo/La/Los/Las acompañamos en el sentimiento/dolor.	You're in our thoughts. / We're with you in your time of pain.

A. ¿Celebración o sufrimiento?

PASO 1.   ¿Con qué expresión asocias cada uno de los siguientes términos?

	¡FELICITACIONES!	LO SIENTO MUCHO.
1. la alegría	☐	☐
2. la angustia	☐	☐
3. la desesperación	☐	☐
4. la diversión	☐	☐
5. el dolor	☐	☐
6. la felicidad	☐	☐
7. la pena	☐	☐
8. la risa (*laughter*)	☐	☐
9. el sufrimiento	☐	☐
10. la tristeza	☐	☐

PASO 2.   Primero, pon las siguientes circunstancias en orden de lo que sería la mejor (1) a la peor (5) para ti. Luego, indica una expresión apropiada para usar con una persona que se encuentra en esa circunstancia.

PON EN ORDEN	EXPRESIÓN APROPIADA
_____ romper (*breaking up*) con el novio / la novia	_____
_____ el nacimiento de un bebé	_____
_____ la adquisición de un nuevo coche	_____
_____ la muerte (*death*) de un pariente	_____
_____ casarse con (*getting married to*) la pareja de tus sueños	_____

B. ¿Qué te pasa?   En parejas, imagínense que son dos viejos amigos (viejas amigas) que no se han visto desde hace mucho tiempo. Tienen que decirse qué les ha pasado en los últimos años —los mejores y peores momentos (pueden inventar momentos falsos también)— y reaccionar.

MODELO: E1: Mi abuela se murió en junio. Estaba muy enferma, así que no nos sorprendió su muerte, pero estamos muy tristes.
E2: Te acompaño en el sentimiento.

CONÉCTATE AL MUNDO HISPANO

En los países donde se habla español, es casi un requisito (*requirement*) expresar **el pésame** a todos los miembros (incluso la pareja, los padres, los hijos y los hermanos) de una familia en la cual alguien se ha muerto. Si es posible, se debe ofrecer el pésame en persona, en un servicio religioso por la persona muerta o en una visita a la casa de la familia. Si no es posible ver a los familiares, una llamada telefónica o una tarjeta escrita a mano son aceptables. Incluso los jóvenes tienen la obligación de buscar la oportunidad de ofrecer el pésame.

Esa actitud representa un contraste con las costumbres estadounidenses. En los Estados Unidos, es más común evitar el tema de la muerte porque puede sentirse incómodo mencionar un tema que parece delicado. El escritor mexicano y ganador del Premio Nobel de Literatura, Octavio Paz, escribió sobre el contraste entre la perspectiva mexicana y la perspectiva estadounidense hacia la muerte en su obra *El laberinto de la soledad*. Paz asegura que las dos culturas se obsesionan con la muerte, pero se manifiesta de dos maneras muy distintas: en una cultura la muerte es una presencia constante y en otra se evita constantemente la realidad de la muerte.

La amistad y el amor
Personal relationships

A. El amor en línea

PASO 1.   Imagínate que has visitado un portal de citas por Internet en español. Contesta las siguientes preguntas que encuentras en el sitio.

1. **Estado civil**
    ☐ **casado/a**
    ☐ **comprometido/a**
    ☐ **divorciado/a**
    ☐ en una **relación**
    ☐ **soltero/a**
    ☐ **viudo/a**

2. La **pareja** ideal debe ser…
    ☐ **abierta**
    ☐ **cariñosa** (muestra afecto)
    ☐ **celosa** (tiene envidia)
    ☐ **comprensiva** (se comprenden / se entienden)
    ☐ **tolerante**

3. La **edad** ideal para…
    • un **noviazgo** (relación romántica) serio entre dos personas que pasan de ser amigos a ser **novios** es a los _____ años.
    • **emanciparse** (**independizarse**) del **nido familiar** (es decir, de sus padres) y **responsabilizarse** es a los _____ años.
    • el **matrimonio** (*marriage*) es a los _____ años.

4. En cuanto al acto de **enamorarse de** (*falling in love with*) otra persona, creo…
    ☐ en el amor a primera vista.
    ☐ que, después de muy poco tiempo, uno sabe si está **enamorado** de otra persona.
    ☐ que el amor crece de una **amistad** (un período de ser amigos) larga.
    ☐ que **casarse con** el el amor de su vida es la expresión mayor del **amor** (*love*).

5. La primera **cita** (*date*) debe ser…
    ☐ una **cita a ciegas** (*blind date*).
    ☐ después de salir varias veces con un grupo de amigos.
    ☐ después de pasar tiempo como amigos.
    ☐ en el momento en que se conocen.

6. ¿Cuánto tiempo debe pasar entre…
    • **conocerse** por primera vez y decir esas palabras mágicas: «**te quiero**» o «**te amo**»? _____
    • ser novios y **comprometerse** (hacer planes para hacerse esposos)? _____
    • comprometerse y **casarse** (hacerse esposos)? _____

7. La **boda** ideal es…
    ☐ grande, cara, en una iglesia y con más de cien personas invitadas.
    ☐ pequeña, en una iglesia y con solo la familia y los amigos más íntimos.
    ☐ los dos novios en un lugar exótico.
    ☐ una boda civil (es decir, no religiosa y con poca ceremonia).

8. Si una persona **rompe con** su esposo/a y el matrimonio termine en **divorcio**…
    ☐ uno de los esposos debe **mudarse** (irse) de la casa.
    ☐ las dos personas deben seguir viviendo en el **hogar** familiar (la casa de la familia).
    ☐ la persona que cuida más a los hijos debe **quedarse** en la casa.

(Continues)

En español…

La pareja is grammatically feminine, but it may refer to either a man or woman when used to mean *partner* and to two men, women, or a mixed couple when used to mean *couple*. The terms **novio** and **novia** can refer to a serious *boyfriend/girlfriend*, an engaged *fiancé/fiancée*, or even an about-to-be-married or recently married *groom/bride*. In general it is easy to recognize the meaning of *groom/bride* because the context of a wedding is usually very clear.

PASO 2. En grupos pequeños, túrnense para hacerse y contestar las preguntas del **Paso 1.** Expliquen sus respuestas.

> **MODELO:** E1: Para ti, ¿cómo es una boda ideal?
>
> E2: Personalmente quiero una boda muy grande, con muchos familiares y todos mis amigos.
>
> E1: Yo prefiero algo más íntimo, con mi familia y mis amigos más íntimos.
>
> E3: No soy religioso/a, así que (*so*) no quiero casarme en la iglesia. Una ceremonia civil sería ideal para mí.

B. A ver: La pareja ideal

Mira y escucha las respuestas de otros miembros del sitio. Mientras miras, completa la información que falta.

PASO 1. Para cada persona que habla, ¿cuál es la edad ideal para casarse?

1. Sabrina, de México

   Más de _____ años

2. Héctor, de México

   De _____ a _____ años

3. Noelia, de España

   De _____ a _____ años

4. Nadia Angélica, de México

   Más o menos a los _____ años

5. Olman, de Costa Rica

   Más de _____ años

6. María Luz, del Perú

   De _____ a _____ años

PASO 2. Para cada persona que habla, ¿cómo es la pareja ideal? Marca todas las respuestas correctas.

1. Mirelle, de México

   ☐ Es cariñosa.
   ☐ Es comprensiva.
   ☐ No es celosa.
   ☐ Quiere a la otra persona.

2. Suny, de Panamá

   ☐ Es comprensiva.
   ☐ Es una persona abierta.
   ☐ No es celosa.
   ☐ Tiene buena comunicación.

3. Víctor, de México

   ☐ Es una persona abierta.
   ☐ Hay respeto mutuo.
   ☐ Te deja ser independiente.
   ☐ Tiene buena relación.

4. Noelia, de España

   ☐ Es cariñosa.
   ☐ Es comprensiva.
   ☐ Quiere a la otra persona.
   ☐ Se comunica bien.

5. Sabrina, de México

   ☐ Acepta a la otra persona.
   ☐ Es cariñosa.
   ☐ Es tolerante.
   ☐ Te deja ser independiente.

6. Anlluly, de Costa Rica

   ☐ Es cariñosa.
   ☐ Es comprensiva.
   ☐ Es honrada.
   ☐ Es sincera.

C. El momento pefecto y la persona ideal

 PASO 1. En grupos de cuatro personas, entrevístense para saber sus ideas sobre casarse y la pareja ideal. Completa la tabla.

Nombre de mi compañero/a	¿Cuál es la edad ideal para casarse?	¿Cuál es su estado civil?	¿Cómo es la pareja ideal?

MODELO: E1: En tu opinión, ¿cuál es la edad ideal para casarse?
E2: Yo creo que entre los 28 y 30 años sería ideal.

 PASO 2. Ahora, dividan su grupo en dos. Cada persona debe hablar con su compañero/a sobre sus opiniones de la pareja perfecta. (**¿Cuáles son sus pasatiempos? ¿Cómo es la personalidad? ¿Cómo es físicamente? ¿Cómo le trata a la pareja?**) ¿A quién conocen Uds. que sería una pareja buena (¡o perfecta!) para uno de los compañeros solteros que entrevistaron? (Si no conocen a nadie, piensen en una persona famosa o de ficción que sería ideal.)

En español...

There are many terms of endearment used throughout the Spanish-speaking world. Here are a few you might come across.

mi amor	my love
mi cariño / mi cari	my dear
cielo	(my) angel (*lit.*, heaven)
corazón	(my) love (*lit.*, heart)
gordito/a	honey (*lit.*, fatty)
mi media naranja	my better half (*lit.*, my half orange)
mi vida	my life
viejo/a	old man/woman

Some of these terms of endearment may seem negative, but they truly are used affectionately among couples in the Spanish-speaking world. While there can be some negative connotation to calling your spouse *old man* or *old lady* in English, this is not necessarily true for the Spanish **viejo/a.** Note also that these words are not necessarily descriptive: someone very thin might be called **gordito** by his partner, and a young woman might be called **vieja.**

COMUN VOCABU **ESTRUCTURA** ATE

 Reciclaje

Review: The present indicative and the infinitive

Completa las conjugaciones del presente de indicativo de los siguientes verbos.

caminar	camin**o**	camin**as**	camin___	camin**amos**	camin___	camin___
correr	corr___	corr___	corr___	corr___	corr**éis**	corr**en**
sal___	sal___	sal**es**	sal___	sal**imos**	sal___	sal___
volver	**vuelv**o	___es	___e	___emos	___éis	___en
ped___	___o	**pid**es	___e	___imos	___ís	___en
pens___	___o	**piens**as	___a	___amos	___áis	___an
casarse	**me** cas**o**	___ cas___	___ cas___	**nos** cas**amos**	**os** cas**áis**	___ cas___

■ Answers to this activity are in **Appendix 2** at the back of your book.

16.1 Los novios no quieren casarse en junio.

Review: The present indicative and the infinitive

Actividades prácticas

A. ¿Eres romántico/a o práctico/a?

PASO 1. Primero, completa las siguientes oraciones con la forma apropiada de los verbos entre paréntesis. Usa el presente de indicativo (la forma **tú** para la pregunta y la forma **yo** para las respuestas) o el infinitivo, como sea apropiado.

PREGUNTA

Cuando _____ (despertarse) en la mañana, ¿qué es lo primero que _____ (pensar)?

RESPUESTAS ROMÁNTICAS

a. _____ (Querer) mucho a mi novio/a.
b. _____ (Amar) mucho a mi esposo/a.
c. _____ (Necesitar) un novio / una novia.

RESPUESTAS PRÁCTICAS

d. _____ (Querer) _____ (ir) al baño.
e. _____ (Tener) hambre.
f. Esta noche _____ (ir) a _____ (acostarse) más temprano.

Ahora, contesta las preguntas.
¿Cuál es la mejor respuesta para ti? _____
¿Es una respuesta romántica o una práctica? _____

PASO 2. En grupos, conversen sobre los primeros pensamientos de Uds. al despertarse. Comparen sus respuestas y escriban un resumen (*summary*) de lo que dicen. En general, ¿Uds. son románticos o son prácticos en sus pensamientos al comienzo del día? **¡Atención!** Acuérdate que si eres parte del grupo, usa la forma **nosotros/as**, pero si no eres parte del grupo, usa la forma **ellos/as**.

> **MODELO:** En general, somos prácticos. Tres de nosotros pensamos que tenemos hambre y solo uno piensa en cuánto ama a su novia.

B. ¿Un rechazo (*rejection*) **o no?**   Cuando uno emprende (*initiates*) una amistad (¡o algo más!) con alguien, siempre existe la posibilidad de rechazo. En esta actividad, vas a ver algunas formas de empezar a hablar con alguien y algunas respuestas posibles.

PASO 1.   Para cada pregunta o exclamación en la primera columna, escoge la mejor respuesta en la segunda columna y complétala con la forma más apropiada del verbo.

PREGUNTAS/EXCLAMACIONES

1. _____ ¿Quieres ir al cine?
2. _____ ¿Me das tu número de teléfono?
3. _____ ¿Dónde vives?
4. _____ ¿Qué vas a hacer este fin de semana?
5. _____ ¿Estás en mi clase de español?
6. _____ ¡Qué guapo eres!

RESPUESTAS

a. No sé. ¿_____ (Tener) planes tú?
b. No, no _____ (ser) estudiante. ¿Tú sí?
c. ¡Gracias! Mira, te _____ (presentar) a mi novia.
d. ¡Muy lejos de ti, _____ (esperar)!
e. Sí. Me _____ (encantar) ir al cine.
f. No. Lo _____ (sentir), pero no _____ (querer) que me llames.

PASO 2.   ¿Cuáles son las respuestas en la segunda columna que se pueden considerar como rechazos?

C. A encontrar la pareja perfecta   Lee los siguientes perfiles (*profiles*) de jóvenes españoles y latinoamericanos. ¿Quién sería buena pareja para quién? ¿Por qué?

MUJERES

Andrea
España

Estudia marketing.
«Me gusta estar con amigos, leer y practicar deporte. Practico gimnasia y pádel, que es un deporte muy parecido al tenis.»

Ximena
Argentina

Trabaja en una agencia de prensa y estudia.
«Me gusta mucho leer y en Buenos Aires hay mucha oferta cultural. Hay mucho cine, exposiciones, recitales… Me gusta mucho reunirme (*get together*) con amigos.»

Laura
Colombia

Estudia artes visuales.
«Pinto. Soy artista y me gusta pintar.»

Nadia Angélica
México

Estudia relaciones internacionales.
«Practico natación, salgo con mis amigos, voy al cine, leo, escucho música y voy a bailar.»

HOMBRES

Adrián
España

Estudia ciencias del deporte.
«Me gusta practicar deporte. Practico fútbol y tenis, pero no me gusta la natación. Me gusta ir al cine. Me gustan las comedias, el drama y las películas de terror.»

Cristián
Argentina

Trabaja como abogado.
«Me gusta jugar al tenis y me gusta salir y divertirme. Salgo con amigos a la noche y voy a cenar. Es buena vida.»

Eduardo
México

Estudia telecomunicaciones.
«Estudio japonés como hobby porque me gusta la cultura japonesa. Soy patinador (*skater*) sobre hielo. Me gustan los tangos y la música electrónica.»

Jahyr
Panamá

Estudia.
«Juego fútbol y me gusta ver fútbol y béisbol en la televisión. También voy al gimnasio. De música me gusta la salsa y también el merengue y el reggae.»

D. Lo mejor y lo peor   Basándote en los ejemplos en la **Actividad C,** crea los siguientes perfiles.

■ un perfil del hombre perfecto / la mujer perfecta
■ un perfil de un hombre / una mujer horrible

Reciclaje

Review: The preterite and imperfect together

PASO 1. Completa las conjugaciones del pretérito de los siguientes verbos.

hablar	hablé	hablaste	habl___	hablamos	hablasteis	habl___
aprender	aprend___	aprendiste	aprendió	aprend___	aprendisteis	aprend___
hacer	hic___	hiciste	___o	hic___	hic___	hic___
ir:	___	fuiste	___		fuisteis	___
llegar:	lleg___	lleg___	llegó	lleg___	lleg___	llegaron
decir:	dije	dij___	dijo	dij___	dijisteis	dij___
tener:	___e	___iste	___o	tuv___	tuv___	tuv___
dormir:	___í	___iste	___ó	dorm___	dorm___	durm___

PASO 2. Ahora completa las conjugaciones del imperfecto de los siguientes verbos.

amar	am___	amabas	am___	amábamos	amabais	am___
comer	comía	com___	com___	com___	com___	com___
ir:	iba	ib___	ib___	íb___	ib___	ib___
ser:	er___	eras	er___	ér___	erais	er___
salir:	sal___	salías	sal___	sal___	sal___	sali___

■ Answers to this activity are in **Appendix 2** at the back of your book.

16.2 Cuando llegaron a la iglesia, los invitados ya los esperaban.

Review: The preterite and imperfect together

Actividades prácticas

A. ¿Te acuerdas?

Se conocieron en la secundaria.

PASO 1. Dos amigas están hablando de cómo se conocieron por primera vez. Primero empareja lo que dice **Amiga 1** con la respuesta de **Amiga 2.** Luego completa las oraciones con el verbo entre paréntesis en *el pretérito*.

AMIGA 1

1. ____ ¿En qué clase te _____ (conocer)?
2. ____ Sí, claro. Y te _____ (preguntar) sobre la tarea, ¿no?
3. ____ ¡Y me _____ (decir) que no! ¿Te acuerdas tú?
4. ____ Sí, la recuerdo bien. Pero luego, Uds. _____ (hablar).
5. ____ ¡Ja, ja, ja, qué chistoso (*funny*)! ¿Por qué _____ (pensar) que yo era buena persona?
6. ____ ¿Con solo una sonrisa (*smile*)? Y entonces, ¿_____ (seguir) con nuestra conversación?
7. ____ ¿Y luego? Te _____ (invitar) a comer con mis amigos, ¿no?
8. ____ ¿Y qué _____ (comer) tú? Seguramente no te acuerdas.

AMIGA 2

a. Sí, y _____ que parecías una buena persona.
b. Claro. Es que _____ (hacer) la tarea con otra amiga y ella me estaba mirando.
c. Lo recuerdas bien. _____ (Ir) con Uds. a un restaurante.
d. Nosotras _____ (conocerse) en la clase de biología. ¿Te acuerdas?
e. No es cierto. Me acuerdo perfectamente: _____ (Pedir) las enchiladas verdes.
f. Pues, te ____ (dar) la tarea y me lo _____ (agradecer).
g. No sé. Creo que porque nos _____ (sonreír).
h. Sí, me _____ (pedir) permitirte ver mi tarea de la noche anterior.

PASO 2. Explícale a un compañero o una compañera cómo conociste por primera vez a una persona importante en tu vida. Tu compañero/a debe hacerte preguntas para sacarte más detalles.

MODELO: E1: Cuando conocí por primera vez a mi entrenador (*coach*) de fútbol, me cayó mal. Ahora es una de las personas más importantes de mi vida.
E2: ¿Por qué te cayó mal? ¿Te acuerdas? ¿Te dijo algo?
E1: Al contrario. No me dijo nada por dos meses. Pero luego me dijo que quería observarme primero.

B. El matrimonio en la civilización inca

PASO 1. Los incas eran una de las grandes civilizaciones en América en la época prehispánica. Sus tradiciones del matrimonio eran parecidas a las europeas, pero no en todos los aspectos. Completa cada oración con el verbo entre paréntesis, conjugándolo en el imperfecto. Luego, decide si cada oración es cierta o falsa para los incas en los tiempos prehispánicos.

¿Cierto o falso?

_____ 1. En general, los jóvenes _____ (casarse) cuando _____ (tener) dieciséis años.

_____ 2. Antes de casarse formalmente, _____ (vivir) juntos para ver si _____ (ser) compatibles.

_____ 3. Los padres del novio _____ (arreglar) el matrimonio con los padres de la novia.

_____ 4. Una vez al año, el gobierno _____ (hacer) una boda en cada pueblo para todos los que _____ (querer) casarse.

_____ 5. Todos _____ (ir) a la iglesia católica del pueblo para asistir a la boda.

_____ 6. La novia _____ (vestirse) de blanco.

_____ 7. Después de la boda oficial, cada familia _____ (hacer) su propia ceremonia en casa.

_____ 8. Durante la boda, el novio _____ (tener) que bailar un vals con la novia.

PASO 2. Ahora, en grupos de tres, creen tres oraciones, dos ciertas y una falsa, sobre el matrimonio en tiempos de sus abuelos. Luego, lean sus oraciones a otro grupo para ver si ellos pueden decir cuál es la oración falsa.

C. Oraciones sobre el amor

PASO 1. Completa cada oración con el verbo en el pretérito (1–4) o en el imperfecto (5–8).

Pretérito

1. «Gerardo y Luz _____ ese día.» (conocerse)

2. «Gerardo _____ (estar) en Las Vegas el 21 de abril.»

3. Gerardo dice: «Cuando éramos estudiantes, yo _____ (enamorarse) de ti, y tú _____ (enamorarse) de mí después.»

4. «Ayer _____ (casarse) Luz y Gerardo.»

Imperfecto

5. «Gerardo y Luz ya _____ (conocerse).»

6. «Luz ya _____ (estar) en Las Vegas el 21 de abril.»

7. Luz dice: «Cuando éramos estudiantes, yo _____ (enamorarse) de ti y tú _____ (enamorarse) de mí.»

8. «Ayer _____ (casarse) Luz y Gerardo.»

Se conocen.

Se enamoran.

Se casan.

PASO 2. Ahora empareja cada oración de arriba (1–8) con la situación más lógica.

SITUACIÓN

_____ a. octubre 2013

_____ b. el 14 de septiembre, 2013: se hablan por primera vez en la clase de biología

_____ c. en Las Vegas: 20, 21, 22, 23 de abril

_____ d. en Las Vegas: 21 de abril

_____ e. el amor: primero Gerardo y luego Luz

_____ f. el amor: Gerardo y Luz, poco a poco y al mismo tiempo

_____ g. Hoy están casados.

_____ h. Hoy no sabemos si están casados o no.

D. La pareja Perón

PASO 1.   Eva y Juan Perón son, sin duda, la pareja política más conocida en toda la historia de Latinoamérica. Se hicieron aún más famosos por la obra de teatro y la película *Evita*. Completa las siguientes oraciones sobre ellos. **¡Atención!** Todas las oraciones están en el pasado, pero tienes que escoger entre el imperfecto y el pretérito.

Juan y Eva Perón

1. Juan _____ (entrar) al Colegio Militar en 1910, cuando Eva no _____ (vivir) todavía.
2. Eva _____ (nacer) en 1919 en una zona rural, cuando Juan ya _____ (ser) militar (*soldier*).
3. Eva _____ (irse) a Buenos Aires en 1935 para trabajar como actriz, pero ella y Juan no _____ (conocerse) todavía. _____ (Conocerse) por primera vez en un concierto organizado por Juan en 1944.
4. Un poco después, Juan _____ (hacerse) vicepresidente, cuando _____ (tener) 48 años.
5. Eva y Juan _____ (casarse) en 1945 y al año siguiente, Juan _____ (hacerse) presidente de Argentina.
6. Eva _____ (empezar) a hacerse muy famosa a nivel mundial por sus discursos (*speeches*) de un gran impacto emocional.
7. Eva _____ (morirse) en 1952 cuando apenas (*barely*) _____ (tener) 32 años.
8. Juan _____ (seguir) como presidente hasta 1955 y después _____ (vivir) muchos años en el exilio.
9. Juan _____ (regresar) a Argentina en 1973 para asumir la presidencia de nuevo. _____ (morirse) en 1974.

PASO 2.   En parejas, hagan una cronología (o «línea de tiempo») de las vidas de Eva y Juan Perón basada en la información en el **Paso 1.** Empiecen en 1910 y terminen en 1974. En un lado de la línea, apunten cada evento o período de la vida de Eva, y en el otro lado, cada evento o período de la vida de Juan.

PASO 3.   Crea una cronología sobre tu propia vida con un mínimo de seis eventos o períodos, y explícasela a tu compañero / compañera. ¡Empieza con el evento más importante: «Nací»!

E. ¡Un desastre!

Cuando uno trata de empezar una relación amorosa con otra persona, las cosas no siempre van muy bien. Usa tu imaginación para terminar la siguiente historia, creando cuatro incidentes desastrosos (*disastrous*) en una noche que iba a ser muy romántica. Para cada incidente, escribe lo que **pasaba** en ese momento y lo que **pasó**.

Salimos a cenar y luego...

¿QUÉ PASABA?	¿QUÉ PASÓ?
1. _____	_____
2. _____	_____
3. _____	_____
4. _____	_____

F. ¿Cómo se conocieron tus padres?

¿Sabes cómo se conocieron tus padres? Cuéntale la historia a un compañero / una compañera e indiquen juntos si eso sería común hoy en día o no y por qué.

MODELO: Mi papá vivía en Fullerton, California. Mi mamá fue a un baile allí con su prima, y allí se conocieron. Eso ya no es muy común ahora, porque ahora nadie va a bailes.

G. Cultura: El matrimonio entre personas del mismo sexo en España

España

PASO 1.   Lee el texto sobre España.

El 3 de julio de 2005, España legalizó el matrimonio entre personas del mismo sexo (es decir, entre dos hombres o dos mujeres). Fue el tercer país del mundo en aprobar una ley[a] similar —después de los Países Bajos (Holanda) y Bélgica[b]— y el primer país en el mundo hispano. El proyecto de ley[c] fue apoyado[d] por el entonces presidente del gobierno, José Luis Rodríguez Zapatero, cumpliendo con[e] una promesa que había hecho durante su campaña electoral. El resultado final fue una reforma al Código Civil: la nueva versión declara que «El matrimonio tendrá los mismos requisitos y efectos cuando ambos contrayentes[f] sean del mismo o de diferente sexo».

Según las encuestas de 2004, un 66 por ciento de los españoles estaban a favor del matrimonio entre homosexuales. Sin embargo, la nueva ley no tenía el apoyo de los grupos más conservadores. El Partido Popular, que tenía la mayoría de los votos en el Senado, argumentó que la homosexualidad era una patología y que tendría un efecto negativo sobre los hijos de una pareja. Sin embargo, esos argumentos se rechazaron[g] y a pesar del veto del Senado, la ley sí fue aprobada por el Congreso, el presidente del gobierno y el rey Juan Carlos I.

Después de que la ley se ratificó, quedaban dos temas importantes por resolver. Uno era si en los matrimonios entre personas del mismo sexo la ley le daría residencia legal en España a un extranjero o una extranjera que se casara con un ciudadano español, incluso si viniera de un país donde el matrimonio homosexual todavía no era legal. Se determinó que sí, que los derechos de esa pareja, incluso la residencia de la persona extranjera, serían reconocidos dentro de España aunque el matrimonio no fuera legal en otros contextos. El otro asunto era «la adopción homoparental». Según la ley, si una pareja lesbiana tuviera un hijo o una hija, la madre no biológica tendría que hacer todos los trámites[h] formales de adopción para ser reconocida legalmente como la madre. Eso no era el caso entre las parejas heterosexuales: si una mujer con hijos se casara con un hombre, el padrastro se reconocería automáticamente como el padre legal de los hijos. Esta desigualdad se resolvió modificando la ley sobre la reproducción asistida, aplicando los mismos derechos legales a las familias homoparentales que tenían ya las familias heteroparentales.

[a]*law* [b]*Belgium* [c]*proyecto… bill* [d]*supported* [e]*cumpliendo… keeping* [f]*parties* [g]*se… were rejected* [h]*paperwork, legal processes*

PASO 2.   Completa las oraciones con la forma apropiada del pretérito o imperfecto del verbo más lógico de la lista. **¡Atención!** No repitas ninguna palabra.

apoyar	dar	existir	legalizar	querer	ser
causar	declarar	hacer	presentar	reformar	

1. Cuando España _____ el matrimonio entre personas del mismo sexo, ya _____ legal en los Países Bajos (Holanda) y Bélgica.
2. José Luis Rodríguez Zapatero _____ cumplir con una promesa que _____ durante su campaña electoral.
3. El Congreso _____ una ley que ya _____ en el Código Civil.
4. Muchos españoles ya _____ el matrimonio entre homosexuales cuando el presidente del gobierno _____ el proyecto de ley al Senado y el Congreso.
5. El Partido Popular _____ que las relaciones homoparentales _____ daño (*harm*) a los hijos.
6. La ley les _____ residencia legal y otros derechos a parejas de países que no habían legalizado el matrimonio homosexual.

PASO 3.   En parejas, contesten las preguntas y explíquense las respuestas.

1. España y el resto del mundo hispano tienen una larga tradición católica, pero en general, hay una separación muy clara entre la religión y la política. ¿Piensas que eso tiene algo que ver (*something to do*) con el hecho de que algunos de estos países (Argentina, España, México, Uruguay) fueron de los primeros en el mundo en legalizar el matrimonio entre personas del mismo sexo?
2. Los cuatro países mencionados, en comparación al resto del mundo hispano, tienen un nivel de desarrollo y un nivel de educación relativamente altos. ¿Piensas que eso también tiene algo que ver?
3. En tu país, ¿la religión tiene mucha o poca influencia en la política? ¿Esto ha tenido un efecto en el debate sobre el matrimonio entre personas del mismo sexo?

↻ Reciclaje

Review: Object pronouns

Empareja el término con la descripción. Luego, completa cada oración con el pronombre de objeto directo (**lo, la** o **los**) o de objeto indirecto (**te, le**). La primera ya se ha hecho.

1. __*b*__ la pareja perfecta
2. _____ tu amigo / amiga
3. _____ el amor
4. _____ el estado civil
5. _____ tu esposo / esposa
6. _____ el novio y la novia

a. _____ regalas algo cuando tienen un aniversario de boda.
b. Muchos *la* buscan, pero no todos *la* encuentran.
c. _____ habla con frecuencia para ver cómo estás.
d. _____ puedes ver en una boda. Son el centro de la atención.
e. Los casados a veces tienen que trabajar para mantener_____ en su matrimonio.
f. _____ tienes que indicar en muchos formularios oficiales.

■ Answers to this activity are in **Appendix 2** at the back of your book.

16.3 Le pidió un divorcio porque ya no lo amaba.

Review: Object pronouns

Actividades prácticas

A. Preguntas y respuestas Vas a escuchar seis preguntas. Escoge la mejor respuesta para cada una.

1. _____ 2. _____ 3. _____ 4. _____ 5. _____ 6. _____

a. Los conocí en una fiesta en tu casa el año pasado.
b. Lo vi en el parque con su hermana.
c. Les hablo por teléfono de vez en cuando y nos mandamos mensajes por Facebook.
d. La queremos tener en Acapulco, pero no sé si podemos ahorrar el dinero.
e. Le dieron un trabajo muy bueno en el banco.
f. Nunca la he visto. ¿Existe o es una fantasía tuya (*of yours*)?

■ The audio files for in-text listening activities are available in the eBook, within Connect Plus activities, and on the Online Learning Center.

B. Un gran problema

PASO 1. Lee esta carta que explica un problema. Luego, completa las posibles soluciones al problema con un pronombre de la lista. **¡Atención!** Algunos pronombres se usan más de una vez.

Para: doctor@amor.com
De: Anónima
Asunto: Dudas

Doctor Amor:

Tengo un gran problema. Ya no quiero seguir con mi novio, pero no sé cómo romper la relación. Lo quería mucho y me parecía muy guapo, pero no sé qué pasó. Últimamente no lo aguanto (*I can't stand him*) y además, ahora me parece muy feo. Me sigue mandando mensajes constantemente, siempre quiere estar conmigo y les cuenta a sus amigos que está locamente enamorado de mí, pero la verdad es que ya no lo quiero en mi vida. ¿Qué hago? No es malo y no quiero lastimarlo (*hurt him*). En el archivo adjunto (*attached*), puse una lista de ideas.

—Anónima

Pronombres preposicionales: él ella
Pronombres de objeto directo e indirecto: le lo me

POSIBLES SOLUCIONES:

1. Decir_____ que sólo quiero ser su amiga.
2. Decir_____ que _____ odio y que ya no _____ quiero ver.
3. Decir_____ que _____ siento mucho, que es muy buena persona, pero _____ parece mejor si terminamos nuestra relación.
4. Ya no hablar_____.
5. Invitar_____ a un restaurante muy caro, cenar allí con _____, decir_____ que voy al baño y luego desaparecer.
6. Presentar_____ a una amiga y esperar que él se enamore de _____.
7. Decir_____ que siempre _____ voy a querer mucho, pero que quiero estar sola por un tiempo.
8. Empezar a vestir_____ muy mal, para que piense que soy muy fea y que _____ deje.
9. Presentar_____ a una amiga y decir_____ que _____ es mi novia y que ya no _____ interesan los hombres.
10. Dar_____ buenísimas recomendaciones como novio en el Internet para que _____ busquen otras mujeres para salir con _____.

PASO 2. En grupos, decidan cuál es la mejor solución de todas y cuál es la peor.

La mejor solución es el número: ____

La peor solución es el número: ____

 PASO 3. Basándose en la mejor solución que escogieron en el **Paso 2**, escriban lo que «Anónima» debería decir **literalmente** cuando hable con el novio.

C. Los muxes de Oaxaca

PASO 1. En el estado de Oaxaca en México, la cultura indígena de los zapotecos es muy fuerte. En esa cultura, existe la tradición del muxe (se pronuncia *MU she*), un hombre que en muchos aspectos lleva la vida de una mujer. Completa las siguientes oraciones sobre los muxes, utilizando un pronombre de objeto (**lo, los, le** o **les**) o un pronombre reflexivo (**se**). Luego, indica cuál de las siguientes oraciones es falsa.

1. En general, a los muxes ____ tratan con respeto en las comunidades zapotecas.
2. A muchos padres ____ gusta tener un hijo muxe porque los hijos muxes no ____ abandonan en tiempos difíciles.
3. Tienen una competencia de muxes cada año y al más bonito ____ dan un premio.
4. Muchos muxes ____ visten de mujeres, pero algunos ____ visten de hombres.
5. A un muxe ____ escogieron como presidente del país en 2008.
6. A muchos niños ____ dan la opción de ser muxe cuando entran a la adolescencia.
7. Mucha gente ____ considera dotados (*gifted*) de un talento artístico especial.
8. En las comunidades zapotecas, ____ puedes ver de vez en cuando vendiendo en el mercado, haciendo artesanía o en otros trabajos tradicionales de mujeres.

 PASO 2. Si pudieras hablar con un muxe, ¿qué le preguntarías? En parejas, creen tres preguntas para ellos.

MODELO: ¿Uds. se casan?
¿Cómo los tratan los demás?

 D. Cómo pueden cuidarse bien el uno al otro   Si uno ama a su pareja y quiere cuidarla bien (mental, física y emocionalmente), ¿qué debe hacer? En grupos pequeños, creen una lista de por lo menos cinco ideas de cómo podrían cuidar a sus parejas y cómo ellos/ellas pueden cuidarlos a Uds. **¡Atención!** Escriban sus ideas en forma del infinitivo.

MODELO: Ayudarlo con la tarea.
Prepararle comida.

 E. La amistad

PASO 1. ¿Qué hace un buen amigo / una buena amiga? En grupos, creen una lista, basada en su experiencia, de las cosas que hacen los amigos / las amigas de verdad (*true*).

MODELO: Los amigos te piden ayuda cuando tienen problemas.

PASO 2. ¿Son iguales las amistades entre los hombres y las amistades entre las mujeres? Creen una lista de algunas diferencias que Uds. han visto entre los hombres y las mujeres en cuanto a (*concerning*) la amistad.

MODELO: Una mujer les pide ayuda mucho a sus amigas. Un hombre no les pide ayuda tanto a sus amigos.

PASO 3. Si encontraron diferencias entre los hombres y las mujeres en el **Paso 2**, ¿piensan que esas diferencias son comunes en todas las culturas?

↻ Reciclaje

Review: The present subjunctive

Completa las conjugaciones del presente de subjuntivo de los siguientes verbos.

amar:	am**e**	am___	am___	am**emos**	am___	am___
hac___:	hag___	hag**as**	hag___	hag**amos**	hag___	hag___
casarse:	**me** case	___ cas___	___ cas___	**nos** cas**emos**	**os** cas**éis**	___ cas___
ser:	___**a**	se___	___	se___	___**áis**	se___
volver:	**vuelv**a	___as	___a	___amos	___áis	___an
tener:	teng**a**	teng___	___a	teng___	___áis	teng___

■ Answers to this activity are in **Appendix 2** at the back of your book.

16.4 Espero que rompa con su novio antes de que se enamore de él.

Review: The present subjunctive

Actividades prácticas

A. Una telenovela Las telenovelas son programas de televisión muy populares en Latino-américa y otras partes del mundo. Se trata de una historia de amor, presentada de una forma sentimental y melodramática.

PASO 1. Lee la siguiente versión muy exagerada de cómo hablan en las telenovelas. Usa los verbos de la lista para completar las oraciones. El primero ya está hecho. **¡Atención!** Algunos verbos están en el indicativo y otros en el subjuntivo.

eres (2x)	se casa (2x)	sea (3x)	te cases
haya	se case	seas	te vayas

MUJER: ¡Quiero que <u>te cases</u> conmigo! ¡Quiero que _____[1] mi esposo!

HOMBRE: ¿Estás loca? No quiero casarme contigo, porque _____[2] muy fea.

MUJER: Es posible que yo _____[3] un poco fea, pero ¡tú eres peor! No creo que _____[4] otro hombre más feo en todo el mundo.

HOMBRE: ¿Pero no entiendes? Me voy a casar con Angélica Antonieta. ¡Necesito que tú _____[5] de mi vida!

MUJER: No pienso que Angélica Antonieta _____[6] tan tonta. Ella dice que _____[7] contigo solo para que la dejes en paz.

HOMBRE: ¡No es cierto! Ella me quiere mucho y hace todo para que yo _____[8] feliz. Si yo le digo a ella que _____[9] conmigo, entonces _____[10] conmigo.

MUJER: ¡Qué idiota _____[11]!

PASO 2. En parejas, escriban un diálogo de telenovela usando el **Paso 1** como modelo.

CONÉCTATE AL MUNDO HISPANO

En muchos países latinoamericanos, la industria televisora es un sector importante de la economía, gracias en parte al enorme éxito internacional de **las telenovelas.** En su temática (*topics*), las telenovelas son parecidas a los «soap operas» de los Estados Unidos, pero en otros aspectos, son parecidas a programas dramáticos, como *Game of Thrones* o *Downton Abbey.* En general, los programas se transmiten (*are broadcast*) por la noche y muchas veces tienen actores muy reconocidos. Atraen (*They attract*) a un público de hombres y mujeres de todas las edades y de todas las clases sociales. A veces parece que el país entero se detiene (*stops*) a la hora indicada para ver su «novela» favorita.

Los países que producen más telenovelas son Argentina, Brasil (en portugués, pero dobladas al español para exportar), Chile, Colombia, México y Venezuela. Pasan los programas no solo en Latinoamérica y España, sino también en otros países de Europa, en Asia y en el Medio Oriente (*Middle East*), con subtítulos, doblados, o hasta con otro equipo de actores. Dos de las telenovelas más famosas internacionalmente son *Los ricos también lloran,* una telenovela mexicana de 1979, y *Yo soy Betty, la fea,* una telenovela colombiana de 1999 a 2001. Esta última fue presentada en su versión original en más de treinta países e hicieron más de veinte versiones con nuevos actores para otros países. La versión norteamericana se llama *Ugly Betty* y estuvo en el aire de 2006 a 2010.

B. William Levy

PASO 1. William Levy es un actor y modelo cubano que inmigró a los Estados Unidos a los 15 años. Durante muchos años, fue uno de los galanes (*leading men*) más conocidos de las telenovelas, sobre todo de las telenovelas mexicanas. Aquí hay unas afirmaciones (*statements*) sobre él que pueden ser ciertas o falsas. Escribe cada afirmación en la categoría correcta para completar la oración. **¡Atención!** En dos de las categorías, tienes que cambiar al subjuntivo el verbo de la afirmación.

William Levy, actor cubano

AFIRMACIONES

Es originario de Cuba.

Tiene problemas para conseguir una novia.

Vive en los Estados Unidos.

Habla bien el inglés y el español.

La mayoría de la gente lo considera muy feo.

Pasa mucho tiempo en diferentes países de Latinoamérica.

Hace mucho ejercicio todos los días.

Es un gran ídolo de las telenovelas.

Se ve (*He looks*) mal sin camisa.

ES VERDAD QUE…	ES POSIBLE QUE…	NO CREO QUE…
_____	_____	_____
_____	_____	_____
_____	_____	_____

PASO 2. Crea una o dos oraciones más sobre Levy para cada una de las categorías. Luego, en grupos pequeños, compartan sus oraciones para ver quién está de acuerdo.

C. La Malinche y Hernán Cortés

La mujer indígena conocida como «Malintzín» o «La Malinche» fue intérprete (*interpreter*) y consejera (*advisor*) diplomática entre los españoles y los aztecas en los tiempos de la conquista de México. Su relación de amor con el conquistador español Hernán Cortés es muy conocida. Completa las siguientes oraciones con la forma apropiada del presente de indicativo o subjuntivo del verbo entre paréntesis. Luego, escribe **M** si la persona que está hablando es La Malinche y **C** si es Cortés. Escribe **M/C** si los dos podrían haber dicho (*could have said*) la oración.

¿M, C o M/C?

1. _____ «Yo nací en España. Hablo español, pero no hablo ninguna lengua indígena de México. Quiero que La Malinche _____ (trabajar) como mi intérprete.»
2. _____ «Yo nací en la frontera (*border*) entre el Imperio azteca y los estados mayas, y por eso hablo náhuatl (la lengua de los aztecas) y maya. Estoy aprendiendo rápidamente el español, porque es necesario que lo _____ (hablar) bien.»
3. _____ «La Malinche y yo vamos a tener un hijo. Quiero que _____ (llamarse) Martín.»
4. _____ «El hijo que tuve con Cortés ya nació. Dicen que _____ (ser) el primer mestizo (*person of mixed race*) de México.»
5. _____ «Ahora me quiero casar con una española. Le voy a decir a La Malinche que _____ (irse).»
6. _____ «Ahora estoy casada con un noble español. No creo que Cortés y yo _____ (volver) a vernos nunca.»
7. _____ «Ahora estoy casado con una española y tengo seis hijos con ella. Creo que ellos _____ (ir) a estar bien, porque les _____ (ir) a dejar mucho dinero en mi testamento para que _____ (tener) todo lo que necesitan.»
8. _____ «Espero que la historia me _____ (tratar [*to treat*]) bien.»

D. ¿Cómo consigues novio/a?

PASO 1. ¿Qué le recomiendas a un amigo / una amiga que quiere conseguir novio/a? Responde con por lo menos tres ideas.

> **MODELO:** Yo te recomiendo que seas simpático/a, que te vistas siempre bien y que te bañes cada día.

PASO 2. Pregúntales a tres compañeros qué recomiendan ellos que uno haga para conseguir novio/a. Apunta las respuestas.

> **MODELO:** ¿Qué recomiendas que uno haga para conseguir novio o novia?

¡Leamos!

Los jóvenes retrasan° su emancipación   *delay*

Antes de leer

El siguiente artículo informa sobre un estudio europeo sobre una tendencia de los jóvenes, pero se concentra en Vitoria, una ciudad en el norte de España, como su punto de referencia.

PASO 1.   Lee el titular (*headline*) del artículo y escoge la mejor respuesta para cada una de las siguientes preguntas.

1. Los jóvenes no se mudan de (*move out of*) la casa de los padres hasta…
   a. casarse.   b. empezar sus estudios universitarios.   c. tener 25 años.

2. La edad promedio (*average*) para casarse es:
   a. 25 años.   b. 30 años.   c. 32 años.

PASO 2.   Ahora, lee el primer subtítulo y escoge los tres factores de la lista que, según el subtítulo, influyen en la decisión de los jóvenes de emanciparse más tarde.

☐ Es más cómodo vivir con los padres que independizarse.
☐ La familia se siente responsable de sus hijos.
☐ Los estudiantes universitarios europeos prefieren vivir con sus padres.
☐ Los precios de los pisos son muy altos.
☐ No hay muchas casas en Vitoria.

A leer

PASO 1.   Lee el artículo del *Diario de Noticias de Álava*.

Los jóvenes retrasan su emancipación hasta la fecha de la boda, en el umbral[a] de los treinta

LA FAMILIA, LA ESCASEZ[b] DE PISOS DE RENTA BAJA Y LA **COMODIDAD** INFLUYEN EN ESTA DECISIÓN

Anglosajones y escandinavos se mudan antes para vivir solos, pero no ocurre lo mismo en los países de tradición católica

R. Ruiz De Gauna
Diario de Noticias de Álava

1 VITORIA. De casa de los padres al hogar conyugal. A diferencia de lo que pudiera parecer,[c] la frase sigue siendo válida. Y es que, a la hora de independizarse, Europa también camina a dos velocidades. Mientras los jóvenes británicos, daneses, suecos o alemanes se mudan de casa a los 25 años, como solteros, para vivir solos, los vascos,

españoles, irlandeses e italianos se resisten a abandonar el nido familiar hasta fijar[d] la fecha de la boda. El matrimonio y la emancipación suelen[e] coincidir en el umbral de los 30.

2 ¿Por qué esas diferencias entre el norte y el sur de Europa? Básicamente son factores culturales, económicos e incluso institucionales los que condicionan la emancipación al matrimonio y hacen que esta se retrase, sin olvidar que por detrás de todos ellos subyacen[f] las raíces[g] del catolicismo.

3 En los países anglosajones y escandinavos, el Estado ejerce un papel activo y directo para garantizar el bienestar de sus ciudadanos. Rol que en los territorios de tradición católica asume la familia, entendiendo que son los padres los responsables del bienestar de sus hijos.

4 La otra cuerda que ata[h] a padres e hijos es la que se deriva del desempleo, la precariedad laboral y los bajos salarios —variables que se han acentuado con la crisis.

[a]*threshold* [b]*lack* [c]*pudiera… might seem* [d]*set* [e]*tend to* [f]*underlie* [g]*roots* [h]*ata… ties*

5 Tras varios años en el mercado de trabajo, alaveses[i] y vascos,[j] en general, logran un empleo estable y mejor remunerado. Ha llegado la hora de mudarse a una vivienda propia y entonces se topan con[k] la cruda realidad: apenas[l] hay alquileres de renta baja y el precio de los pisos en propiedad es prohibitivo para afrontarlo con un único salario. Vitoria se mantiene entre las cinco ciudades con pisos libres más caros y casas de segunda mano que intentan venderse por encima de su valor real. ¿Solución? Casarse, y así poder sumar dos sueldos para afrontar la hipoteca.[m]

[i]*people from the city of Álava (located in the Basque Country)* [j]*Basques (people from the Basque Country)* [k]*topan... to bump into* [l]*barely* [m]*mortgage*

PASO 2. Indica si cada elemento se refiere principalmente a países del *norte* o del *sur* de Europa.

	EL NORTE	EL SUR
1. Después de independizarse, viven con su esposo o esposa.	☐	☐
2. Después de independizarse, viven solos.	☐	☐
3. El Estado garantiza el bienestar.	☐	☐
4. La familia garantiza el bienestar.	☐	☐
5. Se emancipan a los 25 años.	☐	☐
6. Se emancipan a los 30 años.	☐	☐

PASO 3. Indica si cada factor influye en el retraso (*delay*) de la emancipación es cultural o económico.

	FACTOR CULTURAL	FACTOR ECONÓMICO
1. bajos salarios	☐	☐
2. cierta independencia personal	☐	☐
3. el desempleo	☐	☐
4. la religión	☐	☐
5. la vivienda cara	☐	☐

Después de leer

PASO 1. Empareja el párrafo del informe con la idea principal que corresponda.

a. _____ A pesar de tener un puesto de trabajo estable con un buen salario, es difícil poder pagar una vivienda tan cara. Al casarse, los jóvenes pueden unir dos salarios para pagar una vivienda.

b. _____ Con la crisis económica es más difícil que los jóvenes encuentren trabajo estable y que ganen suficiente dinero para independizarse.

c. _____ En el norte se supone que independizarse antes de casarse ayuda a uno a responsabilizarse (con la ayuda del gobierno), mientras que en el sur se supone que son los padres los responsables de sus hijos adultos solteros.

d. _____ Los jóvenes del norte de Europa son más jóvenes cuando se mudan de la casa que los jóvenes del sur.

e. _____ Varios factores influyen en el retraso de la emancipación de los jóvenes en el sur de Europa.

 PASO 2. En grupos, respondan a la pregunta «Donde viven Uds., ¿cuáles son las razones para independizarse de los padres antes de casarse?» Escriban por lo menos cinco razones e intenten ponerlas en orden de prioridad.

¡Escuchemos!

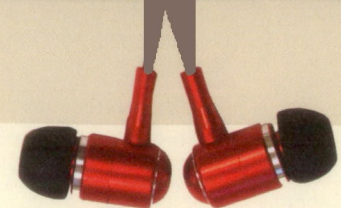

¿Cómo se conocieron?

Antes de escuchar

Indica si conoces a muchas (**M**) o pocas personas (**P**), o si no conoces a nadie (**N**) que haya conocido a su pareja de las siguientes maneras.

____ a través de (*through*) otra persona que conocía a los dos

____ a través de un grupo religioso

____ desde la niñez

____ en colegio (*high school*)

____ por Internet

____ en la calle

____ en otro país

____ en un autobús (u otro transporte)

____ en un bar o restaurante

____ en un lugar de trabajo

¿Cuál es la manera más común de conocer a la pareja? Cuál es la menos común?

A escuchar

Mira y escucha el video en el que los participantes responden a la pregunta, «¿Cómo conoció Ud. a su pareja?». Luego, indica quién dice cada una de las siguientes frases.

Magnolia, de Cuba

Clody, de Argentina

Víctor, de España

María Esther, de México

María Luz, del Perú

Óscar, de Costa Rica

1. _____ «Ahora mi hija tiene dos niños —dos nietos para nosotros.»

2. _____ «Aquí estoy, todavía (me) considero, después de 22 años, enamorada de él.»

3. _____ «Conocí a una sudafricana en la calle y me quedé.»

4. _____ «Él me conoció primero y se flechó (se enamoró) de mí.»

5. _____ «Estaba solo en ese momento. Y entonces ella también estaba sola y acabamos juntos.»

6. _____ «Hace treinta y ocho años que estamos casados.»

7. _____ «Lo conocí en Cuba.»

8. _____ «Me fui de turista a Israel.»

9. _____ «Nos conocimos en… aquí en Barcelona.»

10. _____ «Nos conocimos cuando estábamos los dos estudiando en la universidad.»

11. _____ «Nos conocimos trabajando en una fábrica de ropa.»

12. _____ «Ya nos vamos a tener que morir juntos.»

13. _____ «Yo tenía 19 años, ella tenía 24.»

14. _____ «La vida es lo que te sucede mientras estás ocupado haciendo otros planes.»

Después de escuchar

En una oración completa, describe el comienzo de una relación importante (puede ser relación tuya o la de otras personas).

> **MODELO:** Mi hermana conoció a su esposo cuando él compartía un apartamento con el novio (ahora ex novio) de ella.

¡Escribamos!

La emancipación de los jóvenes estadounidenses

En diferentes culturas, las costumbres asociadas con la emancipación varían mucho según la época histórica, la situación socioeconómica, las tradiciones familiares, la religión y la cultura popular. En esta actividad vas a comparar tu experiencia como joven con las experiencias descritas en la lectura de **¡Leamos!**

Antes de escribir

Escoge dos temas de la lista y apunta algunos elementos relacionados con cada tema que tienes en común con los jóvenes españoles de la lectura, «Los jóvenes retrasan su emancipación», y algunos elementos que no tienes en común con ellos.

TEMAS

la edad de la emancipación	la religión
el matrimonio	la situación económica
la posición política/social	

MODELO:	Semejanzas...	Diferencias...
el matrimonio	*como los vascos, españoles, irlandeses e italianos, mis amigos y yo solemos casarnos a los 30 años*	*no vivimos con los padres hasta casarnos —vivimos con grupos de amigos o con con novios*

	Semejanzas...	Diferencias...
TEMA 1		
TEMA 2		

(Continues)

ESTRATEGIA

Comparing and contrasting

When comparing your situation to that of others, it is important to consider similarities as well as differences. Understanding what you have in common can help you better understand what you don't have in common, and any discussion can be made richer by looking at more than one side. If you contemplate different perspectives by comparing and contrasting them with your own, you can let go of the thought that your worldview is shared by everyone and you will no doubt gain a better understanding of the situations of others as well as a new appreciation of your own.

A escribir

Usando la información de **Antes de escribir,** escribe un ensayo de cuatro párrafos.

☐ En el primer párrafo, explica los dos temas.

☐ En el segundo párrafo, compara y contrasta tu experiencia de uno de los temas con la experiencia de los jóvenes españoles de la lectura.

☐ En el tercer párrafo, compara y contrasta otro tema.

☐ En el último párrafo, concluye el ensayo con una afirmación sobre la comparación entre tú y los jóvenes españoles.

 ## Después de escribir

Revisa tu ensayo. Luego, intercambia ensayos con un compañero / una compañera para evaluarlos. Lee el ensayo de tu compañero/a y decide si ha incluido tanto semejanzas como diferencias con respeto a los dos temas. Lee de nuevo el ensayo con cuidado para revisar los siguientes puntos.

☐ ¿Concuerdan los sujetos y los verbos?

☐ ¿Concuerdan los sustantivos y los adjetivos?

☐ Cuando es apropiado, ¿ha usado las excepciones **mayor, menor, mejor** y **peor**?

☐ ¿Ha usado **que** con **más** y **menos**?

☐ ¿Ha usado **como** con las formas apropiadas de **tan** y **tanto**?

☐ ¿Tiene sentido la conclusión?

Después de revisar el ensayo de tu compañero/a, devuélveselo. Mira tu propio ensayo para ver los cambios que tu compañero/a te recomienda y haz las revisiones necesarias.

¡Hablemos!

Mis primeros días en la universidad

Antes de hablar

Usando el pasado (pretérito e imperfecto), escribe una descripción del comienzo de una relación en la universidad. Luego, usa el presente para describir la relación en este momento.

> **MODELO:** Estaba nerviosa el primer día. Luego, conocí a mi compañera de cuarto y su familia me invitó a cenar con ellos. Fuimos a… . Luego,… . Ahora somos muy buenas amigas.

 ### A hablar

En grupos de tres, comparen sus historias. Luego, formen nuevos grupos de tres y cuenten todas las historias del primer grupo; tienen que contar sus propias historias en primera persona (**yo**) y las historias de los otros estudiantes en tercera persona (**él, ella**). Al final, deben saber nueve historias de los primeros días en la universidad.

Después de hablar

Cuéntale a tu profesor(a) la mejor historia y explícale por qué es la mejor.

Conéctate al cine

Película: *Machuca* (drama, Chile, 2002)
Director: Andrés Wood

Sinopsis:

Es 1973, Gonzalo tiene 11 años, es de una familia de clase media alta y asiste a una escuela privada. Cuando unos niños de los barrios pobres entran a la escuela, Gonzalo se hace amigo de Pedro («Peter») Machuca en su clase de inglés. Visita la casa de Pedro y conoce a su vecina, Silvana, una chica mayor y bastante coqueta (*flirtatious*). Los tres pasan tiempo juntos hasta que estalla el golpe de estado (*coup d'état*), lo que cambia sus vidas para siempre.

Escena (DVD, 01:06:30 to 01:10:02):

Gonzalo, Pedro y Silvana van al cine y luego van a la casa de Pedro. Pedro lee un libro de «el Llanero Solitario» (*The Lone Ranger*). Llega el padre de Pedro, borracho (*drunk*), y empieza a insultar a todos.

Antes de ver

Gonzalo y Pedro son amigos de clases sociales diferentes y de barrios diferentes. ¿Cuáles son algunas diferencias que se encuentran entre barrios y familias de diferentes niveles económicos? Indica tus respuestas y luego explícalas.

- ☐ las calles
- ☐ las casas
- ☐ la comida
- ☐ los espacios exteriores (*outdoor*)
- ☐ los estilos de vestirse
- ☐ las mascotas
- ☐ los padres
- ☐ la seguridad
- ☐ las tiendas

_____

_____

A ver

PASO 1. Lee las **Expresiones útiles** y ve el video. No trates de entender cada palabra, pero escucha con atención. Presta atención a las actitudes y perspectivas de los personajes.

Expresiones útiles	
fome (*Chile*)	boring
tontería	nonsense, something stupid
po (*Chile*)	**pues**
suelta	let go
empresa	business, company
papito	daddy
dueño	owner
adivina	take a guess
ni se va acordar de	won't even remember
curado	drunk (*adj., n.*)
mienten	lie

PASO 2. Ahora indica quién diría cada declaración: Gonzalo, Pedro, Silvana o el padre de Pedro.

1. _____ Me gustaría esta película si hubiera más acción.

2. _____ Si Silvana fuera mi novia, aprendería a bailar con ella.

3. _____ Si los niños no estuvieran leyendo ese libro tonto, me estarían mirando.

4. _____ Viviría en un barrio como este si fuera pobre como ellos.

5. _____ Si no hubiera racismo y represión social en mi país, mi hijo tendría las mismas oportunidades que su amigo.

6. _____ Si mis padres pudieran ver de cerca (*up close*) nuestra amistad, entenderían que las diferencias de clase social no importan (*don't matter*) entre amigos.

7. _____ Si Pedro supiera lo que yo sé, no tendría tantas ilusiones sobre su amistad.

8. _____ Si este señor no estuviera borracho, no estaría diciéndonos la verdad.

Después de ver

En parejas, contesten las siguientes preguntas.

Silvana dice que nunca ha visto una amistad entre un indio y un blanco. Luego, dice que «los niños y los curados no mienten». ¿Por qué dice esto? ¿Estás de acuerdo con sus ideas? Explica.

■ For copyright reasons, the feature-film clips referenced in **Conéctate al cine** have not been provided by the publisher. Each of these films is readily available through retailers or online rental sites such as Amazon, iTunes, or Netflix.

VOCABULARIO

Comunicación

Lo siento mucho. / Cuánto lo siento.	I'm very sorry.
Mi/Nuestro más sentido pésame.	My/Our deepest sympathies.
Te/Le/Les doy/damos el pésame.	My/Our condolences.
Te/Lo/La/Los/Las acompaño en el sentimiento/dolor.	You're in my thoughts. / I'm with you in your time of pain.
Te/Lo/La/Los/Las acompañamos en el sentimiento/dolor.	You're in our thoughts. / We're with you in your time of pain.

Los sustantivos

la amistad	friendship
el amor	love
la boda	wedding
la cita	date; appointment
la cita a ciegas	blind date
el divorcio	divorce
el estado civil	marital status
el hogar	home
el matrimonio	marriage
el nido familiar	parents' home (*lit.*, nest)
el novio / la novia	boyfriend/girlfriend; fiancé/fiancée; groom/bride
el noviazgo	relationship; engagement
la pareja	partner; couple
la relación	relationship

Los adjetivos

abierto/a	open
cariñoso/a	affectionate
casado/a	married
celoso/a	jealous
comprensivo/a	understanding
comprometido/a	engaged; in a serious relationship
divorciado/a	divorced
enamorado/a	in love
en una relación	together; in a relationship
soltero/a	single
tolerante	tolerant
viudo/a	widowed

Los verbos

amar	to love
casarse (con)	to get married (to)
comprometerse	to get engaged; to commit (oneself)
conocerse (zc)	to meet (each other)
emanciparse	to become free/ independent
enamorarse (de)	to fall in love (with)
independizarse (c)	to become independent
mudarse	to move
responsabilizarse (c)	to take responsibility
romper con	to break up with

PARA SABER MÁS

Capítulo 1

1.1 Singular nouns and articles

More about gender of nouns

1. Nouns with the endings **-ción / -sión** (like English *-tion / -sion*) and **-tad / -dad** (like English *-ty*) are generally feminine.

-ción / -sión	la nación (*nation*)
	la solución (*solution*)
	la comprensión (*comprehension*)
	la televisión (*television*)
-tad / -dad	la libertad (*liberty*)
	la ciudad (*city*)
	la universidad (*university*)

2. Feminine nouns that begin with the stressed vowel **a-** use the singular definite article **el** instead of **la.** However, in the plural these feminine nouns do use the expected form **las.**

el agua (*water*)	**las** aguas
el águila (*eagle*)	**las** águilas
el área	**las** áreas

3. Nouns with the ending **-ma** are often masculine. Many of these words are cognates with English.

el clima (*weather*)	el problema	el telegrama
el idioma (*language*)	el programa	el tema (*theme, topic*)
el poema	el sistema	

Capítulo 2

2.1 Adjectives

Adjective placement

1. Descriptive adjectives in Spanish usually follow the noun that they modify.

una mujer **alta**   un libro **blanco**   un estudiante **inteligente**

Some descriptive adjectives, however, occasionally appear before the noun that they modify. **Bueno** and **malo** are two common adjectives that do this, but they are shortened to **buen** and **mal** in the masculine singular form in this case.

un libro **bueno**	un **buen** libro
un día **malo**	un **mal** día
una mesa **buena**	una **buena** mesa
una semana **mala**	una **mala** semana

2. With some adjectives, there is a noticeable difference in meaning depending on their placement. If the adjective follows the noun, it has a literal meaning, but if it precedes the noun, it has a more figurative meaning. This difference is seen clearly in adjectives like **grande, pobre,** and **viejo.** Note that **grande** is shortened to **gran** when it precedes either a masculine or a feminine noun.

	Before the noun	After the noun
grande	una **gran** universidad	una universidad **grande**
	a great university	*a big university*
pobre	un **pobre** hombre	un hombre **pobre**
	a poor (unfortunate) man	*a poor man (without money)*
viejo	un **viejo** amigo	un amigo **viejo**
	a friend for a long time	*a friend who is old*

In English, adjectives always precede the noun, so position cannot differentiate between the above two types of meanings. Context determines whether *an old friend* is intended to mean **un viejo amigo** or **un amigo viejo.**

2.2   The verbs *estar* and *ir*

Using *tener* to express states

The verb **tener,** like **estar,** is often used to express states. **Tener** is used with **calor** (*heat*) and **frío** (*cold*) to say whether someone is hot or cold.

¡**Tengo calor!**	*I'm hot!*
¿No **tienes frío**?	*Aren't you cold?*

To say that someone is hungry or thirsty, use **hambre** (*hunger*) or **sed** (*thirst*).

Elena **tiene hambre.**	*Elena is hungry.*
Tengo sed.	*I'm thirsty.*

A variety of other states may be expressed using **tener,** such as **ganas** (*desire*), **miedo** (*fear*), **prisa** (*haste*), **razón** (*reason*), and **sueño** (*sleepiness*).

Tengo ganas de un café.	*I feel like (having) a coffee.*
¿**Tienes miedo**?	*Are you afraid?*
El profesor **tiene prisa.**	*The teacher is in a hurry.*
¡Ud. **tiene razón**!	*You are right!*
El bebé **tiene sueño.**	*The baby is sleepy.*

With all of these expressions, you can use **mucho/a** or **muchos/as** to express a greater degree of these states.

Tengo **mucho sueño.**	*I'm very sleepy.*
Perdón, tengo **mucha prisa.**	*Sorry, I'm in a big hurry.*

2.3   The verb *gustar*

Nos gusta(n), os gusta(n), les gusta(n)

To say what *we* like, use **nos gusta** or **nos gustan.**

Nos gusta la música.	*We like music.*
Nos gustan las películas.	*We like movies.*

When addressing a group of people as **vosotros/vosotras,** use **os gusta** or **os gustan.**

¿**Os gustan** las clases de biología?	*Do you (pl.) like the biology classes?*

When addressing people as **Uds.,** or when saying what other people (more than one person) like, use **les gusta** or **les gustan.**

¿**Les gusta** el fútbol?	*Do you (pl.) like soccer?*
No **les gusta** la cerveza.	*They don't like beer.*
Les gustan los libros.	*They like books.*

Capítulo 3

3.3 Stem-changing verbs: o → ue

Additional o → ue verbs

1. Here are some other common verbs in Spanish that belong to the **o → ue** family.

contar	*to count; to tell*	¿**Cuento** de uno a diez en español?
		Shall I (Do I) count from one to ten in Spanish?
costar	*to cost*	¿Cuánto **cuesta** el libro?
		How much does the book cost?
encontrar	*to find*	¿Dónde **encuentras** buena comida en la universidad?
		Where do you find good food at the university?
mostrar	*to show*	El mapa **muestra** dónde está la universidad.
		The map shows where the university is.
recordar	*to remember*	No **recuerdo** cómo te llamas.
		I don't remember what your name is.
soler*	*to be in the habit (of)*	Jaime **suele** llegar tarde al trabajo.
		Jaime usually arrives late to work.
volver	*to return*	**Vuelvo** al mismo lugar cada año.
		I return to the same place every year.

2. The verb **jugar** (*to play*) follows the same pattern as the **o → ue** verbs, but it is the **u** that changes to **ue.**

Los niños **juegan** en el parque.	*The children play in the park.*
Jugamos fútbol a las cuatro.	*We play soccer at 4:00.*

3.4 Demonstrative adjectives

The demonstrative adjectives *aquel/aquella/aquellos/aquellas*

In addition to **este/esta/estos/estas** and **ese/esa/esos/esas,** Spanish has a third set of demonstrative adjectives used to indicate something very far away in time or space.

	SINGULAR		PLURAL	
masculino	**aquel** libro	*that book*	**aquellos** libros	*those books*
femenino	**aquella** clase	*that class*	**aquellas** clases	*those classes*

---

*The verb **soler** is very common in Spain, but less so in Latin America.

Aquel/aquella/aquellos/aquellas is similar to English *that,* but it refers to something that is particularly far away or that happened a long time ago.

No me gusta **aquel** libro.	*I don't like that book over there.*
Aquellas clases eran muy difíciles.	*Those classes (back then) were very difficult.*

Spanish thus makes a three-way distinction (**este libro** vs. **ese libro** vs. **aquel libro**) based on distance in time or space, while English makes only a two-way distinction (*this book* vs. *that book*).

Demonstrative pronouns

1. Demonstratives may appear without the noun when the noun has been previously mentioned or is otherwise obvious from the context. In this case, they are called **pronombres demostrativos** (*demonstrative pronouns*).

Esa clase es muy difícil pero **esta** es fácil.	*That class is very difficult but this one is easy.*
Ese es rojo y **este** es azul.	*That one* (masc. sing.) *is red and this one is blue.*
Aquellos son de Honduras.	*Those ones* (across the room) *are from Honduras.*

Traditionally, demonstrative pronouns have been written with an accent mark (**ésta, ése,** and so on) to distinguish them from demonstrative adjectives. It is no longer required, but it is still common.

2. When a demonstrative pronoun refers to the situation in general or something else without a specific name, the neuter (genderless) forms **esto, eso,** and **aquello** are used.

¡**Esto** no me gusta!	*I don't like this (situation in general)!*
¿Qué es **eso**?	*What is that (unknown object)?*

Capítulo 4

4.1 Comparatives

Más de with numerals

In Spanish, when you want to express *more than* (or *less than*) followed by any number, use the construction **más de** (or **menos de**), followed by the number.

¡Elena tiene **más de** treinta primos!	*Elena has more than thirty cousins!*
Todos aquí tenemos **menos de** 25 años.	*All of us here are less than 25 years old.*

Comparatives of equality

1. To say that two people or things are the same with regard to some adjective, use **tan** + *adjective* + **como.**

José Luis es **tan alto como** Margarita.	*José Luis is as tall as Margarita.*
Mis hermanas son **tan inteligentes como** tú.	*My sisters are as smart as you.*

Notice that here the adjective agrees with the subject.

2. To do the same with regard to a noun, use **tanto** + *noun* + **como.**

Tengo **tantos primos como** tú.	*I have as many cousins as you.*
¿Tienes **tanta hambre como** yo?	*Are you as hungry as I am?*

Tanto agrees with the noun in number and gender, so it has four possible forms (**tanto/tanta/tantos/tantas**).

Superlatives

1. You have used **más** to compare one person or thing to another. When preceded by a definite article, **más** expresses the idea of *most.* To express the idea of *least,* use the definite article and **menos.**

María Elena es **la más alta** de todas mis hermanas.	*María Elena is the tallest of all my sisters.*
Jorge es **el más guapo** de la familia.	*Jorge is the best looking in the family.*
Rigoberto y Camila son **los menos altos** de todos mis primos.	*Rigoberto and Camila are the least tall of all my cousins.*

This construction is known as the superlative (**el superlativo**). In English it is expressed with *most* or the ending *-est.*

2. When used with a noun, **más** + *adjective* usually follows the noun.

Carmen es **la abogada más famosa** de Panamá.	*Carmen is the most famous attorney in Panama.*
Marcos es **el estudiante más inteligente** de toda la universidad.	*Marcos is the most intelligent student in the whole university.*
Para mucha gente, el lunes es **el peor día** de la semana.	*For many people, Monday is the worst day of the week.*

When **mejor** and **peor** are used as superlatives, they usually precede the noun.

Mi primo es **el mejor médico** de la ciudad.	*My cousin is the best doctor in the city.*

Expressing things emphatically

1. It is very common in Spanish to attach the suffix **-ísimo** to adjectives to mean *extremely* or *very much.*

¡Elena tiene **muchísimos** primos!	*Elena really has a lot of cousins!*
Mi familia es **grandísima.**	*My family is extremely large.*

If the adjective ends in a consonant, **-ísimo** is simply added to the adjective.

facilísimo *extremely easy*   **dificilísimo** *extremely difficult*

If the adjective ends in a vowel, the vowel is dropped and **-ísimo** is added to the stem.

altísimo *extremely tall*   **delgadísimo** *extremely thin*   **feísimo** *extremely ugly*

When the stem ends in **c, g,** or **z** the spelling is adjusted to preserve the pronunciation of this final consonant. The **c** changes to **qu** (**rico** → **riquísimo**), **g** changes to **gu** (**largo** → **larguísimo**), and **z** changes to **c** (**feliz** → **felicísimo**).

Adjectives with **-ísimo** always agree with the noun they modify in number and gender.

2. In casual speech, there are many other ways to express the idea of *extremely.* One very common way is to use the prefix **super-.**

superfácil *extremely easy*   **superalto** *extremely tall*   **supergrande** *extremely big*

This prefix is common in the spoken language, but is not used in formal written Spanish. It is sometimes written as a separate word.

4.2   Stem-changing verbs: e → *i*

Additional e → *i* verbs

Here are some other common verbs in Spanish that belong to the **e → i** family.

conseguir	*to obtain*	¿Dónde **consigo** una foto de la familia real? *Where can I get a picture of the royal family?*
reír	*to laugh*	Mis papás **ríen** cuando ven la televisión. *My parents laugh when they watch TV.*
sonreír	*to smile*	Mi hermano **sonríe** mucho. *My brother smiles a lot.*

4.3   Stem-changing verbs: e → *ie*

Additional e → *ie* verbs

Here are some other common verbs in Spanish that belong to the **e → ie** family.

cerrar	*to close*	La profesora **cierra** la puerta a las ocho. *The teacher closes the door at 8:00.*
comenzar	*to begin*	El semestre **comienza** en enero. *The semester begins in January.*
entender	*to understand*	Mi mamá no **entiende** que ya no soy niña. *My mom doesn't understand that I'm no longer a little girl.*
perder	*to lose*	Cuando juego con mi hermano, siempre **pierdo.** *When I play with my brother, I always lose.*
preferir	*to prefer*	**Prefiero** caminar. *I prefer to walk.*

Capítulo 5

5.1   Verbs with irregular *yo* forms

More on *saber* and *conocer*

You saw that **saber** can mean *to know* (*a fact*), such as where someone lives or what they study. This can also include knowing an address or phone number, or knowing a poem or the words to a song.

¿**Sabes** el número de teléfono del hospital?   *Do you know the phone number of the hospital?*
Todos **sabemos** la letra de esa canción.   *We all know the words (lyrics) to that song.*

You saw that **conocer** means *to be familiar with* (*someone or something*). When used with reference to a song, for instance, the meaning is very different than **saber.**

¿**Conoces** esa canción?   *Do you know that song? (Are you familiar with it? / Have you heard it before?)*

More irregular verbs with -zco

You saw that the **yo** form of **conocer** is **conozco.** This is part of a larger pattern: verbs whose infinitive ends in **-cer** (or **-cir**) generally take **-zco** in the **yo** form, but are otherwise regular. Here are some other common verbs of this type.

agradecer	to thank; to be grateful for	**Agradezco** su presencia. *I am grateful for your presence (here).*
aparecer	to appear	No **aparezco** en la lista. *I don't appear on the list.*
conducir	to drive	**Conduzco** un auto muy viejo. *I drive a very old car.*
favorecer	to favor; to be partial to	**Favorezco** la idea de crear más parques. *I'm in favor of the idea of creating more parks.*
merecer	to deserve	¡**Merezco** una segunda oportunidad! *I deserve another chance!*
ofrecer	to offer	**Ofrezco** un apartamento en el centro. *I'm offering an apartment downtown.*
parecer	to seem; to look	**Parezco** tonto en esa foto. *I look stupid in that photo.*
pertenecer	to belong	**Pertenezco** a un grupo de estudiantes extranjeros. *I belong to a group of foreign students.*
reconocer	to recognize	No **reconozco** mi ciudad. *I don't recognize my city.*
traducir	to translate	No **traduzco** cuando leo en español. *I don't translate when I read in Spanish.*

5.2 Reflexive verbs

Additional reflexive verbs

Here are some other common reflexive verbs in Spanish. Note that the meanings of reflexive verbs do not necessarily express reflexive action.

alegrarse	to be glad, happy	**Me alegro** cuando veo a mis amigos. *It makes me happy when I see my friends.*
atreverse (a)	to dare (to do something)	¿**Te atreves** a hablar con él? *Do you dare to speak with him?*
encontrarse	to be found, located	La librería **se encuentra** enfrente del museo. *The bookstore is located across from the museum.*
imaginarse	to imagine	**Me imagino** que la tienda del museo es muy grande. *I imagine that the museum store is very big.*
preguntarse	to wonder, ask oneself	**Me pregunto** si hay un cine en ese pueblo. *I wonder if there is a movie theater in that town.*
quedarse	to stay	¿**Te quedas** o te vas? *Are you staying or are you leaving?*
referirse (a)	to refer (to)	Cuando dicen «México», **se refieren** a la ciudad. *When they say "Mexico," they're referring to the city.*

The reciprocal meaning of reflexive verbs

Reflexive verbs with plural subjects can also have a *reciprocal* meaning, corresponding to the English expression *each other*.

Nos vemos los martes en la clase de química.

We see each other on Tuesday in chemistry class.

Marta y Eduardo **se conocen** bien.

Marta and Eduardo know each other well.

The context generally makes it clear whether the intended meaning is reflexive or reciprocal. **Nos vemos,** for example, can have either a reflexive meaning (*we see ourselves*) or a reciprocal meaning (*we see each other*), but in the first example above, the reciprocal meaning is much more likely.

The infinitive after a preposition

Prepositional expressions like the following are a common way to show the relationship between two or more activities.

antes de	*before*	Antes de cenar, quiero bañarme.
		Before having dinner, I want to take a bath.
después de	*after*	Después de nadar, María va a estudiar.
		After swimming, María is going to study.
para	*for, in order to*	Para hablar con mis padres, tienes que hablar español.
		(In order) to speak with my parents, you have to speak Spanish.

In Spanish, the infinitive is used after prepositions. English sometimes uses *-ing* forms of the verb in these cases, but Spanish consistently uses the infinitive.

5.3 *Ser* and *estar* with adjectives

Ser for location of events

1. To say where or when an event *occurs,* use the verb **ser.**

El concierto va a **ser** en el Teatro de la Ciudad.

The concert will be at the City Theater.

La fiesta **es** en la casa de Jaime.

The party is at Jaime's house.

El examen **es** mañana a las ocho.

The exam is tomorrow at 8:00.

2. Use **estar,** in contrast, to say where a person or thing is located.

La calle Torres **está** en el centro.

Torres Street is downtown.

Santiago **está** en Chile.

Santiago is in Chile.

Estamos en la casa de Jaime.

We're at Jaime's house.

In these cases with **estar,** the person or thing that is being described (a street, a city, or a group of people) is located at a particular place, but cannot be said to "occur" there.

Capítulo 6

6.1 The preterite: Regular verbs

Leer, creer, and *oír* in the preterite

The stem of the verbs **leer**, **creer**, and **oír** ends in a vowel (**le**er, **cre**er, **oí**r). Verbs like these take the regular endings in the preterite with one small adjustment: the ending for **él/ella/Ud.** is **-yó** (instead of **-ió**) and the ending for **ellos/ellas/Uds.** is -**yeron** (instead of -**ieron**).

Marta **oyó** que hay un restaurante cubano en el centro.	*Marta heard that there is a Cuban restaurant downtown.*
¿Uds. **leyeron** el libro?	*Did you (pl.) read the book?*
Jaime **creyó** que Luis preparó la cena.	*Jaime thought that Luis prepared the dinner.*

Replacing the **i** with a **y** allows these verbs to avoid having three vowels in a row. For most verbs in Spanish, the stem ends in a consonant (for example, **trabajar**, **aprender**, and **escribir**) and such an adjustment is not necessary.

Ver and *dar* in the preterite

1. For a few verbs in Spanish, the stem consists of a single consonant. The verb **ver** is of this type. Despite its very short stem, the preterite endings attach to **ver** in the usual way, and this verb is regular in the preterite.

Vi mucho pescado en el mercado.	*I saw a lot of fish in the market.*
¿**Viste** la carta?	*Did you see the menu?*
Jorge **vio** la torta.	*Jorge saw the cake.*
¿**Vieron** el restaurante salvadoreño?	*Did you (pl.) see the Salvadoran restaurant?*

Since **vi** and **vio** have only one syllable, a written accent mark is not used (in contrast to forms like **comí** and **comió**).

2. The verb **dar** also has a stem that consists of a single consonant, **d**. It too takes endings in the usual way, but in the preterite, it takes the endings of an **-er/-ir** verb.

Los cocineros **dieron** una clase sobre la comida japonesa.	*The cooks gave a class about Japanese food.*
Dimos una cena para los profesores.	*We gave a dinner for the teachers.*

As with **ver,** the one-syllable forms **di** and **dio** do not require an accent mark.

Capítulo 7

7.3 Pronouns after prepositions

Additional prepositions

1. The preposition **según** is different from other prepositions, because it may be followed by **yo** and **tú** (rather than **mí** and **ti**).

Según yo, Juan es muy buena persona.	*According to me, Juan is a very good person.*
Según tú, vamos a tener un examen mañana.	*According to you, we are going to have an exam tomorrow.*

2. Expressions of location are also sometimes followed by pronouns. Some examples are **cerca de** (*close to*), **lejos de** (*far from*), **delante de** (*in front of*), **detrás de** (*behind*), and **enfrente de** (*across from*).

Vivo **cerca de** ti.	*I live close to you.*
¡Quiero estar muy **lejos de** él!	*I want to be very far from him!*
Robert estaba **delante de** mí.	*Robert was in front of me.*
Miriam estaba **detrás de** él.	*Miriam was behind him.*
Luz estaba **enfrente de** ellos.	*Luz was across from them.*

Stressed possessives

1. The preposition **de** may be used to express possession, as in **la casa de nosotros** (*our house*). Alternatively, a *stressed possessive* (**posesivo tónico**) may be used in place of the phrase with **de**, as in **la casa nuestra.** Here is the full set of stressed possessives.

STRESSED POSSESSIVES	
mío, mía, míos, mías	*my; mine*
tuyo, tuya, tuyos, tuyas	*your; yours* (inform.)
suyo, suya, suyos, suyas	*his, her, your; his, hers, yours* (form.)
nuestro, nuestra, nuestros, nuestras	*our; ours*
vuestro, vuestra, vuestros, vuestras	*your; yours* (inform., pl., Sp.)
suyo, suya, suyos, suyas	*their, your; theirs, yours* (pl.)

In form, stressed possessives are similar, but not identical, to unstressed possessive adjectives (see **1.4**).

2. Stressed possessives are used *after* the noun or when the noun is somewhere else in the sentence (or not present at all). They agree in number and gender with the noun being referred to.

La casa de Uds. es verde, pero la casa **nuestra** es blanca.	*Your* (pl.) *house is green, but our house is white.*
Ese regalo es **mío.**	*That present is mine.*

3. When stressed possessives are used as pronouns, taking the place of the subject or object of the sentence, they have a definite article.

Aquí están mis libros. ¿Dónde están **los tuyos**?	*Here are my books. Where are yours?*
Tu coche es grande. **El mío** es chico.	*Your car is big. Mine is small.*
¿Te gustan tus tarjetas? A mí me gustan **las mías.**	*Do you like your cards? I like mine.*

However, when stressed possessives are used with the verb **ser** to describe the subject, they do not need the definite article.

Este regalo es de Ana. Es **suyo.**	*This gift is Ana's. It's hers.*
¿Esas computadoras son **tuyas**?	*Are those computers yours?*

In either case, all stressed possessives agree in both number and gender with the noun that they refer to.

Capítulo 8

8.1 More irregular preterite forms

Additional irregular preterite forms

The verb **conseguir** (*to obtain; to get*) has **seguir** as its root and is conjugated in the same way in the preterite. Likewise, **despedirse** (*to say good-bye; to take leave*) has **pedir** as its root and is conjugated in the same way.

Here are some other common verbs that change the stem vowel **e** to **i** in the preterite when conjugated in the **él/ella/Ud.** or **ellos/Uds.** forms.

divertirse (ie, i)	*to have fun*	Carmen **se divirtió** mucho en la fiesta.
		Carmen had a lot of fun at the party.
mentir (ie, i)	*to lie*	Carlos **mintió** cuando dijo que tenía 21 años.
		Carlos lied when he said he was 21.
preferir (ie, i)	*to prefer*	Marta **prefirió** comprar el vestido rojo.
		Marta preferred to buy the red dress.
reírse (í, i) (de)	*to laugh* (*at*)	Los niños **se rieron** de la corbata de su padre.
		The children laughed at their father's tie.
repetir (i, i)	*to repeat*	El profesor **repitió** la palabra tres veces.
		The teacher repeated the word three times.
sentirse (ie, i)	*to feel*	Catalina **se sintió** muy contenta cuando vio el anillo.
		Catalina felt very happy when she saw the ring.
sonreír (í, i)	*to smile*	El diseñador **sonrió** cuando mencionaron su ropa en la televisión.
		The designer smiled when they mentioned his clothes on television.
sugerir (ie, i)	*to suggest*	La asistente me **sugirió** una falda más larga.
		The assistant suggested a longer skirt to me.

8.2 The preterite and imperfect together

Comparison of meaning in preterite vs. imperfect

1. You have seen how the preterite can portray an action as having a clear end point. The preterite may also be used to show that an action has a clear beginning point.

María se probó el abrigo y le **gustó** mucho. Cuando vio la foto, Juan **entendió** que la camisa le quedaba mal.

María tried on the coat and liked it a lot. When he saw the picture, Juan understood that the shirt fit him poorly.

Although the meanings of **gustar** and **entender** generally imply ongoing actions, in these sentences, there is a clear point when María begins to like the coat (when she tries it on) and when Juan's understanding begins (when he sees the picture).

2. The preterite forms of **conocer** and **saber** often refer in this way to the beginning point of knowing someone or something. With **conocer,** this is the point of meeting someone, and with **saber,** it is the point of finding something out. In the imperfect, in contrast, the simple state of knowing is referred to, without any specific beginning or ending point.

Pretérito	Imperfecto
Conocí a Francisco cuando éramos niños.	**Conocía** a Francisco cuando éramos niños.
I met Francisco when we were kids.	*I knew Francisco when we were kids.*
Elena **supo** que los zapatos eran caros.	Elena **sabía** que los zapatos eran caros.
Elena found out that the shoes were expensive.	*Elena knew that the shoes were expensive.*

In the preterite, **conocer** and **saber** are sometimes said to change their meaning, but in fact their meaning comes from what they mean normally, together with the regular meaning of the preterite tense.

3. The verbs **poder** and **querer** are similar. Their preterite forms express the beginning or end point of being able and wanting, respectively, while the imperfect forms do not express any clear beginning or end points.

Pretérito	Imperfecto
Ayer **pude** comprar ese vestido negro.	Cuando yo trabajaba, **podía** comprar muchos vestidos.
I was able (I managed) to buy that black dress yesterday.	*When I worked, I could (I had the ability/means, though I may not have actually done it) buy a lot of dresses.*
Mario **quiso** hablar con Ana, pero ella no le hizo caso.	Mario **quería** hablar con Ana, pero nunca llegó.
Mario tried to speak with Ana, but she ignored him.	*Mario wanted (but didn't actually try) to speak with Ana, but she never arrived.*

Poder in the preterite is often translated into English as *to manage to* and **querer** as *to try.* What they both have in common is that some action results (such as, **pude** = *I was able to and actually did it;* **quise** = *I wanted to and actually tried*). When they are used in the negative, they are often translated as *to fail* (*to do something*) and *to refuse,* respectively.

No pude comprar ese vestido negro porque no traía dinero.	*I wasn't able to (failed to) buy that black dress because I didn't have money with me.*
Mario **no quiso** hablar con Ana porque estaba enojado todavía.	*Mario didn't want to (refused to) speak with Ana because he was still mad.*

8.3 Object pronoun placement with infinitives

Double object pronouns

1. Verbs often have both a direct and an indirect object, and both of these objects may be expressed as pronouns. In this case, the indirect object pronoun precedes the direct object pronoun.

Este sombrero es nuevo. **Me lo** dieron ayer.	*This hat is new. They gave it to me yesterday.*
¿Te gusta esta camisa? ¡**Te la** regalo!	*Do you like this shirt? I'll give it to you!*
Necesito esos anillos. ¿**Me los** pasas?	*I need those rings. Will you pass them to me?*

2. The indirect object pronouns **le** and **les** are not used together with direct object pronouns; the form **se** is used instead.

¿Te gustó la falda de María? Yo **se la regalé.**	*Did you like María's skirt? I gave it to her.*
¿La camisa de Jaime? **Se la** dieron por su cumpleaños.	*Jaime's shirt? They gave it to him for his birthday.*
A Ud., ¿qué le parece este abrigo? **Se lo** vendo barato.	*What do you* (form.) *think about this coat? I'll sell it to you cheap.*

3. When reflexive verbs are used with a direct object pronoun, the reflexive pronoun precedes the direct object pronoun.

¿Esa camisa? **Me la** probé pero no me quedó.	*That shirt? I tried it on, but it didn't fit.*
A mi hija le gusta mucho su suéter rojo.	*My daughter really likes her red sweater.*
Se lo pone cada vez que sale.	*She puts it on every time she goes out.*

You will see examples of reflexive verbs with indirect object pronouns in **Estructura 9.3.**

4. Just as with single object pronouns, double object pronouns may either both precede a conjugated verb or both follow and be attached to an infinitive. In the latter case, they are written as a single word with the infinitive, and an accent mark is written to preserve the stress.

¿Esa corbata? **Te la** quiero regalar. (Quiero regalár**tela.**)	*That tie? I want to give it to you.*
¿El suéter de Mario? **Se lo** voy a lavar. (Voy a lavár**selo.**)	*Mario's sweater? I'm going to wash it for him.*
¿El pelo? ¿**Te lo** vas a lavar hoy? (¿Vas a lavár**telo** hoy?)	*Your hair? Are you going to wash it today?*

The relative order of the two pronouns is always the same regardless of whether they precede or follow the verb.

Another use of *lo: Lo* + adjective

To express ideas like *the good thing* or *the bad part,* say **lo bueno** or **lo malo. Lo** may be combined in this way with the masculine singular form of any adjective.

Lo bueno de esos zapatos es que te quedan bien.	*The good thing about those shoes is that they fit you well.*
Lo malo de esa tienda es que es muy cara.	*The bad thing about that store is that it is very expensive.*
Lo difícil es encontrar un abrigo en mi talla.	*The hard part is finding a coat in my size.*

Capítulo 9

9.1   The prepositions *por* and *para*

Additional uses of *por* and *para*

1. The preposition **para** is often used to indicate the organization for which someone works.

Manuel empezó a trabajar **para los hoteles Hilton** el año pasado.	*Manuel began to work for Hilton hotels last year.*
Susana quiere trabajar **para la universidad** después de graduarse.	*Susana wants to work for the university after graduating.*

Para is also used to express a point of comparison.

Para un hotel tan barato, es muy bonito.	*For such an inexpensive hotel, it is very nice.*
Para un norteamericano, Jason sabe mucho de Latinoamérica.	*For an American, Jason knows a lot about Latin America.*

2. The preposition **por** may be used to show a unit of measure, like the English word *per.*

El hotel cuesta cien dólares **por noche.**	*The hotel costs $100 per night.*
El tren va a 120 kilómetros **por hora.**	*The train goes 120 kilometers per hour.*

Por may also be used with verbs of motion to show who or what you are going to pick up along the way.

Mañana paso **por ti** a las ocho.	*Tomorrow I'll come by for you at 8:00.*
Voy **por mi maleta.**	*I'm going for (to get) my suitcase.*

9.3   *Se* for unplanned events

Additional verbs with *se* for unplanned events

1. Some other reflexive verbs that are often used with indirect object pronouns are **irse** (*to go away*), **notarse** (*to be noticeable*), **quebrarse** (*to break*), and **quedarse** (*to stay behind*).

El tren **se me fue.**	*The train left without me.*
Elena dice que está muy nerviosa pero no **se le nota.**	*Elena says she is very nervous, but you can't tell (it isn't noticeable on her).*
¿**Se te quebró** algo?	*Did you break something?*
Las llaves **se me quedaron** dentro del coche.	*I left the keys inside the car.*

In each of these cases, the reflexive verb describes an unintentional action, and the indirect object expresses who is affected by this action.

2. The reflexive verb **hacerse** (*to be/get done*) has the special meaning of *to seem* or *to think* when it is combined with an indirect object pronoun.

Se me hace que el avión va a llegar tarde.	*It seems to me that the plane is going to arrive late.*
Dicen que Cancún es caro. ¿**Se te hace**?	*They say Cancun is expensive. Do you think so?*

Capítulo 10

10.1   The relative pronoun *que*

Que and additional relative pronouns

1. Unlike English *that,* the Spanish relative pronoun **que** is never omitted.

La impresora **que** compré ayer ya está en mi oficina.	*The printer (that) I bought yesterday is already in my office.*

2. **Que** is the most common relative pronoun and may refer either to people or to things. **Quien** (singular) or **quienes** (plural) should be used when referring to people after a preposition.

Ella es la ingeniera **con quien** hablé por teléfono.	*She is the engineer that I spoke with on the phone.*
El señor **a quien** te presenté es el gerente del banco.	*The man that I introduced you to is the bank manager.*
Los ejecutivos **de quienes** vimos una foto en el libro van a venir a la universidad.	*The executives that we saw a picture of in the book are going to come to the university.*

The preposition must always precede the relative pronoun in Spanish. Formal written English is the same (as in, *the engineer with whom I spoke*), but in spoken English, the preposition and the relative pronoun are often separated (as in, *the engineer that I spoke with*).

3. When used as relative pronouns, **que** and **quien/quienes** are not written with accent marks, but when used as question words, they are.

—¿**Qué** vas a leer?   *"What are you going to read?"*
—Voy a leer el libro **que** está en la mesa.   *"I'm going to read the book (that is) on the table."*

—¿**A quién** viste en el trabajo?   *"Who did you see at work?"*
—Vi a la señora **con quien hablaste** ayer.   *"I saw the woman (that) you spoke with yesterday."*

Lo que

Lo que is a very common expression in Spanish. **Lo** here is a pronoun, and **que** introduces the relative clause that follows. **Lo que quiero** thus literally means *that which I want,* but it is more naturally translated as *what I want.*

¡**Lo que** quiero es tener mucho dinero y no tener que trabajar!   *(What) I want (is) to have a lot of money and not have to work!*
Me gusta **lo que** dijiste en la clase.   *I like what you said in class.*
Es interesante **lo que** hacen los arquitectos.   *What architects do is interesting.*

Capítulo 11

11.1 The present perfect

Additional irregular past participles

Here are some other common verbs that have irregular past participles.

INFINITIVE	PAST PARTICIPLE		
abrir	abierto	Han **abierto** la puerta.	*They've opened the door.*
cubrir	cubierto	Hemos **cubierto** la mesa con un mantel.	*We've covered the table with a tablecloth.*
romper	roto	¿Has **roto** la lámpara?	*Have you broken the lamp?*
volver	vuelto	María se fue y no ha **vuelto.**	*María left and hasn't returned.*

Using the past participle as an adjective

Past participles may be used as adjectives, often with the verb **estar.** When they are used as adjectives, they agree in gender and number with the noun that they modify.

La lámpara **está rota.**   *The lamp is broken.*
Los platos ya **están lavados.**   *The dishes are already washed.*
La cocina **está cerrada.**   *The kitchen is closed.*

Using the past participle to form the passive

The past participle may also be used to indicate an action with the verb **ser,** creating a passive construction. The tense of the verb **ser** indicates whether the action is a past, present, or future event.

Las calles **son barridas** cada jueves.   *The streets are swept every Thursday.*
Esta casa **fue construida** en 1982.   *This house was built in 1982.*
El lavaplatos **va a ser instalado** mañana.   *The dishwasher is going to be installed tomorrow.*

The person or thing that is doing the action may be expressed with the preposition **por.**

Los autos fueron lavados **por expertos.**   *The cars were washed by experts.*

The past perfect

The present perfect uses the verb **haber** in the present tense, followed by the past participle. The past perfect (**el pluscuamperfecto**) is the same but uses **haber** in the imperfect tense. It expresses the idea that you had already done something by the time some other event occurred.

Cuando llegó Ana, yo ya **había limpiado** la cocina.
When Ana arrived, I had already cleaned the kitchen.

Cuando yo te vi, ¿ya **habías barrido** el pasillo?
When I saw you, had you already swept the hallway?

11.2   Commands with object pronouns

Nosotros/as commands

1. To say what you want to do with other people as a group, you may use a **nosotros/as** command, equivalent to English sentences with *let's*. The **nosotros/as** command has the same form as the formal **Ud.** command (see **10.3**), but with a **-mos** ending.

Limpiemos la casa.
Let's clean the house.

¡**Pongamos** la comida en la mesa!
Let's put the food on the table!

¡**Cenemos**!
Let's have dinner!

As with formal commands, **nosotros/as** commands use the vowel **e** in the ending for **-ar** verbs and the vowel **a** for **-er** and **-ir** verbs.

2. As with all other command forms, object pronouns (indirect, direct, and reflexive) in **nosotros/as** commands are attached to the end of positive commands and appear as a separate word before negative commands. An accent mark is added to the stressed syllable of a positive command when one or more object pronouns are added.

Limpié**mos**la.
Let's clean it.

¡No **lo** pongamos allí!
Let's not put it there!

When the reflexive pronoun **nos** is attached to a positive **nosotros/as** command, the final **-s** of the verb is dropped.

¡Levanté**mo**nos!
Let's get up!

Senté**mo**nos.
Let's sit down.

3. Unlike other verbs, **ir** uses its present tense form (**vamos**) for the positive **nosotros/as** command. With the reflexive **irse,** the final **-s** is dropped when **nos** is attached.

Vámo**nos**!
Let's go/leave!

4. It is also common to use **vamos a** + *infinitive* to express the idea of *let's*.

Vamos a limpiar la casa.
Let's clean the house.

¡**Vamos a levantarnos** temprano!
Let's get up early!

11.3   The present progressive

The past progressive

In the present progressive, **estar** is in the present tense. However, progressives may also be created with other tenses. It is especially common for **estar** to be in the imperfect.

Estaba limpiando la casa ayer a las ocho.
I was cleaning the house yesterday at 8.

¿**Estabas comiendo** cuando te llamé?
Were you eating when I called you?

Just as the present progressive describes an action in progress in the present, the past progressive describes an action in progress in the past.

Capítulo 12

12.2 The present progressive with object pronouns

The present progressive with double object pronouns

As you saw in **Para saber más 8.3,** verbs sometimes have two objects that are both expressed as pronouns. When the verb is in the present progressive, these object pronouns may either precede **estar** or be attached to the **-ndo** form of the verb, just as with single object pronouns. When attaching either one or two object pronouns to the **-ndo** form, a written accent mark is placed over the vowel where the stress normally falls.

¿La pelota? **Se la** está dando el entrenador. (Está dándo**sela** el entrenador.)	*The ball? The coach is giving it to him/her.*
¿Te gusta esta raqueta? ¡Mariana **me la** está vendiendo a muy buen precio! (¡Mariana está vendiéndo**mela** a muy buen precio!)	*Do you like this racket? Mariana is selling it to me at a really good price!*

The two pronouns must be together, either both before **estar** or both attached to the **-ndo** form.

12.3 The subjunctive: Volition with regular verbs

Additional expressions of volition

Here are some other common verbs and expressions that convey a recommendation, a piece of advice, or a desire, and which are therefore followed by the subjunctive after **que.**

aconsejar *to advise*	**Te aconsejo** que **hables** con tu médico. *I advise you to speak to your doctor.*
exigir *to demand*	**Nos están exigiendo** que **leamos** el libro para el lúnes. *They're demanding that we read the book by Monday.*
insistir en	¡**Insisto** en que **juegues** tenis conmigo! *I insist that you play tennis with me!*
mandar *to order*	**Voy a mandar** que **caminen** un kilómetro al día. *I'm going to order that they walk one kilometer a day.*
permitir	¿**Permiten** que **andemos** en patineta aquí? *Do they allow us to skateboard here?*
preferir	**Prefieren** que **levantemos** pesas por la mañana. *They prefer that we lift weights in the morning.*
prohibir	Nuestro profesor **nos prohibe** que **hablemos** inglés en la clase. *Our teacher prohibits (forbids) us from speaking English in class.*
ser importante	**Es importante** que **duermas** bien todas las noches. *It's important that you sleep well every night.*
ser mejor	**Es mejor** que no **andes** en bicicleta en este clima. *It's better that you don't ride bikes in this weather.*
sugerir	**Te sugiero** que **comas** más fruta. *I suggest that you eat more fruit.*

Capítulo 13

13.1   The subjunctive: Irregular verbs

Additional irregular verbs in the subjunctive

1. In general, verbs that have an irregular stem for **yo** in the present indicative use this same stem in the present subjunctive. The verbs **conocer** (**conozco/conozca**) and **oír** (**oigo/oiga**) are common examples.

Quiero que **conozcas** a mi tía.	*I want you to meet my aunt.*
Es muy importante que Uds. **oigan** la canción de este pájaro.	*It is very important that you (pl.) listen to this bird's song.*

The person/number endings are regular for all verbs in the subjunctive.

2. Some verbs use a special stem for the present subjunctive. **Haber** (**haya**) and **saber** (**sepa**) are common examples of this type of verb.

Es necesario que **haya** un área especial para los pingüinos.	*It is necessary for there to be a special area for the penguins.*
Quiero que **sepas** que cerramos el parque a las siete.	*I want you to know that we close the park at 7.*

3. Verbs that change their stem in the present indicative (such as **poder** [o → ue] and **querer** [e → ie]) do the same in the present subjunctive.

Es importante que las tortugas **puedan** llegar a la playa sin problemas.	*It's important for the turtles to be able to get to the beach without problems.*
¡Quiero que me **quieras**!	*I want you to love me!*

4. Verbs of the **e → i** family, such as **pedir,** undergo this stem-change in all forms of the subjunctive, including the **nosotros** and **vosotros** forms, which do not undergo the change in the indicative.

No es necesario que **pidamos** ayuda.	*It is not necessary for us to ask for help.*
Pedimos ayuda de vez en cuando.	*We ask for help from time to time.*

Similarly, verbs that have an **e → i** or **o → u** change in the preterite, such as **sentirse** or **dormir,** show this same change in the **nosotros** and **vosotros** forms of the present subjunctive. Their regular **e → ie** or **o → ue** change occurs in the other forms.

Es muy importante que **se sientan / nos sintamos** bien en la clase.	*It's very important that you (pl.) / we feel good in class.*
Los médicos recomiendan que **duerman/ durmamos** ocho horas cada noche.	*Doctors recommend that you (pl.) / we sleep eight hours every night.*

Present perfect subjunctive

The present perfect subjunctive (**el presente perfecto de subjuntivo**) is formed with the subjunctive of **haber** and the past participle. It is used in the same contexts as the present subjunctive, but it portrays the event as having happened in the past when the main clause verb is in the present. The English equivalents in these cases may or may not use *have/has.*

Espero que **hayas podido** leer el libro.	*I hope that you have been (were) able to read the book.*
Ojalá que Arturo **haya escuchado** mis consejos.	*I hope that Arturo (has) listened to my advice.*
Es necesario que Uds. **hayan estudiado** antes de hacer el examen.	*It's necessary for you to have studied before taking the test.*

13.2 The subjunctive: Disbelief and uncertainty

The subjunctive in adjective clauses (after nonexistent and indefinite antecedents)

1. You saw in **10.1** that the relative pronoun **que** introduces a clause (called a *relative clause* or *adjective clause*) that gives further information about a noun.

Hay tortugas **que viven en el mar.**   *There are turtles that live in the ocean.*

When the noun being described does not exist or is not known to exist, the relative clause appears in the subjunctive.

No hay ninguna tortuga que **viva** en la nieve. *There is no turtle that lives in the snow.*
¿Aquí hay un parque que **tenga** muchos pájaros? *Is there a park here that has a lot of birds?*

The above relative clauses describe a turtle that does not exist and a park that may not exist.

2. It is especially common to use the subjunctive in relative clauses when the noun being described does not refer to anyone or anything specific.

Los biólogos buscan un animal que **vuele.** *The biologists are looking for an animal that flies. (They don't have any particular animal in mind and there may not even be any.)*

If you want to say that the biologists are looking for a specific animal, use the indicative.

Los biólogos buscan un animal que **vuela.** *The biologists are looking for an animal that flies. (Such an animal exists and they have this animal in mind.)*

3. The use of the subjunctive in relative clauses is in keeping with the core meaning of the subjunctive: to express ideas that may not be true. To describe a noun that may not even exist, you thus use the subjunctive. Since the indicative expresses ideas that are thought to be true, you use it to describe a noun that you think exists.

The subjunctive: Emotion

The subjunctive is used after many verbs and expressions that convey an emotional reaction.

alegrarse *to be happy*	**Me alegro** de que **seas** uno de los mejores estudiantes. *I'm happy that you are one of the best students.*
gustar	**Me gusta** que **estés** en la clase conmigo. *I like it that you're in the class with me.*
lamentar *to regret*	**Lamento** que el sapo dorado ya no **exista.** *I regret that the golden toad doesn't exist anymore.*
molestar *to bother*	¿**Te molesta** que **te digan** «Susie»? *Does it bother you that they call you "Susie"?*
sentir *to be sorry*	**Siento** mucho que **hayan cortado** el árbol. *I'm very sorry that they cut (have cut) down the tree.*
ser bueno/malo	**Es bueno** que **tengan** un parque tan grande en la ciudad. *It's good that they have such a big park in the city.*
ser una lástima *to be a shame*	**Es una lástima** que el bosque **esté** en tan malas condiciones. *It's a shame that the forest is in such bad condition.*
temer	**Temo** que ya no **haya*** muchos pájaros en esta zona. *I'm afraid that there aren't many birds in this area anymore.*

The subjunctive clause describes the situation that the person is reacting to in each of these cases.

---

*Recall that when **haber** is used to express existence, it is always singular.

13.3 The subjunctive: Purpose and contingency

The subjunctive in time clauses

1. Time clauses are introduced by words such as **cuando.** When the time clause refers to an event that has not yet happened, it is in the subjunctive.

Marta se va a poner muy contenta cuando **vea** un cóndor en las montañas.	*Marta will become very happy when she sees a condor in the mountains.* (This hasn't happened yet.)

When the time clause refers to something that happens regularly or that has already happened, it is in the indicative.

Marta se pone muy contenta cuando **ve** un cóndor en las montañas.	*Marta becomes very happy when she sees a condor in the mountains.* (This happens regularly.)

2. **Cuando** is the most common word to introduce a time clause, but some other common expressions are **antes de que, después de que,** and **hasta que.** They all use the subjunctive when describing an event that hasn't happened yet.

Quiero visitar el parque **antes de que** lo **cierren.**	*I want to visit the park before they close it.*
Vamos a hablar **después de que regreses** de tu viaje.	*Let's talk after you return from your trip.*
Tenemos que seguir trabajando **hasta que** las playas **estén** limpias.	*We have to keep working until the beaches are clean.*

Because **antes de que** always refers to an event that hasn't yet happened, it is always followed by the subjunctive.

3. The choice of subjunctive or indicative in time clauses follows from the core meaning of each. The subjunctive is to express ideas that may not be true, so you use the subjunctive in time clauses that refer to a future event. Since the event has not happened yet, there is a chance that it may never happen, and this uncertainty makes the subjunctive appropriate. The indicative is used to express facts or ideas thought to be true, so you use it in time clauses about something that happens regularly or has already happened.

The subjunctive: Additional expressions of contingency

Some other common expressions followed by the subjunctive are **a menos de que** (*unless*), **con tal de que** (*provided that*), and **sin que** (*without*).

Hay muchas hormigas cada año **a menos de que haga** mucho frío.	*There are lots of ants every year unless it is very cold.*
Voy a pasar el día en las montañas **con tal de que me acompañes.**	*I'm going to spend the day in the mountains provided that you accompany me.*
¿Puedes observar a los osos **sin que te vean**?	*Can you observe the bears without them seeing you?*

In all of these cases, the subjunctive clause expresses an event that may not happen.

Capítulo 14

14.1 The past subjunctive

Additional irregular past subjunctive forms

1. The stem of the past subjunctive is always the same as the stem of the preterite, even if the preterite stem is irregular. You have already seen some verbs with irregular past subjunctive forms. Here are more common verbs with irregular stems.

decir	Queríamos que la actriz **dijera** algo interesante en la entrevista.
	We wanted the actress to say something interesting in the interview.
hacer	Era importante que **hicieran** una película sobre la vida del general.
	It was important that they make a movie about the life of the general.
traer	Recomendaban que **trajéramos** un diccionario.
	They recommended that we bring a dictionary.

Note that **decir** and **traer,** whose stems end in **-j,** drop the **i** in the past subjunctive ending. In **6.2,** you saw this same adjustment with the **-ieron** ending of the preterite, as in **dijeron** and **trajeron.** In both cases, this small adjustment makes pronunciation of the verb forms easier.

2. As you saw in **8.1,** some verbs change the stem vowel in the preterite. This change occurs in the past subjunctive also. Here are some common verbs in which stem vowel **e** changes to **i.**

mentir	Yo no quería que me **mintieran.**
	I didn't want them to lie to me.
pedir	No era necesario que los músicos **pidieran** ayuda.
	It wasn't necessary for the musicians to ask for help.
seguir	Era muy importante que los niños me **siguieran** en el museo.
	It was very important that the children follow me in the museum.
servir	Arreglaron esta parte del edificio para que **sirviera** de biblioteca.
	They fixed this part of the building so that it would serve as a library.

3. Here are some common verbs in which the stem vowel **o** changes to **u.**

dormir	Con tanto ruido, era imposible que yo **durmiera** tarde.
	With so much noise, it was impossible for me to sleep late.
morir	No queríamos que la cantante **muriera** en la ópera.
	We didn't want the singer to die in the opera.

The past perfect subjunctive

The *past perfect subjunctive* (**el pluscuamperfecto de subjuntivo**) is formed with the past subjunctive of **haber** (**hubiera, hubieras, …**) followed by the past participle. It has the same basic meaning as the past perfect indicative (for example, **habían salido** [*they had left*]), but it is used in contexts where the subjunctive is required.

Yo esperaba que ya **hubieran salido.**	*I was hoping that they had already left.*
Nadie creía que **hubieras tocado** la guitarra tan bien.	*Nobody believed that you had played the guitar so well.*
Era imposible que **hubiéramos leído** todo el libro para el martes.	*It was impossible for us to have read the whole book by Tuesday.*

14.2   The future

Irregular future forms

The future tense endings are always regular, but some verbs have irregular stems. In addition to those that you have already seen, here are some other common verbs with irregular stems in the future.

querer	querr-	¿**Querrás** venir con nosotros al cine?
		Might you want to come with us to the movies?
saber	sabr-	¿**Sabrá** tocar el violín Gustavo?
		Does Gustavo perhaps know how to play the violin?
valer	valdr-	Ese libro **valdrá** mucho más en el futuro.
		That book will be worth a lot more in the future.

The future perfect

1. The future perfect is formed with **haber** in the future tense followed by the past participle. It is a common way to make conjectures about something that might have happened in the past.

¿**Habrán filmado** esa película en Lima?   *Might they have filmed that movie in Lima?*
¿Borges **habrá entrado** a esta librería?   *Could Borges have entered this bookstore?*

2. You may also use the future perfect to say what will have happened by a certain time.

Para el 2 de julio, Marisela ya **habrá**   *By July 2, Marisela will have already*
   abierto la galería.   *opened the gallery.*

Capítulo 15

15.1   The conditional

Irregular conditional forms

Here are some additional common verbs with an irregular stem in the conditional.

querer	querr-	Yo **querría** acompañarte.
		I would like to go with (accompany) you.
saber	sabr-	Un guatemalteco **sabría** cómo se llama ese pájaro.
		A Guatemalan would know what that bird is called.
valer	valdr-	Mi teléfono **valdría** mucho, pero está roto.
		My phone would be worth a lot, but it's broken.

For many speakers, the conditional form of **querer** (**querría**) is rarely used and the past subjunctive form (**quisiera**) is used instead.

The conditional perfect

The conditional perfect is formed with **haber** in the conditional followed by the past participle. You use it to say what *would have* happened in the past.

Yo **habría viajado** a Uruguay el año pasado,   *I would have traveled to Uruguay last year,*
   pero no tenía suficiente dinero.   *but I didn't have enough money.*
Habría sido buenísimo hablar con los   *It would have been great to speak with the*
   indígenas de la zona en su lengua.   *indigenous people of the area in their*
                                                    language.

15.2 *Si* clauses

The past perfect subjunctive in *si* clauses

1. When a **si** clause refers to a contrary-to-fact event in the past, use the past perfect subjunctive form of the verb (see **Para saber más 14.1**).

Si yo **hubiera sabido** que no tenías dinero, te habría prestado.	*If I had known that you didn't have money, I would have lent you some.*
Si Cristóbal Colón no **hubiera llegado** a América, el mundo sería muy diferente.	*If Christopher Columbus had not arrived in the Americas, the world would be very different.*

2. Many speakers also use this past subjunctive perfect form in place of the conditional perfect.

Hubiera sido buenísimo hablar con los indígenas de la zona en su lengua.	*It would have been great to speak with the indigenous people of that area in their language.*

APPENDIX 1: Verb Charts

A. REGULAR VERBS: SIMPLE TENSES

Infinitive Present Participle Past Participle	INDICATIVE					SUBJUNCTIVE		IMPERATIVE
	Present	Imperfect	Preterite	Future	Conditional	Present	Past	
hablar	hablo	hablaba	hablé	hablaré	hablaría	hable	hablara	habla / no hables
hablando	hablas	hablabas	hablaste	hablarás	hablarías	hables	hablaras	hable
hablado	habla	hablaba	habló	hablará	hablaría	hable	hablara	hablemos
	hablamos	hablábamos	hablamos	hablaremos	hablaríamos	hablemos	habláramos	hablad / no habléis
	habláis	hablabais	hablasteis	hablaréis	hablaríais	habléis	hablarais	hablen
	hablan	hablaban	hablaron	hablarán	hablarían	hablen	hablaran	
comer	como	comía	comí	comeré	comería	coma	comiera	come / no comas
comiendo	comes	comías	comiste	comerás	comerías	comas	comieras	coma
comido	come	comía	comió	comerá	comería	coma	comiera	comamos
	comemos	comíamos	comimos	comeremos	comeríamos	comamos	comiéramos	comed / no comáis
	coméis	comíais	comisteis	comeréis	comeríais	comáis	comierais	coman
	comen	comían	comieron	comerán	comerían	coman	comieran	
vivir	vivo	vivía	viví	viviré	viviría	viva	viviera	vive / no vivas
viviendo	vives	vivías	viviste	vivirás	vivirías	vivas	vivieras	viva
vivido	vive	vivía	vivió	vivirá	viviría	viva	viviera	vivamos
	vivimos	vivíamos	vivimos	viviremos	viviríamos	vivamos	viviéramos	vivid / no viváis
	vivís	vivíais	vivisteis	viviréis	viviríais	viváis	vivierais	vivan
	viven	vivían	vivieron	vivirán	vivirían	vivan	vivieran	

B. REGULAR VERBS: PERFECT TENSES

INDICATIVE					SUBJUNCTIVE	
Present Perfect	Pluperfect	Preterite Perfect	Future Perfect	Conditional Perfect	Present Perfect	Pluperfect
he has ha } hablado hemos comido habéis vivido han	había habías había } hablado habíamos comido habíais vivido habían	hube hubiste hubo } hablado hubimos comido hubisteis vivido hubieron	habré habrás habrá } hablado habremos comido habréis vivido habrán	habría habrías habría } hablado habríamos comido habríais vivido habrían	haya hayas haya } hablado hayamos comido hayáis vivido hayan	hubiera hubieras hubiera } hablado hubiéramos comido hubierais vivido hubieran

C. IRREGULAR VERBS

Infinitive Present Participle Past Participle	INDICATIVE					SUBJUNCTIVE		IMPERATIVE
	Present	Imperfect	Preterite	Future	Conditional	Present	Past	
andar andando andado	ando andas anda andamos andáis andan	andaba andabas andaba andábamos andabais andaban	anduve anduviste anduvo anduvimos anduvisteis anduvieron	andaré andarás andará andaremos andaréis andarán	andaría andarías andaría andaríamos andaríais andarían	ande andes ande andemos andéis anden	anduviera anduvieras anduviera anduviéramos anduvierais anduvieran	anda / no andes ande andemos andad / no andéis anden
caber cabiendo cabido	quepo cabes cabe cabemos cabéis caben	cabía cabías cabía cabíamos cabíais cabían	cupe cupiste cupo cupimos cupisteis cupieron	cabré cabrás cabrá cabremos cabréis cabrán	cabría cabrías cabría cabríamos cabríais cabrían	quepa quepas quepa quepamos quepáis quepan	cupiera cupieras cupiera cupiéramos cupierais cupieran	cabe / no quepas quepa quepamos cabed / no quepáis quepan
caer cayendo caído	caigo caes cae caemos caéis caen	caía caías caía caíamos caíais caían	caí caíste cayó caímos caísteis cayeron	caeré caerás caerá caeremos caeréis caerán	caería caerías caería caeríamos caeríais caerían	caiga caigas caiga caigamos caigáis caigan	cayera cayeras cayera cayéramos cayerais cayeran	cae / no caigas caiga caigamos caed / no caigáis caigan

Infinitive Present Participle Past Participle	INDICATIVE					SUBJUNCTIVE		IMPERATIVE
	Present	Imperfect	Preterite	Future	Conditional	Present	Past	
dar	doy	daba	di	daré	daría	dé	diera	da / no des
dando	das	dabas	diste	darás	darías	des	dieras	dé
dado	da	daba	dio	dará	daría	dé	diera	demos
	damos	dábamos	dimos	daremos	daríamos	demos	diéramos	dad / no deis
	dais	dabais	disteis	daréis	daríais	deis	dierais	den
	dan	daban	dieron	darán	darían	den	dieran	
decir	digo	decía	dije	diré	diría	diga	dijera	di / no digas
diciendo	dices	decías	dijiste	dirás	dirías	digas	dijeras	diga
dicho	dice	decía	dijo	dirá	diría	diga	dijera	digamos
	decimos	decíamos	dijimos	diremos	diríamos	digamos	dijéramos	decid / no digáis
	decís	decíais	dijisteis	diréis	diríais	digáis	dijerais	digan
	dicen	decían	dijeron	dirán	dirían	digan	dijeran	
estar	estoy	estaba	estuve	estaré	estaría	esté	estuviera	está / no estés
estando	estás	estabas	estuviste	estarás	estarías	estés	estuvieras	esté
estado	está	estaba	estuvo	estará	estaría	esté	estuviera	estemos
	estamos	estábamos	estuvimos	estaremos	estaríamos	estemos	estuviéramos	estad / no estéis
	estáis	estabais	estuvisteis	estaréis	estaríais	estéis	estuvierais	estén
	están	estaban	estuvieron	estarán	estarían	estén	estuviera	
haber	he	había	hube	habré	habría	haya	hubiera	
habiendo	has	habías	hubiste	habrás	habrías	hayas	hubieras	
habido	ha	había	hubo	habrá	habría	haya	hubiera	
	hemos	habíamos	hubimos	habremos	habríamos	hayamos	hubiéramos	
	habéis	habíais	hubisteis	habréis	habríais	hayáis	hubierais	
	han	habían	hubieron	habrán	habrían	hayan	hubieran	
hacer	hago	hacía	hice	haré	haría	haga	hiciera	haz / no hagas
haciendo	haces	hacías	hiciste	harás	harías	hagas	hicieras	haga
hecho	hace	hacía	hizo	hará	haría	haga	hiciera	hagamos
	hacemos	hacíamos	hicimos	haremos	haríamos	hagamos	hiciéramos	haced / no hagáis
	hacéis	hacíais	hicisteis	haréis	haríais	hagáis	hicierais	hagan
	hacen	hacían	hicieron	harán	harían	hagan	hicieran	

C. IRREGULAR VERBS (CONTINUED)

Infinitive Present Participle Past Participle	INDICATIVE					SUBJUNCTIVE		IMPERATIVE
	Present	Imperfect	Preterite	Future	Conditional	Present	Past	
ir	voy	iba	fui	iré	iría	vaya	fuera	ve / no vayas
yendo	vas	ibas	fuiste	irás	irías	vayas	fueras	vaya
ido	va	iba	fue	irá	iría	vaya	fuera	vayamos
	vamos	íbamos	fuimos	iremos	iríamos	vayamos	fuéramos	id / no vayáis
	vais	ibais	fuisteis	iréis	iríais	vayáis	fuerais	vayan
	van	iban	fueron	irán	irían	vayan	fueran	
oír	oigo	oía	oí	oiré	oiría	oiga	oyera	oye / no oigas
oyendo	oyes	oías	oíste	oirás	oirías	oigas	oyeras	oiga
oído	oye	oía	oyó	oirá	oiría	oiga	oyera	oigamos
	oímos	oíamos	oímos	oiremos	oiríamos	oigamos	oyéramos	oíd / no oigáis
	oís	oíais	oísteis	oiréis	oiríais	oigáis	oyerais	oigan
	oyen	oían	oyeron	oirán	oirían	oigan	oyeran	
poder	puedo	podía	pude	podré	podría	pueda	pudiera	
pudiendo	puedes	podías	pudiste	podrás	podrías	puedas	pudieras	
podido	puede	podía	pudo	podrá	podría	pueda	pudiera	
	podemos	podíamos	pudimos	podremos	podríamos	podamos	pudiéramos	
	podéis	podíais	pudisteis	podréis	podríais	podáis	pudierais	
	pueden	podían	pudieron	podrán	podrían	puedan	pudieran	
poner	pongo	ponía	puse	pondré	pondría	ponga	pusiera	pon / no pongas
poniendo	pones	ponías	pusiste	pondrás	pondrías	pongas	pusieras	ponga
puesto	pone	ponía	puso	pondrá	pondría	ponga	pusiera	pongamos
	ponemos	poníamos	pusimos	pondremos	pondríamos	pongamos	pusiéramos	poned / no pongáis
	ponéis	poníais	pusisteis	pondréis	pondríais	pongáis	pusierais	pongan
	ponen	ponían	pusieron	pondrán	pondrían	pongan	pusieran	
predecir	predigo	predecía	predije	prediciré	prediciría	prediga	predijera	predice / no predigas
prediciendo	predices	predecías	predijiste	predicirás	predicirías	predigas	predijeras	prediga
predicho	predice	predecía	predijo	predicirá	prediciría	prediga	predijera	predigamos
	predecimos	predecíamos	predijimos	prediciremos	prediciríamos	predigamos	predijéramos	predecid / no predigáis
	predecís	predecíais	predijisteis	prediciréis	prediciríais	predigáis	predijerais	predigan
	predicen	predecían	predijeron	predicirán	predicirían	predigan	predijeran	

C. IRREGULAR VERBS (CONTINUED)

Infinitive Present Participle Past Participle	INDICATIVE					SUBJUNCTIVE		IMPERATIVE
	Present	Imperfect	Preterite	Future	Conditional	Present	Past	
querer queriendo querido	quiero quieres quiere queremos queréis quieren	quería querías quería queríamos queríais querían	quise quisiste quiso quisimos quisisteis quisieron	querré querrás querrá querremos querréis querrán	querría querrías querría querríamos querríais querrían	quiera quieras quiera queramos queráis quieran	quisiera quisieras quisiera quisiéramos quisierais quisieran	quiere / no quieras quiera queramos quered / no queráis quieran
saber sabiendo sabido	sé sabes sabe sabemos sabéis saben	sabía sabías sabía sabíamos sabíais sabían	supe supiste supo supimos supisteis supieron	sabré sabrás sabrá sabremos sabréis sabrán	sabría sabrías sabría sabríamos sabríais sabrían	sepa sepas sepa sepamos sepáis sepan	supiera supieras supiera supiéramos supierais supieran	sabe / no sepas sepa sepamos sabed / no sepáis sepan
salir saliendo salido	salgo sales sale salimos salís salen	salía salías salía salíamos salíais salían	salí saliste salió salimos salisteis salieron	saldré saldrás saldrá saldremos saldréis saldrán	saldría saldrías saldría saldríamos saldríais saldrían	salga salgas salga salgamos salgáis salgan	saliera salieras saliera saliéramos salierais salieran	sal / no salgas salga salgamos salid / no salgáis salgan
ser siendo sido	soy eres es somos sois son	era eras era éramos erais eran	fui fuiste fue fuimos fuisteis fueron	seré serás será seremos seréis serán	sería serías sería seríamos seríais serían	sea seas sea seamos seáis sean	fuera fueras fuera fuéramos fuerais fueran	sé / no seas sea seamos sed / no seáis sean
tener teniendo tenido	tengo tienes tiene tenemos tenéis tienen	tenía tenías tenía teníamos teníais tenían	tuve tuviste tuvo tuvimos tuvisteis tuvieron	tendré tendrás tendrá tendremos tendréis tendrán	tendría tendrías tendría tendríamos tendríais tendrían	tenga tengas tenga tengamos tengáis tengan	tuviera tuvieras tuviera tuviéramos tuvierais tuvieran	ten / no tengas tenga tengamos tened / no tengáis tengan

C. IRREGULAR VERBS (CONTINUED)

Infinitive Present Participle Past Participle	INDICATIVE					SUBJUNCTIVE		IMPERATIVE
	Present	Imperfect	Preterite	Future	Conditional	Present	Past	
traer trayendo traído	traigo traes trae traemos traéis traen	traía traías traía traíamos traíais traían	traje trajiste trajo trajimos trajisteis trajeron	traeré traerás traerá traeremos traeréis traerán	traería traerías traería traeríamos traeríais traerían	traiga traigas traiga traigamos traigáis traigan	trajera trajeras trajera trajéramos trajerais trajeran	trae / no traigas traiga traigamos traed / no traigáis traigan
valer valiendo valido	valgo vales vale valemos valéis valen	valía valías valía valíamos valíais valían	valí valiste valió valimos valisteis valieron	valdré valdrás valdrá valdremos valdréis valdrán	valdría valdrías valdría valdríamos valdríais valdrían	valga valgas valga valgamos valgáis valgan	valiera valieras valiera valiéramos valierais valieran	vale / no valgas valga valgamos valed / no valgáis valgan
venir viniendo venido	vengo vienes viene venimos venís vienen	venía venías venía veníamos veníais venían	vine viniste vino vinimos vinisteis vinieron	vendré vendrás vendrá vendremos vendréis vendrán	vendría vendrías vendría vendríamos vendríais vendrían	venga vengas venga vengamos vengáis vengan	viniera vinieras viniera viniéramos vinierais vinieran	ven / no vengas venga vengamos venid / no vengáis vengan
ver viendo visto	veo ves ve vemos veis ven	veía veías veía veíamos veíais veían	vi viste vio vimos visteis vieron	veré verás verá veremos veréis verán	vería verías vería veríamos veríais verían	vea veas vea veamos veáis vean	viera vieras viera viéramos vierais vieran	ve / no veas vea veamos ved / no veáis vean

Infinitive / Present Participle / Past Participle	INDICATIVE					SUBJUNCTIVE		IMPERATIVE
	Present	Imperfect	Preterite	Future	Conditional	Present	Past	
construir (y) / construyendo / construido	construyo	construía	construí	construiré	construiría	construya	construyera	
	construyes	construías	construiste	construirás	construirías	construyas	construyeras	construye / no construyas
	construye	construía	construyó	construirá	construiría	construya	construyera	construya
	construimos	construíamos	construimos	construiremos	construiríamos	construyamos	construyéramos	construyamos
	construís	construíais	construisteis	construiréis	construiríais	construyáis	construyerais	construid / no construyáis
	construyen	construían	construyeron	construirán	construirían	construyan	construyeran	construyan
creer (y [3rd-pers. pret.]) / creyendo / creído	creo	creía	creí	creeré	creería	crea	creyera	
	crees	creías	creíste	creerás	creerías	creas	creyeras	cree / no creas
	cree	creía	creyó	creerá	creería	crea	creyera	crea
	creemos	creíamos	creímos	creeremos	creeríamos	creamos	creyéramos	creamos
	creéis	creíais	creísteis	creeréis	creeríais	creáis	creyerais	creed / no creáis
	creen	creían	creyeron	creerán	creerían	crean	creyeran	crean
dormir (ue, u) / durmiendo / dormido	duermo	dormía	dormí	dormiré	dormiría	duerma	durmiera	
	duermes	dormías	dormiste	dormirás	dormirías	duermas	durmieras	duerme / no duermas
	duerme	dormía	durmió	dormirá	dormiría	duerma	durmiera	duerma
	dormimos	dormíamos	dormimos	dormiremos	dormiríamos	durmamos	durmiéramos	durmamos
	dormís	dormíais	dormisteis	dormiréis	dormiríais	durmáis	durmierais	dormid / no durmáis
	duermen	dormían	durmieron	dormirán	dormirían	duerman	durmieran	duerman
pedir (i, i) / pidiendo / pedido	pido	pedía	pedí	pediré	pediría	pida	pidiera	
	pides	pedías	pediste	pedirás	pedirías	pidas	pidieras	pide / no pidas
	pide	pedía	pidió	pedirá	pediría	pida	pidiera	pida
	pedimos	pedíamos	pedimos	pediremos	pediríamos	pidamos	pidiéramos	pidamos
	pedís	pedíais	pedisteis	pediréis	pediríais	pidáis	pidierais	pedid / no pidáis
	piden	pedían	pidieron	pedirán	pedirían	pidan	pidieran	pidan
pensar (ie) / pensando / pensado	pienso	pensaba	pensé	pensaré	pensaría	piense	pensara	
	piensas	pensabas	pensaste	pensarás	pensarías	pienses	pensaras	piensa / no pienses
	piensa	pensaba	pensó	pensará	pensaría	piense	pensara	piense
	pensamos	pensábamos	pensamos	pensaremos	pensaríamos	pensemos	pensáramos	pensemos
	pensáis	pensabais	pensasteis	pensaréis	pensaríais	penséis	pensarais	pensad / no penséis
	piensan	pensaban	pensaron	pensarán	pensarían	piensen	pensaran	piensen

D. STEM CHANGING AND SPELLING CHANGE VERBS (CONTINUED)

Infinitive / Present Participle / Past Participle	INDICATIVE					SUBJUNCTIVE		IMPERATIVE
	Present	Imperfect	Preterite	Future	Conditional	Present	Past	
producir (zc, j)	produzco	producía	produje	produciré	produciría	produzca	produjera	produce / no produzcas
produciendo	produces	producías	produjiste	producirás	producirías	produzcas	produjeras	produzca
producido	produce	producía	produjo	producirá	produciría	produzca	produjera	produzcamos
	producimos	producíamos	produjimos	produciremos	produciríamos	produzcamos	produjéramos	producid / no produzcáis
	producís	producíais	produjisteis	produciréis	produciríais	produzcáis	produjerais	produzcan
	producen	producían	produjeron	producirán	producirían	produzcan	produjeran	
reír (i, i)	río	reía	reí	reiré	reiría	ría	riera	ríe / no rías
riendo	ríes	reías	reíste	reirás	reirías	rías	rieras	ría
reído	ríe	reía	rio	reirá	reiría	ría	riera	riamos
	reímos	reíamos	reímos	reiremos	reiríamos	riamos	riéramos	reíd / no riáis
	reís	reíais	reísteis	reiréis	reiríais	riáis	rierais	rían
	ríen	reían	rieron	reirán	reirían	rían	rieran	
seguir (i, i) (g)	sigo	seguía	seguí	seguiré	seguiría	siga	siguiera	sigue / no sigas
siguiendo	sigues	seguías	seguiste	seguirás	seguirías	sigas	siguieras	siga
seguido	sigue	seguía	siguió	seguirá	seguiría	siga	siguiera	sigamos
	seguimos	seguíamos	seguimos	seguiremos	seguiríamos	sigamos	siguiéramos	seguid / no sigáis
	seguís	seguíais	seguisteis	seguiréis	seguiríais	sigáis	siguierais	sigan
	siguen	seguían	siguieron	seguirán	seguirían	sigan	siguieran	
sentir (ie, i)	siento	sentía	sentí	sentiré	sentiría	sienta	sintiera	siente / no sientas
sintiendo	sientes	sentías	sentiste	sentirás	sentirías	sientas	sintieras	sienta
sentido	siente	sentía	sintió	sentirá	sentiría	sienta	sintiera	sintamos
	sentimos	sentíamos	sentimos	sentiremos	sentiríamos	sintamos	sintiéramos	sentid / no sintáis
	sentís	sentíais	sentisteis	sentiréis	sentiríais	sintáis	sintierais	sientan
	sienten	sentían	sintieron	sentirán	sentirían	sientan	sintieran	
volver (ue)	vuelvo	volvía	volví	volveré	volvería	vuelva	volviera	vuelve / no vuelvas
volviendo	vuelves	volvías	volviste	volverás	volverías	vuelvas	volvieras	vuelva
vuelto	vuelve	volvía	volvió	volverá	volvería	vuelva	volviera	volvamos
	volvemos	volvíamos	volvimos	volveremos	volveríamos	volvamos	volviéramos	volved / no volváis
	volvéis	volvíais	volvisteis	volveréis	volveríais	volváis	volvierais	vuelvan
	vuelven	volvían	volvieron	volverán	volverían	vuelvan	volvieran	

Answer key for *Reciclaje, Para empezar,* and *Actividades analíticas*

Capítulo 1

Estructura 1.1

Para empezar: un bolígrafo, una computadora, un diccionario, un libro
Actividades analíticas: 1. una, un, un, una   2. Sí

Estructura 1.2

Para empezar: 1. cinco   2. dos   3. dos   4. cuatro   5. tres   6. dos
Actividades analíticas: 1. **-s:** libro, mochila; **-es:** borrador, mujer   2. estudiantes, meses, universidades, bolígrafos   3. lápices, luces   4. el lápiz, las computadoras, los escritores, la mochila; un gimnasio, unas sillas, una pizarra, unos bolígrafos

Estructura 1.3

Para empezar: 2. f   3. h   4. b   5. g   6. a   7. c   8. d
Actividades analíticas: 1. **él/ella, Ud.:** es, tiene; **ellos/ellas, Uds.:** son, tienen 3b. es, Tiene

Estructura 1.4

Para empezar: 1. d   2. b   3. a   4. c   5. e   **Actividades analíticas:**   1. *my:* mi(s); *your:* tu(s); *our:* nuestro(s)/nuestra(s)

Capítulo 2

Estructura 2.1

Para empezar: 1. g   2. d   3. b   4. f   5. c   6. a   7. e   8. h
Actividades analíticas: 1. altos, alta   4. a. nuevos b. jóvenes c. vieja d. inteligente

Estructura 2.2

Para empezar: 1. b   2. f   3. c   4. a   5. e   6. b, d   7. a, b, c
Actividades analíticas: 1. **tú:** estás, vas; **nosotros:** estamos, vamos   2. está, va

Estructura 2.3

Para empezar: 1. Javier   2. Agustina   3. Pedro   4. nobody   5. Esther
Actividades analíticas: 1. **me gusta (singular):** la música, la biología; **me gustan (plural):** los deportes, los libros   2. Te gustan, Te gusta   3. le gustan, le gusta

Estructura 2.4

Actividades analíticas: 2. **-ar:** bailar, hablar, nadar, usar; **-er:** comer, correr, hacer, leer; **-ir:** dormir

Capítulo 3

Estructura 3.1

Reciclaje: 2. c   3. a   4. b   5. e; a. tiene b. vas c. es d. soy e. está
Para empezar: 1. Javier Bardem   2. Gael García Bernal   3. Gael García Bernal
4. Gael García Bernal, Javier Bardem   5. Gael García Bernal   6. Javier Bardem
7. Gael García Bernal, Javier Bardem   8. Gael García Bernal, Javier Bardem
Actividades analíticas: 1. **yo:** trabajo, leo, vivo; **tú:** trabajas, lees, vives   2. -o   3. -s

Estructura 3.2

Reciclaje: 1. son, falso   2. somos, cierto   3. van, falso   4. están, cierto or falso   5. tienen, cierto   6. vamos, falso

Para empezar: 1. 7 2. 2 3. 8 **Actividades analíticas:** 1. **cenar:** ceno, cenas, cenamos, cenan; **comer:** como, comes, comemos, comen; **vivir:** vivo, vives 2. -e, -á, -e 3. -mos, -is, -n 4. **bailar:** bailas, baila, bailamos, bailan: **correr:** corro, corre, corremos, corréis: **asistir:** asisto, asistes, asistimos, asistís

Estructura 3.3

Reciclaje: 1. ar 2. ar 3. er 4. ar 5. ir 6. er 7. ar 8. er 9. ar 10. ar 11. ar **Para empezar:** pueden tomar café; pueden estudiar medicina; pueden nadar; pueden leer en la biblioteca **Actividades analíticas:** 1. podemos, pueden 2. nosotros/as: podemos; podéis 3. yo: almuerzo, duermo, sueño; **nosotros/as:** almorzamos, dormimos, soñamos

Estructura 3.4

Reciclaje: 1. el 2. la 3. el 4. el 5. el 6. la 7. la 8. el 9. el 10. la 11. la 12. la *words related to time*: la noche, el día, el mes, la semana, la hora, la mañana **Para empezar:** 1. Física 2. martes 3. Salud Pública 4. Química General, Química Orgánica I 5. Química General 6. lunes, jueves **Actividades analíticas:** 2. *sing. m.* ese; *sing. fem.* esa; *pl. m.* esos; *pl. f.* esas 3. este, estas, estos, esta

Capítulo 4

Estructura 4.1

Reciclaje: (*any order*) bonitas, jóvenes, delgadas, ricas **Para empezar:** 1. el rey Felipe 2. la reina Letizia, la reina Sofía 3. el rey Juan Carlos 4. la reina Sofía 5. el rey Felipe, el rey Juan Carlos 6. la princesa Sofía, la princesa Leonor **Actividades analíticas:** 1. más 2. menos rica, menos alta, menos altos

Estructura 4.2

Para empezar: 1. «hola» 2. «diga» 3. «bueno» 4. «hola» 5. «aló» **Actividades analíticas:** 1. dices, decimos, dicen 3. tú: sirves; **nosotros/as:** servimos; **yo:** pido; **ellos/ellas, Uds.:** piden

Estructura 4.3

Para empezar: 1. c 2. d 3. e 4. b 5. a **Actividades analíticas:** 1. queremos, quieren 2. tú: empiezas; **nosotros/as:** empezamos; **yo:** pienso, **él/ella, Ud.:** piensa; **ellos/ellas, Uds.:** piensan

Estructura 4.4

Para empezar: 1. c 2. b, f 3. d, e 4. a 5. h 6. k 7. g 8. l 9. i, j **Actividades analíticas:** 1. **ser:** es, son; **estar:** está, están 2. ...están en diferentes países. 4. a. estar, location b. estar, property that could change c. ser, origin d. ser, identity

Capítulo 5

Estructura 5.1

Reciclaje: 1. Soy, ciudad 2. Voy, campo 3. Soy, campo 4. Estoy, ciudad 5. Tengo, campo 6. Estoy, ciudad **Para empezar:** 1. f, h 2. a, i 3. d 4. c, e 5. g, b 6. d **Actividades analíticas:** 1. hago, traigo, salgo 2. **yo:** tengo, digo; **tú:** vienes; **él/ella, Ud.** tiene, dice; **nosotros/as:** venimos; **ellos/ellas, Uds.:** tienen, dicen 3. oigo, oye

Estructura 5.2

Reciclaje: 1. te llamas 2. Me llamo 3. se llama 4. Se llama 5. te llamas 6. Me llamo **Para empezar:** BIBLIOTECA: dormirse, sentarse; GIMNASIO: (*any four*) afeitarse, bañarse, ducharse, maquillarse, peinarse, vestirse; HOTEL: *any* **Actividades analíticas:** 1. -se 2. **yo:** me baño, me peino; **tú:** te afeitas, te peinas; **él/ella, Ud.:** se baña; **nosotros/as:** nos bañamos, nos peinamos; **vosotros/as:** os peináis; **ellos/ellas, Uds.:** se afeitan

Estructura 5.3

Reciclaje: 1. d 2. a 3. e 4. c 5. b; a. Es b. Está c. Son d. Somos e. Están **Para empezar:** 1. cierto 2. falso 3. falso 4. cierto 5. falso 6. falso 7. falso 8. cierto 9. cierto 10. cierto **Actividades analíticas:** 1. ser, estar 4. a. location b. change c. identity d. intrinsic quality e. origin

Estructura 5.4

Reciclaje: 1. Estos edificios 2. Esta tienda 3. Este muchacho 4. Estas chicas 5. Esta catedral **Para empezar:** 1. cierto 2. falso 3. cierto 4. cierto 5. cierto 6. falso 7. falso 8. cierto 9. cierto 10. falso **Actividades analíticas:** 1. *first row:* algo, algunos, algunas; *second row:* nada, ningún, ninguna 2. a. algunas b. algunos c. ningún d. ninguna

Capítulo 6

Estructura 6.1

Reciclaje: un cocinero profesional: Cocina, Escribe, Trabaja, Aprende; **yo:** (No) Cocino, (No) Escribo, (No) Trabajo, (No) Aprendo **Para empezar, Paso 1:** 1. i 2. f 3. h 5. c 7. d 8. g. 9. e **Paso 2:** 1. b 2. d 3. f 4. a 5. c 6. e **Actividades analíticas: yo:** trabajé, aprendí; **tú:** trabajaste, aprendiste; **él/ella, Ud.:** trabajó, aprendió, escribió 2. **yo:** -í; **tú:** -iste; **nosotros/as:** -amos; **vosotros/as:** -isteis; **ellos/ellas, Uds.:** -aron, -ieron

Estructura 6.2

Reciclaje: 1. Soy 2. hago 3. Digo 4. Voy 5. pongo **Para empezar:** 1. estuvo mal 2. estuvo mal 3. estuvo bien 4. estuvo mal 5. estuvo mal 6. estuvo mal 7. estuvo mal 8. estuvo bien 9. estuvo mal **Actividades analíticas:** 1. Primero fui a la casa equivocada (#1), Fui muy educado (#3) 2. **yo:** dije, hice, puse; **él/ella, Ud.:** estuvo; **tú:** -iste; **nosotros/as:** -imos

Estructura 6.3

Reciclaje: 1. el 2. la 3. la 4. el 5. la 6. el 7. las 8. los 9. la 10. la 11. el 12. el 13. las 14. los 15. la 16. las 17. el 18. los 19. la 20. el; No se puede comer: la cuchara, el cuchillo, la servilleta, las tazas, el tenedor **Para empezar:** 1. P 2. C 3. V 4. C 5. T 6. C 7. P 8. T **Actividades analíticas:** 1. b. la papa c. a mi hermano d. a Marisela 2. b. café, Ana lo toma por la mañana.; c. la fruta, Julián la compró ayer. 5. a. Lo invito a desayunar con nosotros. b. La llevamos a la fiesta.

Capítulo 7

Estructura 7.1

Reciclaje: REGULARMENTE: Hablo, Como, leo, Duermo, voy; **AYER:** Hablé, Comí, leí, Dormí, fui **Para empezar:** 1. cierto 2. cierto 3. cierto 4. falso 5. cierto 6. cierto 7. falso 8. falso **Actividades analíticas:** 2. **tú:** vivías; **nosotros/as:** comíamos, **ellos/ellas, Uds.:** hablaban, comían, vivían 3. **yo:** -ía; **tú:** -abas, -ías; **él/ella, Ud.:** -aba, ía; **nosotros/as:** -ábamos; **vosotros/as:** -íais; **ellos/ellas, Uds.:** -aban, -ían

Estructura 7.2

Reciclaje: 1. la 2. lo 3. los 4. las 5. me **Actividades analíticas:** 1. *sing.:* me, le; *pl:* les 2. his parents, her friends

Estructura 7.3

Reciclaje: 1. los papás 2. la mamá, Ella 3. el hermano, Él 4. el papá, Él 5. el hermano y yo, Nosotros 6. las abuelas, Ellas **Actividades analíticas:** 1. mí

Capítulo 8

Estructura 8.1

Reciclaje, Paso 1: Pasé, regresé, terminé, Estuve, ayudé, Fui, pasamos, Hicimos, comimos, bailamos, Trabajé **Para empezar:** 1. B 2. H 3. H 4. B 5. H 6. H 7. B **Actividades analíticas:** 1. **yo:** serví, vestí; **tú:** seguiste, serviste; **él/ella, Ud.:** pidió, siguió, sirvió, vistió; **nosotros/as:** pedimos, vestimos; **ellos/ellas, Uds.:** pidieron, sirvieron, vistieron 2. **e → i verb forms:** pidió, pidieron; siguió, siguieron; sirvió, sirvieron; vistió, vistieron 3. **yo:** morí; **tú:** dormiste; **él/ella, Ud.:** murió; **nosotros/as:** morimos; **vosotros/as:** dormisteis; **ellos/ellas, Uds.:** durmieron 4. **o → u verb forms:** durmió, durmieron; murió, murieron

Estructura 8.2

Reciclaje: 1. llevabas 2. tenías 3. escogía 4. gustaba 5. lavaba
Para empezar: 1. cierto 2. falso 3. cierto 4. cierto 5. falso 6. cierto 7. cierto
8. falso 9. falso 10. cierto **Actividades analíticas:** 2. 1, 5, 6, 8, 10 4. 7, 9

Estructura 8.3

Reciclaje: 1. e 2. f 3. h 4. b 5. a 6. c 7. d; a. Lo, les b. Los c. Lo
d. Los e. Lo f. Le g. la **Para empezar:** 1. e 2. b 3. a 4. d 5. c
Actividades analíticas: 3. a. Los voy a comprar. c. Lo/Las tengo que comprar. d. La puedo
comprar 4. a. Voy a comprarlos. b. Quiero comprarlos. c. Tengo que comprarlo/las. d. Puedo
comprarla.

Capítulo 9

Estructura 9.1

Reciclaje: 1. De México a Guadalajara 2. De México a Guatemala 4. De México a Nueva
York 5. De México a Santiago 6. De México a Madrid **Para empezar:** 1. b 2. b 3. a
4. b 5. a 6. a 7. a 8. b **Actividades analíticas:** 2. a. para Machu Picchu b. para las
ocho c. para ir a Machu Picchu, para evitar los grandes grupos de turistas d. para tus amigos,
para tu familia, para tu viaje 4. a. por el Valle Sagrado b. por la mañana c. por tren d. por la
gran cantidad de turistas

Estructura 9.2

Para empezar: 1. E 2. M 3. A 4. M 5. E 6. A 7. E 8. E 9. M 10. A 11. M
12. A **Actividades analíticas:** 2. 4, 5, 9; The noun is plural.

Estructura 9.3

Para empezar: 7, 5, 2, 1, 9, 8, 6, 4, 3 **Actividades analíticas:** 1. un café, mi tarjeta de
identificación, un café, el teléfono, el chaleco y los pantalones 2. Se me acabó el dinero,
Se me perdió el pasaporte

Capítulo 10

Estructura 10.1

Reciclaje: EDIFICIOS / INFRAESTRUCTURA: los arquitectos comerciales y residenciales, los
ingenieros civiles y estructurales, una agente de bienes raíces; EDUCACIÓN: una profesora
universitaria; SALUD: un médico especializado en cardiología, las psicólogas clínicas; SEGURIDAD:
un policía motorizado **Para empezar:** 1. C 2. S 3. S 4. S 5. C 6. F 7. C 8. S
9. F 10. S **Actividades analíticas:** 1. que hizo muchos edificios muy famosos en Barcelona
2. sus hijos Carlos, Marco Antonio y Patrick

Estructura 10.2

Reciclaje: 1. g 2. e 3. b 4. f 5. a 6. d 7. c 8. h; a. Escribes b. Haces c. Tomas
d. Cortas, arreglas e. Aceptas, das f. Cuidas g. Apagas h. Llevas **Para empezar:** 7. No te
bañes el día de tu entrevista. ¡Eso te da buena suerte! **Actividades analíticas:** 1. piensa,
aprende, pide; **él/ella/Ud.** form (third person singular of the present indicative) 2. no hables,
no comas 4. haz, pon, sal, ten, ven 7. vístete; no te bañes, no te quedes

Estructura 10.3

Reciclaje: 1. ¿Necesita ayuda? 2. Es el nuevo gerente de la tienda. 3. ¿Sabe cómo hacer
esto? 4. ¿Dónde pone los documentos? 5. ¿Me puede ayudar en algo, por favor? 6. ¿En
qué le puedo ayudar? 7. Le voy a dejar el archivo en su escritorio. 8. ¿Se va después
de la reunión? **Para empezar:** 1. d 2. b 3. c 4. a 5. a 6. d 7. c 8. a
Actividades analíticas: 1. (no) use, (no) oprima; **-ar:** usar, conectar, indicar, comprar;
-er: poner; **-ir:** imprimir 2. (no) usen, (no) coman, (no) opriman 3. *pos. form.:* after and
attached to the verb, cómprela; *neg. form.:* before the verb, no lo use

Capítulo 11

Estructura 11.1

Actividades analíticas: 1. he, hemos   2. lavado, comido, salido; trabajado, aprendido, vivido   3. hecho, He hecho la tarea.; visto, He visto una película.

Estructura 11.2

Reciclaje: 1. La, la   2. los, los   3. Las, las   4. Lo, lo   5. La, la   **Para empezar:**   1. D   2. C   3. C   4. B, C   5. C   6. B   7. D   8. D   9. C, B   10. B, D   11. D   12. C   **Actividades analíticas:**   1. Ponlos en tu dormitorio.; Ponte el pijama verde.   2. No le pongas azúcar al café.; No te pongas el pijama verde.   3. **yo:** límpialo; **Ud.:** no lo limpie; **Uds.:** límpienlo, no lo limpien

Estructura 11.3

Reciclaje: 1. Es   2. Es   3. está   4. está   5. Está   6. es   7. Es   8. Está   9. Es   10. es   **Para empezar:**   1. c   2. j   3. g   4. e   5. d   6. a   7. h   8. b   9. f   10. i   **Actividades analíticas:**   1. *present participles:* cenando, estudiando, escribiendo; *infinitives:* cenar, estudiar, escribir; *present participles:* comiendo, saliendo, ayudando, viendo

Capítulo 12

Estructura 12.1

Reciclaje: **Paso 1:**   1. he caminado   2. he comido   3. he meditado/practicado yoga   4. he dormido   5. he hecho   6. he tomado   **Para empezar:**   1. a   2. f   3. b   4. g   5. e   6. c   7. h   8. d   **Actividades analíticas**   1. reflexive, indirect object   2. I have had to do/make it., Have you been able to answer his/her question (for him/her)?, We have wanted to buy it for a long time.

Estructura 12.2

Reciclaje: 1. Están corriendo.   2. Están caminando.   3. Está nadando.   4. Están boxeando.   5. Está levantando pesas.   6. Está surfeando.   7. Está jugando tenis.   8. Está esquiando   **Para empezar:**   1. e   2. b   3. a   4. g   5. h   6. d   7. f   8. c   **Actividades analíticas:**   1. le está dando, se está haciendo   2. está dándole, está haciéndose

Estructura 12.3

Reciclaje: 1. Tomen agua.   2. Practica yoga.   3. Levanten pesas.   4. Duerme más.   5. Come menos y haz más ejercicio.   6. Corran.   **Para empezar:** La recomendación falsa: 7   **Actividades analíticas:**   1. INDICATIVE: comes, tomas, vives; SUBJUNCTIVE: busques, comas, compres, des, tomes, vivas   2. **-ar** verbs: -e-   **er/-ir** verbs: -a-   3. TOMAR: tomes, tomemos, tomen; COMER: comas, coma, comáis, coman; VIVIR: vivas, vivamos

Capítulo 13

Estructura 13.1

Reciclaje: 1. jaguar   2. Hago, pájaro   3. Tengo, tortuga   4. Soy, tortuga   5. Salgo, jaguar   6. Traigo, pájaro   7. estoy, jaguar   8. Digo, jaguar, pájaro   9. Pongo, tortuga   **Para empezar:**   1. cierto   2. cierto   3. cierto   4. falso   5. cierto   6. falso   7. cierto   8. falso   9. cierto   **Actividades analíticas:**   1. **yo:** ponga, salga, traiga   **tú:** hagas, salgas, tengas   **él/ella, Ud.:** haga, ponga, salga, tenga, traiga   **nosotros/as:** pongamos, tengamos, traigamos   **vosotros/as:** hagáis, salgáis, traigáis   **ellos/ellas, Uds.:** hagan, pongan, tengan   3. **yo:** sea   **tú:** vayas   **él/ella, Ud.:** vaya, sea   **nosotros/as,** seamos   **vosotros/as:** vayáis   **ellos/ellas, Uds.:** vayan, sean

Estructura 13.2

Reciclaje: 1. d   2. a   3. f   4. b   5. c   6. e   **Para empezar:**   1. cierto   2. cierto   3. cierto   4. cierto   5. cierto   6. cierto   7. cierto   8. falso   9. cierto   10. falso   **Actividades analíticas:**   1. esperar que…, no creer que…, es posible que…, no pensar que…   2. They all express the idea that what follows may not be true.

Estructura 13.3

Reciclaje: 1. c   2. e   3. d   4. f   5. a   6. b; a. por   b. para   c. para   d. para   e. por   f. por   **Para empezar:**   2. d   3. g   4. a   5. c   6. e   7. f

Capítulo 14

Estructura 14.1

Reciclaje: 1. hagan 2. a favor del arte, es 3. cierren 4. a favor del arte, tenga
5. a favor del arte, participen 6. tiene **Para empezar:** 1. cierto 2. cierto 3. falso
4. cierto 5. cierto 6. cierto 7. cierto 8. cierto 9. cierto 10. falso
Actividades analíticas: 1. viviera, aprendieras, viviéramos, hablaran, aprendieran
2. **tú:** -aras **él/ella, Ud.:** -iera **nosotros/as:** -áramos **ellos/ellas, Uds.** –aran, -ieran

Estructura 14.2

Reciclaje: a. 3, ar b. 6, er, ar, ir c. er d. er e. 5, ar f. 4, ar g. 2, ar, ar **Para empezar:** 1. e
2. h 3. g 4. a 5. d 6. f 7. b 8. c **Actividades analíticas:** 2. **yo:** estaré **tú:** serás
él/ella, Ud.: estará **nosotros/as:** viviremos **ellos/ellas, Uds.:** serán

Capítulo 15

Estructura 15.1

Reciclaje: 1. b, Erradicaremos 2. e, Haremos 3. f, Resolveremos 4. a, Acabaremos
5. d, Mejoraremos 6. c, Conseguiremos **Para empezar:** 1. g 2. a 3. h 4. e 5. c
6. i 7. d 8. f 9. b *impossible:* f, h **Actividades analíticas:** 2. **yo:** pasaría, iría
tú: serías **él/ella, Ud.:** iría **nosotros/as:** seríamos **vosotros/as:** iríais **ellos/ellas, Uds.:** serían

Estructura 15.2

Reciclaje: *Querían que...:* los niños pudieran asistir a la escuela sin pagar; los trabajadores
descansaran dos días a la semana; las mujeres tuvieran el derecho de votar; la esclavitud
ya no existiera; toda la gente tuviera la libertad de practicar su religión; *No querían que...:*
hubiera guerras; creciera la desigualdad económica; la corrupción estuviera presente en el
sistema jurídico. **Para empezar:** **Paso 1.** a. 4 b. 2 c. 6 d. 5 f. 3 **Paso 2.** Cierto
Actividades analíticas: 1. b. fuera, importarían c. funcionara, tendrían d. pudiera,
funcionaría e. usara, sería f. importara, ganaría 2. **Si...:** past subjunctive / imperfecto de
subjuntivo, **Consecuencia:** conditional/condicional

Capítulo 16

Estructura 16.1

Reciclaje: camina, camináis, caminan; corro, corres, corre corremos; salir, salgo, sale,
salís, salen; vuelves, vuelve, volvemos, volvéis, vuelven; pedir, pido, pide, pedimos, pedís,
piden; pensar, pienso, piensa, pensamos, pensáis, piensan, te casas, se casa, se casan

Estructura 16.2

Reciclaje: **Paso 1.** HABLAR: habló, hablaron; APRENDER: aprendí, aprendimos, aprendieron;
HACER: hice, hizo, hicimos, hicisteis, hicieron; IR: fui, fue, fuimos, fueron; llegar: llegué,
llegaste, llegamos, llegasteis; DECIR: dijiste, dijimos, dijeron; TENER: tuve, tuviste, tuvo, tuvimos,
tuvisteis, tuvieron; DORMIR: dormí, dormiste, durmió, dormimos, dormisteis, durmieron;
Paso 2. AMAR: amaba, amaban; COMER: comías, comía, comíamos, comíais, comían; IR: ibas,
iba, íbamos, ibais, iban; SER: era, era; éramos; eran; SALIR: salía; salía; salíamos; salíais; salían

Estructura 16.3

Reciclaje: 2. c 3. e 4. f 5. a 6. d; a. le c. Te d. Los e. lo f. Lo

Estructura 16.4

Reciclaje: AMAR: ames, amame, améis, amen; HACER: haga, haga, hagáis, hagan;
CASARSE: te cases, se case, se casen; SER: sea, seas, sea, seamos, seáis, sean; VOLVER: vuelvas,
vuelva, volvamos, volváis, vuelvan; TENER: tengas, tenga, tengamos, tengáis, tengan

VOCABULARIO

The following abbreviations are used:

adj. adjective	*inf.* infinitive	*poss.* possessive
adv. adverb	*inform.* informal	*p.p.* past participle
Arg. Argentina	*interj.* interjection	*P.R.* Puerto Rico
C.A. Central America	*inv.* invariable form	*prep.* preposition
Carib. Caribbean	*i.o.* indirect object	*pres. p.* present participle
conj. conjunction	*L.Am.* Latin America	*pron.* pronoun
def. art. definite article	*m.* masculine	*refl. pron.* reflexive pronoun
d.o. direct object	*Mex.* Mexico	*s.* singular
f. feminine	*n.* noun	*S.A.* South America
form. formal	*obj.* (*of prep.*) object (of a	*sl.* slang
gram. grammatical term	preposition)	*Sp.* Spain
ind. art. indefinite article	*pl.* plural	*sub. pron.* subject pronoun

Spanish-English Vocabulary

A

a to (7); at (*with time*); **a base de** based on; **a continuación** following; below; **a escondidas** secretly; **a favor (de)** in favor (of); **a fondo** in depth; **a la plancha** grilled (6); **a la(s)...** at . . . (*time of day*); **a largo plazo** long-term, in the long-term; **a lo largo de** along, throughout; **a mano** by hand; **a mano derecha** on the right; **a mano izquierda** on the left; **a partir de** as of, since; **a pesar de** in spite of, despite; **a pie** on foot; **¿a qué hora... ?** at what time . . . ? (3); **¿a qué se dedica?** what do you (*form. s.*) do (*occupation*)? (4); **¿a qué te dedicas?** what do you (*inform. s.*) do (*occupation*)? (4); **a raíz de** as a result of; **a sus órdenes** at your service; **a ver** let's see; **al aire libre** outdoors; **al ajillo** sautéed with garlic (6); **al cabo de** at the end of; **al contrario** on the contrary; **al final** in the end; **al igual que** just like; **es a la/las...** it's at . . . (3); **está/queda a la derecha** it's on the right/left (5); **está/queda al lado de...** it's beside . . . (5); **un número / una letra a la vez, por favor** one number / letter at a time, please (1); **voy a/al** + *place* I'm going to . . . (2)

abajo below; underneath

abandonar to abandon

abarrotería grocery store

abarrotes: tienda de abarrotes grocery store

abastecedor *m.* grocery store

abastos: tienda de abastos grocery store

abierto/a (*p.p. of* **abrir**) open (16)

abogado/a lawyer (4)

abolir to abolish

abono fertilizer

abrazo hug, embrace; **dar** (*irreg.*) **un abrazo** to hug

abrigado/a bundled up

abrigo coat (8)

abril *m.* April (1)

abrir (*p.p.* **abierto**) to open (6)

absoluto/a absolute

abuelo/a grandfather/grandmother (4); *pl.* grandparents (4)

abulón *m.* (*pl.* **abulones**) abalone

abundar to abound, be plentiful

aburrido/a bored; boring (2); **¡qué aburrido!** how boring! (8)

acá *adv.* here

acabar to finish; to run out of; **acabar de** + *inf.* to have just (*done something*)

academia academy

académico/a academic

acampar to camp

acaso: por si acaso just in case

accesible accessible

acceso access

accesorio accessory (8)

accidente *m.* accident

acción *f.* action; **Día** (*m.*) **de Acción de Gracias** Thanksgiving (7); **película de acción** action movie

aceite *m.* oil (6); **aceite de oliva** olive oil

acentuar (ú) to accentuate

aceptar to accept

acerca de *prep.* about, concerning, regarding

acompañamiento side dish (*food*) (6)

acompañar to accompany; **te/le/les acompaño/acompañamos en el dolor** I'm/we're with you (*inform. s. / form. s. / form. pl.*) in your time of pain (16); **te/le/ les acompaño/acompañamos en el sentimiento** you're (*inform. s. / form. s. / form. pl.*) in my/our thoughts (16)

aconsejable advisable

aconsejar to advise

acontecimiento event, happening

acordarse (ue) (de) to remember (5)

acorde (con) in agreement (with)

acostarse (ue) to go to bed (5)

acostumbrado/a (a) accustomed, used (to)

actitud *f.* attitude

actividad *f.* activity

activista *m., f.* activist

activo/a active; **llevar una vida activa** to lead an active life

acto act

actor *m.* actor (14)

actriz *f.* (*pl.* **actrices**) actress (14)

actuación *f.* acting; performance

actual *adj.* current, present-day

actuar (actúo) to act (14)

acudir (a) to go (to)

acuerdo agreement; **(no) estar** (*irreg.*) **de acuerdo** to (dis)agree

adecuado/a appropriate

adelante forward; **¡adelante!** come on! / let's go! / cheer up! (12)

además *adv.* moreover; **además de** *prep.* besides

adentro inside; **mar adentro** off-shore

adicional additional

adiós good-bye (1)

adivinanza riddle

adivinar to guess

adjetivo *gram.* adjective

administración *f.* administration; **administración de empresas** business administration; **administración de negocios** business administration; **administración de restaurantes** restaurant management

administrar to manage

administrativo/a administrative; **asistente** (*m., f.*) **administrativo/a** administrative assistant (10)
admirar to admire
adolescencia adolescence
adolescente *m., f.* adolescent
¿adónde? where to? (2); **¿adónde va?** where are you (*form.*) going? (2); **¿adónde vas?** where are you (*inform.*) going? (2)
adopción *f.* adoption
adoptar to adopt
adquirir (ie) to acquire
adquisición *f.* acquisition
aduana customs (*at a border*); **agente** (*m., f.*) **de aduanas** customs agent
adulto/a *n., adj.* adult
aeróbico: hacer (*irreg.*) **ejercicio aeróbico** to do aerobics
aerolínea airline
aeropuerto airport (9)
afán *m.* desire, zeal
afectar to affect
afeitarse to shave (5)
aficionado/a fan (12); **ser** (*irreg.*) **aficionado/a (a)** to be a fan (of)
afirmación *f.* statement
afortunado/a lucky
africano/a *n., adj.* African
afrontar to face, confront
afro-uruguayo/a Afro-Uruguayan
afuera *adv.* outdoors
afueras *n. pl.* outskirts; suburbs (5)
agarrar to grab
agave *m.* agave
agavero: alambre (*m.*) **agavero** *dish which features an agave stock on a plate of rice with banana, chicken or beef, and melted cheese*
agencia agency; **agencia de prensa** press agency; **agencia de seguros** insurance agency; **agencia de talentos** talent agency; **agencia de viajes** travel agency
agente *m., f.* agent; **agente de aduanas** customs agent; **agente de bienes raíces** real estate agent (10); **agente de seguros** insurance agent (10); **agente de viajes** travel agent
agosto August (1)
agotador(a) exhausting
agotamiento exhaustion (13); depletion (13)
agotar to sell out; to exhaust; to deplete
agradable pleasant (9)
agradecer (zc) to thank; **te/le/les agradezco por...** I appreciate that you . . . , I thank you for . . . (5)
agradecimiento thanks
agregar (gu) to add
agresivo/a aggressive
agrícola *adj. m., f.* agricultural

agricultor(a) farmer
agricultura agriculture
agroeconomista *m., f.* agroeconomist
agua *f.* (*but* **el agua**) water (6); **agua salada** salt water; **botella de agua** water bottle; **caída de agua** waterfall
aguacate *m.* avocado
aguacero rain shower; downpour
aguadulce *m. typical Costa Rican drink*
aguantar to withstand
ahí there
ahogar (gu) to drown
ahora now; **ahorita** right now
ahorrar to save (13)
aimara *m.* Aymara (*language*)
aire *m.* aire; **al aire libre** outdoors; **contaminación** (*f.*) **del aire** air pollution
ají *m.* chili pepper
ajillo: al ajillo sautéed with garlic (6)
ala *f.* (*but* **el ala**) wing
alambre (*m.*) **agavero** *dish which features an agave stock on a plate of rice with banana, chicken or beef, and melted cheese*
alarmante alarming
alavés, alavesa *n., adj.* from Álava, Spain
albergar (gu) to shelter
albergue *m.* hotel
álbum *m.* album
alcance *m.* reach; **al alcance** within reach
alcanzar (c) to reach; to achieve
alcohólico/a alcoholic
alegrarse (de) to be happy (about)
alegre happy (2)
alegría happiness
alemán *m.* German (*language*)
alemán (*pl.* **alemanes**), **alemana** *n., adj.* German
Alemania Germany
alergia allergy (12); **tener** (*irreg.*) **alergia a** to be allergic to (12)
alérgico/a allergic
alfabetismo literacy
alfabetización *f.* literacy (15); teaching of literacy (15)
alfombra rug
algo something (5); anything
algodón *m.* cotton
alguien someone (5); anyone
algún (alguna/os/as) some (5); any; **algún día** someday; **alguna vez** once; ever; **de alguna manera** in some way; **en algún momento** at some point
aliada *m., f.* ally
alimentar(se) to feed
alimenticio/a food; **cadena alimenticia** food chain
alimento food, foodstuff
alineación *f.* alignment
alistarse to enlist
allá (way) over there
allí there
alma *f.* (*but* **el alma**) soul

almacén *m.* (*pl.* **almacenes**) warehouse; department store (5)
almacenamiento storage
almohada pillow
almorzar (ue) (c) to eat lunch (3)
almuerzo lunch; **preparar el almuerzo** to prepare lunch (4)
aló hello (*telephone greeting*)
alojamiento lodging
alojarse to lodge, stay (hotel)
alpinismo mountaineering
alpinista *m., f.* mountain climber
alpino/a Alpine
alquilar to rent
alquiler *m.* rent
alrededor (de) around
altar *m.* altar
alterado/a altered
alternativa alternative
alternativo/a alternative (14)
altiplano high plateau
alto/a tall (2); **alta costura** haute couture; **en voz alta** out loud; **más alto que** taller than (4); **menos alto que** less tall than (4); **tacones** (*m. pl.*) **altos** high-heeled shoes
alumno/a student
alzar (c) to raise, lift up
amable friendly
amanecer *m.* dawn
amante *m., f.* lover
amar to love (16)
amarillo yellow (2)
Amazonas *m. s.* Amazon (River)
ambicioso/a ambitious
ambiental environmental
ambiente *m.* atmosphere; environment; **medio ambiente** environment (13)
ambos/as both
amenazar (c) to threaten
americano/a American; **fútbol** (*m.*) **americano** football (12); **jugar (ue) (gu) fútbol americano** to play football (12)
amigo/a friend (1)
aminoácido amino acid
amistad *f.* friendship (16)
amo/a master/mistress; **ama** (*f., but* **el ama**) **de casa** housewife (4)
amor *m.* love (16); **canción** (*f.*) **de amor** love song; **Día** (*m.*) **del Amor** Valentine's Day
amplio/a broad
analfabetismo illiteracy (15)
analfabetización *f.* illiteracy
anaranjado/a orange (2)
ancho/a wide (8)
andar *irreg.* to walk; **¡ándale!** come on! *command inform. s.*; **¡ándele!** come on! *command form. s.*; **andar en bicicleta** to ride a bicycle (12); **andar en patineta** to skateboard (12)

andino/a Andean
anécdota anecdote
anglohablante *m., f.* English speaker
anglosajón (*pl.* **anglosajones**), **anglosajona** Anglo Saxon
angustia distress; worry
anhelar to long, yearn for
anidar to nest
anillo ring (8)
animación *f.* animation
animado/a lively (2)
animal *m.* animal; **animal doméstico** pet
¡ánimo! come on! / let's go! / cheer up! (12)
aniversario anniversary
anoche last night
anotación *f.* score
anotar to note
ansioso/a anxious (2)
Antártida Antarctica
antepasado/a ancestor
anterior before
antes *adv.* before (1); **antes de** *prep.* before (1); **antes (de) que** *conj.* before
antes *prep.* before; in front of
antibiótico antibiotic
anticipar to anticipate
antigüedad antiquity
antiguo/a old (5)
antillano/a Antillean (from the Antilles or West Indies)
antioxidante *m.* antioxidant
antipático/a disagreeable (2)
antojarse to feel like, have a craving (9); **se me/te/le/nos/os/les antoja/antojó** + *inf. / s. n.* I / you (*inform. s.*) / he, she, you (*form. s.*) / we / you (*inform. pl.*) / they / they, you (*form. pl.*) feel/felt like + ([*doing*] *something*) (9); **se me/te/le/nos/os/les antojan/antojaron** + *pl. n.* I / you (*inform. s.*) / he, she, you (*form. s.*) / we / you (*inform. pl.*) / they / they, you (*form. pl.*) feel/felt like + *pl. n.* (9)
antojito appetizer
antónimo antonym
antro nightclub
anunciar to announce
anuncio ad; commercial
añadir to add
año year (1); **Año Nuevo** New Year's (7); **año pasado** last year; **cumplir... años** to turn . . . years old (7); **¿cuántos años tienes?** how old are you (*inform.*)? (2); **¿cuántos años tiene?** how old are you (*form.*)? (2); **este año** this year; **¡feliz Año Nuevo!** happy New Year! (7); **tener** (*irreg.*)**... años** to be . . . years old; **tengo** + *number* + **años** I'm + *number* years old (2)
apagar (gu) to turn off
aparato appliance

aparcar (qu) to park
aparecer (zc) to appear
apartamento apartment (5)
aparte: aparte de in addition to; **hoja de papel aparte** separate sheet of paper
apellido surname
apenas barely
aperitivo appetizer (6)
apetecer (zc) (*like* **gustar**) to appeal to
aplastar to flatten
aplicación *f.* application
aplicar (qu) to apply
apodo nickname
apoyar to support
apoyo support
apreciación *f.* appreciation
apreciar to appreciate
aprender (a) to learn (to) (6)
apretado/a tight (8)
apropiado/a appropriate
aprovechar to take advantage of
aproximadamente approximately
apuntar to write down; **apuntarse** to enroll; to add one's name to the list
apuntes *m. pl.* notes (*academic*)
apurarse to hurry
apuro hurry
aquel, aquella that ([way] over there)
aquello that ([way] over there)
aquellos/as those ([way] over there)
aquí here (2)
árabe *m.* Arabic (*language*); *n., adj. m., f.* Arab
árbol *m.* tree (5); **árbol de Navidad** Christmas tree; **copa de los árboles** top of the trees; **tala de árboles** tree cutting (13)
archivo document; file (10)
arcilla clay
ardor *m.* ardor
área *f.* (*but* **el área**) area, region
arena sand
arepa *fried bread made of cornmeal*
argentino/a *n., adj.* Argentine (2)
argumentar to argue
argumento argument (*legal*); plot
arma *f.* (*but* **el arma**) weapon
armado/a armed
armario armoire, closet (11)
armonía harmony
aro hoop; ring
arqueológico/a archeological
arquitecto/a architect (10)
arquitectura architecture (1)
arrecife *m.* reef
arreglar to arrange
arroba @ (at, *in an email address*) (1)
arroz *m.* rice (6); **arroz con leche** rice pudding; **arroz graneado** *fried rice dish*
arruinar to ruin

arte *m.* (*but* **las artes**) art (14); **bellas artes** fine arts; **obra de arte** piece, work of art (14)
artesanal handcrafted; traditional
artesanía crafts (9)
artículo article
artificial artificial; **fuegos artificiales** fireworks (7)
artista *m., f.* artist
artístico/a artistic
asado barbecue, cookout
asado/a roast(ed) (6)
asamblea assembly
ascender (ie) to climb
ascensor *m.* elevator (11)
ascetismo asceticism
asegurar to assure
asequible accessible
asfalto asphalt
así thus; so; **así como** as well as; **así que** therefore, consequently, so
asiático/a Asian
asistente *m., f.* (**administrativo/a**) (administrative) assistant (10)
asistir (a) to attend (2); to go to (*a class, function*)
asma *m.* asthma (12)
asociación *f.* association
aspecto aspect; **tener** (*irreg.*) **buen aspecto** to look good
aspiración *f.* goal
aspiradora vacuum cleaner (11); **pasar la aspiradora** to vacuum (11)
asqueroso/a disgusting
astronauta *m., f.* astronaut
astronómico/a astronomical
asumir to assume
asunto matter
asustar to frighten
atacar (qu) to attack
atar to tie
atención *f.* attention; **poner** (*irreg.*) **atención** to pay attention; **prestar atención** to pay attention
atender (ie) (a) to serve, wait on; to care for
atlántico/a Atlantic; **océano Atlántico** Atlantic Ocean
atleta *m., f.* athlete (12)
atlético/a athletic
atletismo athleticism
atracción *f.* attraction (9)
atractivo attraction
atractivo/a attractive
atraer (*like* **traer**) to draw, attract
atrás *adv.* back, backward; behind
atrevido/a daring
atrocidad *f.* atrocity
atún *m.* tuna (6)
audífonos *pl.* headphones (10)
aula *f.* (*but* **el aula**) classroom (1)
aumentar to increase
aumento increase; gain; **aumento de peso** weight gain

aun *adv.* even

aún *adv.* still, yet

aunque although

austral southern

autobús *m.* (*pl.* autobuses) bus (5)

autóctono/a indigenous

automático/a automatic

autónoma autonomous

autor(a) author; violación (*f.*) de los derechos del autor copyright violation

autoridad *f.* authority

autorización *f.* authorization

avanzar (c) to advance

avenida avenue (5)

aventura adventure; turismo de aventura adventure tourism

aventurero/a adventurous

averiguar to verify

avión *m.* (*pl.* aviones) airplane (9)

avisar to warn

¡ay! *interj.* ah!; oh!; ouch!

ayer yesterday

ayuda help

ayudar to help (13)

azotea roof terrace

azteca *n., adj. m., f.* Aztec

azúcar *m.* sugar (6)

azul blue (2)

B

bacalao codfish, cod

bahía bay

bailar to dance (2)

bailarín (*pl.* bailarines), bailarina dancer (14)

baile *m.* dance (14)

bajar to lower; to download; to go down; to get off (*transportation*); bajar en tirolina to go ziplining (9); bajar de peso to lose weight (12); baje (por esta calle) go down (this street) (*command form. s.*) (5)

bajo/a short (2); Países (*m. pl.*) Bajos Netherlands; planta baja ground floor

balada ballad

balcón *m.* (*pl.* balcones) balcony

ballena whale (13)

ballet *m.* ballet

baloncesto basketball

balsa raft

banca bank

bancario/a banking

banco bank (5)

banda band (14)

bandeja tray, platter

bandera flag (2)

bañarse to bathe (oneself) (5); to take a bath

bañera bathtub (11)

baño bathroom (11); cuarto de baño bathroom (11); traje (*m.*) de baño bathing suit (8)

barato/a inexpensive

bárbaro/a: ¡qué bárbaro! how cool! (8)

barca small boat

barranca ravine

barrer to sweep (11)

barrio neighborhood

basarse (en) to base one's ideas/opinions (on)

base *f.* base; a base de based on; base de datos data base

básico/a basic

básquetbol *m.* basketball; jugar (ue) básquetbol to play basketball (3)

bastante rather, sufficiently; enough

bastar to be enough

bastón *m.* (*pl.* bastones) cane, walking stick

basura trash; correo basura junk mail; no tirar basura don't litter (9); sacar (qu) la basura to take out the trash (11)

basurero/a trash collector

bata robe

batalla battle

batata sweet potato

batidora mixer; blender

bautizar (c) to baptize

bautizo baptism (7)

baya berry

bebé *m., f.* baby

beber to drink; no beber y conducir don't drink and drive (9)

bebida beverage; drink (6)

béisbol *m.* baseball (12); jugar (ue) (gu) béisbol to play baseball (12)

beisbolista *m., f.* baseball player

belga *n., adj. m., f.* Belgian

Bélgica Belgium

belleza beauty

bello/a pretty (2)

bendecido/a blessed

bendición *f.* blessing

benefactor(a) benefactor

beneficiar to benefit

beneficio benefit

berro watercress

besar to kiss

biblioteca library (1)

bicicleta bicycle; andar (*irreg.*) en bicicleta to ride a bicycle (12); bicicleta de montaña mountain bike (9); correr en bicicleta to ride a bicycle

bien *adv.* well; (muy) bien (very) well (1); lo pasé bien I had a good time (7); pasarlo bien to have a good time (7); ¡qué bien! how cool! (8); que le(s) vaya bien may things go well for you (*form. s., pl.*) (12)

bienes raíces *m. pl.* real estate; agente (*m., f.*) de bienes raíces real estate agent

bienestar *m.* well-being

bienvenida *n.* welcome; dar (*irreg.*) la bienvenida to welcome (11); ¡le damos la bienvenida a Ud.! we welcome you (*form. s.*)! (11)

¡bienvenido/a(s)! *adj.* welcome! (11); ser (*irreg.*) bienvenido/a(s) to be welcome (11); usted es (siempre) bienvenido/a you (*form. s.*) are always welcome (11)

bife *m.* steak

bilingüe bilingual (2)

biodiversidad *f.* biodiversity

biografía biography

biología biology (1)

biólogo/a biologist

birria goat meat

bisabuelo/a great-grandfather/great-grandmother (4)

bisturí *m.* scalpel

bitácora digital blog

blanco/a white (2); espacio en blanco blank space; línea en blanco blank; vino blanco white wine (6)

blog *m.* blog (10)

bloguear to blog

bloguero/a blogger (10)

bloqueador (*m.*) solar sunscreen

boca mouth (8)

bocado taste

boda wedding (7); boda civil civil ceremony (*wedding*)

bodega grocery store (*Carib.*)

bofetada slap; dar (*irreg.*) una bofetada to slap

bol *m.* bowl (6)

bola ball

boleto ticket (9)

boliche *m.* bowling

bolígrafo pen (1)

boliviano/a *n., adj.* Bolivian (2)

bolsa bag (8)

bolsillo pocket

bolso purse (8)

bombero, mujer (*f.*) bombero firefighter (10)

bonito/a pretty (2); ¡qué bonita familia! what a beautiful family! (4)

bordado/a embroidered

borracho/a drunk

borrador *m.* eraser (1)

bosque *m.* forest; bosque tropical rainforest (9)

bosquejo outline

botas boots

bote *m.* boat

botella bottle; botella de agua water bottle

botica pharmacy

botón *m.* (*pl.* botones) button

boxear to box (12)

boxeo boxing

boyante prosperous

brazo arm (8)

Bretaña: Gran Bretaña Great Britain

breve *adj.* brief

brindis *m. s., pl.* toast (7)

británico/a *n., adj.* British

brócoli *m.* broccoli (6)
bronce *m.* bronze
bucear to scuba dive (9)
budista *n., adj. m., f.* Buddhist (7)
buen, bueno/a good (2); **buen día** good morning (1); **¡buen provecho!** enjoy your meal!(6); **¡buen viaje!** bon voyage!, have a good trip! (7); **¡buena suerte!** good luck! (7); **buenas noches** good evening/ night (1); **buenas tardes** good afternoon (1); **buenos días** good morning (1); **dar** (*irreg.*) **buena suerte** to bring good luck; **hace buen tiempo** it's nice weather (9); **pasar un buen rato** to have a good time; **¡qué buena idea!** what a good idea!; **¡que tenga(s) un buen día / fin de semana!** have (*form. s. / inform. s.*) a good day/weekend!; **¡que tenga(s) una buena tarde!** have (*form. s. / inform. s.*) a nice afternoon!; **sacar (qu) buenas notas** to get good grades; **tener** (*irreg.*) **buen aspecto** to look good; **tener** (*irreg.*) **buena/mala pinta** to have a good/bad appearance
bufanda scarf
bus *m.* bus
buscador (*m.*) **de Internet** search engine (10)
buscar (qu) to look for (8)
búsqueda search

C

caballero gentleman
caballo horse; **montar a caballo** to ride a horse (3)
cabecera: médico/a de cabecera primary care physician
cabello hair
cabeza head (8)
cable *m.* cable
cabo: al cabo de at the end of
cada *inv.* each, every; **cada vez más** increasingly
cadena chain; **cadena alimenticia** food chain
cadera hip (8)
caer *irreg.* to fall; **caer en** to fall on (*day of the week*); **caerse** to fall down (9)
café *m.* coffee (2); café, coffee shop; *adj.* brown
cafeína caffeine
caída de agua waterfall
caja box
cajero/a cashier (10); teller
calamares *m. pl.* squid (6)
calavera skull
calcetines *m. pl.* socks (8)
calculadora calculator
calcular to calculate
cálculos figures
caldo broth, clear soup (6)
calendario calendar

calentamiento global global warming (13)
calidad *f.* quality
cálido/a warm, hot (9)
caliente hot
calificar (qu) (a) to qualify (for)
callado/a quiet
calle *f.* street (5); **baje/suba (por esta calle)** go down/up (this street) (*command form. s.*) (5)
calor *m.* heat; **hace calor** it's hot (9); **¡qué calor!** it's so hot!
calvo/a bald
calzones *m. pl.* underwear (8)
cama bed (11); **hacer** (*irreg.*) **la cama** to make the bed (11)
cámara camera
camarero/a waiter, waitress (6); server (6)
camarones *m. pl.* shrimp (6)
cambiar to change; **cambiar cheques** to cash checks
cambio change; **cambio climático** climate change
caminar to walk
caminata *n.* walk, hike
camino road; path; **por el camino** on the way
camión *m.* bus
camisa shirt (8)
camiseta t-shirt (8)
campana: pantalones (*m. pl.*) **de campana** bell-bottom pants
campanada peal
campaña campaign
campeón (*pl.* **campeones**), **campeona** champion
campeonato championship
camping: hacer (*irreg.*) **camping** to go camping
campismo camping
campo field; countryside, rural area (5)
campus *m.* campus
Canadá *m.* Canada
canadiense *n., adj. m., f.* Canadian (2)
canal *m.* canal
canas: tener (*irreg.*) **canas** to have gray hair
cancelar to cancel
cáncer *m.* cancer
cancha (athletic) field, court
canción *f.* song; **canción de amor** love song
candidato/a candidate
candombé *m. Afro-Uruguayan music and dance*
canguro kangaroo
cano/a gray-haired
cansado/a tired (2)
cantante *m., f.* singer (14)
cantar to sing (3)
cantautor(a) singer-songwriter
cantidad *f.* quantity
canto singing

cañón *m.* (*pl.* **cañones**) canyon
caótico/a chaotic
capa layer
capacitado/a trained
capital *f.* capital city (5)
capitalismo capitalism
capitán (*pl.* **capitanes**), **capitana** captain
capítulo chapter
caqui: color caqui khaki
cara face (8); **¡qué cara!** what nerve!
característica characteristic
caracterizar (c) to characterize
caramelo candy
carbohidrato carbohydrate
carbón *m.* coal
carga cargo
cargador *m.* charger
cargar (gu) to charge; to load (10); to upload (10); **cargar con** to take on (responsibility)
cargo (political) office; **estar** (*irreg.*) **a cargo (de)** to be in charge (of)
Caribe *m.* Caribbean; **mar** (*m.*) **Caribe** Caribbean Sea
caribeño/a *n., adj.* Caribbean
cariño affection
cariñoso/a affectionate (16)
Carnaval *m.* Carnival (*the festivities in the days preceding Lent*) (7)
carne *f.* (red) meat (6)
carnicería butcher shop (5)
carnitas *Mexican dish made of roasted pork that is sautéed till browned*
caro/a expensive
carpa tent
carrera major (field of study); career; race (12); **carrera de fondo** long-distance race; **¿cuál es tu carrera?** what's your major? (1); **¿cuál es tu correo electrónico?** what is your email (address)? (1); **¿cuál es tu (dirección de) email?** what is your email (address)? (1); **¿cuál es tu número de teléfono?** what is your phone number? (1)
carretera highway (5)
carril *m.* lane
carta letter; menu (6)
casa house (2); **ama** (*f., but* **el ama**) **de casa** housewife (4)
casado/a married (16)
casamiento marriage
casarse (con) to get married (to) (16)
cascada waterfall
cáscara shell; peel
casco helmet (12)
casi *inv.* almost
caso case; **en caso de que** *conj.* in case
casona mansion
casquete *m.* **(polar)** (polar) ice cap
castaño/a brown (2)
catador(a) taster
catarata waterfall (9)
catedral *f.* cathedral (5)

categoría category
categorizar (c) to categorize
catire fair-skinned, fair-haired (*Carib.*)
católico/a Catholic
catorce fourteen
causa cause
causar to cause
cauteloso/a cautious
caverna cavern
cazar (c) to hunt
cazatalentos *inv.* talent scout
cebolla onion (6)
celebración *f.* celebration
celebrar to celebrate (7)
celebridad *f.* celebrity
celeste heavenly; **color** (*m.*) **celeste** light blue
celos: tener (*irreg.*) **celos** to be jealous
celoso/a jealous (16)
celular: (teléfono) celular cell phone
cementerio cemetery
cena dinner; **preparar la cena** to prepare dinner (4)
cenar to eat dinner (3)
censura censorship
centenar *m.* hundred
centígrado/a *adj.* Celsius, centigrade
central central
centro center (5); downtown (5); **centro estudiantil** student center, student union
Centroamérica Central America
centroamericano/a *n., adj.* Central American
cepillarse los dientes to brush one's teeth (5)
cepillo de dientes toothbrush
cerca *adv.* near, nearby, close; **cerca de** close/near to (9)
cereal *m.* cereal
ceremonia ceremony
cerrar (ie) to close (6)
cerro hill
cerveza beer (2)
césped *m.* lawn, grass
ceviche *m. raw fish dish*
chacra small farm
chala husk
chamo kid
champán *m.* champagne (7)
champiñones *m. pl.* mushrooms (6)
chaqueta jacket (8)
charco puddle
charcutería delicatessen
charlar to chat
charrería horsemanship (*Mex.*)
chau good-bye (1)
cheque *m.* check; **cambiar cheques** to cash checks; **cobrar un cheque** to cash a check
chévere cool; **¡qué chévere!** how cool! (8)
chicle *m.* gum
chico/a *n.* guy/girl; *adj.* small (2)

chido/a cool; **¡qué chido!** how cool! (8)
chilaquiles *m. pl. Mexican dish of fried tortilla pieces simmered in salsa or mole and served with cheese and sour cream*
chile *m.* chili pepper (6)
chileno/a *n., adj.* Chilean (2)
chillar to bawl
chimichurri *green sauce used for grilled meat (Arg.)*
chino/a *n.* Chinese person; *adj.* Chinese
chirimoya cherimoya fruit
chispa spark
chistoso/a funny
chivo goat
chocar (qu) con to run into; to bump against
chocolate *m.* chocolate
chofer *m., f.* driver (4)
chorizo sausage (6)
chulo/a cool (*Sp.*); **¡qué chulo!** how cool! (*Sp.*) (8)
chutar to shoot (*a soccer ball*) (*Sp.*)
ciclismo cycling
ciclista *m., f.* cyclist
ciclón *m.* (*pl.* **ciclones**) hurricane
ciego/a *adj.* blind; **cita a ciegas** blind date (16)
cielo sky; heaven
cien one hundred
ciencia science (1); **ciencias políticas** political science (1)
científico/a scientific
ciento one hundred (*used with* 101–199); **por ciento** percent
cierto/a true
cigarrillo cigarette
cinco five
cincuenta fifty
cine *m.* movies (2); movie theater (2); film (*in general*) (2)
cineasta *m., f.* filmmaker
cinematográfico/a *adj.* movie, film
cinta film, movie
cintura waist
cinturón *m.* (*pl.* **cinturones**) belt (8)
circuito circuit
circular to circulate
círculo circle
circunstancia circumstance
ciruela plum
cirugía surgery
cirujano/a surgeon (10)
cita appointment; date (16); **cita a ciegas** blind date (16)
ciudad *f.* city (5)
ciudadano/a citizen
civil civil; **boda civil** civil ceremony (*wedding*); **estado civil** marital status (16); **guerra civil** civil war
civilización *f.* civilization
¡claro que sí! *interj.* of course! (6)
claro/a clear

clase *f.* class (*of students*) (1); class, course (*academic*) (1); **compañero/a de clase** classmate; **salón** (*m.*) **de clase** classroom (1)
clásico/a classic(al) (14)
clasificación *f.* classification
clave *n. f., adj.* key
clic: hacer clic to click (10)
cliente *m., f.* customer
clima *m.* climate; weather
climático/a *adj.* climate; **cambio climático** climate change
climatización *f.* air conditioning
clínica clinic
clóset *m.* (*pl.* **closets**) closet
cobrar un cheque to cash a check
cobre *m.* copper
coche *m.* car (5)
cochi *Nahuatl word meaning to sleep*
cochinillo roast suckling pig (*dish*)
cocina kitchen (11); cuisine
cocinar to cook (3)
cocinero/a cook; chef
codiciado/a sought-after
codo elbow (8)
coger (j) to take (*transportation*) (*Sp.*); **coger a mano derecha/izquierda** to turn right/left (*Sp.*)
cognado *gram.* cognate
cohombro cucumber (*P.R.*)
coincidir to coincide
cola line (*of people*)
colaborar to collaborate
colar (ue) to strain (*liquid*)
colchón *m.* (*pl.* **colchones**) mattress
colección *f.* collection
coleccionar to collect
colectivo bus
colega *m., f.* co-worker, colleague
colegio high school
cólera cholera
colesterol cholesterol
colibrí *m.* (*pl.* **colibríes**) hummingbird
colina hill
collar *m.* necklace (8)
colmado small grocery store (*Carib.*)
colocar (qu) to place
colombiano *n., adj.* Colombian (2)
colonia colony; neighborhood (*Mex.*)
color *m.* color; **color caqui** khaki; **color celeste** light blue; **color verde oliva** olive green; **¿de qué color es?** what color is it? (2)
columna column
com: punto com dot com (*in an email address*) (1)
comadre *f.* godmother of one's child (4); *mother of one's godchild*
comandante *m., f.* commander
comarca region
combatir to fight
combinación *f.* combination

combinar to combine

combustibles (*m. pl.*) **fósiles** fossil fuels

comedia comedy; **comedia musical** musical (*play*)

comedor dining room (11); dining hall

comentar (sobre) to comment (on)

comentario comment

comentarista *m., f.* news anchor

comenzar (ie) (c) to begin; **comenzar a +** *inf.* to begin to + *inf.*

comer to eat (2); **come/coma más** have some more (*command inform. s. / form. s.*) (11); **comer comida mexicana** to eat Mexican food (3); **dar** (*irreg.*) **de comer** to feed; **no dar** (*irreg.*) **de comer** don't feed (*animals*) (9)

comercialización *f.* commercialization

comercializar (c) to commercialize

comestibles *m. pl.* groceries, food (6); **comestibles empaquetados/enlatados** packaged/canned goods (6)

cometer to commit; **cometer un error** to make a mistake

cómico/a funny

comida food (3); (midday) meal (3); **comer comida mexicana** to eat Mexican food (3); **comida rápida** fast food

comienzo *n.* beginning

como like; as; **tal como** just as; **tan... como** as . . . as; **tanto como** as much as; **tanto/a/os/as... como** as much/many . . . as

¿cómo? how? (2); **¿cómo está?** how are you (*form. s.*)? (1); **¿cómo estás?** how are you (*inform. s.*)? (1); **¿cómo se dice... ?** how do you say . . . ? (2); **¿cómo se escribe... ?** how do you spell . . . ? (1); **¿cómo se llama?** what is your name (*form. s.*)? (1); **¿cómo te llamas?** what is your name (*inform. s.*)? (1)

¡cómo no! *interj.* of course! (6)

comodidad *f.* comfort

cómodo/a comfortable

compacto: disco compacto (el CD) compact disc (CD)

compadre *m.* godfather of one's child (4); father of one's godchild

compañero/a companion; friend; classmate; **compañero/a de clase** classmate; **compañero/a de cuarto** roommate

compañía company

comparación *f.* comparison

comparar to compare

compartir to share

competencia competition (12)

competición *f.* competition

competidor(a) competitor

competir (i, i) to compete

competitivo/a competitive

complacer (zc) to please

complejo *n.* complex

complejo/a *adj.* complex

complemento accessory

completar to complete

completo/a complete

complicar (qu) to complicate

componer (*like* **poner**) (*p.p.* **compuesto**) to compose (14)

composición *f.* composition

compositor(a) composer

compostador *m.* composter

comprar to buy (3)

compras: de compras shopping; **ir** (*irreg.*) **de compras** to go shopping (2)

comprender to understand

comprensión *f.* understanding

comprensivo/a understanding (16)

comprobar (ue) to prove

comprometerse to get engaged (16); to commit (*oneself*) (16)

comprometido/a engaged (16); in a serious relationship (16)

compromiso engagement; commitment

compuesto/a (*p.p. of* **componer**) **(de)** composed (of)

computación *f.* computer science

computadora computer (1); **(computadora) láptop/portátil** laptop (computer)

común common

comunicación *f.* communication; communications (*field of study*) (1)

comunicarse (qu) to communicate; **¿me puede comunicar con... ?** can you connect me with . . . ?

comunidad *f.* community

comunista *n., adj. m., f.* communist

comunitario/a community

con with (7); **con frecuencia** often; **¡con mucho gusto!** with pleasure! (6); (very) gladly; **con permiso** excuse me (8); **con tal de que** *conj.* provided that; **con vista a** with a view of; **¿me puede comunicar con... ?** can you connect me with . . . ?

concentrar(se) to concentrate

concepto concept

concha shell

conciencia conscience

consciente conscious (13)

concierto concert (14)

concluir (y) to conclude

conclusión *f.* conclusion

concordancia agreement

concreto: en concreto specifically; in particular

condición *f.* condition

condimento condiment (6)

cóndor *m.* condor

conducir *irreg.* to drive; **no beber y conducir** don't drink and drive (9)

conectar to connect; **conectarse al Internet** to connect to the Internet

conector *m.* connector

conejo rabbit

conexión (*f.*) **(inalámbrica)** (wireless) connection

conferencia conference

confesar (ie) to confess

confianza confidence; trust

conflicto conflict

confundir to confuse

congregarse (gu) to congregate

congreso conference

cónico/a conical

conjugar (gu) to conjugate

conjunto outfit (*clothes*) (8)

conjuro spell

conmemorar to commemorate

conmigo with me (7)

Cono Sur Southern Cone

conocer (zc) to know, be acquainted, familiar with (5); to meet; **conocerse** to meet (each other) (16)

conocimiento knowledge

conquista conquest

conquistador(a) conqueror

consciente conscious; aware

consecuencias consequences

consecutivo/a consecutive

conseguir (*like* **seguir**) to get (10)

consejero/a advisor

consejo (piece of) advice

conservación conservation

conservar to preserve, conserve (13); to keep (13)

consideración *f.* consideration

considerar to consider

consistir (en) to consist (of)

consola console

constipado/a congested (12)

constitucional constitutional

construcción *f.* construction

construir (y) to build

consultar to consult

consumir to consume

consumo consumption

contacto contact; **lentes** (*m. pl.*) **de contacto** contact lenses; **mantenerse** (*like* **tener**) **en contacto con** to stay in touch with; **ponerse los lentes de contacto** to put on contacts (5)

contador(a) accountant

contagiar to infect

contaminación *f.* pollution (5); **contaminación del aire** air pollution

contaminar to pollute

contar (ue) to tell, narrate; to count

contener (*like* **tener**) to contain

contenido content

contento/a happy (2); **ponerse** (*irreg.*) **contento/a** to become happy (5)

conteo count

contestar to answer

contexto context

contigo with you (*inform. s.*) (7)

continente *m.* continent

continuación: a continuación following; below

continuar (continúo) to continue

contra against; **en contra de** against

contraceptivo contraceptive

contrario: al contrario on the contrary; **lo contrario** the opposite

contrastante contrasting

contrastar to contrast
contratar to hire
contrayente *m., f.* party (*of a contract*)
control *m.* control
controlar to control
controversia controversy
controvertido/a controversial
conversación *f.* conversation
conversar to converse
convertir (ie, i) to convert; **convertirse en** to become
conyugal conjugal
cooperar to cooperate
copa drink (*alcoholic*); **copa de los árboles** canopy (*of trees*); **Copa Mundial** World Cup
copiar to copy (10)
coqueto/a flirtatious
coraje *m.* anger, rage; **¡qué coraje!** how frustrating/annoying! (4)
corazón *m.* heart
corbata tie (8)
cordillera mountain range
Corea Korea
coreano/a *n., adj.* Korean
coro choir
coronado/a crowned
corporación *f.* corporation
correcto/a correct
corredor(a) runner
correo mail; **correo basura** junk mail; **correo electrónico** email; **¿cuál es tu correo electrónico?** what is your email (address)? (1); **oficina de correos** post office
correr to run (2); **correr en bicicleta** to ride a bicycle; **correr en el parque** to run in the park (3)
corresponder to correspond
correspondiente corresponding
corrida de montaña mountain running
corrupción *f.* corruption (15)
corrupto/a corrupt
corsé *m.* corset
cortar to cut (10)
Corte (*f.*) **Suprema** Supreme Court
cortés polite
corto/a short (*in length*) (8); **pantalones** (*m. pl.*) **cortos** shorts (8)
cosa thing (1)
cosecha harvest
cosido/a sewn
cosmetólogo/a cosmetologist (10)
costa coast
costal *m.* sack, bag
costar (ue) to cost
costarricense *n., adj. m., f.* Costa Rican (2)
costoso/a expensive
costumbre *f.* custom (7); habit (7)
costura sewing; **alta costura** haute couture
cotidiano/a daily
cráter *m.* crater
crear to create
creativo/a creative

crecer (zc) to grow
creencia belief
creer (y) (*p.p.* creído) to think; to believe (12); **creo que...** I think . . . (15)
crimen *m.* violent crime (15); **lugar** (*m.*) **del crimen** scene of the crime
criminal *m., f.* criminal
criollo/a creole; **pabellón** (*m.*) **criollo** Venezuelan rice and beans dish
crisis *f.* crisis; **crisis económica** economic crisis (15)
cristiano/a Christian (7)
criterio criterion
crítica criticism
criticar (qu) to criticize
crítico/a *n.* critic; *adj.* critical
cruce *m.* crossroads
crucero cruise; cruise ship
crudo/a raw; harsh
cruzar (c) to cross
cuaderno notebook (1)
cuadra (city) block (5)
cuadro square; **de cuadros** plaid
¿cuál(es)? what?; which? (2); **¿cuál es la fecha de hoy?** what is today's date? (1); **¿cuál es tu carrera?** what's your major? (1)
cualificado/a qualified
cualquier *adj.* any
cuando when; **de vez en cuando** once in a while
¿cuándo? when? (2)
cuanto: en cuanto as soon as; **en cuanto a** regarding
cuánto lo siento I'm very sorry (16)
¿cuánto/a(s)? how much?; how many? (1); **¿cuánto tiempo hace que** + *present tense*? how long have you (*done / been doing something*)? (13); **¿cuánto tiempo lleva(s)** + *pres. p.*? how long have you (*form. s. / inform. s.*) (*done / been doing something*)? (13); **¿cuántos años tienes?** how old are you (*inform. s.*)? (2)
cuarenta forty
Cuaresma Lent
cuarto room; **compañero/a de cuarto** roommate; **cuarto de baño** bathroom (11)
cuatro four
cuatrocientos/as four hundred
cubano/a *n., adj.* Cuban (2)
cubierto/a (*p.p. of* **cubrir**) covered
cubierto place setting
cubrir (*p.p.* **cubierto**) to cover
cuchara spoon (6)
cuchillo knife (6)
cuello neck (8)
cuenta account; **darse** (*irreg.*) **cuenta de** to realize (13)
cuento story
cuerda string
cuerdo/a sensible; rational; sane
cuero leather
cuerpo body
cuestión *f.* issue
cuidador(a) curator

cuidar (a, de) to take care of (13)
culantro coriander
culinario/a culinary
culpa fault; blame; **echar la culpa** to blame
cultivar to grow, raise (crop)
culto/a cultured; learned
cultura culture
cumbia *Colombian folk dance now popular throughout Latin America*
cumbre *f.* summit, peak
cumpleaños *s., pl.* birthday (7); **¡feliz cumpleaños!** happy birthday! (7)
cumplir to achieve; **cumplir... años** to turn . . . years old (7)
cuñado/a brother-in-law / sister-in-law (4)
curado/a drunk (*sl.*)
curioso/a curious
curita adhesive bandage
currículum *m.* résumé, curriculum vitae (CV) (10)
curso course (1)
cursor *m.* cursor
cuyo/a whose

D

danés (*pl.* **daneses**), **danesa** *n.* Danish person; *adj.* Danish
danza dance (14)
daño damage (13)
dar *irreg.* to give; **dar a luz** to give birth; **dar buena suerte** to bring good luck; **dar de comer** to feed; **dar el pésame** to give one's condolences; **dar la bienvenida** to welcome (11); **dar un abrazo** to hug; **dar un paseo** to take a walk (9); **dar un paso** to take a step; **dar una bofetada** to slap; **dar una fiesta** to throw a party; **darle vuelta a** to think about (*something*); **darse cuenta de** to realize (13); **darse la mano** to shake hands; **darse prisa** to hurry; **¡le damos la bienvenida a Ud.!** we welcome you (*form. s.*)! (11); **no dar de comer** don't feed (*animals*) (9); **te/le/les doy/damos el pésame** my/our condolences (16)
dato piece of information; *pl.* data; **base** (*f.*) **de datos** database
de of (1); from (1); **de alguna manera** in some way; **de compras** shopping; **de cuadros** plaid; **de dentro a fuera** inside out; **¿de dónde eres?** where are you from?; **de hecho** actually; **de la madrugada** in the early A.M. hours (3); **de la mañana** A.M.; in the morning (3); **de la misma manera** likewise; **de la noche** at night (3); **de la tarde** P.M.; in the afternoon/evening (3); **de lujo** luxury; **de nada** you're welcome (5); **de niño/a** as a child; **¿de parte de quién?** may I ask who's calling?; **¿de qué color es?** what color is it? (2); **¿de qué está hecho/a?** what is it made of?; **de repente** suddenly; **de verdad** really; **de vez en cuando** once in a while; **favor de** + *inf.* please + *inf.*

debajo de below
debate *m.* debate
deber + *inf.* should, must, ought to (*do something*); **debería** + *inf.* should / ought to (*do something*) (13); **debo** + *inf.* I have to / must (*do something*) (6)
debido a because of, due to
débil weak (2)
década decade
decenas *pl.* tens
decente decent
decidir to decide
decir *irreg.* to say (4); to tell (4); **¿cómo se dice... ?** how do you say . . . ? (2)
decisión *f.* decision; **tomar una decisión** to make a decision
declaración *f.* statement
declarar to state
decorar to decorate
dedicarse (qu) (a) to dedicate oneself (to); to work at (job); **¿a qué se dedica?** what do you (*form. s.*) do (*occupation*)? (4); **¿a qué te dedicas?** what do you (*inform. s.*) do (*occupation*)? (4)
dedo finger (8)
defecto de nacimiento birth defect
defender (ie) to defend
definitivamente definitely
deforestación *f.* deforestation
deforestar to deforest
degustación *f.* tasting
degustar to taste (*sample different items for flavor*)
dejar to leave; **dejar de** + *inf.* to stop (*doing something*)
del of the; from the
delante de in front of
delfín *m.* (*pl.* **delfines**) dolphin (13)
delgado/a thin (2)
delicado/a delicate
delincuencia crime
demanda demand (15)
demás the rest; **los/las demás** others; **todo lo demás** everything else
demasiado *adv.* too; too much
demasiado/a *adj.* too; *pl.* too many
democracia democracy (15)
democrático/a democratic
demostrar (ue) to show
demostrativo/a *gram.* demonstrative
denominación *f.* designation
dentista *m., f.* dentist (10)
dentro inside; **de dentro a fuera** inside out; **dentro de** inside; within, in
departamento apartment
dependencia dependency
depender (de) to depend (on)
dependiente *m., f.* clerk
deporte sport (2); **hacer** (*irreg.*) **deportes** to play sports; **practicar (qu) un deporte** to play a sport (3)
deportista *m., f.* athlete
deportivo/a *adj.* sporting, sports

depositar to deposit
depresión *f.* depression (12)
derecha *n.* right side; **a la derecha (de)** to the right (of); **coger (j) a mano derecha** to turn right (*Sp.*); **doble/gire a la derecha** turn right (*command form. s.*) (5); **quedar a la derecha** to be on the right
derecho right (*prerogative*); law (*field of study*); *adv.* straight ahead; **derecho humano** human right (15); **siga derecho** go / keep going / continue straight (*command form. s.*) (5); **violación** (*f.*) **de los derechos del autor** copyright violation; **violar los derechos humanos** to violate human rights
derivarse (de) to derive (from)
dermatológico/a dermatological
derramar to spill
derretimiento melting
derrocar (qu) to overthrow
desaparecer (zc) to disappear
desarrollar to develop
desarrollo development (15)
desastre (*m.*) **natural** natural disaster (15)
desayunar to eat breakfast (3)
desayuno breakfast; **preparar el desayuno** to make/prepare breakfast (4)
descalzo/a barefoot
descansar to rest (11)
descarga download
descargar (gu) to download (10)
descender (ie) (de) to descend (from)
describir to describe
descripción *f.* description
descubrir (*p.p.* **descubierto**) to discover
descuido carelessness
desde *prep.* from; since; **desde hace** + *period of time* for + period of time
desear to wish; to want; **le(s) deseo mucha suerte** I wish you (*form. s., pl.*) luck (12)
desechable disposable
desecho (orgánico) (organic) waste
desempleo unemployment (15)
desencadenar to trigger; to unleash
deseo wish
desequilibrio imbalance (13)
desesperación *f.* desperation
desfile *m.* parade (7); **desfile de moda** fashion show (8)
desgarrador(a) heartbreaking
desgraciadamente unfortunately
deshacer (*like* **hacer**) (*p.p.* **deshecho**) to dissolve; to undo (10)
desierto desert
desigualdad *f.* inequality (15)
deslizar (c) to slide
desmayarse to faint (12)
desordenado/a disorganized; messy
despacho office
despedida farewell, good-bye (7)
despejado/a clear (*weather*); **está despejado** it's clear (*sky*) (9)
despejarse to clear up (*weather*)

despensa pantry (11)
despertarse (ie) to wake up (5)
después *adv.* afterwards; **después (de)** after (1); **después (de) que** *conj.* after
destacado/a renowned
destilería distillery
destino destination
destreza skill
destrozado/a destroyed
destrucción *f.* destruction
destruir (y) to destroy
desventaja disadvantage
desviarse (me desvío) to change course
detallado/a detailed
detalle *m.* detail
detallista *m., f.* detail-oriented
detective *m., f.* detective
deteriorar to deteriorate
deterioro deterioration (13)
determinar to determine
detrás de behind; **está/queda detrás de...** it's behind . . . (5)
deuda debt; **deuda externa** foreign debt (15)
devolver (*like* **volver**) (*p.p.* **devuelto**) to return
día *m.* day (1); **algún día** someday; **buen día** good morning (1); **buenos días** good morning (1); **Día de Acción de Gracias** Thanksgiving (7); **día de entre semana** weekday (3); **Día de la Independencia** Independence Day (7); **Día de las Madres** Mother's Day; **Día de los Muertos** Day of the Dead (7); **Día de los Padres** Father's Day; **Día de los Reyes Magos** Three Kings' Day; Epiphany (Adoration of the Magi) (7); **Día de Todos los Santos** All Saints' Day; **Día del Amor** Valentine's Day; **día festivo** holiday; **días entre semana** weekdays; **hoy en día** today; these days; **¡que tenga(s) un buen día!** have a nice day (*form. s. / inform. s.*)!; **son las doce del día** it's noon; **todo el día** all day (3); **todos los días** every day (3)
diagnóstico diagnosis
diálogo dialogue
diamante *m.* diamond
diario newspaper
diario/a daily; **rutina diaria** daily routine
dibujar to draw
dibujo drawing
diccionario dictionary (1)
dicho/a aforesaid
diciembre December (1)
dictadura dictatorship (15)
diecinueve nineteen
dieciocho eighteen
dieciséis sixteen
diecisiete seventeen
diente *m.* tooth; *pl.* teeth (8); **cepillarse los dientes** to brush one's teeth (5); **cepillo de dientes** toothbrush; **lavarse los dientes** to brush one's teeth
dieta diet; **estar** (*irreg.*) **a dieta** to be on a diet

dietética dietetics

diez ten; **son diez para las nueve** it's 8:50 (3); **son las nueve menos diez** it's 8:50 (3)

diferencia difference

diferente different (1)

difícil difficult (2); hard

dificultad *f.* difficulty

difunto/a *n., adj.* deceased

digestión *f.* digestion

digestivo/a digestive

digitalizado/a digitalized

dinero money; **ganar dinero** to make money; **sacar (qu) dinero** to withdraw money

dios *m. s.* god; **Dios** God

diplomático/a diplomatic

dirección *f.* address; *pl.* instructions; **¿cuál es tu (dirección de) email?** what is your email (address)? (1); **¿cuál es tu/su profesión?** what is your (*inform. s. / form. s.*) profession? (4)

directo/a direct

director(a) de marketing director of marketing (10)

dirigir (j) to direct (14)

discapacitado/a disabled

disciplina discipline

disco record; **disco compacto** compact disc; **disco duro** hard drive (10)

discriminación *f.* discrimination (15)

disculpar to excuse, pardon; **disculpa/ disculpe** excuse me (*command inform. s. / form. s.*) (3); **disculpen** excuse me (*command form. pl.*) (8)

discurso speech

diseñador(a) designer (8); **diseñador(a) gráfico/a** graphic designer (10)

diseñar to design

diseño design (1)

disfraz *m.* (*pl.* **disfraces**) costume (7)

disfrazado/a disguised

disfrutar de + *n.* to enjoy (*something*) (9)

dislocarse (qu) to dislocate

disminución *f.* decrease (13); reduction

disminuir (y) to diminish

disponer (*like* **poner**) (*p.p.* **dispuesto**) **de** to have available

disponible available

dispositivo device

dispuesto/a ready, prepared; willing; **estar** (*irreg.*) **dispuesto** to be ready/willing (10)

distancia distance

distinguir (distingo) to distinguish

distribuidor(a) distributor

distrito district

diversidad *f.* diversity

diversión *f.* fun

diverso/a diverse

divertido/a fun

divertirse (ie, i) to have fun (7); **¡diviértete!/ ¡diviérta(n)se!** have fun! (*command inform. s. / form. s., pl.*) (11); **me divertí mucho** I had a lot of fun (7)

dividir to divide

división *f.* division

divorciado/a divorced (16)

divorcio divorce (16)

doblar to turn; **doble a la derecha/ izquierda** turn (to the) right/left (*command form. s.*) (5); **no doblar** do not turn (9)

doble *m.* double

doce twelve; **son las doce del día** it's noon

doctor(a) doctor (4)

doctorado doctorate

documento document

dólar *m.* dollar

doler (ue) (*like* **gustar**) to hurt (12); to ache

dolor *m.* pain (12); **te/le/les acompaño/ acompañamos en el dolor** I'm/we're with you (*inform. s. / form. s. / form. pl.*) in your time of pain (16)

doméstico/a domestic; **animal** (*m.*) **doméstico** pet

dominante dominant

dominar to dominate

domingo Sunday (3); **Domingo de Pascua** Easter Sunday; **Domingo de Ramos** Palm Sunday

dominicano/a *n., adj.* Dominican (2); **República Dominicana** Dominican Republic

donar to donate

donde where

¿dónde? where? (2); **¿de dónde eres?** where are you (*inform. s.*) from? (1); **¿de dónde es usted?** where are you (*form. s.*) from? (1); **¿dónde está/queda... ?** where is . . . ? (5); **¿dónde vive(s)?** where do you (*form. s. / inform. s.*) live? (1)

dormir (ue, u) to sleep (2); **dormirse** to fall asleep (5)

dormitorio bedroom (11)

dorso: nadar de dorso to do the backstroke

dos two; **dos veces** twice (3); **son las dos y cuarto** it's 2:15 (3)

doscientos/as two hundred

drama *m.* drama

dramático/a dramatic

drástico/a drastic

droga drug

ducha shower (11)

ducharse to take a shower (5)

duda doubt; **poner** (*irreg.*) **en duda** to call into question; **sin duda** without (any) doubt (14)

dueño/a owner (10)

dulce *adj.* sweet (6)

dulces *m. pl.* sweets; candy

duquesa duchess

duración *f.* length

durante during

durar to last

durazno peach

duro/a hard; **disco duro** hard drive (10)

DVD *m.* DVD

E

echar to throw; to add; **echar de menos** to miss; **echar la culpa** to blame

ecología ecology

ecológico/a ecological (13)

ecologista *m., f.* ecologist

economía economy; economics (1)

económico/a economic; economical; **crisis** (*f.*) **económica** economic crisis (15)

ecoturismo ecotourism

ecuatoriano/a *n., adj.* Ecuadorian (2)

edad *f.* age

edificio building (5)

editar to edit; to publish

editor(a) editor

editorial *m.* editorial

educación *f.* education

educado/a polite

educar (qu) to teach, educate

educativo/a educational

efecto effect

Egipto Egypt

egoísta *m., f.* selfish

egresado/a (de) graduate (of)

ejecutivo/a executive (10)

ejemplo example; **por ejemplo** for example

ejercer (z) to exercise

ejercicio exercise; **hacer** (*irreg.*) **ejercicio** to work out (2)

el *def. art. m. s.* the (1)

él *sub. pron.* he; *obj. of prep.* him

elaboración *f.* production

elaborar to manufacture, produce

elección *f.* election (15)

electricidad *f.* electricity

eléctrico/a electrical

electrónico/a electronic; **correo electrónico** email; **¿cuál es tu correo electrónico?** what is your email (address)? (1)

elefante *m.* elephant

elegante elegant

elegir (i, i) (j) to choose; to elect

elemento element

eliminar to eliminate

élite *f.* elite

ella *sub. pron.* she; *obj. of prep.* her

ellos/as *sub. pron.* they; *obj. of prep.* them

elogiado/a praised

elogio praise

email *m.* email (10); **¿cuál es tu (dirección de) email?** what is your email (address)? (1)

emancipación *f.* emancipation

emancipar(se) to become free/ independent (16)

embarazo pregnancy

embarcar (qu) to embark

embargo: sin embargo nevertheless

emblemático/a emblematic

emigrante *m., f.* emigrant

emoción *f.* emotion; **¡qué emoción!** how exciting!

emocional emotional

emocionante exciting

empacar (qu) to pack

empaquetado/a packaged; **comestibles** (*m. pl.*) **empaquetados** packaged goods (6)

emparejar to match

empate *m.* tie (*score*)

empezar (ie) (c) to begin (4); to start; **empezar a** + *inf.* to begin to (*do something*) (4)

empleado/a employee (10)

empleo job; employment; **solicitar un empleo** to apply for a job (10)

emprender to undertake, start

empresa corporation; business; **administración** (*f.*) **de empresas** business administration

empresarial *adj.* business

empresario/a business person (10)

empujar to push; push (9)

en in (1); on; at (1); **caer** (*irreg.*) **en** to fall on (*day of the week*); **en algún momento** at some point; **en caso de que** (*conj.*) in case; **en concreto** specifically; in particular; **en contra de** against; **en el punto de mira** in the crosshairs; **en general** in general; **en mi opinión...** in my opinion . . . (15); **en negrita** boldface; **en particular** in particular; **¿en qué puedo servirle(s)?** how may I help you (*form. s., pl.*)? (10); **en total** in all; **en una relación** together (16); in a relationship (16); **en voz alta** out loud; **está/queda en la esquina de... y...** it's on the corner of . . . and . . . (5)

enagua petticoat

enamorado/a (de) in love (with) (16)

enamorarse (de) to fall in love (with) (16)

encandilar to dazzle

encantado/a nice to meet you, enchanted (10)

encantar (*like* **gustar**) to like very much, love; to delight (7)

encender (ie) to turn on (*appliance*); to light

encerrar (ie) to enclose; to circle

enclavado/a nestled

encontrar (ue) to find

encuentro encounter

encuesta survey

energía energy; **energía eólica** wind energy

enero January (1)

énfasis *m.* emphasis; **poner** (*irreg.*) **énfasis** to emphasize

enfermarse to get sick

enfermedad *f.* illness (12)

enfermero/a nurse (10)

enfocado/a focused

enfocarse (qu) (en) to focus (on)

enfrentarse (a) to confront

enfrente de *prep.* in front of / facing; **está/queda enfrente de...** it's facing / in front of . . . (5)

engañar to deceive

engordar to gain weight

¡enhorabuena! congratulations! (7)

enlace *m.* (web) link

enlatado/a canned; **comestibles** (*m. pl.*) **enlatados** canned goods (6)

enojado/a angry (2)

enorme enormous

ensalada salad (6); **ensalada mixta** tossed salad

ensayar to rehearse

ensayo rehearsal

enseñanza teaching

enseñar to teach (7); **enseñar a** + *inf.* to teach to (*do something*)

ensuciar to dirty

entablar to initiate

entender (ie) to understand

entonces so; then, next

entrada entrance

entrar to enter; **no entrar** do not enter (9)

entre *prep.* between; among; **entre semana** during the week; **días de entre semana** weekdays

entregar (gu) to turn in; to deliver

entrenador(a) coach (12); trainer (12)

entrenamiento training

entrenar to train

entretenimiento entertainment

entrevista interview

entrevistar to interview (10)

entusiasmo enthusiasm

enviar (envío) to send

eólico/a: energía eólica wind energy

episodio episode

época era

equilibrado/a balanced

equilibrio balance

equinoccio equinox

equipaje *m.* baggage (9)

equipo team (12)

equis *f.* × (*letter*)

equivocación: por equivocación by mistake

equivocado/a mistaken; wrong

erradicar (qu) to eradicate

error *m.* mistake; **cometer un error** to make a mistake; **error ortográfico** spelling mistake

escala scale; layover; stop (9); **hacer** (*irreg.*) **escala** to have a layover; to make a stop (9)

escalada rock/mountain climbing (9); **hacer** (*irreg.*) **escalada** to go rock climbing (9)

escalar to climb

escalera stairs (11)

escalofríos chills

escándalo scandal

escandinavo/a Scandinavian

escanear to scan

escáner *m.* scanner (10)

escapar to escape

escasez *f.* shortage

escena scene

escenario setting; stage

escenografía set (*film*); scenery (*theater*)

escéptico/a skeptical

esclavitud (*f.*) **(infantil)** (child) slavery (15)

esclavo/a slave

escoger (j) to choose (7)

escolar *adj.* school

escondido/a hidden; **a escondidas** in secret

escribir (*p.p.* **escrito/a**) to write (7); **¿cómo se escribe... ?** how do you spell . . . ? (1)

escrito/a (*p.p. of* **escribir**) written

escritor(a) writer (10)

escritorio desk (1)

escritura writing

escuchar to listen (3)

escuela school (3); **escuela militar** military school; **escuela primaria** elementary school; **escuela privada** private school; **escuela secundaria** high school; **escuela tele-secundaria** distance high school

esculpir to sculpt

escultura sculpture (14)

ese/a *adj.* that (3)

esencial essential

esfuerzo force

eso that (*neuter*)

esos/as *adj.* those (3)

espacio space; **espacio en blanco** blank space

espalda back

España Spain

español *m.* Spanish (*language*)

español (*pl.* **españoles**), **española** *n.* Spaniard (2); *adj.* Spanish

espárragos *pl.* asparagus

especia spice

especial special

especialidad *f.* specialty

especialista *m., f.* specialist

especializarse (c) (en) to specialize (in); to major (in)

especie *f.* species, kind (13); **especie en peligro de extinción** endangered species

específico/a specific

espectacular spectacular

espectáculo show

espectador(a) spectator

espejo mirror (11)

esperanza hope

esperar to hope (for) (12); to wait (for) (12)

espíritu *m.* spirit

espiritual spiritual

esposo/a husband/wife (4)

espuma foam

esquí *m.* skiing

esquiador(a) skier

esquiar (esquío) to ski (12)

esquina corner; **está/queda en la esquina de... y...** it's on the corner of . . . and . . . (5); **siga hasta llegar a la esquina de...** go / keep going / continue until you (*command form. s.*) reach the corner of . . . (5)

establecer (zc) to establish

establecimiento establishment

establo barn; stable

estación *f.* station; season (1)

estacionar to park; **no estacionar** no parking (9)

estadio stadium (12)

estado state; **estado civil** marital status (16); **Estados Unidos** United States; **golpe** (*m.*) **de estado** coup d'état

estadounidense *n.* U.S. citizen, American; *adj.* of/from the United States of America (2)

estallar to erupt

estampilla stamp

estancia stay

estar *irreg.* to be (2); **¿cómo está(s)?** how are you (*form. s. / inform. s.*)? (1); **¿de qué está hecho/a?** what is it made of?; **¿dónde está... ?** where is . . . ? (5); **está a la derecha/izquierda** it's on the right/left (5); **está al lado de / detrás de / enfrente de / en la esquina de... y ...** it's next to / behind / facing, in front of / on the corner of . . . and . . . (5); **está despejado** it's clear (*sky*) (9); **está lloviendo** it's raining (9); **está nevando** it's snowing (9); **está nublado** it's cloudy (9); **¡está padre!** that's cool! (8); **estar a cargo de** to be in charge of; **estar a dieta** to be on a diet; **estar dispuesto** to be ready/willing (10); **estar (pasado) de moda** to be (un)fashionable; **(no) estar de acuerdo** to (dis)agree

este/a *adj.* this (3); **baje/suba por esta calle** go down/up this street (*command form. s.*) (5)

estereotipo stereotype

estética aesthetics

estilo style

estirarse to stretch

esto this (*neuter*)

estos/as these (3)

estómago stomach

estornudar to sneeze

estrategia strategy

estrecho/a narrow

estrella star (14)

estrés *m.* stress

estribillo chorus, refrain

estricto/a strict

estrofa verse

estructura structure

estudiante *m., f.* student (1)

estudiantil *adj.* student; **centro estudiantil** student center, student union

estudiar to study (2); **¿qué estudias?** what do you study?; what's your major? (1)

estudio study

estufa stove (11)

estupendo/a stupendous (2); **¡qué estupendo!** how cool! (8)

étnico/a ethnic

Europa Europe

europeo/a European

evaluar to evaluate

evento event

evidencia evidence

evitar to avoid

exacto/a exact

exagerado/a exaggerated

examen *m.* exam (1)

excelente excellent (2)

excesivo/a excessive

exclamación *f.* exclamation

excluir (y) to exclude

exclusivo/a exclusive

excremento excrement

excursión *f.* excursion; tour

excusa excuse

exiliado/a exiled

exilio exile

existencia existence

existente existing

existir to exist

éxito success; **tener** (*irreg.*) **éxito** to be successful

exitoso/a successful

exorcista *m., f.* exorcist

exótico/a exotic

expandir(se) to expand

expansión *f.* expansion

experiencia experience

experimentar to experience

experto/a expert

explicación *f.* explanation

explicar (qu) to explain

exploración *f.* exploration

explorar to explore

explotar to exploit; to develop (13)

exportador(a) exporter

exportar to export

exposición *f.* exposition

expresar to express

expresión *f.* expression

exquisito/a exquisite

extendido/a widespread

extensión *f.* extension

externo/a external; **deuda externa** foreign debt (15)

extinción *f.* extinction; **especie** (*f.*) **en peligro de extinción** endangered species

extinto/a extinct

extraer (*like* **traer**) to extract

extranjero abroad (9)

extraño/a strange

extremadamente extremely

extremo/a extreme

extrovertido/a extroverted (2)

F

fábrica factory

fabricación *f.* production

fabuloso/a fabulous

fácil easy (2)

facilitar to facilitate

factor *m.* factor

factura bill

facultad *f.* school (*of a university*)

falda skirt (8)

fallar to fail

fallecer (zc) to die, pass away

fallo error, mistake

falso/a false

falta lack

faltar to be lacking

fama fame; reputation; **tener** (*irreg.*) **fama de** to be known for

familia family; **¡qué bonita familia!** what a beautiful family! (4)

familiar *adj.* family; **nido familiar** parents' home (16); **planificación** (*f.*) **familiar** family planning

famoso/a famous

fantasía fantasy

fantástico/a fantastic

farmacia pharmacy

faro lighthouse

fascinado/a fascinated

fascinante fascinating

fascinar (*like* **gustar**) to fascinate (7); to like very much, love (7)

fauno faun

favor *m.* favor; **a favor (de)** in favor (of); **favor de no fumar** please don't smoke (9); **por favor** please; **un número / una letra a la vez, por favor** one number/letter at a time, please (1)

favorito/a favorite

fax *m.* fax

febrero February (1)

fecha date; **¿cuál es la fecha de hoy?** what is today's date? (1)

felicidad *f.* happiness; **¡felicidades!** congratulations! (7)

felicitación *f.* greeting; wish; **¡felicitaciones!** congratulations! (7)

felicitar to congratulate (7); **te felicito/felicitamos** I/we congratulate you (7)

feliz (*pl.* **felices**) happy (2); **¡feliz Año Nuevo!** happy New Year! (7); **¡feliz cumpleaños!** happy birthday! (7); **¡feliz Navidad!** Merry Christmas! (7)

femenino/a feminine

fenomenal phenomenal; awesome; **¡qué fenomenal!** how cool! (8)

fenómeno phenomenon

feo/a ugly (2); **¡qué feo/a!** how ugly! (4)

feria fair

ferrocarril *m.* railroad

festival *m.* festival

festivo/a festive, celebratory; **día** (*m.*) **festivo** holiday

ficción *f.* fiction

fiebre *f.* fever (12); **tener** (*irreg.*) **fiebre** to have a temperature

fiesta party (2); **dar** (*irreg.*) **una fiesta** to throw a party; **hacer** (*irreg.*) **una fiesta** to throw a party; **irse** (*irreg.*) **de fiesta** to party

fiestero/a party-loving
figura figure
figurar to figure
fijarse to pay attention to
fijo/a fixed, set
fila row
filarmónico/a philharmonic
film *m.* movie
filmar to film
filmografía filmography
filosofía philosophy (1)
filtro filter
fin *m.* end; **fin de semana** weekend (3); **organización** (*f.*) **sin fines de lucro** nonprofit organization (15); **por fin** finally; **¡que tenga(s) un buen fin de semana!** have (*form. s. / inform. s.*) a nice weekend!
final *m.* end; **al final** in the end
finalmente finally
financiamiento financing
financiero/a financial
firma signature
firmar to sign
física physics (1)
flaco/a thin (2)
flamenco *music of Andalusia and southern Spain*
flan *m.* (baked) custard (6)
flecharse to fall in love
flexibilidad *f.* flexibility
flor *f.* flower (7)
Florida: Pascua Florida Easter (7)
fluorescente fluorescent
fogata bonfire
folclor *m.* folklore
folclórico/a folk (9)
folleto brochure
fomentar to encourage, promote
fondo background; bottom; fund; **a fondo** in depth; **carrera de fondo** long-distance race; **recaudar fondos** to raise funds
forma form; shape; **mantenerse en forma** to stay in shape
formación *f.* formation; (academic) training; education
formar to form
formato format
fórmula formula
formular to formulate
formulario form
fortalecer (zc) to strengthen
forzar (ue) (c) to force
fósil *m.* fossil; **combustibles** (*m. pl.*) **fósiles** fossil fuels
foto *f.* photo; **sacar (qu) fotos** to take photos
fotocopia photocopy
fotografía photograph
fotógrafo/a photographer (10)
fractura fracture (12)
fracturarse to fracture
fragancia fragrance
francés *m.* French (*language*) (1)

francés (*pl.* **franceses**), **francesa** *n.* French person; *adj.* French
Francia France
franquear to go through
frase *f.* phrase; sentence
frecuencia frequency; **con frecuencia** often
frecuente often
fregadero kitchen sink (11)
frente *m.* front; *adv.* **frente a** facing
fresa strawberry (6)
frijoles *m. pl.* beans (6)
frío cold(ness); *adj.* cold; **hace frío** it's cold (9); **¡qué frío!** how cold! (4); **tener** (*irreg.*) **(mucho) frío** to be (very) cold
frito/a fried (6); **papas fritas** french fries
frontera border (15)
fronterizo/a *adj.* border
fruta fruit (6)
frutería fruit store
frutilla strawberry (*Arg.*)
fuego fire; **fuegos artificiales** fireworks (7)
fuente *f.* fountain; source
fuera *adv.* outside; **de dentro a fuera** inside out
fuerte strong (2); heavy (*food*)
fuerza force; strength; **fuerzas militares** military forces
fumar to smoke; **favor de no fumar** please don't smoke (9)
función *f.* function
funcionamiento functioning
funcionar to function, work
fundación *f.* foundation
fundar to found
funeral *m.* funeral
fútbol *m.* soccer; **fútbol americano** football (12); **jugar (ue) (gu) fútbol** to play soccer (3); **jugar (ue) (gu) fútbol americano** to play football (12)
futbolista *m., f.* soccer player
futuro future
futuro/a future

G

gabinete *m.* cabinet
gafas *pl.* (*eye*) glasses
galán *m.* (*pl.* **galanes**) leading man
galería gallery
gallina hen
gallo rooster; **gallo pinto** *rice and beans dish of Nicaragua and Costa Rica*; **pico de gallo** *uncooked salsa made of chopped tomato, onion, and jalapeños*
galón *m.* (*pl.* **galones**) gallon
ganadería ranching
ganador(a) winner
ganar to win (12); **ganar dinero** to earn (*income*), to make money
ganas: tener (*irreg.*) **ganas de** + *inf.* to feel like (*doing something*); **¿tiene(s) ganas de** + *n./inf.*? do you (*form. s. / inform. s.*) feel like . . . ? (6)
garantía guarantee

garantizar (c) to guarantee
gasolina gasoline
gastar to spend (9)
gastronomía gastronomy
gastronómico/a gastronomic
gato/a cat (4)
gazpacho *cold tomato soup of southern Spain*
gel *m.* gel
generación *f.* generation; **generación de relevo** upcoming generation
generar to generate
género gender; genre, type (14)
generoso/a generous
genético/a genetic
gente *f.* people
geoglifo geoglyph
geografía geography
geográfico/a geographic
geométrico/a geometric
gerente *m., f.* manager (10)
gigante *adj. m., f.* gigantic
gimnasia gynamastics
gimnasio gym(nasium) (1); **ir** (*irreg.*) **al gimnasio** to go to the gym (3)
gira tour
girar to turn; **gire a la derecha/izquierda** turn (to the) right/left (*command form. s.*) (5); **no girar** do not turn (9)
glaciar *m.* glaciar
glamoroso/a glamorous
global global; **calentamiento global** global warming (13); **Sistema** (*m.*) **de Posicionamiento Global (SPG)** Global Positioning System (GPS)
globalización *f.* globalization
gobernador(a) governor
gobernante *m., f.* leader, ruler
gobernar (ie) to govern
gobierno government
gol *m.* goal; **marcar (qu) un gol** to score a goal; **meter un gol** to score a goal
golazo: ¡qué golazo! what a goal!
golf *m.* golf
golfista *m., f.* golfer
golpe (*m.*) **de estado** coup d'état
gordo/a fat (2)
gorra (baseball) cap (8)
gorro knitted hat (8)
gracias thank you (1); **gracias por** + *n./verb* thank you for . . . (5); **Día** (*m.*) **de Acción de Gracias** Thanksgiving (7); **muchas/muchísimas gracias** thank you very much (5); **no, gracias** no, thank you (6); **sí, gracias** yes, please (5)
gracioso/a funny (2)
grado degree (*temperature*)
graduación *f.* graduation (1)
graduarse (me gradúo) (de) to graduate (from)
gráfico/a graphic; **diseñador(a) gráfico/a** graphic designer (10)
gramática grammar

gran, grande large, big (2); great; **Gran Bretaña** Great Britain

graneado: arroz (*m.*) **graneado** *fried rice dish*

granizo hail

granja farm

grano grain

grappamiel *f. alcoholic beverage of Uruguay*

grasa fat

grasiento/a greasy

gratis *inv.* free (*of charge*)

grave serious

gripe *f.* flu

gris gray (2)

gritar to shout

grupo group; band

guacamayo macaw

guagua bus (*Carib.*)

guanábana soursop

guantes *m. pl.* gloves (8)

guapo/a handsome; good-looking; **¡qué guapo/a!** how handsome/beautiful! (4)

guaraní *m. indigenous language of S.A.*

guardar to keep; to save (8)

guatemalteco/a *n., adj.* Guatemalan (2)

guay: ¡qué guay! how cool! (8)

guayabera *lightweight shirt worn in tropical climates*

guerra war (15); **guerra civil** civil war

guía *m., f.* guide (9); **guía naturalista** nature guide (4)

guion script

guisado stew (6)

guita dinero *sl.*

guitarra guitar; **tocar (qu) la guitarra** to play the guitar (2)

guitarrista guitarist

gustar to be pleasing; **¿le gusta** + *activity*? do you (*form. s.*) like + *inf.*? (2); **¿le gustaría** + *inf.*? would you (*form. s.*) like (*to do something*)? (9); **me gusta** + *inf./n.* I like + *inf./n.* (2); **me gustaría** + *inf.* I would like (*to do something*) (9); **no me gusta** + *inf./n.* I don't like + *inf./n.* (2); **¿te gusta** + *activity*? do you (*inform. s.*) like + *inf.*? (2); **¿te gustaría** + *inf.*? would you (*inform. s.*) like (*to do something*)? (9)

gusto like, preference; *pl.* likes; **¡con mucho gusto!** with pleasure! (6); **mucho gusto** nice to meet you (1)

H

haber *irreg.* (*inf. of* **hay**) there is, there are (1); **no hay de qué** you're welcome (5); **(no) hay que** + *inf.* you (don't) have to / it's (not) necessary to (*do something*) (12)

hábil skillful

habilidad *f.* ability

habitación *f.* bedroom

habitante *m., f.* inhabitant

hábitat *m.* habitat

hábito habit

hablar to speak (2); to talk (3); **hablar por teléfono** to talk on the phone (3)

hacer *irreg.* (*p.p.* **hecho**) to do (3); to make (5); **¿cuánto tiempo hace que** + *present tense*? how long have you (*done / been doing something*)? (13); **desde hace** + *period of time* for + period of time; **hace** + *time expression* + *present tense* I've been (*doing something*) for + time (13); **hace buen tiempo** it's nice weather (9); **hace (mucho) calor** it's (very) hot (*weather*) (9); **hace (mucho) frío** it's (very) cold (*weather*) (9); **hace mal tiempo** it's bad weather (9); **hace (mucho) sol** it's (very) sunny (9); **hace** + *time expression* + **que** + *present tense* to have been (*doing something*) for (*time*); **hace** + *time expression* + **que** + *preterite* to have (done *something*) (*time*) ago; **hace (mucho) viento** it's (very) windy (9); **hacer camping** to go camping; **hacer clic** to click (10); **hacer deportes** to play sports; **hacer ejercicio aeróbico** to do aerobics; **hacer ejercicio** to work out (2); **hacer escala** to have a layover; to make a stop (9); **hacer escalada** to go rock climbing (9); **hacer kayak** to go kayaking; **hacer la cama** to make the bed (11); **hacer la maleta** to pack a suitcase (9); **hacer la tarea** to do homework (3); **hacer ruido** to be noisy; **hacer senderismo** to go hiking; **hacer snorkel** to go snorkeling (9); **hacer un recorrido** to take a trip / go on a tour (9); **hacer una fiesta** to throw a party; **hacerse de voluntario** to volunteer; **¿qué tiempo hace?** what's the weather like? (9)

hacia toward

hambre *f.* (*but* **el hambre**) hunger (15); **tener** (*irreg.*) **hambre** to be hungry

hamburguesa hamburger (2)

harina flour (6)

hasta *adv.* until; even; *prep.* until; **hasta luego** see you later (1); **hasta mañana** see you tomorrow (1); **hasta pronto** see you soon (1); **hasta que** (*conj.*) until; **siga hasta llegar a (la esquina de)...** go / keep going / continue (*command form. s.*) until you reach (the corner of) . . . (5)

hechizo spell

hecho *n.* fact, event; **de hecho** actually

hecho/a (*p.p. of* **hacer**) made; **¿de qué está hecho/a?** what is it made of?

helado ice cream (6)

helicóptero helicopter

hembra female

hemisferio hemisphere

heredar to inherit

heredero/a heir

herencia inheritance

herida wound (12); injury (12)

hermanastro/a stepbrother/stepsister (4)

hermano/a brother/sister (4); *pl.* siblings

hermoso/a pretty (2); beautiful

héroe *m.* hero

herramienta tool

hervor *m.* boil (*liquid*)

heteroparental *family made up of opposite-sex parents and their children*

hielo ice; **patinar sobre el hielo** to ice skate; **patinaje** (*m.*) **sobre el hielo** ice skating

hijastro/a stepson/stepdaughter (4)

hijo/a son/daughter (4); *pl.* children; **hijo/a único/a** only child (4)

hinchazón *f.* (pl. **hinchazones**) swelling (12)

hipermercado large supermarket (6)

hipocondríaco/a hypochondriac

hipoteca mortgage

hipotético/a hypothetical

hispano/a Hispanic

hispanohablante *n. m., f.* Spanish-speaker; *adj. m., f.* Spanish-speaking

historia history (1)

histórico/a historical (14)

hogar home (16); **sin hogar** homeless

hoja de papel sheet of paper (1)

hola hi; hello (1)

Holanda Holland

Hollywoodense *n., adj.* of or pertaining to Hollywood

hombre *m.* man (1)

hombro shoulder (8)

homenaje *m.* tribute

homoparental *family made up of same-sex parents and their children*

hondureño/a *n., adj.* Honduran (2)

hongos *m. pl.* mushrooms (6)

honor *m.* honor

hora hour; time; **¿a qué hora... ?** at what time? (3); **¿qué hora es?** what time is it? (3)

horario schedule

hormiga ant

hormiguero anthill

horno oven (11)

horrible horrible (2)

hospital *m.* hospital (5)

hotel *m.* hotel (9)

hoy today; **¿cuál es la fecha de hoy?** what is today's date? (1); **hoy en día** today; these days; **hoy es...** today is . . . (1)

huarache *m.* sandal

hueso bone

huevo egg (6); **huevos motuleños** *Yucatan dish of fried eggs over black beans and a fried tortilla*

huitlacoche *m.* corn smut

humanidad *f.* humanity; *pl.* humanities (1)

humanitarismo humanitarianism

humano/a human; **derecho humano** human right (15); **violar los derechos humanos** to violate human rights

humedad *f.* humidity
húmedo/a humid
humillar to humiliate
humorístico/a humorous
huracán *m.* (*pl.* **huracanes**) hurricane (13)

I

iceberg *m.* iceberg
idea idea (1); **¡qué buena idea!** what a good idea!
identidad *f.* identity
identificar(se) (qu) to identify (oneself)
idioma *m.* language
idiosincrasia idiosyncrasy
idiota *m.* idiot
iglesia church (5)
ignorar to ignore
igual same (1); igual; **al igual que** just like; **igual que** just like; **sin igual** unequaled
igualdad *f.* equality (15)
igualmente likewise (1)
ilegal illegal
ilegítimo/a illegitimate
ilógico/a illogical
ilusión *f.* dream; hope
imagen *f.* (pl. **imágenes**) image
imaginación *f.* imagination
imaginar to imagine
imaginario/a imaginary
imitar to imitate
impacto impact
impensado/a unexpected
imperfecto *gram.* imperfect
imperialismo imperialism
imperio empire
imponer (*like* **poner**) (*p.p.* **impuesto**) to impose
importación *f.* importation
importancia importance
importante important
importar (*like* **gustar**) to matter (7); to be important; **sin importar** regardless of
imposible impossible
impresión *f.* impression
impresionante impressive
impreso/a (*p.p. of* **imprimir**) printed
impresora printer (10)
imprimir (*p.p.* **impreso**) to print
impulsar to motivate
impureza impurity
inalámbrico/a wireless; **conexión** (*f.*) **inalámbrica** wireless connection
inauguración *f.* inauguration
inaugurado/a inaugurated
inca *n. m., f.* Inca; *adj. m., f.* Incan
incapacitado/a disabled
incidente *m.* incident
incienso incense
inclinarse (por) to lean (toward)
incluir (y) to include
incluso/a including
incorporar to incorporate
incrementar(se) to increase

indefinido/a indefinite
independencia independence; **Día** (*m.*) **de la Independencia** Independence Day (7)
independiente independent
independizarse (c) to become independent (16)
indicación *f.* indication; instruction
indicar (qu) to indicate
índice *m.* index; rate
indiferente indifferent
indígena *n. m., f.* native (indigenous) person (15); *adj. m., f.* indigenous
indigente indigent
indio/a *n., adj.* Indian
individuo individual
industrializarse (c) to industrialize
inesperado/a unexpected
infantil *adj.* child, children's; **esclavitud** (*f.*) **infantil** child slavery (15)
infección *f.* infection (12)
inferior inferior; lower
infierno hell
infinitivo *gram.* infinitive
inflable inflatable
inflar to inflate
influencia influence
influir (y) to influence
influyente influential
información *f.* information
informar to inform
informática computer science
informe *m.* report
infraestructura infrastructure (15)
ingeniería engineering (1)
ingeniero/a engineer (4)
Inglaterra England
inglés *m.* English (*language*) (1)
inglés (*pl.* **ingleses**), **inglesa** *n.* English person; *adj.* English
ingrediente *m.* ingredient
ingresos *pl.* income
iniciar to begin
inicio beginning
injusticia injustice
inmaduro/a immature
inmediatamente immediately
inmigración *f.* immigration
inmigrante *m., f.* immigrant (15)
inmigrar to immigrate
innovación *f.* innovation
inodoro toilet (11)
inseguridad *f.* insecurity
inseguro/a insecure
insistir (en) to insist (on)
insomnio insomnia (12)
inspeccionar to inspect
inspiración *f.* inspiration
inspirar to inspire
instalar to install
institucional institutional
instrucción *f.* instruction
instructor(a) instructor

instrumento instrument; **tocar (qu) un instrumento** to play an instrument
insultar to insult
integrar to integrate
inteligente intelligent (2)
intenso/a intense
intentar to try (to)
interacción *f.* interaction
intercambio exchange
interés *m.* (*pl.* **intereses**) interest
interesante interesting (2)
interesar (*like* **gustar**) to interest (7)
interior interior; **ropa interior** underwear (8)
internacional international; **relaciones** (*f. pl.*) **internacionales** international relations (1)
Internet *m.* Internet (10); **buscador** (*m.*) **de Internet** search engine (10); **conectarse al Internet** to connect to the Internet
interno/a internal
interpretar to interpret; **interpretar un papel** to play a role/part (14)
intérprete *m., f.* interpreter
interrumpir to interrupt
intersección *f.* intersection
íntimo/a intimate
intrínsico/a intrinsic
introducción *f.* introduction
introvertido/a introverted (2)
inundación *f.* flood (13)
inundar(se) to flood
inventar to invent
inversión *f.* investment
inversionista *m., f.* investor
investigación *f.* research
invierno winter (1); **Juegos Olímpicos de invierno** Winter Olympics
invitación *f.* invitation
invitado/a guest
invitar to invite (7); **invitar** + **a** + *inf.* to invite (*to do something*)
iPad *m.* iPad
ir *irreg.* to go (2); **ir a** + *inf.* to be going to (*do something*) (2); **ir al gimnasio** to go to the gym (3); **ir de compras** to go shopping (2); **irse** to leave, to go away (5); **irse de fiesta** to party; **¿adónde va(s)?** where are you (*form. s. / inform. s.*) going? (2); **que le(s) vaya bien** may things go well for you (*form. s., pl.*) (12); **voy a/al** + *place* I'm going to . . . (2)
irlandés (*pl.* **irlandeses**), **irlandesa** *n.* Irish person; *adj.* Irish
isla island
Italia Italy
italiano/a *n., adj.* Italian
itinerario itinerary
izquierda left; **a la izquierda** on the left; **a mano izquierda** on the left; **coger (j) a mano izquierda** to turn left (*Sp.*); **doble/ gire a la izquierda** turn (to the) right/left (*command form. s.*) (5); **quedar a la izquierda** to be on the left

J

jaguar *m.* jaguar
jalar to pull; pull (9)
jalisciense *adj.* of or pertaining to Jalisco, Mex.
jamaicano/a *n., adj.* Jamaican
jamón *m.* ham (6)
Jánuca *m.* Hanukah (7)
japonés *m.* Japanese (*language*)
japonés (*pl.* **japoneses**), **japonesa** *n.* Japanese person; *adj.* Japanese
jarabe (*m.*) **para la tos** cough syrup
jardín *m.* (*pl.* **jardines**) garden (5)
jeans *m. pl.* jeans (8)
jefe/a boss (10)
jerarquía hierarchy
Jerusalén Jerusalem
jirafa giraffe
jitomate *m.* tomato (*Mex.*)
joven *n. m., f.* (*pl.* **jóvenes**) young person (1); *adj.* young (2)
joyería jewelry; jewelry store
joyero/a jeweler
jubilación *f.* retirement
judío/a *n.* Jewish person, Jew; *adj.* Jewish (7)
juego game; **Juegos Olímpicos (de invierno/verano)** (Winter/Summer) Olympics (12)
jueves *m.* Thursday (3)
juez(a) *n.* judge (10)
jugador(a) player (12)
jugar (ue) (gu) to play (*a game, sport*) (2); **jugar básquetbol** to play basketball (3); **jugar béisbol** to play baseball (12); **jugar fútbol** to play soccer (3); **jugar fútbol americano** to play football (12); **jugar tenis** to play tennis (12); **jugar videojuegos** to play video games (3); **jugar voleibol** to play volleyball (12)
jugo juice (6)
juicio trial
julio July (1)
junio June (1)
juntarse (con) to hang out (with); to get together (with)
junto a along with
juntos/as together
jurídico/a judicial
justicia justice; **sala de justicia** courtroom (10)
justificar (qu) to justify
justo/a fair (15)
juvenil young; youthful
juventud *f.* youth
juzgar (gu) to judge

K

kayak *m.* kayak (9); **hacer** (*irreg.*) **kayak** to go kayaking
kilo(gramo) kilo(gram) (1)
kilómetro kilometer
kiosko kiosk (5)
koala *m.* koala

kuna *n. m., f.* member of the Kuna group; *adj. m., f.* of or pertaining to the Kuna indigenous group of Panama

L

la *def. art. f. s.* the (1); *d.o. pron. f. s.* you (*form.*), her, it (6)
laberinto labyrinth
labio lip (8)
laboral *adj.* work-related
lácteo/a *adj.* dairy; **productos lácteos** dairy products (6)
lado side; **al lado** beside; **al otro lado de** on the other side of; **de un lado al otro** from one side to the other; **dejar a un lado** to leave aside; **por otro lado** on the other hand; **por un lado** on one hand
ladrón (*pl.* **ladrones**), **ladrona** thief
lago lake
lágrima tear
lamentablemente sadly, unfortunately
lamentar to regret
lamento lament; moan, cry
lámpara lamp (11)
lanzador(a) pitcher (*baseball*)
lanzar (c) to launch; to throw, pitch
lápiz *m.* (*pl.* **lápices**) pencil (1)
láptop: (computadora) láptop laptop (computer) (10)
largo/a long (2); **a largo plazo** long-term, in the long-term; **a lo largo de** along, throughout
largometraje *m.* feature film
las *def. art. f. pl.* the (1); *d.o. pron. f. pl.* they, you (*form.*) (6); **a la(s)...** at ... (*time of day*)
lastimar(se) to injure (oneself) (12)
Latinoamérica Latin America
latinoamericano/a *n., adj.* Latin American
lavabo bathroom sink (11)
lavadora washing machine (11)
lavandería laundromat
lavaplatos *m. s., pl.* dishwasher (11)
lavar to wash (4); **lavar el suelo** to wash the floor (11); **lavar la ropa** to wash clothes (4); **lavar los platos** to wash dishes (4); **lavarse las manos** to wash one's hands (5); **lavarse los dientes** to brush one's teeth
le *i.o. pron.* him, her, you (*form. s.*) (7); **¿en qué puedo servirle?** how may I help you? (10); **le acompaño/acompañamos en el dolor** I'm/we're with you in your time of pain (16); **le acompaño/acompañamos en el sentimiento** you're in my/our thoughts (16); **le agradezco por...** I appreciate that you . . . , I thank you for . . . (5); **¡le damos la bienvenida a Ud.!** we welcome you! (11); **le deseo mucha suerte** I wish you luck (12); **le doy/damos el pésame** my/our condolences (16); **¿le gusta** + *activity*? do you (*form.*) like + *inf.*? (2); **¿le gustaría** + *inf.*? would you like (*to do something*)? (9); **que le vaya bien** may things go well

for you (12); **quiero presentarle a...** I'd like you to meet . . . (10); **se le antoja/antojó** + *inf. / s. n.* they, you feel/felt like ([*doing*] *something*) (9); **se le antojan/antojaron** + *inf. s. n.* they, you feel/felt like + *pl. n.* (9)
leche *f.* milk (6); **arroz** (*m.*) **con leche** rice pudding
lechuga lettuce (6)
lector(a) reader
lectura reading
leer (y) (*p.p.* leído) to read (2); **leer el periódico** to read the newspaper (3)
legalizar (c) to legalize
lejano/a distant
lejos (de) far (from) (9)
lema *m.* slogan
lengua tongue; language
lenguado sole (*fish*)
lenguaje *m.* language
lenteja lentil
lentes *m. pl.* glasses (8); **lentes de contacto** contact lenses; **ponerse** (*irreg.*) **los lentes / los lentes de contacto** to put on glasses/contacts (5)
lentillas contact lenses
lento/a slow (2)
león (*pl.* **leones**), **leonesa** lion; **león marino** sea lion (13)
leprosario leper colony
les *i.o. pron.* them, you (*form. pl.*) (7); **¿en qué puedo servirles?** how may I help you? (10); **les acompaño/acompañamos en el dolor** I'm/we're with you in your time of pain (16); **les acompaño/acompañamos en el sentimiento** you're in my/our thoughts (16); **les agradezco por...** I appreciate that you . . . , I thank you for . . . (5); **les deseo mucha suerte** I wish you luck (12); **les doy/damos el pésame** my/our condolences (16); **que les vaya bien** may things go well for you (12); **quiero presentarles a...** I'd like you to meet . . . (10); **se les antoja/antojó** + *inf. / s. n.* they/you feel/felt like ([*doing*] *something*) (9); **se les antojan/antojaron** + *inf. pl. n.* they/you feel/felt like + *pl. n.* (9)
letra letter; **una letra a la vez, por favor** one letter at a time, please (1)
levantador(a) de pesas weightlifter
levantar to raise, lift; **levantar pesas** to lift weights (12); **levantarse** to get up (5)
leve *adj.* light
ley *f.* law; **violar la ley** to break the law
libanés (*pl.* **libaneses**), **libanesa** *n.*, Lebanese person; *adj.* Lebanese
Líbano Lebanon
libertad *f.* freedom (15)
libre free; **al aire libre** outdoors; **tiempo libre** free time
librería bookstore (1)
libro book (1); **libro de texto** textbook
licenciado/a graduate; attorney
licenciatura degree (Bachelor's)

licopeno lycopene
licor *m.* liquor
licorería liquor store
líder *m., f.* leader
liga league
ligado/a tied, bound
ligero/a light
lima lime
limitar to limit
límite *m.* limit
limón *m.* (*pl.* **limones**) lemon (6); lime (6)
limpiar to clean (4)
limpio/a clean
lince *m.* lynx
lindo/a pretty (2); **¡qué lindo/a!** how cute/pretty! (4)
línea line; **línea en blanco** blank (line)
lino linen
lío trouble, mess: **¡qué lío!** what a mess! (4)
líquido liquid
Lisboa Lisbon
lisina lysine
lista list
listo/a ready
literatura literature (14)
llamada (phone) call
llamar to call; **llamarse** to be called (1); **¿cómo se llama?** what is your name (*form. s.*)? (1); **¿cómo te llamas?** what is your name (*inform. s.*)? (1); **me llamo** my name is (1)
llanero/a plainsman, plainswoman
llanto sobbing, weeping
llanura plain
llave *f.* key (1)
llavero keychain
llegar (**gu**) to arrive (5); **siga hasta llegar a (la esquina de)...** go / keep going / continue (*command form. s.*) until you reach (the corner of) . . . (5)
llenar to fill
lleno/a full
llevar to wear (8); to bring (8); to carry; to take; **¿cuánto tiempo lleva(s)** + *pres. p.***?** how long have you (*form. s. / inform. s.*) (*done / been doing something*)? (13); **llevar una vida activa** to lead an active life; **llevo** + *time expression* + *pres. p.* I've been (*doing something*) for + *time* (13)
llover (**ue**) to rain; **está lloviendo** it's raining (9); **llueve** it's raining (9)
lluvia rain
lluvioso/a rainy
lo *d.o. pron. m. s.* you (*form.*) (6); him; it (6); **cuánto lo siento** I'm very sorry (16); **lo contrario** the opposite; **lo siento** I'm sorry (7); condolences (7); **lo siento mucho** I'm very sorry (16)
lobo wolf
localidad *f.* locality
localizar (**c**) to locate
loco/a crazy (2)
lógico/a logical

Londres London
loro parrot (13)
los *def. art. m. pl.* the (1); *d.o. pron. m.* they (6); *d.o. pron. m. pl.* you (*form. pl.*) (6)
lotería lottery; **sacar** (**qu**) **la lotería** to win the lottery
luchar to fight
lucir (**zc**) to wear, to dress up (8); to shine (8)
lucrativo/a lucrative
lucro: organización (*f.*) **sin fines de lucro** nonprofit organization (15)
lúcuma lucuma (*fruit*)
luego then, afterward, next; **hasta luego** see you later (1)
lugar *m.* place (5); **lugar del crimen** scene of the crime
lujo: de lujo luxury
luna moon
lunes *m.* Monday (3)
luz *f.* (*pl.* **luces**) light; **dar** (*irreg.*) **a luz** to give birth

M

macerar to tenderize
macho male
madera wood
madrastra stepmother (4)
madre *f.* mother (4); **Día** (*m.*) **de las Madres** Mother's Day
madrina godmother
madrugada early morning; dawn; **de la madrugada** in the early A.M. hours (3)
madurez *f.* maturity
maestría Master's degree; **sacar** (**qu**) **una maestría** to get a Master's (degree)
maestro/a teacher
mágico/a magic
mago: Día (*m.*) **de los Reyes Magos** Three Kings Day; Epiphany (Adoration of the Magi) (7)
maillot *m.* (sports) jersey
maíz *m.* corn (6)
mal *adv.* poorly; **lo pasé mal** I had a bad time (7); **(muy) mal** (very) bad (1); **pasarlo mal** to have a bad time (7)
mal, malo/a *adj.* bad (2); **hace mal tiempo** it's bad weather (9); **¡qué malo!** that's terrible! (8); **sacar** (**qu**) **malas notas** to get bad grades; **tener** (*irreg.*) **mala pinta** to have a bad appearance; **verse** (*irreg.*) **mal** to look bad
maldición *f.* curse
maleta suitcase (9); **hacer** (*irreg.*) **la maleta** to pack a suitcase (9)
malgastar to waste (13)
mamá mother (4)
manchar to stain; **mancharse** to get dirty
mandar to order; to send
mandato command
manejar to drive
manera way; **de la misma manera** likewise
manga sleeve
mango mango (6)

manifestación *f.* protest
manifiesto manifest
mano *f.* hand (8); **a mano** by hand; **a mano derecha/izquierda** on the right/left; **coger** (**j**) **a mano derecha/izquierda** to turn right/left (*Sp.*); **darse** (*irreg.*) **la mano** to shake hands; **lavarse las manos** to wash one's hands
mantener (*like* **tener**) to maintain; **mantenerse en contacto (con)** to stay in touch (with); **mantenerse en forma** to stay in shape
mantequilla butter (6)
manzana apple (6); city block (*Sp., S.A.*)
mañana tomorrow; morning; **de la mañana** in the morning, A.M. (3); **hasta mañana** see you tomorrow (1); **por la mañana** (*generally*) during the morning (3)
mapa *m.* map
mapuche *n. indigenous person of south-central Chile and southwestern Argentina*
mapuey *m. tropical tuber*
maquillarse to put on makeup (5)
máquina machine
mar *m.* sea (13); **mar adentro** off-shore
maracuyá passion fruit
maratón *m.* (*pl.* **maratones**) marathon
maravilloso/a marvelous (2)
marca brand (8)
marcar (**qu**) to mark; to score; **marcar un gol** to score a goal
margen *m.* (*pl.* **márgenes**) margin
marido husband (4)
marino/a *adj.* sea; **león** (*m.*) **marino** sea lion (13)
mariposa butterfly
mariscos *m. pl.* seafood (6)
marítimo/a *adj.* maritime
marketing *m.* marketing
marrón brown (2)
Marruecos Morocco
martes *m.* Tuesday (3)
marzo March (1)
más more; **cada vez más** increasingly; **come/coma más** have some more (*command inform. s. / form. s.*) (11); **más alto que** taller than (4); **más de** + *number* more than + *number*; **más** + *adj.* **que** more (-er) + *adj.* than (4); **mi/nuestro más sentido pésame** my/our deepest sympathies (16)
masa dough
máscara mask
mascota pet (4)
masculino/a masculine
masivo/a mass
máster *m.* Master's (program, degree)
masticar (**qu**) to chew
matar to kill
mate *m. strong tea of South America*
matemáticas *pl.* math (1)
materia subject (1)
material *m.* material

materno/a maternal
matrícula tuition
matricularse to enroll
matrimonio marriage (16)
máximo/a maximum
maya *n., adj. m., f.* Mayan
mayo May (1); **el primero de mayo** the first of May (1);
mayor older (4); oldest; greater; greatest
mayoría majority
mayormente principally
mayúscula capital (letter), uppercase
mazcora ear of corn; cob
me *d.o. pron.* me (6); *i.o. pron.* to/for me (7); *refl. pron.* myself; **me gusta** + *inf./n.* I like + *inf./n.* (2); **me gustaría** + *inf.* I would like (*to do something* (9); **¿me puede comunicar con... ?** can you connect me with . . . ?; **no me gusta** + *inf./n.* I don't like + *inf./n.* (2); **se me antoja/antojó** + *inf. / s. n.* I feel/felt like + ([*doing*] *something*) (9); **se me antojan/antojaron** + *pl. n.* I feel/felt like + *pl. n.* (9)
mearse *sl.* to wet/pee oneself
mecánico/a *n., adj.* mechanic
medialuna croissant
medianoche *f.* midnight; **es medianoche** it's midnight (3)
medias *pl.* stockings
medicado/a medicated
medicina medicine
médico/a doctor (4); **médico/a de cabecera** general practitioner
medio *n.* medium; means; *pl.* mass media; **medio ambiente** environment (13); **medio de transporte** means of transportation
medio/a *adj.* half; middle; average; **es la una y media** it's 1:30 (3); **media naranja** better half; **y media** half past (*the hour*)
medioambiental environmental (13)
mediocampo mid-field
mediocre mediocre
mediodía *m.* noon; **es mediodía** it's noon (3);
meditar to meditate
Mediterráneo Mediterranean
medusa jellyfish
megaestrella superstar
mejillón *m.* mussel
mejor better (4); best
mejorar to improve
mellizo/a fraternal twin
melocotón *m.* peach
melodramático/a melodramatic
memoria memory; **memoria USB** memory card/stick (10); **tarjeta de memoria** memory card
memorizar (c) to memorize
mencionar to mention
menor younger (4); youngest; less; least
menos less; least; minus; **menos** + *adj.* + **que** less + *adj.* than (4); **menos alto que** less tall than (4)

mensaje *m.* message; **mensaje recordatorio** reminder
mensual monthly
mente *f.* mind
mentir (ie, i) to lie
menú *m.* menu
mercado (outdoor) market (5)
merendar (ie) to have a snack (6)
merienda snack (6)
merluza hake
mes *m.* month (1)
mesa table (1)
mesita de noche nightstand (11)
mesoamericano/a *n., adj.* Meso-American
mestizo/a of mixed race (European and native American)
meta goal
metabólico/a metabolic
metal *m.* metal
meter to put, place; **meter un gol** to score a goal
metro subway (5); meter
metrópoli *f.* metropolis
metropolitano/a metropolitan
mexicano/a *n., adj.* Mexican (2); **comer comida mexicana** to eat Mexican food (3)
mezcla mix
mezclar(se) to mix, blend
mí *obj. of prep.* me; **para mí** for me (7); for me (personally) (15)
mi(s) *poss. adj.* my; **en mi opinión...** in my opinion . . . (15); **mi más sentido pésame** my deepest sympathies (16); **mi nombre es** my name is (1)
micro bus (*C.A. and S.A.*)
microempresa micro-business
microfinanza micro-finance
micrófono microphone (10)
microondas *m. s., pl.* microwave (11)
microproducto micro-product
miedo fear; **tener (irreg.) miedo** to be afraid
miedoso/a easily frightened
miel *f.* honey
miembro member
mientras while
miércoles *m.* Wednesday (3)
mil (one) thousand
militar *n. m., f.* soldier; **escuela militar** military school; **fuerzas militares** military forces
milla mile
millón *m.* million
minería mining
minibús *m.* small bus
minifalda miniskirt
minimizar (c) to minimize
mínimo minimum
miniserie *f.* miniseries
minuto minute
mío/a(s) *poss. adj.* my; *poss. pron.* (of) mine
mira: en el punto de mira in the crosshairs

mirar to look at; to watch (3); **mirar la televisión** to watch television (3)
misa mass
misión *f.* mission
mismo/a same; **de la misma manera** likewise
misquito *indigenous group of Central America*
misterio mystery
misterioso/a mysterious
místico/a *n., adj.* mystic
mitad *f.* half
mixteco/a *n., adj.* Mixtec (*an indigenous group of Mex.*)
mixto/a mixed; **ensalada mixta** tossed salad
mochila backpack (1)
moda fashion; style; **desfile** (*m.*) **de moda** fashion show (8); **estar** (*irreg.*) **(pasado) de moda** to be (un)fashionable (8); **la última moda** the latest fashion
modalidades *f. pl.* manners
modelo model
módem *m.* (*pl.* **módems**) modem (10)
moderado/a moderate
moderno/a modern (5)
modificar (qu) to modify
modistería dressmaker's shop
modo way; manner; means; **modo de transporte** means of transportation
mojar to wet
mola *embroidered panel used in the typical clothing of Kuna women in Panama*
molestar (*like* **gustar**) to bother (7)
molestia bother; **si no es molestia** if it's not a bother (6)
momento moment; **en algún momento** at some point
monarquía monarchy
monitor *m.* monitor
mono monkey (13)
montaña mountain (9)
montar to ride; **montar a caballo** to ride a horse (3); **montar en bicicleta** to ride a bicycle
montón: un montón a lot
monumento monument
morado/a purple (2)
morder (ue) to bite
moreno/a *n.* brunet(te); *adj.* dark brown (*hair, eyes*) (2)
moretón *m.* (*pl.* **moretones**) bruise (12)
morir(se) (ue, u) (*p.p.* **muerto**) to die (8)
mosaico mosaic
mostrar (ue) to show
motivado/a motivated (2)
moto(cicleta) motorcycle
motuleño: huevos motuleños *Yucatan dish of fried eggs over black beans and a fried tortilla*
mover(se) (ue) to move (*motion*)
móvil *m.* cell phone

movimiento movement

muchacho/a boy, girl

mucho *adj.* much; a lot; *adv.* a lot; **me divertí mucho** I had a lot of fun (7)

mucho/a a lot (of); *pl.* many; **¡con mucho gusto!** with pleasure! (6); **le(s) deseo mucha suerte** I wish you (*form. s., pl.*) luck (12); **lo siento mucho** I'm very sorry (16); **¡mucha suerte!** good luck! (12); **muchas/muchísimas gracias** thank you very much (5); **mucho gusto** nice to meet you (1); **mucho tiempo** a long time (13)

mudarse to move (*residence*) (16)

mueble *m.* piece of furniture

muerte *f.* death

muerto/a (*p.p. of* **morir**) to die; **Día** (*m.*) **de los Muertos** Day of the Dead (7)

mujer *f.* woman (1); wife (4); **mujer bombero** female firefighter (10); **mujer policía** policewoman

mulato/a mulatto

múltiples *pl.* multiple

multitud *f.* multitude

mundial *adj.* world; **Copa Mundial** World Cup

mundo world

municipalidad *f.* municipality

municipio municipality

muñeca wrist; doll

muñeco doll

mural *m.* mural

murga *typical song of Carnival celebrations in Uruguay and Arg.*

músculo muscle

museo museum (5)

música music (2)

músico *m., f.* musician

musulmán (*pl.* **musulmanes**), **musulmana** *n., adj.* Muslim (7)

mutuo/a mutual

muy very; **muy bien** very well (1); **muy mal** very bad (1)

N

nacer (zc) to be born (6)

nacimiento birth (7); **defecto de nacimiento** birth defect

nación *f.* nation; **Naciones Unidas** United Nations

nacional national

nacionalidad *f.* nationality

nacionalista *m., f.* nationalist

nacionalizado/a nationalized

nada nothing (5); not anything; **de nada** you're welcome (5)

nadar to swim (2); **nadar de dorso** to do the backstroke

nadie no one (5); nobody, not anybody

náhuatl *m.* Nahuatl (*language of the Aztecs*)

naranja orange (6); **media naranja** better half

narcotráfico drug trafficking (15)

nariz *f.* (*pl.* **narices**) nose (8)

narración *f.* narration

narrar to narrate

natación *f.* swimming (12)

nativo/a native

natural natural; **desasatre** (*m.*) **natural** natural disaster (15); **recurso natural** natural resource (13)

naturaleza nature (9)

naturalista *adj.* nature; **guía** (*m., f.*) **naturalista** nature guide (4)

náuseas *pl.* nausea (12); **tener** (*irreg.*) **náuseas** to feel nauseous

náutico/a nautical

navegable navigable

navegador *m.* browser; **navegador web** web browser

navegante *m., f.* sailor

navegar (gu) to navigate

Navidad *f.* Christmas (7); **árbol** (*m.*) **de Navidad** Christmas tree; **¡feliz Navidad!** Merry Christmas! (7)

navideño/a *adj.* Christmas

necesario/a necessary

necesidad *f.* necessity

necesitar to need

negativo/a negative

negociar to negotiate

negocio business; **administración** (*f.*) **de negocios** business administration

negrita: en negrita boldface

negro/a black (2)

nervioso/a nervous

nevar (ie) to snow; **está nevando** it's snowing (9); **nieva** it's snowing (9)

ni neither; nor; **ni... ni** neither . . . nor

nicaragüense *n., adj. m., f.* Nicaraguan (2)

nido nest; **nido familiar** parent's home (16)

nieto/a grandson, granddaughter (4)

ningún/ninguna none, no (not one, not any) (5)

niñez *f.* childhood

niño/a small child; boy/girl; **de niño/a** as a child

nivel *m.* level (15)

no no (1); **¡cómo no!** *interj.* of course! (6); **favor de no fumar** no smoking, please (9); **no beber y conducir** don't drink and drive (9); **no doblar** do not turn (9); **no entrar** do not enter (9); **no estacionar** no parking (9); **no fumar** no smoking (9); **no girar** do not turn (9); **no, gracias** no, thank you (6); **no hay de qué** you're welcome (5); **no hay que** + *inf.* you don't have to / it's not necessary to (*do something*) (12); **no pasar** do not enter (9); **no pisar (el césped)** stay off / do not walk on (the grass) (9); **no puedo** I can't (8); **no tirar basura** don't litter (9); **no vale la pena** it's not worth it; **si no es molestia** if it's not a bother (6)

noble *m.* noble, aristocrat; *adj.* noble

noche *f.* night; **buenas noches** good evening/night (1); **de la noche** at night (3); **por la noche** (*generally*) during the night (3); **toda la noche** all night (3)

Nochebuena Christmas Eve (7)

Nochevieja New Year's Eve (7)

nombrar to name

nombre *m.* name; **mi nombre es** my name is (1)

nominación *f.* nomination

nominar to nominate

nopalitos *pl. dish made with the leaves of prickly pears*

noreste *m.* northeast

normal normal

noroeste *m.* northwest

norte *m.* north

norteamericano/a *n., adj.* North American (2)

Noruega Norway

noruego/a *n., adj.* Norwegian

nos *d.o. pron.* us (6); *i.o. pron.* to/for us (7); *refl. pron.* ourselves; **se nos antoja/antojó** + *inf. / s. n.* we feel/felt like + ([*doing*] *something*) (9); **se me/te/le/nos/os/les antojan/antojaron** + *pl. n.* we feel/felt like + *pl. n.* (9)

nosotros/as *sub. pron.* we; *obj. of prep.* us

nota grade (*academic*); note; **nota de agradecimiento** thank-you note; **sacar (qu) buenas/malas notas** to get good/back grades

notar to note

noticia piece of news; *pl.* news

novecientos nine hundred

novela novel

noveno/a ninth

noventa ninety

noviazgo relationship (16); engagement (16)

noviembre *m.* November (1)

novio/a boyfriend/girlfriend (16); fiancé(e) (16); groom/bride (16)

nublado/a cloudy; **está nublado** it's cloudy (9)

núcleo nucleus

nuera daughter-in-law (4)

nuestro/a(s) *poss. adj.* our; *poss. pron.* our, of ours; **nuestro más sentido pésame** my/our deepest sympathies (16)

nueve nine; **son diez para las nueve** it's 8:50 (3); **son las nueve menos diez** it's 8:50 (3)

nuevo/a new (2); **Año Nuevo** New Year's (7); **¡feliz Año Nuevo!** happy New Year! (7); **Nueva York** New York

nuez *f.* (*pl.* **nueces**) nut; walnut

número number; shoe size (8); **¿cuál es tu número de teléfono?** what is your phone number? (1); **un número a la vez, por favor** one number at a time, please (1)

nunca never (3)

nutrición *f.* nutrition
nutriente *m.* nutrient
nutritivo/a nutritious

O

o or
objetivo/a objective
objeto object
obligación *f.* obligation
obligar (gu) to force
obligatorio/a obligatory
obra work; **obra de arte** piece, work of art (14); **obra de teatro** play (14)
obrero/a worker, laborer
observación *f.* observation
observador(a) observer
observar to observe
obtener (*like* **tener**) to obtain
océano ocean; **océano Atlántico** Atlantic Ocean; **océano Pacífico** Pacific Ocean
ochenta eighty
ocho eight
ochocientos/as eight hundred
octavo/a eighth
octubre *m.* October (1); **el quince de octubre** October fifteenth (1)
ocupación *f.* occupation
ocupado/a busy
ocupar to occupy
ocurrir to occur
odiar to hate
oeste *m.* west
ofensivo/a offensive; **volante** (*m., f.*) **ofensivo/a** offensive midfielder
oferta supply (15); offer (15)
oficial official
oficina office (1); **oficina de correos** post office
oficio trade (*profession*)
ofrecer (zc) to offer
oír *irreg.* to hear (5); to listen to (*music, the radio*) (5); **oye...** listen . . . (*command inform. s.*); **oiga...** listen . . . (*command form. s.*); **oigan...** listen . . . (*command form. pl.*)
ojalá (que) I hope (that)
ojo eye (8)
oleoducto oil pipeline
oler *irreg.* to smell
Olímpicos: Juegos (*pl.*) **Olímpicos (de Invierno/Verano)** (Winter/Summer) Olympics (12)
oliva olive; **aceite** (*m.*) **de oliva** olive oil; **color** (*m.*) **verde oliva** olive green
olla pot, pan
olor *m.* scent, odor
olvidar(se) to forget (9)
once eleven
onda wave
opción *f.* option
ópera opera (14)
operación *f.* operation
operático/a pertaining to opera

opinar to think; to have/express an opinion
opinión *f.* opinion; **en mi opinión...** in my opinion . . . (15)
oportunidad *f.* opportunity
oportuno/a opportune
optar (por) to opt (for)
optimista *m., f.* optimist; *adj.* optimistic (2)
opuesto/a opposite
oración *f.* sentence
orden *m.* order; *f.* order (*command, legal*); **a sus órdenes** at your (*form. s., pl.*) service
oreja ear (8)
orgánico/a organic; **desecho orgánico** organic waste
organismo organism; body
organización *f.* organization; **organización sin fines de lucro** nonprofit organization (15)
organizar (c) to organize
orgullo pride
orgulloso/a proud
oriental Oriental; Eastern
oriente *m.* east
origen *m.* origin
originario/a native
originarse to begin
orilla shore
oro gold
orquesta orchestra (14)
orquídea orchid
ortografía spelling
ortográfico/a *adj.* spelling; **error** (*m.*) **ortográfico** spelling mistake
os *d.o. pron.* (*Sp.*) you (*inform. pl.*) (6); *i.o. pron.* (*Sp.*) to/for you (*inform. pl.*) (7); *refl. pron.* (*Sp.*) yourselves (*inform. pl.*); **se os antoja/antojó** + *inf. / s. n.* you (*inform. pl.*) feel/felt like + ([*doing*] something) (9); **se os antojan/antojaron** + *pl. n.* you (*inform. pl.*) feel/felt like + *pl. n.* (9)
oscuro/a dark
oso (polar) (polar) bear (13)
ostra oyster
otoño autumn, fall (1)
otro/a other, another; **otra vez** again
ozono ozone

P

pabellón (*m.*) **criollo** *Venezuelan rice and beans dish*
paciencia patience
paciente *m., f.* patient
pacífico/a *adj.* Pacific; **océano Pacífico** Pacific Ocean
padecer (zc) to suffer
pádel *m.* paddle tennis
padrastro stepfather (4)
padre *m.* father (4); *pl.* parents (4); **Día** (*m.*) **de los Padres** Father's Day; **¡está padre!** that's cool! (8); **¡qué padre!** how cool! (8)
padrino godfather

pagar (gu) to pay
página page; **página web** web page (1)
país *m.* country (3); **Países Bajos** Netherlands; **País Vasco** Basque Country
paisaje *m.* scenery, landscape (9)
pájaro bird (13)
palabra word
palacio palace
palestino/a *n., adj.* Palestinian
paleta palette
pan *m.* bread (6); **pan tostado** toast
panadería bakery (6)
panameño/a *n., adj.* Panamanian (2)
panamericano/a Pan-American
panel (*m.*) **(solar)** (solar) panel
panorámico/a panoramic
pantalla monitor (10); screen (10)
pantalón *m.* pants; *pl.* pants (8); **pantalones cortos** shorts (8); **pantalones de campana** bell-bottoms
panteón *m.* mausoleum
papa potato (6); **papas fritas** french fries
papá *m.* father (4)
papel *m.* paper; role, part (*in a movie or play*) (14); **hoja de papel** sheet of paper (1); **interpretar un papel** to play a role/part (14)
paquete *m.* package
Paquistán *m.* Pakistan
paquistaní *n., adj. m., f.* Pakistani
par *m.* pair (*objects*)
para (intended) for (7); **para** + *inf.* in order to (*to do something*); **para mí** for me (7); for me (personally) (15); **para que** so that; **para servirle** at your (*form. s.*) service (10); **para ti** for you (*inform. s.*) (7); **servir (i, i) para** to be good at/for (*doing something*) (4); **son diez para las nueve** it's 8:50 (3); **son las nueve menos diez** it's 8:50 (3)
paradisíaco/a idyllic
paradójico/a paradoxical
paraguas *m. s., pl.* umbrella (8)
paraguayo/a *n., adj.* Paraguayan (2)
parapente *m.* paragliding
parar to stop
parásito parasite
parecer (zc) (*like* **gustar**) to seem (7); **parecerse (a)** to resemble; **¿qué te/le parece(n)** + *n./inf.*? how about (*inform. s. / form. s.*) . . . ? (6)
parecido/a (a) similar (to)
pared *f.* wall
pareja pair; partner (16); couple (16)
pariente *m., f.* relative (4)
París Paris
parlamentario/a parliamentary
parlante *m., f.* loudspeaker
parlar to chatter
parque *m.* park (5); **correr en el parque** to run in the park (3)
párrafo paragraph

parrilla grill

parte *f.* part; **de parte de** from; on behalf of; **¿de parte de quién?** may I ask who's calling?

participante *m., f.* participant

participar to participate

particular: en particular in particular

partido game (12); match (12)

partir: a partir de as of, since

pasado past; **estar** (*irreg.*) **pasado/a de moda** to be unfashionable (8)

pasado/a last; **año pasado** last year; **semana pasada** last week

pasaporte *m.* passport (9)

pasar to spend (*time*); to happen; **lo pasé bien/mal** I had a good/bad time (7); **no pasar** do not enter (9); **pasa/pase(n)** come in / go ahead (*command inform. s. / form. s., pl.*) (8); **pasar la aspiradora** to vacuum (11); **pasar por** to go through; **pasar un buen rato** to have a good time; **pasarlo bien/mal** to have a good/bad time (7); **¿puedo pasar?** excuse me / may I pass by/enter? (8); **¿qué te/le pasa?** what's happening with you? (*inform. s. / form. s.*) (1); what's the matter? (1)

pasatiempo pastime

Pascua Easter (7); **Domingo de Pascua** Easter Sunday; **Pascua de Resurrección** Easter (7); **Pascua Florida** Easter (7)

pasear to tale a walk, stroll; **sacar** (**qu**) **a pasear** to walk (*dog*)

paseo walk, trip (9); **dar** (*irreg.*) **un paseo** to take a walk (9)

pasillo hallway (11)

paso step; **dar** (*irreg.*) **un paso** to take a step

pasta pasta (6)

pastel *m.* pastry; cake

pastilla pill

patada kick

patata potato (*Sp.*)

paterno/a paternal

patinador(a) skater

patinaje *m.* skating; **patinaje sobre el hielo** ice skating

patinar to skate; **patinar sobre el hielo** to ice skate

patines *m. pl.* skates (12)

patineta skateboard (12); **andar** (*irreg.*) **en patineta** to skateboard (12)

patología disease

patrocinador(a) sponsor

patrocinar to sponsor

paz *f.* peace (15)

pecho chest (8)

pechuga breast

pedacito small piece

pedir (i, i) to ask for (4); to order

pedo *n.* fart

pedorrear to fart

peer (y) to fart

pegar (gu) to paste (10); **pegarse** to bump

peinarse to brush/comb one's hair (5)

película movie; film (2); **película de acción** action movie; **película de terror** horror film (2)

peligro danger (13); **especie** (*f.*) **en peligro de extinción** endangered species

peligroso/a dangerous (15)

pelo hair (2)

pelota ball (12)

pelotero/a baseball player

peluquería (hair) salon

pena embarrassment; shame; **(no) vale la pena** it's (not) worth it

peña *venue for musical and other artistic performances (S.A.)*

pendiente *m.* earring (8); *adj.* pending

pensamiento thought

pensar (ie) (en) to think (about) (12); **pensar** + *inf.* to intend, plan to (*do something*)

peor worse (4)

pepino cucumber (6)

pequeño/a small (2)

pera pear

percusionista *m., f.* percussionist

perdedor(a) loser

perder (ie) to lose; to miss

perdón excuse me (8)

perdonar to forgive; **perdona/perdone(n)** excuse me (*command inform. s. / form. s., pl.*) (8)

perejil *m.* parsley (6)

perezoso/a lazy (2)

perfeccionar to perfect

perfecto/a perfect

perfil *m.* profile

perfume *m.* perfume

perico parakeet

perímetro perimeter

periódico newspaper; **leer** (**y**) **el periódico** to read the newspaper (3)

periodista *m., f.* journalist (4)

periodo period (*of time*)

permiso permission; **con permiso** excuse me (8)

permitir to permit

pernoctar to spend the night

pero *conj.* but

perro dog (4)

perseguir (*like* **seguir**) to chase; to pursue

persona person; *pl.* people

personaje *m.* character (*in a movie, play or novel*) (14); celebrity, well-known person (14)

personalidad *f.* personality

perspectiva perspective

pertenecer (zc) (a) to belong (to)

pertenencias *pl.* belongings

peruano/a *n., adj.* Peruvian (2)

pesado/a boring; difficult; heavy; **¡qué pesado!** how annoying! (8)

pésame: dar (*irreg.*) **el pésame** to give one's condolences; **mi/nuestro más sentido pésame** my/our deepest sympathies (16); **te/le/les doy/damos el pésame** my/our condolences (16)

pesar to weigh; **a pesar de** in spite of, despite

pesas weights (12); **levantar pesas** to lift weights (12)

pesca fishing

pescadería fish market (6)

pescado fish (*food*) (6)

pesero bus (*Mex.*)

pesimismo pessimism

pesimista *m., f.* pessimist; *adj.* pessimistic (2)

pésimo/a awful; **¡qué pésimo!** that's awful! (8)

peso weight; **aumento de peso** weight gain; **bajar de peso** to lose weight (12) **subir de peso** to gain weight (12)

petróleo petroleum, oil

petrolero/a *adj.* oil; petroleum

pez *m.* (*pl.* **peces**) fish (*animal*) (4)

pianista *m., f.* pianist

picadura bite; sting

picante spicy (6)

picar (qu) to bite; to chop, mince

pico peak; beak; **pico de gallo** *uncooked salsa made of chopped tomato, onion, and jalapeños*

pie *m.* foot (8); **a pie** on foot

piel *f.* skin (2)

pierna leg (8)

pijama *m.* pijama (8)

pimienta pepper (*spice*) (6)

pimiento pepper

pinchar to click (*computer, Sp.*)

pingüino penguin (13)

pinta appearance; **tener** (*irreg.*) **buena/ mala pinta** to have a good/bad appearance

pintar to pain

pinto: gallo pinto *rice and beans dish of Nicaragua and Costa Rica*

pintor(a) painter (4)

pintura paint; painting (14)

piña pineapple (6)

pirámide *f.* pyramid

piraña piranha

pisar to step on; **no pisar (el césped)** stay off / do not walk on (the grass) (9)

piscina swimming pool (11)

piso floor; apartment (*Sp.*)

pista clue

pitisalé *m.* salted meat of Dominican Republic and Haiti

pizarra chalkboard (1); whiteboard (1)

placer *m.* pleasure; **es un placer** nice to meet you (10); it's a pleasure (10)

plagio plagiarism

plan *m.* plan

plancha: a la plancha grilled (6)

planeación *f.* planning
planear to plan
planeta (*m.*) **(Tierra)** planet (Earth) (13)
planificación *f.* planning; **planificación familiar** family planning
planta plant; floor; **planta baja** ground floor; **primera/segunda/tercera planta** second/third/fourth floor (11)
plástico plastic
plata silver
plataforma platform
plátano banana (*Mex.*) (6); plantain
platillo dish
plato dish; plate (6); **lavar los platos** to wash dishes (4); **plato principal** main course
playa beach (2)
plaza plaza (5)
plazo: a largo plazo in the long run
pliegue *m.* pleat
pluma pen
población *f.* population
pobre poor (2)
pobreza poverty (15)
poco/a few; (a) little; **un poco (de)** a little bit (of)
poder *n. m.* power
poder *irreg.* to be able, can (3); **¿en qué puedo servirle(s)?** how may I help you (*form. s., pl.*)? (10); **¿me puede comunicar con... ?** can you connect me with . . . ?; **no puedo** I can't (8); **¿puede repetir... ?** can you (*form. s.*) repeat . . . ? (1); **¿puedo pasar?** excuse me; may I pass by/enter? (8); **sí, se puede** yes we can; it can be done (12)
poema *m.* poem
poesía poetry (14)
polar polar; **casquete** (*m.*) **polar** polar cap; **oso polar** polar bear
polémico/a controversial
policía *m., f.* police officer (4); *f.* police (*force*); **mujer** (*f.*) **policía** policewoman
polinesio/a Polynesian
política politics; policy
político/a *n.* politician (15); *adj.* political; **ciencias** (*pl.*) **políticas** political science; **proceso político** political process (15)
pollo chicken (6)
pólvora powder
pomelo grapefruit (*Sp., Arg.*)
poner *irreg.* (*p.p.* **puesto**) to put (5); to place; **poner atención** to pay attention; **poner en duda** to call into question; **poner énfasis** to emphasize; **ponerse** to put on (*an article of clothing*) (5); **ponerse** + *adj.* to become/get + *adj.* (5); **ponerse contento/a** to become happy (5); **ponerse los lentes / los lentes de contacto** to put on glasses/ contacts (5)
pop *adj.* pop (*music, culture*) (14)
popularizar (c) to make popular

por about; because of; through; for; by; **baje/suba por esta calle** go down/up this street (*command form. s.*) (5); **gracias por** + *n./verb* thank you for . . . (5); **por ejemplo** for example; **por equivocación** by mistake; **por favor** please; **por fin** finally; **por la mañana** (*generally*) during the morning (3); **por la noche** (*generally*) during the night (3); **por la tarde** (*generally*) during the afternoon/evening (3); **por primera vez** the first time; **¿por qué?** why? (2); **por si acaso** just in case; **¡por supuesto!** of course! (6); **un número / una letra a la vez, por favor** one number / letter at a time, please (1)
porcentaje *m.* percentage
porción *f.* portion; serving
porque because
portarse to behave
portátil: (computadora) portátil laptop (computer)
portero/a building manager; doorman
portuario/a *adj.* port
portugués *m.* Portuguese (*language*)
portugués (*pl.* **portugueses**), **portuguesa** *n., adj.* Portuguese
porvenir *m.* future
posada inn
posgrado graduate (study)
posibilidad *f.* possibility
posible possible
posición *f.* position
posicionamiento: Sistema (*m.*) **de Posicionamiento Global (SPG)** Global Positioning System (GPS)
positivo/a positive
posponer (*like* **poner**) (*p.p.* **pospuesto**) to postpone
posgrado (*or* **postgrado**) graduate (study)
postre *m.* dessert (6)
potencial potential
práctica practice
practicar (qu) to practice (3); **practicar yoga** to do yoga (3); **practicar un deporte** to play a sport (3)
práctico/a practical
precariedad *f.* uncertainty
precaución *f.* precaution
precio price
precioso/a pretty (2)
preciso/a precise
precolombino/a Pre-Columbian
predador *m.* predator
predicción *f.* prediction
predisposición *f.* predisposition
preferencia preference
preferido/a preferred; favorite
preferir (ie, i) to prefer
pregunta question
preguntar to ask (7)
prehispánico/a pre-Hispanic
premio prize

prenda article of clothing
prender to turn on (*appliance*)
prensa: agencia de prensa press agency
preocupado/a worried
preocupar(se) to worry
preparación *f.* preparation; training
preparar (el desayuno / el almuerzo / la cena) to prepare (breakfast/lunch/ dinner) (4); **prepararse** to get ready, prepare oneself
preparativos *pl.* preparations
preposición *f. gram.* preposition
presentación *f.* presentation
presentador(a) presenter
presentar to present; to introduce; **quiero presentarle(s) a...** I'd like you (*form. s., pl.*) to meet . . . (10); **quiero presentarte a...** I'd like you (*inform. s.*) to meet . . . (10)
preservar to preserve
presidencia presidency
presidente, presidenta president
prestar to lend; **prestar atención** to pay attention; **prestarse a** to lend oneself to
prestigioso/a prestigious
presupuesto budget
pretérito *gram.* preterite
prevención *f.* prevention
prevenir (*like* **venir**) to warn
previo/a previous, prior
prieto/a dark
primaria: escuela primaria elementary school
primavera spring (*season*) (1)
primer, primero/a first; **por primera vez** the first time; **primer piso / primera planta** second floor (11); **primero de mayo** first of May (1)
primo/a cousin (4)
princesa princess
principal main; **plato principal** main course (*of a meal*)
príncipe *m.* prince
principio *n.* beginning
prisa: darse (*irreg.*) **prisa** to hurry; **tener** (*irreg.*) **prisa** to be in a hurry
privado/a private; **escuela privada** private school
privatización *f.* privatization
privatizar (c) to privatize
privilegiado/a privileged
probador(a) tester
probar (ue) to try; to test; **probarse** to try on (8)
problema *m.* problem; **problema social** social problem (15)
problemático/a problematic
proceloso/a stormy
procesar to process
procesión *f.* procession
proceso process; **proceso político** political process (15)
producción *f.* production
producir (*like* **conducir**) to produce

producto product; **productos lácteos** dairy products (6)

profesión *f.* profession (4); **¿cuál es tu/su profesión?** what is your (*inform. s. / form. s.*) profession? (4)

profesional profession

profesor(a) professor (1)

profundidad *f.* depth

profundo/a deep

progenitor(a) parent

programa *m.* program

programador(a) programmer (10)

progresar to progress

progresivo/a progressive

progreso progress

prohibir (prohíbo) to prohibit

promedio average

prometedor(a) promising

prometer to promise

promoción *f.* promotion

promover (ue) to promote

pronombre *m. gram.* pronoun

pronóstico del tiempo weather forecast

pronto soon; **hasta pronto** see you soon (1)

propiedad *f.* property

propio/a own, one's own

proponer (*like* **poner**) (*p.p.* **propuesto**) to propose

propósito purpose

prosperidad *f.* prosperity

protagonista *m., f.* protagonist (14)

protección *f.* protection

protector(a) protective

proteger (j) to protect (13)

proteína protein

protestar to protest

provecho: ¡buen provecho! enjoy your meal! (6)

proveer (y) (*p.p.* **proveído**) to provide

provincia province

provisión *f.* provision; *pl.* supplies

provocar (qu) to provoke

próximo/a next

proyecto project

proyector *m.* projector (1)

prueba quiz

psicología psychology (1)

psicólogo/a psychologist (4)

psiquiatra *m., f.* psychiatrist

pub *m.* pub, bar

publicar (qu) to publish

publicidad *f.* publicity

público/a public; **transporte** (*m.*) **público** public transportation (5)

pueblo town (5)

puente *m.* bridge (5)

puerco pig; pork (6)

puerta door (1)

puertorriqueño/a *n., adj.* Puerto Rican (2)

pues *conj.* well; since

puesto job; position; stand; **conseguir** (*like* **seguir**) **un puesto** to get a job/position (10)

pulmón *m.* lung

pulpa pulp

pulpería small grocery store

pulsera bracelet (8)

punto point; **en el punto de mira** in the crosshairs; **punto com** dot com (*in an email address*) (1)

puñado handful

purificador(a) purifying

purificar(se) (qu) to purify (oneself)

puro/a pure; **¡pura vida!** cool! (8)

Q

que that, which; who; **hasta que** *conj.* until; **que le(s) vaya bien** may things go well for you (*form. s., pl.*) (12); **¡que tenga(s) un buen día!** have (*form. s. / inform. s.*) a good day! (12); **¡que tenga(s) un buen fin de semana!** have (*form. s. / inform. s.*) a nice weekend!; **¡que tenga(s) una buena tarde!** have (*form. s. / inform. s.*) a nice afternoon!; **que yo sepa** as far as I know; **ya que** since

¿qué? what? (2); which?; **¿a qué hora... ?** at what time . . .? (3); **¿a qué se dedica?** what do you (*form. s.*) do (*occupation*)? (4); **¿a qué te dedicas?** what do you (*inform. s.*) do (*occupation*)? (4); **¿en qué puedo servirle(s)?** how may I help you (*form. s., pl.*)? (10); **¿qué estudias?** what do you study?; what's your major? (1); **¿qué hora es?** what time is it? (3); **¿qué tal?** how are you? (1); **¿qué te/le parece(n)** + *n./inf.*? how about (*inform. s. / form. s.*) . . . ? (6); **¿qué te pasa?** what's happening with you (*inform. s.*)?; what's the matter? (1); **¿qué tiempo hace?** what's the weather like? (9)

¡qué... ! what . . . !; **¡qué** + *adj.*! how + *adj.*! (4); **¡qué** + *adj.* + *n.*! what + *adj.* + *n.*! (4); **¡qué** + *n.*! how/what + *n.*! (4); **¡qué aburrido!** how boring! (8); **¡qué bárbaro!** how cool! (8), awesome!; **¡qué bien!** how cool! (8); **¡qué bonita familia!** what a beautiful family! (4); **¡qué buena idea!** what a good idea!; **¡qué calor!** it's so hot!; **¡qué cara!** what nerve!; **¡qué chévere!** how cool! (8); **¡qué chido!** how cool! (8); **¡qué chulo!** how cool! (8); **¡qué coraje!** how frustrating/annoying! (4); **¡qué emoción!** how exciting!; **¡qué estupendo!** how cool! (8); **¡qué fenomenal!** how cool! (8); **¡qué feo/a!** how ugly! (4); **¡qué frío!** how cold! (4); **¡qué golazo!** what a goal!; **¡qué guapo/a!** how handsome/beautiful! (4); **¡qué guay!** how cool! (8); **¡qué lindo/a!** how cute/pretty! (4); **¡qué lío!** what a mess! (4); **¡qué malo/a!** that's terrible! (8); **¡qué padre!** how cool! (8); **¡qué pesado!** what a pain!, how annoying! (4); **¡qué pésimo!** that's awful! (8); **¡qué poca vergüenza!** what nerve!; **¡qué**

rabia! how frustrating/annoying! (4); **¡qué rico/a!** how delicious! (4); **¡qué vergüenza!** how embarrassing!

quechua *m.* Quechua (*language*)

quedar to remain, to be left; to be located; **¿dónde queda... ?** where is . . . ? (5); **queda a la derecha/izquierda** it's on the right/left (5); **queda al lado de / detrás de / enfrente de / en la esquina de... y ...** it's next to / behind / facing, in front of / on the corner of . . . and . . . (5); **quedarle** to fit (8); **quedarse** to stay (5)

quehacer *m.* chore

quemadura *n.* burn; **quemadura de sol** sunburn (9)

quemar to burn

querer *irreg.* to want (4); **querer** + *inf.* to want (*to do something*) (4); to love; **¿quiere(s)** + *n./inf.*? would you (*form. s. / inform. s.*) like . . . ? (6); **quiero presentarle(s) a...** I'd like you (*form. s., pl.*) to meet . . . (10); **quisiera** + *inf.* I would like (*to do something*) (10)

querido/a dear; **ser** (*m.*) **querido** loved one

queso cheese (6)

quetzal *m.* quetzal bird

quiché *adj. m., f.* of or pertaining to the Quiche Mayan group of Guatemala

quichua *n. m., f.* Quechua

¿quién(es)? who? (2); whom?; **¿de parte de quién?** may I ask who's calling?

quieto/a calm, still

química chemistry (1)

quince fifteen; **el quince de octubre** October fifteenth (1)

quinceañera *15th birthday celebration for girls* (7); *young woman celebrating her fifteenth birthday*

quinientos/as five hundred

quinta farm; country house

quinto/a fifth

quitar(se) to remove, take off

quizá(s) *adv.* perhaps, maybe (14)

R

rabia anger; fury; **¡qué rabia!** how frustrating/annoying!

racismo racism (15)

radio *f.* radio (*medium*)

raíz *f.* (*pl.* **raíces**) root; **a raíz de** as a result of; **bienes** (*m. pl.*) **raíces** real estate; **agente** (*m., f.*) **de bienes raíces** real estate agent

rama branch

ramo: Domingo de Ramos Palm Sunday

rana frog

rancho ranch

rango rank

rap *m.* rap music

rapanui *m. language of the Rapa Nui people of Easter Island*

rapero/a rapper

rapidez *f.* (*pl.* **rapideces**) speed

rápido *adv.* quickly
rápido/a fast (2); **comida rápida** fast food
raqueta racket (12)
rarámuri *m., f.* of or pertaining to the Tarahumara people of northwestern Mexico
raro/a strange
rascacielos *m. s., pl.* skyscraper (5)
rastafari *adj. m., f.* Rastafarian
ratificar (qu) to ratify
rato while, short time; **pasar un buen rato** to have a good time
ratón *m.* mouse (10)
raza race
razón *f.* reason; **no tener** (*irreg.*) **razón** to be wrong; **tener** (*irreg.*) **razón** to be right
razonable reasonable
reacción *f.* reaction
reaccionar to react
real royal; real
realidad *f.* reality
realismo realism
realizar (c) to achieve, attain
rebaja sale (8); **estar** (*irreg.*) **de rebajas** on sale, at a reduced price
rebelde *m., f.* rebel
rebeldía rebellion
recalar en to end up at
recaudar fondos to raise funds
recepción *f.* reception
receta recipe
rechazar (c) to reject
rechazo rejection
recibir to receive
reciclaje *m.* recycling (13)
reciclar to recycle (13)
recién *adj.* recent
recinto (universitario) campus
recipiente *m.* recipient
reclutar to recruit
recoger (j) to pick up
recolectar to gather; to harvest
recomendable recommendable
recomendación *f.* recommendation
recomendar (ie) to recommend (12)
reconocer (zc) to recognize
reconocido/a famous
reconocimiento recognition
reconstrucción *f.* reconstruction
récord *adj. m., f.* record
recordar (ue) to remember
recordatorio/a: mensaje (*m.*) **recordatorio** reminder
recorrer to traverse
recorrido tour; **hacer** (*irreg.*) **un recorrido** to take a trip / go on a tour (9)
recreación *f.* recreation
recrear to recreate
recto/a straight; **siga recto** go straight (*command form. s.*) (5)
recuerdo memory; souvenir (9)
recuperar to recuperate

recurrir to turn to; to resort to
recurso resource; **recurso natural** natural resource (13)
red *f.* network; Internet; **red social** social network (10)
reducir (like **conducir**) to reduce
reelección *f.* reelection
reelegir (i, i) (j) to reelect
reescribir (*p.p.* **reescrito**) to rewrite
referencia reference
referéndum *m.* referendum
referirse (ie, i) (a) to refer (to)
reflejar to reflect
reforma reform
refrán *m.* saying, proverb
refresco soda (6)
refugio refuge
regalar to give as a gift (7)
regalo gift
regañar to scold
reggae *m.* reggae
reggaetón *m.* reggaeton
región *f.* region
registrarse to register; to check in
regla rule
regresar to return (3)
regreso return
rehusar (rehúso) to refuse
reina queen
reintroducir (like **conducir**) to reintroduce
reírse (me río, i) (de) to laugh (about)
relación *f.* relationship (16); **en una relación** together (16); in a relationship (16); **relaciones internacionales** international relations (1)
relacionado/a (con) related (to)
relajante relaxing
relajar(se) to relax
relativamente relatively
relevo: generación (*f.*) **de relevo** upcoming generation
religión *f.* religion
religioso/a religious
relleno/a stuffed (*culin.*)
reloj *m.* clock (1); watch (1)
remoto/a remote
remover (ue) to stir
remunerado/a remunerated
renegar (ie) (gu) de to reject
renombre *m.* renown
renovación *f.* renovation
renovar (ue) to renovate
renta rent
rentar to rent
renunciar (a) to resign
repartir to deliver; to distribute
repelente *m.* repellent
repente: de repente suddenly
repetir (i, i) to repeat (4); **¿puede repetir... ?** can you (*form. s.*) repeat . . . ? (1)
repleto/a full
reportaje *m.* report
reportar to report

representante *m., f.* representative; *adj.* representative
representar to represent
represión *f.* repression
reprochar to reproach
reproducción *f.* reproduction
reproducir (like **conducir**) to reproduce
reptil *m.* reptile
república republic; **República Dominicana** Dominican Republic
requerir (ie, i) to require
requisito requirement
resentido/a resentful; bitter
reserva reserve; reservation
reservado/a reserved (2)
resfriado *n.* cold (*illness*) (12)
residencia residence
residente *m., f.* resident; *adj.* resident
residir to reside
residuo waste
resistencia resistance
resistir to resist
resolver (ue) (*p.p.* **resuelto**) to resolve
respecto: al respecto on this/that matter
respetar to respect
respeto respect
respetuoso/a respectful
responder to respond
responsabilidad *f.* responsibility
responsabilizarse (c) to take responsibility (16)
responsable responsible
respuesta answer
restar (*like* **gustar**) to remain, to be left
restaurante *m.* restaurant (5); **administración** (*f.*) **de restaurantes** restaurant management
resto rest
resultado result
resumen *m.* (*pl.* **resúmenes**) summary
resumir to summarize
resurrección *f.* resurrection; **Pascua de Resurrección** Easter (7)
retirarse to go away; to go to bed
reto challenge
retocado/a retouched
retrasar to delay
retraso delay
retrato portrait
reunión *f.* meeting
reunirse (me reúno) (con) to meet (with); to get together (with)
revelar to reveal
revisar to review
revisión *f.* revision
revista magazine
revolución *f.* revolution
rey *m.* king; **Día** (*m.*) **de los Reyes Magos** Three Kings Day; Epiphany (Adoration of the Magi) (7)
rico/a rich (2); delicious; **¡qué rico/a!** how delicious! (4)
ridículo/a ridiculous
riesgo risk

río river
riqueza richness
risa laughter
ritmo rhythm
rito rite; ritual
ritual *m.* ritual
rival *m.* rival
robar to rob
rock rock (*music*) (14)
rocoso/a rocky
rodaje *m.* filming, shooting (*movie*)
rodar to film, shoot (*movie*)
rodeado/a (de) surrounded (by)
rodilla knee (8)
rodillera knee pad/guard
rojo/a red (2)
rol *m.* role
romance *m.* romance
romántico/a romantic
romper(se) (*p.p.* **roto**) to break (9); **romper con** to break up with (16)
ropa clothes, clothing; **ropa interior** underwear (8); **lavar la ropa** to wash clothes (4)
rosado/a pink (2)
rostro face
roto/a (*p.p. of* **romper**) broken
rubio/a blond (2)
rudo/a rough
ruido noise (5)
ruinas *pl.* ruins
rural rural (5)
ruso/a *n., adj.* Russian
ruta route
rutina (diaria) (daily) routine

S

sábado Saturday (3)
sabana savannah
saber *irreg.* to know (5); **saber** + *inf.* to know how to (*do something*); **que yo sepa** as far as I know
sabroso/a tasty
sacar (**qu**) to take out, withdraw; **sacar a pasear** to walk (*dog*); **sacar buenas/malas notas** to get good/bad grades; **sacar dinero** to withdraw money; **sacar fotos** to take photos; **sacar la basura** to take out the trash (11); **sacar la lotería** to win the lottery; **sacar una maestría / un doctorado** to get a master's/doctorate (degree)
saco suit jacket
sacudir to dust (11)
safari: ir (*irreg.*) **de safari** to go on a safari
sagrado/a sacred
sal *f.* salt (6)
sala living room; **sala de clase** classroom; **sala de justicia** courtroom
salado/a *adj.* salt, salty; **agua** (*f., but* **el agua**) **salada** salt water
salar *m.* salt flat
salario salary
salir *irreg.* to leave (*a place*) (5); to go out (5); **salir con** to date

salmón *m.* salmon
salón *m.* living room (11); **salón de clase** classroom (1)
salsa salsa; sauce (6)
saltar to jump
salto waterfall
salud *f.* health
saludable healthy
saludar to greet
saludo greeting
salvadoreño/a *n., adj.* Salvadoran (2)
san, santo/a *n.* saint; **Día** (*m.*) **de Todos los Santos** All Saints' Day; **Semana Santa** Holy Week (7)
sandalias sandals (8)
sándwich *m.* sandwich
saneamiento sanitation
sano/a healthy
sapo toad (13)
satisfactorio/a satisfactory
se *refl. pron.* yourself (*form.*); himself/herself; itself; yourselves (*form. Sp.; inform./form. elsewhere*); themselves
secar(se) (**qu**) to dry (oneself)
sección *f.* section
seco/a dry
secretario/a secretary (10)
sector *m.* sector
secuela effect, consequence
secundario/a secondary; **escuela secundaria** high school
sed *f.* thirst; **tener** (*irreg.*) **sed** to be thirsty
sedentario/a sedentary
segmento segment
seguido/a one after the other
seguir (**i, i**) (**g**) to follow (4); to continue; to keep on going; **siga derecho/recto** go / keep going / continue straight (*command form. s.*) (5); **siga hasta llegar a (la esquina de)...** go / keep going / continue (*command form. s.*) until you reach (the corner of) . . . (5)
según according to
segundo *n.* second
segundo/a second; **la segunda planta / piso** the third floor (11)
seguridad *f.* safety (15); security (15)
seguro *n.* insurance; **agencia de seguros** insurance agency; **agente** (*m., f.*) **de seguros** insurance agent
seguro/a sure
seis six
seiscientos/as six hundred
selección *f.* selection; team
seleccionar to select, choose
selva jungle (13)
semana week; **día** (*m.*) **de entre semana** weekday; **fin** (*m.*) **de semana** weekend (3); **¡que tenga(s) un buen fin de semana!** have (*form. s. / inform. s.*) a nice weekend!; **semana pasada** last week; **Semana Santa** Holy Week (7); **una vez a la semana** once a week

sembrar (**ie**) to sow, plant
semejante similar
semejanza similarity
semifinal *f.* semifinal
senado senate
sencillez *f.* simplicity
sencillo/a simple
senderismo: hacer (*irreg.*) **senderismo** to go hiking
sendero path
sentarse (**ie**) to sit down (5); **¡siéntate/ siénte(n)se!** sit down / have a seat (*command inform. s. / form. s., pl.*)! (11)
sentido *n.* sense
sentido/a *adj.* heartfelt; **mi/nuestro más sentido pésame** my/our deepest sympathies (16)
sentimental emotional
sentimiento emotion, feeling; **te/le/les acompaño/acompañamos en el sentimiento** you're (*inform. s. / form. s. / form. pl.*) in my/our thoughts (16)
sentir (**ie, i**) to regret; to feel sorry; **cuánto lo siento** I'm very sorry (16); **lo siento** I'm sorry (7); condolences (7); **sentirse** to feel (*an emotion*)
señal *f.* sign
señalar to mark; to point at
señor (Sr.) *m.* man; Mr.; sir
señora (Sra.) woman; Mrs.; ma'am
señorita (Srta.) young woman; Miss; Ms.
separar to separate
septiembre *m.* September (1)
sequía drought (13)
ser *m.* being; **ser querido** loved one
ser *irreg.* to be (1); **¿cuál es la fecha de hoy?** what is today's date? (1); **¿de dónde eres/ es?** where are you (*inform. s. / form. s.*) from? (1); **¿de qué color es?** what color is it? (2); **eres** you are (*inform. s.*) (1); **es** he/ she is / you (*inform. s.*) are (1); **es a la(s)...** it's at . . . (3); **es la una** it's 1:00 (3); **es la una y media** it's 1:30 (3); **es medianoche** it's midnight (3); **es mediodía** it's noon (3); **hoy es...** today is . . . (1); **mi nombre es** my name is (1); **¿qué hora es?** what time is it? (3); **ser aficionado/a (a)** to be a fan (of); **ser bienvenido/a(s)** to be welcome (11); **si no es molestia** if it's not a bother (6); **somos** we are (1); **son** you (*form. pl.*) / they are; **son diez para las nueve** it's 8:50 (3); **son las doce del día** it's noon; **son las dos y cuarto** it's 2:15 (3); **son las nueve menos diez** it's 8:50 (3); **soy** I am (1); **soy de...** I'm from . . . (1); **Ud. es (siempre) bienvenido/a** you (*form. s.*) are always welcome (11)
serie *f.* series
serio/a serious (2)
servicio service (9)
servilleta napkin (6)
servir (**i, i**) to serve (4); to be useful (4); to work (function) (4); **¿en qué puedo**

servirle(s)? how may I help you (*form. s., pl.*)? (10); **para servirle** at your (*form. s.*) service (10); **servir para** to be good at/for (*doing something*) (4); **¡sírvete/ sírva(n)se!** help yourself (*command inform. s. / form. s., pl.*)! (11)

sesenta sixty

setenta seventy

sexo sex

shorts *m. pl.* shorts

si if; **si no es molestia** if it's not a bother (6)

sí yes (1); **¡claro que sí!** *interj.* of course! (6); **sí, gracias** yes, please (5); **sí, se puede** yes, we can / yes, it can be done (12)

siempre always (3); **Ud. es (siempre) bienvenido/a** you (*form. s.*) are always welcome (11)

sierra mountain

siete seven

siglo century

significado meaning

significar (qu) to mean; to signify

siguiente following

silla chair (1)

sillón *m.* armchair (11)

simbólico/a symbolic

símbolo symbol

simpático/a nice (2)

simular to simulate

simultáneo/a simultaneous

sin without (7); **organización** (*f.*) **sin fines de lucro** nonprofit organization (15); **sin duda** without (any) doubt (14); **sin hogar** homeless; **sin igual** unequaled; **sin importar** regardless of

sincero/a sincere

sinfónica symphony

singular *m. gram.* singular

sino (but) rather; **sino que** *conj.* but (rather)

sinónimo synonym

síntoma *m.* symptom (12)

sistema *m.* system; **Sistema de Posicionamiento Global (SPG)** Global Positioning System (GPS)

sitio site; place; **sitio web** website

situación *f.* situation

situado/a located

SMS *m.* text messaging (*abbrev. for Short Message Service*)

snorkel *m.* snorkeling (9); **hacer** (*irreg.*) **snorkel** to go snorkeling (9)

snowboard *m.* snowboard

sobre *prep.* about (7); on, above (7); on top of; over

sobremesa after-dinner conversation

sobresaliente outstanding

sobresalir (*like* **salir**) to stand out

sobrevivir to survive

sobrino/a nephew/niece (4)

social social; **problema** (*m.*) **social** social problem (15); **red** (*f.*) **social** social network; **trabajador(a) social** social worker (10)

sociedad *f.* society

socio/a member; partner

socioeconómico/a socioeconomic

sociología sociology

sociólogo/a sociologist (4)

sofá *m.* sofa (11)

sofisticado/a sophisticated

sol *m.* sun; **hace (mucho) sol** it's (very) sunny (9); **tomar el sol** to sunbathe (9); **quemadura de sol** sunburn (9)

solar solar; **bloqueador** (*m.*) **solar** sunscreen (9); **panel** (*m.*) **solar** solar panel

soldado soldier

soleado/a sunny

soledad *f.* solitude; loneliness

solemnidad *f.* solemnity

solicitar (un empleo / un trabajo) to apply for (a job) (10)

sólido/a solid

solista *m., f.* soloist

solo *adv.* only

solo/a *adj.* alone (2)

soltar (ue) to let loose

soltero/a single (*not married*) (16)

solución *f.* solution

solucionar to solve, resolve

sombrero hat (8)

sombrilla parasol

someter to submit

sondeo poll

sonido sound

sonoro/a sonorous

sonreír(se) (*like* **reír**) to smile

sonrisa smile

soñar (ue) (con) to dream (about) (3)

sopa soup (6)

soportar to stand

sorprender to surprise

sorprendido/a surprised

sospecha suspicion

sospechoso/a suspect, suspicious

sostenible sustainable (13)

sótano basement (11)

su(s) *poss. adj.* his, hers, its, your (*form. sing., pl.*), their

suave soft

subir (a) to go up; to get on (*a vehicle*); to raise; **suba (por esta calle)** go up (this street) (*command form. s.*) (5); **subir de peso** to gain weight (12)

subjuntivo *gram.* subjunctive

subrayar to underline

subyacer (zc) to underlie

suceder to happen; to occur

sucesión *f.* succession

sucio/a dirty

Sudáfrica South Africa

sudafricano/a *n., adj.* South African

Sudamérica South America

sudamericano/a *n., adj.* South American

sueco/a *n.* Swede; *adj.* Swedish

suegro/a father-in-law / mother-in-law (4)

sueldo salary

suelo floor; **lavar el suelo** to wash the floor (11)

sueño dream; **tener** (*irreg.*) **sueño** to be sleepy

suerte *f.* luck; **¡buena suerte!** good luck! (7); **dar** (*irreg.*) **buena suerte** to bring good luck; **le(s) deseo mucha suerte** I wish you (*form. s., pl.*) luck (12); **¡mucha suerte!** good luck! (12); **¡suerte!** good luck! (12)

suéter *m.* sweater (8)

suficiente enough

sufrimiento suffering

sufrir (de) to suffer (from) (12)

sugerencia suggestion

sugerir (ie, i) to suggest

sujetador *m.* bra (8)

sujeto *gram.* subject

sumar to add

sumergir (j) to immerse, submerge

suministrar to supply, provide

suministro supply

suntuoso/a sumptuous, luxurious

súper *m.* supermarket (2)

superficie *f.* surface

supermercado supermarket (2)

superstición *f.* superstition

supervisar to supervise

suponer(se) (*like* **poner**) (*p.p.* **supuesto**) to suppose

supremo/a supreme; **Corte** (*f.*) **Suprema** Supreme Court

suprimir to delete, erase

supuesto: ¡por supuesto! of course! (6)

sur *m.* south

sureño/a southern

surfear to surf (12)

surfista *m., f.* surfer

surrealista *adj. m., f.* surreal

suscripción *f.* subscription

suspender to suspend

suspenso suspense

sustantivo *gram.* noun

suyo/a(s) *poss. adj.* your (*form.*); his, her, its, their; *poss. pron.* (of) your, his, her, it, their; (of) yours (*form.*), hers, its, theirs

T

tabla table, chart

tableta tablet (10)

tachar to cross out

tacones (*m. pl.*) **(altos)** high-heeled shoes (8)

tailandés (pl. **tailandeses**), **tailandesa** *n., adj.* Thai

tal such, such a; **con tal de que** *conj.* provided that; **¿qué tal?** how are you? (1); **tal como** just as; **tal vez** maybe, perhaps (14)

tala de árboles tree cutting (13)

talar to cut down

talento talent; **agencia de talentos** talent agency

talentoso/a talented

talla clothing size (8)

taller *m.* workshop

tamal *m.* tamale

tamaño size

también also

tampoco neither, not either

tan *adv.* so; as; **tan... como** as . . . as; **tan pronto como** as soon as

tanto/a *adj.* as much, so much; such a; *pl.* so many; as many; **tanto/a(s)... como** as much/many . . . as; **tanto como** as much as

tapar to cover

tapir *m.* tapir (*large mammal of C.A. and S.A.*)

taquillero/a: una película taquillera box-office success (*film*)

tarahumara *n., adj. m., f.* Tarahumara (*see* **rarámuri**)

tardar to delay; to be late

tarde *f.* afternoon; *adv.* late; **buenas tardes** good afternoon (1); **de la tarde** in the afternoon/evening (3); **por la tarde** (*generally*) during the afternoon/evening (3); **¡que tenga(s) una buena tarde!** have (*form. s. / inform. s.*) a nice afternoon!

tarea homework (1); **hacer (irreg.) la tarea** to do homework (3)

tarjeta card (7); **tarjeta de memoria** memory card

tasa rate; **tasa de natalidad** birthrate

taxi *m.* taxi (5)

taxonómico/a taxonomical

taza coffee cup (6)

te *d.o. pron.* you (*inform. s.*) (6); *i.o. pron.* to/for you (*inform. s.*) (7); *refl. pron.* yourself (*inform. s.*); **¿Cómo te llamas?** What's your name? (1); **quiero presentarte a...** I'd like you (*inform. s.*) to meet . . . (10); **te acompaño/acompañamos en el dolor** I'm/we're with you in your time of pain (16); **te acompaño/acompañamos en el sentimiento** you're in my/our thoughts (16); **¿te gusta + activity?** do you like + *inf.*? (2); **te agradezco por...** I appreciate that you. . . (5); **te doy/ damos el pésame** my/our condolences (16); **te felicito/felicitamos** I/we congratulate you (7); **¿te gustaría + inf.?** would you like (*to do something*)? (9)

té *m.* tea

teatro theater (5); **obra de teatro** play (14)

techo roof (11)

teclado keyboard (10)

técnico/a *n.* technician; *adj.* technical

tecnología technology

tecnológico/a technological

tejo *Colombian sport played by throwing a metal plate or disk at a target to try to hit paper triangles filled with gunpowder*

tela cloth, fabric

telecomunicaciones *f. pl.* telecommunication

telefónico/a *adj.* telephone

teléfono (móvil) (cellular) telephone (10); **¿cuál es tu número de teléfono?** what is your phone number? (1); **hablar por teléfono** to talk on the phone (3)

telenovela soap opera

tele-secundaria: escuela tele-secundaria distance high school

televisión *f.* television (*medium*); **mirar la televisión** to watch television (3)

televisor *m.* television set (11)

temático/a themed

temer to fear

temperatura temperature

templado/a temperate

temporada season

temprano *adv.* early

tendencia tendency; trend (8)

tenedor *m.* fork (6)

tener *irreg.* to have (1); **¿cuántos años tiene(s)?** how old are you (*form. s. / inform. s.*)? (2); **no tener razón** to be wrong; **¡que tenga(s) un buen día** have (*form. s. / inform. s.*) a nice day!; **¡que tenga(s) un buen fin de semana!** have (*form. s. / inform. s.*) a nice weekend!; **¡que tenga(s) una buena tarde!** have (*form. s. / inform. s.*) a nice afternoon!; **tenemos** we have (1); **tener alergia a** to be allergic to; **tener buen aspecto** to look good; **tener buena/mala pinta** to have a good/bad appearance; **tener celos** to be jealous; **tener éxito** to be successful; **tener fama de** to be known for; **tener fiebre** to have a temperature/ fever; **tener ganas de + inf.** to feel like (*doing something*); **tener hambre** to be hungry; **tener miedo** to be afraid; **tener (mucho) frío** to be (very) cold; **tener náuseas** to feel nauseous; **tener prisa** to be in a hurry; **tener que + inf.** to have (*to do something*) (4); **tener razón** to be right; **tener sed** to be thirsty; **tener sueño** to be sleepy; **tener tos** to have a cough; **tener voz y voto** to have a say; **tengo** I have (1); **tengo + number + años** I'm + *number* + years old (2); **tiene** he/she has; you (*form s.*) have (1); **tienen** they/you (*form. pl.*) have (1); **tienes** you (*inform. s.*) have (1); **¿tiene(s) ganas de + n./inf.?** do you (*form. s. / inform. s.*) feel like . . . ? (6)

tenis *m.* tennis (12); *pl.* tennis shoes (8); **jugar (ue) (gu) tenis** to play tennis (12)

tenista *m., f.* tennis player

tequila *m.* tequila

tequilero/a *adj.* tequila

tercer(o/a) third; **la tercera planta / el tercer piso** the fourth floor (11)

terminación *f. gram.* ending

terminar to finish

término term

termita termite

terraza terrace (11)

terreno land

territorio territory

terror *m.* terror; **película de terror** horror movie

terrorismo terrorism

testamento will

testigo *m., f.* witness

textear to text (10)

textil *m.* textile

texto text; text message; **libro de texto** textbook

textura texture

ti *obj. of prep.* you (*inform. s.*); **para ti** for you (*inform. s.*) (7)

tibio/a lukewarm

tico/a *n., adj.* Costa Rican (*sl.*)

tiempo time; weather; **¿cuánto tiempo hace que + present tense?** how long have you (*done / been doing something*)? (13); **¿cuánto tiempo lleva(s) + pres. p.?** how long have you (*form. s. / inform. s.*) (*done / been doing something*)? (13); **hace buen/mal tiempo** it's good/bad weather (9); **mucho tiempo** a long time (13); **¿qué tiempo hace?** what's the weather like? (9); **tiempo libre** free time

tienda store (5); **tienda de abarrotes** grocery store; **tienda de abastos** grocery store

tierra earth, soil (13); **planeta (m.) Tierra** planet Earth (13)

tímido/a shy

tinta ink

tinto: vino tinto red wine (6)

tío/a uncle/aunt (4); *pl.* uncles and aunts

típico/a typical

tipo type, kind

tirado/a stranded

tiranía tyranny (15)

tirar to throw (away) (8); **no tirar basura** don't litter (9)

tirolina zip line; **bajar en tirolina** to go ziplining (9)

titulado/a graduate

titular *m.* headline

título title

tobillo ankle; **torcerse (ue) (c) (el tobillo)** to sprain (one's ankle) (12)

tocar (qu) to touch; **tocar la guitarra** to play the guitar (2); **tocar un instrumento** to play an instrument

todavía still

todo *n.* everything; everyone (3); all of us (3); **todo lo demás** everything else

todo/a *adj.* all (3); every; **Día (m.) de Todos los Santos** All Saints' Day; **toda la noche** all night (3); **toda la vida** all my/ your/his/her life, all our/your/their lives (13); **todo el día** all day (3); **todos los días** every day (3)

tolerancia tolerance

tolerante tolerant (16)

tomar to take; to drink; **tomar el sol** to sunbathe (9); **tomar una decisión** to make a decision

tomate *m.* tomato (6)

tonto/a silly, foolish

toparse con to run into

topografía topography

torcedura sprain (12)

torcerse (ue) (c) (el tobillo) to sprain (one's ankle) (12)

torero/a bullfighter

toronja grapefruit (*L.Am.*)

torpe clumsy

torre *f.* tower

torta cake (6); sandwich (*Mex.*)

tortilla potato omelet (*Sp.*); *thin unleavened cornmeal or flour pancake (Mex.)*

tortuga turtle (13)

tortuguero/a *adj.* turtle

tos *f.* cough (12); **jarabe** (*m.*) **para la tos** cough syrup; **tener** (*irreg.*) **tos** to have a cough

tostado/a toasted; **pan** (*m.*) **tostado** toast

tostar (ue) to toast

total total; **en total** in all

tóxico/a toxic

trabajador(a) *n.* worker; **trabajador(a) social** social worker (10); *adj.* hard-working (2)

trabajar to work (3)

trabajo work (2); job; **conseguir** (*like seguir*) **un trabajo** to get a job/position (10); **solicitar un trabajo** to apply for a job (10)

tradición *f.* tradition

tradicional traditional

traducción *f.* translation

traducir (*like* **conducir**) to translate

traer *irreg.* to bring (5); to carry (5)

tráfico traffic (5)

tragedia tragedy

traje *m.* suit (8); formal gown (8); **traje coctel** cocktail dress; **traje de baño** bathing suit (8)

trámite *m.* step; procedure

tranquilidad *f.* tranquility, peace, calm (5)

tranquilo/a tranquil (2), peaceful, calm

transbordador *m.* ferry

transecuatoriano/a trans-equatorial

transformar(se) to transform, change into

transición *f.* transition

tránsito traffic

transmitir to transmit

transnacional transnational

transparencia transparency

transportar to transport

transporte *m.* transportation (5); **medio/ modo de transporte** means of transportation; **transporte público** public transportation (5)

tras *prep.* after

trasfondo background

trasladarse to move

traslado transfer

tratamiento treatment

tratar de + *inf.* to try to (*do something*)

trato agreement; contract

traumático/a traumatic

través: a través de across; through; throughout

trece thirteen

treinta thirty

tremendo/a tremendous

tren *m.* train (9)

tres three

trescientos/as three hundred

tribunal *m.* court (10)

tributo tribute

trigo wheat

trigueño/a light brown (2)

trilingüe trilingual

triplicarse (qu) to triple

triste sad (2)

tristeza sadness

triunfo triumph

tropical tropical; **bosque** (*m.*) **tropical** rainforest (9)

trozo piece

tú *sub. pron.* you (*inform. s.*); **¿y tú?** and you (*inform. s.*)? (1)

tu(s) *poss. adj.* your (*inform. s.*)

tumba tomb

turbulento/a turbulent

turismo tourism; **turismo de aventura** adventure tourism (9)

turista *m., f.* tourist

turístico/a *adj.* tourist

turnarse to take turns

turquesa turquoise

tuyo/a(s) *poss. adj.* your (*inform. s.*); *poss. pron.* of yours (*inform. s.*)

tzotzil *m. Mayan language spoken by the Tzotzil people*

U

u or (*used instead of* **o** *before words beginning with* **o** *or* **ho**)

ubicación *f.* placement; location

último/a last, final; **la última moda** the latest fashion; **la última vez** the last time

ultramaratón *m.* ultra marathon

ultramaratonista *m., f.* ultra marathon runner

umbral *m.* threshold, beginning

un, uno/a one; *ind. art.* a, an (1); *pl.* some (1); **es la una** it's 1:00 (3); **es la una y media** it's 1:30 (3); **una vez** once (3); **una vez a la semana** once a week

único/a only; unique; **hijo/a único/a** only child

unidad *f.* unit

unido/a united; **Estados** (*pl.*) **Unidos** United States; **Naciones** (*f. pl.*) **Unidas** United Nations

unión *f.* union

unirse (a) to join

universidad *f.* university (1)

universitario/a *adj.* (of the) university; **recinto universitario** campus

urbano/a urban (5)

urgente urgent

uruguayo/a *n., adj.* Uruguayan (2)

usar to use (2); to wear

USB: memoria USB memory card/stick (10)

uso use

usted (Ud.) *sub. pron.* you (*form. s.*); *obj.* (*of prep.*) you (*form. s.*); **¡le damos la bienvenida a Ud.!** we welcome you (*form. s.*)! (11); **Ud. es (siempre) bienvenido/a** you are always welcome (11); **¿y usted?** and you? (1)

ustedes (Uds.) *sub. pron.* you (*form. pl.*); *obj.* (*of prep.*) you (*form. pl.*)

útil useful

utilidad *f.* usefulness, utility

utilizar (c) to use

uva grape

V

vacaciones *f. pl.* vacation

vacante *m.* opening

vainilla vanilla

valer *irreg.* to be worth; **(no) vale la pena** it's (not) worth it; **vale** OK (*Sp.*)

válido/a valid

valor *m.* value, worth

valorar to value, appreciate

vals *m.* waltz

vampírico/a *adj.* vampire

variación *f.* variation

variar (varío) to vary

variedad *f.* variety

varios/as several

varón *m.* son; boy; male

vasco/a *n., adj.* Basque; **País** (*m.*) **Vasco** Basque Country

vaso (drinking) glass (6)

vecindario neighborhood

vecino/a neighbor

vegetación *f.* vegetation

vegetariano/a vegetarian

vehículo vehicle

veinte twenty

veinticinco twenty-five

veinticuatro twenty-four

veintidós twenty-two

veintinueve twenty-nine

veintiocho twenty-eight

veintiséis twenty-six

veintitrés twenty-three

veintiún, veintiuno/a twenty-one

vela candle

velocidad *f.* speed

vencer (z) to defeat; to overcome

vendedor(a) vendor

vender to sell

veneno poison

venezolano/a *n., adj.* Venezuelan (2)

venir *irreg.* to come (5)

venta sale

ventaja advantage

ventana window (1)

ver *irreg.* (*p.p.* **visto**) to see (7); **a ver** let's see; **verse mal** to look bad

verano summer (1); **Juegos Olímpicos de Verano** Summer Olympics

verdad *f.* truth; **de verdad** really

verdadero/a true

verde green (2); **color** (*m.*) **verde oliva** olive green

verdulería greengrocer; vegetable market (6)

verdura vegetable (6)

vergüenza shame; embarrassment; **¡qué poca vergüenza!** what nerve!; **¡qué vergüenza!** how embarrassing!

vestido dress (8)

vestir (i, i) to dress (8); **vestirse** to get dressed (5)

vez *f.* (*pl.* **veces**) time (3); **a veces** sometimes, at times; **alguna vez** once; ever; **cada vez más** increasingly; **de vez en cuando** once in a while; **dos veces** twice (3); **la última vez** the last time; **otra vez** again; **por primera vez** the first time; **tal vez** maybe, perhaps (14); **un número / una letra a la vez, por favor** one number/letter at a time, please (1); **una vez** once (3); **una vez a la semana** once a week

viajar to travel (9)

viaje *m.* trip (9); **agencia de viajes** travel agency; **agente** (*m.*, *f.*) **de viajes** travel agent; **¡buen viaje!** bon voyage!, have a good trip! (7)

vicepresidente/a vice president

vida life; **llevar una vida activa** to lead an active life; **¡pura vida!** cool! (8); **toda la vida** all my/your/his/her life, all our/ your/their lives (13)

videojuego videogame; **jugar (ue) (gu) los videojuegos** to play videogames (3)

videollamada video call

viejo/a old (2)

viento wind; **hace (mucho) viento** it's (very) windy (9)

viernes *m.* Friday (3)

vinagre *m.* vinegar (6)

vínculo tie, link

vino (blanco, tinto) (white, red) wine (6)

violación *f.* violation; **violación de los derechos del autor** copyright violation

violar to violate; **violar la ley** to break the law; **violar los derechos humanos** to violate human rights

violencia violence (15)

violento/a violent

virgen *m.*, *f.* virgin

visión *f.* vision

visita visit (9)

visitante *m.*, *f.* visitor

visitar to visit (9)

vista view; **con vista a** with a view of

visto/a (*p.p. of* **ver**) seen

vitamina vitamin

viudo/a widowed (16), widower/widow

vivienda housing

vivir to live (3); **¿dónde vive(s)?** where do you (*form. s. / inform. s.*) live? (1); **vivo en** + *place* I live in + *place* (1)

vocabulario vocabulary

vocalista *m.*, *f.* vocalist

volante (*m.*, *f.*) **ofensivo/a** offensive midfielder

volar (ue) to fly

volcán *m.* volcano

voleibol *m.* volleyball (12); **jugar (ue) (gu) voleibol** to play volleyball (12)

voluminoso/a voluminous

voluntariado volunteerism

voluntario volunteer; **hacerse** (*irreg.*) **de voluntario** to volunteer

volver (ue) (*p.p.* **vuelto**) to return (3)

vomitar to vomit (12)

vómito *n.* vomit

vomitona *adj.* vomiting

vorazmente voraciously

vos *sub. pron.* you (*inform. s. C.A., S.A.*)

vosotros/as *sub. pron.* you (*inform. pl. Sp.*); *obj. of prep.* you (*inform. pl. Sp.*)

votar to vote

voto vote; **tener** (*irreg.*) **voz y voto** to have a say

voz *f.* (*pl.* **voces**) voice; **en voz alta** out loud; **tener** (*irreg.*) **voz y voto** to have a say

vuelo flight

vuelta return; **darle** (*irreg.*) **vuelta a** to think about (*something*)

vuelto/a (*p.p. of* **volver**) returned

vuestro/a(s) *poss. adj.* your (*inform. pl. Sp.*); *poss. pron.* your, of yours (*inform. pl. Sp.*)

W

web *m.* web; **navegador web** web browser; **página web** web page (1); **sitio web** website

WIFI *m.* WiFi (10)

Y

y and (1); **y media** half past (*the hour*); **¿y tú?** and you (*inform. s.*)? (1); **¿y usted?** and you (*form. s.*)? (1)

ya already; **ya no** no longer; **ya que** *conj.* since

yate *m.* yacht

yerno son-in-law (4)

yo *sub. pron.* I; **que yo sepa** as far as I know

yoga *m.* yoga; **practicar (qu) el yoga** to do yoga (3)

yogur *m.* yogurt (6)

York: Nueva York New York

yuca cassava, manioc

Z

zanahoria carrot

zapatería shoe store

zapatilla tennis shoe

zapato shoe (8)

zapoteca Zapotec

zona area; zone

zumo juice (*Sp.*)

CREDITS

TEXT CREDITS

INDEX

Note: There are two parts to this index. The Grammar Topics include a vocabulary list. The Cultural Topics index includes references to Spanish speaking nations as well as cultural features.

GRAMMAR TOPICS

a
to clarify who is affected by unplanned events, 272
emphasizing **gustar** and similar verbs, 210
with indirect objects, 206
abbreviated words, 38
abrir, past participle, 490
adjectives
agreement in gender and number, 46
cognates, 43
colors, 42
demonstrative, 86
with **estar** or **ser**, 50
hair color and complexion, 42
placement, 476
changes in meaning, 477
possessive, 25–26
synonyms for frequently used, 41
See also descriptive adjectives
afeitarse, 141
age, 36
ago, 171
al, 37, 38
algo, 150
alguno/a/os/as, 150
alphabet, Spanish, 10, 10n
i latina and **y griega**, 11n
ll and **rr**, 10n
w, 11
andar, uses, 337
antojarse, 271
aprender
past participle, 327
past subjunctive, 413
preterite tense, 171
tú commands, 300
aquel/aquella/aquellos/aquellas, 478–479
articles
definite, 17
gender, 476
indefinite, 16–17
asistir, present tense, 79
asking questions, question words, 50
asking where someone is going, 38
auxiliary verbs
estar in present progressive, 146, 336, 362
See also **haber**
ayudar, present participle, 336

bailar, present tense, 79
bañarse, 141
to become, 146
body, parts of, 226
bueno, 105
placement, 476
buscar, present subjunctive, 365

calendars, 73
capitalization
days of the week, 73
months, 13
cenar
present progressive, 336
present tense, 78
cognates
adjectives, 43
o → ue cognate pairs, 83
true and false, 13
colors, 42
comer
imperfect, 201
past participle, 326
present tense, 78
present progressive, 336
present subjunctive, 365
tú commands, 300
Ud./Uds. commands, 304
command forms, 300
making polite invitations, 318
nosotros/as commands, 491
with object pronouns, 332–333, 491
"opposite" vowel in, 300, 301, 303
subjunctive compared, 367
See also **tú** commands; **Ud./Uds.** commands
comparatives, 105
of equality, 479–480
más de with numerals, 479
comprar, present subjunctive, 365
conditional perfect tense, 497
conditional tense, 436
irregular forms, 497
congratulations, 194
conjecture, future to express, 418
conocer
irregular **yo** form, 137, 481–482
preterite and imperfect forms, 487
uses, 137, 481
contigo / conmigo, 210
contractions, **al** and **del**, 37, 38
contrary-to-fact situations, 439–440
correr, present tense, 79
creer, preterite, 484
cuando, 495
¿cuántos... hay?, 14
cubrir, past participle, 490

daily routines, 69–70
dar
indirect object pronouns, 206
la bienvenida a, 316
past subjunctive, 414
present subjunctive, 365
preterite, 484
dates, 14
deber, declining politely with, 162
debería + *infinitive,* 379
decir
conditional tense, 436
future, 418

past participle, 327
present subjunctive, 366, 387
present tense, 108–109, 136, 366
preterite tense, 175
tú commands, 301
definite articles, 17
plural, 19
with superlatives, 106
del, 37, 38
demonstrative adjectives, 86
aquel/aquella/aquellos/aquellas, 478–479
demonstrative pronouns, 479
descriptive adjectives, 41
colors, 42
placement, 476–477
synonyms for frequently used, 41
de to express possession, 485
diminutives, 58
directions, asking for and giving, 127
direct object pronouns, 179
commands with, 332–333
double object pronouns, 487–488
forms, 179
placement with commands, 305
placement with infinitives, 241
present perfect, 358
present progressive, 362
direct objects, 178–179
doler, 354
dormir, preterite tense, 231
double object pronouns, 487–488
present progressive with, 492

él, written accent mark, 25
empezar
present tense, 112
preterite tense, 172
en, 210
en caso de que, 394
escribir
past participle, 327
present progressive, 336
preterite tense, 171
tú commands, 300
ese/esa/esos/esas, 86
esperar, present subjunctive with, 366
estar
with adjectives, 144–145
compared to **ser**, 50, 115, 145
formation, 49, 116
future tense, 418
for greetings, 7
for location, 115, 144
of person or thing, 483
past subjunctive, 413
present progressive, 146, 336–337, 362
preterite tense, 175
uses, 50, 115, 144–145
with verbs ending in **-ndo**, 146
versus **ser** in present progressive, 337
weather expressions with, 258

este/esta/estos/estas, 86
estudiar, present progressive, 336

food and meals, 71, 90
setting the table, 167
vocabulary, 164–166
formal speech, 5
addressing those whose names you do not know, 317
asking for directions, 127
introductions, 4
Ud./Uds. commands, 304–305
use of **Ud./Uds.**, 304n
future perfect tense, 497
future tense, 417–418
forms, 418
irregular verb forms, 497
uses, 417–418

gender, 16
adjectives, 46
indefinite articles, 16–17
nouns, 476
good-byes, 9
wishing someone well, 348
good luck, wishing someone, 347–348
greetings, 2–3
asking people how they are, 7
gustar, 39
emphasis with **a**, 210
indirect object pronouns, 206
infinitives with, 54–55
object pronouns with, 53
singular and plural, 52–53
uses, 477–478
verbs similar to, 210, 354
te/le gustaría + infinitive, 253

haber
conditional perfect tense, 497
conditional tense, 436
future, 418
imperfect, 202
past perfect subjunctive, 496
past perfect tense, 491
present perfect, 326
present perfect subjunctive, 493
hablar
imperfect, 201
past subjunctive, 413
tú commands, 300
hace + time expression, 171, 380
¿Cuánto tiempo hace que...?, 380
hacer
conditional tense, 436
future, 418
past participle, 327
present perfect, 326
present tense, 136
preterite tense, 175
subjunctive, 387
tú commands, 301
weather expressions with, 258

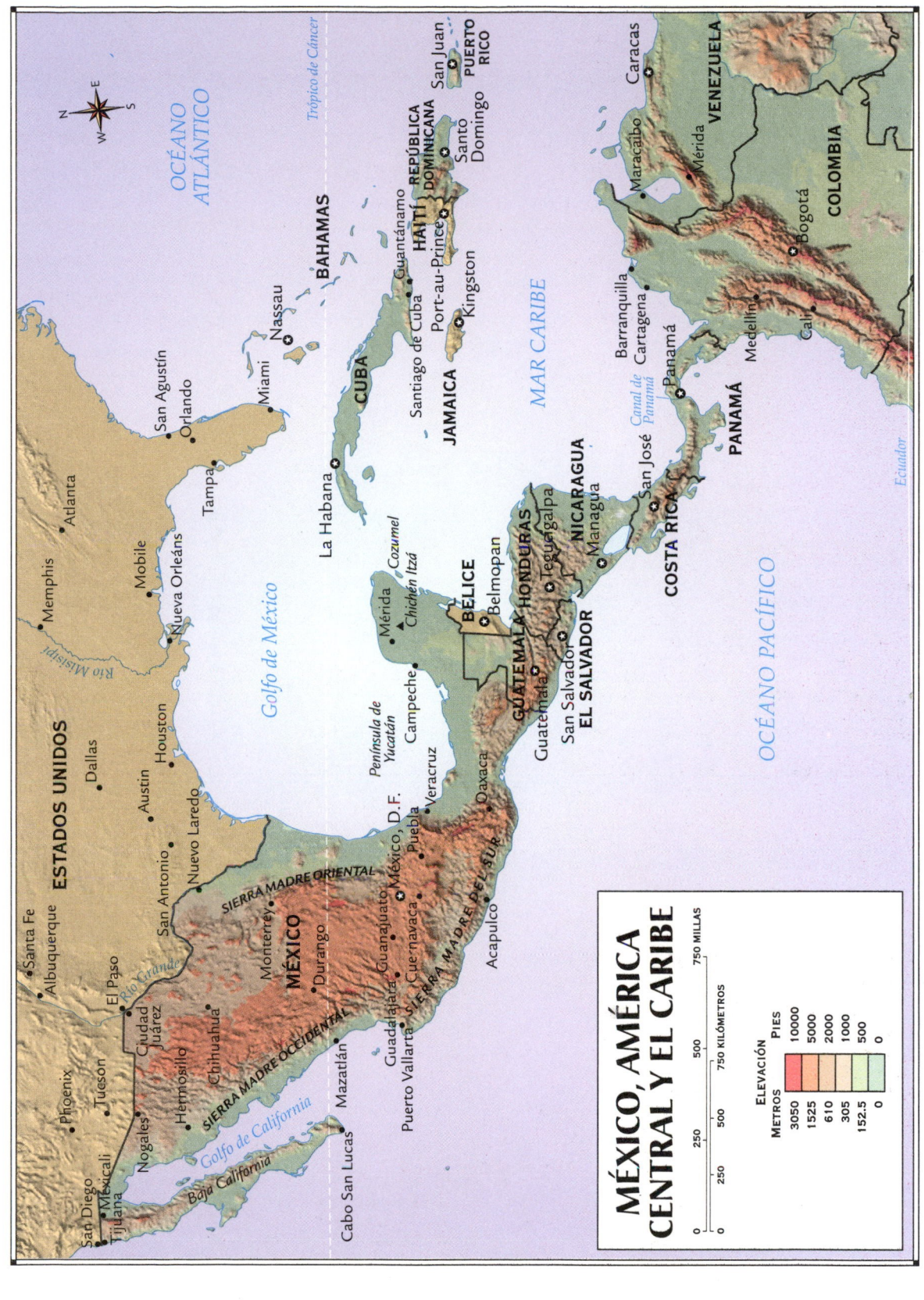

MÉXICO, AMÉRICA CENTRAL Y EL CARIBE

AMÉRICA DEL SUR

NICARAGUA

MAR CARIBE

COSTA RICA

PANAMÁ

Barranquilla

Maracaibo

Caracas

Río Orinoco

VENEZUELA

Georgetown

GUYANA

Paramaribo

Cayenne

GUAYANA FRANCESA

SURINAM

OCÉANO ATLÁNTICO

Medellín

Bogotá

Cali

COLOMBIA

Quito

ECUADOR

Guayaquil

Manaus

Río Amazonas

Belém

Ecuador

OCÉANO PACÍFICO

PERÚ

Lima

Machu Picchu

Cuzco

C O R D I L L E R A   D E   L O S   A N D E S

Lago Titicaca

BOLIVIA

La Paz

Sucre

Arequipa

BRASIL

Brasília

Recife

OCÉANO PACÍFICO

Isla Pinta

Isla Marchena

Isla San Salvador

Isla Santa Cruz

Isla Isabela

Isla San Cristóbal

Puerto Baquerizo Moreno

ISLAS GALÁPAGOS (ECUADOR)

0   100 MILLAS

0   100 KILÓMETROS

Antofagasta

PARAGUAY

Asunción

Puerto Iguazú

São Paulo

Rio de Janeiro

Trópico de Capricornio

CHILE

Río Paraná

0   8 MILLAS

0   8 KILÓMETROS

Cabo Cummings

Hanga Roa

Mataveri

Cabo Sur

OCÉANO PACÍFICO

ISLA DE PASCUA (CHILE)

Valparaíso

Córdoba

Rosario

URUGUAY

Santiago

ARGENTINA

Buenos Aires

Montevideo

Río de la Plata

OCÉANO ATLÁNTICO

Concepción

Bahía Blanca

San Carlos de Bariloche

OCÉANO PACÍFICO

Estrecho de Magallanes

Islas Malvinas

Punta Arenas

Tierra del Fuego

Cabo de Hornos

AMÉRICA DEL SUR

0   250   500   750 MILLAS

0   250   500   750 KILÓMETROS

ELEVACIÓN

METROS		PIES
3050		10000
1525		5000
610		2000
305		1000
152.5		500
0		0